ENCYCLOPEDIA OF RUSSIAN WOMEN'S MOVEMENTS

ENCYCLOPEDIA OF RUSSIAN WOMEN'S MOVEMENTS

Edited by
Norma Corigliano Noonan
and
Carol Nechemias

GREENWOOD PRESS
Westport, Connecticut • London

Library of Congress Cataloging-in-Publication Data

Encyclopedia of Russian women's movements / edited by Norma Corigliano Noonan and Carol Nechemias.
p. cm.
Includes bibliographical references and index.
ISBN 0–313–30438–6 (alk. paper)
1. Feminism—Russia (Federation)—Encyclopedias. 2. Feminism—Soviet Union—Encyclopedias. 3. Feminism—Russia—Encyclopedias. 4. Feminists—Russia (Federation)—Biography. 5. Feminists—Soviet Union—Biography. 6. Feminists—Russia—Biography. I. Noonan, Norma C. II. Nechemias, Carol, 1947–
HQ1665.15.E5 2001
305.42'0947—dc21 00–061046

British Library Cataloguing in Publication Data is available.

Library of Congress Catalog Card Number: 00–061046
ISBN: 0–313–30438–6

First published in 2001

Greenwood Press, 88 Post Road West, Westport, CT 06881
An imprint of Greenwood Publishing Group, Inc.
www.greenwood.com

Printed in the United States of America

The paper used in this book complies with the Permanent Paper Standard issued by the National Information Standards Organization (Z39.48–1984).

10 9 8 7 6 5 4 3 2 1

For Thomas S. Noonan, my husband and friend, who has been there for me in good times and bad, and for our parents, Toby and Herbert Nechemias and Amelia Corigliano and the late Domenic Corigliano, in gratitude for their lifelong support.

Contents

Acknowledgments ix

Introduction: Russian Women's Movements of the Nineteenth and Twentieth Centuries xi

Chronology of Russian Women's Movements in Historical Context xiii

Part I: Women's Movements from the Nineteenth Century to the Revolutions of 1917 1

Part II: Women's Movements in the Soviet Era, 1917–1991 125

Part III: Women's Movements in the Transitional and Post-Soviet Eras, 1985– 195

Glossary of Abbreviations and Major Terms 373

Selected Bibliography 379

Index 385

Contributors 397

Acknowledgments

In thanking people who have assisted in the development and production of any work, one always runs the risk of forgetting someone. First of all, special thanks to Nita Romer and others on the staff of the Greenwood Publishing Group for their careful work in developing the project and the individual authors, who devoted considerable time and effort to their essays, patiently making revisions to fit the needs of this work. It is also important to remember Russian friends and colleagues who answered frequent questions about specific points and movements in which they were involved.

Norma Noonan is grateful to International Research and Exchanges Board (IREX) for the short-term travel grant awarded to her in 1998, which assisted her in her research trip to Moscow and St. Petersburg to interview individuals and survey some newer organizations and developments. She appreciated the sabbatical leave from Augsburg College in the academic year 1998–1999, which made it possible to devote extensive time to the project. She also wants to thank her husband, Thomas S. Noonan, and her son, Thomas R. Noonan, who patiently stood by during the long process of writing, editing, and reediting countless entries and encouraged her efforts. Special thanks are also due to friends in Moscow and St. Petersburg, who, through E-mail, patiently answered questions about evolving place-names and terms, especially Zoia Molokova and Elena Zdravomyslova. In Norma Noonan's four trips during the 1990s, Larisa Vasil'eva and Elvira Ershova were of incredible help in working her way through the labyrinth of Russian women's groups. Many other Russian friends were helpful in getting information and in making contacts, and their assistance will be forever embedded in her memory.

Carol Nechemias wishes to express her appreciation for the warm support that she has received over the years from Russian friends, especially Elena Kochkina, Nadezhda Shvedova, and Mariia Zolotukhina. Without their encouragement and assistance, it would have been difficult to pursue research on contemporary women's issues. Her work on this project drew on information and insights from research conducted during the 1990s. She is deeply appreciative of support from the American Political Science Association, which awarded her a research grant in 1995, and from IREX for the short-term travel grant awarded in 1994. A short-term grant from the Kennan Institute in 1995 facilitated research focusing on women's involvement in parliamentary politics.

Introduction: Russian Women's Movements of the Nineteenth and Twentieth Centuries

This relatively brief volume encompasses almost 200 years but with special focus on developments since 1985. During the past two centuries, Russian women's movements have taken many forms. There is no single Russian women's movement, either past or present. In the 1990s, in particular, with new opportunities to create nongovernmental associations, one finds an abundance of women's movements, moving in diverse and sometimes even opposite directions.

In organizing this volume, we identified three distinct periods: the nineteenth century and early twentieth century prior to the Bolshevik Revolution of 1917 (Part I); the Soviet period, 1917–1991 (Part II); and the transitional era and post-Soviet movements, 1985–) (Part III). Wherever a movement or person transcended or encompassed more than one period, we used our judgment as to the best placement of the entry. A number of developments that began during Perestroika (1985–1991) but continued and evolved in the post-Soviet era have been placed into Part III.

In selecting entries for inclusion, we used a rather comprehensive definition of women's movements. Any group that purported to support or advance improvements in the status of women was included. Individuals who advanced the status of women in some way, even if they personally were not directly involved in women's movements, were considered for inclusion.

In our desire to create an encyclopedia of Russian women's movements, we recognized that one could not possibly cover all existing organizations. Some selectivity was necessary in choosing organizations, and some omissions have occurred, however carefully we tried to include all significant groups.

Because of the extensive published works on women in pre-1917 Russia, the work does not cover all possible groups or individual women. With a rare exception, the coverage begins with the late nineteenth century. For both prerevolutionary Russia and the Soviet era, we included important groups, while recognizing that, because of space constraints, we were not fully comprehensive. Also, entries on some famous historic figures may seem shorter than justified, but those figures have been widely described elsewhere, often in separate monographs.

Our emphasis is on the post-Soviet era, but even there, we cannot claim to cover all possible groups, as hundreds of women's organizations now exist. As editors we endeavored to select important groups and, in some cases, organized our presentation of women's organizations by localities in order to present a coherent view of women's movements in cities such as Ekaterinburg and Vladimir. Women's movements in the post-Soviet era were, and are, as volatile and elusive as Russian politics generally. Women's movements encompass a great variety of organizations, groups, and actions; late twentieth-century Russia reflected a situation in which movements were fluid, diverse, and fragmented. Political movements prominent in the early 1990s barely, or no longer, existed by 2000, while new organizations continued to emerge. Women's organizations mirror the larger society with respect to the ephemeral character of many groups.

The book uses the Library of Congress system of transliteration, even though this may occasionally produce some alien results. Well-known cities, such as Yaroslavl, appear as Iaroslavl. In a few cases, Russian authors protested at the transformation of their own names into a style unfamiliar to them. With well-known political figures such as Boris Yeltsin, we used the popular way of spelling names, rather than, in this case, El'tsin.

Another problematic area was the *otchestvo*, or patronymic. For some lesser-known historic figures, the patronymic was not available, and indeed in some cases only an initial or initials were available. In the contemporary period, some feminists have protested the use of the patronymic as a vestige of patriarchal society and have refused to use it. Russian society itself may be in transition about the use of the patronymic, as Russia becomes more Westernized. Former Prime Minister Viktor Chernomyrdin broke with tradition when he did not use a patronymic, shocking many in the older generation. Younger people seem less inclined to use the *otchestvo* among their peers, reserving it for their professors or for the older generation as a sign of respect.

In writing about individual women, the authors and the editors endeavored to include information about their early lives, but, unfortunately, such information was not universally available. As with any work, contradictions were discovered in dates and incidents even in well-researched publications. While this may occur more often with historical figures, even with contemporary individuals and movements, there are often conflicting data about when a movement began or when it was officially registered or where its branches exist. In the post-Soviet era, most groups were affected by the hardships of the transition; especially after the financial and economic crisis of 1998, the outreach of numerous groups was severely curtailed. The decline of some groups in the late 1990s in no way detracts from their overall contributions and efforts but has to be noted as part of the turmoil of the post-Soviet, Russian experience.

Chronology of Russian Women's Movements in Historical Context

The following is a chronology of persons and organizations in this work associated with Russian women's movements within the larger context of Russian and Soviet history. Some general movements and individuals or organizations for which there are no dates are not included.

1805–1863	Volkonskaia, Mariia
1817–1852	Herzen, Natal'ia
1822–1895	Stasova, Nadezhda
1825	Decembrist revolt
1825–1855	Reign of Nicholas I
1830s–1850s	Decembrist women active in Siberia
1835–1897	Trubnikova, Mariia
1835–1912	Filosofova, Anna
1843–1918	Suslova, Nadezhda
1844–1934	Breshko-Breshkovskaia, Ekaterina
1848–1932	Shabanova, Anna
1849–1902	Davydova, Aleksandra
1849–1919	Zasulich, Vera
1850s–1870s	*Niglistki* (Women Nihilists)
1850–1916	Shapir, Ol'ga
1852–ca. 1922	Pokrovskaia, Mariia
1852–1942	Figner, Vera
1854–1881	Perovskaia, Sof'ia

1854–1938	Shchepkina, Ekaterina
1855–1881	Reign of Alexander II
1857–1933	Zetkin, Klara
Ca. 1860s–ca. 1910s	Bogel'man, Sof'ia
1861	Emancipation of serfs
1861–1864	Land and Freedom (*Zemlia i volia*) movement
1863	N. Chernyshevskii, *What Is to Be Done?*
1863–1879	*Zhenskaia Izdatel'skaia artel'* (the Women's Publishing Artel)
1864–1944	Ariian, Praskov'ia
1865–1913	Mirovich, Zinaida
1866–1934	Chekhova, Mariia
1866–1937	Lesnevskaia, Antonina
1869–1939	Krupskaia, Nadezhda
1869–1962	Tyrkova, Ariadna
1870s	Higher education for women; women's medical courses developed
Ca. 1870s–ca. 1917	Kal'manovich, Anna
Ca. 1870s–ca. 1917	Ruttsen, Liudmila
Ca. 1870s–ca. 1920	Muravieva, Aleksandra
1871	Women permitted to practice pharmacy
1871–1956	Panina, Sof'ia
1872–1952	Kollontai, Aleksandra
1873–1874	"Going to the people" movement (*khozhdenie v narod*)
1873–1966	Stasova, Elena
1875–1920	Armand, Inessa
1875–1947	Shishkina-Iavein, Poliksena
1876–1879	Populist Land and Freedom (*Zemlia i volia*) organization
1876–1921	Samoilova, Konkordiia
1877–1878	Russo-Turkish War
1879–1883	People's Will (*Narodnaia volia*) movement—terrorist group
1881	Alexander II assassinated

1881–1894	Reign of Alexander III
1884–1941	Spirodonova, Mariia
1886–1900	Higher educational programs for women closed, except Bestuzhev Courses
1889–1920	Bochkareva, Mariia
1889–1969	Artiukhina, A.
1894–1917	Reign of Nicholas II
1895–1917	Russian Women's Mutual Philanthropic Society (*Russkoe zhenskoe vzaimno-blagotvoritel'noe obshchestvo*)
1895–1927	Reisner, Larisa
1899–1915	*Pervyi zhenskii kalendar'* (First Women's Calendar)
1900–ca. 1914	Russian Society for the Protection of Women (*Rossiiskoe obshchestvo zashchity zhenshchin*)
1904–1917	*Zhenskii Vestnik* (*Women's Herald*)
1905–1907	Revolutionary activity leading to reforms and establishment of the Duma
1905–1908	*Soiuz ravnopraviia zhenshchin* (Women's Equal Rights Union)
1905–1917	*Zhenskaia Progressivnaia Partiia* (Women's Progressive Party)
1907–1909	*Soiuz Zhenshchin* (*Union of Women*)—journal
1907–1917	*Liga ravnopraviia zhenshchin* (League for Women's Equal Rights)
Dec. 1908	First All-Russian Women's Congress
1910	All-Russian Congress for the Struggle against the Trade in Women
1911	Right to higher education in medical, pedagogical, and other higher education establishments granted to women
1914–1917	Women's military movement
1914–1918	World War I
Feb./Mar. 1917	February Revolution: Overthrow of tsarist regime and establishment of Provisional Government
July 1917	Women granted suffrage
Aug. 1917	Women's Military Congress

Oct./Nov. 1917	October or Bolshevik Revolution: Establishment of communist-led government, headed by V. I. Lenin
1917–1918	Women's military units in World War I, including Women's Death Battalion
1917–1920	Professional Union of Home Employees (*Professional'nyi soiuz domovykh sluzhashchikh*)
1918	First All-Russian Congress of Women Workers
1918–1930	Narpit (Union of People's Food Service and Dormitory Workers), large organization composed primarily of women
1918–1991	Komsomol
1919	Coeducation established in universities
1919–1930	*Zhenotdel* (Women's Department of the Communist Party)
1920	Establishment of Komsomol, communist youth league
1920	Legalization of abortion
1921–1928	New Economic Policy (NEP)
1922–1953	J. V. Stalin, General Secretary of the Communist Party
1923	Kollontai appointed first female ambassador from USSR
1924	Death of Vladimir I. Lenin
1929–1932	Collectivization of agriculture
1930	*Zhenotdel* (Women's Department of the Communist Party) abolished
1932–1999	Gorbacheva, Raisa
1934–1941	*Obshchestvennitsa* movement
1934–	Ershova, Elena
1934–	Sal'e, Marina
1935–	Vasil'eva, Larisa
1936–1955	Abortions banned in USSR
1937–1938	Height of Stalinist terror
1940–	Fedulova, Alevtina
1940–	Voznesenskaia, Iuliia
1941–1945	World War II (Great Fatherland War)
1943–	Mamonova, Tatiana
1944–	Dement'eva, Natal'ia
1944–	Klimantova, Galina

1946–1998	Starovoitova, Galina
1947–	Pivnenko, Valentina
1948–	Lakhova, Ekaterina
1948–	Trofimova, Elena
1949–	Matvienko, Valentina
1949–	Shvetsova, Liudmila
1950–	Regent, Tatiana
1951–	Dmitrieva, Tatiana
1953	Death of J. V. Stalin
1953–	Pamfilova, Ella
1953–	Savkina, Irina
1953–	Zdravomyslova, Elena
1953–1964	N. S. Khrushchev, First Secretary of the Communist Party
1954–	Lipovskaia, Ol'ga
1955	Abortion again legalized
1955–	Khakamada, Irina
1956–	Bronevich, Valentina
1956–1991	Soviet Women's Committee (*Komitet sovetskikh zhenshchin*)
1957–	Arbatova, Mariia
1958–	Dmitrieva, Oksana
1958–	Posadskaia, Anastasiia
1958–ca. 1991	*Zhensovety* (women's councils)
1960–	Liborakina, Marina
1960–	Temkina, Anna
1964–1982	L. I. Brezhnev, General Secretary of the Communist Party
1979–1980	Publication of samizdat *Al'manakh zhenshchinam i o zhenshchinakh* (*Almanac for Women and about Women*)
1979–ca. 1984	Woman and Russia, first independent feminist organization in USSR
1980–1983	*Mariia*, club of religious feminists
1985–1991	M. S. Gorbachev, General Secretary of the Communist Party of the Soviet Union (CPSU); era of reform begins

1988–	Institute for Development of International Business (St. Petersburg)
1988–1990	LOTOS
1989–	Committee of Soldiers' Mothers of Russia (*Komitet soldatskikh materei Rossii*)
1989–	Committee, "The Soldier's Mother," St. Petersburg
1989–	International League of Women Writers
1990s	Establishment of gender research centers; rapid growth of independent women's organizations
1990–	Disabled Russian Women's movement
1990–	FALTO/SAFO
1990–	Femina (Tatarstan)
1990–	International Women's Center Gaia
1990–	*Missiia* (Moscow)
1990–	Moscow Center for Gender Studies
1990–	Mother's Right Fund
1990–	SAFO (St. Petersburg)
1990–	Union of Disabled Women (St. Petersburg)
1990–	Women in Global Security (WINGS)
1990–	Women's Union of Russia
Ca. 1990–	Scientific Center "Women and Russia" (St. Petersburg)
Ca. 1990–	Women and Business in Russia (St. Petersburg)
Ca. 1990–	Women's Club-Café "*Sudarynia*" (St. Petersburg)
1991	Dissolution of USSR, December 31, 1991
1991	First Independent Women's Forum, Dubna
1991–	St. Petersburg Association of University Women, VERA
1991–	St. Petersburg Association of Widows and Their Families, Valita
1992	Second Independent Women's Forum, Dubna
1992–	Association of Women in Law Enforcement, St. Petersburg
1992–	Association of Women Journalists
1992–	Baikal' Regional Union, "Angara"
1992–	Institute "Woman and Management" (St. Petersburg)

1992–	Russian Federation established
1992–	St. Petersburg Center of Gender Issues
1992–	Union of Soviet Women of Leningrad and Leningrad Oblast
1992–	Women and Development Association
1992–	Women's Congress of the Kola Peninsula
1992–	Women's League/Women's Initiative
1993–	Commission on Women, Family, and Demography
1993–	Consortium of Women's Nongovernmental Associations
1993–	"Women of the Don" Union
1993–	Women of Russia bloc created to contest Duma elections
1994–	Association of Crisis Centers for Women (*Assotsiatsiia krizichnykh tsentrov*)
1994–	The Information Center of the Independent Women's Forum (*Informatsionnyi tsentr nezavisimogo foruma*)
1994–	*Sovremennaia zhenshchina* (Moscow)
1995–	Karelian Center for Gender Studies
1995–	Women's Humanitarian Collegium (St. Petersburg)
1996	Valentina Bronevich elected the first female governor in the Russian Federation
1996–	All-Russian Sociopolitical Movement of Women of Russia (*Obshcherossiiskoe obshestvenno-politicheskoe dvizhenie zhenshchin Rossii*)
1996–	Association for the Advancement of Women in Science and the Humanities (AAWISH)
1996–	Ivanovo Center for Gender Research (see Ivanovo)
1996–	Women's Information Network
1997	Charter of Women's Solidarity
1997–	Commission on Improving the Status of Women (CISW)
Dec. 1998	Conference marking the Ninetieth Anniversary of the First All-Russian Women's Congress
2000–	Vladimir Putin elected President of the Russian Federation

PART I

WOMEN'S MOVEMENTS FROM THE NINETEENTH CENTURY TO THE REVOLUTIONS OF 1917

From the early nineteenth century until the October Revolution of 1917, when the Soviet political system was established, tsarist Russia witnessed the development of many women's groups and movements. A characteristic of women's movements prior to 1917 was their great diversity. Women's movements encompassed a myriad of directions, from women in medicine, to women terrorists, from intellectual women who tried to escape the confines of the prescribed roles of wives and mothers, to revolutionaries who tried to change society. All the movements and groups were born in the idea of the need for change, but there was no consensus from generation to generation and from group to group about what forms change should take. Both reform and revolutionary groups emerged. The reform groups wanted to improve the status of women within the tsarist system, whereas the revolutionaries sought to overthrow the system. Some sought reforms for all women; others, for selected groups of women. Some movements focused primarily on the upper and middle classes; others, on the disadvantaged classes. Some groups had a philanthropic orientation, whereas others wanted to affect women's legal status. Women's struggle to obtain education and pursue careers was a major part of most groups' agenda. A few movements, such as the Marxist revolutionary groups that arose at the end of the century, sought to change the entire society and assumed that women would benefit along with other oppressed groups.

The women who headed the organizations were as diverse as the movements. Some women focused on equal rights under the law and the right to vote. Others wanted to expand women's career opportunities. Still others sought the liberation of women and men from the oppressive restraints that they perceived in Russia. The actors in the prerevolutionary movement were usually highly educated members of the gentry or the emerging middle class. Although most movements appeared to be dominated by women from the privileged classes, women from humble circumstances often took the initiative to improve their lot as well. The organizational skills and efforts that Russian women demonstrated over 100 years ago were impressive, especially given the societal constraints and their limited resources. The dedication of the nineteenth-century women provides inspiration for people in the contemporary world who believe that they can and should do more but do not know quite how to begin.

Our goal in this section is to present selected examples of various types of women's efforts, organizations, and movements that existed before 1917 as a prelude to developments in the Soviet era. The pre-1917 experience, along with the Soviet era, provides a context for understanding the Russian situation in the post-Soviet era and in the early twenty-first century. The Russian heroines described in this work travailed under adverse conditions. Adversity was the norm of Russian reality in the lives and efforts of the groups and individuals studied in the nineteenth century, as well as in the Soviet and post-Soviet periods.

Part I of this volume does not attempt to encompass every group or movement, but only some representative groups in order to provide a context and background for later women's movements in the Soviet and post-Soviet periods. The pre-Soviet period has been chronicled in many excellent published works, ranging from Richard Stites' classic, *The Women's Liberation Movement in Russia*, to biographies of prominent women activists and revolutionaries, such as Barbara Clements' *Bolshevik Feminist* and Jay Bergman's *Vera Zasulich*, as well as monographs of women journalists, physicians, pharmacists, and other groups. In selecting movements, organizations, and individuals for inclusion in this first section of the work, the editors were guided by a desire to select representative groups, present current research, and highlight some of the most outstanding figures. The single most important criterion was whether the movements, groups, or individuals acted to improve women's situation and status.

Because of the space allocation for the entire volume, it was necessary to limit discussion of the earlier movements in order to give adequate coverage for recent movements and groups, about which little or nothing has been written in published works in the West. As a result, some relatively important early figures and movements may not be included. This first part of our work may be viewed as a sampler of nineteenth-century developments rather than an all-inclusive work.

A

All-Russian Congress for the Struggle against the Trade in Women (1910)

A conference convened by the Russian Society for the Protection of Women (RSPW) in 1910 to focus public attention on the problems of prostitution and to combat the trade in women. The congress attracted many members of educated society, including tsarist officials, aristocrats, doctors, and even a few workers, and resulted in an attack on government regulation of prostitution.

The *Rossiiskoe obshchestvo zashchity zhenshchin* (Russian Society for the Protection of Women, or RSPW) in 1910 convened a conference in St. Petersburg to call attention to the problems of prostitution and to highlight ways to oppose the trade in women. The All-Russian Congress for the Struggle against the Trade in Women met from April 21 to April 25, 1910, in St. Petersburg with about 300 attendees. Two-thirds of those in attendance were women, many of whom were affiliated with feminist and philanthropic organizations. Professionals from various fields as well as government officials were also present. The proceedings centered on the themes of the origins of prostitution, its prevention, the international trade in women, saving "fallen women," and state regulation of prostitution. Most of the resolutions addressed economic issues and public education about venereal disease and sexual abstinence. Some of the resolutions called for greater public action. Participants, for example, called for free medical clinics for patients with sexually transmitted diseases. The Congress urged increased penalties for involvement in sexual trafficking, reflecting the view that women entered into prostitution only after having been enticed or coerced, rather than from choice. The Congress also recommended prosecution of men who bought sex from prostitutes.

The educated public's repugnance against the state's practice of issuing licenses to street prostitutes and brothels in exchange for medical and police surveillance was also addressed in resolutions. Participants voted unanimously to recommend the end of state licensing for brothels. Most participants also opposed licensing street prostitutes, but there was disagreement about the role of regulation. Those who supported regulation argued that regular medical inspections and the mandatory treatment of prostitutes with venereal disease were the only way to protect public health. The opponents of regulation had a more convincing case. The majority of Congress participants endorsed a resolution denouncing regulation as contrary to sanitary goals and as a method of increasing the number of prostitutes, enslaving women to prostitution, a demoralizing influence, and an insult to women's human dignity. The Congress fulfilled its role in raising public consciousness and in promoting measures to limit prostitution.

Cross-reference: Russian Society for the Protection of Women (RSPW).

Suggested Readings

Bernstein, Laurie. *Sonia's Daughters: Prostitutes and Their Regulation in Imperial Russia*. Berkeley: University of California Press, 1995.

Bernstein, Laurie. " 'A Necessary Institution in the Capitalist World': Socialists and Workers Consider Prostitution." *Russian History/Histoire Russe* 23, nos. 1–4 (1996): 179–196.

Trudy pervogo vserossiiskogo s"ezda po bor'be s torgom zhenshchinami i ego prichinami proiskhodivshchogo v S.-Peterburge 21 do 25 aprelia 1910 goda (Works of the First All-Russian Congress for the Struggle against the Trade in Women and Its Causes), vols. 1–2. St. Petersburg: Tipo-Litografiia S.-Peterburgskoi Odinochnoi Tiur'my, 1911–1912.

Laurie Bernstein

Ariian, Praskov'ia Naumovna Belenkaia (1864–1944)

The driving force behind the establishment of the St. Petersburg *Pervyi zhenskii politekhnicheskii institut* (First Women's Technical Institute, (1906–1924). She also founded, edited, and published the *Pervyi zhenskii kalendar' (First Women's Calendar)* from 1899 to 1915.

Praskov'ia Naumovna Belenkaia was born in St. Petersburg in 1864 (some sources list her birth date as 1865). Admitted to the physics-mathematics section of the Bestuzhevskie Higher Courses for Women, she finished with the third graduating class of the courses in 1884 but did not officially graduate, perhaps because of her political activity. The courses were a hotbed of radicalism, and, like a number of other feminist activists, Ariian was a student radical.

Ariian supported herself as a translator and journalist, traditional occupations for educated Russian women, while also seeking to integrate her work with her ideals. She wrote for a range of publications, including the *Birzhevaia vedomosti (The Stock Market Gazette)*, the *Sputnik zdorov'ia (The Health Guide)*, the *Vestnik blagotvoritel'nosti (The Philanthropy Bulletin)*, and *Iskusstvo i zhizn' (Art and Life)*. After finishing the Bestuzhev Courses, she was one of the organizers of the day-care center *Detskaia Pomoshch'* (Children's Aid) for children of workers in St. Petersburg, where she worked for ten years. The Bolshevik activist Elena Stasova was among her coworkers.

In 1899 she founded the *Pervyi zhenskii kalendar' (First Women's Calendar)*, single-handedly compiling, editing, and publishing this compendium of religious, health, employment, and education information for women every year until 1915. The *Calendar* contained biographical sketches of Russian feminists, radical activists, and literary figures, with accompanying photos. It also chronicled the activities of the major feminist organizations, such as the *Russkoe zhenskoe vzaimno-blagotvoritel'noe obshchestvo* (Russian Women's Mutual Philanthropic Society), including photos of the society's facilities, and the *Liga ravnopraviia zhenshchin* (the League for Women's Equal Rights). Feminist congresses, such as the 1908 *Pervyi vserossiiskii zhenskii s"ezd* (First All-Russian Women's Congress) and the *Pervyi vserossiiskii s"ezd po obrazovaniiu zhenshchin* (First All-Russian Congress on Women's Education), held from December 26, 1912, to January 4, 1913, received detailed coverage. The *Calendar* is a significant historical source of information about Russian feminists and other female social activists and literary figures of the nineteenth and early twentieth centuries. Ariian recruited a wide range of contributors to the *Calendar*, including the writer Maksim Gor'kii, the radical activist Vera Figner, the artist Ilia Repin, and the psychologist Vladimir M. Bekhterev.

Ariian traveled widely. Working in the archives of Swiss universities, she gathered data about Russian women studying abroad for the *Calendars* of 1899 and 1912. After a trip to Japan, she published articles about the Women's University in Tokyo and the status of Japanese women in the *Calendars* of 1904 and 1905. News about the international women's movement was a regular part of the *Calendar*.

The *Calendar* dwelled on a range of issues affecting women. Prominent among them was health, both physical and mental. Each issue contained nutritional advice and pointers about general cleanliness and behavior. The 1912 *Calendar*, for example, included the article *"Nervnost' i meryi dlia bor'by s nei"* (Nervousness and Methods of Fighting It).

Ariian was perhaps best known as the initiator and driving force in the establishment of the *Pervyi zhenskii politekhnicheskii institut* (First Women's Technical Institute). She tirelessly lobbied the government for permission to open a program initially called *Vysshie zhenskie politekhnicheskie kursy* (Women's Higher Polytechnical Courses), did the fund-raising necessary to sustain the new venture, hired the staff, and even rented the initial space, an apartment, in her own name. When the courses opened on January 15, 1906, they were the first in the world to train women engineers. Ariian remained committed to providing educational opportunities for workers of both sexes. In the same year that the Women's Polytechnical Courses began, she won permission to open an evening school for workers in the Narva Gate section of St. Petersburg. Despite government harassment, closings, and arrests of students, the school lasted ten years.

Although never imprisoned for her activity, Ariian maintained ties with those who had been incarcerated for their opposition to the tsarist regime. From 1907 to 1917 she was an active member of the support group for prisoners in the notorious Schlusselburg Fortress near St. Petersburg. Given her connections to radical political groups, it is curious that the focus of Ariian's feminist activity was with the most conservative of the women's groups, the Russian Women's Mutual Philanthropic Society. Ariian's activism included speaking and writing for the society, working in its library, and chairing the committee researching the conditions of women's work in Russia.

After the October Revolution, Ariian seemed to have a nervous breakdown, but she recovered. She complained privately to friends about the lip service that the Bolsheviks paid to woman's rights. In the 1930s she conducted courses for workers at the Kirov factory, lecturing on Pushkin. In 1942, during the siege of Leningrad, she was evacuated to Piatigorsk and then to Tashkent, where she died in 1944.

Cross-references: Pervyi zhenskii kalendar', Russian Women's Mutual Philanthropic Society (*Russkoe vzaimno-blagotvoritel'noe obshchestvo*), Elena Stasova.

Suggested Readings

Ariian, Praskov'ia N., ed. *Pervyi zhenskii kalendar'*. 1899–1915.

Edmondson, Linda Harriet. *Feminism in Russia, 1900–1917.* Stanford, CA: Stanford University Press, 1984.

Goldberg, Rochelle (Ruthchild). "The Russian Women's Movement, 1859–1917." Ph.D. Diss., University of Rochester, 1976.

Stites, Richard. *The Women's Liberation Movement in Russia: Feminism, Nihilism, and Bolshevism, 1860–1930.* Princeton, NJ: Princeton University Press, 1978, 1991.

Rochelle Goldberg Ruthchild

B

Bochkareva, Mariia Leont'eva (1889–1920)

An officer in the Russian army and women's military leader during World War I. She served three years in the rank and file from the beginning of the war, was decorated twice for acts of bravery, and was promoted to senior noncommissioned officer (NCO). After the February 1917 Revolution, Bochkareva initiated the creation of, and became the commander of, the First Russian Women's Battalion of Death in 1917 and was promoted to lieutenant. She was internationally renowned as a female officer and hero.

Mariia Bochkareva (née Frolkova) was born to a peasant family in Novgorod in European Russia but soon after moved to Tomsk in Siberia. Hard physical labor and brutality characterized her early life. At age fifteen she married Afanasi Bochkarev to escape an abusive and alcoholic father, but her husband turned out to be no different. She later ran off with a petty criminal named Iakov Buk. Life with Buk also proved to be difficult, as he was similarly inclined to violence while intoxicated. When war broke out in 1914, she left Buk and returned to Tomsk with the desire to serve her country on the battlefield. She decided to enlist in the local reserve regiment but was denied admittance because women were forbidden to serve in the active army. The commander facetiously suggested that she send a telegram to the tsar for permission to enlist, and Bochkareva took him up on the offer. Surprisingly, the tsar responded positively to Bochkareva's request, and she was accepted into the unit. She fought with this unit for three years, achieving the rank of senior noncommissioned officer, and was awarded two St. George's medals for acts of bravery.

In May 1917 Bochkareva was discovered by Duma President Mikhail Rodzianko, who took her to Petrograd. Both were distressed over the deteriorating condition of the army following the February Revolution and believed that the heroism of women soldiers could provide inspiration for those wavering in their support. Bochkareva and other women pressed the government to organize women into combat units. The Minister of War, Alexander Kerenskii, consented and thus began the formation of the First Russian Women's Battalion of Death.

Kerenskii named Bochkareva the commander of the unit and promoted her to sublieutenant. The unit initially attracted around 2,000 women, but Bochkareva's strict discipline and crude style drove away many women, and, as a result, the battalion retained only about 300 women. The unit was sent to the front after a month's training and fought in one battle, after which she was promoted to lieutenant. Although the female soldiers performed well in combat, they had little support from men in the army, who had virtually given up fighting. Antiwar sentiment had grown so strong in the Russian army that many male soldiers perceived the women, who desired to continue fighting, as the enemy; hence, it became dangerous for the women to remain at the front. After the Bolsheviks seized power in late October, the battalion was forced to disband.

Bochkareva returned to Petrograd in November 1917 and was immediately arrested. Her sex and peasant origin initially spared her from execution. She went to the British Consulate in Petrograd for protection. The British ambassador gave her 500 rubles to travel to the United States and Great Britain to solicit allied aid for the struggle against the Bolsheviks. Bochkareva became an international celebrity, as Western and Russian journalists lauded her as a patriotic heroine dedicated to defending her nation while many shirked this responsibility. She arrived in Washington in May 1918 and met with President Woodrow Wilson. Her emotional plea for American intervention in Russia left the president in tears, and he promised to send aid. Bochkareva then went to Great Britain and was given an audience with the king, who advised her to return home and continue her work there. She returned to Russia through Archangel in August 1918 and spent the next year lingering around Allied Headquarters in the Northern Territories. Neither the officers of the Allied and Russian White forces nor the local residents approved of this woman soldier, and she was sent back to Tomsk in October 1919. There she attempted to aid the White forces under the command of Admiral Kol'chak by forming a women's medical detachment, but she was unsuccessful, and the Whites were soon driven out of the region by the Red Army. In January 1920 she was arrested by the Bolsheviks and found guilty of being an "enemy of the worker-peasant republic." She was sentenced to death and executed on May 16, 1920.

Cross-references: Women's Military Movement of World War I, Women's Military Units of World War I.

Suggested Readings

Abraham, Richard. "Mariia L. Bochkareva and the Russian Amazons of 1917." In *Women and Society in Russia and the Soviet Union*, edited by Linda Edmondson, 124–144. Cambridge: Cambridge University Press, 1992.

Botchkareva [*sic*], Maria. *Yashka: My Life as Peasant, Officer, and Exile*. As set down by Isaac Don Levine. New York: Frederick Stokes, 1919.

Drokov, S. V. "*Organizator Zhenskogo Batal'ona Smerti*" (The Organizer of the Women's Battalion of Death). *Voprosy Istorii (Problems of History)* 7 (1993): 164–169.

"*Protokolii doprosov organizatora Petrogradskogo zhenskogo batal'ona smerti.*" (Records of the Interrogation of the Organizer of the Petrograd Women's Battalion of Death). *Otechestvennye Arkhivy (Archives of the Fatherland)* 1 (1994): 52–66.

Laurie Stoff

Bogel'man, Sof'ia Zakharovna (ca. 1860s–ca. 1910s)

Editor and publisher of the St. Petersburg weekly *Zhenshchina* (1907–1909, 1913–1916), a woman's magazine focused on the complexity of a woman's life and her multiple roles in the family and in society at large.

Little is known about Sof'ia Bogel'man's early life. She was married to Isaac Abramovich Bogel'man, a member of the middle-class Jewish intelligentsia permitted to live in St. Petersburg as a registered "Merchant of the Second Guild" with voting rights as an "Individual Honorary Citizen." His company, *Narodnaia Pol'za* (Popular Well-Being), founded in 1897, operated one of the largest printing and publishing establishments in the capital, filling annual government contracts for religious, legal, financial, and pedagogical print jobs in addition to publishing traditional works of literature and popular science. By the time Sof'ia Bogel'man received authorization to launch her unique and highly ambitious women's weekly in mid-1907, Isaac Bogel'man chaired the Council of the Society of Owners of Printing Works in St. Petersburg. At that time, the family lived in a colorful art nouveau apartment house at 147 Nevskii Prospect, part of the thriving district just north of the Moscow Railroad Station. Sof'ia had already raised four sons, having seen them through the university and into their professional careers as a printer-publisher, a dentist, a lawyer, and an engineer-architect.

The journal *Zhenshchina* consisted of twelve separate sections, including *Zhenshchina-Grazhdanka* (The Woman Citizen), *Zhenshchina Vrach* (The Woman Physician), *Detskii Mir* (Children's World), and *Poslednye Mody* (The Latest Fashions). Taking pride in her role as editor, Sof'ia Bogel'man noted in the "Chronicle" section of *Zhenshchina-Grazhdanka* (December 15, 1907) that there were already "quite a few—about 30" women editors and publishers in Russia. She commented further that "in each case the woman is responsible for editorial policy only when she is also the publisher or is one of a group of publishers. If the publisher is male, the editor is never a woman." Subsequently, under the rubric of famous quotes, she cited John Stuart Mill's words: "Who can say how many original ideas expressed by male writers originated with their wives?" (February 1, 1908). Although Sof'ia Bogel'man was a firm advocate of women's equality in education, the law, and the workplace, she understood woman's role as "citizen" as one of her multiple functions. Bogel'man emphasized the centrality of "knowledge" for a woman as her "weapon" to assure both her family's strength and the future of Russian society. Advertisements aimed at subscribers for the second year of the magazine emphasized every woman's four primary functions: "Woman as Mother—Citizen—Wife—Housekeeper." Bogel'man's commitment to the women's movement was clear. For example, no less than ten issues referred to the First All-Russian Women's Congress in the year leading up to the event; and the magazine published the full program in June 1908, the original date set for the Congress, which was postponed until December 1908. Equal in strength to her dedication to women's equality was Bogel'man's firm editorial policy regarding the family. Among the magazine's various illustrated sections, the one entitled *Detskii Mir (Children's World)* expanded during the life of the magazine, gradually comprising alternate issues for younger children one week and older children the next. Included were stories, games, and amusements about and for children as well as articles on child raising, education, popular science, ethnography, and travel. Rubrics of popular medicine and hygiene were subsumed under a section called *Zhenshchina-Vrach (Woman-Doctor)*, while several different sections contained practical guidance for raising fruits and vegetables, caring for birds and other domestic animals, and even advice on how to identify adulterated food products in the market. Another section, the Domestic Encyclopedia, was filled with useful advice on all branches of housekeeping and homemaking, while *Poslednye Mody (Latest Fashions)* offered information on the latest fashions and provided patterns for women's and children's clothing and for handicrafts and toys. Each section was later marketed in book form when the magazine collapsed in mid-1909 as a result of bankruptcy proceedings against Isaac Bogel'man by the St. Petersburg Commercial Court after his firm lost some major government contracts and could no longer meet its debts.

It is unclear what happened to Sof'ia Bogel'man after 1910, when she twice applied for authorization to reopen the magazine. Although it finally reemerged in 1913–1916 in a more commercially viable and simplified format, edited and published by her husband, her editorial policies were basically maintained under three different male editors. They attempted to adapt to a significantly changed audience and market, competing with the new women's magazines founded by Moscow businessmen beginning in 1910.

Cross-references: First All-Russian Women's Congress (1908), Women's Periodical Publishing in Late Imperial Russia 1860–1905, Women's Periodicals in Early Twentieth Century Russia.

Jane Gary Harris

Breshko-Breshkovskaia, Ekaterina Konstantinovna (1844–1934)

Early propagandist among Russian peasantry who became a prominent populist and a founder and leader of the Socialist Revolutionary Party. Breshko-Breshkovskaia was a well-known fund-raiser in the United States, supported by some of the leading American feminists, who idealized her as the "grandmother" of the Russian Revolution.

Ekaterina Konstantinovna Verigo was born on January 13 (some sources say February 3) 1844, into a wealthy, aristocratic family in the village of Ivano in Vitebsk province. She was given a liberal education by her broad-minded, but ineffective, father and instruction in the social message of the Gospels by her religious mother. With the emancipation of the serfs in 1861, Ekaterina committed herself to serving the peasants. Certain that they could fulfill their great potential through education, she opened a school and for two years struggled to teach them. Realizing that the peasants would benefit more from economic and political reforms than from education, in 1863 she closed her school, went to St. Petersburg, and immersed herself in liberal intellectual life. Returning home in 1866 as a pragmatist devoted to reform, she again established a school for peasants and in 1869 married Nikolai Breshko-Breshkovskii, a well-educated neighbor who assisted her efforts. Together they established an agricultural school on his estate and became active in the local zemstvo (district council).

In 1871 wary authorities curtailed liberal activities in the district and placed Ekaterina and her family under surveillance. This thwarting of peaceful reform confounded Breshko-Breshkovskaia, who decided that, if legal means were prohibited, she would resort to illegal ones. When her husband refused to support her, the pregnant Breshko-Breshkovskaia left him and joined her widowed sister in Kiev. In this hub of youthful radicalism, their quarters soon became the nucleus of the famous Kiev Commune. In mid-pregnancy Breshko-Breshkovskaia went to St. Petersburg to widen her contacts and participated in debates between Lavrovists, who advocated education and propaganda leading to gradual reform, and Bakuninists, who favored instigating revolution among the "people" as soon as possible. Despite her desire to promote education, her volatile nature was drawn to the Bakuninists' doctrine of bold action. In the spring of 1872, she returned to Kiev, gave her baby son to her brother's wife, and started her career as a master of disguise: artificially aging her face and hands with acid, she "went to the people." In September 1874 she was arrested and sent to the Petropavlovsk Fortress, where she remained until 1878. She was tried at the Trial of the 193, a tsarist show trial intended to expose revolutionary propagandists as members of an evil extremist fringe. She received the maximum sentence for a woman: five years of hard labor followed by Siberian exile, the first Russian woman (with four others) subjected to such punishment.

When she was permitted to return to European Russia in 1896, Breshko-Breshkovskaia first sought out her son, Nikolai, a conservative writer who wanted nothing to do with the revolutionary mother who had abandoned him more than two decades earlier. After this rebuff she returned to education and agitation among the peasants, going underground in Minsk to organize libraries and illegal imports of revolutionary literature. After fleeing to Saratov in 1900 to escape the police, she played a vital role in creating the Socialist Revolutionary Party (SR) and organizing its printing operations. In 1903 she again outwitted police, who had captured her comrades, by escaping abroad, and the next year she made a well-publicized tour of the United States to raise funds for the SR Party. She became friendly with the leaders of the woman's suffrage movement, who considered her a model emancipated woman. She did not join the suffrage movement, however, explaining that in Russia political rights were denied to all.

When the 1905 Revolution broke out, Breshko-Breshkovskaia rushed back to Russia, but until 1907 she spent much of her time avoiding capture. That year, at the age of sixty-five, she began her second exile in Siberia, where she met and developed a close friendship with Aleksandr Kerenskii. An attempted escape resulted in exile to the far north but was changed to the less frigid Minusinsk due to American public pressure.

In 1917 Breshko-Breshkovskaia returned from exile in a triumphal procession arranged by Kerenskii, whom she uncritically supported as the best hope for political and social justice. As a legendary revolutionary figure and right-wing leader of the SRs, she was featured at all major assemblies supporting the Provisional Government. She openly advocated women's rights and endorsed military service for women, who were badly needed in the war that she and Kerenskii championed. When Vladimir I. Lenin took power in November 1917, Breshko-Breshkovskaia went underground to propagandize for the Constituent Assembly, and in 1918 she again went to America to raise money. Her reception there was mixed. Although she was famous as *babushka* (grandmother) of the Russian Revolution and although her pro-war agitation had strong support from Americans, her violent anti-Bolshevism dismayed many of her radical friends. Like most people, they did not understand her enigmatic character: ultraradical Bakuninist flamboyance, coupled with a basically Lavrovist disposition that placed the welfare of the people, especially the peasants, above factional authority.

While she was in America, events once more overtook Breshko-Breshkovskaia. As the Bolsheviks began to win the Civil War, she realized that she could not return to Russia and went into exile in Czechoslovakia in 1919, where the president of the republic welcomed her. Supported by American friends, she returned to her first love, education, establishing two schools for Russian orphans. When she died in 1934, tributes were published throughout the West. In the country that she had so passionately tried to serve, however, her name had slipped into virtual oblivion.

Suggested Readings

Blackwell, A. S., ed. *The Little Grandmother of the Russian Revolution: Reminiscences and Letters*. Boston, 1918.

Breshko-Breshkovskaia, Katerina. *Hidden Springs of the Russian Revolution: Personal Memoirs*, edited by Lincoln Hutchinson. Stanford, CA: Stanford University Press, 1931.

Good, Jane E., and David R. Jones. *Babushka: The Life of the Russian Revolutionary Ekaterina K. Breshko-Breshkovskaia (1844–1934)*. Newtonville, MA: Oriental Research Partners, 1991.

Kerensky, Alexander. "Catherine Breshkovsky, 1844–1934." *The Slavonic and East European Review* 13 (1934–1935): 428–431.

Klawa N. Thresher

C

Chekhova, Mariia Aleksandrovna Argamakova (1866–1934)

Founder of the *Soiuz ravnopraviia zhenshchin* (Women's Equal Rights Union), editor of the journal *Soiuz zhenshchin (Union of Women)* from 1907 to 1909, and President of the Moscow branch of the *Liga ravnopraviia zhenshchin* (League for Women's Equality).

Mariia Argamakova was born January 18, 1866, to a gentry family in St. Petersburg. She came from a family of educators; both her maternal and paternal grandfathers were teachers, as was her father. Mariia attended *gimnaziia* (gymnasiums) and then teachers' preparatory courses, beginning her pedagogical career even before graduating with a specialization in mathematics. She established her own school in 1889 and the next year married fellow educator Nikolai Chekhov.

Theirs was a companionate marriage, the ideal of the Russian intelligentsia of the time, and the two sought to live their ideals in the Russian countryside. From 1890 until 1904, Mariia and Nikolai Chekhov resided in regional towns and cities, establishing day and Sunday schools, ministering to victims of the 1891 famine, and raising five children. Moving to Moscow in 1904, they became active participants in the Liberation movement and the Teachers Union.

One of the founders of the *Soiuz ravnopraviia zhenshchin* (Women's Equal Rights Union) in 1905, Chekhova was its secretary and a member of the organization's Central Bureau, along with her husband. Her ties with the provinces aided the organization's outreach to women outside Moscow and St. Petersburg, and by 1906 the Union boasted a membership of 8,000 to 10,000 with chapters throughout the Russian Empire.

In addition to her involvement with the Women's Equal Rights Union, Chekhova taught courses for workers and helped organize the first Moscow children's club. From 1906 to 1910 Mariia and Nikolai lived in St. Petersburg, where Mariia kept up her activism in the Women's Union. She also joined the *Russkoe zhenskoe vzaimno-blagotvoritel'noe obshchestvo* (Russian Women's Mutual Philanthropic Society), organized petition campaigns for women's suffrage to the Second Duma, and participated in the 1908 Women's Congress, the 1910 Women's Education Congress, and the 1910 Congress to Combat Prostitution. She served as editor of the Women's Union journal, *Soiuz zhenshchin (Union of Women)* from 1907 to 1909.

When the Women's Equal Rights Union disintegrated and its journal ceased publication in 1909, Mariia Chekhova found a new venue for her feminist activity as president of the Moscow branch of the *Liga ravnopraviia zhenshchin* (League for Women's Equal Rights). Much of her activity continued to be in St. Petersburg. She participated in the League-organized Women's Education Congress, held in St. Petersburg December 1912–January 1913, and joined the lobbying for suffrage and equal rights with the conservative Third and Fourth Dumas. The women's lobbying efforts won modest victories with the passage of changes in passport, marriage, and inheritance legislation. Chekhova also continued her educational work, initiating a course in preschool education at the Moscow Teachers' Courses, becoming the head of the preschool education section of the Moscow Pedagogical Circle, and organizing a day-care center for the children of students at the Higher Courses for Women.

After the February 1917 Revolution and the formation of the Provisional Government, the League successfully lobbied with other feminists for women's right to vote; with its July 1917 suffrage law Russia was the first large country to do so. Chekhova continued to promote feminist political involvement, prompting a split at the All-Russian Congress of Women held in April 1917 but leading to the creation of the Republican Union of Democratic Women's Organizations. Chekhova was on the League's electoral list for the Constituent Assembly, along with League President Poliksena Shishkina-Iavein, historian Ekaterina Shchepkina, political activist Ekaterina Kuskova, historian and zemstvo statistician Aleksandra Efimenko, and Aleksandra Kalmykova, a supporter of "legal Marxism."

Mariia Chekhova and her husband remained in Russia after the Bolshevik Revolution. Nikolai Chekhov became a prominent Soviet educator. With feminist organizations banned, Mariia Chekhova devoted herself to educational activity and to writing of her memoirs, which were never published but can be found in the Moscow City Historical Archive. Chekhova died in 1934, her significance as a feminist pioneer consigned by the Soviets to the dustbin of history.

Cross-references: First All-Russian Women's Congress (1908), *Liga ravnopraviia zhenshchin* (League for Women's Equal Rights), Russian Women's Mutual Philanthropic Society *(Russkoe zhenskoe vzaimno-blagotvoritel'noe obshchestvo), Soiuz ravnopraviia zhenshchin* (Women's Equal Rights Union), *Soiuz zhenshchin* (Union of Women).

Suggested Readings

Ariian, Praskov'ia N. "M. A. Chekhova." *Pervyi zhenskii kalendar' na 1912 god* (The First Women's Calendar). St. Petersburg: 1912, 8–11.

Edmondson, Linda Harriet. *Feminism in Russia, 1900–1917*. Stanford, CA: Stanford University Press, 1984.

Goldberg, Rochelle (Ruthchild). "The Russian Women's Movement 1859–1917." Ph.D. Diss., University of Rochester, 1976.

Grishina, Zoia V. "*Dvizhenie za politicheskoe ravnopravie zhenshchin v gody pervoi Rossiiskoi revoliutsii*" (The Movement for Women's Political Equal Rights in the Years of the First Russian Revolution). *Vestnik Moskovskogo universiteta (Moscow University Herald*). Ser. 8 *Istoriia (History)*, no. 2 (1982): 33–42.

Grishina, Zoia V. "*Zhenskie organizatsii v Rossii (1905 g.-fevral'/mart 1917 g)*" (Women's Organizations in Russia [1905–1917]. *Kandidat* Diss., Moscow State University, 1978.

Mirovich, N. (Z. S. Ivanova). *Iz istorii zhenskago dvizheniia v Rossii (From the History of the Women's Movement in Russia)*. Moscow: Tipografia T-va. I. D. Sytina, 1908.

Soiuz zhenshchin (Union of Women) journal. St. Petersburg, 1907–1909.

Stites, Richard. *The Women's Liberation Movement in Russia: Feminism, Nihilism, and Bolshevism, 1860–1930*. Princeton, NJ: Princeton University Press, 1978, 1991.

Rochelle Goldberg Ruthchild

D

Davydova, Aleksandra Arkad'evna (1849–1902)

Beginning in the late 1880s, the literary salon of Aleksandra Arkad'evna Davydova provided a gathering place for many of the literary figures of the day. Especially important for Russian women's history, Davydova's salon provided an atmosphere that welcomed and encouraged women to take on significant roles as publishers and writers.

Born into a noble family in 1849, Aleksandra Arkad'evna Gorzhanskaia in her early life followed a full, yet predictable, path for someone of her social origins. Aleksandra was well educated, earning the certificate of "domestic teacher" at the end of her schooling. She married the famous cellist and conservatory director Karl Iul'evich Davydov and, as a result, was well known in St. Petersburg high society. In the mid-1880s Davydova began to take an interest in the publishing world and became the secretary of the journal *Severnyi vestnik (Northern Herald)*; the journal was published by Anna Mikhailovna Evreinova, who was Russia's first female to hold a law degree, which she earned at the University of Leipzig. By the late 1880s Davydova began to host meetings and discussions, which attracted literary figures such as Nikolai Konstantinovich Mikhailovskii, Gleb Ivanovich Uspenskii, Dmitrii Sergeevich Merezhkovskii, Nikolai Minskii (pseudonym of Nikolai Maksimovich Vilenkin), Iuliia Bezrodnaia (pseudonym of Iuliia Ivanovna Iakovleva), and A. I. Volynskii (pseudonym of Akim Lvovich Flekser). The relationships fostered at this salon proved to be among the more important literary connections for the 1890s. The salon provided aspiring writers and publishers a place to meet and discuss ideas with some of the established literary voices of the period. Davydova, for example, developed a very close relationship with Mikhailovskii, who had worked on *Severnyi vestnik* and who encouraged Davydova in her desire to found a journal. In 1892 she began *Mir Bozhii (God's World)* as a children's journal and asked well-known pedagogue Victor Petrovich Ostrogorskii to join as the editor. Letters from Davydova to Ostrogorskii reveal the fact that she was not content simply to cover the financial and business aspects of the journal. Although she never attempted to become a writer, Davydova insisted on playing a significant role in the editorial decisions of the publication. She was overwhelmingly concerned with the journal and applied herself to tasks, such as the study of English, that she felt would improve her ability to work at a literary enterprise. Davydova's vision of publishing as an appropriate and useful role for women can be seen in her insistence that Ostrogorskii take her ideas seriously. The editor nearly abandoned the venture over the issue of editorial control.

Davydova's encouragement of women in publishing extended to her own family. Her daughter Lidiia worked diligently for *Mir Bozhii*, serving as a correspondent to the 1899 International Women's Congress in London, among other activities. Davydova's younger, adopted daughter, Maria, married the famous literary figure Aleksandr Ivanovich Kuprin, who worked on *Mir Bozhii*, as well as its successor, *Sovremennyi mir (Contemporary World).*

Not only was the idea for *Mir Bozhii* born in Davydova's salon, but Mikhailovskii's plan to begin a new literary journal also evolved in this setting. That dream was realized in 1892 with the founding of *Russkoe bogatstvo (Russian Wealth).* In addition, at these literary evenings Davydova introduced Liubov' Gurevich to Volynskii and other key figures in the production of the *Severnyi vestnik.* Gurevich developed a vision to support her own writing and that of others through a publishing undertaking. She became a shareholder of *Severnyi vestnik* in 1891 and published it until the journal's demise in 1898. Her relationship with Volynskii continued through the work of *Severnyi vestnik* as he increasingly controlled the journal's editorial policies. *Severnyi vestnik* served as an important early publisher of symbolist writers.

Besides being instrumental in the formation of three major journals of the 1890s, Davydova's salon helped to integrate aspiring writers, both male and female, with the noted literati of the day. Although women writers and publishers of the 1890s had not yet begun to reach full acceptance by their male counterparts, the Davydova circle nonetheless encouraged the significant involvement of women in periodical publishing of this period.

Cross-reference: Women's Periodical Publishing in Late Imperial Russia (1860–1905).

Suggested Readings

Gurevich, Liubov'. "*Istoria 'Severnogo vestnika'* " (The History of *Severnyi vestnik*). In *Russkaia literature XX veka, 1890–1910 (Russian Literature of the Twentieth Century, 1890–1910)*, edited by S. A. Vengerov, 235–264. Moscow: T-va "Mir," 1914.

Gurevich, Liubov'. "Liubov Iakovlevich Gurevich." In *Pervye literaturnye shagi (First Literary Steps)*, edited by F. F. Fidler, 181–198. Moscow: Literary fond, 1911.

Kuprina-Iordanskaia, M. *Gody molodosti (Years of Youth)*. Moscow: Khudozhestvennaia literatura, 1966.

Pimenova, Emiliia Kirillovna. *Dni minuvshie (Days of the Past)*. Leningrad, 1929.
Volynskii, A. "*Russkie zhenshchiny* [L. Ia. Gurevich]" (Russian Women [L. Ia. Gurevich]). *Zhizn' isskustva (Life of Art)*, 6 (1924): 17–19.

Rhonda Clark

Decembrist Women in Siberia in the 1830s–1850s

Although much has been written about the *Dekabristy* (Decembrists), the men of noble birth who revolted against the autocracy of Nicholas I in 1825, much less is known about the significant role that the Decembrist women played in Siberia in the aftermath of their husbands' unsuccessful revolution and exile.

A rich literature has been devoted to the *Dekabristy* (Decembrists), those men of noble birth who in December 1825 revolted against Tsar Nicholas I's autocracy and sought the establishment of a constitutional monarchy and the abolition of serfdom. Although the young officers failed, they became heroes in the eyes of Russians committed to reform and even won fame abroad. While their political trial resulted in several death sentences, most of the young men received sentences of lifelong banishment to Siberia. Many of the wives and sisters of these conspirators voluntarily accompanied their loved ones into Siberian exile. In contrast to the men, the Decembrist women have received little attention from historians, perhaps because, unlike the later female activists in the *narodnichestvo* (populism) and anarchist movements, they stood in the shadow of their husbands and brothers as apolitical figures who lacked political consciousness or a political program.

The Decembrist men had not shared their political plans with their wives. Aristocratic society in European Russia had clearly demarcated spheres for men and women, with political discussion and participation as a male prerogative. Ironically, exile in remote Siberia offered the Decembrist women a form of emancipation, an opportunity to step into the gap that their husbands had vacated. In her memoirs the most prominent of these women, Mariia Volkonskaia, told how she became aware of the immense sacrifices that she and others would have to make in the struggle for her country's liberty and how a feeling of great pride came over her.

Volkonskaia and other Decembrist women worked arduously to carry out reforms and struggle against the tsarist bureaucracy. While their activities frequently received praise as a form of altruism appropriate to the traditional role of women, it should be pointed out that these women broke with their former passive role and escaped from the "Golden Cage" associated with the lifestyle of aristocratic women. They lost titles, privileges, civil rights, and finally the right to see their children, left behind in European Russia.

Volkonskaia characterized Siberia as a descent to "total darkness" and was determined to promote reforms. The Decembrist women pushed for the improvement of conditions in Siberian prisons and in Siberia as a whole: the first hospitals, orphanages, and primary schools were established, for European settlers as well as for the indigenous peoples of Siberia. The wives of merchants, especially those in the cities, were encouraged to participate. The isolated wives of political criminals became the core of social life in Siberia. Thanks to their ideas and funds, Irkutsk received a theater and a concert hall, and the city of Chita acquired an Academy of Sciences. Lectures, open for men and women, were given on natural sciences, history, and literature. The birth of the Siberian intelligentsia took place.

The women never boasted of their heroic deeds and have suffered from oblivion and neglect at the hands of historians. Nonetheless, later female activists like Vera Figner regarded the Decembrist women as a shining example of the awakening of women's consciousness and the redefining of women's role in Russian society. Decades later, in the 1890s and, above all, in 1905, the year of the first Russian Revolution, the autocracy banished women to Siberia. In contrast to the Decembrist women, the new exiles—Maria Spiridonova, Fania Kaplan, Anastasiia Bizenko, Irina Kachovskaia—sought to overthrow the hated autocracy through terrorism rather than reform.

Cross-references: Vera Figner, Mariia Volkonskaia.

Suggested Readings

Figner, Vera Nikolaevna. *Zhëny dekabristov (The Wives of the Decembrists).* Moscow: *Izdatel'stvo vsesoiuznogo obshchestva Politkatorzhan i Ss.-poselentsev*, 1925.

Mazour, Anatole Gregory. *Women in Exile: Wives of the Decembrists.* Tallahassee, FL: Diplomatic Press, 1975.

Sutherland, Catherine. *The Princess of Siberia: The Story of Maria Volkonsky and the Decembrist Exiles.* New York: Farrar, Straus, Giroux, 1984.

Volkonskaia, Mariia. *Pis'ma kniagini Marii N. Volkonskoi iz Sibiri, 1827–1831gg (Princess Maria N. Volkonskaia's Letters from Siberia, 1827–1831).* Moscow: Izdanie Sabashnikovykh, 1915.

Volkonskaia, Mariia. *Zapiski (Memoirs).* St. Petersburg: Izdatel'stvo Benke, 1906.

Eva-Maria Stolberg

F

Figner, Vera Nikolaevna (1852–1942)

Prominent populist, revolutionary, and memoirist who was recognized by her comrades as an ethical touchstone and by the next generation as a role model and who was co-opted by the Bolsheviks as a revolutionary icon. Her memoirs are one of the most valuable sources about the revolutionary movement in Russia.

Born on July 7, 1852, into an old, aristocratic family in Kazan province, Vera Figner was the eldest of six children (four girls, two boys), of whom three became staunch revolutionaries as young women. Her father, a state forester, was a strong-tempered disciplinarian, while her mother, fifteen years his junior, was a meek, religious woman. A peasant nanny, later idealized by Figner, played an important role in raising the children. Figner was tutored at home before studying at the Rodionovskii Institute for Young Noble Ladies in Kazan. She broadened its narrow education by reading widely, and from Nikolai Alekseevich Nekrasov, Russia's leading civic poet, she adopted a motto that became the basis of her personal creed: "match your deeds to your words." As she became more aware of the reality of peasant lives, Figner sought a way to ameliorate their suffering and decided on medicine, but her father refused to let her go abroad to study. After marrying Aleksei Filippov in 1870, Figner convinced him to give up his judicial career and accompany her to Zurich. Soon after beginning her medical studies there in 1872, she joined a women's group that later became the Frichi Circle, whose members avidly read socialist literature and discussed social problems. The group quickly became a revolutionary organization for propagating socialist ideas. When the tsarist government, alarmed by rising revolutionary propaganda, barred further study in Zurich, Figner decided to study in Berne, leaving her apolitical husband behind.

In 1875 Figner had to make a difficult decision: whether to continue her studies or return to Russia, where recent arrests had decimated populist groups. She decided to give up her dream of becoming a doctor for the greater goal of socialism, which she could spread while working as a *fel'dsher* (medical assistant). At first assigned to organizational work, in the spring of 1877 Figner began working as a *fel'dsher* in Samara. Like most populists she had never truly seen "the people" and began to question whether one could propagandize people living in such wretched conditions. She persevered, and after her work was cut short by a wave of police arrests in the fall, she moved to Saratov. With her sister Evgeniia she organized a school for peasant children and evening readings for parents.

After police suspicions again curtailed her work in the spring of 1879, Figner became receptive to active revolutionary operations. When the *Zemlia i volia* (Land and Freedom) organization splintered in June 1879, she joined its terrorist faction, *Narodnaia volia* (the People's Will), which advocated political terror rather than peaceful propaganda. Strongly opposed to secret societies, Figner at first resisted joining its Executive Committee, the closed, decision-making body. Once it was decided to execute Alexander II, she dedicated her life to this goal. After the tsar's assassination on March 1, 1881, most Executive Committee members were arrested or fled abroad. As the sole remaining member, Figner felt a duty to her comrades and to the new generation of revolutionaries and zealously attempted to revive *Narodnaia volia*. Betrayed by one of her former coconspirators, she was arrested on February 10, 1883.

During her almost two-year imprisonment in the Petropavlovsk Fortress in St. Petersburg, Figner wrote her confessions, which she used when she was the center of attention at the Trial of the 14, involving members of *Narodnaia volia*. More importantly, this document was preserved in the prison archives and in the 1920s was used as the basis for the first volume of her memoirs, one of the most complete accounts of the revolutionary movement of the 1870s and early 1880s. Figner's death sentence was commuted to life imprisonment in Schlusselburg Fortress, the dreaded tsarist prison near St. Petersburg. Her twenty years in the island prison, where she relieved oppression by writing poetry, are related in *Kogda chasy zhizni ostanovilis' (When the Clock of Life Stopped)*, the second part of her three-volume memoirs. After her unexpected release in 1904, Figner began the life chronicled in her third volume, *Posle Shlussel'burga (After Schlusselburg)*.

In 1905 Figner began publishing articles to educate the masses about the important issues of the day and used unsolicited funds sent by well-wishers to work among "the people," one of whom burned down her ancestral home in 1906. With her nerves shattered and still subjected to repression and harassment by the authorities, she went into voluntary exile in Europe in 1907. She devoted herself to the revolutionary movement of the 1870s, memorializing in numerous articles and collections the revolutionaries' ideals and their struggle against despotism. She also committed herself to helping all Russian political fighters, founding the Committee to Help Russia's Political Prisoners, writing brochures about them, and raising funds by lecturing.

Figner returned to Russia in February 1915 and, after receiving full freedom of movement at the end of 1916, immediately went to Petrograd, where she witnessed the developments of 1917. She gave moral support to feminist organizations and on March 20, 1917, rode at the head of one of the largest mass rallies ever staged in Russia. But she did not become an active feminist; she continued to focus her energy on helping and commemorating old comrades and political prisoners. Although she later served in minor positions, she was disappointed in the revolution's results and did not join the Russian Communist Party/Bolsheviks (RKP/B) after the November Revolution.

Unlike many of her former comrades, Figner did not emigrate; she felt compelled to share the people's fate and to work on their behalf through education and personal charity. Some felt that she betrayed her ideals by not emigrating and/or actively opposing the government. The Soviet government, moreover, capitalized on her presence and distorted her image, leading many to believe that she was a Communist. Figner herself did not give up her guiding principles and in 1932 publicly and forcefully refused to join a Soviet society of political prisoners because it did not denounce the trials in which innocent people were being convicted and killed. She continued to inspire the young, one of whom, Zoia Rukhadze, invoked her name as she faced a German firing squad during World War II. When the Germans threatened Moscow in 1941, Figner refused evacuation, telling the authorities to worry about the living. She died the next year, at the age of ninety, and was buried with honor at Novodevichii Cemetery in Moscow. Her three-volume memoirs remain as her legacy and are one of the most important documents about the Russian revolutionary movement of the second half of the nineteenth century.

Cross-references: Higher Education for Women, Sof'ia Perovskaia, Women's Medical Courses.

Suggested Readings

Broido, Vera. *Apostles into Terrorists: Women and the Revolutionary Movement in the Russia of Alexander II*. New York: Viking, 1977.

Engel, Barbara Alpern, and Clifford Rosenthal, eds. and trans. *Five Sisters: Women against the Tsar*. New York: Knopf, 1975.

Figner, Vera Nikolaevna. *Memoirs of a Revolutionist*. 1927. Introduction by Richard Stites. DeKalb: Northern Illinois University Press, 1991.

Figner, Vera Nikolaevna. *Polnoe sobranie sochinenii v shesti tomakh (Complete Collected Works in Six Volumes)*. Moscow: Izdatel'stvo vsesoiuznogo obshchestva politkatorzhan i ssyl'no-poselentsev, 1932.

Figner, Vera Nikolaevna. *Vospominaniia* (Memoirs). Moscow: Izdatel'stvo sotsial'no ekonomicheskoi literatury *'Mysl'*, 1964.

Pavliuchenko, E. A. *Vera Figner*. Moscow: Gosudarstvennoe uchebno-pedagogicheskoe izdatel'stvo ministerstva prosveshcheniia RSFSR, 1963.

Klawa N. Thresher

Filosofova, Anna Pavlovna (1835–1912)

A pioneer feminist activist and a driving force behind the establishment of the first Russian Higher Courses for Women, the Bestuzhev Courses, shelters for abused and abandoned women and children, the *Russkoe zhenskoe vzaimno-blagotvoritel'noe obshchestvo* (Russian Women's Mutual Philanthropic Society), and other major prerevolutionary Russian feminist initiatives, such as the 1908 First All-Russian Women's Congress.

Born to an old Moscow aristocratic family, Anna Diaghileva was the eldest daughter among nine children and was educated at home. At age eighteen, she married Vladimir Filosofov, seventeen years her senior and on his way to a high-ranking bureaucratic career. Between 1858 and 1872, Filosofova had at least six children, several miscarriages, and possibly one or two stillbirths.

Childbearing did not seem to affect Filosofova's health, and her financial resources made it possible to employ servants to care for her children. One year after the birth of her first child, Filosofova, rejecting the life of a society "butterfly," met Mariia Trubnikova at the latter's salon. The two, together with Nadezhda Stasova, formed a "triumvirate" responsible for many of the early Russian feminist efforts in charity and education.

Among their projects were the *Obshchestvo dostavlenniia deshëvykh kvartir i drugikh posobii nuzhdaiushchimsia zhiteliam S-Peterburga* (Society for Cheap Lodging and Other Aid to the Needy Residents of St. Petersburg), which gave shelter to abused and abandoned women. As President of the Society for most of the years between 1859 and 1879, Filosofova led the development of its services to include a school, dormitories, cafeterias, a child-care center, and a store; her fund-raising efforts greatly increased the organization's budget and resources. Committed to projects aimed at economic self-sufficiency for women, she supported radical efforts to remake society; she was a charter member of the women's publishing artel. Filosofova supported Peter Lavrov's short-lived *Obshchestvo zhenskogo truda* (Society for Women's Work), which could not survive the conflicts between the "aristocrats" and "nihilists" in its membership. She was also rumored to have helped the anarchist Peter Kropotkin to escape his Russian jail and go into exile.

Filosofova was best known for her efforts on behalf of higher education for women. She tirelessly lobbied tsarist officials to approve the establishment of the Bestuzhev and other women's courses and then headed up fund-raising for the Bestuzhev Courses. She continued to campaign against those who, fearing female radicalism, sought to shut down the courses.

Filosofova was a founding member of the *Russkoe zhenskoe vzaimno-blagotvoritel'noe obshchestvo* (Russian Women's Mutual Philanthropic Society), which was modeled on U.S. women's clubs. She, along with Mutual Philanthropic Society President Dr. Anna Shabanova, was among the chief organizers of the 1908 All-Russian Women's Congress. An honorary Vice President of the International Council of Women, her dream, to join Russian feminists in a National Council of Women, was defeated at the 1908 Congress. Filosofova remained active until her death at age seventy-seven in 1912.

Cross-references: First All-Russian Women's Congress (1908), Higher Education for Women, Russian Women's Mutual Philanthropic Society *(Russkoe zhenskoe vzaimno-blagotvoritel'noe obshchestvo)*, Anna Shabanova, Nadezhda Stasova, Mariia Trubnikova.

Suggested Readings

Dudgeon, Ruth Arlene Fluck. "Women and Higher Education in Russia, 1855–1905." Ph.D. Diss., George Washington University, 1975.

Edmondson, Linda Harriet. *Feminism in Russia, 1900–1917.* Stanford, CA: Stanford University Press, 1984.

Goldberg, Rochelle. "The Russian Women's Movement 1859–1917." Ph.D. Diss., University of Rochester, 1976.

Johanson, Christine. *Women's Struggle for Higher Education in Russia 1855–1900.* Kingston and Montreal: McGill-Queen's University Press, 1987.

Sbornik pamiati Anny Pavlovny Filosofovoi (Collected Memoirs of Anna Pavlovna Filosofova). Vol. 1: A. V. Tyrkova, *Anna Pavlovna Filosofova i eia vremia (Anna Pavlovna Filosofova and Her Times*) Petrograd: M. O. Vol'f, 1915. *Vol. 2: Stat'i i materialy (Articles and Materials).* Petrograd: P. Golike and A. Vil'borg, 1915.

Shabanova, Anna. *Ocherk zhenskogo dvizheniia v Rossii (Essay on the Women's Movement in Russia).* St. Petersburg: *Prosveshchenie*, 1912.

Stites, Richard. *The Women's Liberation Movement in Russia: Feminism, Nihilism and Bolshevism, 1860–1930.* Princeton, NJ: Princeton University Press, 1978, 1991.

Valk, S. N., et al., eds. *Sankt-Peterburgskie visshie zhenshie (Bestuzhevskie) kursy (1878–1910): Sbornik statei (The St. Petersburg Higher (Bestuzhev) Courses [1878–1919]: A Collection of Essays).* Leningrad: Leningrad University Press, 1965.

Rochelle Goldberg Ruthchild

First All-Russian Women's Congress (December 10–16, 1908)

A congress organized by Russian feminists to publicize the plight of Russian women, lobby for equal rights, and unify the movement. Under the watchful gaze of police censors, the Congress sessions showcased a wide range of perspectives and information about Russian women, but socialist opposition ultimately thwarted the drive to create a national women's council.

The idea for the congress originated with Dr. Anna Shabanova, head of the *Russkoe zhenskoe vzaimno-blagotvoritel'noe obshchestvo* (Russian Women's Mutual Philanthropic Society). After much negotiation with tsarist officials, the gathering was scheduled for June 1905, but the 1905 Revolution and subsequent government repression delayed it until 1908. The final Congress Organizing Committee reflected the spectrum of feminist groups, including representatives from the Mutual Philanthropic Society (Shabanova, Anna Filosofova, Olga Shapir, Evgeniia Chebysheva-Dmitrievna, and Evgeniia Avilova), *Soiuz ravnopraviia zhenshchin* (Women's Equal Rights Union) activists Liudmila von Ruttsen, Mariia Chekhova, Ekaterina Shchepkina, and Mariia Blandova, and Dr. Mariia Pokrovskaia from the *Zhenskaia progressivnaia partiia* (Women's Progressive Party).

Of the 1,053 women and a few men who registered for the Congress, held in the St. Petersburg City Hall, the vast majority came from the tsarist capital.

There were a small group from Moscow, smaller groups from provincial cities, largely from Ukraine, and one delegate, Ekaterina Vasilievna Bakunina, from the United States. Participants reflected the urban social spectrum, including society ladies and women workers, but the largest number were *intelligentki*, educated women students and professionals, especially doctors and teachers.

The workers' group included unaffiliated trade union activists as well as members of the socialist parties. Many responded favorably to the opportunity to publicize their plight; the group prepared ten talks for the Congress and vowed to attend the entire event. Aleksandra Kollontai, then a Menshevik, worked tirelessly to ensure workers' group participation but was able to attend only half of the Congress before fleeing abroad to avoid arrest. Despite some efforts by the organizers, no peasant women attended.

The program was divided into four main sections, the first on enlightenment (*prosvetitel'nyi*) and philanthropy, the second on the economy and ethics in the family and society, the third on women's political and civil situation, and the fourth on women's education. The meeting format was uniform, consisting of the presentation of papers, discussion, and voting on resolutions. Topics included temperance, coeducation, women's culture, women workers, free love, feminism in other countries, motherhood, prostitution, the applicability of the Pankhursts' militant suffrage tactics to Russia, women's moral superiority, peasants, domestic servants, women's consciousness, and the political structure. Meeting attendance was restricted to Congress registrants. Long lines of police stationed themselves at the entrances to the meeting halls. In the sessions, police censors throttled comments about the Orthodox Church, Stolypin's policies, or other critiques of the tsarist regime. Nevertheless, the Congress sessions involved a great deal of wide-ranging debate. The discussions about the final resolutions for the Congress revealed deep divisions among the delegates. The goal, especially dear to Filosofova, of creating a National Council of Russian Women that would affiliate with the International Council of Women, was not realized; workers' group representatives objected to even symbolic unification of women across classes. The fear of government reaction led Congress planners to offer a watered-down resolution on voting rights, endorsing limited suffrage. This prompted a walkout by the workers' group.

The Congress did not achieve its goal of uniting the women's movement, nor did it revitalize women's organizations. The *Soiuz ravnopraviia zhenshchin* (Women's Equal Rights Union) was moribund by the time of the conference; other groups remained small. Nevertheless, it drew attention to women's issues, and the Congress proceedings provide a comprehensive portrait of the multiplicity of the movement, chief feminist concerns, and conflicts of the time.

Feminism has often united its enemies across the political spectrum. In the post-Soviet period, feminism has been derided by communists as bourgeois and by capitalists and ultranationalists as a Soviet relic. Nevertheless, feminist activists, seeking to reclaim their history and heritage in post-Soviet Russia, commemorated the ninetieth anniversary of the 1908 Congress with a conference in

Moscow on December 9–10, 1998, featuring lectures about the history and current context of the Russian women's movement. A book entitled *Zhenskoe dvizhenie v kontekste rossiiskoi istorii (The Women's Movement in the Context of Russian History)* was published in 1999, featuring the presentations at the conference.

Cross-references: Mariia Chekhova, Anna Filosofova, Aleksandra Kollontai, *Liga ravnopraviia zhenshchin* (League for Women's Equal Rights), Mariia Pokrovskaia, Russian Women's Mutual Philanthropic Society (*Russkoe zhenskoe vzaimno-blagotvoritel'noe obshchestvo*), Anna Shabanova, Olga Shapir, Liudmila von Ruttsen, *Soiuz ravnopraviia zhenshchin* (Women's Equal Rights Union), (*Zhenskaia progressivnaia partiia*) (Women's Progressive Party).

Suggested Readings

Barybina, T., et al., eds. *Zhenskoe dvizhenie v kontekste rossiiskoi istorii (The Women's Movement in the Context of Russian History).* Moscow: Izd. "Eslan," 1999.

Edmondson, Linda Harriet. *Feminism in Russia, 1900–1917.* Stanford, CA: Stanford University Press, 1984.

Edmondson, Linda Harriet. "Russian Feminists and the First All-Russian Congress of Women." *Russian History* 3 (1976), Part II: 123–149.

Goldberg, Rochelle (Ruthchild). "The Russian Women's Movement 1859–1917." Ph.D. Diss., University of Rochester, 1976.

Grishina, Zoia V. *"Dvizhenie za politicheskoe ravnopravie zhenshchin v gody pervoi Rossiiskoi revoliutsii"* (The Movement for Women's Political Equal Rights in the Years of the First Russian Revolution). *Vestnik Moskovskogo universiteta (Moscow University Herald).* Ser. 8 *Istoriia (History)*, no. 2 (1982): 33–42.

Grishina, Zoia V. *"Zhenskie organizatsii v Rossii, 1905 g.-fevral'/mart 1917 g"* (Women's Organizations in Russia, 1905–February/March 1917). *Kandidat's* Diss., Moscow State University, 1978.

Kal'manovich, A. A. *Pretenzii k zhenskomu dvizheniiu voobshche i k pervomu vserossiiskomu zhenskomu s"ezdu v chastnosti. Neskol'ko slov o knige g-zhi Kollontai: Sotsial'nie osnovy zhenskago [sic] voprosa (The Aspersions of the Women's Movement in General and of the First All-Russian Women's Congress in Particular: A Few Words on Kollontai's Book: The Social Bases of the Woman Question.* St. Petersburg, 1910.

Kollontai, A. M. *Selected Writings.* With introduction and commentaries by Alix Holt. New York: Norton, 1977.

Kollontai, A. M. *Sotsial'nie osnovy zhenskogo voprosa (Social Bases of the Woman Question).* St. Petersburg: *Znanie*, 1909.

Kollontai, A. M. "*Zhenshchina-rabotnitsa na pervom feministkom kongresse v Rossii*" (The Woman Worker at the First Feminist Congress in Russia). *Golos sotsial-demokrata (The Voice of the Social-Democrat)* 12 (March 1909): 6–7.

Kuskova, E. D. "*Zhenskii vopros i zhenskii s"ezd*" (The Woman Question and the Women's Congress). *Obrazovanie (Education)* (January–February 1909): 33–43, 74–99.

Mirovich, N. "*Pervyi vserossiiskii zhenskii s"ezd*" (First All-Russian Women's Congress). *Vestnik Evropy (The Herald of Europe)* (January 1909): 411–415.

Sbornik pamiati Anny Pavlovny Filosofovoi (Collected Memoirs of Anna Pavlovna Filosofova). Vol. 1: A. V. Tyrkova, *Anna Pavlovna Filosofova i eia vremia (Anna*

Pavlovna Filosofova and Her Times). Petrograd: M. O. Vol'f, 1915. *Vol. 2: Stat'i i materialy (Articles and Materials)*. Petrograd: P. Golike and A. Vil'borg, 1915.

Shabanova, Anna. *Ocherk zhenskogo dvizheniia v Rossii (Essay on the Women's Movement in Russia)*. St. Petersburg: Prosveshchenie, 1912.

Stites, Richard. *The Women's Liberation Movement in Russia: Feminism, Nihilism, and Bolshevism, 1860–1930*. Princeton, NJ: Princeton University Press, 1978, 1991.

Trudy pervogo vserossiiskogo zhenskogo s"ezda pri Russkom zhenskom obshchestve v Sankt-Peterburge 10–16 Dekabria, 1908 (Proceedings of the First All-Russian Woman's Congress of the Russian Women's Society in St. Petersburg, 10–16 December 1908). St. Petersburg, 1909.

Tyrkova, A. V. "Pervyi zhenskii s"ezd" (First Women's Congress). *Zarnitsy: Literaturno-politicheskii sbornik*, no. 2 (1909): 172–209.

"Women's Congress of 1908." In *The Modern Encyclopedia of Russian and Soviet History*, edited by Joseph Wieczynski, vol. 44, 30–31. Gulf Breeze, FL: Academic International Press, 1987.

Zhenskoe dvizhenie v kontekste rossiiskoi istorii (The Women's Movement in the Context of Russian History). Moscow: Izd. "Eslan," 1999.

Rochelle Goldberg Ruthchild

H

Herzen, Natal'ia Alexandrovna (born Zakharina) (1817–1852)

The wife of Alexander Herzen; a member of the intelligentsia generation of the 1840s and a follower of George Sand.

Born in 1817, Natal'ia Alexandrovna Herzen (born Zakharina) was a member of the Russian intelligentsia generation of the 1840s and the wife of Alexander Herzen. The illegitimate daughter of wealthy landlord Alexander Iakovlev, Natal'ia spent her first seven years living among dozens of half siblings, who were, like herself, the children of her father and numerous serf women on the estate. When the old patriarch died in 1824, his wealthy, childless sister, Princess Mariia Khovanskaia, chose to take Natal'ia as her ward. In her childhood reminiscences, Natal'ia describes her childhood in her aunt's Orthodox home as loveless, isolated, and bitter. Her friendship-turned-romance with her cousin Alexander Herzen brought Natal'ia relief from the loneliness and misery of her aunt's house.

The friendship between Natal'ia and Alexander blossomed into a passionate romance during their several-year correspondence. Despite the objections of their families, the two cousins eloped in May 1838. Their first year of marriage was spent in Vladimir, Russia, where Alexander was serving a sentence of internal exile for his Polish sympathies. During their first year of happy marriage, Alexander found himself influenced by Natal'ia's religious faith, and love for his wife inspired Alexander with a deep faith in, and love of, God. Natal'ia loved her husband, and they shared a passionate connection, at once religious and physical. Once they returned to Moscow the following year, the marital spell was broken, and tensions mounted. Over the course of their fourteen-year marriage, Natal'ia bore two children, who lived until adulthood, and a deaf-mute son, who tragically drowned in a boating accident while still a child.

Natal'ia Herzen was a member of a generation of Russian intellectuals who embraced the theories of George Sand's cult of love and sought to emulate Sand's ideas in their own lives. Influenced by Sand's philosophies of love, sexual passion, and marital fidelity, many Russian intellectuals of the 1840s asked themselves the same question on the subject of fidelity that the hero of Sand's novel *Jacques* asked: Why was it considered sinful to betray one's own heart? They answered that it was not a sin. On the contrary, they believed that love—whether marital or extramarital, romantic or carnal—was a higher calling not to be ignored. Like many in her generation, therefore, Natal'ia Herzen attempted to find fulfillment and self-realization through passionate connections outside her marriage. Natal'ia's romantic friendship with Natal'ia Tuchkova, whom she met in Italy in 1848 while the Herzens were living in Europe, illustrates her embracing of these ideals. Natal'ia Tuchkova, the eighteen-year-old daughter of a landowner from Penza (and future wife of Alexander Herzen's childhood friend Nicholas Ogarev) was traveling with her family in Europe when they met the Herzen family. During the next few months in Italy and France, the two Natal'ias grew very close and rhapsodized over their feelings for each other. In their correspondences, the two women declared their love and devotion to one another; calling each other by pet names (Natal'ia Herzen's affectionate name for her friend was Consuelo, after a heroine in one of Sand's novels) and signing letters with exclamations of love.

Their romantic friendship, however, faded into the background when Natal'ia Herzen embarked on a carnal love affair with German Romantic poet and close family friend Georg Herwegh. The happiness of the triangular friendship of Alexander, Natal'ia, and Georg Herwegh did not last long. Natal'ia and Herwegh carried on a yearlong love affair, sanctioned by the philosophies of Sand and kept secret from Alexander. When Alexander accidentally discovered the liaison, husband and wife eventually reconciled. Natal'ia was sickly and weak from worry and numerous stillborn births and died soon after in 1852. The tragic life story of Natal'ia Herzen illustrates the difficulties facing women of her generation who, with few outlets for political and social emancipation, attempted to free themselves through exalted romantic and sexual liaisons.

Cross-reference: The Decembrist Women.

Suggested Readings

Carr, Edward Hallett. *The Romantic Exiles: A Nineteenth-Century Portrait Gallery*. Cambridge: MIT Press, 1981.

Engel, Barbara Alpern. *Mothers and Daughters: Women of the Intelligentsia in Nineteenth-Century Russia*. Cambridge: Cambridge University Press, 1983.

Herzen, Alexander. *My Past and Thoughts: The Memoirs of Alexander Herzen*. Vols. 1–4. London: Chatto and Windus, 1968.

Herzen, Alexander. *Sobranie sochinenii v tridtsati tomakh (Collected Works in Thirty Volumes)*. Moscow: Akademia nauk, 1954–1965.

Malia, Martin. *Alexander Herzen and the Birth of Russian Socialism, 1812–1855*. Cambridge: Harvard University Press, 1961.

Miliukov, Pavel. *Iz istorii russkoi intelligentsii (From the History of the Russian Intelligentsia)*. Hattiesburg, MS: Academic International Press, 1970.

Rebecca Friedman

Higher Education for Women in Nineteenth- and Early Twentieth-Century Russia

The nineteenth-century Russian women's movement involved a lengthy struggle to obtain access to higher education. By 1917 Russian women had largely succeeded in obtaining the right to higher education.

Beginning in the 1860s with efforts first to attend the universities, then, when the university statute of 1863 excluded them, to organize their own educational institutions, women gradually succeeded in creating women's universities and other higher educational institutions and in gaining rights for graduates nearly equal to those of men. By 1913–1914 some 40,000 women were studying in higher educational institutions in Russia, more than in any other country except the United States. Finally, during World War I, women obtained access to the universities, but only to the vacancies not filled by qualified men.

In the 1860s the Russian government rejected petitions from women and their supporters for admission to the universities on equal terms with men, for the establishment of women's divisions within the universities, and for the creation of separate women's universities. In 1872 to stem the flow of Russian women to foreign universities, the government relented and allowed the establishment of higher courses for women in Moscow (Guerrier Courses) and Courses for Learned Midwives (renamed Women's Medical Courses in 1876) in St. Petersburg. Four years later the government announced that courses would be permitted in all the university cities, and courses were established in Kazan in 1876 and in St. Petersburg (Bestuzhev Courses) and Kiev in 1878. Petitions for courses in Kharkov, Odessa, and Warsaw were ignored following a secret government decision in 1879 not to allow more women's courses because of the increased student disturbances and political terrorism.

The original *vysshie zhenskie kursy* (Higher Courses for Women) were not recognized as state higher educational institutions, granted their graduates no rights, and lacked government funding. Organized and run by women and those university professors who supported them, they relied on tuition and public donations for funding and utilized university facilities or those of other educational institutions. Generally, they had two faculties—humanities and natural sciences/mathematics—in which university professors taught the same courses as in the universities.

In the reaction following the assassination of Alexander II in 1881, all the Higher Courses for Women were closed except the Bestuzhev Courses, which were saved by a direct appeal to the tsar but only in a truncated form, which raised questions about their status as a higher educational program. Study of the natural sciences was eliminated, enrollment was sharply limited, the number of Jewish students was restricted, students were required to live in dormitories or at home, and the state now appointed the director, although it continued to refuse to provide funding for the courses.

From the mid-1890s, higher educational opportunities began to expand again for women as the Bestuzhev Courses escaped from many of the restrictions imposed in 1889. The St. Petersburg Women's Medical Institute (a state institution) opened in 1897, Higher Courses for Women reopened in Moscow in 1900, pedagogical institutes for women were established in St. Petersburg and Odessa in 1903, and a women's agricultural institute was established in St. Petersburg in 1904. A few private institutions with specialized curricula were also permitted.

With the revolutionary upheaval of 1905, the universities were granted autonomy. Together with some of the technological institutes, universities opened their doors to women, only to have them closed again in 1908 by order of the Minister of Education. Despite this setback, higher education for women flourished in the period 1905–1914. The program of women's courses expanded, adding the faculties of law, medicine, commerce, and economics to the traditional humanities and natural sciences. The government authorized more than thirty new higher educational institutions for women during that decade. Higher Courses for Women were opened in Kiev, Odessa, and Kazan in 1906, in Kharkov in 1907, in Tiflis and Iuriev in 1908, in Warsaw and Novocherkassk in 1909, and in Tomsk in 1910. The St. Petersburg Women's Polytechnical Institute was organized in 1906. Women's medical institutes were opened in Odessa in 1909 and Kharkov in 1910, and medical faculties were added to the women's courses in Moscow and Kiev. Commercial ventures in higher education for women increased in number and range, but only a very few attempted a full university program. Two major public coeducational institutions opened their doors: the Psycho-Neurological Institute in St. Petersburg and the Shaniavskii Municipal University in Moscow. The Commercial Institutes authorized in 1906 by the Ministry of Trade and Industry were also coeducational. With expansion in the number and range of institutions, the number of women enrolled increased as well: from 2,500 women students in 1900/1901, to 5,500 in 1904/1905, to 38,000 in 1913/1914.

As the number of Higher Courses for Women increased and as their quality improved, the government was forced to come to terms with the question of the rights to be granted to graduates. This issue had already been settled before 1905 for the graduates of the St. Petersburg Women's Medical and Pedagogical Institutes, who gained rights nearly equal to those of male graduates except for the right to state service and admission to the Table of Ranks. The law of December 19, 1911, defined the terms under which graduates of Higher Courses for Women would be admitted to the state examination, which would entitle them to all the rights and privileges of university graduates except state service and entrance into the Table of Ranks. Women now were given full access to university degrees, and the established women's courses operated as de facto universities, although the state continued to deny them the use of that name.

Cross-reference: Women's Medical Courses.

Suggested Readings

Dudgeon, Ruth A. "Women and Higher Education in Russia, 1855–1905." Ph.D. Diss., George Washington University, 1975.

Johanson, Christine. *Women's Struggle for Higher Education in Russia, 1855–1900.* Kingston and Montreal: McGill-Queens University Press, 1987.

Likhacheva, Elena A. *Materialy dlia istorii zhenskago obrazovanii v Rossii (Materials for the History of Women's Education in Russia).* 2 vols. St. Petersburg: M. M. Stasiulevich, 1899, 1901.

Pervye zhenshchiny-inzhenery (The First Women Engineers). Leningrad: Lenizdat, 1967.

Valk, S. N., ed. *Sankt-Peterburgskie vysshie zhenskie (Bestuzhevskie) kursy, 1878–1918 gg (The St. Petersburg Higher Women's (Bestuzhev) Courses, 1878–1918).* Leningrad: Leningrad University Press, 1973.

Ruth A. Dudgeon

K

Kal'manovich, Anna Andreevna (late nineteenth century–early twentieth century)

A feminist activist from Saratov, Kal'manovich was among the first to speak out publicly for women's equal political rights in the period right before the 1905 Revolution. One of the few Jewish women active in the movement, she steered an independent course between women's rights advocates aligned with liberal or socialist parties and was among the strongest supporters of the militant tactics of the British suffragists, attending a number of international suffrage congresses.

Anna Andreevna Kal'manovich in her public activity moved from philanthropy in the 1890s to radical feminism by the time of the 1905 Revolution in Russia. In 1893 she founded the Saratov Hebrew Society for the Care of the Sick (*Saratovskoe evreiskoe popechitsel'stvo o bol'nikh*), remaining its President until 1904, founded a children's committee, and served as liaison to the local poverty aid society before becoming immersed in feminist work. She gave her first public speech, a report on the 1904 International Woman Suffrage Association (IWSA) Congress originally written for Mariia Pokrovskaia's *Zhenskii vestnik*, in December 1904. In this speech, Kal'manovich displayed key elements of her feminist politics, such as her interest in, and ties to, the international feminist movement, her advocacy of an independent feminism, distinct from male politics, and her proud self-description as a feminist.

Kal'manovich was married to Samuil Eremeevich Kal'manovich, a prominent defense lawyer involved in many of the major political trials up to and during the 1905 Revolution. Barely escaping an attack on their apartment in 1905 by the far-right, anti-Semitic Black Hundreds, the Kal'manoviches fled Saratov and soon after left Russia. The family's two-year exile in Switzerland gave Anna Kal'manovich the opportunity to strengthen her contacts with foreign feminists and develop her talents as a public speaker. She lectured about the women's movement to Russian groups in Geneva, Lausanne, and Zurich and took part in a debate about women's rights organized by professors at the University of Geneva.

Upon her return to Russia, Kal'manovich took part in the *Soiuz ravnopravniia zhenshchin* (Women's Equal Rights Union) meetings, wrote for the leading feminist periodicals (*Soiuz zhenshchin* and *Zhenskii vestnik*), and lectured. Her most notable and controversial lecture was at the 1908 All-Russian Women's Congress. Entitled "*Zhenskoe dvizhenie i otnosheniia partii k nemu*" (The Women's Movement and How the Parties Relate to It), it marked one of the clearest arguments by a Russian feminist for the importance of gender as a separate category of oppression. To Kal'manovich, women, like the proletariat, were an oppressed class and, like any other oppressed group, had to fight for their own liberation. Facing vocal opposition from socialists and liberals, Kal'manovich, citing her husband and sons, decried those who called her a man-hater and declared herself a "patriot for women."

After the 1908 Women's Congress, Kal'manovich and many other Women's Union activists, such as Mariia Chekhova, Zinaida Mirovich, Liudmila Ruttsen, and Ariadna Tyrkova, joined the *Liga ravnopraviia zhenshchin* (League for Women's Equal Rights), continuing their feminist agitation as the democratic hopes kindled by the 1905 Revolution faded farther from view. Kal'manovich spoke at the First All-Russian Congress on the Struggle with Prostitution *(Pervyi Vserossiiskii S"ezda po borbe s torgom zhenshchinami).* She countered both government representatives defending state regulation of prostitution and Marxists claiming that prostitution was an outgrowth of capitalism, arguing for attention to the gender discrimination inherent in this vice and for the abolition of tsarist regulation of prostitution.

During this time Kal'manovich intensified her interest in the militant tactics of English feminists such as the Pankhursts. Her pamphlet *Suffrazhistki i suffrazhetki (Suffragists and Suffragettes)* was published in 1911, and her translation of Christabel Pankhurst's condemnation of men's immorality appeared in 1914. Kal'manovich's fate after the 1917 Bolshevik Revolution is not known.

Cross-references: First All-Russian Women's Congress (1908), *Liga ravnopraviia zhenshchin* (League for Women's Equal Rights), *Soiuz ravnopraviia zhenshchin* (Women's Equal Rights' Union).

Suggested Readings

Edmondson, Linda Harriet. *Feminism in Russia 1900–1917.* Stanford, CA: Stanford University Press, 1984.

Goldberg, Rochelle (Ruthchild). "The Russian Women's Movement 1859–1917." Ph.D. Diss., University of Rochester, 1976.

Grishina, Zoia V. *"Dvizhenie za politicheskoe ravnopravie zhenshchin v gody pervoi Rossiiskoi revoliutsii"* (The Movement for Women's Political Equal Rights in the Years of the First Russian Revolution). *Vestnik Moskovskogo universiteta (Moscow University Herald).* Ser. 8 *Istoriia (History)*, no. 2 (1982): 33–42.

Grishina, Zoia V. *"Zhenskie organizatsii v Rossii, 1905 g.-fevral'/mart 1917 g"* (Women's Organizations in Russia, 1905–February/March 1917). Abstract of a *kandidat*'s Diss., Moscow State University, 1978.

Kal'manovich, Anna Andreevna. *Otchet o zhenskom mezhdunarodnom kongresse 1904g. (Report on the 1904 International Congress).* Saratov: G. K. Shel'gorn, 1905.

Kal'manovich, Anna Andreevna. *Pretenzii k zhenskomu dvizheniiu voobshche i k I-mu Vserossiiskomu zhenskomu s"ezdu v chastnosti (Aspersions on the Women's Movement in General and on the First All-Russian Women's Congress in Particular).* St. Petersburg, 1910.

Kal'manovich, Anna Andreevna. *Suffrazhistki i suffrazhetki (Suffragists and Suffragettes).* St. Petersburg: N.p., 1911.

Kal'manovich, Anna Andreevna. *Zhenskoe dvizhenie i ego zadachi (The Woman's Movement and Its Aims).* St. Petersburg: Rabotnik, 1908.

Kal'manovich, Anna Andreevna. *Zhenskoe dvizhenie i otnoshenie partii k nemu (The Woman's Movement and the Attitude of the Parties to It).* St. Petersburg: B.M.Vol'f, 1911.

Pankhurst, Christabel. *Strashnyi bich i sredstvo ego unichtozhii (The Great Scourge and How to End It).* Translated by Anna Andreevna Kal'manovich. St. Petersburg: N.p., 1914.

Stites, Richard. *The Women's Liberation Movement in Russia: Feminism, Nihilism, and Bolshevism, 1860–1930.* Princeton, NJ: Princeton University Press, 1978, 1991.

Rochelle Goldberg Ruthchild

L

Lesnevskaia, Antonina Boleslavna (1866–1937)

One of the first Russian women pharmacists, Lesnevskaia contributed to women's education and the professionalization of pharmacy in late imperial Russia. An entrepreneur with considerable political acumen, she exemplified what determined women could achieve before the revolutions of 1917.

Antonina Boleslavna Lesnevskaia was born in the town of Makar'ev, Kostroma province, in 1866, where her maternal grandparents had been exiled after the Polish uprising of 1830–1831. She received her elementary education at the school attached to the Roman Catholic Church of St. Catherine in St. Petersburg and her secondary education in Warsaw. She qualified as a governess in 1886. Bored with teaching and being a governess after only a few years and keen to assist her physician father, Lesnevskaia became a pharmacy apprentice in 1889, the year after pharmacy was opened to women. She passed her assistant pharmacist examination at the Military Medical Academy in St. Petersburg in 1893. After serving in four more pharmacies and taking additional university courses as an extern, she qualified for her Provizor degree in 1898 at the Military Medical Academy. In 1900 Lesnevskaia passed the examination for the *Magistr* (Master's) degree, but there is no record of a thesis.

Lesnevskaia worked well with male pharmacists, who supported her when she applied for permission to open her own pharmacy. The Medical Council of the Ministry of Internal Affairs approved her request with unusual alacrity, waiving the rules, that tied the number of pharmacies to strict population quotas, to allow Lesnevskaia to establish her pharmacy in 1901. Lesnevskaia's *Pervaia zhenskaia apteka* (First Women's Pharmacy) was located in a choice section of St. Petersburg, at #32 Nevskii Prospekt, across the courtyard from St. Catherine's Church. The pharmacy was entirely staffed by women—reputedly the first such pharmacy in the modern world. It had state-of-the-art equipment and attracted international attention.

In 1903 Lesnevskaia established a women's pharmacy school connected to her all-women's pharmacy. As such she not only contributed to women's education but also helped professionalize pharmacy. Some 387 women were trained in Lesnevskaia's school by 1913. Two subsequently received the learned title *Magistr* and became prestigious pharmacologists.

Lesnevskaia was a pharmacist and proprietor above all. She advocated woman's rights and participated in the First All-Russian Women's Congress in 1908. She also sympathized with workers; in her autobiography, she blamed both pharmacy owners and staff pharmacists for the class conflict then rending the pharmacy corporation *(soslovie)*. She defended her business, however, from attacks, whether by male or feminist socialists.

Having established a seven-hour workday and two shifts in her pharmacy, additionally providing lodging, she opposed her workers' strike in the fall of 1905, drafting her students to break the strike. When they refused, she closed her school until September 1906, despite a threatened lawsuit.

Lesnevskaia similarly fought the attempt of the Society for the Preservation of Women's Health, sponsored by noblewoman Princess Ol'denburgskaia and headed by woman physician Volkova, to establish a pharmacy near hers that would dispense medicine free or at a discount to poor women. Lesnevskaia complained to tsarist officials that, since Russian pharmacies were normally required to dispense medicine at government-established prices, the Society's pharmacy would constitute unfair competition. Officials agreed with her and ordered the Society to found their pharmacy elsewhere. The Society's pharmacy failed in a few years due to poor management, vindicating Lesnevskaia's sounder financial principles.

Tsarist officials respected her. In 1914, when tuition did not cover her school's operating costs, Lesnevskaia requested and received funds from the Minister of Finance, Peter Bark. In 1916 the Ministry of Internal Affairs and the Ministry of Education designated her school a higher pharmacy institute.

Soviet authorities also respected her. In 1918, upon Lesnevskaia's petition, Professor S. A. Przhibytek, a member of the Scientific Section of the Pharmacy Commission in the new Soviet Commissariat of Health *(Narkomzdrav)*, and the Commissariat of Public Enlightenment defended her pharmacy and school from nationalization. Nevertheless, they were nationalized in the summer of 1918.

Polish, Catholic, and a contributor to Polish charities, Lesnevskaia was, nevertheless, loyal to the tsarist government. In 1919, after her school and pharmacy were nationalized, she fled to Warsaw, where, to support her mother, siblings, and their families, she opened a pharmacy on one of the main boulevards in 1932. She died in 1937.

Cross-references: First All-Russian Women's Congress (1908), Higher Education for Women, Women Pharmacists in Late Imperial Russia (1871–1917).

Suggested Readings

Broido, Eva. *Memoirs of a Revolutionary*. Translated by Vera Broido. London: Oxford University Press, 1967.

Conroy, Mary Schaeffer. *In Health and in Sickness: Pharmacy, Pharmacists and the*

Pharmaceutical Industry in Late Imperial, Early Soviet Russia. Boulder, CO: East European Monographs, distributed by Columbia University Press, 1994.

Conroy, Mary Schaeffer. "Women Pharmacists in Russia before World War I: women's emancipation, feminism, professionalization, nationalism, and class conflict." In *Women and Society in Russia and the Soviet Union*, edited by Linda Edmondson, 48–72. Cambridge: Cambridge University Press, 1992.

Lesnevskaia, Antonina B. *Po neprotorennoi doroge (Along an Unbeaten Road)*. St. Petersburg: Tipografiia A. Smolinkskii, 1901.

Mary Schaeffer Conroy

Liga ravnopraviia zhenshchin (League for Women's Equal Rights) (1907–1917)

The single most important Russian feminist organization spearheading the fight for women's equal rights after the 1908 Women's Congress until the October 1917 Revolution.

The League's charter was approved by the St. Petersburg city government on March 6, 1907. Its founders were from the ruling class, generally wives, widows, or daughters of officials. As stated in its charter, the League's purpose was the "attainment by all women of political and civil rights identical with the rights of Russian male citizens, with the goal of improving the legal and economic situation of women." Although League members collected signatures for suffrage petitions to the Second Duma in 1907, it was not until after the 1908 Women's Congress that the League showed real signs of life. By that time, many former activists in the *Soiuz ravnopraviia zhenshchin* (Women's Equal Rights Union) joined and rose to prominence in the League. These included Ekaterina Shchepkina, who became head of the organization's speakers' bureau, Anna Kal'manovich, Zinaida Mirovich, Liudmila Ruttsen, Ariadna Tyrkova, and Olga Vol'kenshtein.

Mariia Chekhova, a founder of the Union and editor of its journal, *Soiuz zhenshchin (Union of Women)*, spoke about her reasons for joining the League in her inaugural address as President of the organization's St. Petersburg chapter in January 1909. The League, to Chekhova, combined the best of both types of women's organizations, those whose goals were directed at philanthropy, education, and/or mutual aid and those that were purely political. Most important, the League was legal, a significant advantage in a repressive period when many veterans of the 1905 Revolution sought shelter in legally chartered groups. Like the Women's Equal Rights Union, the League sought political rights and the unification of all Russian feminist groups. Like the Russian Women's Mutual Philanthropic Society, the League restricted membership to women and was governed by a council. The sixteen members of the League's governing council served three-year terms. In an effort to ensure continuity, stability, and control, four of the seats had to be filled by the organization's founders. Funding for the League's operations came from dues, investments, benefits, and bequests.

Chekhova moved to Moscow in 1910. The new League President, Poliksena

Shishkina-Iavein, a St. Petersburg physician, led the St. Petersburg chapter until its demise after the October Revolution. Like others in the organization's leadership, she was part of the democratic intelligentsia, largely formed of teachers, journalists, and doctors, which spearheaded all the major liberal and left political organizations in this period.

The League was a small organization, its membership generally between 1,500 and 2,000, mostly centered in its Moscow and St. Petersburg chapters, with smaller chapters in Kharkov and Tomsk. Its relatively small size did not help the organization achieve unity. The Moscow and St. Petersburg sections often operated autonomously and at times directly conflicted. This was especially true in 1911 after a bitter dispute over charges of anti-Semitism between Zinaida Mirovich, the accused, and Mariia Raikh, the accuser, caused Mirovich and her allies, backed by the St. Petersburg section, to leave the Moscow League. Conflict in the St. Petersburg League between the organization's founders and newer members flared up in 1913, when the rule giving the founders four seats on the executive council was abolished.

Despite the internal struggles, League members were active in lobbying and educational outreach efforts from 1910 to 1917. Joining members of the Russian Women's Mutual Philanthropic Society, they won passage in 1912 and 1914, respectively, of bills equalizing inheritance rights and removing the despised passport restrictions for married women. Suffrage remained at the top of the League's agenda, but attempts to enact such legislation proved unsuccessful. Both the Third and Fourth Dumas, elected on the basis of more restrictive voting laws than those of their predecessors, were dominated by parties not known for their sympathy for women's rights. Nevertheless, some League-supported bills won majorities in the Duma, only to be vetoed by the even more conservative State Council. Measures providing for women's suffrage in *volost* (district) zemstvos and abolishing restrictions for women lawyers met this fate. Bills for universal suffrage without distinction of sex were unsuccessfully introduced in the Third and Fourth Dumas, opposed by legislators and government ministers fearing "the admiration of women for revolutionary ideals" and the affront to tsarist "manners and morals." In one coalition effort, the League joined the Bolsheviks in promoting legislation for the appointment of female factory inspectors; this passed the Duma in 1916.

The League utilized other legal opportunities to rally support, organizing meetings and congresses. The most important of these was the *Pervyi vserossiiskii s"ezd po obrazovaniiu zhenshchin* (First All-Russian Congress on Women's Education), held in St. Petersburg from December 26, 1912, to January 4, 1913, about four years after the First All-Russian Women's Congress. Such gatherings provided good opportunities for rallying public opinion. Those attending the Education Congress represented a broad range of liberal-left activists, from Kadet Ariadna Tyrkova, to Bolshevik Praskov'ia Kudelli. Resolutions passed at the Congress included calls for coeducation, autonomy for educational institutions, and the elimination of nationality restrictions.

With the outbreak of World War I, many feminists rallied to the war effort. The League summoned the "daughters of Russia" to a "women's mobilization" similar to that advocated by the suffragist Christabel Pankhurst in England. Although she advocated support for Russians fighting in the war, Shishkina-Iavein also supported feminist peace initiatives, entertaining a delegation from the International Committee of Women for Permanent Peace, an outgrowth of the 1915 women's peace congress at The Hague.

The February 1917 Revolution, sparked by female workers' demonstrations commemorating International Women's Day, revitalized the League and resulted in its most significant achievement. The cause around which the League rallied support was the failure of the Provisional Government and the Soviets to support the immediate enactment of woman suffrage. The organization stepped up its activity, organizing public meetings and distributing feminist literature all over the Russian Empire. On March 20 the League launched one of the first mass demonstrations after the February Revolution. Approximately 40,000 women, led by Shishkina-Iavein and revolutionary heroine Vera Figner in an automobile flanked by female guards riding white horses, marched from the City Duma to the State Duma, demanding action on women's suffrage. Two days later a delegation including Shishkina-Iavein, Vera Figner, Anna Miliukova, Mariia Pokrovskaia, Anna Shabanova, and Ariadna Tyrkova won assurances from Prince L'vov, head of the Provisional Government, to include women in the suffrage statute. With the law's passage a few weeks later, Russia became the first major power to give women the vote.

Fresh from its victory on suffrage, the League continued to push for change throughout 1917. The organization's efforts to form a nationwide feminist coalition resulted in the creation of the *Respublikanskii soiuz demokraticheskikh zhenskikh organizatsii* (Republican Union of Democratic Women's Organizations) at a League-organized Women's Congress held in Moscow in April. The coalition united liberals and socialists, mostly Mensheviks. The Bolsheviks present left the congress in protest. Immediately after the October Revolution, the League was still active and sponsored a feminist slate that polled 5,310 votes in the Constituent Assembly elections. The slate was a mix of feminists, socialists, and liberals and included Shishkina-Iavein, Mariia Chekhova, Ekaterina Shchepkina, Ekaterina Kuskova, L. M. Gorolits-Vlasova, an instructor at the Women's Medical Institute, Bestuzhev Courses graduate and legal Marxist Aleksandra Kalmykova, and the ethnographer and Bestuzhev Courses graduate professor Aleksandra Efimenko.

The last evidence of League activity is a 1918 leaflet entitled "Appeal of the All-Russian League for Women's Equal Rights," exhorting women to defend their motherland against both foreign invaders and the Bolsheviks.

Cross-references: Mariia Chekhova, Anna Kal'manovich, Zinaida Mirovich, Liudmila Ruttsen, Ekaterina Shchepkina, *Soiuz ravnopraviia zhenshchin* (Women's Equal Rights Union), Ariadna Tyrkova.

Suggested Readings

Edmondson, Linda Harriet. *Feminism in Russia 1900–1917*. Stanford, CA: Stanford University Press, 1984.

Goldberg, Rochelle (Ruthchild). "The Russian Women's Movement 1859–1917." Ph.D. Diss., University of Rochester, 1976.

Grishina, Zoia V. *"Dvizhenie za politicheskoe ravnopravie zhenshchin v gody pervoi Rossiiskoi revoliutsii"* (The Movement for Women's Political Equal Rights in the Years of the First Russian Revolution). *Vestnik Moskovskogo universiteta (Moscow University Herald)*. Ser. 8 *Istoriia (History)*, no. 2 (1982): 33–42.

Grishina, Zoia V. *"Zhenskie organizatsii v Rossii (1905g.-fevral'/mart 1917 g.)" (Women's Organizations in Russia (1905–February/March 1917)*. Abstract of a *kandidat*'s Diss., Moscow State University, 1978.

Ruthchild, Rochelle. "League of Equal Rights for Women." In *Modern Encyclopedia of Russian and Soviet History*, edited by Joseph Wieczynski, vol. 19, 88–92. Gulf Breeze, FL: Academic International Press, 1981.

Stites, Richard. *The Women's Liberation Movement in Russia: Feminism, Nihilism, and Bolshevism, 1860–1930*. Princeton, NJ: Princeton University Press, 1978, 1991.

Rochelle Goldberg Ruthchild

M

Mirovich, Zinaida Sergeevna Ivanova (aka N. Mirovich and Zinaida Mirovich) (1865–1913)

Feminist activist, historian, critic, writer, and translator. One of the founders of the Women's Equal Rights Union.

Like many other feminist activists, Zinaida Ivanova, daughter of a Moscow superintendent of schools, took advantage of recently available higher education opportunities for women, graduating from the exclusive and pioneering Guerrier Courses in 1897. Soon after graduation, she married and also began work as a freelance writer, one of the few career opportunities for educated women in this period.

Although she sometimes used the male pseudonym N. Mirovich, Ivanova often focused on topics related to the *zhenskii vopros* (woman question). She wrote about the French revolutionary heroine Madame Roland and the playwright Henrik Ibsen; her interest in Ibsen led her to translate his best-known plays. At the end of the nineteenth-century, when the fear of radicalism in Russia made articles about the French Revolution difficult to publish, she turned to publicist writing and lecturing, speaking, for example, in Moscow and several provincial towns about British feminism. Fluent in six languages and a seasoned world traveler, she attended several international women's gatherings, including the 1899 International Congress of Women in London and the 1904 and 1906 International Woman Suffrage Alliance Congresses in Berlin and Copenhagen, respectively. At the 1906 Congress, she held delegates spellbound describing the events of the 1905 Revolution. An Anglophile, she spent much time in England, spoke several times at suffrage rallies in Hyde Park, and translated John Stuart Mill's *On the Subjection of Women*.

When women's political rights became a possibility during the 1905 Revolution, Mirovich was among the founders of, and spoke at, the First Organizational Congress of the Women's Equal Rights Union in Moscow in May 1905. She attended subsequent Women's Union congresses, lectured and wrote in favor of equal rights and suffrage, and in 1908 published one of the few sources for the history of the Russian movement, *Iz istorii zhenskogo dvizheniia v Rossii (From the History of the Women's Movement in Russia).* At the 1908 Women's Congress in St. Petersburg, the largest such gathering in prerevolutionary Russia, Mirovich was among the most militant feminists, advocating tactics similar to those of English suffragists like the Pankhursts, with whom she was personally connected, and arguing for women's unity across party lines.

Mirovich continued her feminist activity in the years of repression after the 1905 Revolution and after the Women's Union dissolved. She joined other activists such as Mariia Chekhova and Olga Bervi-Kaidanova in the *Liga ravnopraviia zhenshchin* (League for Women's Equal Rights) in 1910, spoke at the 1912 Congress on Women's Education, and continued to attend international feminist congresses. Her last years were marred by a dispute with Mariia Raikh, along with Mirovich a delegate to the 1911 Stockholm International Woman Suffrage Alliance Congress. Raikh charged Mirovich with anti-Semitism, an accusation backed by the Moscow League's board. Mirovich hotly disputed Raikh's charge and resigned from the League, causing a split that seriously weakened the organization. Although Mirovich's activism in Russia declined, she continued her close contacts with British feminists until her death in 1913.

Cross-references: Mariia Chekhova, First All-Russian Women's Congress (1908), *Liga ravnopraviia zhenshchin* (League for Women's Equal Rights), *Soiuz ravnopraviia zhenshchin* (Women's Equal Rights Union).

Suggested Readings

Ariian, Praskov'ia N. "Z. S. Mirovich." In *Pervyi zhenskii kalendar' na 1914 god*, edited by Praskov'ia N. Ariian, opposite p. 306i. St. Petersburg, 1914.

Edmondson, Linda Harriet. *Feminism in Russia 1900–1917.* Stanford, CA: Stanford University Press, 1984.

Goldberg, Rochelle (Ruthchild). "The Russian Women's Movement 1859–1917." Ph.D. Diss., University of Rochester, 1976.

Grishina, Zoia V. *"Dvizhenie za politicheskoe ravnopravie zhenshchin v gody pervoi Rossiiskoi revoliutsii"* (The Movement for Women's Political Equal Rights in the Years of the First Russian Revolution). *Vestnik Moskovskogo universiteta (Moscow University Herald).* Ser. 8 *Istoriia (History),* no. 2 (1982): 33–42.

Grishina, Zoia V. *"Zhenskie organizatsii v Rossii, 1905 g.-fevral'/mart 1917 g"* (Women's Organizations in Russia, 1905–February/March 1917). Abstract of a *kandidat*'s Diss., Moscow State University, 1978.

Kizevetter, A. A. "Pamiati Zinaidy Sergeevny Mirovich." *Russkaia mysl'* 9 (1913): 140–141.

Mirovich, N. (Z. S. Ivanova). *Iz istorii zhenskago dvizheniia v Rossii (From the History of the Women's Movement in Russia).* Moscow: Tipografiia T-va. I. D. Sytina, 1908.

Ruthchild, Rochelle. "Mirovich, N." *In Dictionary of Russian Women Writers*, edited by Marina Ledkovsky, Charlotte Rosenthal, and Mary Zirin, 431–432. Westport, CT: Greenwood Press, 1994.

Stites, Richard. *The Women's Liberation Movement in Russia. Feminism, Nihilism, and Bolshevism*. Princeton, NJ: Princeton University Press, 1978, 1991.

Rochelle Goldberg Ruthchild

Muravieva, Countess Aleksandra Zakharovna (late nineteenth–early twentieth centuries; dates of birth and death not available)

Editor and publisher of the St. Petersburg woman's monthly Damskii Mir (Ladies' World) (1907–1918) and the annual supplement *Damskii Mir Kalendar' (Ladies' World Calendar*) (1910–1917).

Very little is known about the personal life of Aleksandra Zakharovna Muravieva, other than that she was married to Count Leonid Leonidovich Muraviev, who served with the state railroad administration, that they had at least one son, and that they lived in St. Petersburg at 173 Fontanka. For six years, 1898–1903, Muravieva was associated with *Vestnik inostrannoi literatury (Herald of Foreign Literature)*, where her numerous translations of contemporary prose from French, German, and English were published. Her translations of excerpts from Prevost's trilogy of *Lettres de Femmes (Letters of Women)* (1892–1897), which were acclaimed for their portrayal of "the feminine soul" of society women, appeared in 1898–1899; these were followed by the translation of his novel, *Lea*, an exploration of the pointed contemporary issue of the relationship between women's education and women's independence. In addition to works depicting women's psychology and contemporary mores, Muravieva translated works of humor, including dramatic works by Arthur Schnitzler, and tales and stories by Guy de Maupassant and Otto Erich Hartleben. Throughout 1905, Muravieva edited and published the magazine *Baian*, founded the same year by A. I. Osipov, to which she also contributed translations from German and English. Experience gained from both periodicals undoubtedly influenced her decision to start her own magazine, *Damskii Mir (Ladies' World)*, whose first issue appeared in February 1907 and which lasted into early 1918. Although it was begun as a deluxe fashion magazine produced at first by print works specializing in arts publishing, Muravieva soon recognized the need to tailor her publication to the complex needs of her audience of educated society women. To that purpose, both the *Herald of Foreign Literature* and *Baian* served as a source of contributors and staff for *Damskii mir*. Poets, critics, translators, and associates of Muravieva's, such as Anna Boane, Olga Chiumina, and Izabella Grinevskaia, as well as the art critic O. Bazankur, became familiar names on the roster of her new magazine as its initial format and horizons expanded. Translations by such popular European writers of the day as Marcel Prevost, Mathilde Serao, and August Strindberg were included, along with Russian writings by Vera Kryzhanovskaia (Rochester), Teffi (Nadezhda Aleksandrovna Lokhvitskaia), Nikolai Breshko-Breshkovskii, Anna Mar, and Vera Rudich, among others. Anna Boane reviewed the latest works by women writers, including Evdokiia Nagrodskaia's *Gnev Dionysa (Wrath of Dionysius)* (1911), Karin Mikhaelis' *Opas-*

nyi vek (Dangerous Age) (1911), stories by Anna Mar (1912), and essays by Aleksandra Kazina (1912).

Muravieva's education, curiosity, and fluency in several European languages allowed her to keep abreast of developments in the worlds of fashion, society, and the arts as well as the worlds of education, health and sports, and later even politics. For example, while most fashion magazines turned to Paris for inspiration, Muravieva's magazine also included fashions from London and New York, especially in coats and suits. In addition, her Anglophile sentiments were undoubtedly expressed in her interest in "five o'clock tea," "picnics," English-style summer cottages, and automotive sport. She also included stories about remarkable Englishwomen, such as Jesse Akkerman, "who circled the globe five times" as head of the Girls Realm Guild (founded in 1900), an international society for the improvement of the lives of young women. There is no information about Muravieva after her magazine closed in early 1918.

Cross-references: *Pervyi zhenskii kalendar'*, Women's Periodicals in Early Twentieth-Century Russia, Women's Periodical Publishing in Late Imperial Russia (1860–1905).

Jane Gary Harris

N

Niglistki (Women Nihilists) (late 1850s to early 1870s)

Whether mathematicians educated in Europe, young wives in fictitious marriages, or members of translating collectives, nihilist women of the 1860s were cultural revolutionaries who refused to participate in the polite world of their parents. Instead, they insisted on total equality with men and attempted to reorganize the structure of work and home, and many devoted themselves to medicine and science. They were a generation of women who were influenced by the intelligentsia's embracing of George Sand in the 1840s and who, in turn, inspired the populist and anarchist women of the next generation in the 1880s.

Vera Pavlovna, the protagonist of Nikolai Chernyshevskii's 1863 novel, *What Is to Be Done?*, in many respects, is a prototypical female nihilist, or *niglistka*. She speaks frankly to her unwanted suitors, rejects feminine dress and coquettish mannerisms, enters into a fictitious marriage with her brother's tutor in order to escape the "cellar" of her parental home, works at a laundry collective, and devotes herself to the study of medicine. The term *niglistka* (nihilist woman), a term used by sympathizers and critics alike, encompassed accomplished scientists as well as schoolgirls with short hair who smoked, and by the 1870s the word *niglistka*, along with its masculine counterpart "nihilist," had become synonymous with assassin.

In the late 1850s and early 1860s a distinct group of young urban and provincial women appeared on the political landscape who were united not by a coherent political program but rather by their rejection of social conventions, embodied in their mothers and most of their female contemporaries.

By shedding outward signs of femininity—dress, mannerism, and comportment—nihilist women hoped to achieve some measure of equality with men. Their "revolt in dress" translated into a costume of dark-colored, loose-fitting shirts and blouses without frills that covered their bodies up to their necks. Their hair was shortly cropped, and they smoked. In her reminiscences of childhood, renowned mathematician and nihilist-sympathizer Sofia Kovalevskaia described the nihilist awakening of her elder sister Anna (Aniuta) Korvin-Krukovskaia.

Kovalevskaia wrote of how her sister began to dress simply in plain colors and became resentful of gentry social activities, from balls to visiting neighbors. Unconcerned with mannerisms, from daintiness to sentimentality, required of young ladies by respectable gentry society, *niglistki* spoke openly and directly and refrained from emotional melodramatic scenes.

Niglistki rejected traditional marital ties and instead entered into "new marriages" or "fictitious marriages." Under this arrangement, women would marry not for love, but rather in the name of freedom from conventional female roles and obligations. Fictitious marriages were a means for women to achieve independence from parental supervision and the social expectations imposed on them. In these partnerships with men, *niglistki* were not concerned with sexual freedom, but rather with freedom from all sexuality—whether the demands of their husbands or their own desires. In theory, new marriages would allow women not only the freedom from their own libidos as well as the libidos of others but also the opportunity to leave their parental homes, travel abroad, and attend institutions of higher learning. The life of Sofia Kovalevskaia (born Korvin-Krukovskaia), the first European woman to receive her doctorate in mathematics, illustrates the potential freedom gained—also the degree of personal happiness lost—in "new" marital arrangements. Her fictitious marriage (September 1868) to V. O. Kovalevskii, a bright, young geologist and translator, permitted Kovalevskaia the chance to study in Heidelberg with world-renowned European scientists. In 1880, after many years of marital unhappiness and professional hiatus, she became the first woman in Europe to occupy a university chair (in Stockholm). These legal, yet often unconsummated and loveless, arrangements—with friends, tutors, and other acquaintances—did not always lead to women's emancipation. In her memoirs, a contemporary observer, E. N. Vodovozova, cataloged possible negative outcomes from such fictional unions. One such story involves a young girl who enters into a "new marriage" in order to secure a passport to study abroad. Once there, her fictitious husband declares that he is in love with another and that she must return home for the divorce. In the meantime, the husband and his lover have had two children out of wedlock. The experiences of women in these arrangements were fraught with tensions between the theory of women's independence and the constraints that they encountered in practice.

Many *niglistki* tried not only to restructure their personal lives but also to change their work lives. In the years following the emancipation of the serfs, women in unprecedented numbers traveled by themselves to urban centers in order to find work. Rents, however, were high, and jobs were difficult to secure. Some women, inspired by Chernyshevskii's 1863 novel, *What Is to Be Done?*, found refuge in the nascent artel/commune movement. The novel, as many contemporaries observed, had a huge influence on the whole generation. Residential communes based on nihilist ideals sprang up even before the publication of Chernyshevskii's novel. In 1862, for instance, Arthur Benni, an Englishman born in Poland, organized a residential and work commune in the Grech lodgings for women translators in St. Petersburg. The Grech Commune, though, soon failed because its members spent their time debating politics, such as the "woman question," instead of working. Created in the shadow of Chernyshevskii's Vera Pavlovna, the Znamenskaya Commune was one of the generation's longest-lasting residential communes. Located in a large apartment on Znamenskaia Street in St. Petersburg, the commune was organized by Vasily Sleptsov, a radical writer interested in social experimentation, and lasted about a year and a half. While each of the fourteen members—seven men and seven women—had his or her own separate bedroom, together they shared expenses, preparation of meals, and housework. During the year and a half of this residential experiment, the members of this small group of upper-class personalities encountered many obstacles—including personal disagreements, inability to pay the bills, and their inexperience in scrubbing the floors. Despite such difficulties, artels and communes proliferated in Moscow and St. Petersburg in the 1860s, reaching faddish proportions. By the 1870s, however, the artel movement increasingly became associated with a radical underground movement, which foreshadowed populist and anarchist activities of later decades.

Nihilist women of the 1860s attempted to challenge cultural norms and inspire new social relationships between the sexes. Yet, in their search for equality, they encountered many obstacles: not only gaps in theory and practice but also inherent difficulties in the theories themselves. Even in the most radical of living arrangements or in the rejection of social convention, as historian Linda Edmondson suggests, *niglistki* looked to the men in their lives as agents of change and, in so doing, failed to escape the world of inequality produced by notions of sexual difference.

Cross-reference: Higher Education for Women.

Suggested Readings

Broido, Vera. *Apostles into Terrorists: Women and the Revolutionary Movement in the Russia of Alexander II.* New York: Viking Press, 1977.

Brower, Daniel R. *Training the Nihilists: Education and Radicalism in Tsarist Russia.* Ithaca, NY, and London: Cornell University Press, 1975.

Chernyshevskii, Nikolai. *What Is to Be Done?* Translated by Michael R. Katz. Ithaca, NY: Cornell University Press, 1989.

Edmondson, Linda Harriet. "Women's Emancipation and Theories of Sexual Difference in Russia, 1850–1917." In *Gender Restructuring in Russian Studies*, edited by Marianne Liljeström, Eila Mäntysaari, and Arja Rosenholm, 39–52. Tampere, Finland: University of Tampere, 1993.

Engel, Barbara Alpern. *Mothers and Daughters: Women of the Intelligentsia in Nineteenth-Century Russia.* Cambridge: Cambridge University Press, 1983.

Kovalevskaia, Sofia. *A Russian Childhood.* New York: Springer-Verlag, 1978.

Stites, Richard. *The Women's Liberation Movement in Russia: Feminism, Nihilism, and Bolshevism, 1860–1930.* Princeton, NJ: Princeton University Press, 1978, 1991.

Vodovozova, E. N. *Na zare zhizni: memuarnie ocherki i portrety (At the Dawn of Life: Memoir Essays and Portraits).* Moscow: Khudozhestvennaia literatura, 1987.

Rebecca Friedman

P

Panina, Countess Sof'ia Vladimirovna (1871–1956)

Heiress, philanthropist, and founder of the Ligov People's House (*Ligovskii Narodnyi Dom*) in St. Petersburg, Panina was also one of the founders of the Society for the Protection of Women and the only female minister in the Provisional Government cabinet. Put on trial by the Bolsheviks in 1917, she became a member of the Kadet National Center in South Russia during the Civil War and emigrated in 1920.

Sof'ia Panina was born into two families of great wealth and influence. Her maternal grandfather, General Sergei Ivanovich Mal'tsev, owned an industrial empire employing more than 100,000 workers. Count Viktor Nikitich Panin, her paternal grandfather, served as minister of justice for more than twenty-five years and was one of the richest serf owners in the country. A family drama during Panina's childhood had a profound effect on her views and activities as an adult. Widowed after only two years of marriage, in 1878 her mother Anastasiia Panina fell in love with Ivan Il'ich Petrunkevich, one of the founders of the constitutional liberal movement against the autocracy. They married in 1882, while Petrunkevich was still serving a sentence of exile as a political criminal. Fearing that Anastasiia was using her daughter's considerable inheritance to finance revolutionary activity, her mother-in-law Countess Natal'ia Panina obtained Imperial consent to take her eleven-year-old granddaughter away from her mother. Sof'ia was placed in an elite boarding school for noble girls, the Catherine Institute in St. Petersburg. The custody battle and the injustice against her mother shaped Panina as a strong-minded progressive committed to social and, eventually, political reform.

Panina's life in early adulthood explored several different paths. Marriage in 1890 to the young officer Alexander Polovtsov thrust her into Petersburg high society. When she came of age in 1892, she became one of Russia's wealthiest women. After a few years, however, Panina successfully sued for divorce, possibly because Polovtsov was a homosexual. Reassuming her maiden name, she never remarried. In the late 1890s, she attended the Higher Courses for Women in St. Petersburg, which functioned as a women's college.

According to Panina herself, the turning point in her life was meeting a Petersburg schoolteacher, Aleksandra Vasil'evna Peshekhonova, in 1891. The two women first collaborated to establish a cafeteria for Peshekhonova's pupils, who lived in one of the poorest districts of the capital. The cafeteria was the base from which, over the course of the next twelve years, Panina's social work among the Petersburg poor expanded and flourished. In 1903 she built the Ligov People's House, which ran a day care center, reading rooms and libraries for adults and children, a cafeteria and tea room, instructional workshops, evening classes for adults, and a theater. Funded entirely by Panina and constituting the heart of her public activity until 1917, the People's House served as a model for similar institutions elsewhere in Russia.

Panina also participated in other philanthropies and reform movements, among which was the antiprostitution Russian Society for the Protection of Women (1900). She headed the committee that sought to prevent prostitution by assisting young working women and subsidized the Society's hostel for them. As this work suggests, Panina cared deeply about the victimization of women; but like many other progressive Russians, she dedicated herself to improving the lives of the underprivileged without regard to their sex and seems to have assigned a higher priority to education and social progress than to women's rights.

Despite her stepfather's and mother's intense involvement in the liberal opposition movement, Panina remained aloof from politics until the February 1917 Revolution granted women the right to vote. In the spring of 1917 Panina was elected to the Petrograd City Council and the Central Committee of the liberal Constitutional Democratic (Kadet) Party. She also became the only female member of the Provisional Government cabinet when she was appointed Assistant Minister of State Welfare in May, then Assistant Minister of Education in July.

After the Bolsheviks seized power in November 1917, Panina, one of the few members of the Provisional Government still at liberty, organized resistance to the coup by encouraging civil servants to strike. Her house became an underground Kadet center. Arrested in late November 1917 as an enemy of the people, Panina was accused of theft for refusing to transfer funds that she controlled at the Ministry of Education to the Bolsheviks. Her trial on December 10, 1917, was the first before the Bolsheviks' new Revolutionary Tribunal. A dramatic speech by a worker and former visitor to the Ligov People's House in defense of "Citizeness Panina" and her service to Russia's lowest classes forced the Tribunal to modify the trial's previously scripted outcome. It found Panina guilty but, conceding her popularity and social contribution, limited her punishment to the obligation to give the Bolsheviks the Ministry of Education funds. When she refused, Panina was returned to prison, where she remained until friends raised enough money to ransom her from incarceration just before Christmas 1917.

In 1918 Panina fled Petrograd for the south of Russia, where she joined other members of the Kadet Central Committee working with the anti-Bolshevik forces under General Anton Denikin. From this time her constant companion was Nikolai Ivanovich Astrov, another Kadet leader who had been mayor of Moscow during 1917. Panina and Astrov spent most of the war in Ekaterinodar with Denikin. In the summer of 1919, empowered as Denikin's representatives, they traveled to Paris and met with French leaders in an unsuccessful attempt to obtain greater Allied support for the Whites. Returning to southern Russia in September, they fled the country permanently in March 1920, joining the ranks of thousands of other penniless White Russian refugees. Although they never married, Panina and Astrov were deeply attached to each other and lived together until his death in 1934. In emigration, first in Switzerland and then in Czechoslovakia, Panina and Astrov played leading roles in refugee relief and émigré organizations. In Prague, where they lived from 1925, Panina founded and directed the principal émigré community and cultural center, the *Russkii ochag* (Russian Hearth). With the Nazi takeover of Czechoslovakia imminent, she left Europe in late 1938 for the United States. Working with the Tolstoy Foundation to assist refugees created by World War II, she lived in New York until her death in 1956.

Cross-references: Russian Society for the Protection of Women, Higher Education for Women.

Suggested Readings

Panina, S. V. "*Na Peterburgskoi okraine*" (On the Outskirts of St. Petersburg). Parts 1 and 2. *Novyi zhurnal* 48 (1957): 163–196, and 49 (1957): 189–203.

Panina, S. V., et al. *Narodnyi dom (The People's House)*. Petrograd, 1918.

Raeff, Marc. *Russia Abroad: A Cultural History of the Russian Emigration 1919–1939*. New York: Oxford University Press, 1990.

Rosenberg, William G. *Liberals in the Russian Revolution: The Constitutional Democratic Party, 1917–1921*. Princeton, NJ: Princeton University Press, 1974.

Adele Lindenmeyr

Perovskaia, Sof'ia L'vovna (1854–1881)

A prominent populist who became a model of the revolutionary woman. A primary force in assassination attempts on Alexander II, she took charge of the final successful attack on March 1, 1881. For this she became the first female political activist in Russian history to be executed.

Sof'ia Perovskaia was born on September 1, 1854 (some sources say 1853), into an old, aristocratic family in St. Petersburg, where her father was the governor-general. Her father's tyranny fostered her ardent love for her timid mother and antagonism for her father, as well as an aversion to men in general. As was typical for aristocratic girls, she was educated by tutors and a German governess. In the aftermath of Karakozov's attempt on the tsar's life and her brother Vasilii's involvement in student disturbances, her father lost his post in 1866. The family's straitened circumstances led the women in the family to withdraw to their small estate in the Crimea. Here Perovskaia furthered her education by reading books from her grandfather's library and, especially, radical materials provided by her brother.

When the family returned to St. Petersburg in 1869, Perovskaia eagerly enrolled in the recently opened Alarchin Courses, evening lectures for women that supplemented their superficial education without conferring degrees. She made friends with other young noblewomen and began attending book discussion groups, where she was exposed to new ideas and debated issues related to political economy and the "woman question." Perovskaia felt strongly about the importance of women's autonomy and became a vehement supporter of separate groups for women in order to avoid male domination. Her father disapproved of her activities, and when he forbade visits by her friends, she escaped his domination by fleeing to Kiev in the fall of 1870. She returned after a few months when family pressure persuaded her father to give Sof'ia her own legal documents. While this gave her virtual independence, it cut her off from her family. To avoid her father, who did not want to see her, she visited her mother by using the servants' entrance.

The perspective of Perovskaia and her friends from the Alarchin Courses changed as they became more aware of the suffering that surrounded them. They dropped their separatist stance, and in the spring of 1871 Perovskaia and her friends joined with a male student commune, forming what later became known as the Chaikovskii Circle. Devoted to the development of the people, the group became one of the main sources of the "going to the people" movement, dedicated to spreading propaganda among the lower classes. Perovskaia enthusiastically took up its ideological mission, as well as the task of keeping house for the revolutionaries. She set the tone for the life of the commune, insisting on serious, puritanical relations of complete equality between men and women.

In 1872 she "went to the people," first teaching and then vaccinating the peasants against smallpox. She walked from village to village, shared the peasants' wretched living conditions, and gradually began to propagandize and distribute revolutionary literature. The following spring she conducted propaganda among workers in St. Petersburg but was arrested in the winter of 1874. After a six-month imprisonment she was bailed out by her father but was soon summoned to the Trial of the 193. Although a show trial, this was perhaps the most important political trial in tsarist Russia, involving participants of the "going to the people" movement. Perovskaia was released despite her principled refusal to defend herself but was rearrested shortly thereafter while attempting to liberate political prisoners. On the way to administrative exile, she escaped and began her existence as an "illegal."

At the end of 1878 she returned to St. Petersburg, where Vera Zasulich's acquittal, despite shooting the city's governor-general, had legitimated terrorism for many revolutionaries. Perovskaia, a fervent populist, vainly tried to forestall the breakup of the group's secret revolutionary society, *Zemlia i volia* (Land and Freedom). After it split into two factions, she continued to work with both. Her decision to join *Narodnaia volia* (the People's Will), the terrorist group planning the assassination of Alexander II, probably was influenced by Andrei Zheliabov, the handsome, charismatic peasant who had become the party's leader. Perovskaia, the strong feminist and admitted man-hater, was, according to Vera Figner, "swept off her feet." She joined him in the Executive Committee, the party's decision-making body, and participated in two attempts on the tsar's life during the next year. With Zheliabov, she was in charge of the third and final attempt. After he was arrested two days before the planned attack on March 1, 1881, Perovskaia took sole command. When the tsar took an alternate route on his weekly ride to the riding academy, she calmly activated a backup plan, strategically placing the bomb throwers to react to her signals. Although the first bomb was hurled too late, the second mortally wounded the tsar and the revolutionary who threw it.

After the assassination, Perovskaia was consumed with freeing Zheliabov, with whom she had lived as man and wife, and ignored her friends' urging to escape abroad. She was arrested on March 10 and at the trial was sentenced to die by hanging. She spent much of her remaining time consoling her mother, assuring her that she did not regret her fate. When she was hanged on April 3 with four of her coconspirators, Perovskaia became the first female activist to be executed by the tsarist government.

Cross-references: Vera Figner, Vera Zasulich.

Suggested Readings

Asheshov, Nikolai. *Sof'ia Perovskaia: Materialy dlia biografii i kharakteristiki (Sof'ia Perovskaia: Materials for a Biography and Characterization).* St. Petersburg: Gosudarstvennoe izdatel'stvo, 1920.

Figner, Vera. "Sof'ia Perovskaia." *Byloe (The Past)* 4–5, nos. 10–11 (April 1918): 3–11.

Footman, David. *Red Prelude: The Life of the Russian Terrorist Zheliabov.* New Haven, CT: Yale University Press, 1945.

Segal, Elena. *Sof'ia Perovskaia.* Moscow: "*Molodaia Gvardiia,*" 1962.

Klawa N. Thresher

Pervyi zhenskii kalendar' (The First Women's Calendar, or PZhK) (1899–1915)

The first almanac or general handbook of its kind devoted to information pertaining to all aspects of women's lives. It served both as an annually updated compendium of information and as a resource for journalists, feminists, and women in general, providing signed and unsigned articles and reports on topics of significance to the women's movement.

Pervyi Zhenskii Kalendar' (The First Women's Calendar), edited and published by Praskov'ia Naumovna Ariian, was begun in 1899 and saw its last issue during World War I in 1915. It was financed primarily through advertisements, which obviously increased with the PZhK's appeal and circulation over the decade and a half of its existence. Published annually, this remarkable calendar or, perhaps more appropriately, almanac grew steadily and became the primary handbook for women seeking information about every kind of resource pertaining to women and their families; it included the five religious calendars and their holidays in use in the Russian empire (Orthodox, Roman Catholic, Lutheran, Jewish, and Muslim) and girls' names (Orthodox, Lutheran, and Catholic), detailed information about the Russian Imperial Family, and the official times of the changing of the seasons and of the raising of the bridges. This was followed, in the first three issues, by the publication of all the laws pertaining to women in Russia: "The Rights and Obligations of Women according to Russian Law," accompanied by models for petitions as well as other documents and forms and the addresses for filing them. Essential information was continuously updated and published in subsequent issues of the PZhK. Certain volumes also contained basic demographic analyses of the city of St. Petersburg, including women's employment statistics, the ethnographic makeup and literacy levels of the city, birthrates and mortality rates, and even the number and characteristics of women with library cards. Each year data were included on educational and job opportunities, and health and medical resources, as well as on the Russian charity societies, such as the Russian Women's Mutual Philanthropic Society and women's clubs and organizations of interest to women. With respect to education, updated information was published annually about kindergartens and Sunday schools, private and public elementary and high schools, commercial schools, schools for music, the arts, trades, and handicrafts, special schools for the deaf, and so on. Other listings included Higher Courses for Women in St. Petersburg and Moscow, Medical Courses, and Teacher Training Courses, as well as the universities abroad that accepted women. In addition, information was provided on how to apply, along with models of application forms.

Under its rubric "From the Past and Present," PZhK also published biographies and obituaries of famous Russian and foreign women from the past and present, a history of the women's movement abroad and in Russia, and honored anniversaries of famous women and events in women's history, such as the founding of the Bestuzhev Higher Courses for Women. Illustrations were often included in this section as well. Later it also published a list of foreign women's magazines dealing with the women's movement and a list of Russian and foreign women's magazines.

Other types of information that appeared in every issue included pertinent addresses: post offices, employment bureaus, especially for governesses and servants, shelters for wet nurses, birthing homes, and private rooming houses and public shelters for pregnant women as well as for poor working women and for young male as well as female students. It also provided lists of women's organizations, sources of private support for orphans, and resources for other needy women and young working girls, as well as lists of annually updated medical and legal resources such as clinics, hospitals, and birthing homes, advice for mothers in caring for newborns, advice on family nutrition and hygiene, and information on new discoveries in medicine and the health sciences. Not only did Ariian's PZhK have a direct influence on its readers, providing data and information used by many of the women's magazines and some magazines of general interest as well, but it served as a model for other almanacs of its kind, such as the *Damskii Mir Kalendar' (Women's World Calendar)*, begun in 1910 and published annually through 1917 as a special supplement for that magazine's annual subscribers. Contributors included well-known members of the Russian wom- en's organizations, feminists, women doctors, teachers, and journalists, and a variety of legal, educational, and other experts. Although most sections of the almanac were unsigned, the bulk of the articles included in the section "From the Past and Present" carried bylines.

Cross-references: Praskov'ia N. Ariian, Higher Education for Women, Russian Women's Mutual Philanthropic Society.

Jane Gary Harris

Pokrovskaia, Mariia Ivanovna (1852–1922?)

Physician, feminist activist, and editor and publisher of the feminist journal *Zhenskii vestnik (Women's Herald)*, 1904–1917, the longest-running feminist publication in the history of Russia. Pokrovskaia was also a founder of the first Russian women's political party, the Women's Progressive Party, in 1905.

Born in 1852 in the district town of Nizhnyi Lomov in Penza Guberniia to a family of the gentry class, Pokrovskaia was educated at home. At age eighteen, in 1870, she took and passed the exam for home tutor, taught for a while in a girls' school in Teminkov, Tambov Guberniia, and in 1876 was admitted to medical school. Upon graduation in 1881, she began work as a *zemskii vrach'* (zemstvo doctor), treating the rural population in Pskov Guberniia. She left the countryside, moving to St. Petersburg in 1888.

Russian sources offer conflicting information about Pokrovskaia's medical activity in St. Petersburg. Some say that she gave up her practice and engaged in laboratory research and writing about public health. The Soviet scholar E. Ia. Belitskaia cited her as a pioneering woman physician, working for the city administration in treating the urban poor. Pokrovskaia's fictionalized account, *Kak ia byla gorodskim vrachom dlia bednykh: Iz vospominanii zhenshchiny-vracha (How I Became a City Doctor for the Poor: From the Reminiscences of a Woman Doctor)*, published in 1903, appears to have autobiographical elements.

Whether as a practitioner or researcher or both, Pokrovskaia proved a prolific lecturer and author of articles and pamphlets about public health. Her first lectures and writing about disease, living conditions, and access to water among the peasants whom she treated appeared in the journal *Vrach' (Physician)* and in the publications of the *Russkoe obshchestvo okhraneniia narodnago zdraviia* (Russian Society for the Preservation of Public Health). Her pamphlets (thirteen published by 1902) included advice on how to keep a clean house, raise healthy children, instill "healthy habits," and understand the connection between hygiene and health.

Pokrovskaia crusaded vigorously against prostitution, especially the Russian medical-police inspection system that certified prostitutes. In pamphlets and lectures she protested against legalized prostitution as exploitation of women, as the cause of disease, and as the corruption of the Russian people.

She is best known as the founder of one of the first women's political parties in the world, the *Zhenskaia Progressivnaia Partiia* (Women's Progressive Party) and as the editor and publisher of the *Zhenskii Vestnik (Women's Herald)*, the feminist journal, which she sustained almost single-handedly from 1904 to 1917, compiling it in her two-room apartment and financing it primarily through her modest personal resources. The journal is an excellent source of information about Russian women in those years and reflects Pokrovskaia's wide-ranging interests. It contains articles about Russian and international feminism, violence against women, prostitution, poverty, class and socialism, campaigns for suffrage and equal rights, free love, sex, and the activities of the Women's Progressive Party and Club.

After the February 1917 Revolution Pokrovskaia was among the feminist delegates who met with Prince L'vov, head of the Provisional Government, in their successful plea for woman suffrage. Pokrovskaia continued to publish *Zhenskii vestnik* until the Bolshevik Revolution in 1917. Little is known about the activities of this feminist pioneer after the October Revolution. Her voice silenced, she remained in Russia and is believed to have died in 1922.

Cross-references: First All-Russian Women's Congress (1908), Russian Women's Mutual Philanthropic Society (*Russkoe zhenskoe vzaimno-blagotvoritel'noe obshchestvo*), *Soiuz ravnopraviia zhenshchin* (Women's Equal Rights Union), *Zhenskaia progressivnaia partiia* (Women's Progressive Party), *Zhenskii vestnik (Women's Herald)*.

Suggested Readings

Ariian, Praskov'ia N. "Mariia Ivanovna Pokrovskaia." *Pervyi zhenskii kalendar' na 1905 god*. 1905; 394–396.

Belitskaia, E. Ia. *"Poliklinicheskaia pomoshch' v dorevoliutsionnom Peterburge i uchastie v nei zhenshchin vrachei"* (Polyclinic Assistance in Pre-Revolutionary St. Petersburg and the Participation of Women Physicians). *Sovetskoe zdravookhranenie (Soviet Health)* 10 (October 1972): 64–68.

Cook, Kathrine Schach. "Women's Progressive Party." In *Modern Encyclopedia of Russian and Soviet History*, edited by Joseph Wieczynski, vol. 44, 36–41. Gulf Breeze, FL: Academic International Press, 1987.

Edmondson, Linda Harriet. *Feminism in Russia, 1900–1917*. Stanford, CA: Stanford University Press, 1984.

Edmondson, Linda Harriet. "Mariia Pokrovskaia and *Zhenskii vestnik*: Feminist Separatism in Theory and Practice." In *An Improper Profession: Women, Gender and Journalism in Late Imperial Russia*, edited by Jehane Gheith and Barbara Norton. Durham, NC: Duke University Press, in press.

Edmondson, Linda Harriet. "Women's Rights, Civil Rights and the Debate over Citizens in the 1905 Revolution." In *Women and Society in Russia and the Soviet Union*, edited by Linda Edmondson, 77–100. Cambridge: Cambridge University Press, 1992.

Pokrovskaia, Mariia Ivanovna. *Kak ia byla gorodskim vrachom dlia bednykh. Iz vospominanii zhenshchiny-vracha (How I Became a City Doctor for the Poor. From the Memoirs of a Woman Doctor).* St. Petersburg, 1903.

Ruthchild, Rochelle G. "Writing for Their Rights. Four Feminist Journalists: Mariia Chekhova, Liubov' Gurevich, Mariia Pokrovskaia, and Ariadna Tyrkova." In *The Improper Profession: Women and Journalism in Late Imperial Russia*, edited by Jehane Gheith and Barbara Norton. Durham, NC: Duke University Press, in press.

Stites, Richard. *The Women's Liberation Movement in Russia: Feminism, Nihilism, and Bolshevism, 1860–1930.* Princeton, NJ: Princeton University Press, 1978, 1991.

Rochelle Goldberg Ruthchild

R

Russian Society for the Protection of Women (RSPW) (*Rossiiskoe obshchestvo zashchity zhenshchin*) (1900–ca. 1914)

The society developed in response to a European-wide movement to combat prostitution and the trade in women. At its height, the RSPW sponsored programs in all the major cities of the Russian Empire, both to prevent women from turning to prostitution and to wean prostitutes from their trade. The RSPW succeeded in bringing the issue of prostitution to the public's attention, particularly with its sponsorship of a 1910 congress on prostitution. It also provided important services to urban women in the working class. A moralistic and condescending attitude toward prostitutes and prostitution, as well as a refusal to challenge the social and economic status quo limited the society's success.

The origins of the *Rossiiskoe obshchestvo zashchity zhenshchin* (Russian Society for the Protection of Women, or RSPW) date from 1899, when several state officials, feminists, and female philanthropists attended the London Congress on the White Slave Traffic. Along with their European counterparts, they established grounds for international cooperation in fighting the trade in women. Upon their return, the Russian representatives adhered to the guidelines of the London Congress by forming a committee in St. Petersburg and petitioning to gain official recognition. The Russian bureaucracy approved their petition quickly because of the petitioners' elite social rank. The Ministry of Internal Affairs permitted Princess Evgeniia Ol'denburgskaia, a relative of the tsar, to organize an agency focusing on prostitution. In the words of the RSPW's first annual report, the organization sought "to assist in the protection of girls and women from the danger of being enticed into debauchery and to return already fallen women to an honest life." By 1905 RSPW affiliates operated in Aleksandrovsk, Vilna, Kiev, Minsk, Odessa, Riga, Sevastopol, Rostov-on-the-Don, and Kharkov, but St. Petersburg remained the heart of RSPW activities.

The RSPW in St. Petersburg provided an umbrella under which a wide array of various philanthropic activities and services addressed the needs of urban women in the lower classes. Its Department of Prevention, funded by Princess

Elena Saksen-Al'tenburgskaia, built a dormitory on Ligovskaia Street in St. Petersburg, at which women could stay for a reasonable five kopecks a day and dine in the subsidized cafeteria. The Department of Prevention hoped that their dormitory would provide women newly arriving in St. Petersburg with an alternative to flophouses which, according to the RSPW, were frequented by drunks, vagrants, prostitutes, and pimps. The Department of Prevention also advertised RSPW services in St. Petersburg's railroad stations and in third-class train wagons in an attempt to keep new female arrivals from falling into the hands of unscrupulous recruiters who might lure them into brothels. Recognizing that many of the women who arrived in St. Petersburg from the countryside could not read, the RSPW posted volunteers at these stations as well. The RSPW's Investigative Department managed a small dormitory, dispensed medical aid, assisted women in finding jobs, and rendered financial assistance. It also sent patrons and staff out to local work sites to assess conditions and find out from bosses and managers how the female employees were being treated. Another RSPW program leased and sold sewing machines at reasonable rates in order to allow women to go into business independently as seamstresses. An RSPW sewing workshop on Zhukovskaia Street employed young women who sold their goods in an RSPW store.

In 1903 the RSPW established a facility known as the Shelter for women in desperate circumstances and former prostitutes. Located on Nevskii Prospect, the Shelter housed twenty-five women, all of whom took turns doing housework, laundering, cooking, and scrubbing floors. The Shelter supplied its residents with legal and employment assistance, clothing, shoes, and even money for their dowry. In the countryside, the RSPW's Department of Charity for Unwed Mothers organized a rural compound. Its sponsor, Elizaveta Kalacheva, hoped that her facility would enable single mothers to support themselves and their children. A 600-ruble annual grant from the Ministry of Agriculture went toward instructing the residents in poultry breeding, gardening, and agronomy. Similarly, the countess Mariia Orlova-Davydova established an RSPW labor colony for girls from the ages of eleven to fifteen who were defined as at risk of becoming prostitutes. In a large wooden house on St. Petersburg's outskirts, the colony provided the girls with training in simple trades and supplied them with chickens, cows, and a garden.

The Department for the Care of Jewish Girls of the City of St. Petersburg also operated under RSPW auspices. Baron Goratsii Gintsburg, a prominent St. Petersburg Jew, sponsored programs designed to educate and entertain Jewish girls and women. Saturday meetings involved instruction not only in Russian, Hebrew, Yiddish, the Torah, history, geography, literature, and arithmetic but also in music and dancing. In addition, Gintsburg's branch financed cultural, recreational, and social services, including trips to museums and exhibitions, a summer camp, an employment agency, a cafeteria, a library, and two dormitories.

In 1910 the RSPW convened nearly 300 feminists, physicians, tsarist bureaucrats, gentry, liberals, and even a few socialist workers for the All-Russian Congress for the Struggle against the Trade in Women and Its Causes. Although conflicts arose at the congress between the five socialist workers in attendance and the majority of participants, the congress took an important stand in relation to tsarist policies toward prostitution. A regulatory policy dating back to 1843 permitted prostitutes who underwent regular police and medical inspections and brothel keepers who adhered to specific rules to ply their trade in the Russian Empire without legal interference. Public sentiment against regulated prostitution had grown since the turn of the century, but only at the 1910 congress did it coalesce as a united front. Congress participants unanimously demanded the abolition of brothels, which they denounced as "dens of depravity," and the overwhelming majority of participants came out against any form of government-sponsored regulation.

Despite the congress vote, the RSPW refused to go on record as opposing government policy. In 1912 it called for the abolition of state-licensed brothels, but not for an end to regulating street prostitution. In 1901 the RSPW's Department for the Struggle against the Enticement of Women into Depravity had managed to convince the Ministry of Internal Affairs to raise the minimum age of brothel prostitutes to twenty-one. In 1909 it urged passage of a bill in the Duma to prosecute "flesh traders" but never directed its energies toward comprehensive legislation. In fact, the RSPW participated in the system that licensed prostitutes, supplying volunteers who interviewed women registering as prostitutes and submitting proposals for only a reform of St. Petersburg's regulatory agency in 1912.

The RSPW had little success at drawing prostitutes away from their trade. RSPW members viewed prostitution as white slavery that all women would abandon, if given the opportunity, and thereby missed a crucial point. For poor women in the Russian Empire, prostitution served as a viable, albeit unfortunate, economic alternative. The "honest work" proffered by RSPW programs yielded salaries well below subsistence, whereas prostitution usually paid quite well.

Preventive programs accomplished more, in that they provided girls and women with housing, jobs, financial assistance, and even social support. But good intentions were not always enough. For example, most single mothers in Kalacheva's compound were illiterate and could not benefit from the agronomy lessons. Although the Investigative Department spoke with bosses about women's ill treatment and investigated sexual harassment at the workplace, it did not urge women to organize in defense of their economic interests. The RSPW never challenged the socioeconomic realities of female labor, and its members did not join forces with the Russian opposition that argued something more had to be done in autocratic Russia.

In February 1914 the RSPW requested permission from the Ministry of Internal Affairs to organize a second Russian conference on prostitution. The RSPW also anticipated St. Petersburg's role as host of the proposed sixth international congress against the trade in women to be held in 1916. War prevented further efforts in international cooperation and halted the RSPW's philanthropic and political activities. In 1914 the RSPW published what turned out to be its final yearly report.

Cross-reference: All-Russian Congress for the Struggle against the Trade in Women (1910).

Suggested Readings

Bernstein, Laurie. *Sonia's Daughters: Prostitutes and Their Regulation in Imperial Russia*. Berkeley: University of California Press, 1995.

Congress on the White Slave Traffic: Transactions of the International Congress on the White Slave Trade. London: Office of the National Vigilance Association, 1899.

Rossiiskoe obshchestvo zashchity zhenshchin v 1900 i 1901 gg (Russian Society for the Protection of Women in 1900 and 1901). St. Petersburg, 1902.

Rossiiskoe obshchestvo zashchity zhenshchin v 1913 g (Russian Society for the Protection of Women in 1913). St. Petersburg, 1914.

Stites, Richard. *The Women's Liberation Movement in Russia: Feminism, Nihilism, and Bolshevism, 1860–1930*. 2d ed. Princeton, NJ: Princeton University Press, 1991.

Trudy pervogo vserossiiskogo s"ezda po bor'be s torgom zhenshchinami i ego prichinami proiskhodivshchogo v S.-Peterburge s 21 do 25 aprelia 1910 goda (Works of the First All-Russian Congress for the Struggle against the Trade in Women and Its Causes). Vols. 1–2. St. Petersburg, 1911–1912.

Laurie Bernstein

Russian Women's Mutual Philanthropic Society (*Russkoe zhenskoe vzaimnoblagotvoritel'noe obshchestvo*) (1895–1917)

Modeled after U.S. women's clubs, the Society blended traditional philanthropic and educational activity with lobbying for woman's rights.

The impetus for the founding of the Society came from Anna Nikolaevna Charnotskaia, who, in a notice in a conservative St. Petersburg newspaper on October 17, 1893, called on Russian women to organize a women's society in commemoration of the day five years before when Tsar Alexander III and his family escaped injury in a train accident. Through a friend, Charnotskaia obtained the charter of the New England Women's Club. The charter, providing for a strong Board of Directors, allowing men to be associate members, and committing the group "to promote social enjoyment and general improvement," served as the model for the Russian society's first organizational statute.

Tsarist officials rejected the group's initial application for legal status; regulations of the time stipulated that only women's organizations with a philanthropic goal could be approved. Finally, with the help of highly placed contacts, the society won acceptance in May 1895, its awkward name reflecting the compromises necessary to give it life.

By the time the Society was approved, its women-only membership included many feminist activists. Nadezhda Stasova became its first President. When Stasova died within the year, Anna Filosofova, Honorary President until her death in 1912, nominally shared the Society's leadership with Anna Shabanova, the Society's second President.

Shabanova, an 1860s radical imprisoned for her membership in the Ivanova Dressmaking Workshop, channeled her energies after her release into medicine and feminism. One of the first graduates of the St. Petersburg Women's Medical Academy and a respected pediatrician, she led the Mutual Philanthropic Society until the Bolshevik Revolution in October 1917. Her strong leadership style and the compromises made to win government approval caused resentment, especially in the Society's early years, when those who considered themselves "democratic feminists" left.

Nevertheless, the Society, housed at 18 Spasskaia Street in St. Petersburg for most of its existence, reached a membership of 2,000 by 1900, becoming the major feminist organization of the pre-1905 period. Seeking to appeal to women of all classes, the Society offered both charitable and educational services, operating dormitories for women with and without children, a cafeteria, and an employment service. The Society's Children's Section supplied clothes and linen to poor children, operated a child-care center for working women, aided victims of flood and famine, and organized lectures on the "physical, intellectual and moral upbringing of children."

Services aimed at self-development and educating women for the skills of the new female service class included courses in bookkeeping, typing, and foreign languages, as well as a lecture series. Tsarist authorities kept a close watch on the Society's activities, ending the lecture series in 1901 after a talk on N. Minskii's play *Al'ma*, noted for its sympathetic portrayal of lesbianism.

Seeking international ties, the Society affiliated with the International Council of Women (ICW), at the time the only major global women's organization. Shabanova and other members attended the Council's international congresses. The ICW honored Russian feminist efforts by naming Filosofova an Honorary Vice President and encouraging the establishment of a Russian National Council of Women. This became Filosofova's cause for the rest of her life; it was thwarted by a combination of official government suspicion and splits within the women's movement.

By 1905 the Society's membership had slipped below 1,000, but the 1905 Revolution, which gave birth to the *Soiuz ravnopravnosti zhenshchin* (Women's Equal Rights Union) and the *Zhenskaia progressivnaia partiia* (Women's Progressive Party), also energized the Society. Shabanova led the Society's efforts in petitioning zemstvo and urban local governments, national officials, and thousands of public and private organizations as well as intense personal lobbying for woman suffrage and equal rights. Despite all of this activity, not until the end of 1906 did the Society formally set up a Suffrage Section.

Overshadowed at the height of the revolutionary surge of 1905–1906, the society survived when other, more radical feminist groups, such as the Women's Equal Rights Union, dissolved. Shabanova and Filosofova, in particular, spearheaded efforts to organize a Russian women's congress, in the hope of unifying all segments of the Russian women's movement. First proposed by Shabanova in 1902, the Congress finally came into being in 1908. Its organizing committee included representatives from the society, the Equal Rights Union, and the Women's Progressive Party. Held in St. Petersburg and attracting over 1,000 women and a few men, the congress left a rich legacy of information about Russian women and the feminist movement. The delegates were unable to unify around a National Council of Women, and some members of the small socialist delegation walked out.

After 1908 the Society's membership again declined, dropping to about 600 in 1913. Scaling back its legislative agenda considerably, the Society remained in the forefront of the few initiatives on woman's rights that did become law. The Society succeeded in winning passage of a law equalizing inheritance rights in 1912 and a law ending the provision that wives be registered in their husbands' passports in 1914. Such initiatives reflected the concerns of the Society's relatively privileged and well-educated members and had little relevance to the masses of women, but they must also be understood in the context of the conservative backlash repressing and inhibiting more sweeping demands for change within the legal political framework.

With the outbreak of World War I in August 1914, the Society's efforts turned toward mobilizing women to support the war effort and prove their worth to the nation. Shabanova spearheaded the establishment of a Society committee to aid war victims and the establishment of a hospital for wounded soldiers. She was not unsympathetic, however, to international feminist peace efforts and sent the women who organized The Hague Peace Congress in February 1915 her sincere wishes for their success.

Shabanova still sought to create a unified Russian women's organization, and at the end of 1916 the Society, along with other women's groups, drafted a statute for the *Vserossiiskoe zhenskoe obshchestvo* (All-Russian Women's Society). With the war weakening government authority, Shabanova renamed the Society the National Council of Women and affiliated it with the ICW in early 1917 before the February Revolution, thus finally fulfilling Filosofova's dream. After the February Revolution the council was sanctioned by the Provisional Government, but by the time it met in December 1917 the Bolsheviks had seized power. In the period between the February and October Revolutions, Shabanova and the Society continued to promote the cause of woman's rights, participating in the largest woman's rights demonstration in Russian history on March 19, 1917. Two days later, Shabanova represented the Society as part of a feminist delegation to Prince L'vov, the Provisional Government's premier, and heard him pledge his support for woman suffrage, which became law within a few days.

The Mutual Philanthropic Society, along with most other independent civic organizations, ceased existence soon after the October Bolshevik Revolution.

Cross-references: Anna Filosofova, First All-Russian Women's Congress (1908), Anna Shabanova, *Soiuz ravnopravii zhenshchin* (Women's Equal Rights Union), *Zhenskaia progressivnaia partiia* (Women's Progressive Party).

Suggested Readings:

Edmondson, Linda Harriet. *Feminism in Russia, 1900–1917.* Stanford, CA: Stanford University Press, 1984.

Goldberg, Rochelle (Ruthchild). "The Russian Women's Movement 1859–1917." Ph.D. Diss., University of Rochester, 1976.

Grishina, Zoia V. "*Dvizhenie za politicheskoe ravnopraviia v gody pervoi Rossiiskoi revoliutsii*" (The Movement for Women's Equal Political Rights in the Years of the First Russian Revolution [1905]). *Vestnik Moskovskogo universiteta (Bulletin of Moscow University)*, ser. 8 *Istoriia (History)*, no. 2 (1982): 33–42.

Grishina, Zoia V. "*Zhenskie organizatsii v Rossii (1905g.-fevral'/mart 1917 g*" (Women's Organizations in Russia (1905–February/March 1917)." Ph.D. Diss., Moscow State University, 1978.

Shabanova, Anna. *Ocherk zhenskago dvizheniia v Rossii (Outline of the Women's Movement in Russia).* St. Petersburg: Prosveshchnie, 1912.

Stites, Richard. *The Women's Liberation Movement in Russia: Feminism, Nihilism, and Bolshevism, 1860–1930.* Princeton, NJ: Princeton University Press, 1978, 1991.

Rochelle Goldberg Ruthchild

Ruttsen (or Von-Ruttsen), Liudmila Nikolaevna (n.d.)

Organizer of a zemstvo congress in her native Kursk, Ruttsen initiated the founding meeting of the *Soiuz ravnopraviia zhenshchin* (Women's Equal Rights Union) in Moscow in February 1905. She was a member of the Women's Union Central Bureau, wrote for its journal *Union of Women (Soiuz zhenshchin)*, and attended and spoke at the 1908 Women's Congress.

Liudmila Ruttsen was among those early twentieth-century Russian feminist activists about whom we know little but who apparently played a key role in the woman's rights movement. An early participant in zemstvo congresses in her native Kursk, Ruttsen had links to the Kadet Party; she was the sister of A. N. Ruttsen, a founding member of the party.

According to Mariia Chekhova, Ruttsen gathered a small group together in Moscow in February 1905 in the "cozy living room" of N. A. Gol'tseva, an organizer of the Prechistenskie Courses, the first Russian "Workers University." This small group consisted of teachers, doctors, and social activists, about twenty in all, and included one man, Nikolai Chekhov. As the revolutionary fervor of 1905 swept over Russia, the group grew rapidly until it was clear that a larger organizational framework was necessary.

Ruttsen attended the Women's Union's founding congress May 8–11, 1905, as part of its Central Bureau and took an active part in the congress and in Union activities. She wrote pamphlets, such as *Ravnopravnost' zhenshchin (Women's Equality)*, lectured, and wrote for the union journal, *Soiuz zhenshchin (Union of Women)*. Ruttsen lectured about the Englishwomen's movement at the 1908 Women's Congress. She harshly criticized the militants' "extremely aggressive character in relation to the government," called their tactics wrong, and explained them partly as reflecting the after effects of the suffragists' harsh imprisonment. Sister feminist Zinaida Mirovich spoke at the same session and praised the English suffragists' tactics.

At the end of 1909, with the demise of the Women's Union complete and the *Union of Women* publishing its last issue, Ruttsen and other former activists joined the *Liga ravnopraviia zhenshchin* (League for Women's Equal Rights). Ruttsen's fate after the Bolshevik Revolution is not known.

Cross-references: Mariia Aleksandrovna Chekhova, First All-Russian Women's Congress (1908), Zinaida Mirovich, *Soiuz ravnopraviia zhenshchin* (Women's Equal Rights' Union), *Soiuz zhenshchin* (Union of Women).

Suggested Readings

Edmondson, Linda Harriet. *Feminism in Russia, 1900–1917.* Stanford, CA: Stanford University Press, 1984.

Edmondson, Linda Harriet. "Women's rights, civil rights and the debate over citizens in the 1905 Revolution." In *Women and Society in Russia and the Soviet Union*, edited by Linda Edmondson, 77–100. Cambridge: Cambridge University Press, 1992.

Goldberg, Rochelle (Ruthchild). "The Russian Women's Movement 1859–1917." Ph.D. Diss., University of Rochester, 1976.

Grishina, Zoia V. "*Dvizhenie za politicheskoe ravnopravie zhenshchin v gody pervoi Rossiiskoi revoliutsii*" (The Movement for Women's Political Equal Rights in the Years of the First Russian Revolution). *Vestnik Moskovskogo universiteta (Moscow University Herald)*. Ser. 8, *Istoriia (History)*, no. 2 (1982): 33–42.

Grishina, Zoia V. "*Zhenskie organizatsii v Rossii, 1905 g.-fevral'/mart 1917 g*" (Women's Organizations in Russia, 1905–February/March 1917). Abstract of a *kandidat*'s Diss., Moscow State University, 1978.

Mirovich, N. (Z. S. Ivanova). *Iz istorii zhenskago dvizheniia v Rossii.* Moscow: Tipografiia T-va, I. D. Sytina, 1908.

Ruttsen, L. *Ravnopravnost' zhenshchin (Equality of Women).* Moscow: Lissner and Sobko, 1907.

Stites, Richard. *The Women's Liberation Movement in Russia: Feminism, Nihilism, and Bolshevism, 1860–1930.* Princeton, NJ: Princeton University Press, 1978, 1991.

Rochelle Goldberg Ruthchild

S

Samoilova, Konkordiia Nikolaevna (born Gromova) (1876–1921)

A revolutionary and activist among women workers before and after the Bolshevik Revolution.

Konkordiia Gromova was born in Irkutsk in 1876. Her father was a priest in the Orthodox Church. In 1894 she completed a gymnasium for girls and in 1896 entered the Bestuzhev Courses for women in order to become a teacher. While in the teacher training program, she became active in the student movements. In 1901 as a result of participating in a student protest movement, she was arrested and expelled from school. In 1902 she moved to Paris, where she enrolled in the *Vol'naia Russkaia shkola obshchestvennykh nauk* (Free Russian School of Social Sciences). Lecturers at the School included V. I. Lenin and Iuri Martov. In 1903 she joined the Bolshevik faction of the Russian Social Democratic Labor Party (RSDLP/B). Returning to Russia, over the next few years she worked as a propagandist for the revolutionary cause in the Tver, Odessa, Rostov, Lugansk, and Moscow committees of the RSDLP/B under the pseudonym Natasha. About 1906 she began a relationship with Arkadi A. Samoilov, and they were officially married in 1913, after overcoming a number of legal obstacles so that she could reside with him in St. Petersburg. Samoilov was also a propagandist in the party. The marriage was a happy one, and they had two children.

At the end of 1912, Samoilova became a secretary of the editorial board of the party's newspaper, *Pravda*, and later part of the editorial staff of the journal *Rabotnitsa (Working Woman)*. Her expertise about women workers, developed during the years before the Bolshevik Revolution, was put to use shortly after the revolution. In November 1917 Samoilova, together with Alexandra Kollontai and K. Nikolaeva, organized the First Conference of Women Workers in Petrograd. The conference sought to attract the sympathy of women workers. In 1918 she helped to organize the First All-Russian Congress of Women Workers. She also assisted in the establishment of government and party departments concerned with the problems of women workers. After her husband's death, she no longer wanted to live in his native Petrograd and sought an assignment far away from where they had lived together. As an organizer for *Zhenotdel*, she worked with women in various regions, especially in the Ukraine.

In 1920–1921 she became the head of the political department of the ship *Krasnaia zvezda (Red Star)*, which stopped at every city along the Vol'ga to propagandize the Bolshevik cause among the population. Samoilova also had a special purpose in going on this mission. She wanted to find the grave of her husband, who had died of typhoid fever in early 1919. Later she was persuaded to undertake one more trip on the *Krasnaia zvezda*; during that trip in 1921, she was appalled by the conditions that she witnessed en route. She herself contracted cholera and died in Astrakhan, shortly before she was scheduled to return to Moscow to work in *Zhenotdel*.

During her brief life, Samoilova became known as an advocate for women workers, and most of her reputation rests on that work. Her life was cut short by fatal disease, as was often the case during the turbulent civil war.

Cross-references: Aleksandra Kollontai, Higher Education for Women, *Zhenotdel*.

Suggested Readings

Clements, Barbara Evans. *Bolshevik Women*. Cambridge: Cambridge University Press, 1997.

Kudelli, P. *K. N. Samoilova—Gromova ("Natasha"), 1876–1921*. Leningrad: Priboi, 1925.

Putilovskaia, N. "K. N. Samoilova." In *Slavnie Bolshevichki (Glorious Bolshevik Women)*, edited by E. D. Stasova. Moscow: Gospolitizdat, 1958.

Stites, Richard. *The Women's Liberation Movement in Russia: Feminism, Nihilism and Bolshevism, 1860–1930*. Princeton, NJ: Princeton University Press, 1979, 1991.

Vinogradova, S. F. "*Zhizn', otdannaia revoliutsionnoi rabote*" (Living for Revolution). In *Leningradki: Vospominaniia: Ocherki. Dokumenty (Leningradites: Memoirs, Essays, Documents)*. Leningrad: Lenizdat, 1969.

Liudmila Zhukova

Shabanova, Anna Nikolaevna (1848–1932)

Pediatrician, advocate for children, activist in the women's movement, and leader in women's organizations, including the Women's Mutual Philanthropic Society.

Anna Nikolaevna Shabanova was born in 1848 in Smolensk to a gentry family. While in her teens, her family suffered severe economic reverses, and she worked as a governess to support herself. Despite her family's difficult financial circumstances, Shabanova was determined to continue her studies. She went to Moscow in the 1860s, where she joined the Ishutin circle, a hard-core group of nihilists who were involved in an unsuccessful attempt on the tsar's life in 1866. Her involvement in the circle's communal and propaganda work resulted in her arrest in 1866; she was kept in solitary confinement for six months.

After her release, Shabanova returned to Smolensk. There she organized an unsuccessful petition signed by 400 women to allow women to attend Smolensk University. Undeterred, she applied to the Medical-Surgical Academy, where some women had been studying as auditors. Despite the assistance of the well-known writer Mikhail E. Saltykov-Schedrin and the prominent physiologist Ivan M. Sechenov, she was not admitted. In 1870 with the help of a stipend from Saltykov-Schedrin, she enrolled in Helsingfors (Helsinski) University, supporting herself with translation work and returning home in the summers to earn money. When the Higher Women's Medical Courses opened in St. Petersburg in 1872, she transferred into the second-year class in 1873 and graduated in 1878. Influenced by the lectures of Professor Karl A. Raukhfus, she made pediatrics her specialty.

As a pediatrician, Shabanova left her early political agitation behind and turned her reformist impulses to improving children's lives. Shabanova initially worked in the children's clinic of Nikolaevskii military hospital in St. Petersburg, assisting women medical students. At the same time, Dr. Raukhfus, her former professor, invited her to work as a staff physician at his clinic in the Ol'denburg Children's Hospital in St. Petersburg. Shabanova worked at the clinic for the rest of her life, eventually becoming a senior hospital physician and continuing on as a consultant well into her eighties. One of Shabanova's major accomplishments was the establishment of the Society for the Treatment of Chronically Ill Children. Chemist and composer A. P. Borodin contributed the proceeds from one of his concerts to the cause. Assisted by Borodin's and other private contributions, she opened a children's clinic at Gatchina in 1882 and in 1900 opened a second clinic at Vindava.

Shabanova was also intimately involved in women's issues and founded the *Zhenskoe vzaimno-blagotvoritel'noe obshchestvo* (Russian Women's Mutual Philanthropic Society) in 1895, the first woman's rights organization in Russia. She also participated in the international women's movement as a member of the League of Struggle for the Rights of Women. In 1899 she was elected chair of the International Women's League of Peace, which collapsed with the advent of World War I. In 1908 she participated in the organization of the First All-Russian Women's Congress. In 1917 she became president of the Russian National Council of Women, which was the Russian division of the International Women's Congress.

Shabanova had wide-ranging interests and worked tirelessly for causes in which she believed. She published extensively and attended professional congresses both at home and abroad. Prior to her death in 1932, she was honored by the new socialist Union of Doctors, and the library at Raukhfus Hospital in St. Petersburg was named for her. In 1928 she received a medal as a Hero of Labor and in 1929 was chosen as a member of the American Academy of Social Sciences in Philadelphia. In her own time she was as well known as the first Russian woman doctor, Nadezhda Prokof'evna Suslova, due to her affiliations with various women's organizations, her overseas travels, and her tireless work on behalf of children.

Cross-references: Higher Education for Women, Mariia Pokrovskaia, Ol'ga Shapir, Russian Women's Mutual Philanthropic Society, Women's Medical Courses.

Suggested Readings

"*A. N. Shabanova: K eiu portretu*" (Portrait of A. N. Shabanova). *Zhenskoe Delo (Women's Affairs)* no. 3 (1910): 2–3.

Pavluchkova, A. V. "*Pervaia Zhenshchina-pediatr, geroi truda A. N. Shabanova*" (The First Woman Pediatrician, Labor Hero A. N. Shabanova). *Fel'dsher i akusherka (Physician's Assistant and Midwife)* 40 (1975): 41–42.

Shabanova, Anna. "*Dva goda v Gel'singforskom universitete*" (Two Years at Helsingfors University). *Vestnik Evropy (Messenger of Europe)* 2 (1888): 289–310.

Shabanova, Anna. "*Iz pervykh let zhenskogo meditsinskogo obrazovaniia v Rossii: Vospominaniia zhenshchiny-vracha pervogo vypuska*" (The First Years of Women's Medical Education in Russia: Memoirs of a Woman Doctor from the First Graduating Class). In *K svetu: nauchno-literaturnyi sbornik (Toward the Light: Scientific-Literary Collection)*, 289–310. St. Petersburg, 1904.

Shabanova, Anna. *O mezhdunarodnykh zhenskikh kongressakh (On the international Women's Congress)*. St. Petersburg, 1897.

Shabanova, Anna. *O podanii pervoi pomoshchi v neschastnykh sluchaikh do pribytiia vracha (Providing First Aid in Accidents until the Arrival of a Doctor)*. St. Petersburg, 1897.

Shabanova, Anna. *Obzor deiatelnosti detskoi lechebnitsy v Gatchine (Survey of the Activities of the Gatchina Children's Clinic)*. St. Petersburg: Gokike, 1887.

Shabanova, Anna. *Ocherk zhenskogo dvizheniia v Rossii (An Essay on the Women's Movement in Russia)*. St. Petersburg, 1912.

Shabanova, Anna. "*Zhenskoe vrachebnoe obrazovanie v Rossii*" (Women's Medical Education in Russia). *Istoricheskii Vestnik (Historical Messenger)*, 131, no. 3 (1913): 952–961.

Tuve, Jeanette. *The First Russian Women Physicians*. Newtonville, MA: Oriental Research Partners, 1984.

Michelle DenBeste

Shapir, Ol'ga Andreevna (née Kislaikova) (1850–1916)

A well-known nineteenth-century writer and one of the leaders and theorists of Russian liberal feminism.

Ol'ga Kislaikova was born in Oranienbaum, near St. Petersburg, on September 10 (22), 1850. Her father was a military official in the commandant's headquarters in Oranienbaum. In 1865 she completed Alexandrovskaia gymnasium in St. Petersburg with a gold medal, signifying that she was the top student in her class. Like many young women in the 1860s and 1870s, Ol'ga attended public lectures, such as the Vladimirskie Courses, and participated in intellectual circles. The Vladimirskie Courses were free and one of Russia's first educational initiatives on behalf of women. Although supported by her family, Ol'ga wanted to earn a living on her own. She did translations and wrote short articles for the newspapers *Birzhevye vedomosti (Stock-Exchange News)* and *Novoe vremia (New Times).*

In 1871, when Ol'ga turned twenty-one, she announced her independence to her family. She began to manage the Vasileostrovsky Library, one of the libraries of Aleksandr Cherkesov, a well-known owner of libraries and bookstores in St. Petersburg and Moscow. In 1872 she married Lazar Shapir, a former student of the Medical-Surgical Academy in St. Petersburg, who had been exiled to Novgorod for participation in the Nechaev Affair. Sergei Nechaev was a revolutionary who led the group *Narodnaia rasprava* (Popular Punishment). When the government took action against the group, Nechaev fled abroad, but his followers were tried and convicted. Ol'ga managed to get permission for her husband to complete his education, and she supported the family during this time, which was atypical of women of her time but characteristic of her. During her entire life, she violated standard norms and stereotypes. After graduation from the Surgical Academy in St. Petersburg in 1874, her husband worked as a rural doctor in Saratov *guberniia* (region). In Saratov province, she turned her attention to writing. Her first novel, *Na poroge zhizne (On the Threshold of Life)*, was published in 1879. The themes in her works were popular among Russian intellectuals. Topics like the female world, relations between men and women, the spiritual suppression of women, and the aspirations of downtrodden people to improve their life resonated with the intelligentsia.

In the 1880s and 1890s Ol'ga Shapir became a popular and fashionable writer. Everything she wrote was published both in magazines and in book form. Ol'ga returned to St. Petersburg in 1881 with her two children and immediately became engaged in supporting other writers and assisting in the development of women's activities. In 1895 she joined the newly created *Russkoe zhenskoe vzaimno-blagotvoritel'noe obshchestvo* (Russian Women's Mutual Philanthropic Society). Within the Society she at various times served as manager of its Commission on Fundraising, manager of the Society's *Otdel referatov* (Department of Abstracts), and member of the governing Council that determined the policies of the organization in its early stages. The Department of Abstracts was the theoretical arm of the Society, and members presented their research on women's issues at sessions convened by the department. She considered the Society a female club, which would gather women with shared views, discuss women's problems, and develop strategies for the organization and for the women's movement as a whole. She opposed the Society's involvement in charitable works, preferring to promote a political agenda.

Rivalry existed between Shapir and Anna N. Shabanova, one of the women who established the Society in 1895 and served as its chair throughout its entire existence. Anna Shabanova was an administrative leader, whereas Shapir was an intellectual leader who was charismatic and had enormous prestige. Because of her disagreement about the Society's role in charitable projects, Shapir resigned from the Council but continued to work in the Suffrage Department of the Society, which was planning for the First All-Russian Women's Congress.

In 1905 Shapir also joined the *Soiuz ravnopraviia zhenshchin* (Women's Equal Rights Union), a women's political organization dedicated to securing suffrage. Inspired by the first Russian Revolution of 1905, this organization took part in acts of open civil disobedience, together with the left-wing political parties and organizations.

Shapir was a good public speaker and was adept at business and respected among the Russian *ravnopravki* (equal rights feminists). Shapir's articles and speeches, which advocated women's equality, established her as a theorist of one direction of Russian feminism, which she labeled "feminism of distinction." She believed that men and women were different and that women should not aspire to the uniform standards established by men. Women could not and should not be the same as men, but the differences between men and women should not be a cause for inequality. For Shapir, the purpose of the women's movement was to establish the equality of distinction. From her perspective, it would take more than changing laws to alter women's status since inequality was deeply embedded in society, its laws, customs, and cultural traditions. She believed that the women's movement had to change both political institutions and gender consciousness in society. Shapir's liberal feminism was unusual for her era. She considered gender inequality the central problem of human society and believed that all other public conflicts were derived from the basic conflict of inequality of the sexes.

At the First All-Russian Women's Congress in 1908, Shapir declared that women had to cherish the female experience in history. Her report, "Ideals of the Future," maintained that the female experiences and perceptions were important for humankind and its development and were no less significant than men's experiences.

Although Shapir's theoretical works were known only among a narrow circle of Russian feminists, her fictional works gave her a broader audience in society. Through fiction, Shapir tried to change the cultural stereotypes of women and to counter the ideals of female passivity, obedience, and self-renunciation. In this respect, she challenged the traditions of Russian literature. In her novels a new, positive image of a Russian woman was contrasted with the traditional image. Shapir wrote about women who succeeded in the public sphere and achieved high positions in society. Her heroines revealed feelings of pragmatism, professionalism, and self-sufficiency. Shapir rejected self-sacrifice as the norm for Russian women. She defined women's emancipation as the achievement of self-realization and self-respect. She condemned the idea that women should subordinate their interests to those of the family and promoted the unconditional right of women to participate in public life.

After the Congress, she continued to work in the Suffrage Department of the Russian Women's Philanthropic Society. The department drafted legislative and administrative proposals about women's participation in local government and about woman's rights to an inheritance and to live separately from their spouses. Some of these proposals were adopted by the State Duma.

Shapir resigned in 1912 because of illness and died on July 13 (26), 1916, in St. Petersburg; she was buried in the Literatorskie Mostki of Volkovskii Orthodox Cemetery.

Cross-references: Russian Women's Mutual Philanthropic Society, Anna Shabanova, *Soiuz ravnopraviia zhenshchin* (Women's Equal Rights Union).

Suggested Readings

Iukina, Irina. "*Doktor Anna Shabanova.*" In *Kharizmaticheskie Lichnosti v Istorii Rossii (Charismatic Persons in Russia's History*, edited by I. I. Rogozin, 80–86. St. Petersburg: Petrovskaia Academy of Arts and Sciences, 1997.

Iukina, Irina. "*Ol'ga Shapir—ideolog rossiiskogo feminizma*" (Ol'ga Shapir as a Russian Ideologist of Feminism). In *Iz istorii zhenskogo dvizheniia v Rossii (From the History of Women's Movement in Russia)*, edited by O. R. Demidova, 116–127. St. Petersburg: Nevskii Institute of Language and Culture, 1998.

Iukina, Irina. "*Zabytaia Feministka Ol'ga Shapir*" (Forgotten Feminist Ol'ga Shapir). In *Materialy konferentsii provedennoi 30-ogo maia 1996 goda v Moskve* "Zhenshchina i kul'tura" (*Materials of the Conference, "Woman and Culture," Moscow, May 30, 1996*), edited by E. I. Trofimova, 20–39. Moscow: Information Center of Independent Women's Forum, 1997.

Kazakova, Irina. "Ol'ga Andreevna Shapir." In *Dictionary of Russian Women Writers*, edited by Marina Ledkovsky, Charlotte Rosenthal, and Mary Zirin, 577–580. Westport, CT: Greenwood Publishing Group, 1994.

Shabanova, A. (Anna Nikolaevna). *Ocherk zhenskogo dvizheniia v Rossii (Story of Women's Movement in Russia*. St. Petersburg: Tip. *Obrazovanie*, 1912.

Shapir, Ol'ga. "*Idealy budeshego*" (Ideals of the Future). In *Trudy pervogo vserossiiskogo zhenskogo s'ezda pri Russkom Zhenskom obshestve v Sankt-Peterburge, 10–16 Dek., 1908 (Works of the First All-Russian Women's Congress*), 895–898. St. Petersburg: Russian Women's Mutual Philanthropic Society, 1909.

Shapir, Ol'ga. "*Obrashchenie k chlenu Gosudarstvennoi Dumy L. Petrazhickomu*" (Official Appeal to a Member of the State Duma Lev Petrazhitchky). (An unpublished document.) St. Petersburg: Department of Manuscripts of the Russian National Library, Fund #844. Archive of O. Shapir, Document #186.

Shapir, Ol'ga. "*Zhenskoe bespravie*" (Women's Inequality). *Birzhevye Vedomosti (Exchange Sheets*) (July 16, 1916): 2–3.

Irina Yukina (Iukina)

Shchepkina, Ekaterina Nikolaevna (1854–1938)

Historian, journalist, and activist, Shchepkina was one of the founders of the Women's Equal Rights Union. She was a teacher at the Bestuzhevskie Higher Courses for Women. She also wrote many articles and books about Russian history.

Ekaterina Nikolaevna Shchepkina was born into a family of scholars and academics. Among her siblings and cousins were several noted historians and linguists. Shchepkina attended the Guerrier Courses in Moscow and then the Bestuzhevskie Higher Courses for Women in St. Petersburg. She was a protégé of the director, Bestuzhev, through whom she met some of the leading male intellectuals of the day, including Fëdor Dostoevskii and Vladimir Solov'ev. Shchepkina taught history at the Bestuzhevskie Courses in 1895–1896 and 1898–1899. Beginning in 1890, she taught history in classes for workers at the *Imperatorskoe Technicheskoe Obshchestvo* (Imperial Technical Society).

In February 1905 Shchepkina was one of the founders of the Women's Equal Rights Union. When the St. Petersburg section of the Union foundered in factional conflict, Shchepkina, along with Liubov'Gurevich and the Union's secretary, Mariia Chekhova, kept that branch of the organization afloat. When some members sought to depoliticize the Union, Shchepkina strongly supported the policy of political involvement, arguing that the goal of woman's equal rights was "political to the core." Shchepkina took part in the 1908 All-Russian Women's Congress, lecturing in a session about peasant women on the topic "*Trud i zdorov'e krest'ianki*" (The Work and Health of the Peasant Woman) and arguing that peasant women endured a double oppression as both peasants and women.

The Women's Equal Rights Union was defunct by the time of the All-Russian Women's Congress in December 1908. Key activists, searching for a vehicle to continue the fight for woman's equal rights, found it in the *Liga ravnopraviia zhenshchin* (League for Women's Equal Rights). The League, unlike the Union, was legally registered at its founding in March 1907 and able to operate publicly in a period of increased police surveillance and repression. Shchepkina became head of the League's lecture bureau. The activist Mariia Chekhova served as President; Liubov Gurevich, Anna Kal'manovich, Liudmila Ruttsen, and Ariadna Tyrkova-Williams were also active.

Shchepkina remained active in the League and in 1917 was one of ten candidates on the organization's electoral list for the Constituent Assembly. Others on the league list included its President, Poliksena Shishkina-Iavein, Mariia Chekhova, Marxist and feminist E. D. Kuskova, historian Alexandra Efimenko, and populist and advocate for "legal Marxism" A. Kalmykova.

A prolific writer, she published two historical monographs, stories from Russian history for Sunday School students, a Russian history textbook, and articles for several "thick" journals about women's history and the current situation of women in Russia. Shchepkina contributed articles to both of the leading feminist journals, *Soiuz zhenshchin (Union of Women*) and *Zhenskii vestnik (Women's Herald*).

Like many others, Shchepkina's family was torn apart by the October Revolution. Her twin brother, the Kadet Nikolai N. Shchepkin, was executed by the Bolsheviks in 1919 for counterrevolutionary activity. Her younger brother, the historian Evgenii N. Shchepkin, actively supported the Bolshevik Revolution but died in 1920, his health shattered by the privations of the Civil War. In the early 1920s Shchepkina continued to write for publication. In 1921, at the age of sixty-seven, she published a history of the women's movement during the French Revolution, with a critical introduction by the leading Bolshevik women's activist, Alexandra Kollontai. Her next project, an article about the

Women's Equal Rights Union, was to appear in *Byloe (The Past)*, but in 1926 this journal ceased publication. Little is known about Shchepkina's life after this. She died in 1938 at the age of eighty-four.

Cross-references: Mariia Chekhova, Higher Education for Women, Anna Kal'manovich, *Liga ravnopraviia zhenshchin* (League for Women's Equal Rights), Liudmila Ruttsen, *Soiuz ravnopraviia zhenshchin* (Women's Equal Rights Union), *Soiuz zhenshchin* (Union of Women), Ariadna Tyrkova, *Zhenskii vestnik (Women's Herald*).

Suggested Readings

Edmondson, Linda Harriet. *Feminism in Russia 1900–1917*. Stanford, CA: Stanford University Press, 1984.

Goldberg, Rochelle (Ruthchild). "The Russian Women's Movement 1859–1917." Ph.D. Diss., University of Rochester, 1976.

Grishina, Zoia V. "Dvizhenie za politicheskoe ravnopravie zhenshchin v gody pervoi *Rossiiskoi revoliutsii* (The Movement for Women's Political Equal Rights in the Years of the First Russian Revolution)." *Vestnik Moskovskogo universiteta (Moscow University Herald)*. Ser. 8 *Istoriia (History)*, no. 2 (1982): 33–42.

Grishina, Zoia V. "*Zhenskie organizatsii v Rossii, 1905 g.-fevral'/mart 1917 g*" (Women's Organizations in Russia, 1905–February/March 1917). Abstract of a *kandidat*'s Diss., Moscow State University, 1978.

Shchepkina, Ekaterina N. *Iz istorii zhenskoi lichnosti v Rossii (From the History of Women's Personality in Russia)*. St. Petersburg, 1914.

Shchepkina, Ekaterina N. "*Pamiati dvukh zhenshchin-vrachei*" (The Memories of Two Women Doctors). *Obrazovanie (Education)* 5–6 (1896): Part I, 92–137.

Shchepkina, Ekaterina N. "*Vospominaniia i dnevniki russkikh zhenshchin*" (The Reminiscences and Diaries of Two Russian Women). *Istoricheskii vestnik (The Historical Herald)* 8 (1914): 536–55.

Shchepkina, Ekaterina N. *Zhenskoe dvizhenie v gody Frantsuzskoi revoliutsii, s obrashcheniem k chitateliu A. Kollontai (The Women's Movement in the Years of the French Revolution, with an Introduction to the Readers by A. Kollontai)*. Peterburg (Petrograd): Gosudarstevennoe izdatel'stvo, 1921.

Shchepkina, Ekaterina N. "*Zhenskoe naselenie Peterburga*" (The Female Population of Petersburg). *Obrazovanie* 5–6 (1897): 218–232.

Stites, Richard. *The Women's Liberation Movement in Russia: Feminism, Nihilism, and Bolshevism, 1860–1930*. Princeton, NJ: Princeton University Press, 1978, 1991.

Rochelle Goldberg Ruthchild

Shishkina-Iavein, Poliksena Nesterovna (1875–1947)

Physician, activist and feminist, and a leader of the League for Women's Equality before 1918.

Poliksena Shishkina was born in Nikolaev in 1875 into the family of a musical conductor in the military in 1875. Shishkina was among the first to graduate from the St. Petersburg Women's Medical Institute in 1904. In 1900 she married Georgi Iulievich Iavein, a professor at the Medical-Surgical Academy in St. Petersburg.

Shishkina-Iavein belonged to the third generation of feminist activists in the Russian women's movement. These Russian women, born at the end of the 1860s and early 1870s, were the first Russian women not part of royalty to succeed in politics. They included Ariadna Tyrkova, Sofia Panina, Anna Miliukova, Elena Stasova, Aleksandra Kollontai, Nadezhda Krupskaia, and Inessa Armand. Although the life of liberal women politicians developed dramatically, they were displaced from the political stage by the revolutionary events surrounding 1917.

The achievements and popularity of Poliksena Shishkina-Iavein were connected with the *Liga ravnopraviia zhenshchin* (League for Women's Equality). The League was initially established in March 1907 to promote political and civil rights for women. Shishkina-Iavein became the League's chair in 1910 at a difficult time for the movement. The magazine *Union of the Women*, printed in St. Petersburg in 1907–1909, had closed. Its former editor and chair of the League, Mariia Chekhova, disappointed and tired in defeat, left St. Petersburg for Moscow.

The vigorous activity of Russian feminists in the highly political *Soiuz ravnopraviia zhenshchin* (Women's Equal Rights Union) to obtain the right to vote for everyone and to coordinate their efforts with revolutionary groups had not achieved the anticipated results. The idea of the equality of women did not have support among the wider population.

At the time that Shishkina-Iavein became the chair of the League, the feminists' participation in a left-wing coalition was reconsidered, and the feminists concluded that the women's movement had to be an independent political force. It had to define its own strategic purposes and develop a theory and methods of struggle. The League of Women's Equality moved away from the idea of democracy for all and sought to represent only the political and economic interests of women in society. As chair of the League, P. Shishkina-Iavein changed the organization's goals to focus its efforts on the pursuit of woman suffrage. She encouraged the publishing and educational activities of the League. The number of members in the organization grew from 219 in 1910, to 1,235 in 1915. New branches of the League opened in Tomsk and Ekaterinburg. Shishkina-Iavein considered legislative activity the only way to achieve social change; therefore, the Council of the League increased its attention to the State Duma's actions. Any proposed bill in the Duma was subjected to gender examination in the League. The League defended women's interests, directing inquiries, protests, and feedback to the State Duma if a law appeared to affect women's interests negatively. The Russian feminists avoided class distinctions, considering themselves obliged to work on behalf of all women. For example, in 1910 the League directed a petition to the State Council concerning the government's bill on land reform, which modified the 1906 land reform of Petr A. Stolypin. The feminists were worried that, if adopted, the new law would violate woman's rights, especially the rights of peasant women. In their petition, the League offered concrete measures to protect the rights of peasant women.

The League managed to become a persistent influence on Duma proceedings. Pressure from the League compelled the Third State Duma (1907–1912) to consider bills about divorce, separate residences of spouses, the right of women to practice law, and woman suffrage. Shishkina-Iavein, together with a member of the State Duma, Aleksandr Ivanovich Shingarev, developed the government bill canceling state regulation of prostitution. The state regulation of prostitution limited the rights of prostitutes, who could not carry internal passports, required of other citizens, but only special "yellow tickets," which did not bear the full rights of citizenship.

The League at various times also initiated discussion about granting women who had certain property qualifications the right to elect rural and urban self-management officials. On this issue, the League departed from its position on universal suffrage for women. Although the Russian women's movement criticized the League for favoring special interests, Shishkina-Iavein thought its position was appropriate. If the League could not achieve universal suffrage for women, it could at least advance voting rights for some groups.

The League's legislative initiatives were widely publicized at public assemblies, meetings, and public debates, which attracted women from different social strata, politicians, and the mass media. The reports and speeches were printed and were distributed in big cities and in the provinces. Shishkina-Iavein's speech, *"Zhenshchina-glasnyi"* (Woman-Politician), issued in Petrograd in 1917, reflected the passion of the League's meetings.

The beginning of World War I turned the League's activity from politics to charity, such as opening public canteens, hospitals, and shelters for women and children. Shishkina-Iavein not only was involved as an organizer but also taught medical courses and worked as a physician in soldiers' hospitals.

Led by Shishkina-Iavein, the League of Women's Equality became the largest and most active female political organization in Russia. The League organized the women's protest in 1917, when it discovered that the program of the Provisional Government did not include woman suffrage. The League's appeal in support of woman suffrage to the Revolutionary Council of Workers' and Soldiers' Deputies and to the Ministerial Council of the Provisional Government did not produce any results. Shishkina-Iavein and other League activists decided to organize protests. About ninety women's organizations and groups joined the League. The League's Council officially handed a resolution to the Provisional Government on March 4 (17), 1917, demanding woman suffrage.

The appeal to the women of Petrograd to unite in the struggle for political freedom was posted and actively distributed in the streets, sent to women's organizations, factories, and women's educational institutions. Mass meetings were held at which Shishkina-Iavein was one of the featured speakers. The League's Council organized a woman's demonstration on March 19 (April 1), 1917, in which about 40,000 women participated. Shishkina-Iavein and the well-known revolutionary Vera Figner rode in an automobile in the center of the demonstration.

At the State Duma building, Shishkina-Iavein made a speech expressing women's demands for equal human rights. By evening, Prince Lvov, head of the Provisional Government, acquiesced to the women's demands. On March 21 (April 3), 1917, a delegation of well-known Russian feminists, including Shishkina-Iavein, Ariadna V. Tyrkova, Anna. N Shabanova, Mariia I. Pokrovskaia, and Anna S. Miliukova, met with Prince Lvov. They received assurances that women would receive the right to vote and could participate in electing the Constituent Assembly in November–December 1917. Although the election ballots were later destroyed by the Bolshevik government, it is believed that Ariadna V. Tyrkova was elected. The Constituent Assembly met briefly in January 1918 before it was disbanded by the Bolshevik government. In 1918 all rival parties and political organizations were abolished by the Soviet government. Shishkina-Iavein and her husband went to Estonia, which gained its independence after the revolutions of 1917, but he died soon afterward, and she was not permitted to practice medicine in Estonia. Eventually, she returned to the USSR and worked as a physician. She lived through the blockade of Leningrad during World War II and died in 1947. Shishkina-Iavein was buried in Nikolski Cemetery in St. Petersburg.

Cross-references: Inessa Armand, Mariia Chekhova, Vera Figner, *Liga ravonopravlia zhenshchin* (the League for Women's Equality), Aleksandra Kollontai, Nadezhda Krupskaia, Sofia Panina, Russian Women's Mutual Philanthropic Society, Anna Shabanova, Ol'ga Shapir, *Soiuz ravnopraviia zhenshchin*, Elena Stasova, Ariadna Tyrkova.

Suggested Readings

Aivazova, S. *"Gendernye issledovaniia: perechityvaia A. Kollontai"* (Gender Research: Rereading A. Kollontai). In *Formirovanie gernoi kul'tury i studentcheskoi molodëzhei (The Formation of Gender Culture in Student Youth)*, edited by E. V. Mashkova, 40–43. Naberezhnye Chelny: Femina, 1995.

Edmundson, Linda Harriet. *Feminism in Russia, 1900–1917*. Stanford, CA: Stanford University Press, 1984.

Iukina, Irina. *"Doktor Shabanova"* (Dr. Shabanova). In *Kharizmaticheskie lichnosti v istorii Rossii (Charismatic People in the History of Russia)*, edited by I. I. Rogovin, 80–86. St. Petersburg: Petrovskaia Academy of Science and Arts, 1997.

Shishkina-Iavein, P. *Zhenshchina-glasnyi (Woman Politician)*. Petrograd: Liga Ravnopraviia zhenshchin, 1917.

Zakuta, O. *Kak v revolutsionnoe vremia Vserossiiskaia Liga Ravnopraviia zhenshchin dobivalas' izbiratel'nykh prav dlia russkikh zhenshchin (How in a Revolutionary Period the League for Women's Equality Achieved Suffrage for Russian Women)*. Petrograd: Izdanie Vserossiiskoi Ligi ravnopravliia zhenshchin, 1917.

Irina Yukina (Iukina)

Soiuz ravnopraviia zhenshchin (Women's Equal Rights Union) (1905–1908)

The largest feminist organization in the history of Russia, which arose after the 1905 Revolution but collapsed in the repressive reaction that followed the revolutionary fervor.

Organized during the revolutionary events of 1905, the *Soiuz ravnopraviia zhenshchin* (Women's Equal Rights Union) was the major force for lobbying for woman suffrage and equal rights within the overall movement against the tsarist autocracy, among liberal and socialist parties, and in the Duma. Union members were largely progressive women professionals. Outreach to urban working-class and peasant women proved difficult, and the Union foundered in the repression following 1905.

Founded in Moscow in February 1905 by a group of about thirty women professionals, including Mariia Chekhova, Zinaida Mirovich, zemstvo activist Liudmila von Ruttsen, educator Emiliia Vakhterova, and historian Ekaterina Shchepkina, the Women's Equal Rights Union was formed in reaction to the indifference of liberals and the Left to women's issues. Union members fought to include woman's rights among the central concerns of the Liberation movement, in keeping with the ideals of such early Russian radicals as Alexander Herzen and Nikolai Chernyshevskii. The members' efforts gained them inclusion; the Women's Union was one of the fourteen unions represented at the founding congress of the Union of Unions in Moscow in May 1905.

The union organization featured a Central Bureau at the top, local committees and local bureaus in the middle, and local chapters at the base. Membership was open to men; one man, N. V. Chekhov, Teachers Union activist and husband of Women's Union founder Mariia Chekhova, was elected to the organization's Central Bureau. There were considerable autonomy and a wide range of political perspectives among Women's Union chapters. Some were dominated by socialists; others, by liberal Kadets. Socialists active in the Union included Socialist Revolutionary Ol'ga Vol'kenshtein, Menshevik Margarita Margulies, and Bolshevik Anna Gurevich; Kadets included Anna Miliukova and, later, Ariadna Tyrkova. The Union never sought to become a legal organization because of members' philosophical objections and the slim chances of official approval. The organization's lack of legal status crippled its activity even more as government repression increased in the aftermath of the 1905 Revolution.

Throughout its existence, the Women's Union maintained contact with the international feminist movement. Union delegates such as Zinaida Mirovich attended International Woman Suffrage Alliance Congresses, reporting on the ups and downs of the organization and the feminist movement in general in Russia.

Women's Union activity in 1905–1906 included extensive lobbying. Such efforts were directed first at other unions, municipal government, and zemstvo organizations and then at the Dumas. Struggles to convince those in newly forming unions to include woman suffrage were generally successful; by mid-1905 only the professors and the zemstvo unions held out. The Union of Unions included woman's rights provisions two months after its founding, with future Kadet Party leader Paul Miliukov casting the lone dissenting vote. After a sit-in at their Central Bureau office, the zemstvo and town representatives endorsed woman suffrage. At the liberal Kadet Party's first congress in October 1905, Kadet leader Miliukov and his wife, Anna, publicly clashed on the issue of woman suffrage. In deference to Miliukov, the successful woman suffrage resolution was made nonbinding. Kadet Women's Union members successfully won a mandatory woman suffrage plank at the party's second congress in January 1906 after an impassioned speech by writer Ariadna Tyrkova, a Women's Union and Kadet activist.

The Union's period of greatest militancy coincided with the height of general revolutionary activity in 1905, from the October general strike through the Moscow uprising in December. Union members marched in demonstrations, maintained barricades, and served as medics during the Moscow uprising. At the Union's October Delegate Congress, members endorsed a resolution allying with the socialist parties and voted almost two to one to boycott the Duma elections. By the time the First Duma convened in April 1906, union members more sympathetic to Russia's first parliament were in control.

At the request of some Duma representatives, four union members, Shchepkina, Liubov Gurevich, Ol'ga Klirikova, and Gromnitskaia, made specific recommendations for revamping the legal code to incorporate woman's equal rights, but the Duma was dissolved before any action could be taken. Although the Women's Union along with other feminist organizations deluged the Second Duma with woman's rights petitions, Trudovik representatives presented a union suffrage resolution to the Duma, and the Kadets presented similar proposals, the Second Duma never took up the issue. The Third and Fourth Dumas, much more conservative than their predecessors, were even more hostile to woman's rights. In a turnabout, Paul Miliukov, now a Kadet Duma deputy, presented a woman suffrage proposal to the Fourth Duma in February 1913, with no success. By this time, the Women's Union was long since defunct.

At its height at the end of 1905 and the beginning of 1906, the Women's Union boasted 8,000 members, with chapters in Moscow, St. Petersburg, and many provincial cities. In 1907, when the union launched its journal, *Soiuz zhenshchin (Union of Women)*, most of the provincial chapters had disbanded or been closed as the tsarist repression gathered strength. By the time the journal ended publication in December1909, the Women's Union had ceased to exist.

Cross-references: Mariia Chekhova, Zinaida Mirovich, Liudmila Ruttsen, *Soiuz zhenshchin* (Union of Women), Ariadna Tyrkova.

Suggested Readings

Edmondson, Linda Harriet. *Feminism in Russia, 1900–1917*. Stanford, CA: Stanford University Press, 1984.

Edmondson, Linda Harriet. "Women's Rights, Civil Rights and the Debate over Citizens in the 1905 Revolution." In *Women and Society in Russia and the Soviet Union*, edited by Linda Edmondson, 77–100. Cambridge: Cambridge University Press, 1992.

Goldberg, Rochelle (Ruthchild). "The Russian Women's Movement, 1859–1917." Ph.D. Diss., University of Rochester, 1976.

Grishina, Zoia V. "Dvizhenie za politicheskoe ravnopravie zhenshchin v gody pervoi *Rossiiskoi revoliutsii* (The Movement for Women's Political Equal Rights in the Years of the First Russian Revolution). *Vestnik Moskovskogo universiteta (Moscow University Herald)*. Ser. 8, *Istoriia (History)*, no. 2 (1982): 33–42.

Grishina, Zoia V. *"Zhenskie organizatsii v Rossii, 1905 g.-fevral'/mart 1917 g."* (Women's Organizations in Russia, 1905–February/March 1917). Abstract of a *kandidat*'s Diss., Moscow State University, 1978.

Mirovich, N. (Zinaida Sergeevna Ivanova). *Iz istorii zhenskago dvizheniia b Rossii (From the History of Women's Movement in Russia)*. Moscow: Tipografia T-va. I. D. Sytin, 1908.

Orlovskaia, M. V. *O zhenskom dvizhenii v Rossii (On the Women's Movement in Russia)*. St. Petersburg, 1911.

Ravnopravie zhenshchin: Tret'ii s"ezd soiuza ravnopravnosti zhenshchin. Otchety i protokoly 1906 g. (The Equal Rights of Women: Third Congress of the Women's Equal Rights Union) Reports and Protocols, 1906. St. Petersburg: *Ia. Trei*, 1906.

Stites, Richard. *The Women's Liberation Movement in Russia: Feminism, Nihilism, and Bolshevism, 1860–1930*. Princeton, NJ: Princeton University Press, 1978, 1991.

Rochelle Goldberg Ruthchild

Soiuz zhenshchin (Union of Women) (1907–1909)

A feminist journal connected to the *Soiuz ravnopraviia zhenshchin* (Women's Equal Rights Union). A useful source of information about Russian feminism and especially the views of the journal's editor, Mariia Chekhova, in the period of repression that followed the Revolution of 1905.

The first issue of *Soiuz zhenshchin (Union of Women)* appeared in the summer of 1907, when the tide of women's activism, connected to the hopes and expectations aroused by the 1905 Revolution, had largely dissipated. The Women's Equal Rights Union was reeling from government repression, and most of its provincial chapters had closed. Nevertheless, the journal positioned itself as the voice of the new women's movement in Russia.

Mariia Aleksandrovna Chekhova edited the journal in St. Petersburg throughout its existence, with five issues published the first year and twelve issues annually for the subsequent two years. Issues were between sixteen and forty pages each; the press run was 1,000. No fashion advertising appeared; the ads were primarily for other journals, such as the *Theosophical Review, Health Resort News*, and the *Public School Teacher*.

In the first issue, Chekhova reaffirmed the feminist commitment to woman's equal rights and especially the vote, as the first necessary step on the path to female liberation. In its almost exclusive focus on politics, *Soiuz zhenshchin* initially differed from Pokrovskaia's *Zhenskii vestnik*, which covered a wide range of subjects outside the traditional political sphere but related to women.

Soiuz zhenshchin covered the activities of the Women's Union and other feminist organizations in lobbying for woman's rights in the Duma, including petitions, meetings, and the mobilization of peasant and proletarian women. Articles in the journal rejected feminist separatism, or those who sought to win woman's rights outside the framework of the overall political struggle in Russia, to win gains for themselves without regard for others. Equally forcefully, Mariia Chekhova and other contributors argued that woman's rights had to be included in the political agenda of the Liberation movement. Chekhova was quite open in advocating socialism as the system that would truly liberate women and end all forms of exploitation, but she opened the pages of the journal to a wide spectrum of feminist writers, including the more separatist Anna Andreevna Kal'manovich, the Kadet Ariadna Vladimirovna Tyrkova, the literary critic and former editor of the thick journal *Northern Herald (Sever'nyi vestnik)* Liubov Iakovlevna Gurevich, and the socialist revolutionary Olga Akimovna Vol'kenshtein. *Soiuz zhenshchin* reported on the activities of the Women's Progressive Party, the political rival of the Women's Equal Rights Union, but dismissed its program as utopian and Mariia Pokrovskaia, its leader, as an airy idealist.

Government repression effectively suppressed the Liberation movement and increased the sense of isolation of feminists like Chekhova who sought to maintain alliances with the larger movement. By the end of 1907 Chekhova, disillusioned by the lack of real support from other segments of the Liberation movement, advocated the view that the political liberation of women must be up to women themselves. External repression was matched by internal repression. As *Soiuz zhenshchin* struggled, Chekhova also sought to explain the lack of support from women themselves, criticizing the internalized oppression and self-negation that kept women from political participation. Nevertheless, the journal maintained its monthly publication schedule, reporting on the 1908 Women's Congress, international feminism, and the demise of its sponsoring organization, the Women's Union.

Chekhova gave up trying to keep *Soiuz zhenshchin* afloat, and the journal ceased publication at the end of 1909. Its feminist financial backers had dwindled, its subscription base had shrunk, and Chekhova transferred much of her own energy to a new, more moderate, and legally chartered organization, the *Liga ravnopraviia zhenshchin* (League for Women's Equality).

Cross-references: Mariia Aleksandrovna Chekhova, First All-Russian Women's Congress (1908), *Liga ravnopraviia zhenshchin* (League for Women's Equal Rights), Ariadna Vladimirovna Tyrkova, *Soiuz ravnopraviia zhenshchin* (Women's Equal Rights Union), *Soiuz zhenshchin* (Union of Women).

Suggested Readings

Ariian, Praskov'ia N. "M. A. Chekhova." In *Pervyi zhenskii kalendar' na 1912 god*, edited by Praskov'ia N. Ariian, 8–11. St. Petersburg, 1912.

Edmondson, Linda Harriet. *Feminism in Russia, 1900–1917*. Stanford, CA: Stanford University Press, 1984.

Edmondson, Linda Harriet. "Women's rights, civil rights and the debate over citizens in the 1905 Revolution." In *Women and Society in Russia and the Soviet Union*, edited by Linda Edmondson, 77–100. Cambridge: Cambridge University Press, 1992.

Goldberg, Rochelle (Ruthchild). "The Russian Women's Movement 1859–1917." Ph.D. Diss., University of Rochester, 1976.

Grishina, Zoia V. *"Dvizhenie za politicheskoe ravnopravie zhenshchin v gody pervoi Rossiiskoi revoliutsii"* (The Movement for Women's Political Equal Rights in the Years of the First Russian Revolution). *Vestnik Moskovskogo universiteta (Moscow University Herald).* Ser. 8 *Istoriia (History),* no. 2 (1982): 33–42.

Grishina, Zoia V. *"Zhenskie organizatsii v Rossii, 1905 g.-fevral'/mart 1917 g."* (Women's Organizations in Russia, 1905–February/March 1917). Abstract of a *kandidat*'s Diss., Moscow State University, 1978.

Mirovich, N. (Z. S. Ivanova). *Iz istorii zhenskago dvizheniia v Rossii (From the History of the Women's Movement in Russia).* Moscow: Tipografiia T-va I.D. Sytina, 1908.

Ruthchild, Rochelle G. "Writing for Their Rights. Four Feminist Journalists: Mariia Chekhova, Liubov' Gurevich, Mariia Pokrovskaia, and Ariadna Tyrkova." In *The Improper Profession: Women and Journalism in Late Imperial Russia,* edited by Jehane Gheith and Barbara Norton. Durham, NC: Duke University Press (in press).

Stites, Richard. *The Women's Liberation Movement in Russia: Feminism, Nihilism, and Bolshevism, 1860–1930.* Princeton, NJ: Princeton University Press, 1978, 1991.

Rochelle Goldberg Ruthchild

Spiridonova, Mariia Aleksandrovna (1884–1941)

A prominent revolutionary and member of the Socialist Revolutionary Party (SRs) before 1917, she later became an opponent of the Soviet government and suffered greatly before her death in 1941.

Mariia Spiridonova was born on October 16, 1884, in Tambov into a family that was part of the nobility. She graduated from a women's gymnasium in 1901 and worked in the office staff of the Tambov Provincial Nobleman's Assembly. She became part of the Socialist Revolutionary (SR) Party in 1900 and joined its military combat unit. In 1906 she volunteered to kill G. N. Luzhenkovskii, whom the SRs had condemned to death for organizing the notorious Black Hundreds organization in Tambov and for his cruel reprisals against the peasants. Luzhenkovskii was wounded and died twenty-four days later. Spiridonova was arrested, interrogated, and brutalized, causing a public outcry against the violent treatment of women.

In 1906 Spiridonova published an open letter in the newspaper *Rus* that attracted considerable public attention, and progressive society labeled her the "Russian Joan of Arc." Spiridonova was tried for her terrorist act and condemned to death, but her sentence was commuted to life imprisonment. In 1917, after serving eleven years of her penal sentence in Siberia, Spiridonova received political amnesty from the Provisional Government in 1917. She went to Petrograd, where she became a leading activist in the SR movement. She was selected to serve on the Petrograd city committee of the SR Party and on the editorial board of the Left-SR newspaper the *Flag of Labor*. In September 1917 she was elected as deputy to the Petrograd Council.

During the revolutionary days of November 1917, Spiridonova undertook the task of trying to win the support of the majority of the peasants at the Extraordinary and Second All-Russian Congress of Peasant Deputies. Spiridonova had developed into a persuasive orator and publicist in her defense of peasant interests. John Reed in his famous book, *Ten Days That Shook the World*, called her the "most influential and popular woman in Russia."

After the October Revolution, Spiridonova changed her position sharply. She went from cooperation with the victorious Bolsheviks to the opposition in 1918. The change in her position resulted from doubts about the Brest–Litovsk Peace Treaty and questions about the way the Soviet government was treating the peasantry.

In June 1918 the Central Committee of the SR Party decided to protest the Brest–Litovsk Peace Treaty by organizing terrorist acts against leading representatives of the German government. Spiridonova organized the murder of the German ambassador, V. Mirbach, in Moscow. As part of the SR rebellion, she was involved in the arrest of Felix Dzerzhinskii on July 6, 1918. The SR rebellion was defeated on July 7, 1918. Spiridonova's political activism ended, and she faced a new life of imprisonment, alternating with treatments in sanitariums and hospitals and exile in Kaluga province and Samarkand. In February 1937 she was again arrested and executed on September 11, 1941, in Orel province.

A revolutionary activist of some note, Spiridonova achieved success as a defender of the peasants prior to, and in the early days after, the Bolshevik Revolution, but her differences with the Bolsheviks led to rapid termination of her political activism.

Suggested Readings

Bezberezh'ev, S. V. "Mariia Aleksandrovna Spiridonova." *Voprosy istorii*, no. 9 (1990): 65–81.

Meshcheriakova, Iu, and A. Rybakova. " *'Blazhennaia' Mariia: Novye dokumenty i biografii M. A. Spiridonovoi, 1884–1941*" (Holy Mary: New Documents toward the Biography of M. A. Spiridonova). In *Neizvestnaia Rossiia XX vek (The Unknown Russia, 20th Century)*, vol. 2, 9–56. Moscow: *Istoricheskoe nasledie*, 1992.

Reed, John. *Ten Days That Shook the World*. New York: Bone and Liveright, 1919.

Stites, Richard. *The Women's Liberation Movement in Russia*. Princeton, NJ: Princeton University Press, 1978, 1991.

Ulam, Adam. *The Bolsheviks: The Intellectual and Political History of the Triumph of Communism in Russia*. Cambridge: Harvard University Press, 1998.

Vladimirov, V. *M. Spiridonova*. Moscow: Tip. Poplavskogo, 1906.

Liudmila Zhukova

Stasova, Nadezhda Vasil'evna (1822–1895)

A leader of the first wave of Russian feminists, responsible for major philanthropic, self-help, and educational initiatives, including the Bestuzhevskie Higher Courses for Women. A founder and the first president of the *Russkoe zhenskoe vzaimno-blagotvoritel'noe obshchestvo* (Russian Women's Mutual Philanthropic Society).

Nadezhda Vasil'evna Stasova was born June 12, 1822, in Tsarskoe selo, the location of the tsar's summer residence. Her family was well placed: her father was the court architect and a close friend of Tsar Alexander I, and Nadezhda (meaning "hope") was the tsar's godchild. Stasova was the fourth of seven children. Her older sister Sofiia and Nadezhda were the only girls. When Stasova was nine, her mother died in the cholera epidemic of 1831.

At an early age, Stasova was aware of the unequal treatment of women, as she encountered stereotypes about girls' "empty-headedness" and inferiority and recalled how she was raised to fit such notions. Despite or because of societal expectations, Stasova showed an iron will and an ability to transform adversity into strength. In her late twenties, already old by the standards of the day, she became engaged to a Guards officer with whom she was deeply in love. At the last moment he broke the engagement and married another woman. Devastated, Stasova had a nervous breakdown and lapsed into insanity. The family doctor treated her with hypnosis, and during trances she dictated her own prescriptions in Latin, which she had never studied. When she recovered, Stasova vowed never to marry and to begin an entirely new life. At first she directed her energies toward her family. But with the death of her sister Sofiia in 1858, Stasova decided to devote herself to "a universal family."

Stasova was among the women recruited by Mariia Vasil'evna Trubnikova at her feminist salon. She was intimately involved in many of the key feminist ventures from 1859 to 1895. The ventures had as their chief goals to provide women with the tools for economic self-sufficiency, through education, work opportunities, and, in some cases, shelter. These needs became more acute with the emancipation of the serfs in 1861, as single gentry women could no longer be supported within the "nest of gentlefolk," and unattached peasant women were also less likely to find economic sustenance in the villages.

In 1859 Stasova, along with Anna Filosofova, Mariia Trubnikova, and her sister Vera Ivasheva, was a founder of the *Obshchestvo dostavleniia deshevykh kvartir i drugikh posobii nuzhdaiushchimsia zhiteliam S-Peterburga* (Society for Cheap Lodging and Other Aid to the Needy Residents of St. Petersburg). Trubnikova had the idea of renting apartments for needy women, many of whom had been deserted by their husbands. The organization sought to move beyond traditional philanthropy by encouraging self-help and skills training among its recipients. Over time the society's services grew to include a school for working mothers, cafeterias, a child-care center, a store, dormitories, and a clothing workshop employing 300–500 women workers, mostly making uniforms for the War Ministry.

Stasova was a key figure in the Women's Publishing Cooperative. Aiming to provide "useful and stimulating reading for the upcoming generation," from 1863 to 1879 the cooperative published fourteen books, from *The Tales of Hans Christian Andersen*, to Louisa May Alcott's *Little Women*. Working closely with

Mariia Trubnikova, Stasova was responsible for dealing with the printers, binders, and suppliers.

Not all the feminists' endeavors were as successful as the Society for Cheap Lodgings and the Publishing Cooperative. The Society for Women's Work, proposed by the then-reformer Petr Lavrov and the feminist Anna Nikolaevna Engel'gardt, was to serve as an employment agency for women. Although it won the support of feminist leaders, and its charter was approved in 1865, the society foundered on the conflict between the older activists and the younger *nigilistki* (nihilist women) and never opened.

Stasova actively assisted efforts at expanding educational opportunities for women. She and Trubnikova were prominent in the Sunday school movement, founded to provide free education to adults of all social classes, with sessions on Sunday to enable workers to attend. Stasova worked in a women's Sunday school, opened in August 1860, but the movement proved short-lived as all Sunday schools were closed by government decree in 1862. In 1868 Stasova, Evgeniia Konradi, and Trubnikova drafted and presented a petition, signed by 400 women, to the rector of St. Petersburg University, seeking lectures and courses for women at the university. After years of struggle with the tsarist government, which feared that educating women would lead them to become revolutionaries, in 1873 women's medical courses opened, and in 1878 the Bestuzhevskie Higher Courses for Women finally opened. To aid the courses, which received inadequate funding from the government, Stasova, Filosofova, Trubnikova, and others formed societies designed to help needy students.

Stasova, along with Varvara Tarnovskaia and other women, feminists and nonfeminists alike, organized an exhibit highlighting Russian women's intellectual and cultural achievements for the 1893 Chicago World's Fair. The cultural part arrived intact; the intellectual section was mysteriously lost.

Stasova's final venture combined the twin thrusts of education and philanthropy. She was the first President of the *Russkoe zhenskoe vzaimnoblagotvoritel'noe obshchestvo* (Russian Women's Mutual Philanthropic Society). The Society, modeled on U.S. women's clubs that combined social advocacy with self-development, borrowed heavily from the charter of the New England Women's Club for its organizational statute. Government insistence that women's organizations have a philanthropic purpose led to the Society's rather clumsy name. Stasova lived to see the Society's charter approved in 1895 but died soon after. The Society served as a bridge to the more overtly political woman's rights groups that emerged during the 1905 Revolution and as a training ground for some feminist activists such as Praskov'ia Ariian and Liubov' Gurevich.

Stasova never wrote her autobiography; the major source for information about her life is an extensive biography written by her brother, the noted art and music critic Vladimir V. Stasov, and published four years after her death.

Cross-references: Praskov'ia Naumovna Ariian, Anna Pavlovna Filosofova, Higher Education for Women, Russian Women's Mutual Philanthropic Society

(*Russkoe zhenskoe vzaimnoblagotvoritel'noe obshchestvo*), Mariia Vasil'evna Trubnikova, *Zhenskaia izdatel'skaia artel'* (Women's Publishing Artel).

Suggested Readings

Bulanova-Trubnikova, Olga K. *Tri pokoleniia (Three Generations).* Moscow and Leningrad: Gosudarstvennoe Izdatel'stvo, 1928.

Dudgeon, Ruth Arlene Fluck. "Women and Higher Education in Russia 1855–1905." Ph.D. Diss., George Washington University, 1975.

Goldberg, Rochelle (Ruthchild). "The Russian Women's Movement 1859–1917." Ph.D. Diss., University of Rochester, 1976.

Johanson, Christine. *Women's Struggle for Higher Education in Russia, 1855–1900.* Kingston and Montreal: McGill University Press, 1987.

Johnson, W.H.E. *Russia's Educational Heritage.* Pittsburgh: Carnegie Press, 1950.

Likhacheva, Elena. *Materialy dlia istorii zhenskago obrazovaniia v Rossii (Materials for the History of Women's Education in Russia).* 4 parts in 2 vols. St. Petersburg: 1890–1893.

Sbornik pamiati Anny Pavlovny Filosofovoi (Collected Remembrances of Anna Pavlovna Filosofova). Vol. 1: Ariadna V. Tyrkova, *Anna Pavlovna Filosofova i eë vremia (Anna Pavlovna Filosofova and Her Times).* Petrograd: M. O. Vol'f, 1915. Vol. 2: *Stat'i i materialy (Articles and Materials).* Petrograd: P. Golike i A.Vil'borg, 1915.

Stasov, Vladimir V. *Nadezhda Vasil'evna Stasova: vospominaniia i ocherki (Memoirs and Essays).* St. Petersburg: Tipografiia M. Merkusheva, 1899.

Stites, Richard. *The Women's Liberation Movement in Russia: Feminism, Nihilism, and Bolshevism, 1860–1930.* Princeton, NJ: Princeton University Press, 1978, 1991.

Rochelle Goldberg Ruthchild

Suslova, Nadezhda Prokofievna (1843–1918)

Author, physician, nihilist, and the first Russian woman doctor.

Women in Russia began clamoring for higher education in the 1860s. Many women audited courses at the universities, and some attended special Higher Courses for Women. One such woman, Nadezhda Suslova, at first audited courses and then, hoping for more than just casual study, traveled to Zurich; several years later, after successfully completing a course in medicine, she became known as the first modern Russian woman to receive a medical degree from an accredited university.

Suslova began her life as the daughter of a freed serf. She was born in 1843 to forward-thinking parents who subscribed to such progressive journals as *Sovremennik (The Contemporary One)* and encouraged their daughters to read and become educated. When Suslova's father received a promotion and was sent to manage one of Count Sheremetev's estates near Moscow in 1854, Nadezhda and her sister Apollinaria were sent to a boarding school for noble girls. At the school they studied foreign languages, music, and a smattering of math and science. Although they often felt alienated from the other girls due to their own background as daughters of a former serf, the girls did receive a rudimentary education.

At the beginning of the 1860s, Nadezhda went to St. Petersburg and began auditing courses at St. Petersburg University. There she became involved in the *Zemlia i volia* (Land and Freedom) movement. In 1861 she requested admission to the St. Petersburg Medical Surgical Academy as an auditor. Although her request was granted, new rules forbade women from attending the school, and all women currently studying at the Academy were forced to go elsewhere. One exception was made for Varvara Kashevarova-Rudneva, who had a special scholarship and planned to serve the Bashkir women upon her graduation. During her time in St. Petersburg, Suslova also experimented with writing and contributed several stories to *Sovremennik*. In 1865 she decided that medicine was her true vocation, and she traveled to Zurich to study medicine.

Suslova was originally admitted to the University of Zurich as an auditor, but after studying for a while, she requested and received admittance to the examinations. In February 1867 she matriculated into the university and became the first woman to enter Zurich University as a full student. In August of that year she took and passed her exams. Then she traveled to Graz, Austria, where her friend and mentor Ivan Sechenov, a well-known physiologist, was working. There she performed the research for her dissertation on the significance of the lymph nodes in the human body. She successfully defended her dissertation on December 14, 1867, to a packed hall of students, professors, and curious onlookers. According to all accounts, she performed beautifully, and her success was written up in newspapers across Europe.

While in Zurich, Suslova met Frederick Erisman, a renowned physician who was beginning his illustrious work in the growing field of hygiene. In February 1868 Erisman and Suslova were married, and the following year Erisman joined Suslova in her private practice in St. Petersburg. They worked together and published several articles on hygiene. In 1874 they divorced after a period of estrangement. The year before, the secret police had started proceedings against both Erisman and Suslova because of their involvement with radical groups, but the charges against Suslova were ultimately dropped. Erisman, however, left Russia and was not allowed to return, straining what was apparently an already difficult relationship.

In 1885 Suslova married a professor of histology, A. E. Golubev. With her new husband she moved to the Crimea, where she continued to practice medicine until the end of her life. She died in 1918.

Cross-references: Higher Education for Women, Mariia Pokrovskaia, Anna Shabanova, Women's Medical Courses.

Suggested Readings

Bonner, Thomas Neville. "Rendezvous in Zurich: Seven Who Made a Revolution in Women's Medical Education, 1864–1874." *Journal of the History of Medicine* 44 (January 1989): 7–27.

DenBeste-Barnett, Michelle. "Earnestly Working to Improve Russia's Future: Russian Women Physicians." Ph.D. Diss., Southern Illinois University, 1997.

Meijer, J. M. *Knowledge and Revolution: The Russian Colony in Zurich (1870–1873).* Assen, Netherlands: Van Gorcum, 1955.

Smirnov, Alexander. *Pervaia russkaia zhenshchina-vrach (The First Russian Woman Doctor).* Moscow: Medgiz, 1960.

Tuve, Jeanette. *The First Russian Women Physicians.* Newtonville, MA: Oriental Research Partners, 1984.

Michelle DenBeste

T

Trubnikova, Mariia Vasil'evna (1835–1897)

A pioneer feminist activist whose ideas inspired the work of the triumvirate (Trubnikova, Anna Pavlovna Filosofova, and Nadezhda Vasil'evna Stasova) in establishing cooperative self-help ventures for women and the Bestuzhevskie Higher Courses for Women.

Mariia Trubnikova was born in Siberia, the daughter of the exiled Decembrist Vasilii Ivashev and his wife, Camille LeDantieux, who was the youngest daughter of the Ivashev family's French governess. When Mariia was five, her mother died in childbirth. Her grief-stricken father died one year later. She and her younger sister Vera were taken in by a wealthy aunt, Princess Khovanskaia, and given an excellent education, equal to that of the boys in the household and including history, natural science, philosophy, and several European languages.

At the age of nineteen, Mariia married Konstantin Trubnikov, a young government official who impressed her by his liberalism and quotations from the populist writer Alexander Herzen. Trubnikov soon abandoned provincial government service for St. Petersburg, where he became an investor and publisher of the newspaper *Birzhevye Vedomosti (Stock Exchange News).* The move to the tsarist capital proved fortuitous for Trubnikova, who already considered the "woman question" central and was corresponding with leading European feminists such as the French activist Jenny d'Hericourt. Starting the first Russian salon exclusively for women, she went about finding like-minded recruits for her cause. Among those who responded were Anna Pavlovna Filosofova and Nadezhda Vasil'evna Stasova.

The three, known as the triumvirate, spearheaded much feminist activity until almost the end of the century. By the accounts of her contemporaries, Trubnikova was the "nerve center" for their major initiatives in philanthropy, women's higher education, and self-help, all aimed at helping women achieve economic independence. The first of their endeavors, begun in 1859 and officially chartered in 1861, was the *Obshchestvo dostavleniia deshevykh kvartir i drugikh posobii nuzhdaiushchimsia zhiteliam S-Peterburga* (Society for Cheap Lodging and Other Aid to the Needy Residents of St. Petersburg). Trubnikova, perhaps anticipating her own future, had the idea of renting apartments for needy women, many of whom had been deserted by their husbands, and she was the Society's first President. The organization sought to move beyond traditional philanthropy by encouraging self-help and skills training among its recipients. Over time the Society's services expanded to include a school for working mothers, cafeterias, a child-care center, a store, dormitories, and a clothing workshop employing 300 to 500 women workers, mostly making uniforms for the War Ministry.

Promoting the notion of women's self-help further, Trubnikova conceived of a women's publishing cooperative, closed to men, with all the work done by women, from artwork and translation, to printing, binding, and book sales. Aiming to provide "useful and stimulating reading for the upcoming generation," from 1863 to 1879 the cooperative published fourteen books, from *The Tales of Hans Christian Andersen*, to Louisa May Alcott's *Little Women*. Trubnikova was involved in many aspects of the cooperative's operation, from editing, to recruiting new members, to bookkeeping. Nevertheless, even before its dissolution, the cooperative showed its founders the limits of small-scale attempts to uplift women, and they turned toward endeavors with greater potential for training in self-sufficiency, such as higher education.

In 1867 Evgeniia Konradi initiated what was to be the feminists' most successful effort when she petitioned a congress of natural scientists to support women's higher education. The congress rejected the petition, and Konradi in despair contacted Trubnikova. A group, including Trubnikova, Stasova, Konradi, and leading professors such as Dmitri Ivanovich Mendeleev and Ivan Parfen'evich Borodin, met in Trubnikova's apartment and resolved to petition the rector of St. Petersburg University for women's access to higher education. Once again, Trubnikova proved to be a catalyst for a movement that, after a complicated struggle, resulted in the opening of the Bestuzhevskie Higher Courses for Women in St. Petersburg in 1878.

Although her husband assisted the operation of the women's publishing cooperative, Trubnikova's marriage soured as Konstantin lost her inheritance through bad investments and as his liberalism proved limited. Konstantin and his friends openly scorned women's emancipation, associating it with radical nihilism; he considered his wife's social activism harmful to his business interests, and he strayed consistently enough to have a second family. Finally, in 1876 the couple definitively split up, and Trubnikova and her four daughters left. With few resources, she supported herself and her children by translating and writing articles for newspapers and journals.

Trubnikova was plagued by deteriorating physical and mental health in the last part of her life. In 1869 she left for an extended period of treatment abroad in Nice and Switzerland. Devastated by the suicide of her friend, the radical activist Alexander A. Serno-Solov'evich, and by the continued effects of her illness, she nevertheless used her time abroad to strengthen contacts with such admirers of the Russian feminists as John Stuart Mill, the English feminist Josephine Butler, and the French feminist writer Andre Leo (aka Leodile Champseix, 1824–1900).

She was devastated again in 1880 by the arrest of her oldest daughter, Olga, and her friend Evgeniia Figner and the execution of another friend, Aleksandr Aleksandrovich Kviatkovskii, for revolutionary activity and in 1881 was hospitalized for a year. This was the end of her feminist activity. She spent the last years of her life, from 1882 to 1897, living with her daughter Mariia, Mariia's husband, and their children on their estate in Vladimir province.

Cross-references: Anna Pavlovna Filosofova, Higher Education for Women, Nadezhda Vasil'evna Stasova, *Zhenskaia Izdatel'skaia Artel'* (The Women's Publishing Artel).

Suggested Readings

Bulanova-Trubnikova, Olga K. *Roman dekabrista: dekabrist V. P. Ivashev i ego semia: iz semeinogo arkhiva. Istoriko-revoliutsionnaia biblioteka zhurnala "Katorga i ssylka" (The Story of a Decembrist: The Decembrist V. P. Ivashev and His Family: From the Family Archive. The Historical-Revolutionary Library of the Journal, "Prison and Exile").* Book 6. Moscow: Vsesoiuznoe obshchestvo politicheskikh katorzhan i ssylno-poselentsev, 1925.

Bulanova-Trubnikova, Olga K. *Tri pokoleniia (Three Generations).* Moscow and Leningrad: Gosudarstvennoe Izdatel'stvo, 1928.

Dudgeon, Ruth Arlene Fluck. "Women and Higher Education in Russia 1855–1905." Ph.D. Diss., George Washington University, 1975.

Goldberg, Rochelle (Ruthchild). "The Russian Women's Movement 1859–1917." Ph.D. Diss., University of Rochester, 1976.

Stasov, Vladimir V. *Nadezhda Vasil'evna Stasova: vospominaniia i ocherki.* St. Petersburg: Tipografiia M. Merkusheva, 1899.

Stites, Richard. *The Women's Liberation Movement in Russia: Feminism, Nihilism, and Bolshevism, 1860–1930.* Princeton, NJ: Princeton University Press, 1978, 1991.

Rochelle Goldberg Ruthchild

Tyrkova, Ariadna (1869–1962)

A feminist and Kadet activist, journalist, and writer. A member of the Kadet Central Committee (1906–1917) and the organizing committee for the First All-Russian Women's Congress (1908). Tyrkova was editor of the newspaper *Russkaia molva (Russian Talk)* and Kadet representative on the Petrograd City Council in 1917.

Ariadna Tyrkova, born into an old, landed, gentry family from Novgorod province, was one of seven children; her older brother Arkadii was exiled to Siberia for revolutionary activity connected with the assassination of Tsar Alexander II. Tyrkova numbered among her school friends Nadezhda Krupskaia, and both went on to study at the Bestuzhev Higher Courses for Women. Tyrkova dropped out after one year to marry the naval architect Arkadii Borman. At the age of twenty-seven, Tyrkova separated from her husband and, seeking financial sustenance for herself and her two young children, Arkadii and Sofiia, turned to writing. She at first used the male pseudonym Vergezhskii and then switched to her own name.

Tyrkova's political activism began with her connection to the émigré journal *Osvobozhdenie (Liberation)*. One of a handful of female contributors, in 1903 she ran afoul of the tsarist police when attempting to smuggle the journal into Russia from Finland and fled abroad to escape prison. During her exile she met her future second husband, the British journalist Harold Williams. Returning to Russia in November 1905, she gained attention for her speech at the January 1906 Kadet Congress, advocating woman suffrage in the face of the opposition of Kadet leader Paul Miliukov. Her outspokenness won Tyrkova a seat on the Kadet Central Committee, on which she was the only woman from 1906 to 1917. She was very conscious of her role as a token woman in the party leadership and the condescending way in which she was often treated.

Tyrkova took part in feminist activity of the period through speaking and writing and affiliation with the Women's Equal Rights Union. She wrote for the Women's Union journal *Soiuz zhenshchin (Union of Women)* and also authored woman's rights pamphlets. She served on the organizing committee for the 1908 First All-Russian Women's Congress, and participated in the debates, admonishing the delegates to eschew separatism and adopt more mainstream positions. She served on the editorial bureau for the Congress and chaired its final general session, at which a group of Bolshevik-led women workers walked out in protest against the consensus politics of the Congress organizers. She also authored a biography of the pioneer feminist Anna Filosofova and edited a volume of reminiscences of Filosofova, published in Petrograd in 1915.

After the February 1917 Revolution, she published the pamphlet *Osvobozhdenie zhenshchiny (Woman's Liberation)* and took part in the large April 1917 woman suffrage demonstration in Petrograd. Together with Mariia Pokrovskaia, Anna Shabanova, and Poliksena Shishkina-Iavein, Tyrkova was part of the delegation meeting with Prince L'vov, head of the Provisional Government, after the demonstration. The Provisional Government's proclamation of woman suffrage made Russia the first large country to give women the right to vote. Tyrkova continued to work both for woman's rights and as a Kadet activist throughout 1917. She won a seat as a Kadet representative on the Petrograd City Council in the summer of 1917. Running as a Kadet candidate for the Constituent Assembly in two districts, she was defeated in her home district in Novgorod by Leon Trotsky.

Tyrkova left Russia in March 1918. She and her husband returned to Russia in 1919 as part of the English legation. She actively supported the Whites in the civil war and had to flee back to London in March 1920. Harold Williams was foreign editor of the *Times* of London from 1922 until he died in 1928.

In the early 1950s, following her son, she emigrated to the United States, living briefly in New York before settling in Washington, D.C. She continued to write, in total publishing eleven books in Russian and English as well as many magazine and newspaper articles in Russian, French, and English. Her works included an autobiographical trilogy, a biography of Harold Williams, polemics against the Bolsheviks, and *Zhizn' Pushkina (The Life of Pushkin)*, reflecting her long study of Russia's premier poet. In her memoirs, she played down her feminist activity.

Cross-references: First All-Russian Women's Congress, Higher Education for Women, Nadezhda Krupskaia, Mariia Pokrovskaia, Anna Shabanova, Poliksena Shishkina-Iavein, *Soiuz ravnopraviia zhenshchin* (Women's Equal Rights Union).

Suggested Readings

Borman, Arkadii. *A. V. Tyrkova-Williams po eë pis'mam i vospominaniiam syna (A. K. Tyrkova-Williams through Her Letters and the Reminiscences of Her Son)*. Washington, DC: Luven, 1964.

Edmondson, Linda Harriet. *Feminism in Russia, 1900–1917*. Stanford, CA: Stanford University Press, 1984.

Kaznina, O. A. "Tyrkova, Ariadna Vladimirovna." In *Dictionary of Russian Women Writers*, edited by Marina Ledkovsky, Charlotte Rosenthal, and Mary Zirin, 675–677. Westport, CT: Greenwood Press, 1994.

Norman, Anita. "Ariadna Tyrkova-Williams." *Russian Review* 21, no. 3 (July 1962): 277–281.

Stites, Richard. *The Women's Liberation Movement in Russia: Feminism, Nihilism, and Bolshevism, 1860–1930*. Princeton, NJ: Princeton University Press, 1978, 1991.

Tyrkova-Williams, Ariadna. "The Cadet Party." *Russian Review* 12 (1953): 173–186.

Tyrkova-Williams, Ariadna. *Cheerful Giver: The Life of Harold Williams*. London: P. Davies, 1935.

Tyrkova-Williams, Ariadna. *Na putiakh k svobode (On the Paths to Freedom)*. New York: Izd. im. Chekhova, 1952.

Tyrkova-Williams, Ariadna. *Pod"em i krushenie (Rise and Fall)*. Paris: N.p., 1956.

Tyrkova-Williams, Ariadna. *To, chego bol'she ne budet (That Which Will Be No More)*. Paris: Vozrozhdenie, 1954.

Rochelle Goldberg Ruthchild

V

Volkonskaia, Mariia Nikolaevna (1805–1863)

The most famous of the Decembrist wives who followed their husbands into Siberian exile.

Mariia Volkonskaia was the fifth child born into an important Russian noble family on the estate of Boltishka in the Ukraine. Her father, Nikolai Nikolaevich Raevskii, was a famous general who served in the Napoleonic War (1812–1815), and her mother, Sophia, was a great-granddaughter of the renowned scientist Mikhail Lomonosov. The empress Catherine the Great had arranged the marriage of Mariia's parents, and the Raevskiis enjoyed the special confidence of Tsar Alexander I. Mariia received an education typical of that for noble daughters of her era and led the life of a privileged member of the aristocracy.

Mariia's marriage, like that of her parents, was an arranged one. Her father chose Sergei Volkonskii, his adjutant. In 1825, a few months before the Decembrists' uprising, Mariia married Volkonskii. This choice had great consequences for Mariia's life, as Volkonskii figured among the young, noble officers who rose in revolt against Tsar Nicholas I's autocracy in December 1825. Their demands for a constitutional monarchy and the abolition of serfdom were repulsed, and Volkonskii, like many of his fellow conspirators, was banished to Siberia for life. Although Mariia had known nothing about her husband's plans, she did not hesitate to follow him into exile and spent the next twenty-eight years in Siberia. During this lengthy period, Mariia Volkonskaia became prominent, along with her friend Ekaterina Trubetskaia, the French wife of the Decembrist Sergei Trubetskoi, as an advocate for better living conditions for the exiles. She took on a variety of causes. She sent petitions to the notorious head of the tsarist police administration in St. Petersburg, General Benckendorff, deploring conditions in Siberian prisons; she used her patronage and her influence on the Governor-General of Eastern Siberia, Murav'ev-Amurskii, to encourage the building of schools and a theater in Irkutsk. She also took an interest in the indigenous peoples of Siberia like the Buriats and the Ostiaks, admiring their intelligence and independence. Her house in Irkutsk became the cultural center not only for the Decembrists but also for the city as a whole. Next to the wife of the Governor-General, she was the most prominent grande dame in the "outback" of Siberia. Mariia laid special emphasis on enlightenment, working at the grassroots levels in towns and villages in Siberia, an approach to change that contrasted with the political hotheadedness of the Decembrist men, although she never openly criticized her husband's and his colleagues' former revolutionary activity.

In 1855, after the death of Tsar Nicholas I and the general amnesty issued by his successor, Alexander II, Mariia and her husband returned to European Russia. Although Mariia could have returned anytime before, she had chosen not to leave her work of enlightenment in Siberia. Siberia was, indeed, her destiny.

Volkonskaia died in 1863 on the Raevskii estate in Voronkii in the Ukraine. She left a significant legacy. The people in Siberia called her the "Princess of Siberia," the great Russian poet Alexander Pushkin devoted a poem to her, and she became the heroine of many Russian folk ballads. Numerous editions of her memoirs appeared in late Imperial Russia and the Soviet era. Today a rich collection of her letters and autobiographical notes is stored in the Decembrist Museum in Irkutsk, in the Pushkin Museums in St. Petersburg and Moscow, and in the British Library.

Cross-reference: Decembrist Women.

Suggested Readings

Mazour, Anatole Gregory. *Women in Exile: Wives of the Decembrists.* Tallahassee, FL: Diplomatic Press, 1975.

Novosil'tseva, Tatiana. "*Rasskazy iz proshlogo: Kniaginia Mariia Nikolaevna Volkonskaia*" (Stories from the Past: Princess Mariia Nikolaevna Volkonskaia). *Russkaia Starina* 6 (1878): 336–342.

Sutherland, Catherine. *The Princess of Siberia: The Story of Maria Volkonsky and the Decembrist Exiles.* New York: Farrar, Straus, Giroux, 1984.

Volkonskaia, Mariia. *Pis'ma kniagini Marii N. Volkonskoi iz Sibiri, 1827–1831gg (Princess Maria N. Volkonskaia's Letters from Siberia, 1827–1831).* Moscow: Izdanie Sabashnikovykh, 1915.

Volkonskaia, Mariia. *Zapiski (Memoirs).* St. Petersburg: Izd.Benke, 1906.

Volkonskii, Mikhail. *Zapiski kniagini Marii Nikolaevny Volkonskoi (The Notes of Princess Maria Nikolaevna Volkonskii).* St. Petersburg: Benke, 1906.

Eva-Maria Stolberg

W

Women Pharmacists in Late Imperial Russia (1871–1917)

Women pharmacists helped professionalize pharmacy, made medical breakthroughs, and improved public health. Pharmacy offered women financial independence, an interesting career, and, for Jews and Poles, assimilation.

Women were allowed to own pharmacies throughout the nineteenth century. Only in 1871, however, were they permitted to practice pharmacy and then only in women's medical facilities. Following women's petitions to the Ministry of Internal Affairs, which regulated medical education and practice, to permit general practice, in 1882 Tsar Alexander II, despite closing most women's medical courses, instructed government agencies to establish procedures. In 1888 the Ministry of Internal Affairs opened all levels of pharmacy practice to women.

From the first, women pharmacists in Russia were virtually equal to male counterparts. Entrance requirements were identical: four years of women's *gimnaziia* or an equivalent education and passing a Latin examination, necessary for medical terminology. In 1900 women graduates of church schools were admitted as pharmacy apprentices. A three-year apprenticeship in a qualified pharmacy and passing an examination entitled women, like males, to become Assistant Pharmacists. A further three-year practicum, two years of university courses, and passing a second examination allowed women to become fully qualified pharmacists or *Provizor*s. Women could become *Magistry* (Masters) of Pharmacy after two additional years of university courses and a thesis. Although all could own pharmacies, only *Provizor*s, either male or female, could manage fully outfitted pharmacies, designated as *normal'naia apteka* (normal pharmacy) under Russian law; these were limited by population, prescription turnover, and other criteria. Women Assistant Pharmacists, like their male counterparts, were confined to managing partially outfitted village pharmacies, such as those run by the zemstvos.

Since women could not attend universities in late imperial Russia, the first eager aspirants studied with university professors and used university labs as externs. Some met obstacles, but others received generous assistance from male colleagues and government officials. Special women's pharmacy courses opened in the first decade of the twentieth century.

The first women pharmacists included Anna Mikhailovna Makarova, who passed the examination for Assistant Pharmacist at Kiev University in 1892, and Antonina Boleslavna Lesnevskaia, who received the Assistant Pharmacist title in 1893. She, Zinaida Akker, Stanislavna Doviaglo, A. I. Levitan, and A. P. Gal'perin-Vogava received the *Provizor* degree in 1898. Ol'ga Evgen'evna Gabrilovich was the first woman to receive the *Magistr* degree, in 1906.

Before World War I there were 500 or more women pharmacists and pharmacy students out of 10,000 in the field. In 1910 there were eighty-five women *Provizor*s and 4,724 male *Provizor*s. About five women attained the highest degree, *Magistr*. About one-third of the women pharmacists, like their male counterparts, were Polish, and another third were Jewish, for university quotas for Jews rose to 20 percent for pharmacists (versus 3 to 10 percent for university quotas generally), and Jewish students—and sometimes pharmacists—could live outside the Pale of Settlement.

Some women pharmacists managed zemstvo pharmacies or privately owned village pharmacies. Many worked in pharmacies, pharmaceutical laboratories, or pharmaceutical firms. Almost one-third of women *Provizor*s managed normal pharmacies. Antonina Lesnevskaia claimed that women and male pharmacists' remuneration was equal.

The handful of women *Magistry* in the early twentieth century performed and published significant research on major pharmacological and public health problems. Some were affiliated with the prestigious Institute of Experimental Medicine in St. Petersburg. Zemstvos hired Ol'ga Gabrilovich to study a serious, widespread disease, distinct from ergotism, caused by spores in rye bread; Liubov' Nikolaevna Lavrova did seminal research on preventing arteriosclerosis following massive injections of adrenalin, a therapy then used; L. A. Kovaleva researched the effect of *fotin* on human breathing and phosphorous preparations, specifically lecithin, on oxidization in animals. The latter two graduated from Antonina Lesnevskaia's pharmacy school. Women pharmacists, like their male counterparts, covered the political spectrum. Some were Mensheviks or Bolsheviks, serving as officers of provincial and district organizations, journalists, and labor organizers. Others opposed strikes and revolution. A few particularly raised pharmacy education and standards. All the women pharmacists advanced health care and women's career opportunities.

Cross-references: Higher Education for Women, Antonina Lesnevskaia, Women's Medical Courses.

Suggested Readings

Broido, Eva. *Memoirs of a Revolutionary*. Translated by Vera Broido. London: Oxford University Press, 1967.

Conroy, Mary Schaeffer. *In Health and in Sickness: Pharmacy, Pharmacists and the Pharmaceutical Industry in Late Imperial, Early Soviet Russia*. Boulder, CO: East European Monographs, distributed by Columbia University Press, 1994.

Conroy, Mary Schaeffer. "Women Pharmacists in Russia before World War I: women's emancipation, feminism, professionalization, nationalism, and class conflict." In *Women and Society in Russia and the Soviet Union*, edited by Linda Edmondson, 48–76. Cambridge: Cambridge University Press, 1992.

Mary Schaeffer Conroy

Women's Medical Courses (1872–1887; 1897–1917)

A term encompassing Courses for Learned Midwives, Higher Women's Medical Courses, and the Women's Medical Institute in late nineteenth-century Russia.

During the 1870s education for women became an important part of the "woman question" in Russia. One of the most significant victories for women involved the opening of the St. Petersburg Medical-Surgical Academy to women in 1872. Beginning in the late 1850s, women had been allowed to attend some Russian universities and the Medical-Surgical Academy as auditors. In 1864 this possibility was abruptly terminated, and only one woman, Varvara Kashevarova-Rudneva, remained at the Medical-Surgical Academy because the Governor of Orenburg Province had given her a special scholarship so that, after graduation, she could serve Bashkir women, who were forbidden by religious law to see male doctors. She graduated in 1863 but never fulfilled her obligation to Orenburg province. Kasherarova's failure to fulfill her obligation caused a stir among opponents of medical education for women, who argued that she had used this as a pretext to obtain an education. According to Kasherarova, Orenburg province did not have any zemstvos (local government organs) or women's hospitals, and, therefore, the only place to serve would have been a military hospital. Since service in the military hospital would have entitled her to a military position, official rank in the Russian civil service, and all the privileges of male physicians, she was not allowed to serve there.

Other women received their medical education abroad, due to the lack of opportunities at home. In 1867 Nadezhda Prokovievna Suslova became the first Russian woman to graduate from a European medical school; another woman, Mariia Bokova, followed in 1871. By 1873 seventy-seven Russian women were studying in Zurich as well as at a few other European universities.

Concerned that so many women were studying abroad, the Russian government issued a decree in 1873 ordering all women to return home by January 1, 1874, or risk exclusion from educational and employment opportunities. To encourage women studying abroad to return and to appease Russian women, who had been agitating for years for higher educational opportunities, the government initiated courses for learned midwives at the Medical-Surgical Academy in St. Petersburg on November 2, 1872. The program, designed to admit seventy students a year for four years' study, allowed women to earn the degree of learned midwife. Students had to have a gymnasium diploma, permission of their parents or husband, and evidence of loyalty from the police before admission; they also had to be at least twenty-two years old and pass an entrance examination on gymnasium subjects.

The curriculum was a demanding one. The first-year course covered physics, chemistry, botany, anatomy, and histology. Second-year students studied medical chemistry, physiology, pathology, epidemiology, and pharmacology. Third-year students took pathological anatomy and histology, midwifery, women's and children's diseases, surgery and bandaging, nerve and eye diseases, and internal diseases. Fourth-year students attended courses on surgical midwifery and gynecology, as well as clinics on midwifery, women's and children's diseases, syphilis, and skin diseases. Anna Nikolaevna Shabanova, an early medical student, described the negative rumors and gossip that clouded the experience of the first women medical students, including the rumor that the women students cut up corpses at night and carried internal organs in their pockets. Rumors soon ceased, and educated society generally supported the women. Wealthy patronesses set up inexpensive cafeterias for the students, and small groups of women supporters established scholarship funds.

In 1876 the medical courses were expanded to five years, and the name was changed to *Vysshie zhenskie vrachebnye kyrsi* (Higher Women's Medical Courses). The students moved to Nikolaevskii Military Hospital, which was reorganized as an institution separate from the Medical-Surgical Academy. The first class graduated in 1877 but received only certificates stating that they had passed the exams and were qualified to treat women and children. In June 1880 women were finally permitted to receive the title of woman doctor; women had the right to practice but were not officially listed on the Table of Ranks or government pensions. After graduating about 700 women, the courses were closed by an imperial *Ukaz* (decree) of August 5, 1882. Alexander II's death in 1881 and the resignation of Dmitri Alekseevich Miliutin from the Ministry of War led to the appointment of a more conservative Minister of War, Pëtr S. Vannovskii. Vannovskii decided that the Higher Women's Medical Courses did not belong at the Medical-Surgical Institute, which was under the ministry's jurisdiction. The courses were left without institutional affiliation or sponsor. The St. Petersburg City Duma agreed to assume responsibility for the courses if a sponsor could be found, but opposition from conservative elements in the government kept the courses closed until 1897. Even successful fund-raising efforts by private citizens and a press campaign, including letters from supporters such as the writer Ivan S. Turgenev, could not change the situation.

Women and their supporters continued to agitate for educational opportunities for women. Speakers at medical conferences urged the government to reconsider its position on women physicians, citing Russia's desperate need for more medical personnel. Articles in the press praised the achievements of women doctors during wartime and their work in zemstvos as proof of their ability and the need to train female health care workers.

After years of petitions, fund-raising efforts, and conversations with sympathizers, in 1895 Nicholas II agreed to the creation of a Women's Medical Institute with a five-year course of study. In 1897 the Higher Women's Medical Courses were reorganized and reopened as the Women's Medical Institute (WMI), with graduates entitled to the degree of woman doctor. The institute attracted talented professors from St. Petersburg University and the Medical-Surgical Academy. The new medical courses featured an expanded curriculum that included anatomy, physics, chemistry, hygiene, and midwifery and introduced new subjects such as toxicology and the study of mineral water and water healing. Courses in ophthalmology, mental diseases, and surgery were also required. The new Women's Medical Institute became the first Russian medical school to mandate a course, taught by Danilo Kirilovich Zabolotnyi, in the new science of Bacteriology and a course in professional hygiene, taught by Dmitri P. Nikolskii.

The ambiguous nature of women's status was finally cleared up in 1898, when the State Council approved an order expanding the rights of women doctors, thus entitling them to pensions and state salaries but not *chin* (ranking on the Table of Ranks) or honorary service medals. In May 1904 the Women's Medical Institute became part of the official state educational system with an operating budget financed by the state, reducing tuition to the same amount paid by university students. Staff at the institute could be awarded civil service rank. The first graduating class in 1902 contained 112 students. By 1906, 1,635 students had enrolled at the WMI, and its success led to women's medical institutes' opening in Moscow, Kiev, Odessa, Kharkov, Kazan, Dorpat, and Ekaterinoslav. After the 1917 Revolution, the institute continued to operate and became a coeducational medical school. It was later renamed the Leningrad Medical Institute.

In the years before the Revolutions of 1917, the popularity of medical courses may have stemmed from the paucity of professional opportunities available to women. Other than medicine, the most likely career possibility for a woman was to become a governess or teacher. As early as 1871, women could practice as pharmacists in women's medical facilities, but they did not earn the right to general practice until 1888. Russian women supporters of medical courses used these bleak prospects to their advantage, claiming that some women must support themselves and that the government should provide suitable opportunities for them to do so.

Women graduates of the medical courses worked in a variety of capacities throughout the Russian Empire, especially in the zemstvos and city municipal organs. About 20 percent of the women graduating between 1876 and 1906 published in leading medical journals, such as *Vrach (Physician)* and *Meditsinskii vestnik (Medical Messenger)*. During the 1877 Russo-Turkish War, students from the Women's Medical Institute served as nurses and assistants and sometimes as surgeons in the war zone. A large contingent of women physicians served in World War I. Women graduates became an integral part of the debate over the character of Russian medicine in the late nineteenth and early twentieth centuries. Both male and female physicians were concerned about issues such as whether medicine would become a for-profit enterprise and how to give physicians more control over medical administration and licensing standards. Women attended national and local medical congresses and carried out valuable research.

Cross-references: Higher Education for Women, Mariia Pokrovskaia, Anna Nikolaevna Shabanova, Women Pharmacists in Late Imperial Russia.

Suggested Readings

DenBeste-Barnett, Michelle. "Earnestly Working to Improve Russia's Future: Russian Women Physicians." Ph.D. Diss., Southern Illinois University, 1997.

Engel, Barbara Alpern. "Women Medical Students in Russia, 1872–1882." *Journal of Social History* 12 (1979): 394–415.

Gertsenshtein, G. M. "*Zhenskie vrachebnye kursy i zhenshchiny-vrachei*" (Women's Medical Courses and Women Doctors). *Real'naia entsiklopediia meditsinskikh nauk (Practical Medical Encyclopedia)* 7 (1893): 221–227.

Johanson, Christine. *Women's Struggle for Higher Education in Russia, 1855–1900.* Kingston and Montreal: McGill-Queen's University Press, 1987.

Tuve, Jeanette. *The First Russian Women Physicians.* Newtonville, MA: Oriental Research Partners, 1984.

Michelle DenBeste

Women's Military Congress (August 1–4, 1917)

A meeting of women representatives from various military and quasi-military women's groups as well as individual women involved in the war effort from all over Russia. The congress, held in Petrograd, convened with the purpose of establishing order and control over the disparate activities women were carrying out for the war effort, with a specific focus on the women's military movement.

World War I saw an unprecedented level of participation by Russian women. Not only did thousands of women work in war-related industry, as nurses, and in auxiliary services, but thousands became involved in the front-line hostilities as combatants as well. Women across the country organized groups to provide assistance to the war effort. After the February Revolution, women began working for the extension of their participation in the war effort in every area, including combat. Flooded with requests asking for creation of all-female military units, the Ministry of War of the Provisional Government acquiesced in late May 1917 and undertook the process of forming women's combat and auxiliary units. Other units were formed unofficially by local women's quasi-military groups. By midsummer there were dozens of official and unofficial units. The Women's Military Congress was a gathering of representatives from these women's military and quasi-military organizations, as well as a number of individual women participating in war-related activities. The congress opened on August 1, 1917, at the Nikolaevskii Engineering School in Petrograd and lasted until August 4. Ol'ga K. Nechaeva, the head of the Russian army's Commission on Women's Labor Service, chaired the congress. The "grandmother" of the Russian revolutionary movement, Ekaterina Breshko-Breshkovskaia, was also present and was voted honorary chair by the delegates. The aim of the congress was to determine the exact numbers of women serving the war effort and in what capacity they were doing so, both as part of the many different voluntary associations and as individuals. These women were offering their services in a variety of war-related areas, from combat, to medical assistance, but much of this work was a grassroots, impromptu effort. The congress sought to coordinate their activities and bring them under the authority of a central agency, the Women's Military Union of Petrograd. The organization was supposed to consolidate the members and activities of women's military organizations all over the country.

The congress was also concerned with the unfavorable response of some elements of Russian society toward women in military service, particularly toward female combat participation. The women were especially troubled by their negative image within the male military establishment and conservative quarters. The congress leadership urged women soldiers to demonstrate their effectiveness and value to the Russian military as well as to the Provisional Government. Testimonials were read from those who had seen women perform well in combat in order to buoy the spirits of the delegates. Breshko-Breshkovskaia lauded the women soldiers for their bravery and told them to ignore derision and insults from cowardly men. The representatives at the congress also called for female military volunteers to receive the same rights as male volunteers and draftees.

Cross-references: Ekaterina Breshko-Breshkovskaia, Women's Military Movement of World War I, Women's Military Units of World War I.

Suggested Readings

Stites, Richard. *The Women's Liberation Movement in Russia: Feminism, Nihilism, and Bolshevism, 1860–1930.* Princeton, NJ: Princeton University Press, 1978, 1991.

Stoff, Laurie S. "Russian Women in Combat: Female Soldiers of the First World War." M.A. Thesis, University of Kansas, 1995.

"*Zhenskii voennyi s"ezd*" (The Women's Military Congress). *Rech' (Speech)* (August 2, 1917): 3; (August 3, 1917): 4; (August 6, 1917): 4

Laurie Stoff

Women's Military Movement of World War I (1914–1917)

During World War I, there was extensive participation of thousands of women in military activities in Russia, including combat. The movement culminated in the creation of segregated women's military formations in the spring and summer of 1917, both under the auspices of the Provisional Government and by grassroots women's organizations.

From the very start of the hostilities of World War I in the summer of 1914, thousands of women in Russia joined the war effort on the front lines. Most served in auxiliary and medical capacities, but many actually joined the fighting as combatants. During the first three years of the war, most women participated in the fighting as individuals or in small groups, gaining entrance into the active army by disguising themselves as young men. Many fought undetected in the trenches until they were wounded and examined by medical personnel. A few, however, were accepted into the ranks as women. It is estimated that there were nearly 1,000 such women. After the February Revolution, which deposed tsarist rule, there was a resurgence of patriotic feeling and activity in Russia. Various quarters of society, from veterans, to students, expressed the desire to aid newly "free" Russia to defeat its enemies. Women were no exception to this volunteer spirit, and many began to press the new Provisional Government to give them a greater role in the war effort. A number of women, including several female veterans of the war, appealed to the Ministry of War to utilize the energies and abilities of women by organizing them into female military formations. Some members of Russian society questioned the viability of women's combat units. Others, including the Minister of War, Alexander Kerenskii, the Duma President, Mikhail Rodzianko, and the Supreme Commander of the Russian Army, Aleksei Brusilov, believed that women soldiers at the front would have propaganda value and would inspire war-weary male troops to resume fighting by reminding them of their duty to defend the homeland. Kerenskii gave permission for the organization of the First Russian Women's Battalion of Death, under the command of veteran woman soldier Mariia Bochkareva, in late May 1917. Shortly thereafter, he authorized the formation of three additional women's combat units and eleven communications detachments. The creation of these official units inspired many other women to join the war effort. Requests for combat participation poured into the Ministry of War from individuals and groups of women from all around the country. Women's military and quasi-military organizations sprang up in many of Russia's major cities, including Petrograd, Moscow, Kiev, Odessa, Kharkov, Poltava, Minsk, Saratov, Ekaterinburg, Tashkent, Simbirsk, Viatka, Perm, and Ekaterinodar. Authorization from the Ministry of War to form the official women's units was often interpreted as a carte blanche for action by women's organizations. These groups began creating their own, nongovernmentally sanctioned women's military formations, with the intention of joining the front-line fighting. Although the government appreciated the sentiments of these women, it was concerned about the formation of military units over which it did not have direct control. Military officials were often confused and frustrated when they encountered such unauthorized formations, especially in the absence of official procedures regarding the women's military movement. These units often presented themselves to local commanders requesting inclusion in active regiments, but without instructions from higher authorities, command personnel did not know what to do with the units. The sporadic and grassroots manner in which such formations were generated precluded their systematic utilization. The military authorities had no way of determining whether such units were properly trained, armed, and equipped and what their aims and loyalties were. The government tried to consolidate all these efforts by bringing them under the supervision of the Main Directorate of the General Staff and standardizing their formation. They forbade the formation of any women's military units outside the army's authority. The efforts were unsuccessful; they did not end the unofficial organization of such units, nor did they bring the unauthorized units under the army's control. The government could not accommodate all the women who wanted to serve. Unofficial women's units continued to mushroom around the country through the summer and fall of 1917. By August 1917 so many women were involved in military endeavors that a Women's Military Congress was convened in Petrograd, with the purpose of bringing the disparate efforts of women around the country under centralized control. The congress also failed in its attempt to control the unwieldy women's military movement.

After the Bolshevik Revolution in October 1917, the new Soviet authorities ordered the women's units to disband. When the Bolshevik government declared its intention of withdrawing Russia from the war, there was little reason for these formations to remain in existence. Furthermore, the Bolsheviks regarded them as hostile forces, since they had sworn loyalty to the Provisional Government, and they were particularly concerned about armed bands of women roaming the streets. The desire to fight did not disappear among these women, and many went on to fight on both sides of the Civil War.

Cross-references: Mariia Bochkareva, Women's Military Congress, Women's Military Units of World War I.

Suggested Readings

Griese, Ann Eliot, and Richard Stites. "Russia: Revolution and War." In *Female Soldiers: Combatants or Noncombatants? Historical and Contemporary Perspectives*, edited by Nancy Loring Goldman, 61–84. Westport, CT: Greenwood Press, 1982.

Ivanova, Iu. N. "*Problem khvatalo i bez nikh no . . .*" (There Were Enough Problems without Them, but . . .). *Voenno-Istoricheskii Zhurnal (The Military-Historical Journal)* 6 (1994): 75–77.

Senin, A. S. "*Zhenskie batal'ony i voennye komandy v 1917 godu*" (The Women's Battalions and Military Units of 1917). *Voprosy Istorii (Problems of History)* 10 (1987): 176–182.

Stites, Richard. *The Women's Liberation Movement: Feminism, Nihilism, Bolshevism, 1860–1930*. Princeton, NJ: Princeton University Press, 1978, 1991.

Stoff, Laurie S. "Russian Women in Combat: Female Soldiers of the First World War." M.A. Thesis, University of Kansas, 1995.

Laurie Stoff

Women's Military Units of World War I (1917–1918)

The segregated, all-female combat and auxiliary units formed between the February and October Revolutions by the Russian Provisional Government and private women's groups in a last-ditch effort to inspire the mass of war-weary soldiers to continue fighting the war until victory could be achieved.

The Russian women's military units of World War I were created in the spring and summer of 1917. After the February Revolution, a number of women pressured the government to expand female participation in the war effort, in particular to form sexually segregated military units from women volunteers.

High-ranking members of the government and of the military, including the Duma President, Mikhail Rodzianko, the Minister of War, Alexander Kerenskii, and the Supreme Commander of the Russian Army, Aleksei Brusilov, believed that female soldiers would have propaganda value and that their example would revitalize the weary, demoralized Russian army. In essence, the women's units were intended to shame the men into continuing to fight. At the end of May 1917 Kerenskii authorized the formation of the First Russian Women's Battalion of Death in Petrograd. He placed Mariia Bochkareva, a seasoned noncommissioned officer who had seen three years of combat, in command of the unit. In June Kerenskii approved the organization of two additional women's combat units in Petrograd and Moscow, as well as four separate communications detachments. Authorization from the government for the formation of women's military units provided the impetus for private women's organizations to form their own quasi-military units. In an attempt to satisfy popular demand and bring these units under its control, the Ministry of War expanded the number of women's military formations. A fourth combat battalion was designated in Ekaterinodar, created from a preexisting, grassroots unit made up of Cossack women. Seven additional communications units were formed in Kiev and Saratov, again employing the already existing women's units in those cities. These extensions failed to end the impromptu, unofficial organization of quasi-military units of women volunteers, and the government found it impossible to control such formations. The formation and implementation of the official women's units also proved problematic. There was no consensus among the military administration as to the potential value of female soldiers, and this, coupled with the severe shortages from which the nation was then suffering, meant that the army made only a halfhearted commitment to the project. Therefore, the women's units received inadequate attention and assistance from the military administration. By August 1917 there was a growing inclination in the military establishment to discontinue the organization of women for combat purposes. Since the First Russian Women's Battalion of Death failed to inspire a renewed fighting spirit in the men, the military questioned the value of the women's units. In particular, the government found it difficult to justify the allocation of badly needed resources to such an unreliable project. At the end of the summer, the authorities ended assistance to the units but allowed them to exist.

When the Bolsheviks seized power in October 1917, the women's units were still in existence. The First Russian Women's Battalion of Death, commanded by Bochkareva, was at the front but soon disbanded. The Moscow battalion had begun to disintegrate as early as September, as many of its members left the unit. Just prior to disbanding, however, about 500 volunteers were sent to the front at their own request but without the knowledge or permission of the military authorities. The Petrograd battalion was intact, but its only action was its involvement in the defense of the Winter Palace during the October Revolution. On October 24 the Provisional Government summoned the women's unit to the Winter Palace to provide defense against the Bolsheviks. Only a small company of the women's unit actually participated in the defense, and the numerically superior Bolshevik forces quickly overwhelmed them. Once in power, the Bolshevik government ordered the official dissolution of any remaining women's military formations on November 30. Members of the Petrograd and Ekaterinodar battalions lingered in their camps until early 1918 and then finally dispersed. Some women who had served in these units went on to fight on both sides of the civil war.

Cross-references: Mariia Bochkareva, Women's Military Movement.

Suggested Readings

Botchkareva [*sic*], Maria. *Yashka: My Life as Peasant, Officer, and Exile.* As told to Isaac Don Levine. New York: Frederick A. Stokes, 1919.

Griese, Ann Eliot, and Richard Stites. "Russia: Revolution and War." In *Female Soldiers: Combatants or Noncombatants? Historical and Contemporary Perspectives*, edited by Nancy Loring Goldman, 61–84. Westport, CT: Greenwood Press, 1982.

Ivanova, Iu. N. "*Problem khvatalo i bez nikh no . . .*" (There Were Enough Problems without Them, but . . .). *Voenno-Istoricheskii Zhurnal (The Military-Historical Journal)* 6 (1994): 75–77.

Senin, A. S. "*Zhenskie batal'ony i voennye komandy v 1917 godu*" (The Women's Battalions and Military Units of 1917). *Voprosy Istorii (Problems of History)* 10 (1987): 176–182.

Stoff, Laurie S. "Russian Women in Combat: Female Soldiers of the First World War." M.A. Thesis, University of Kansas, 1995.

Laurie Stoff

Women's Periodical Publishing in Late Imperial Russia (1860–1905)

Encouraged by the reforms of Alexander II in the 1860s, a broader, open forum to discuss women's issues emerged, particularly in the periodical press. Under the rubric of the "woman question," periodicals debated proper roles for women in Russian society. In later decades attempts to further woman's rights through periodicals aimed at a female audience often met with economic and governmental challenges. Women also tried to further their economic and literary positions by working in periodical presses as editors, publishers, writers, translators, correspondents, typesetters, and office managers.

The early 1860s saw the emergence of the "woman question," a fascination with issues of women's education and role in society. Concurrently, a marked increase in periodical publishing, in response to the relaxed censorship rules of Alexander II, helped stimulate the debate over women's roles. These issues emerged in the press, in large part, as a response to a series of articles by the noted poet, writer, and publicist Mikhail Larionovich Mikhailov, which appeared from 1859 to 1865. The most dominant voices of the written debate were male; their forum was the political-literary "thick" journal, voluminous periodicals that provided an arena for political debates in late nineteenth-century Russia. Specialized publications aimed at a female audience also began to turn their attention to these questions. *Razsvet (Daybreak*, 1859–1862) is an early example of a women's literary magazine that published articles discussing women's education. More serious were the journals *Damskii vestnik (Ladies' Herald*, 1860, two issues only) and *Zhenskii vestnik (Women's Herald*, 1866–1868). These early journals experienced governmental antagonism not only toward the topic of woman's rights but also against women's direct participation in the production of such ideas. Although earlier women's journals officially had been run by males, in the case of *Zhenskii vestnik*, a woman, Anna Borisovna Messarosh, requested permission both to publish and to edit the journal. The censor allowed Messarosh to become the publisher but dictated that a male be the official editor registered with the censorship office. Official editors were legally responsible for ideas printed in journals and could incur fines or jail time. This consideration probably precipitated the censor's directive, but other women had been allowed to edit journals before 1866. The sensitive topic of the journal clearly played into the denial of Messarosh as editor. The editorial staff of *Zhenskii vestnik*, comprising males and females, was closely tied to the coworkers of the defunct *Russkoe slovo (Russian Word)* and *Slovo (Word)*, both of which had been closed by the government. The journal thus invited close scrutiny from the censor.

The decades following the 1860s saw the evolution of women activists who increasingly turned toward revolutionary ideals. The vast majority of magazines aimed at women in this period dealt with fashion and traditional female roles. Efforts to publish specialized journals on women's education and social roles often met with economic difficulties and governmental opposition. The writer Mariia Savel'evna Skavronskaia Boguslavskaia met with a great deal of financial difficulty in publishing her journal *Drug zhenshchin (Women's Friend*, 1882–1884). Boguslavskaia founded *Drug zhenshchin* with an emphasis on education, statistics on working women, histories of women in other countries, and religion. Boguslavskaia applied to be the official editor and publisher with the financial and literary support of journalist and writer Anna Ivanovna Volkova. The journal was approved, but in 1882 Boguslavskaia appealed to the censor for money to cover paper and printing costs. She noted that her financial problems stemmed from a small subscriber base but that she had hopes of the journal's eventual success. She argued for governmental support to save the journal by emphasizing its religious content, but this attempt to wed governmental concerns and women's issues was denied. By 1884 the enterprise had experienced sufficient governmental and economic pressure to necessitate its closure.

The best example of the financial difficulties experienced by those trying to publish women's journals was the writer Aleksandra Nikolaevna Peshkova-Toliverova. (Toliverova was a pseudonym; she was also known as Iakobi by marriage.) Her journal *Zhenskoe delo (Women's Cause*, 1899–1900) was the most interesting Russian feminist journal of the late nineteenth century. Containing articles on women's movements in other countries, legal questions, and women's work, the journal reflected an avid interest on the part of Peshkova-Toliverova and her writing staff in educating Russian women on women's issues abroad. After two years, Peshkova-Toliverova changed the journal to a news-oriented *Novoe delo (New Affairs)*, aimed at a general audience. Her letter of explanation to the readers diagnosed her efforts to found a feminist journal in Russia as premature.

Despite such difficulties, late nineteenth-century Russian women utilized journalism to advance their vision of a larger role for women in society. Of particular note is the fact that over 230 women in Russia from 1860 to 1905 became official publishers or editors of periodicals. Twenty-five percent of the periodicals that they published provided reading material for the young or discussed pedagogy, with particular emphasis on teaching children values. Some perceived children's publishing as an "acceptable" forum for a woman's voice. Women publishers and editors also worked on a wide variety of other topics, especially from the 1880s onward. Women published periodicals with varied topics such as insurance, sports, advertising, music, drama, politics, and literature. Of special note were individuals like Evgeniia Ivanovna Konradi, who worked as a writer, publicist, social activist, newspaper publisher, and translator. Konradi published articles on the education of women in *Zhenskii vestnik*, wrote for other women's pedagogical journals, and contributed articles to *Zhenskoe delo* and the thick journal *Russkaia mysl' (Russian Thought)*. At one point, Konradi published the St. Petersburg newspaper *Nedelia (Week)*. She embodied the interlocking roles played by women in publishing in late nineteenth-century Russia. Many who had concerns about women's issues but were not radicals or revolutionaries voiced their views in the publishing arena. The determined, yet frustrated, efforts of these women to express their ideas paved the way for a new generation of women in the early twentieth century. With the freeing of most publications from strict censorship in 1905, women were no longer forced to conform to government restrictions in their writing and publishing efforts.

Cross-references: A. A. Davydova, Women's Periodicals in Early Twentieth-Century Russia, *Zhenskaia izdatel'skaia artel'* (Women's Publishing Artel).

Suggested Readings

Altaev, Al (M. V. Iamshchikova). "*Moi starye izdateli (Iz vospominanii)*" (My Former Publishers [from Memoirs]). In *Kniga, Issledovaniia i materialy (The Book: Research and Materials)*, edited by N. A. Letova and B. D. Letova, vol. 26, 154–182. Moscow: Kniga, 1973.

Clark, Rhonda Lebedev. "Forgotten Voices: Women in Periodical Publishing of Late Imperial Russia, 1860–1905." Ph.D. Diss., University of Minnesota, 1996.

Lisovskii, N. M. *Bibliografiia russkoi periodicheskoi pechati, 1703–1900 (A Bibliography of the Russian Periodical Press, 1703–1900)*. Petrograd: 1915. Reprint, 2 vols., Moscow: Literaturnoe obozrenie, 1995.

Marks, Carolyn R. " 'Provid[ing] Amusement for the Ladies': The Rise of the Women's Magazine in the 1880s." In *An Improper Profession: Women, Gender and Journalism in Late Imperial Russia*, edited by Barbara T. Norton and Jehanne M. Gheith. Durham, NC: Duke University Press (in press).

Stites, Richard. *The Women's Liberation Movement in Russia: Feminism, Nihilism, and Bolshevism, 1860–1930*. Princeton, NJ: Princeton University Press, 1978.

Tishkin, G. A. *Zhenskii vopros v Rossii: 50–60-e gody XIX v (The Woman Question in Russia: The 1850s and 60s)*. Leningrad: Izdatel'stvo leningradskogo universiteta, 1984.

Rhonda Clark

Women's Periodicals in Early Twentieth-Century Russia

Russian women's periodical literature has never been given its due as a significant cultural institution, even though the early twentieth century witnessed a burgeoning interest in the publication of magazines dedicated to women's domestic, social, and civil concerns. Almost two dozen new women's magazines were founded between the turn of the century and the Revolution of 1917, revealing a broad spectrum of ideas, values, and aspirations.

For many reasons, the contributions of Russian women to journalism and to women's periodicals have been ignored for many years. "Women's activities," by definition, whether they involved ministering to one's own family or to society's poor, creating fashions and toys at home, establishing women's organizations outside the home, or advocating equality in the marriage bed or equal opportunity in education, politics, the law, and the workplace, received far less attention than men's accomplishments. Socially as well as politically, woman's place was clearly associated with her domestic duties, not with policies of editorial boards or the publishing industry. Until very recently, Western and Soviet scholarship severely biased the study of journalism of the prerevolutionary period and almost completely ignored women's publications. Although the majority of women's periodicals were short-lived, approximately two dozen new women's magazines were founded between 1900 and 1917, and there was also a significant increase in the number of women writers, translators, critics, and journalists whose work appeared on their pages. These publications are a major resource and record for chronicling, categorizing, and tracing with accuracy the variety and scope of women's domestic, social, and civil roles, thought processes, and activities, all of which helped to shape the Russian women's movement and Russian cultural life in general in the decades prior to the Revolutions of 1917.

The four most successful magazines edited and published by women during the first decade of the twentieth century appeared in St. Petersburg: *Zhenskii vestnik (Women's Herald*, 1904–1917), *Damskii mir (Ladies' World*, 1907–1918), *Soiuz zhenshchin (Union of Women*, 1907–1909), and *Zhenshchina (Woman*, 1907–1909, 1913–1916). They illustrate not only the variety of women's concerns but also the intensity of their expression in the years bracketing the first Russian Revolution of 1905 and, subsequently, the First All-Russian Women's Congress convened in December 1908. While none of these magazines, except perhaps *Damskii mir*, could claim to be a commercial success, by the beginning of the following decade, well-established Moscow businessmen, having recognized the potential of women's periodicals and taking their cues from the successes and failures of their female predecessors, started up their own more commercially competitive women's magazines. These included *Zhenskoe delo (Women's Cause*, 1910–1917), *Zhurnal dlia xoziaek (Magazine for Housewives*, 1912–1926), and *Zhurnal dlia zhenshchin (Magazine for Women*, 1914–1926).

Dr. Mariia I. Pokrovskaia's *Zhenskii vestnik* was the first Russian women's magazine edited and published by a woman and devoted to the cause of women in Russia to last more than two years. Its first issue appeared in September 1904 and was followed by ten issues a year through 1917. Pokrovskaia's experience practicing medicine in the slums of the Russian capital and authoring numerous pamphlets on public health greatly influenced the content of her periodical, which almost immediately became the voice of her newly formed Women's Progressive Party, organized in 1905. Editorials, articles, and fiction, in particular, her "Psychological Sketches" of Russian women, were all aimed at raising women's political and social consciousness. Her first editorial emphasized the magazine's feminist goal of improving the lot "not only of women of the intelligentsia, but also of women of all backgrounds." Containing no illustrations, no articles on fashion or personal appearance, no advice on household management, and few advertisements, it focused on the cultural and political significance of women's issues beyond the home in theoretical and practical terms; among the concerns discussed were reforms in health, hygiene, education, the legal system (especially laws pertaining to women), politics, and the workplace, as well as moral appeals for temperance and a campaign against prostitution. Prominent feminists and doctors constituted the staff of the journal. Although its circulation was limited, articles were cited in other women's periodicals, such as *Zhenshchina* and even the short-lived *Zhenskaia mysl' (Women's Thought*, 1909–1910), produced in Kiev. By 1907 three other magazines edited and published by women were established in St. Petersburg. They spanned much of the political and social spectrum, from the upper-class, Anglophile monthly *Damskii mir*, edited and published by Countess Aleksandra Zakharovna Muravieva, advertised as a deluxe magazine of "fashion, literature and woman's life in both the domestic and social spheres," through the suffragist monthly *Soiuz zhenshchin*, to the politically conscious, but family-oriented, middle-class weekly *Zhenshchina*.

After a slow start, Muravieva's *Damskii mir* continued to bring her readers the latest fashion news from abroad but expanded its coverage of women's culture. Muravieva's many years as a translator for *Vestnik inostrannoi literatury (Herald of Foreign Literature*) and prior experience as editor and publisher of the short-lived *Baian* may have helped her modify her project, increase circulation, and acquire more advertisements. After trying different printers, she contracted with A. S. Suvorin, whose association may have helped her magazine increase its distribution. Moreover, by 1908–1909 many new rubrics and contributors were added; besides advice on fashion, personal hygiene, and housekeeping, there were sections on poetry and fiction (including the most popular writers of the day such as Anna Mar), book and arts reviews, and a "mail box" as well as an "occult mail box." Almost every issue contained a "portrait" of a famous woman, honoring her achievements in a feature article often accompanied by the cover illustration. These "portraits" included representatives of high society and charitable organizations, celebrities from the theater, art, and music, and visiting foreign women writers, artists, or travelers. Music and theater reviews were written by the well-known critic Anna Matova, who became a permanent staff member, and arts reviews were by O. Bazankur, an associate from Muravieva's days on *Baian*. Anglophile in its leanings, certain rubrics were borrowed directly from contemporary British women's periodicals, and its fashion reviews were more international than those of other magazines that focused only on Paris. By 1911 some women's political issues were included, initiated by the publication of an article by a Serbian feminist and the editor's request for readers' comments, and by 1913 new rubrics included "Contemporary Life" and quotes by famous historical figures about women. The war years emphasized women's contributions to the war effort and value to the nation.

Soiuz zhenshchin was edited and published by the political activist and schoolteacher Mariia Ivanovna Chekhova and dedicated "to the struggle for equal rights for women and, above all, for her right to vote." Chekhova's sixteen years in the provinces, raising a large family and working as a rural schoolteacher, proved invaluable when, on her return to St. Petersburg in 1906, she became a founding member and secretary of the *Soiuz ravnopraviia zhenshchin* (Union of Equal Rights for Women). Until 1910, when she moved to Moscow, she edited the union's magazine, *Soiuz zhenshchin*. Established in mid-1907 as a suffragist publication, with the political goal of obtaining the vote for women, it also printed articles on various aspects of the women's movement. It defined its goals broadly as "spreading the idea of equal rights for women among the reading public, developing theoretical positions on improving the economic, social and legal situation of women, and providing a forum for the expression of ideas on tactics for women activists." Regarding its function as informational, it focused its nonradical approach to woman's rights on "uniting all women." Run on a tight budget that utilized the financial as well as literary contributions of its staff, it was not a commercial venture. Its minimal advertisements were for a few books and magazines. Based on membership and contribution figures, its circulation was about 1,000; however, its articles were often cited or reprinted by other magazines.

Indeed, both Pokrovskaia's and Chekhova's magazines provided material for Bogel'man's *Zhenshchina*, founded in November 1907. Sophia Bogel'man defined its primary goal as promoting family strength through knowledge. In addition to calling for women's equality in education, the legal system, the family, and the workplace, in a grand rhetorical flourish its advertisements proclaimed the woman as the backbone of both family and nation; however, because woman has been so "burdened," her civic duty can be fulfilled "only if the necessary weapon is put at her disposal: knowledge." Hence, the magazine's goal was "to arm every woman with essential knowledge." Although this highly ambitious periodical lasted barely two years under her editorship, being a weekly, it produced four times as much copy as the monthlies. Moreover, its format was unique, for each week subscribers would receive a half dozen individual, two- to eight-page sections of the magazine, edited separately and distributed bimonthly. The format suggested the highly complex nature of its subject by invoking the entire gamut of roles that a woman was called upon to play: as citizen, wife, mother, homemaker, nutritionist, doctor, teacher, caregiver, and so on. Each section was duly named and introduced by its own symbolic cover, for example, *Zhenshchina–Grazhdanka* (Woman–Citizen), *Zhenshchina–Zhena* (Woman–Wife), *Zhenshchina–Mat'* (Woman–Mother), *Zhenshchina–Khoziaika* (Woman–Housewife), *Zhenshchina–Vrach* (Woman–Doctor), *Detskii Mir* (Children's World), *Domashnye zhivotnye* (Domestic Animals), and *Poslednye mody* (Latest Fashions). Although closed in 1909 due to her husband's bankruptcy, there is evidence of at least two attempts to restart it in 1910. It is unclear why and how her husband revived it after a five-year hiatus as a less ambitious, but commercially viable, bimonthly, which lasted until mid-1916, despite World War I.

The single Moscow periodical initiated by a woman before 1910 was edited by Elena Ivanovna Kippar, director of a school for seamstresses. It was first known as *Domashnaia portnikha (Domestic Seamstress*, 1906–1908), but after a year of seeking its proper niche, it changed its format and name to *Zhenskoe bogatsvo (Women's Wealth*, 1908–1909) and then to *Zhenskii mir (Women's World*, 1909–1911).

By the second decade of the new century, St. Petersburg's women editors and publishers found themselves in competition with Moscow's business establishment. Recognizing the commercial potential of women's periodicals, Lev Mikhailovich Rodionov produced his first issue of *Zhenskoe delo (Women's Cause)* in 1910; Aleksandr Viktorovich Lobanov began his highly successful *Zhurnal dlia xoziaek (Magazine for Housewives)* in 1912. The *Zhurnal dlia zhenshchin (Magazine for Women)* emerged in 1914, published by the stock corporation Anons. All three lasted through 1917, with the latter two continuing well into 1926, following a four-year hiatus during the civil war (1918–1922). The experienced entrepreneurs not only continued the most popular rubrics of the earlier magazines but also did not hesitate to introduce commercial ploys to expand sales and circulation. Competition became so great that by early 1915 Lobanov, whose low-cost, left-leaning magazine bragged a readership of upward of 150,000, charged *Zhurnal dlia zhenshchin* with plagiarism. Among the major changes introduced by these male editors was increased, but rather bland, patriotic coverage of women's social and political issues, especially on the achievements of the women's movement, as well as more timely coverage of the arts, including the serialization of fiction and articles by the most popular women writers of the day, such as Anastasiia Verbitskaia, Evdokiia Nagrodskaia, and

Anna Mar. *Zhenskoe delo*, for example, covered the latest fashions, provided up-to-date reviews of the latest art exhibitions and theatrical and musical productions, and during the war sought solace in the idea that "it is a holy sacrifice for our sins." It offered a nonradical stand on feminist issues, reporting on the latest activities and supporting the initiatives of the *Russkoe Zhenskoe Vzaimnoblagotvoritel'noe Obshchestvo* (Russian Women's Mutual Philanthropic Society) and the *Rossiiskaia Liga Ravnopraviia Zhenshchin* (League of Equal Rights). The *Zhurnal dlia xoziaek*, in order to appeal to more subscribers, opened a mail-order service for Parisian cosmetics and proposed the establishment of a school to train women to form their own small business cooperatives.

With the exception of *Rabotnitsa* (*Working Woman*, 1914; 1917–), the most politically left of the women's periodicals, the women's magazines expressed interest in social change to bring about civil and political equality and predicated their hopes for the future on some kind of constitutional government rather than revolution. Established with a male editor, Feliks Vasilievich Martsinkevich, and female publisher, D. F. Petrovskaia, *Rabotnitsa* finally saw its first issue of 12,000 copies in St. Petersburg on International Women's Day, 1914. *Rabotnitsa* was launched, however, only after four years of debate over whether socialist women workers needed anything more than a "women's page" in *Pravda*. Arguing that the "woman question" was but "one aspect" of the general social question, the male-dominated RSDLP opposed a separate women's publication as a waste of funds. Closed in mid-1914 after only seven issues, it was revived in Moscow in 1917 and later designated as the Russian Communist Party/Bolshevik's (RCP/B) official women's magazine.

Some older fashion magazines also persisted, with some breaks, through the early war years, such as *Modnyi svet* (*The World of Fashion*, St. Petersburg, 1868–1916) and *Modnyi kur'er (The Fashion Messenger*, St. Petersburg, 1899–1916). Other women's magazines founded in the early twentieth century that lasted for at least one issue or up to several years included *Zhenskoe delo (Women's Cause*, St. Petersburg, 1899–1900), *Khoziaika (Homemaker*, St. Petersburg, 1901–1903), *Zhurnal akusherstva i zhenskikh boleznei (Journal of Midwifery and Women's Diseases*, St. Petersburg, 1901–1916), *Khoziaika (Homemaker*, St. Petersburg, 1908), *Zhenskaia mysl' (Women's Thought*, Kiev, 1909–1910), *Damskii listok (Ladies' Page*, St. Petersburg, 1910), *Mir zhenshchiny (Women's World*, Moscow, 1912–1916), *Zhenshchina (Woman*), which became *Sovremennaia Zhenshchina (Contemporary Woman*, Warsaw, 1913–1914), *Zhenshchina i voina (Woman and War*, Moscow, 1915), *Zhenshchina i Khoziaika (Woman and Homemaker*, Moscow, 1916), and *Khoziaika (Homemaker*, Petrograd, 1916).

Detailed information regarding the commercial and publishing history of the women's periodicals seems nonexistent or perhaps was never considered significant enough to preserve. Soviet scholarship emphasized only magazines with a "socialist" agenda, ignoring one of the major characteristics of early twentieth-century periodical publishing: the wonderfully broad spectrum of coverage. As a significant prerevolutionary cultural institution, Russian women's magazines can now be viewed as reflecting the prevailing spectrum of traditional feminine values, habits, and aspirations and as providing a forum for airing women's concerns and shaping new feminine and contemporary feminist ideals. On the other hand, by the second decade of the twentieth century, the commercial potential of these cultural vehicles was realized, and they were recognized as a formidable business enterprise. This fact had serious implications for the women editors and publishers, who found themselves in competition with their more entrepreneurial male counterparts.

Cross-references: Sophia Zakharovna Bogel'man, Mariia Aleksandrovna Chekhova, First All-Russian Women's Congress (1908), *Liga ravnopravii zhenshchin* (League of Women's Equal Rights), Countess Alexandra Zakharovna Muravieva, Mariia Ivanovna Pokrovskaia, *Soiuz ravnopravii zhenshchin* (Women's Equal Rights Union), Women's Mutual Philanthropic Society, Women's Periodical Publishing in Late Imperial Russia, 1860–1905, Zhenskaia progressivnaia partiia (Women's Progressive Party).

Suggested Readings

Clark, Rhonda Lebedev. "Forgotten Voices: Women in Periodical Publishing of Late Imperial Russia, 1860–1905." Ph.D. Diss., University of Minnesota, 1996.

Edmondson, Linda Harriet. *Feminism in Russia, 1900–1917*. Stanford, CA: Stanford University Press, 1984.

Gheith, Jehanne M., and Barbara T. Norton, eds. *An Improper Profession: Women, Gender and Journalism in Late Imperial Russia*. Durham, NC: Duke University Press (in press).

Marsh, Rosalind, ed. *Gender and Russian Literature: New Perspectives*. Cambridge: Cambridge University Press, 1996.

Martinsen, Deborah A., ed. *Literary Journals in Imperial Russia*. Cambridge: Cambridge University Press, 1997.

Stites, Richard. *The Women's Liberation Movement in Russia: Feminism, Nihilism, and Bolshevism, 1860–1930*. Princeton, NJ: Princeton University Press, 1978, 1991.

Jane Gary Harris

Z

Zasulich, Vera Ivanovna (1849–1919)

Prominent Russian revolutionary of the late nineteenth and early twentieth centuries, best known for her 1878 shooting of General Trepov, which made her a world celebrity and in Russia legitimated terrorism as a means of opposing tyranny.

Vera Zasulich was born on July 27, 1849, to impoverished noble parents on the family estate in Smolensk province. After her father died when she was three, she was sent to live with aunts at a nearby estate. Although she spent most of her childhood with them, she did not feel complete approval there or at home. Throughout her life she remained a reserved and timid woman, continually seeking acceptance but having difficulty establishing relationships. She studied with a governess until she was fifteen, when she was sent to a *pensionat* (boarding school) in Moscow to prepare her for becoming a governess. Zasulich abhorred the idea of being a governess and resented others' making plans for her future. Exposed to the ideologies of the revolutionary intelligentsia in Moscow, her personal feelings of injustice gradually began to evolve into social consciousness.

After completing her education in 1867, Zasulich first worked as a clerk in Serpukhov and then in seamstress and bookbinding artels in St. Petersburg, where she also taught Sunday literacy classes. That winter she met Sergei Nechaev, whose use of her as a courier led to her arrest and imprisonment in 1869. While no charges were filed, she was imprisoned for two years, released, rearrested, and put under administrative exile until 1875. Her treatment during this period transformed Zasulich from a rhetorical revolutionary into a real one. As soon as her exile ended, she went to Kiev, joined the revolutionary group *Iuzhnye buntari* (Southern Rebels), and assumed an "illegal" existence.

In July 1877 she was disturbed by the flogging of E. A. Bogoliubov, a young political prisoner in St. Petersburg. Like most educated revolutionaries, Zasulich considered corporal punishment as the greatest shame and resolved to shoot General Trepov, the city's governor. Expecting to pay with her life but fearing repercussions for the defendants in the imminent Trial of the 193, the famous tsarist show trial involving participants in the "going to the people" movement, she waited to act until after they were sentenced. Although she only wounded Trepov in January 1878, her trial and acquittal made her an instant celebrity and, to some extent, legitimated terrorism, which heretofore had been heatedly debated by Russian revolutionaries. This distressed Zasulich. In contrast to radicals such as Vera Figner and Sof'ia Perovskaia, who later came to believe in terror as a political weapon, Zasulich felt that terrorism was justifiable only as a gesture of conscience. She wanted to raise the moral consciousness of her nation and expose Russian officials' bestiality to the world. Zasulich was acquitted by jury, which in Russia could acquit on the basis of "conscience," and thus judged her character and motives rather than her actions. To escape rearrest, Zasulich immediately went into hiding and fled to Switzerland two weeks later. Except for surreptitious visits to Russia in 1879 and 1899, she lived abroad until the general amnesty of 1905 made it possible for her to return.

In Western Europe Zasulich could mix with other radicals and contribute to the revolutionary movement, which further enhanced her stature. After *Zemlia i volia* (Land and Freedom) broke up, during a clandestine trip to Russia in 1879 she joined its nonterrorist faction, *Chernyi peredel* (Black Repartition), which saw the peasantry as the basic revolutionary force and favored propaganda. She later became associated with the terrorist faction *Narodnaia volia* (the People's Will) as president of the Foreign Section of its *Krasnyi krest* (Red Cross), aiding political prisoners and exiles. After falling under the influence of Georgi V. Plekhanov, with whom she worked for most of the remainder of her revolutionary life, in 1883 Zasulich joined him in forming the first Russian Marxist organization, *Osvobozhdenia truda* (Liberation of Labor). The next year she suffered a loss whose void was never filled when Lev Deich, the comrade with whom she had lived as man and wife, was arrested and exiled to Siberia, where he later married a fellow prisoner. Plekhanov and his wife, Rosalia, supported her during this difficult time and became her closest friends. She lived with them in exile and helped nurse Plekhanov through a serious battle with tuberculosis, even traveling to France in 1889 to care for him. Although Plekhanov was fond of, and respected, Zasulich, he was autocratic by nature, and, without Deich to support her, his influence on her became even greater. Although she disagreed with his negative estimation of the peasantry and the *obshchina* (the peasant commune), in the 1890s she became increasingly more Marxist in outlook, acknowledging the supremacy of the proletariat in the revolutionary struggle.

After living in England from 1894 to 1897, Zasulich returned to Switzerland and began editing publications for the Union of Russian Social Democrats Abroad, a branch of the Liberation of Labor, which published literature for distribution in Russia. When she secretly returned to Russia in the winter of 1899–1900 and met Vladimir I. Lenin, both were positively impressed. She later reluctantly agreed to serve as editor of *Iskra* (the *Spark*), the party newspaper, mainly to mediate between Plekhanov and Lenin. In 1903 Lenin removed Zasulich from the paper's editorial board during the conflict that split the party into the Bolsheviks and Mensheviks. Zasulich became one of the leaders of the Mensheviks and edited the new Menshevik *Iskra*, where she attacked Lenin's authoritarian views—the only time that she criticized a fellow socialist in print. She favored solidarity among revolutionaries over ideological perfection, and when Lenin's "Jacobinism," his ruthless authoritarianism, undermined her ideal of a broadly based political community, she became his adversary.

While abroad, Zasulich spent most of her time translating, editing, and writing, especially philosophical critiques. Although she expressed some interesting theoretical insights, she was not a theorist, mainly using Marxist methodology to analyze social and literary questions. She also was not a feminist. Although sympathetic to discrimination against women, like most socialists she was convinced that in Russia, where rights were denied to all, the "woman question" could be resolved only within the overall framework of socialism. Her early opposition to what she considered sexually divisive movements within the Party may have softened with time, and, shortly after returning to Russia in 1905, she addressed the *Obshchestvo vzaimopomoshchi rabotnits* (Society for the Mutual Aid of Working Women).

The failure of the Revolution of 1905 brought a virtual end to Zasulich's active participation in revolutionary politics. As a member of the right wing of the Mensheviks, she even broke with Plekhanov, reconciling with him only after the outbreak of World War I. A strong advocate of Russia's support of France and England, in the winter of 1918–1919 Zasulich was evicted by Bolshevik soldiers from the Writer's Home, where she had lived since 1909, earning a meager income by writing, translating, and editing. She had suffered for years from the tuberculosis that she probably had contracted when caring for Plekhanov in the 1880s and died on May 8, 1919, just weeks before Plekhanov. They were buried next to each other in St. Petersburg's Volkhov Cemetery in a section for distinguished writers and political thinkers. Ironically, although she wrote extensively for the Marxists and in 1901 wrote an article condemning terrorism as a political weapon, she is remembered more as a terrorist than as a Marxist scholar.

Cross-references: Vera Figner, Aleksandra Kollontai, Sofia Perovskaia.

Suggested Readings

Bergman, Jay. *Vera Zasulich: A Biography*. Stanford, CA: Stanford University Press, 1983.

Broido, Vera. *Apostles into Terrorists: Women and the Revolutionary Movement in the Russia of Alexander II*. New York: Viking, 1977.

Deich, Lev. "Vera Ivanovna Zasulich." Introductory biographical sketch. In *Revoliutsionery iz burzhuaznoi sredy: V. I. Zasulich (Revolutionaries from the Bourgeois Milieu: V. I. Zasulich)*. St. Petersburg: Gosudarstvennoe izdatel'stvo, 1921.

Engel, Barbara Alpern, and Clifford Rosenthal, eds. and trans. *Five Sisters: Women against the Tsar*. New York: Knopf, 1975.

Noonan, Norma C. "Zasulich, Vera Ivanovna." In *The Modern Encyclopedia of Russian and Soviet History*, edited by Joseph L. Wieczynski, vol. 45, 186–189. Gulf Breeze, FL: Academic International Press, 1987.

Klawa N. Thresher

Zhenskaia Izdatel'skaia Artel' (the Women's Publishing Artel) (1863–1879)

A workers' cooperative formed in St. Petersburg to provide women employment opportunities in the publishing industry; it is also referred to as the Society of Women Translators.

The *Zhenskaia izdaltel'skaia artel'* (Women's Publishing Artel) was formed in the 1860s, a decade that saw the appearance of many charitable societies and *arteli* (workers' cooperatives) in Russia. Many of these organizations, such as the Society for Inexpensive Lodgings, were designed to provide moral and economic support to women seeking new educational and work opportunities. Feminist leaders in this period viewed philanthropy as a vehicle to better the position of women in society. The Women's Publishing Artel was unique in its specific focus on educated women who were capable of pursuing employment in the publishing industry. Two well-known advocates of woman's rights of the 1860s, Nadezhda Vasil'evna Stasova and Maria Vasil'evna Trubnikova, founded the *Artel'* in 1863. The founders wanted the *Artel'* to provide work for women as translators, editors, proofreaders, illustrators, and other occupations associated with publishing. Theoretically, women from any social background would be welcome to join, although there was a membership fee required. In order to make membership a possibility for all, it was agreed that one could pay the fee by working at the *Artel'*. Original members of the group included N. A. Belozerskaia, A. N. Engel'gardt, A. P. Filosofova, M. G. Ermolova, E. G. Beketova, M. S. Ol'khina, V. N. Rostovtseva, A. G. Markelova, V. I. Pechatkina, P. S. Stasova, M. A. Menzhinskaia, V. V. Ivasheva, A. F. Shakeva, O. N. Butakova, E. A. Shtakenshneider, A. N. Shul'govskaia, and others. The *Artel'* embodied two main ideals in its activities: supporting woman's rights to jobs in the publishing sector and producing books of concern to the organizers, namely, instructive reading material for children and adults. The *Artel'* immediately began working toward both goals, employing up to fifty persons in the first years of operation. The organization began its efforts in 1863 with the publication of the *Polnoe sobranie skazok Andersena* (*Complete Collection of Andersen's [Hans Christian] Tales*). A favorable review in *Sovremennik* (*The Contemporary*) noted the fact that this collection was produced entirely by the work of women. The success of the first book was followed by translations of works by scientists such as Charles Darwin and Hermann Wagner. The print run ranged from 1,200 to 2,400 copies per volume.

By 1868 the number of paid employees of the *Artel'* shrank to approximately thirty per year, but the membership was determined to continue its work. The group had experienced difficulty from the beginning with gaining official government recognition of their right to exist and publish. Although the *Artel'* had been able to publish its works by using one member, Trubnikova, as the official editor, the members wanted more latitude over increasing both membership and publications. The application to be recognized as a publishing artel by the government was formally denied in 1868, however, so from this period forward, Stasova and Trubnikova took legal responsibility upon themselves for any governmental objections raised to their work. Publications appeared under the firm name of "Trubnikova and Stasova," instead of the previous label "A Publication of Women Translators." Since some publications of the artel had already attracted the attention of the government censors, Trubnikova and Stasova assumed a tremendous responsibility in order to allow publication to continue. The work of the artel continued into the 1870s but began to flounder as a result of economic difficulties and the increasing absence of its founders. In 1869 Trubnikova left the country for two years to seek treatment for an illness, and Stasova spent more than five years abroad in the 1870s. The members of the *Artel'* voted to disband in 1879. The unique nature of this organization in late nineteenth-century Russian women's history cannot be overstated, for it provided women access to a full range of occupations in the publishing industry. The *Artel'* also marked a high point in the Russian feminism of the 1860s, which focused on bettering women's lives through education and mutual support in organized societies.

Cross-references: A. A. Davydova, Women's Periodical Publishing in Late Imperial Russia (1860–1905), Women's Periodicals in Early Twentieth-Century Russia.

Suggested Readings

Barenbaum, I. E. "*Iz istorii russkikh progressivnykh izdatel'stv 60-x—70-x godov XIX veka: Zhenskaia izdatel'skaia artel' M. V. Trubnikovoi i N. V. Stasovoi*" (From the History of Russian Progressive Publishers of the 1860s and 70's: The Women's Publishing Artel of M. V. Trubnikova and N. V. Stasova). In *Kniga, issledovaniia i materialy* (*The Book: Research and Materials*), vol. 11, 223–241. Moscow: Kniga, 1965.

Lindenmeyr, Adele. *Poverty Is Not a Vice: Charity, Society, and the State in Imperial Russia*. Princeton, NJ: Princeton University Press, 1996.

Stasov, Vladimir Vasilevich. *Nadezhda Vasil'evna Stasova: vospominaniia i ocherki* (*Nadezhda Vasil'evna Stasova: Memoirs and Essays*). St. Petersburg, 1899.

Rhonda Clark

Zhenskaia Progressivnaia Partiia (Women's Progressive Party) (1905–1917)

One of the first women's political parties in the world. It was founded in the aftermath of the 1905 Russian Revolution.

The *Zhenskaia progressivnaia partiia* (Women's Progressive Party, hereafter WPP), the second Russian feminist political entity to be born in 1905, was the brainchild of Mariia Ivanovna Pokrovskaia, who announced her intention to form the party at a meeting of the *Russkoe zhenskoe vzaimno-blagotvoritel'noe obshchestvo* (Russian Women's Mutual Philanthropic Society). Thirty-three women attended the gathering on December 15, 1905, at which the party was formed, but conflict arose between those who wanted to focus exclusively on equal rights and those who wanted a general political platform. The latter group, to which Pokrovskaia belonged, prevailed. The next month Pokrovskaia's *Zhenskii vestnik (Women's Herald)* published the platform of the new party. In many respects, the WPP's goals resembled those of the *Soiuz ravnopraviia zhenshchin* (Women's Equal Rights Union); they had similar demands for civil and political liberties, equal rights in all spheres, an end to legalized prostitution, the elimination of the unfair distribution of wealth and fair wages, and the destruction of militarism. It differed significantly in its advocacy of a constitutional monarchy and in limiting its membership to women.

Considered more "antimale" than other feminist organizations, the WPP actually sought more legal sanction from the male power structure than did the Union. As the spheres of possible political action narrowed after 1905, the WPP applied for legal permission to operate and was allowed to open a club in St. Petersburg in December 1906, which became the focus of party activities. Like the Union, the Women's Progressive Party focused primarily on lobbying the male representatives of the Duma to support woman's rights; its members were equally embittered at the failure of the major liberal and left parties to do more than give lip service to the political rights of women. Pokrovskaia, the Party's leader, envisioned the WPP as akin to a loyal opposition to the Duma parties, but it never achieved a critical mass and had no serious support outside the capital. Furthermore, the repressive conditions in Russia made the kind of militant activism engaged in by small groups of British and U.S. feminists impossible even in the unlikely situation that WPP members would choose to use them.

The WPP remained small, its activities mainly focused in its Club. There was a flurry of activity in 1912–1913, when members organized several well-attended meetings at the end of 1912, after a woman suffrage bill had been introduced unsuccessfully in the Fourth Duma. At the end of 1916, the WPP Petrograd Club joined with other women's groups in forming the *Vserossiiskoe zhenskoe obshchestvo* (All-Russian Women's Society), slated to meet at the end of 1917 but swept away by the revolutionary events of that year. Mariia Pokrovskaia was among the feminist delegation that persuaded the Provisional Government to grant Russian women suffrage soon after the February overthrow of the tsar. The WPP and its club ceased activity after the October 1917 Bolshevik Revolution.

Cross-references: First All-Russian Women's Congress (1908), Mariia Ivanovna Pokrovskaia, Russian Women's Mutual Philanthropic Society (*Russkoe zhenskoe vzaimno-blagotvoritel'noe obshchestvo*), *Soiuz ravnopraviia zhenshchin* (Women's Equal Rights Union), *Zhenskii vestnik (Women's Herald).*

Suggested Readings

Ariian, Praskov'ia N. "Mariia Ivanovna Pokrovskaia." In *Pervyi zhenskii kalendar' na 1905 god*, edited by Praskov'ia N. Ariian, 394–396. St. Petersburg, 1905.
Cook, Kathrine Schach. "Women's Progressive Party." In *Modern Encyclopedia of Russian and Soviet History*, edited by Joseph Wieczynski, vol. 44, 36–41. Gulf Breeze, FL: Academic International Press, 1987.
Edmondson, Linda Harriet. *Feminism in Russia, 1900–1917*. Stanford, CA: Stanford University Press, 1984.
Edmondson, Linda Harriet. "Mariia Pokrovskaia and *Zhenskii vestnik*: Feminist Separatism in Theory and Practice." In *An Improper Profession: Women, Gender and Journalism in Late Imperial Russia*, edited by Jehane Gheith and Barbara Norton. Durham, NC: Duke University Press (in press).
Edmondson, Linda Harriet. "Women's rights, civil rights and the debate over citizens in the 1905 Revolution." In *Women and Society in Russia and the Soviet Union*, edited by Linda Edmondson, 77–100. Cambridge: Cambridge University Press, 1992.
Ruthchild, Rochelle G. "Writing for Their Rights. Four Feminist Journalists: Mariia Chekhova, Liubov' Gurevich, Mariia Pokrovskaia, and Ariadna Tyrkova." In *The Improper Profession: Women and Journalism in Late Imperial Russia*, edited by Jehane Gheith and Barbara Norton. Durham, NC: Duke University Press (in press).
Stites, Richard. *The Women's Liberation Movement in Russia*. Princeton, NJ: Princeton University Press, 1978, 1991.

Rochelle Goldberg Ruthchild

Zhenskii Vestnik (*Women's Herald*) (1904–1917)

The longest-running Russian feminist periodical, which was edited and published by Mariia Ivanovna Pokrovskaia. It is an excellent source for information about Russian women and the domestic and international women's movements.

The feminist physician Mariia Pokrovskaia first published *Zhenskii vestnik* (*Women's Herald*) in September 1904, seeking to create a journal exclusively devoted to discussion of the *zhenskii vopros* ("woman question"), to news about women of all classes, and to information about women in other countries. With the exception of mid-1907 to the end of 1909, when *Soiuz zhenshchin (Union of Women)* was published, *Zhenskii vestnik* was the only consistent source of feminist news and information in Russia.

The journal remained primarily Pokrovskaia's; she edited and published it almost single-handedly from her modest, two-room apartment in St. Petersburg. At times discouraged by *Zhenskii vestnik*'s small circulation (no more than 500) and the hostility of men and women to her efforts, Pokrovskaia persisted. A majority of the journal's articles seem to have been penned by her, although others did contribute writing and translations. In the January1906 issue of the journal, Pokrovskaia listed twenty-two contributors and helpers, including Praskov'ia Ariian, editor and publisher of the *Pervyi zhenskii kalendar' (First*

Women's Calendar), the writer Ol'ga Shapir, and Professor Levinson-Lessing of the Bestuzhev Higher Courses for Women.

Zhenskii vestnik reflected Pokrovskaia's eclectic interests from the beginning. The first issue included an article about matriarchy in early European history, an Olive Schreiner story in translation, a survey of women journalists in other countries, a discussion of the wartime roles of women, including information about Slavic Amazons, and the history of New York's Women's Public Health Association. Subsequent issues addressed such topics as women's access to education, disease prevention, the plight of peasant women, woman's rights in the Russian empire, comparisons of the status of women in other countries, violence against women, sex roles, marriage, divorce, free love, and the oppressive nature of housework.

Zhenskii vestnik became a vehicle for Pokrovskaia's crusade against prostitution and the legalized Russian medical-police inspection system, as well as for reports about the activities of the *Zhenskaia progressivnaia partiia* (Women's Progressive Party). The party program was published in the January 1906 issue, and news about the party and its activities in support of woman's rights, especially the right to vote, was often featured in the journal.

Zhenskii vestnik totaled between 128 and 384 pages annually and was published monthly except in summer for fourteen years, from 1904 to 1917. The prolific Pokrovskaia articulated a position closest to what is now considered radical feminist. She insisted on the primacy of women's oppression, chastising the Left for ignoring women and children in strike actions and generally paying lip service to equality, liberals for failing to support woman suffrage, and conservatives for perpetuating outmoded stereotypes about women's inferiority.

With the advent of World War I, the pages of *Zhenskii vestnik* included stories about war as opportunity for women alongside those describing the excesses of male militarism. Pokrovskaia extolled the patriotic work of suffragists in other countries and female military heroism, while continuing to emphasize the importance of woman's rights and hailing the formation of the *Zhenskii ekonomicheskii soiuz* (Women's Economic Union) to combat wartime inflation.

Zhenskii vestnik appeared through most of 1917, hailing the February Revolution and reporting on the Provisional Government's law granting suffrage to women, Mariia Bochkareva's Women's Battalion, and the effects of the war on women. It ceased publication after the Bolshevik Revolution, a casualty of Bolshevik hostility to feminism and overall Bolshevik repression of the independent press.

Cross-references: Praskov'ia N. Ariian, Mariia Bochkareva, Higher Education for Women, *Pervyi zhenskii kalendar' (First Women's Calendar)*, Mariia Ivanovna Pokrovskaia, Ol'ga Shapir, *Soiuz zhenshchin (Union of Women), Zhenskaia progressivnaia partiia* (Women's Progressive Party).

Suggested Readings

Ariian, Praskov'ia N., ed. "Mariia Ivanovna Pokrovskaia." *Pervyi zhenskii kalendar' na 1905 god*, 1905:394–396.

Edmondson, Linda Harriet. *Feminism in Russia, 1900–1917*. Stanford, CA: Stanford University Press, 1984.

Edmondson, Linda Harriet. "Mariia Pokrovskaia and *Zhenskii vestnik*: Feminist Separatism in Theory and Practice." In *An Improper Profession: Women and Journalism in Late Imperial Russia*, edited by Jehane Gheith and Barbara Norton. Durham, NC: Duke University Press (in press).

Edmondson, Linda Harriet. "Women's Rights, Civil Rights and the Debate over Citizens in the 1905 Revolution." In *Women and Society in Russia and the Soviet Union*, edited by Linda Edmondson, 77–100. Cambridge: Cambridge University Press, 1992.

Goldberg, Rochelle (Ruthchild). "The Russian Women's Movement 1859–1917." Ph.D. Diss., University of Rochester, 1976.

Grishina, Zoia V. "*Dvizhenie za politicheskoe ravnopravie zhenshchin v gody pervoi Rossiiskoi revoliutsii*" (The Movement for Women's Political Equal Rights in the Years of the First Russian Revolution). *Vestnik Moskovskogo universiteta* (*Moscow University Herald*). Ser. 8 *Istoriia* (*History*), no. 2 (1982): 33–42.

Grishina, Zoia V. "*Zhenskie organizatsii v Rossii, 1905 g.-fevral'/mart 1917 g*" (Women's Organizations in Russia, 1905–February/March 1917). Abstract of a *kandidat*'s Diss., Moscow State University, 1978.

Ruthchild, Rochelle G. "Writing for Their Rights. Four Feminist Journalists: Mariia Chekhova, Liubov' Gurevich, Mariia Pokrovskaia, and Ariadna Tyrkova." In *The Improper Profession: Women and Journalism in Late Imperial Russia*, edited by Jehane Gheith and Barbara Norton. Durham, NC: Duke University Press (in press).

Stites, Richard. *The Women's Liberation Movement in Russia: Feminism, Nihilism, and Bolshevism, 1860–1930*. Princeton, NJ: Princeton University Press, 1978, 1991.

Rochelle Goldberg Ruthchild

PART II

WOMEN'S MOVEMENTS IN THE SOVIET ERA, 1917–1991

Although the Soviet Era (1917–1991) lasted over seventy years, it produced fewer and less varied Russian women's movements than either the Tsarist Era or the Transitional and Post-Soviet Eras (1985–).

The goal of the Soviet leadership over the years was to direct societal development into prescribed directions. Although there were women's organizations and women's efforts, especially early in the Soviet era, homogenization during the Stalin era erased most of the diversity of the efforts. In the post-Stalin period, there were a few notable developments, such as the creation of the *zhensovety* (women's councils) in the Khrushchev years and the incipient, but crushed, dissident women's movements in St. Petersburg (then Leningrad) in the Brezhnev years.

Not until the Gorbachev years (1985–1991) does one witness the emergence of informal associations and the nascent development of nongovernmental associations. The brief era known as perestroika gave birth to a number of new organizations. Those organizations created in the late 1980s, which continued into the post-Soviet era, are included in Part III of this volume since they are viewed as part of the transition to the new Russia.

Despite limitations imposed by the Soviet government and the Communist Party of the Soviet Union (CPSU), the movements, actors, and organizations of the Soviet period have a character of their own and are no less interesting than those that came before or after. The special attention given to mobilizing women at selected periods within the Soviet era reflects ways in which the Soviet government made use of women's talents and energy to implement some of its goals. The mobilization of women to assist in the improvement of social conditions took various forms, each important and unique in its time and place.

Although formally committed to equality of men and women from its earliest days, the Soviet government fell short of making women's equality a reality.

From the 1920s onward, one perceives the struggle to transform legal equality into reality. Quotas for parliamentary representation and local government underlay some of the goals. Eventually, as with many other social policies, there was resigned acceptance of the gap between professed goals and reality. In the Soviet era, women's equality was proclaimed but never fully realized, and that legacy underlies many of the struggles that women have faced, and continue to face, in the post-Soviet era.

A

Armand, Inessa (born Elizaveta Fedorovna d'Heubenville) (1875–1920)

One of the best-known revolutionary women in Russia, a close friend of V. I. Lenin and his wife, Nadezhda Krupskaia, and the first head of *Zhenotdel.* A Frenchwoman raised in Russia who became identified with Russia and its revolutionary cause, Armand was one of the most intriguing of the revolutionaries.

Inessa Armand was born in Paris in 1875. Her real name was Elizaveta d'Heubenville, and her father was French. After her parents' death, she was sent to Russia to live with her aunt, who was employed as a tutor by the Armands, a well-to-do Moscow family. Inessa was treated as a member of the family and even married one of the sons, E. A. Armand. They had five children, but the marriage ended in 1903, although they remained on friendly terms, and he continued to support her financially. She had a long love affair with her brother-in-law Vladimir Armand, which ended only with his death in 1909.

Inessa's socialist leanings developed while she was still in her twenties. She initially gravitated toward the Tolstoy movement, which was pacifist in orientation, and later became a socialist. In 1904, while living abroad, she became familiar with the views of Vladimir Ilich Lenin and at some point decided to become affiliated with his Bolshevik faction of the Russian Social Democratic Labor Party (RSDLP). She also had strong feminist inclinations, which did not always ingratiate her with other socialists.

Like many other prominent socialists in the years before 1917, her life included a combination of exile in Siberia and exile abroad in Western Europe. Her children lived with their father, and Inessa, often lonely after Vladimir Armand's death, sought friendship among the community of revolutionaries living in exile abroad. During her time abroad, Inessa completed her formal education in 1910 with a degree in political economy and history from the University of Brussels. Among her closest friends in Western Europe were V. I. Lenin and Nadezhda Krupskaia, who, like Armand, were dedicated revolutionaries. Armand was a beautiful woman, and over the years there has been much speculation that Lenin fell in love with her. Since Lenin's wife was notably plain and more a helpmate than a romantic partner, the myth of a romance between Lenin and Armand has persisted. One letter from Armand to Lenin, uncovered in recent years in Russian archives, suggested an affectionate relationship but is not decisive proof of a love affair. On the other hand, it is believed that much of their correspondence was destroyed and that those letters published in Lenin's *Collected Works* were carefully edited to remove the more personal comments. Krupskaia was also close to Armand, and they remained friends both before and after the revolution.

In the prerevolutionary years, Armand was part of Lenin's inner circle in Europe, and he trusted her with important assignments. In 1912 Armand was sent back to Moscow to serve as his representative on the Bolshevik newspaper *Pravda*. She was soon arrested, sent into exile, then freed to return to Europe again. She also performed several assignments on his behalf at international conferences during World War I. Barbara Evans Clements has hypothesized that women may have found it easier to work with Lenin than did men and were more likely to acquiesce to his exacting demands. As a result, women were more likely to be trusted to represent him at various times.

In 1917 Armand returned to Russia and worked in Moscow for both the party and the government after the Bolshevik Revolution. She was in charge, for a time, of the *sovnarkhoz* (economic council) of the Moscow *guberniia*'s *Soviet* (council). Active in the planning for the *Pervyi vse-rossiiskii s"ezd rabotnits* (First All-Russian Congress of Woman Workers) in 1918, Armand was Lenin's choice to head *Zhenotdel* (the women's department of the RCP/B) when it was created in 1919. Although Aleksandra Kollontai was perhaps the best-known woman in the Soviet government, she was later in her commitment to Bolshevism than was Armand. Although Lenin and Armand disagreed on issues from time to time, he trusted her to carry out sensitive assignments, and from his perspective, serving as head of *Zhenotdel* was a task that required someone whom Lenin trusted implicitly. Lenin, although a supporter of women revolutionaries, distrusted the whole idea of a separate women's organization. *Zhenotdel*, situated within the RCP/B, was a compromise between no women's organization at all and a separate women's organization.

Armand worked tirelessly at her new assignment in *Zhenotdel*, as well as other responsibilities during the Civil War. Exhausted from overwork, in 1920 she was ordered to take a vacation. She traveled to southern Russia, where she contracted cholera and died. Lenin was visibly affected by her death, adding further fuel to the rumors about their relationship. Krupskaia offered assistance and protection to Armand's five children during the volatile civil war; as young aristocrats, they might not have fared well in the revolutionary climate.

Armand's legacy is difficult to assess since she worked in the government for only two years before her death. She worked diligently at all the important assignments given to her, but her brief tenure prior to her death makes her contribution to the Soviet system and to the development of women's issues hard to evaluate. She had an important influence on Lenin, and he on her, and one can perhaps attribute some of Lenin's willingness to entrust important positions to women to the confidence that he had in her ability and that of other dedicated Bolshevik women. Unlike Kollontai, Armand never had a major clash with the Bolshevik leadership, probably because of her close friendship with Lenin, even though she occasionally disagreed with Lenin's policies both before and after the Bolshevik Revolution. What would have been her fate had she outlived Lenin can never be known.

Cross-references: First All-Russian Congress of Women Workers (*Pervyi vserossiiskii s"ezd rabotnits*), Aleksandra Kollontai, Nadezhda Krupskaia, *Zhenotdel*.

Suggested Readings

Clements, Barbara Evans. *Bolshevik Women*. Cambridge: Cambridge University Press, 1997.

Elwood, R. C. *Inessa Armand: Revolutionary and Feminist*. Cambridge: Cambridge University Press, 1992.

McNeal, Robert H. *Bride of the Revolution: Krupskaya and Lenin*. Ann Arbor: University of Michigan Press, 1972.

Noonan, Norma. "Inessa Armand." In *The Soviet Union: A Biographical Dictionary*, edited by Archie Brown, 18–19. London: Weidenfeld and Nicolson, 1990.

Sokolov, Boris. *Armand i Krupskaia: Zhenshchiny vozhdia (Armand and Krupskaia: The Women of the Leader)*. Smolensk: Rusich, 1999.

Stites, Richard. *The Women's Liberation Movement in Russia: Feminism, Nihilism and Bolshevism, 1860–1930*. Princeton, NJ: Princeton University Press, 1978, 1991.

Volkogonov, Dmitri. *Autopsy of an Empire: The Seven Leaders Who Built the Soviet Regime*. New York: Free Press, 1998.

Norma Corigliano Noonan

Artiukhina, Aleksandra Vasil'evna (born Afanasenkova) (1889–1969)

A worker, political activist, and revolutionary who became the head of *Zhenotdel* (1925–1930) and was one of the key women administrators in the 1920s.

Aleksandra Afanasenkova was born on October 25, 1889, into a working-class family. Artiukhina attended a three-year primary school and then learned to become a seamstress. She began working at twelve to help support the family. She also had to help raise her younger brothers and sisters, since some members of her family, including her mother, were imprisoned and exiled for socialist political activities, such as attending meetings and participating in worker strikes. In 1903 the police searched their apartment for forbidden pamphlets, which her mother had hidden. Aleksandra's mother was blacklisted, excluded from working in the local factories, and moved to St. Petersburg to find work in a textile factory. Sometime later, Aleksandra followed her mother and found work in the same factory. The 1905 Revolution in St. Petersburg radicalized the already politically socialized Aleksandra. She became acquainted with Bolshevik ideas. In 1908 she joined the textile workers union in St. Petersburg and in 1910, at the age of twenty-one, became a member of the Bolshevik faction of the RSDLP. She continued her work in the metalworkers' factory, *Aivaz,* in St. Petersburg, where she entered the metalworkers' union. Although men dominated the organization, she became a member of this Bolshevik-dominated trade union and in 1913 became part of its leadership.

Artiukhina worked for the journal *Rabotnitsa (Working Woman)* when it began in 1913, but, shortly afterward, she was arrested and exiled to Siberia. In February 1917 she returned to her birthplace in Tver' province and worked for the Bolsheviks. At the time of the October 1917 Revolution Artiukhina lived in St. Petersburg. In 1918 she attended the *Pervyi vse-rossiiskii s"ezd rabotnits* (First All-Russian Congress of Women Workers) and during the Civil War (1918–1920) served on the Ukrainian front.

Very little is known of her personal life or her marriage. Her husband's name, which she adopted, unlike many revolutionaries of her time, was Mikhail Artiukhin. It is not known when she married him, but their careers progressed together.

Artiukhina's work on behalf of women began before the Bolshevik Revolution and continued after the civil war. In 1923 she began to work for *Zhenotdel* in Tver, and in 1924 Artiukhina moved to Moscow to work in the headquarters of the *Zhenotdel* (Women's Department of the RCP/B, later Communist Party of the Soviet Union, CPSU). A year later, she was appointed the director of *Zhenotdel*, the third woman to hold this post after the dismissal of the influential Aleksandra Kollontai in 1922. From 1925 to 1930, she directed *Zhenotdel* until its elimination in 1930. She was one of the few leaders of *Zhenotdel* who came from working-class origins. Artiukhina pursued an activist agenda and expanded the outreach and influence of *Zhenotdel* in Russia. Her most important contribution as head of *Zhenotdel* involved strengthening of the *delegatki* (delegates') program. The *delegatki* were trained as transmission belts between women and the Communist Party. Artiukhina devoted her efforts to enhancing this aspect of *Zhenotdel* outreach, established by her predecessors. Artiukhina faced significant opposition to the very existence of *Zhenotdel* in the late 1920s and did her best to save the organization from its critics within the Party. Although a loyal Party member, she opposed the CPSU's termination of *Zhenotdel* in 1930; she believed that an organization for women workers was still crucial, but her voice did not prevail.

After the demise of *Zhenotdel*, she taught classes from 1931 to 1934 for the Central Committee of the Workers' and Peasants' Inspectorate. She served as head of the Union for Cotton Production from 1934 to 1941 and as director of a textile mill from 1941 until her retirement in 1951. After Stalin's death, she spoke out on what the Party had done for women's rights after the October revolution but also reminded people how much women had done for the new Bolshevik state. She died in Moscow on April 7, 1969.

Artiukhina was a revolutionary and a working-class woman concerned about women's interests in the revolution but also convinced of the need for men and women to work together in the proletarian movement. After the Bolshevik Revolution, she adhered to the official Bolshevik position that eliminating the formal conditions of suppression would liberate women and did not seriously challenge the CPSU's decision to abolish *Zhenotdel* in 1930, even though she personally realized that *Zhenotdel* was still necessary.

Cross-references: First All-Russian Congress of Working Women (*Pervyi vserossiiskii s"ezd rabotnits), Zhenotdel.*

Suggested Readings

Artiukhina, A. V., L. I. Gus'kova, M. O. Levkovich, and V. N. Nikolaeva, eds. *Oktyabrem rozhdennye (Born in October)*. Moscow: Politicheskaia literatura, 1967.

Artiukhina, A. V., A. I. Vakurova, A. I. Nuchrat, and E. A. Popova, eds. *Zhenshchiny v revoliutsii (Women of the Revolution)*. Moscow: Politicheskaia literatura, 1959.

Clements, Barbara Evans. *Bolshevik Women*. Cambridge: Cambridge University Press, 1997.

Fieseler, Beate. "The Making of Russian Female Social Democrats, 1890–1917." *International Review of Social History* 34, no. 2 (1989): 193–226.

Goldman, Wendy. "Industrial Politics, Peasant Rebellion and the Death of the Proletarian Women's Movement in the USSR." *Slavic Review* 55, no. 1 (1996): 46–77.

Vsegda s vami: Sbornik posviashchennyi 50-letiiu zhurnala "Rabotnitsa" (Always with You: A Collection Dedicated to the Fiftieth Anniversary of the Journal "Working Woman"). Moscow: Pravda Publishing House, 1964.

Wood, Elizabeth. *The Baba and the Comrade: Gender and Politics in Revolutionary Russia*. Bloomington: Indiana University Press, 1997.

Carmen Scheide

F

Family Protection and Women's Well-Being under Communism and Later (1917–)

State protection for the family, its coherence, and members' rights vacillated between radical reform and reaction and between liberalization and sheer deterioration in the Soviet era and later. The fluctuations in protection reflected shifts in leadership and ideology, the changing regimes' conflicted motivations, and the frequently turbulent Soviet setting. Surviving all changes, a persistent patriarchal bias contributed to women's political and social subordination, their double burden as workers and mothers, and the impunity of their abusers.

The Bolshevik overthrow of the post-tsarist Provisional Government of March–November 1917 shifted governmental goals from moderate liberal reform to the "withering away of the family" as a "stronghold of reaction." To that end, the new government set out to loosen the social hold of religion and to emancipate women. But the government rejected the doctrines of free love and communal feeding and child rearing advocated by radical women's advocates. If love is like drinking a glass of water when you're thirsty, Lenin argued in his retort to the women's liberationist, Alexandra Kollontai, who would want to drink from a glass greasy with many lips? Besides, abolishing the family conflicted with the regime's reliance on it for child rearing and its members' mutual support, as stipulated in family legislation of 1917 and 1918.

At the same time, the 1918 family code signaled new principles of freedom of marriage, state secular regulation of marriage and the family, equality of children born in and out of wedlock, family ties based on affection, not material advantage, and freedom of divorce. The new law replaced religious marriage and divorce with their simple civil registration. The law stipulated the equality of women and men in all family relations. Women's advocacy to ensure this was hampered by the Bolsheviks' insistence that women's liberation would come with the socialist revolution and not by any autonomous efforts of women outside the leadership of the Communist Party and the Council of People's Commissars headed by Lenin. That, in part, accounts for the short life and limited authority of the *Zhenotdel* (Women's Department) of the Central Committee.

The peak of legal radicalism in 1926 reflected the Bolsheviks' ambivalence toward the family in the USSR (Union of Soviet Socialist Republics formed December 30, 1922). On the one hand, new union republic family codes recognized de facto (common-law) marriage and divorce, as well as divorces by simple mailed notification, often called "postcard divorces." These policies further eroded the protection of women in two ways: leaving them without paternal support, although unemployment affected women and mothers especially, and encouraging some farmers to take "wives for the season" and dump them after harvest time.

The concessions of NEP (the New Economic Policy) to private farming and commerce in 1921 and restoration of the right of inheritance in 1926 strengthened family ties. They had been badly shaken not so much by radical family policy as by the violence, economic ruin, and famine during the Civil War, 1918–1921, which produced up to 7 million homeless waifs (*besprizorniki*). There could be little chance of family protection under such conditions, whatever the intentions of the Bolsheviks.

Stalin's victory in the four-year power struggle after Lenin's death on January 21, 1924, led to his "revolution from above" of forced-rate heavy industrialization, plus agricultural collectivization and massive deportations (1929–1933), terrible famine in the Ukraine and Western Siberia (1932–1933), and a new terror of political Purges between December 1934 and 1938. Collectivization robbed millions of peasant family households of NEP's temporary protection as productive units and produced a new wave of child homelessness.

A "great retreat" during the 1930s reflected the shift of ideological goals from the "withering away" of the state and law and family, to the strengthening of the socialist state and family. As women's employment and independence increased, abandonment by their husbands became less threatening, and divorce from abusive spouses became more feasible. But a 1936 law aimed to curb divorces by requiring both parties to be present at the registration of divorce and by setting higher fees, rising for each divorce.

The regime's new obstacles to divorce reflected its return to a traditional ideal of the family as nurturer of children and fertile procreator of the new generation. To increase the birthrate, the government banned abortion of the first child in 1935 and all nontherapeutic abortions in 1936. It increased birth allowances and the capacity of nurseries and kindergartens. Pro-natalism and patriarchalism peaked in the edict of July 8, 1944. The government responded to the depletion of the population, especially males, in the Purges of the 1930s and Great Patriotic War. The government intended to boost birthrates while protecting the registered family from the consequences of males' extramarital, yet demographically crucial, procreative activities among the unmarried surplus of fertile women. The 1944 decree denied recognition to extramarital paternity by banning both voluntary acknowledgment and paternity suits. Many women preferred to have children out of wedlock rather than no family of their own. These single, "lonely" mothers could choose between very modest state child supports or placing the children in state orphanages. Married fathers had parental obligations only during and after marriage and only toward children born in wedlock.

Under the 1944 decree, divorce became a cumbersome and very expensive procedure in two courts, which was reminiscent of the prerevolutionary Orthodox divorce in two church hearings. Stage 1 required an attempted reconciliation in local courts. Following a mandatory paid publication of notice in a local newspaper between court hearings, stage 2 brought the trial proper to the next level of city or regional courts. Perhaps this deterred some family breakup, but it certainly drew back the protection of the law from many women involved in unregistered family breakups.

To stimulate fertility further, the 1944 decree increased birth payments and added progressively larger monthly grants beginning with the birth of the fourth, instead of the seventh, child as previously. It awarded Mother Heroine medals to women raising ten surviving children. Stalin's concern for the family as a reproductive unit did not prevent him from causing a new mounting death toll through the 1944 deportations of ethnic minorities, such as the North Caucasian Chechens, the Crimean Tatars, and the Volga Germans. Stalin's paranoia led him to further swell the "fatherless generation" by sending to labor camps as alleged traitors the prisoners of war (POWs) and forced laborers returning from defeated Germany.

After Stalin's death on March 3, 1953, the post-Stalin "thaw" under General Secretary Nikita Khrushchev (1953–1964) continued Soviet contradictions in the protection of the family and of women. Khrushchev ended in 1954 the criminal penalties for women having abortions and lifted the abortion ban altogether in 1955 because of the harm to women caused by illegal abortions. Increases in pensions helped families cope with old age, even while attacks on "unearned income" and the ownership of illegally large dacha homes struck at material ties.

The cultural thaw permitted some frank writing about the problems of children of the "fatherless generation." It tolerated the emergence in 1954 of a movement led by women lawyers and other professionals for reform of "anti-Leninist" family law. Divorce courts liberalized their interpretation of marriages broken beyond repair. But Khrushchev, the author of the 1944 family decree, blocked legal reform.

Khrushchev tried to protect the family from the influences of religion in a campaign attacking church attendance, enforcing criminal sanctions against parents who took part in the organized religious instruction of children, and depriving the offenders of parental rights. Some young women in regions of Islamic and other traditional cultures found protection from their parents in the state's enforcement of bans on "survivals of local customs" such as bride abduction, bride-price, and attempts to bar daughters from the education made available to them by the Soviet state. To compete with religious influences in family life, Khrushchev introduced new "civil rituals" such as rites of passage marking births, receipt of internal passports at age sixteen, and marriage. He opened "wedding palaces" and shops for brides and newlyweds.

The period of Leonid Brezhnev's leadership, 1964–1982, has been associated with "stagnation" and reaction. Indeed, it brought the repression of nonconformist writers and the resulting emergence of a dissident movement for human rights. Ideological repression continued its intrusion into the family in matters of religion, but rarely to protect women from abuse. Under the surface, economic decline continued, concealed by imports of cheap grain and rising foreign indebtedness. But social calamity was yet to come for Soviet families. Meanwhile, for conformist families and would-be parents, life became materially more secure and legally less constrained under Brezhnev than under Khrushchev. Brezhnev permitted the liberalization of family law. A 1965 reform facilitated divorce by allowing the civil registration of uncontested divorces without custody disputes and by simplifying contested divorces in one people's court hearing, without publication, with fees lower than before. Official divorce rates promptly soared. For women, the majority among those seeking divorce, it provided a way of legally recognized escape from unfaithful, alcoholic, and abusive husbands.

The basic law on marriage and the family of 1968 incorporated the 1965 divorce law reforms. Under the 1968 law, an unwed mother could expect that her child would have a legally recognized father, whether born in or out of wedlock. The law restored voluntary acknowledgment of paternity. It again allowed paternity suits, though not simply on the basis of biological paternity, as allowed up to 1944. Paternity suits could be brought only in cases of proven cohabitation of mother and putative father and with proof that he acknowledged his paternity. Biological paternity alone creates no parental obligations.

Brezhnev's new benefits package initiated in 1981 stimulated birthrates noticeably. It added optional, partly paid maternity leaves of up to one year from childbirth, plus an extra six months' unpaid leave beyond that, extended mothers' sick-child leaves and vacations, and increased birth and monthly grants to mothers of middle-sized families. The regime passed these quite popular pronatalist measures to stimulate births among Russian and other non-Muslim, European nationalities. The fertility of these groups had been falling ever further behind that of the Muslims of Central Asia especially. The new family policies did nothing to improve means of family planning, which continued to rely heavily on abortions, because of the inadequacies of counseling and the scarcity of contraceptive devices.

The advocacy of woman's rights and the reforms in family protection mentioned here occurred only with the approval of the Communist Party. The KGB closed down the sole independent women's advocacy group, Woman and Russia, in 1980, sending its leaders into exile, where Tatiana Mamonova remained in touch with the nascent Russian women's movement. The repression of

Women and Russia occurred with little more than a rustle of protest among dissidents.

General Secretaries Iurii Andropov (1982–1984) and Konstantin Chernenko (1984–1985) carried over Brezhnev's family policy. Under Mikhail Gorbachev (1985–1991), a new openness (glasnost) fostered women's advocacy and research on issues of gender relations and rights. But Gorbachev's remarks on the sacred role of women as keepers of the hearth and faltering attempts at economic reform, plus the growing unrest and separatism in several union republics, hardly created a favorable setting for family protection, nor did discrimination in hiring, women's disproportionate share of the new unemployed, and the unhampered sexual objectification of employed women.

Setbacks to women's equality carried over into the post-Soviet successor states, including the Russian Federation. So did the rise in infant mortality and the drop in birthrates and in life expectancy, especially among men, for whom it dropped to around fifty-seven years in the Russian Federation, compared with women's life expectancy of around seventy.

This statistical plunge in life expectancy to a Third World level reflected a near-collapse in health care, daily tensions, and men's alcoholism and heavy smoking. Life's growing difficulties undermined cohesion of the already vulnerable family. So did the widespread nonpayment of state wages and pensions. There were two divorces for every three marriages. Rising numbers of abandoned and homeless children were symptomatic of the worsening family disorganization and social hardships. Spousal abuse rose; murders of wives by their partners in the Russian Federation reached 15,000 a year by the later 1990s, or half the total of murder victims. Police remained slow to intervene in domestic violence.

The only increases in family protection after the breakup of the USSR appeared as various women's research, charitable, and advocacy initiatives, including the Soviet Committee of Soldiers' Mothers, a movement formed during the war in Afghanistan (1979–1989). One offspring, the Committee of Soldiers' Mothers of Russia, sought to lessen the hardships suffered by the young conscripts during the brutal war in Chechnia of 1994–1996 and to expose the ongoing abuses of soldiers revealed in the high peacetime annual death rate of around 5,000 due to suicides, brutal hazing, illness, dire poverty, and even starvation in the ranks.

There were no clear winners in the family after communism, except for the youth starting afresh, for all those who valued the new freedom above the new disruptions, and for a minority of families that adapted successfully to the difficult and changing times. Among those left behind, a vast majority of less affluent families and the men, women, and children in them suffered consequences of reduced social protection and family breakdown.

Cross-references: Committee of Soldiers' Mothers of Russia, Legal Equality in the 1920s, Tatiana Mamonova, Women and Russia, *Zhenotdel*.

Suggested Readings

Buckley, Mary, ed. *Perestroika and Soviet Women.* Cambridge: Cambridge University Press, 1992.

Geiger, H. Kent. *The Family in Soviet Russia.* Cambridge: Harvard University Press, 1968.

Goldman, Wendy Z. *Soviet Family Policy and Social Life, 1917–1936.* New York: Cambridge University Press, 1993.

Juviler, Peter. *Freedom's Ordeal: The Struggle for Human Rights and Democracy in Post-Soviet States.* Philadelphia: University of Pennsylvania Press, 1998.

Juviler, Peter. "The Urban Family and the Soviet State: Emerging Contours of a Demographic Policy." In *The Contemporary Soviet City*, edited by Henry W. Morton and Robert C. Stuart, 84–112. Armonk, NY: M. E. Sharpe, 1984.

Schlesinger, Rudolf, ed. *Changing Attitudes in Soviet Russia: The Family in the U.S.S.R. Documents and Readings.* London: Routledge and Kegan Paul, 1949.

Peter Juviler

First All-Russian Congress of Women Workers (*Pervyi vse-rossiiskii s"ezd rabotnits*, aka the Congress of Peasant and Working Women or the First All-Russian Congress of Women Workers and Peasants) (1918)

The first major nonparty congress for women held in postrevolutionary Russia in November 1918. The fact that V. I. Lenin addressed the congress and not long afterward created *Zhenotdel* (the Women's Department of the Communist Party) enhanced its significance.

Following the Bolshevik Revolution of November 1917, the Bolshevik Party proclaimed new rights and responsibilities for women, which was only the first step toward their full emancipation. The new leadership was now presented with the task of informing women of their new status as well as encouraging them to participate in public life. A number of female activists, prominent in the pre–World War I efforts to organize women workers, particularly Inessa Armand, Aleksandra Kollontai, Nadezhda Krupskaia, Klavdiia Nikolaeva, and Konkordiia Samoilova, played a decisive role in obtaining official approval for the creation of new organizational mechanisms to organize women. Several small conferences of women were held in the postrevolutionary months immediately preceding the congress. Although only 300 delegates were expected, more than 1,147 working and peasant women dressed in native costumes from far-reaching regions of Soviet Russia converged upon the Kremlin Hall of Unions in Moscow in November 1918 to attend the *Pervyi vse-rossiiskii s"ezd rabotnits* (First All-Russian Congress of Women Workers).

The Congress took place before official approval had actually been granted for the creation of special organizations for work among women. V. I. Lenin, the leader of the new Soviet regime, addressed the women and was greeted with wild enthusiasm. Lenin outlined the measures that the Soviet government had already taken to improve the status of women and encouraged women to play a more active political role. Seven issues were at the heart of the Congress's agenda: (1) women workers in Soviet Russia, (2) the relationship between the family and the Bolshevik government, (3) social policies on behalf of women, (4) the international proletarian revolution and the woman worker, (5) organization, (6) the struggle against prostitution, and (7) the housing question.

As a result of the Congress, Commissions for Agitation and Propaganda among Working Women were established. The Commissions were reorganized in 1919 as *Zhenotdel* (the Women's Department) of the Central Committee Secretariat, under the leadership of Inessa Armand.

Cross-references: Inessa Armand, Aleksandra Kollontai, Nadezhda Krupskaia, Konkordiia Samoilova, *Zhenotdel*.

Suggested Readings

Buckley, Mary. *Women and Ideology in the Soviet Union*. Ann Arbor: University of Michigan Press, 1989.

Heitlinger, Alena. *Women and State Socialism: Sex Inequality in the Soviet Union and Czechoslovakia*. Montreal: McGill-Queen's University Press, 1979.

Lapidus, Gail. *Women in Soviet Society: Equality, Development, and Social Change*. Berkeley: University of California Press, 1978.

Cheri C. Wilson

G

Gorbacheva, Raisa Maksimovna (born Titarenko) (1932–1999)

Educator and wife of Mikhail S. Gorbachev, the last General Secretary of the Communist Party of the Soviet Union (CPSU) and the last President of the USSR. Viewed in the West as a new kind of Soviet first lady because of her visible presence and style, she was not highly regarded in the USSR. She very likely, however, influenced Gorbachev's position on women's issues.

Raisa Maksimovna Gorbacheva is a problematic figure in the study of Russian women's movements, since she did not participate in any women's movements, nor did she seem to embrace women's issues. During her husband's tenure as General Secretary of the CPSU (1985–1991) and president (1988–1991), women's issues appeared to have more official attention than at any other time since the 1920s. It was well known that he consulted her on political and economic issues, since he admitted it publicly to journalists. Therefore, it seems likely that she influenced his perception of women's issues.

There has always been considerable mystery surrounding Raisa's early life and background. In her autobiography, she refers to quite an ordinary life. She was born Raisa Maksimovna Titorenko in Rubtsovsk, a town in western Siberia on January 5, 1932. Her father had gone to Siberia to work on building the Siberian railway system. Raisa was the oldest of three children. She graduated from secondary school as a gold medalist, which enabled her to attend Moscow State University, one of the most prestigious institutions in the USSR. There she met young Mikhail Gorbachev, a fellow student, at a dance, and the two fell in love instantly. They married in early 1953, while still students, and completed their studies during the transitional period after the death of J. V. Stalin.

After graduation in 1955, Raisa and her husband moved to Stavropol, the region of his birth, and there Gorbachev began his political career, first in the Komsomol and then in the CPSU. Raisa worked as a teacher and continued her studies. She received the *kandidat*'s degree in Sociology in 1967, after completing a study of the peasantry in Stavropol. Her findings were apparently valuable to Gorbachev in his development of agricultural policy for the region.

Although her life in Stavropol was relatively tranquil, the increasing prominence of her husband's career began to move them into the political spotlight. Once Gorbachev became First Secretary of the Communist Party of the Stavropol region, he had de facto entered national politics in the USSR. Since the Stavropol area had a number of spas favored by the Soviet leadership, the Gorbachev family became acquainted with some of the top leaders who vacationed at the spas. The most significant friendship formed was with Iuryi Andropov, a member of the Politburo and head of the KGB, who was looking for young, talented Party leaders to recruit for his own future political entourage. As a protégé of Andropov, Gorbachev was invited to Moscow in 1978 to serve in the Secretariat of the CPSU as the secretary in charge of agriculture, one of the most politically volatile areas of the Soviet economy. Raisa obtained an appointment at Moscow State University and continued to teach until after Gorbachev became General Secretary.

Raisa Gorbacheva first drew international attention when Gorbachev visited England in 1984. She was attractive, stylish, and articulate. Her every step was followed. Media interest in her grew with each trip, and after Gorbachev became general secretary, she received a great deal of attention at the Geneva Summit of 1985 and the Reykjavik Summit of 1986. The new first lady of Soviet politics was glamorous and willing to discuss issues with the media. She shattered the traditional image of the Soviet leader's wife: in the background, stout, and dowdy. With a wardrobe created by the some of the young Soviet designers, Raisa abroad was a walking advertisement for a new style in Soviet politics.

At home, there was a different reaction to her. The Soviet economy was in the doldrums, after the relatively prosperous Brezhnev years, in which oil and gold exports and arms sales had masked the deepening economic crisis. Soviet women, struggling to survive amid the burdens of their everyday life, did not appreciate her glamour and wardrobe changes. Although people realized that the families of the leadership lived at a higher standard than that of the general population, this was the first time that a first lady publicly demonstrated the lifestyle differences. Furthermore, her views on politics were not appreciated either by the Party or by the population generally, since it had never been a Soviet tradition for wives to reveal their views publicly or appear to influence their husbands. Not since Nadezhda Krupskaia, V. I. Lenin's wife, had any Soviet leader's wife had a prominent career, and Krupskaia had not expressed her views except on educational issues, the area in which she worked after the revolution.

Gorbacheva was not involved in the informal women's movements that emerged in the late 1980s and early 1990s, nor was she a prominent voice in the Soviet Women's Committee, which became more assertive in the Gorbachev era. Her influence behind the scenes would be impossible to gauge. She did speak with some influential women and ask them to support Gorbachev's efforts to transform society but remained officially apart from any women's movements.

After the 1991 attempted coup against Gorbachev, she became ill and virtually disappeared from public life. In the late 1990s she was diagnosed with leukemia and died on September 20, 1999. She was given a dignified funeral in Moscow and laid to rest amidst global reflections on her role as first lady.

Cross-references: Nadezhda Krupskaia, Women in the Communist Party of the Soviet Union.

Suggested Readings

Gorbachev, Raisa. *I Hope*. New York: HarperCollins, 1991.

Noonan, Norma C. "Raisa Maksimovna Gorbacheva." In *The Gorbachev Encyclopedia*, edited by Joseph L. Wieczynski, 186–193. Salt Lake City, UT: Charles Schlacks Jr., 1993.

Sheehy, Gail. *Gorbachev: The Man Who Changed the World*. New York: HarperCollins, 1990.

Vasil'eva, Larisa Nikolaevna. *Kremlëvskie zheny (Kremlin Wives)*. Moscow: Vagrius, 1992.

Norma Corigliano Noonan

K

Kollontai, Aleksandra Mikhailovna (1872–1952)

Revolutionary, feminist, civic activist, and diplomat. One of the most famous women associated with the Russian revolutionary movement and the most prominent feminist of the early Soviet period, Kollontai served the Soviet system in several roles, including *Zhenotdel*, and later was the first woman Ambassador of the USSR.

Aleksandra Mikhailovna Domontovich was born in St. Petersburg on March 19, 1872, into a relatively affluent family. Her father was a general, and her mother strongly believed in education for her children. Aleksandra received an excellent education but also acquired some radical ideas of women's role in society from her tutor, Mariia Strakhova. At twenty-one Aleksandra married her cousin Vladimir Kollontai, and they had a son, Mikhail (Misha), but the marriage was not happy, and they separated. With help from her parents, Aleksandra continued to study and do research in Russia and Switzerland in order to become a writer. She considered herself a Marxist by twenty-six, although her interpretation of Marxist theory was less orthodox than that of most of her contemporaries. She saw Marxism as a means to develop personal freedom and choice, freeing one from the bonds of traditional society. She joined the Russian Social Democratic Labour Party (RSDLP) and loosely identified with the Menshevik faction.

As a writer, Kollontai's first works were on children and on workers. Later she turned her attention to the "woman question," as the Marxists labeled it. Her treatise "The Social Bases of Feminism" was published in 1909. Kollontai's feminism was Marxist, growing out of her study of Engels and Bebel, but set her apart from most Russian Marxists, who considered feminism an alien concept. Kollontai tried to organize socialist women and met with considerable opposition among her fellow Marxists.

Her views on women differed from those of most other Marxist women. She supported, in a general sense, the Russian Marxist notion that revolution would free both men and women. At the same time, she was an advocate of what she termed the "new woman," an independent being free from traditional constraints on women and free to determine her own destiny. In 1916, however, she wrote an essay, "Society and Maternity," which was more compatible with the views of Russian Marxists, perhaps in response to pressure or the realization that she should respond to the perceived needs of the movement. Kollontai's ideas also challenged traditional sexual mores. Kollontai herself lived according to her personal values and was often criticized for her behavior, especially after the Bolshevik Revolution.

Kollontai attended the First All-Russian Women's Congress held in December 1908, together with other Marxist women. Her prepared speech was delivered by a friend, since Kollontai was, at that time, dodging the tsarist police because of her political activities; in the speech she argued against feminism and advocated radical reform. She included a list of demands to improve conditions for women workers. She also expressed concern for maternity conditions. Her written speech emphasized areas she held in common with other Marxists and not her more unconventional views on love and life.

During World War I, Kollontai cooperated with the Bolsheviks and supported Lenin in the Bolshevik Revolution of 1917. After the revolution, Kollontai became Commissar (Minister) for Social Welfare in the new Soviet government, working on policies to benefit women and children. Her tenure was brief but may well have established the precedent of having a woman head, or play a leading role in, the ministry dealing with social and family issues in the Soviet era and afterward. Kollontai's resignation was probably due to a combination of her love affair with Pavel Dybenko, an ambitious Soviet sailor much younger than herself, and her growing disagreement with the direction of Soviet policies. She and Dybenko were married in 1918, but the marriage was short-lived. Her son, Misha, strongly objected to the union, as did other friends, who could not conceive of the aristocratic and well-educated Kollontai with a mere sailor. Dybenko rose quickly in the Soviet system but was purged in the 1930s.

In 1920 Kollontai accepted Lenin's invitation to head *Zhenotdel* (the Women's Department), of the Russian Communist Party/B after the death of Inessa Armand. At *Zhenotdel*, she did as much for women as possible within the constraints established by the Party. Kollontai also participated in the Workers' Opposition bloc within the Party. Her role in the opposition, her vigorous leadership on the "woman question," and lingering questions about her personal life led the Party to seek another assignment for her. Too prominent simply to be dismissed and retired, Kollontai was given a diplomatic assignment.

Kollontai was appointed Ambassador to Norway (1923–1926) and then briefly Ambassador to Mexico (1926–1927). In 1927 she returned to Norway until 1930 and then was appointed Ambassador to Sweden (1930–1945). She was the first woman to serve as a Soviet ambassador; her appointments, although significant, effectively removed her from Soviet politics. In her early years in Scandinavia, there was little work to do, and she turned her attention to writing several political novels, in which the female protagonists were dedicated revolutionaries, while the men selfishly pursued their own goals under the guise of revolutionary commitment.

Except for occasional trips home, Kollontai remained in diplomatic work until 1945, despite seriously deteriorating health. Kollontai's diplomatic skills were considerable, and she served as a mediator in the Soviet–Finnish War of 1939–1940. She served in Sweden during World War II, even though she suffered a stroke in 1942 and never fully recovered. In 1945, in ill health, Kollontai returned to Moscow, where she served nominally as an adviser to the Ministry of Foreign Affairs but was actually retired. In her last years, she lived quietly in Moscow and devoted her time to writing her memoirs until her death in 1952. She was outwardly loyal to Stalin's regime but able to have little impact on policy. A devoted mother, she used her influence to keep Misha near her during and after the war and obtained an early retirement for him because of his poor health.

Kollontai remained an idealist for most of her life, believing in the communist dream, even though it had been compromised and betrayed. Occasionally, the facade of optimism cracked, and one saw the tormented woman beneath, whose revolutionary hopes and friends had perished at the hands of Stalin.

In the USSR, until about 1990 Kollontai was known primarily for her revolutionary and diplomatic work. Her writings, especially her feminist views, were suppressed from the late 1920s onward. In contrast, among Western feminists, she was well known as a Russian feminist. After the early years of Soviet power, she did not have great influence on Soviet social policy. In the post-Soviet era, there has been a rediscovery of her views among those studying women's history and women's studies.

Cross-references: First All-Russian Women's Congress of 1908, *Zhenotdel*.

Suggested Readings

Clements, Barbara. *Bolshevik Feminist*. Bloomington: Indiana University Press, 1979.

Farnsworth, Beatrice. *Aleksandra Kollontai: Socialism, Feminism, and the Bolshevik Revolution*. Stanford, CA: Stanford University Press, 1980.

Kollontai, Aleksandra M. *Selected Writings*. Introduction and Commentaries by Alix Holt. New York: Norton, 1977.

Noonan, Norma C. "Two Solutions to the Zhenskii Vopros in Russia and the USSR—Kollontai and Krupskaia: A Comparison." *Women and Politics* 11, no. 3 (1991): 77–99.

Stites, Richard. *The Women's Liberation Movement in Russia*. Princeton, NJ: Princeton University Press, 1978, 1991.

Norma Corigliano Noonan

Komsomolka (pl. *komsomolki*) (1918–1991)

Female member(s) of the youth league established in Moscow one year after the 1917 Bolshevik Revolution and disbanded at the end of the Soviet era in

1991. Although active in the Komsomol, young women rarely achieved leadership positions within the organization.

Originally named the *Rossiiskii kommunistichesii soiuz molodëzhi* (Russian Communist Youth League), the organization experienced two name changes during its first decade of existence. Shortly after Lenin's death in 1924 the Bolshevik leader's name was incorporated, and in 1926 it became the *Vsesoiuznyi Leninskii kommunisticheskii soiuz molodëzhi* (All-Union Leninist Communist Youth League, or VLKSM). After that it was generally known as the Komsomol.

The membership of the Komsomol comprised teenagers and young people in their twenties known as *komsomol'tsy*, the plural of the masculine *komsomolets*. At the beginning, young women, or *komsomolki*, constituted only a small portion of that membership and were almost nonexistent within its leadership. At the League's founding congress in 1918, only nine of the 176 delegates were women, and only two of these nine were among the twenty-two members elected to the League's first Central Committee. At the Second Congress (1919), three *komsomolki* were elected to the governing body, but at the Third (1920) there were no identifiable women's names among the seventeen elected.

Young women were active in the Russian revolutionary movement and World War I, and many joined the Komsomol and underwent military training during the Civil War. After the Civil War ended, the level of the women's sociopolitical consciousness, rather than their military expertise, became an issue for the Komsomol leaders.

In 1920 at the League's Second Congress, women were described as the "most backward element" of Russian society. The Komsomol was to be their vehicle to enlightenment. By 1924, with women constituting only 15 percent of the membership, it was clear that the majority of young women were not taking advantage of the opportunity for sociopolitical education offered by the Youth League. A membership drive was launched, and within the next two years the number of *komsomolki* rose by 4 percent. No effort was made to equalize the male–female ratio in Komsomol's leadership, and the League remained a male-dominated organization despite the *komsomolki*'s vigorous participation in social projects.

Throughout the 1920s, despite the *komsomolki*'s military activities during the civil war and their advanced sociopolitical education, female League members were primarily involved in pursuits traditionally reserved for women, at home and in the League. Their most important task involved the members of the Komsomol's junior youth organizations. While many Young Pioneer and Little Octobrist cell leaders were male, it was expected that the *komsomolki* would participate in the sociopolitical and moral training of those who would follow them into the League and perhaps eventually into the Communist Party. The traditional nurturing aspect of this task was highlighted by Nadezhda Krupskaia, who informed "working girls" attending the League's Sixth Congress (1924) that "bringing up the children to be fighters for Communism" was one of their major responsibilities. Many parents, however, were reluctant to surrender their children to the influence of the Komsomol.

Despite propaganda efforts to show that the Youth League was a positive influence, its poor public image hampered the *komsomolki*'s efforts during the 1920s to enlighten the Soviet Union's future citizens. In the countryside, where prerevolutionary customs and ideas persisted, many parents feared the Komsomol's influence on their daughters. Those fears were fueled not only by the nontraditional attire and attitudes adopted by many *komsomolki* but also by widespread stories regarding prostitution and sexual misconduct. Devising strategies to improve its public image became a league priority.

In an effort to placate those parents who believed that women's emancipation equaled sexual promiscuity and that the Komsomol offered too many opportunities for premarital intimacy, the league promoted "Red Weddings" to replace the traditional religious rite. This strategy did little to improve the general impression that the bulk of society had of *komsomolki*. More successful was officially published fictional literature that depicted the *komsomolka* as a paragon of virtue and Soviet social consciousness and established her as a model for young women. The fact that many new Soviet heroines were League members who demonstrated behavior and values acceptable to the more traditional members of Soviet society improved the *komsomolka*'s public image. It was not long, however, before that image underwent a further metamorphosis.

The industrialization campaign that accompanied Stalin's first *Piatiletka* (Five-Year Plan), which actually lasted from 1929 to 1932, required Soviet young women to involve themselves in less traditional pursuits in both rural and urban settings. To stimulate their interest and participation, *komsomolki* were regaled with images of celebrated women Stakhanovites. Since female "shock workers" were generally as unpopular as their male counterparts, young women who emulated them were often verbally or physically abused. Sometimes *komsomolki* were murdered, especially in areas where the Youth League threatened a strong patriarchal system; many *komsomolki* ignored the dangers, however, and energetically participated in *Piatiletka* projects.

One of the Komsomol's primary tasks in the early 1930s was to further the forced collectivization of agriculture that accompanied Stalin's industrialization drive. Rural *komsomol'tsy*, both male and female, encouraged their parents to enter the collective farms and assisted in rooting out "enemies of the State," including priests and *kulaki* (relatively wealthy peasants). By this time it was obvious that *komsomolki* could play a prominent role in creating a modern socialist state, and in 1934 the Communist Party of the Soviet Union (CPSU) issued a directive urging all young women to become involved in building socialism by joining the Youth League.

By the Tenth VLKSM Congress in 1936, over one-third of all *komsomol'tsy* were women. This was a significant increase over 1928, when they constituted less than one-quarter of the membership, but still below Party and League goals.

Two areas where the ratio was particularly low—the rural sector and among the national minorities—were specifically targeted for recruitment.

There was no acknowledgment of factors that made League membership less than attractive for many young women. Since men constituted the vast majority of its leaders, Komsomol membership brought few opportunities for women's advancement within the League. There was even less hope they would be welcomed into the Party, which limited their opportunities to enter the Soviet elite.

Some young women recognized that the skewed male–female ratio of the league membership might be a springboard to marriage, but the persistent traditionalism of the male majority often jettisoned even these ambitions. While male *komsomol'tsy* were urged to treat women with respect, especially those who distinguished themselves in the *Piatiletka*, the beliefs and behavior of the average *komsomolets* were often based on traditional values, which had nothing to do with Stakhanovite-ism. Young men often criticized *komsomolki* for being too masculine in appearance and actions, and their respect for women shock workers was often superseded by a cult of femininity and motherhood that totally ignored the *komsomolki*'s social and military service record. The Kremlin leaders, however, were aware that young women could play a major role in an international war, which they believed to be inevitable, and in the spring of 1941 the Party called for the mobilization of all female citizens into "war work." During World War II, many *komsomolki* maintained essential services on the home front, distributing food and fuel to the elderly and sick and performing various humanitarian tasks as members of the Red Cross and Red Crescent organizations. Others took the places of their absent male cohorts in factories and on collective farms, while others were directly involved in civil defense.

During the 1930s, many *komsomolki* had been introduced to military life in aviation schools and paramilitary clubs, where they learned to be pilots, parachutists, and snipers. During the first months of the war, many *komsomolki* transported military supplies, worked in military traffic control, and were trained in the use of antiaircraft armaments. In 1942 the military potential of Soviet young women was formally recognized by the Party and the Soviet military commanders.

With the establishment of their own military unit, the Komsomol Red Army women's volunteer brigade, more than 8,000 *komsomolki* rushed to enlist in the army or the navy, and over 7,000 joined the Stalingrad Corps of Air Defense. By the end of the war, approximately 400,000 *komsomolki* had joined the fight against Hitler's forces. As members of the Soviet armed forces, they worked in communications and medical divisions and served as tank drivers, navigators, and pilots. While women were often initially treated with disdain by many of their male counterparts, most proved to be competent military personnel, and many were rewarded with promotions.

As officers, *komsomolki* were generally respected, but their responsibilities usually tended to be more organizational than military in nature. Comrade-Sergeant *Komsomolka*'s duties might include organizing a Youth League cell within her military unit or simply drafting all eligible nonmembers into the league. She was expected to use her propagandist skills to broaden the Komsomol's membership and to ensure that the morale of her comrades did not falter, especially when someone died in battle.

Serving as apparent equals, *komsomolki* were susceptible to the same dangers as their brothers-in-arms, and many young women did not survive the war. In the air they were gunned down by enemy planes; as ground soldiers or civilians they were shot, bombed, tortured, and raped; and at least one died at the hands of a Nazi hangman. By the end of the war, 100,000 *komsomolki* had been decorated in recognition of their service to the motherland. With the end of the war, however, came the end of the *komsomolki*'s "Amazon" era.

In the postwar period, despite a popular belief that their wartime participation had finally and unequivocally achieved women's equality in the Soviet Union, *komsomolki* continued their ongoing battle for sociopolitical and personal emancipation in new fields. Under Khrushchev, they took part in the "Virgin Lands" program, which sought to exploit the potential of the vast plains of Kazakhstan. Although praised by the state for their postwar social participation and many achievements, they made little progress climbing the ladder of league success—except in the classroom.

During the late 1960s and early 1970s, schoolteachers often placed girls in positions of authority over boys, ostensibly because of their superior organizational skills. This became a matter of concern for Soviet social scientists, who believed the *komsomolka*'s increasing preeminence to be contrary to the natural order of male–female relationships and even a threat to the very structure of Soviet society. Domineering *komsomolki*, they asserted, undermined the masculine pride and natural supremacy of young men and helped turn the latter into mama's boys or hooligans.

Ignoring the social scientists' concerns, Party and league leaders continued to voice their own concerns regarding women's insufficient involvement in both organizations. Paradoxically, however, throughout the 1970s the CPSU continued to accept more *komsomol'tsy* than *komsomolki* as Party members. Even though women constituted at least half of the League's membership, the reins of the Komsomol leadership remained firmly in male hands. After more than half a century, very little had changed for the *komsomolki*.

In 1979 a special issue of a women's magazine, *Krest'ianka (Peasant Woman)*, was published to celebrate the VLKSM's sixtieth birthday and honor its female members. Its articles highlighted the *komsomolka*'s participation in Stalin's drive to modernize the Soviet Union in preparation for the Great Fatherland War (World War II), her achievements and sacrifices during that war, her participation in the labor force throughout the League's history, and particularly her involvement with the Young Pioneers. Although the magazine proclaimed the *komsomolki*'s significance for Soviet history, it ignored her continuing subservience to the male hierarchy of the League and the CPSU.

During the 1980s Mikhail Gorbachev's glasnost policy gave Soviet young women access to feminist writings that had previously been available only through the underground press. A significant number of *komsomolki* began to voice their concerns about the manner in which the Party used the League to control every aspect of their lives. Although in the 1980s the Komsomol was the source of approximately 70 percent of the new members of the CPSU, young women began to question the role of the League in their own lives. Many decided that perhaps the League was not the path to the shining future that had been promised them and declined to become *komsomolki*. This weakened the VLKSM's hold over Soviet young women and became part of the larger process that led to the disintegration of the Soviet Union and the concomitant collapse of both the CPSU and its youth organization.

Cross-references: Obshestvennitsa, Zhenotdel, zhensovety.

Suggested Readings

Attwood, Lynne. *The New Soviet Man and Woman: Sex-Role Socialization in the USSR*. Bloomington: Indiana University Press, 1990.

Fisher, Ralph Talcott, Jr. *Pattern for Soviet Youth: A Study of the Congresses of the Komsomol, 1918–1954*. New York: Columbia University Press, 1959.

Gorsuch, Anne E. " 'A Woman Is Not a Man': The Culture of Gender and Generation in Soviet Russia, 1921–1928." *Slavic Review* 55, no. 3 (Fall 1996): 636–660.

Riordan, Jim, ed. *Soviet Youth Culture*. Bloomington: Indiana University Press, 1989.

Tirado, Isabel A. *Young Guard! The Communist Youth League, Petrograd 1917–1920*. New York: Greenwood, 1988.

R. Connie Wawruck-Hemmett

Krupskaia, Nadezhda Konstantinovna (1869–1939)

Educator, revolutionary and publicist, and the wife of Vladimir Il'ich Lenin (Ul'ianov), the first head of the Soviet government and leader of the Bolshevik movement, which came to power in 1917. Krupskaia was instrumental in defining early Bolshevik policy toward women.

Nadezhda Krupskaia was born in St. Petersburg in 1869, the daughter of an army officer who was demoted while she was a child. Nadezhda had an impoverished childhood; she began study at the university but dropped out. A Marxist by twenty-one, she taught in the workers' evening and weekend schools in St. Petersburg in the 1890s. Through Marxist circles, she met the aspiring revolutionary and lawyer Vladimir Il'ich Ul'ianov, who used the revolutionary name V. I. Lenin, and they became friends. Lenin gave lectures to her classes, which are reputed to be Lenin's first real contact with workers. When Lenin was exiled to Siberia for his political activity, the friendship continued, and he invited Krupskaia to join him. To do this, she had to become his fiancée, and they were married in Siberia.

Their life in Siberia was tranquil. Lenin read and did research, and Krupskaia first wrote about women's role in the postrevolutionary society. Her work, published in 1901, bore Lenin's influence as well as her own and became the basis for Bolshevik policy on women. How much her views on women were shaped by Lenin remains an open question, since her views were developed when they lived in relative isolation and were each other's principal intellectual companion. Krupskaia's theory on the "woman question" focused on the worker–mother, whose life and working conditions the revolutionaries hoped to improve. The concern did not extend to all women, but only to women workers. On the one hand, she argued that work outside the home would free women from household burdens, but, on the other hand, like all good Marxists, Krupskaia believed that only the revolution could liberate women. She was interested in the family and in children and did not challenge traditional social mores, unlike her more flamboyant contemporary Aleksandra Kollontai. She was socially much more conservative than Kollontai and a strong believer in the role of the family.

From 1901 to 1917 Krupskaia and Lenin lived in exile in Western Europe, where she served as his assistant. During this period their marriage survived some problems, including intrusive relatives and Lenin's alleged romance with Inessa Armand. After the Bolshevik Revolution, Krupskaia worked primarily in the development of Soviet educational policy for children and adults and in the development of the Soviet library system. Like most other prominent revolutionary women, Krupskaia played a role in *Zhenotdel* in the 1920s and thus continued to influence Soviet policy toward women, but her primary focus was the education of children, which she considered crucial for the future of society. Her lifelong interest in children never abated, and she reportedly regretted that she and Lenin had had no children.

During Lenin's protracted illness (1922–1924), she was his principal contact with the outside world. She frequently had to deal with Joseph Stalin, the general secretary of the Communist Party and the Politburo's emissary to Lenin during this period. Under Politburo policy, Lenin, who was very ill, was not supposed to be involved in official work. Lenin, with her help, managed to do some writing during his illness. Krupskaia found Stalin so rude and unbearable that she wrote a letter of complaint to Lev Kamenev, another Politburo member. Lenin, aware of Stalin's behavior, was prompted in early 1923 to write in his "Last Testament" that Stalin should be dismissed from his post. From this time onward, Stalin saw her as an enemy, and that influenced his subsequent behavior toward her.

Krupskaia's life was difficult after Lenin's death in 1924. She lived in a small apartment in the Kremlin and was closely watched by Stalin, Lenin's successor, who feared her influence in society as Lenin's widow. After the Central Committee decided not to publish Lenin's "Last Testament," Krupskaia wanted to do so herself. Stalin threatened to produce another woman who would swear that she, not Krupskaia, was Lenin's true wife if she dared to publish Lenin's famous "Last Testament." She also objected to memorialization of Lenin in a mausoleum and the naming of cities and places for him, all of which she believed Lenin would have opposed. Although Krupskaia believed that no one could speak for Lenin, she, nonetheless, actively opposed policies that she believed were not in the spirit of Lenin in the early years after his death. She cooperated with the opposition bloc within the Central Committee in 1924–1926 but broke with them in late 1926, when she recognized that they could do little to change the policies of the Central Committee, which was increasingly under Stalin's control. Gradually, her influence waned, and she became a passive icon who was showcased on special holidays.

From 1929 to 1939 she was Deputy Commissar (Minister) of the Commissariat for *Narkompros* (Education), a member of the Central Committee of the Communist Party of the Soviet Union (CPSU) (1927–1939), and an honorary member of the Academy of Sciences. As an educator, she objected to some of the directions in Soviet educational policy but, nevertheless, acquiesced. Stalin used her to good effect on important holidays such as March 8, International Women's Day, when she was encouraged to make public speeches. She worked until the very last days of her life. She died after a brief illness on February 27, 1939, the day after her seventieth birthday, and her ashes were placed in the Kremlin Wall.

A plain woman with few affectations, her philosophy of life was both simple and dogmatically Marxist. Because of her self-effacing personal style and low profile, her role has been underestimated in the West, but she unquestionably had a strong influence on Lenin, and vice versa. Krupskaia viewed women as mothers and workers, simplistically merging Marxist and traditional Russian views of women. In the late 1920s and 1930s she made a number of speeches about women, but there was little new or creative in them. She regretted that women still bore the brunt of family obligations, urging the expansion of public services to alleviate women's burdens. She advocated various measures that society could take to help women, but none of these departed from a traditional mind-set about women's basic roles in life. Her conception of the worker–mother remained a cornerstone of public policy throughout the Soviet era. Her belief in the importance of political socialization in education also played an important role in the Soviet approach to education for both children and adults.

Cross-references: Alexandra Kollontai, *Zhenotdel*.

Suggested Readings

Krupskaia, N. K. *Sobranie sochinenii (Collected Works)*. Moscow, 1930–1934.

McNeal, Robert H. *Bride of the Revolution*. Ann Arbor: University of Michigan Press, 1972.

Noonan, Norma C. "Two Solutions to the Zhenskii Vopros in Russia and the USSR—Kollontai and Krupskaia: A Comparison." *Women and Politics* 11, no. 3 (1991): 77–99.

Sokolov, Boris. *Armand i Krupskaia: Zhenshchiny vozhdia (Armand and Krupskaia: The Leader's Women)*. Smolensk: Rusich, 1999.

Vasilieva, Larissa. *Kremlin Wives*. New York: Arcade Press, 1992.

Norma Corigliano Noonan

L

Legal Equality in the 1920s, Women's Pursuit of

Although prevented from organizing an independent women's movement in the early years after the Bolshevik Revolution, Soviet women pressed the regime to deliver on its promise of gender equality. While Soviet women articulated their understanding of legal equality, evidence indicates that women began to develop a sense of their own interests, interests that did not wholly coincide with those set from above. By the end of the 1920s, when the number of complaints increased and received press attention, the dispute resolution system had limited resolution of women's grievances. Stalin's ascendance subsequently stifled debate and removed mechanisms for women to challenge the Party's definition and pursuit of women's interests.

The Bolshevik Revolution promised women's deliverance from the social and legal inequalities of the tsarist regime. By granting Soviet women the right to vote, the Bolsheviks set a standard of equality and provided demonstrative evidence for touting the virtues of the Bolshevik Revolution. Subsequent statutory restrictions prohibiting women from night work, overtime work, underground work, and other labor considered dangerous to women's health catered to women's special needs as actual or potential mothers. This legislation was among the most progressive in the world and offered further evidence that the regime supported gender equality in the workplace. These measures also suggested that law had a significant role in securing that equality. The Bolsheviks nurtured this myth of legal equality for women; official rhetoric, disseminated through agitation and propaganda designed to stimulate women's support for Bolshevik power, trumpeted these advances along with the general proclamation prohibiting workplace discrimination on the basis of sex.

As Bolsheviks prohibited any separate women's movement, and because the legal system did not provide for—and the Soviet woman's nascent legal consciousness did not conceive of—strategic litigation campaigns in the public interest, women's efforts to secure legal equality cannot be characterized as a formal or official movement. For an appreciable number of women, socialization into the Bolshevik state included development of a distinct female "interest." As the 1920s progressed, many women articulated their interests by filing petitions and formal complaints with unions, Communist Party officials, and other factory, state, and Party agencies and dispute resolution forums. Working women in this period nurtured a budding legal consciousness, giving form to what procedural and substantive legal equality meant for them in Soviet society.

Women characterized their legal claims in terms sanctioned by the regime, which professed support for workers and women. Some women fought for the proper allocation of maternity benefits, seeking remedy from employers who technically complied with the law but in such a way as to discriminate against women workers. For example, some factories placed the rest area for nursing women so far from where the women worked that they could not get there, nurse, and return to the shop floor in the allotted break time, thereby eliciting demerits for tardiness. Some complained that managers refused to hire women or tended to dismiss pregnant women and mothers of young children. Other women challenged sexually coercive and abusive behavior of bosses, coworkers, and labor exchange officials, characterizing their injuries as "disparaging treatment" (*preobrezhitel'noe otnoshenie*) toward workers. Such behavior, they argued, was a violation of women's legal equality (*ravnopravie*) and health and safety; was offensive to communist morality and violated workers' rights, and constituted unlawful activity in violation of collective labor agreements and the law.

Although the Soviet system denied women the opportunity to advance their legal claims collectively, complaints about disparaging treatment and violence against women in the workplace increased as the decade advanced. With the advent of production meetings (*proizvodstvennye soveshchaniia*) and the criticism/self-criticism campaign, the number of women filing grievances and complaints swelled. At production meetings, where workers were urged to point out problems and inefficiencies in the workplace, women took the floor to demand equal treatment. Women petitioned for benefits or better working conditions and also sought that employers and others who violated woman's legal rights be held accountable by the Communist Party of the Soviet Union (CPSU) or the administrative authorities.

By the late 1920s, however, the chances of redress diminished. The fluid legal regime of the early 1920s, which gave judges more latitude, allowing them to plug the many lacunae in Soviet law and to be more receptive to women's novel claims, ceased to exist. The disintegration of the rule of law reduced women's chances for receiving legal remedy for "disparaging treatment" (i.e., sexual harassment) or other workplace indignities. With no clear hierarchy of dispute resolution mechanisms, women filed their complaints with multiple authorities. This practice, along with poor communication and the prohibition against a separate women's movement, prevented women from creating a critical mass to force change. Since gender equality was not a high priority of the regime, bureaucrats, arbiters, and union and Party officials could ignore women's complaints in favor of issues perceived to be more pressing. During the Purges of the 1930s, however, a harassment allegation might conveniently trigger an investigation and purge of the accused, perhaps his workplace as well.

The number of grievances dropped off markedly once Stalin declared the "woman question" "solved" in 1930. As the CPSU increasingly determined the meaning of laws and statutes, debates were squelched, and judges and other arbiters had no opportunity to issue legal decisions not sanctioned at the highest levels. By 1934, with the dissolution of the *Biuro zhalob* (Complaint Department) of the Workers' and Peasants' Inspectorate (*Rabkrin*) and the onset of the Purges, women ceased to pursue work-related claims in the public arena. Discussion of women's equality was limited to the Central Committee line of the CPSU, and any chance for women to define or press for their own independent interests was crushed.

Cross-references: Family Protection, *Zhenotdel*.

Suggested Readings

Goldman, Wendy Z. *Women, the State and Revolution*. New York: Cambridge University Press, 1993.

Granik, Lisa. "The Trials of the *Proletarka (Proletarian Woman)*." In *Reforming Justice in Russia*, edited by Peter Solomon, 131–167. New York: M. E. Sharpe, 1997.

Koenker, Diane P. "Men against Women on the Shop Floor in Early Soviet Russia: Gender and Class in the Socialist Workplace." *American Historical Review* 100, no. 5 (December 1995): 1438–1464.

Wood, Elizabeth. *The Baba and the Comrade: Gender and Politics in Revolutionary Russia*. Bloomington: Indiana University Press, 1997.

Lisa Granik

M

Mamonova, Tatiana Valentinovna (1943–)

Poet, essayist, and painter, Tatiana Mamonova was the motivating force behind Woman and Russia, the first independent feminist organization in the Soviet Union, which she organized with several other Leningrad women in 1979. Mamonova was exiled from the Soviet Union because of her role in Woman and Russia's publishing and organizing activities. She has continued her work as a Russian feminist in exile both in Europe and in the United States.

Tatiana Mamonova was born in the Iaroslavl (Yaroslavl) region, to which her parents had been evacuated during World War II, but raised in Leningrad. Like many activists in Russia's unofficial culture, she had initially dutifully pursued a technical career but began to question Soviet policies after the Soviet Union invaded Czechoslovakia in 1968. In her twenties Mamonova first attended, but did not graduate from, pharmacy school (1961–1964), then worked at the Leningrad television station for two years (1967–1968) and at the Leningrad journal *Aurora* from 1969 to 1972. As she began to write more of her own poetry and to draw, Mamonova became active in Leningrad's nonconformist circles. The sexism and indifference of those groups to women's issues, as well as her personal experiences with maternity wards and motherhood under Soviet conditions (she gave birth to a son in 1975), prompted her to organize the Soviet Union's first independent feminist group, *Zhenshchina i Rossiia* (Woman and Russia). The samizdat (self-published) *Al'manakh zhenshchinam i o zhenshchinakh (Almanac for Women and about Women)*, published by the group in December 1979, included articles on social and religious issues affecting women in late Soviet society, as well as poetry and prose. After the first issue of the *Al'manakh*, the group split in two, creating a larger, religious wing, *Mariia*, and a smaller, secular wing under Mamonova's leadership. Even after the split, the almanac continued to be published under Mamonova's editorship, and articles from its issues have been translated into eleven languages in twenty-two countries.

As a result of her feminist activism, Mamonova was one of numerous intellectuals and artists (relatively few of them women) who were forced to leave the Soviet Union in the early 1980s. After being expelled in 1980 with loss of all rights of Soviet citizenship, she lived in Paris for several years. Since 1984 she has lived in the United States.

Life outside the Soviet Union has not stopped Mamonova from continuing her activist work in various forums and media. In 1984 she edited *Women and Russia*, a collection of English translations of articles selected from the *Almanakh*. Essays in the collection examined the disproportionately heavy burden of labor and family support faced by Russian women, revealed the role of some of Russian culture's "foremothers," and reported on women in Soviet prisons, as well as on other social and literary topics. *Women and Russia* was well received and attracted attention in the West as the first contemporary volume to present women's issues from the point of view of Russian women themselves. Mamonova also served on the international advisory panel of *Ms.* magazine (which had been among the first in the West to recognize the group Woman and Russia), lectured widely on women's issues, and published several collections of her essays (often accompanied by her own illustrations) on Russian women's culture. Her two collections of essays, *Russian Women's Studies* and *Women's Glasnost versus Naglost*, received mixed reviews: some respondents object to their superficiality and to Mamonova's tendency to make sweeping judgments.

Although she visited Russia several times since 1990, Mamonova considered herself a "citizen of the world" and actively promoted global women's causes. In 1993 she founded a new "ecofeminist" almanac, *Woman and Earth*, which was published both on-line and in hard copy. The almanac also had a video production company focusing on interviews with prominent feminists. Copies of the magazine and videos were made available to Eastern Europe and Russia at no cost. *Woman and Earth* also sponsored film festivals and global ecological travel and kept an active Web page that was largely run by Mamonova.

Cross-references: Mariia, Woman and Russia (*Zhenshchina i Rossiia*).

Suggested Readings

Holt, Alix. "The First Soviet Feminists." In *Soviet Sisterhood*, edited by Barbara Holland, 237–265. Bloomington: Indiana University Press, 1985.

Mamonova, Tatiana. "Freedom and Democracy: Russian Male Style." In *Radically Speaking: Feminism Reclaimed*, edited by Diane Bell and Renate Klein, 441–447. North Melbourne, Victoria (Australia): Spinifex Press, 1996.

Mamonova, Tatiana. *Russian Women's Studies: Essays on Sexism in Soviet Culture*. New York: Pergamon Press, 1989.

Mamonova, Tatiana. *Women's Glasnost versus Naglost*. Westport, CT: Bergin & Garvey, 1994.

Mamonova, Tatiana, ed. *Women and Russia: Feminist Writings from the Soviet Union*. Boston: Beacon Press, 1984.

Morgan, Robin. "The First Feminist Exiles from the U.S.S.R." *Ms.*, November 1980: 49–56, 80–83, 102, 107–108.

Noonan, Norma C. "Tat'iana Valentinovna Mamonova." In *Dictionary of Russian*

Woman Writers, edited by Marina Ledkovsky, Charlotte Rosenthal, and Mary Zirin, 401–403. Westport, CT: Greenwood Press, 1994.

Ruderman, Florence. Review of *Russian Women's Studies: Essays on Sexism in Soviet Culture. Society* 27, no. 4 (May/June 1990): 108–110.

Ruthchild, Rochelle. "Sisterhood and Socialism: The Soviet Feminist Movement." *Frontiers* 7, no. 2 (1983): 4–12.

"Woman and Russia: Soviet Women Speak." *Spare Rib*, no. 6 (1981): 26–27, 34.

Natasha Kolchevska

Mariia (aka Maria) (1980–1983)

A club formed by several religious feminists who had initially been involved with the Woman and Russia collective in 1979, then broke with that group's founder, Tatiana Mamonova and its smaller secular wing in 1980. Its founders later went into exile but continued their contacts with Soviet dissidents.

Three women—Tatiana Mikhailovna Goricheva, the group's main philosopher; Iuliia Nikolaevna Voznesenskaia; and Natal'ia Malakhovskaia—established the *Mariia* club. Together they published six issues of an almanac, *Mariia*, in Paris (first issue, 1980) and subsequently in Paris and Frankfurt. In addition to organizing conferences on feminism and spirituality and writing for their almanac in the early 1980s, all three contributed articles to various Russian émigré Christian journals.

Disapproving of what they saw as Western feminism's excessive focus on gender equality, the *Mariia* group sought to develop a uniquely Russian form of feminism based on the role of the Virgin Mary in Orthodox Christianity. They looked to historical models of the Orthodox Church as a sanctuary for women and to a psychological model that emphasized the emotional, rather than the intellectual, strengths of women. The compassion and suffering of Mary the Mother of God, rather than the feminine wisdom of Sophia, was their source of inspiration. Goricheva, who contributed an article to each issue of *Mariia*, delineated the significance of the Mother of God for modern women. Other sections of the almanac addressed issues such as motherhood and the breakup of the family. Voznesenskaia, who had been imprisoned in the 1970s, edited a section on women religious dissidents who were serving prison sentences for their beliefs.

Several other samizdat anthologies of religious feminist writings, *Dalëkie-blizkie (Those Near and Far)* and *Nadezhda (Hope)*, were inspired by the group, but the *Mariia* club broke up in 1983. Goricheva went on to study theology at the St. Sergius Theological Institute in Paris from 1981 to 1984 and continued to write and articulate the religious vein of Russian feminism. In 1990 she returned to Russia; as of the late 1990s, she worked for a Christian publishing house based in St. Petersburg and Germany.

For women living under late Soviet communism, the absence of spirituality may have led women to see Mary the Mother of God as a welcome alternative to communist heroes and the emphasis on the material aspects of life. *Mariia*, with its focus on woman's essential qualities and on a Christian feminism to the exclusion of non-Christians, also reflected the often dissonant priorities of Western and Russian feminism. The views of this religious club were no more welcome in the USSR of the early 1980s than were the feminist views of Mamonova.

Cross-references: Tatiana Mamonova, Iuliia Voznesenskaia, Woman and Russia (*Zhenshchina i Rossiia*).

Suggested Readings

Buckley, Mary. "Soviet Religious Feminism as a Form of Dissent." *Journal of the Liberal Arts* (Fall 1986): 5–12.

Goricheva, Tatiana. "*Razmyshleniia o sbornike Nadezhda*" (Thoughts about the *Nadezhda* Anthology). *Posev*, no. 2 (1982): 58–60.

Holt, Alix. "The First Soviet Feminists." In *Soviet Sisterhood*, edited by Barbara Holland, 237–265. Bloomington: Indiana University Press, 1985.

Morgan, Robin. "The Russian Women's Movement." *Ms*. (November 1990): 49–56, 80–83, 102, 107–108.

Neginsky, Rosina. "Tatiana Mikhailovna Goricheva." In *Dictionary of Russian Woman Writers*, edited by Marina Ledkovsky, Charlotte Rosenthal, and Mary Zirin, 221–223. Westport, CT: Greenwood Press, 1994.

Ruthchild, Rochelle. "Sisterhood and Socialism: The Soviet Feminist Movement." *Frontiers* 7, no. 2 (1983): 4–12.

Voronina, Ol'ga. "The Mythology of Women's Emancipation in the USSR as the Foundation for a Policy of Discrimination." In *Women in Russia: A New Era in Russian Feminism*, edited by Anastasiia Posadskaya, 37–54. London: Verso, 1994.

Natasha Kolchevska

N

Narpit (Union of People's Food Service and Dormitory Workers) (*Professional'nyi soiuz rabotnikov narodnogo pitaniia i obshchezhitii*) (1918–1930)

The largest organization of service workers in the Soviet Union during the 1920s. Composed primarily of women, its members represented a wide range of occupations, which included tea shop, restaurant, shashlik-house and cafeteria workers, poolhall, bowling alley, and casino workers, hotel staff, rest-home staff, kvass sellers, and cooks. Eventually, the majority of Narpit's membership consisted of domestic workers, which undermined the union's credibility and precipitated challenges to Narpit's status as a legitimate workers' organization.

Formed in June 1918, Narpit, the Union of People's Food Service and Dormitory Workers, was first called the *Professional'nyi soiuz rabochikh i sluzhashchikh traktirnogo promysla* (Professional Union of Workers and Employees of the Food and Beverage Industry). It was constituted from various smaller organizations of waiters and cooks whose existence dated back to the tumultuous events of 1905. On May 3, 1919, it was officially renamed the Union of People's Food Service and Dormitory Workers in response to the changing nature of Soviet society. There were fewer private cafés, restaurants, and taverns and more public cafeterias. This new appellation represented Narpit's attempt to assume its place with other workers' groups. These efforts were threatened in 1920, when the All-Russian Central Council of Trade Unions (VTsSPS) required Narpit to absorb several dismantled unions, the most controversial of which was the *Professional'nyi soiuz domovykh sluzhashchikh* (Professional Union of Home Employees), mainly composed of domestic servants.

Narpit's leadership strenuously resisted the admission of domestics on the grounds that they were a backward legacy from the prerevolutionary period whose inclusion would dilute the proletarian character of the union, cause internal tension, and divert scarce resources and services away from the general membership. Despite these objections, domestic servants were incorporated into the membership in 1920. Although initially a negligible number, they accounted for an increasing percentage of the union's membership, reaching over 65 percent by 1927. In 1924 domestic servants were officially renamed domestic workers. The presence of domestic workers in the union strengthened its numbers and coffers, but it undermined the union's credibility, precipitating challenges to Narpit's status as a legitimate workers' union. In 1930 Narpit underwent a further metamorphosis, including a change of name and purpose, shedding all domestic, hotel, and dormitory workers to dedicate itself solely to people's food service.

At the grassroots level, Narpit was organized throughout the Soviet Union into a series of small, manageable groups intended to be responsive to its members' concerns. Any enterprise with twenty-five or more Narpit workers was entitled to form its own local committee. Domestic workers, usually one per household, were grouped by the streets where their establishments were located.

To join Narpit, a candidate was required to submit a formal application to the local committee along with a paybook showing three months of consecutive employment in one of the many eligible occupations and to complete a questionnaire on her background. These documents were presented at a general union meeting. If approved, the applicant was given a membership card. Domestic workers, who were often new arrivals from the countryside, were considered a transient group and more likely to make fraudulent applications in order to collect union benefits. Thus, every domestic was also required to demonstrate a minimum of six months of service with an employer and to provide a corroborating statement from the housing management committee attesting to residence and place of employment.

To remain in good standing, Narpit members were expected to fulfill certain responsibilities, including regular payment of dues. Entrance dues to the union were a half day's wage, and monthly dues were 2 percent of one's total monthly salary, including noncash remuneration such as room and board. Failure to pay could result in suspension and even expulsion from the union.

In 1921 the Tenth Party Congress adopted the New Economic Policy (NEP). In describing the role of unions in a workers' state, the new policy prescribed that unions function both as agents of the state and as advocates of their members' interests. Unions had to enforce official policies and improve the cultural and political level of their members, while safeguarding their members from exploitation by the state and individual private employers. To fulfill this dual role and provide a wide range of services, local branches of Narpit generated revenue from union dues, compulsory employer contributions, and fees for issuing wage books and negotiating employment contracts. Narpit attempted to assist its members by resolving workplace conflicts and, for those who had fallen on hard times, by providing access to unemployment insurance, emergency loans, and even temporary accommodations. It also campaigned to have all members, particularly domestic workers, conclude formal contracts with their employers cementing the terms of their employment.

In pursuit of cultural enlightenment, local committees of Narpit sponsored excursions to concerts, the cinema, and the theater, as well as field trips to museums and historical sites. Narpit also attempted to combat illiteracy, which was pervasive among its female members; free evening classes were established that were designed to educate both the partially literate and the completely illiterate. Along with liquidating illiteracy, safeguarding economic interests, and heightening cultural awareness, one of Narpit's primary goals was cultivating political consciousness. It sought to instill in its members a sense of activism and to encourage them to play a greater role in union activities. Despite its efforts and numerous national campaigns, Narpit was plagued by poor participation from its primarily female membership. Local branches did not understand that women's low level of activism was not necessarily due to backwardness and laziness. The double burden of work and family weighed women down and did not allow them the luxury of taking part in events, often inconveniently scheduled in inaccessible locations, poorly promoted, and of little relevance to their immediate problems.

Narpit fell victim to the dual role that it and other trade unions were expected to play during the 1920s and was attacked from all sides. Members assailed it for failing to protect them adequately against exploitation in the workplace. Employers repeatedly accused local union branches of overzealousness and even of resorting to intimidation and extortion in order to impose employment contracts, to ensure the prompt payment of wages, and to obtain employer contributions to the union's coffers. Narpit's relations with central union authorities fared no better. In the eyes of officialdom, Narpit could not rise above the stigma of the dubious proletarian credentials of its membership and the lackluster level of activism among its female constituents.

It would be a gross simplification to assess Narpit's contributions solely on the basis of its inability to fulfill the dual role demanded of it and the resulting criticism to which it was subjected. For members employed in larger establishments such as cafeterias, rest homes, dormitories, and hotels, Narpit functioned like any other trade union serving individuals working in clearly defined units who were readily organized and monitored and whose interests were more easily represented to the employer. The challenge that Narpit faced with domestic workers, however, was complex in light of their continued, but anomalous, employment in the postrevolutionary period. The progress that Narpit made with this unwieldy group of members—either in protecting their interests or in ensuring their compliance with state and party programs and policies—was no less significant because of its limitations.

Cross-reference: Professional Union of Home Employees.

Selected Readings

Bogomazova, Z. A. *Domashniaia Rabotnitsa (The Domestic Worker).* Moscow: VTsSPS, 1928.

Chase, William J. *Workers, Society, and the Soviet State: Labor and Life in Moscow 1918–1929.* Chicago: University of Illinois Press, 1987.

Halle, Fannina. *Women in Soviet Russia*. London: Routledge, 1933.

Hatch, John B. "Labor and Politics in NEP Russia: Workers, Trade Unions and the Communist Party in Moscow, 1921–1926." Ph.D. Diss., University of California, Irvine, 1985.

Orlovsky, Daniel. "The Hidden Class: White-Collar Workers in the Soviet 1920s." In *Making Workers Soviet: Power, Class and Identity*, edited by Lewis H. Seigelbaum and Ronald Grigor Suny. Ithaca, NY: Cornell University Press, 1994.

Wood, Elizabeth A. *The Baba and the Comrade: Gender and Politics in Revolutionary Russia*. Bloomington: Indiana University Press, 1997.

Wood, Elizabeth A. "Gender and Politics in Soviet Russia: Working Women under the New Economic Policy, 1918–1928." Ph.D. Diss., University of Michigan, 1991.

Rebecca Spagnolo

O

Obshchestvennitsa Movement (1934–1941)

A movement that involved civic-minded "wife-activists" in voluntary educational, cultural, and social service work in the new Soviet industrialized settlements of the 1930s. Women's initial efforts to improve living and working conditions in the settlements were systematized by the Party and trade unions; the movement culminated in a series of conferences in 1936 and 1937 and ended with the 1941 German invasion.

According to official Soviet sources, the movement of *obshchestvennitsy* (civic-minded women) began in 1934, when Heavy Industry Commissar Grigorii Ordzhonikidze, inspecting Urals factories, noticed flower beds planted in front of a substation. Inquiring, he discovered that this was the handiwork of a manager's wife, Klavdiia Surovtseva. Appalled by abysmal living conditions in the new industrial settlements under his purview, Ordzhonikidze perceived that Surovtseva's initiative might serve as an example for otherwise nonemployed managers' and engineers' wives; he publicized her efforts and fostered a unionwide movement of wife-activists.

While there is some truth to this "founding myth," the movement had significant antecedents. Primary among these were efforts to organize army officers' wives. From 1930 to 1932 the army's Political Administration held three "All-Army Conferences of Commanders' Wives," urging involvement in educational and social work, particularly in the campaign to collectivize daily life. In addition, working-class housewives were recruited to similar ends by the *Zhenotdel* in the 1920s and by trade unions and political departments during the 1920s and early 1930s and undertook ventures of their own, including *subbotniki* and competitions for the cleanest apartment. Tasks such as overseeing cafeterias, kindergartens, and cultural clubs and mobilization methods paralleled those of the *obshchestvennitsa* movement.

Furthermore, other managers' and engineers' wives sought to improve their surroundings during the early Five-Year Plans. Although Surovtseva's efforts were the first to draw official attention, a poultry farm established in 1933 by

Evgeniia Vesnik, a factory manager's wife in the Ukraine, was equally renowned. In fact, Vesnik, an articulate former opera singer, served as a symbol for the movement. At about the same time, wives established nurseries and playgrounds in Magnitogorsk and libraries near the oil fields of Sakhalin.

In early 1934, prior to Ordzhonikidze's encounters with Surovtseva and Vesnik, the union that represented managers and technical workers (the All-Union Intersectional Bureau of Engineers and Technicians of the All-Union Central Council of Trade Unions, or VMBIT VTsSPS) expressed concern about two issues that would ultimately converge in the *obshchestvennitsa* movement: the high turnover among male industrial specialists due to poor living conditions and the need to mobilize the wives of these specialists into the labor force. When Ordzhonikidze began to promote volunteer work among wives, the VMBIT endorsed his initiative with a resolution in early 1936 that praised the movement, designated the wives' council as the appropriate form of organization for its activities, and called for a national conference of wives from heavy industry to be held in Moscow in May 1936.

The *obshchestvennitsa* movement entered a new phase in its development with the All-Union Conference of Wives of Executives and Engineering-Technical Workers in Heavy Industry. Organized by the Commissariat of Heavy Industry and the Central Council of Trade Unions (VTsSPS), the conference was held at the Kremlin May 10–12, 1936, and was attended by over 3,000 delegates and guests, including such high-level officials as Ordzhonikidze, Viacheslav Molotov, Kliment Voroshilov, and Joseph Stalin. Some sixty women related their experiences as wife-activists seeking to promote a uniquely Soviet "culture of daily life," and conference proceedings were well publicized in the press.

The conference had been preceded by a series of regional meetings, dating back to mid-1935, and was followed by both regional and industry-specific meetings, which were designed to spread information about, and promote, the movement. Among the largest, most publicized was the December 1936 conference of army officers' wives. Convened in the Kremlin and attended by nearly 1,500 delegates and by numerous dignitaries, the conference recalled all-army wives' meetings of the early 1930s, while consciously emulating the format and tone of the civilian wives' conferences.

The May 1936 conference was marked by the creation of a journal, *Obshchestvennitsa*, published by the Commissariat of Heavy Industry. With two other official women's magazines, *Rabotnitsa (Woman Worker)* and *Krest'ianka (Peasant Woman)*, already in publication, the new journal marked the official recognition of a third category of Soviet woman. The journal featured articles and letters from activists describing their work, propaganda and agitation material, reports on the international situation, and instructional articles on child care, sewing, beauty, and icons of official Soviet high culture, such as Pushkin.

In the wake of the May and December all-union conferences, the *obshchestvennitsa* movement became a nationwide phenomenon, with wives' councils established in industrial enterprises and military districts from major urban centers to new industrial settlements, as well as in union republics and the Soviet far north and east. The movement expanded to encompass sectors outside heavy industry and the military. Wives' councils were formed, and conferences were held, for example, on light industry, forestry, academe, trade, and state farms, although apparently not on collective farms. The wives' movement was also active in the transport sector, particularly during Kaganovich's tenure as People's Commissar of Transportation, although a much-heralded, 1937 all-union conference seems to have been aborted due to a purge of the Commissariat of Transportation.

By 1936 the movement was defined primarily in terms of the relatively well educated wives of industrial specialists and Stakhanovites, but, in many cases, the wives of rank-and-file workers also participated. The wives' councils were generally divided into brigades or sections responsible for different areas of factory life. The variety of sections varied from council to council, but the most common were devoted to supervising children's institutions such as nurseries, kindergartens, and schools. Other sectors were commonly devoted to improving stores and cafeterias, ameliorating sanitary conditions in workers' dormitories and barracks, liquidating illiteracy, and conducting cultural and educational work through clubs, circles, and other activities. Another goal of the movement was to prepare wives to replace their husbands in production in the event of war and to participate in defense themselves. Some wives studied for skilled professions, and many participated in military or physical training, learning to ski, drive trucks, shoot rifles, ride horses and bicycles, and parachute.

Although the movement achieved a nationwide scope by 1936, male industrial managers and union officials often regarded the wives' activities as a nuisance, refusing to allocate funding for their projects or ignoring the councils altogether. The wives sometimes faced hostility from workers in the various institutions where they volunteered their services. As with other "mass" phenomena of the Stalin era, the *obshchestvennitsa* movement combined genuine idealism and coerced participation, and many groups reported difficulties in maintaining a large and active cohort. Ordzhonikidze appeared to be the wives' primary sponsor, and after his death in early 1937 the VTsSPS cut funding to the wives' councils. The Purges also took their toll on the movement, as many wives of the industrial elite, including Vesnik, were arrested along with their husbands.

During the late 1930s the movement pursued several new initiatives as the Soviet Union prepared for war. By 1938 *obshchestvennitsy* were focusing more closely on training women to replace men in production in the event of war. This campaign dovetailed into the "masculine professions" movement of the late 1930s, in which women, including *obshchestvennitsy*, qualified for professions that previously had been exclusively male. The wives also educated workers about the 1938 labor discipline campaign and organized job-training courses for working-class women in industry during the final prewar years. The nationwide movement disintegrated following the Nazi invasion in 1941, but some local councils survived into the war and postwar years.

The activities of *obshchestvennitsy* corresponded, in some respects, to social service work undertaken by women in other times and places. Wife–activists were sometimes accused of resembling prerevolutionary "ladies bountiful." Although establishing sewing circles for working women and providing toys for children echoed bourgeois philanthropy, the movement's leaders repudiated this association, and there were important differences. Prerevolutionary charity was often linked to the Orthodox Church, and the imperial state obstructed development of secular charitable associations. In contrast, the wife–activists of the 1930s were actively sponsored by the Soviet regime. Furthermore, few prerevolutionary women translated charitable work into broader public roles, whereas the *obshchestvennitsa* movement made a claim, however tenuous, for social and political legitimacy on the basis of social welfare work.

Some comparison can be made with the emergence of the homemaker and mother as a role model and quasi-public figure in interwar Western Europe. Rooted in turn-of-the-century social work movements and pro-natalism, interwar women's organizations in England, France, Italy, and Germany purported, in different ways, that fulfilling "natural" motherly and wifely duties allowed women to realize a civic obligation and contribute to state and societal well-being. It is unclear whether any similarities to Soviet developments were due to conscious emulation, and there were significant, unique aspects to the Soviet case. The emphasis on Soviet women's workforce participation during the 1930s contrasted sharply with the attempts of depression-ridden European nations to remove women from the paid labor force. Furthermore, the continued Soviet expression, however rhetorical, of a commitment to equal rights and opportunities for women was not echoed in Western Europe.

The *obshchestvennitsa* movement helped to stabilize the labor force during the era of industrialization. Labor turnover was rampant in the mid-1930s, due, in large part, to poor living conditions at many industrial enterprises. Working in cafeterias, dormitories, and day-care centers, wives addressed these "daily life" problems, while restricting their activities primarily to the "feminine" sphere of reproductive labor. Party and industrial officials, in effect, mobilized this cohort of well-educated wives as a corps of unpaid social workers. The volunteers at times were even called "the wives of the nation," reflecting their contribution to the larger society.

The movement's representational significance was considerable: the *obshchestvennitsa* joined the woman worker and collective farmer as a variant of the "new Soviet woman." Official approval of the *obshchestvennitsa* signified overt recognition of the continuing importance of domestic life and its connection to state and Party priorities. It also demonstrated a shift away from the earlier understanding of women's emancipation as predicated solely upon workforce participation and the socialization of the domestic sphere. Through participation in social, cultural, and educational work, housewives in the *obshchestvennitsa* movement could also be considered "builders of socialism."

Cross-references: Zhenotdel, Zhensovety, Zhensovety in the Soviet Army.

Suggested Readings

Buckley, Mary. "The Untold Story of *Obshchestvennitsa* in the 1930's." *Europe-Asia Studies* 48, no. 4 (1996): 569–586.

Fitzpatrick, Sheila. *The Cultural Front*. Ithaca, NY: Cornell University Press, 1992.

Kashkina, Irina Valentinovna. "*Materialy Tsentral'nogo Muzeia Revoliutsii SSSR po istorii dvizhenia zhen-obshchestvennits. 1934–1941 gg*" (Materials of the Central Museum of Revolution of the USSR on the History of the Obshchestvennitsa Movement). In *Formy i metody nauchno-prosvetitel'skoi raboty muzeev: Sbornik nauchnykh trudov. Tsentrl'nyi muzei Revoliutsii SSSR* (*Forms and Methods of Scientific-Educational Work of Museums: A Collection of Scientific Works*), 74–77. Moscow: Izdatel'stvo TsMR SSSR, 1986.

Kashkina, Irina Valentinovna, "*Privlechenie sovetskikh zhenshchin k obshchestvenno poleznomu trudu v perekhodnyi ot kapitalizma k sotsializmu period, 1917–1937: Istorigrafia problemy*" (Drawing Soviet Women into Socially Useful Work during the Transition from Capitalism to Socialism, 1917–1937: Historiography of the Problem). *Vestnik Moskovskogo universiteta (Moscow University Herald)* Seria 8. *Istoriia*, no. 2 (1987): 26–36.

Neary, Rebecca Balmas. "Mothering Socialist Society: The Movement of Wife–Activists and the Soviet Culture of Daily Life, 1934–1941." *The Russian Review* 58 (July 1999): 396–412.

Rebecca Balmas Neary and Thomas G. Schrand

P

Professional Union of Home Employees (*Professional'nyi soiuz domovykh sluzhashchikh*) (1917–1920)

Formed in March 1917, this union survived only three years before being dismantled and incorporated into other larger organizations, most notably the *Professional'nyi soiuz rabotnikov narodnogo pitaniia i obshchezhitii* (Professional Union of People's Food Service and Dormitory Workers). Despite its small size and short life span, the Union of Home Employees represented a continuation of activism among domestic servants who had begun, even before the Revolution of 1905, to organize themselves both locally and nationally.

The *Professional'nyi soiuz rabotnikov narodnogo pitaniia i obshchezhitii* (Professional Union of People's Food Service and Dormitory Workers), originally called the *Professional'nyi soiuz domashnei prislugi* (Professional Union of Domestic Servants), garnered its primarily female membership from the prerevolutionary domestic service groups in cities and towns, such as St. Petersburg, Moscow, Ekaterinoslav, Simbirsk, Kiev, and Tiflis. Numbered among its ranks were parlor maids, laundry maids, kitchen maids, nursery maids, nannies, wet nurses, and maids-of-all-work. In January 1918 the union's name was changed to the Professional Union of Home Employees, and the once exclusively domestic-service organization absorbed smaller, more disparate groups of caretakers, janitors, drivers, electricians, plumbers, doorkeepers, and even some tailors and dressmakers to broaden its membership base and enhance its viability.

At the local level, the Union of Home Employees was divided into small groups in urban locations, where there were sufficient concentrations of domestic servants and other member occupations. Dramatic urban depopulation during the Civil War along with significant changes in housing conditions and domestic lifestyles resulted in a decline in the number of employed domestic servants and other home workers. Nonetheless, the union continued to attract members from these traditionally marginalized occupations, doubling the number of its branches between 1918 and 1919.

The primary goal of the Union of Home Employees was to establish and enforce norms regulating the employment of a previously unregulated and frequently exploited segment of the population. One of the union's most significant achievements was the creation of a standardized wage scale based on job classifications. Introduced in September 1919 and revised annually, this wage scale determined the salaries of all occupations in the union, according to clearly defined criteria, including a minimum living amount, the nature and difficulty of the work, noncash benefits, and geographic region. The union also introduced procedures governing the employment, dismissal, and resignation of its members, as well as mechanisms for resolving workplace conflicts.

In addition to attempting to normalize relations in the workplace with uniform standards, the Union of Home Employees campaigned to secure certain basic requirements regarded as essential to placing its members on an equal footing with other workers. Of particular concern were endless workdays and lack of respect in the workplace. The union demanded for its members a nine-hour workday with an hour for lunch, an eight-hour day on Saturdays and the day before holidays, overtime pay and time off on Christmas and Easter, a five-hour day on other holidays, and a half day free on alternate Sundays. Union members insisted that they be addressed in the polite form at work, using the pronoun *vy* (you) rather than the more familiar *ty* (thou).

The union's efforts to normalize their situation in the workplace did not always result in compliance on the part of the employer. More often than not, local union committees met with outright refusal from employers and little support from official authorities. Local branches of the Union of Home Employees did not allow resistance to diminish their zeal; they frequently responded with a level of organization, cohesion, and militancy believed impossible from domestic servants and workers. For example, in June 1917 domestic servants in various cities throughout the country marched in the streets and succeeded in securing their demands through a determined campaign of picketing and strike action. Though calls for salary increases were ignored, the servants' ten-day strike resulted in employers' agreeing to limit the workday, provide regular time off each month and for major holidays, and create mechanisms for resolving workplace conflicts. They agreed to pay additional compensation to nonresident domestic servants in lieu of room and board. Although these gains were more honored in the breach than in the observance, they formed the cornerstone of subsequent union achievements.

The union was most effective in its efforts to secure the rights of its members in the workplace, to improve their economic position, to monitor their living conditions, and to combat illiteracy. The Union of Home Employees also undertook to instill a sense of activism and political consciousness in its membership by circulating pamphlets, bulletins, prescriptive short stories, and the union's own journal, which was designed to keep members informed of union activities and assist in recruiting new members. Moreover, the union oversaw the construction of small, local reading libraries, as well as coordinating cultural excursions to theaters, museums, and the cinema. Grassroots union groups held evening lectures, specifically to address questions of politics and economics, and they continually attempted to motivate members to play a greater role in union activities, committees, and clubs.

The Union of Home Employees was disbanded in May 1920, and its members were apportioned among other unions. The All-Russian Central Council of Trade Unions (VTsSPS) divided the union's assets and most of its membership between Narpit (the Union of People's Food Service and Dormitory Workers) and the *Soiuz rabotnikov kommunal'nogo khoziaistva* (Union of Municipal Workers). Other groups required to absorb its remaining, disparate members were the *Soiuz narodnogo obrazovaniia* (Union of People's Education), the *Soiuz transportnykh rabochikh* (Union of Transport Workers), and the *Soiuz shveinoi promyshlennosti* (Garment Industry Union).

These organizations resented the dismantling and forced absorption of the Union of Home Employees, despite the prospect of new members and additional revenue for their own organizations. In particular, the Union of People's Food Service and Dormitory Workers questioned the legitimacy of the Union of Home Employees' status as a workers' group. Domestic servants, doormen, and janitors were seen as a backward legacy from the prerevolutionary period whose presence would dilute the proletarian character of the new unions. The legacy of this short-lived union, however, continued in an embryonic system of rights and regulations, unprecedented for this traditionally marginalized workforce.

Cross-reference: Narpit (Union of People's Food Service and Dormitory Workers).

Selected Readings

Bogomazova, Z. A. *Domashniaia Rabotnitsa (The Domestic Worker.)* Moscow: VTsSPS, 1928.

Engel, Barbara Alpern. *Between the Fields and the City: Women, Work and Family in Russia, 1861–1914.* Cambridge: Cambridge University Press, 1994.

Kelly, Catriona. " 'Who'll Clean the Boots Now?' Servants and Social Anxieties in Late Imperial St. Petersburg." *Europa Orientalis* 16, no. 2 (1997): 9–34.

Koenker, Diane P., and William G. Rosenberg. *Strikes and Revolution in Russia, 1917.* Princeton, NJ: Princeton University Press, 1989.

Rustemeyer, Angela. *Dienstboten in Petersburg und Moskau, 1861–1917 (Domestic Service in Petersburg and Moscow.)* Stuttgart: Steiner, 1996.

Wood, Elizabeth A. "Gender and Politics in Soviet Russia: Working Women under the New Economic Policy, 1918–1928." Ph.D. Diss., University of Michigan, 1991.

Rebecca Spagnolo

R

Reisner, Larisa (1895–1926)

A writer, political journalist, and Bolshevik activist before the 1917 Revolution and in the early years after the revolution.

Larisa Reisner was born on May 13, 1895, in Lublin, Poland, the first child of Ekaterina Aleksandrovna Pachnovoi, who was descended from Polish aristocrats, and Mikhail Reisner, a sociologist and jurist of Baltic origins. In 1898 the family moved to Tomsk. Reisner was a committed member of the Russian Social Democratic Labor Party (RSDLP), from its inception in 1898. Because of his political activity, in 1903 Reisner and his family were forced to emigrate; they went to Berlin, where he continued his political work. Among the family's friends were the revolutionary theorists August Bebel and Karl Liebknecht. In 1905 and 1906 the Reisner family lived in Paris. Larisa's early life was influenced by her father's political views and by her determined mother, who ran the household. After the Revolution of 1905, Russia entered a period of liberalization, and in 1906 the Reisner family moved back to St. Petersburg.

From 1906 to 1913 Larisa attended D. T. Prokov'eva's private grammar school for girls. The famous writer Leonid Andreev also tutored her. Young women could not attend the universities but could attend Higher Classes for Women. She matriculated at the Psycho-Neurological Institute in St. Petersburg in 1913 and became part of the first class to complete a coeducational, university-level program there. During the same period, Larisa also audited classes in the Law and Philology Departments at St. Petersburg University. She continued her interest in literature and published her first poems in 1910. In 1912–1913 her two books about portrayals of Ophelia and Cleopatra in Shakespeare's dramas were printed by the publisher *Nauka i Zhizn* (Science and Life) in Riga, and in 1913 her play *Atlantida* was published in the *Almanakh "Shipovnik"* (*wild rose*). Larisa wanted to be a journalist and worked briefly with her father in 1915 editing the newspaper *Rudin* until a lack of funds terminated publication. She also worked for several editorial offices, during which time she met Maksim Gorki. Socialized by her father at an early age, during her youth she had visited several workers' clubs. After the February 1917 Revolution, she sympathized with the Bolshevik faction of the RSDLP and became an active Bolshevik after the October Revolution. For a short time she worked with Anatolii Lunacharskii on an inventory of the tsars' art treasures in the St. Petersburg Hermitage. From 1918 to 1920 she worked as a Secretary of the Communist Party organization of the Volga fleet, heading its intelligence department. During the Civil War she met Leon Trotsky, whose military leadership she admired. In 1921 she became part of the Left Opposition, which objected to NEP (New Economic Policy), a policy that she considered a step backward toward capitalism.

Larisa's career as a journalist continued after the revolution. She wrote newspaper reports from the civil war, collected later in a book, *Front*, published in 1928. Together with her husband, Fedor Raskol'nikov, whom she met in the Volga Fleet and married in 1918, she traveled to Afghanistan from 1921 to 1923. Raskol'nikov was a member of the first Soviet diplomatic mission, while Reisner worked as a journalist, sending stories about Afghanistan to several Soviet newspapers, including *Izvestiia (News)*. In 1925 *Afghanistan*, a book of her articles, was published. In 1923 she and her husband separated, and Larisa returned to Moscow. They divorced in 1924.

In her role as a political journalist, Reisner went to Hamburg to observe the workers' uprisings there. In Berlin in 1923 she met the revolutionary Karl Radek, who became her companion until her death from typhus in 1926. In 1924–1925 Larisa traveled through the industrial regions of the Urals, the Don Basin, and Belorussia. She wrote about the workers and their living conditions in a volume, *Ugol' zhelezo i zhivye liudi* (Coal, Iron, and Real People), published in 1925. In 1925 she traveled to Germany for her health, but instead of staying in a Wiesbaden spa, she visited Berlin and Dessau, collecting material for articles about Germany. Returning to Moscow, she taught Russian literature at Sun Yat-Sen University for a short while before her death.

Larisa was an emancipated woman with a highly developed sense of self. She witnessed and participated in the Bolshevik Revolution, primarily through her writing. She embodied the new Soviet woman but never stepped outside the boundaries of accepted roles for women in the revolutionary intelligentsia. Her former husband, Raskol'nikov, left the Soviet Union in the late 1920s and migrated to England. Karl Radek was a victim of the Purges in the 1930s. Larisa herself was forgotten for many years.

Suggested Readings

Porter, Cathy. *Larisa Reisner*. London: Virago, 1988.
Reisner, Larisa. *Afghanistan*. Moscow: Gosizdat, 1925.
Reisner, Larisa. *Front*. Moscow: Krasnaia nov', 1928.
Reisner, Larisa. *Izbrannoe (Selected Works)*. Moscow: Sovetskii pisatel', 1965.
Reisner, Larisa. *Ugol' zhelezo i zhivye liudi (Coal, Iron, and Real People)*. Moscow: Gosizdat, 1926.

Solovei, Eleanora. *Larisa Reisner: Ocherk zhizni i tvorchestva (Larisa Reisner: An Essay on Her Life and Work)*. Moscow: Sovetskii pisatel', 1969.
Zeide, Alla, "Larisa Reisner: Myth as Justification for Life." *Russian Review* 51, no. 3 (April 1992): 72–87.

Carmen Scheide

S

Soviet Women's Committee (SWC) (*Komitet Sovetskikh zhenshchin*) (1956–1991)

An organization that represented the USSR at international conferences, interacted with women's groups abroad, and served as a propaganda mouthpiece for the Communist Party of the Soviet Union (CPSU).

The *Komitet Sovetskikh zhenshchin* (Soviet Women's Committee, or SWC) grew out of the Soviet Women's Anti-Fascist Committee, founded in 1941 to rally women against Nazi aggression. Its first president, Valentina Grizodubova, was a pilot heroine of World War II. After the war, the Soviet Women's Anti-Fascist Committee represented the USSR at international women's meetings, presenting itself and the Soviet government as champions of peace. In 1956 the organization was renamed the Soviet Women's Committee and served primarily as the Soviet state's propagandist on women's issues. Until its monopoly was broken by the emergence of independent women's organizations during Perestroika, the SWC was the only organization at the all-union level that could speak on behalf of women.

Through most of its history, SWC was an elite organization with no links to rank-and-file Soviet women. SWC functioned as a propaganda tool, actively involved with international and regional women's organizations as well as peace groups. These linkages included the Women's International League for Peace and Freedom, United Nations agencies, and the Forum for a Nuclear Free World. At home, the SWC hosted women's delegations from abroad and conducted a variety of international summits and roundtables. The SWC stressed that Soviet women had achieved equality and greater happiness than women elsewhere. SWC published the magazine *Soviet Woman*, which began in 1945, appeared in fourteen languages, and was distributed in more than 140 countries.

While the emphasis during the Cold War era was on international contacts, the role of the SWC began to shift under Gorbachev, who urged that the *zhensovety* (women's councils) be revitalized and that the SWC turn its attention toward domestic issues and assume an active role vis-à-vis these organizations.

In 1986 Valentina Tereshkova, the first woman to fly in space, stepped down after serving as SWC's head since 1968. Her long term in office reflected her role as an international symbol of women's achievements in the USSR. Zoia Pukhova, who had achieved fame in the 1970s as a textile mill director and then served in top state positions in Ivanovo oblast, took over the reins of SWC. She delivered hard-hitting speeches calling for protective legislation that would move women out of arduous and heavy physical labor, the improvement of maternal and infant health, and ending night shifts for women. She also pointed out that men were far more likely than women to move up career ladders. Although her rhetoric was traditional, in the sense of stressing protective legislation for women, her criticisms of women's working conditions were sharply worded and went beyond what was typical of the past. In the 1989 elections to the USSR Congress of People's Deputies (CPD), the SWC was awarded seventy-five uncontested seats (one-third of CPD seats were allocated to public organizations) in recognition of its official status as the key voice of Soviet women. State sponsorship of public organizations was, however, in its waning days, and the SWC soon faced the challenge of making the transition to an independent women's organization.

In 1990 Alevtina Fedulova, who had worked with the Soviet Peace Committee and the Pioneers, succeeded Pukhova as head of SWC. She had served as vice president of SWC since 1987 and played a key role in shifting the organization's activities toward domestic concerns. Programs were established to retrain unemployed women, to teach women how to start businesses, and to provide consultation services for economic, family, and psychological problems. Fedulova oversaw the transformation of the SWC into the Women's Union of Russia (WUR), one of the most important independent women's organizations in the Russian Federation in the 1990s.

Cross-references: Alevtina Fedulova, Women's Union of Russia (WUR), *Zhensovety*.

Suggested Readings

Nechemias, Carol. "Democratization and Women's Access to Legislative Seats: The Soviet Case, 1989–1991." *Women & Politics*, 14, no. 3 (1994): 1–18.

Pukhova, Z. P. *"Zhenskoe dvizhenie i Perestroika v SSSR"* (The Women's Movement and Perestroika in the USSR). In *Zhenshchiny v sovremennom mire (Women in the Contemporary World)*, edited by V. V. Liubimova, 58–64. Moscow: Nauka, 1989.

Racioppi, Linda, and Katherine O'Sullivan See. *Women's Activism in Contemporary Russia*. Philadelphia: Temple University Press, 1997.

Carol Nechemias

Stasova, Elena Dmitrievna (1873–1966)

A prominent figure in the Bolshevik movement who occupied a variety of positions in the Soviet government and the international communist movement.

Although not identified with advocacy of women's issues, she was one of the highest-ranking women officials in the Soviet system.

Elena Stasova was born on October 30, 1873, in St. Petersburg, the daughter of D. V. Stasov, a famous Russian lawyer and political activist. After completing the gymnasium, she taught, together with Nadezhda Krupskaia, in the special Sunday schools for workers. In 1898 she joined the Russian Social Democratic Labor Party (RSDLP) and also began to work for the *Soiuz bor'by za osvobozhdenie rabochego klassa* (Union for the Liberation of the Working Class). Beginning with 1901, she was a contributor to the party's newspaper, *Iskra* (the *Spark*) and worked for the RSDLP under various pseudonyms, including *Absolut*, Varvara Ivanovna, Delta, Knol', and *Tscapla* (Heron), in several regions of the Russian empire, including Orel, Kiev, Smolensk, Moscow, Minsk, Vilnius, and Tbilisi. She was arrested numerous times and spent the years 1913 to 1916 in exile in Eniseiskaia Province in Siberia.

Beginning in February 1917, she worked as a secretary of the RSDLP/B Central Committee. At first she was its only secretary, functioning, more or less, as V. I. Lenin's secretary before the revolution. After the revolution, she was part of the newly created Secretariat of the Russian Communist Party/Bolsheviks until 1926. She was a candidate member of the Central Committee of the RSDLP/B and then a member of the Central Committee of the RCP/B from 1918 to 1920.

She organized the first *S"ezd narodov vostoka* (Congress of the Peoples of the East) in 1920. In 1921 she began working for the Comintern, and from 1927 to 1937 she was an official of the International Organization of Relief to Fighters for the Revolution (MOPR) and head of its Soviet branch. In 1934 she participated in the formation of the Anti-War and Anti-Fascist Women's Committee.

From 1938 until her retirement in 1946, she was an editor of the journal *International Literature*, published in English and French.

Stasova remained an active Communist Party member for her entire career and participated in seven congresses of the CPSU. She received four Orders of Lenin. One of the last survivors of the Bolshevik Revolution, she died on December 31, 1966, in Moscow and was buried in Red Square near the Kremlin Wall in recognition of her longtime contribution to the communist cause.

Cross-reference: Nadezhda Krupskaia.

Suggested Readings

Abramov, A. *U Kremliovskskoi steny (Near the Kremlin Wall).* Moscow: Politizdat, 1974.

Izbakh, A. A. *Tovarisch Absolut (Comrade Absolute).* Moscow: Znanie, 1963.

Lipilin, V. G. *Absolut: Dokumental'nyi rasskaz o E. D. Stasovoi (Absolute: A Documentary Account of E. D. Stasova).* Leningrad: Lenizdat, 1990.

Stasova, E. D. *Stranitsy zhizni i bor'by (Pages of Life and Struggle).* 3d ed. Moscow: Politizdat, 1988.

Liudmila Zhukova

V

Voznesenskaia, Iuliia Nikolaevna (1940–)

Poet, novelist, essayist, and human rights activist. An important Leningrad participant in Soviet nonconformist culture of the 1960s and 1970s and cofounder of Woman and Russia, later *Mariia*.

Although her father and husband were both loyal Communists, Iuliia Voznesenskaia broke away from official Soviet culture in her thirties and became an active organizer of unofficial publications, poetry readings, and art exhibitions in Leningrad. In 1979 Voznesenskaia cofounded the Leningrad feminist group Woman and Russia, which published a *samizdat* almanac with the same name from 1979 until early 1981. Voznesenskaia belonged to the religious branch of *Zhenshchina i Rossiia* (Woman and Russia), which broke with the more socially minded secular wing in 1980 to form its own group, the *Mariia* club. Voznesenskaia edited the second issue of *Mariia*, the club's almanac, in 1980. The KGB's interest in Woman and Russia and *Mariia* led to Voznesenskaia's forced emigration in 1980. Even before that she had been no stranger to prison and exile, having been arrested in 1964 and 1976 for organizing and editing several unofficial collections of writings on literary and social topics. Not one to abide by government sentences, in 1977, while serving a five-year term of exile, Voznesenskaia illegally returned to Leningrad and was sentenced to two years in a labor camp. Her personal experience and interest in the fate of fellow prisoners explain her many contributions on women political prisoners in nonofficial Soviet publications in the late 1970s and 1980s. These were collected and published in an English-language volume, *Letters of Love*, in 1989.

Although highly respected among dissident writers for the underground poetry that she wrote during the late Soviet era, Voznesenskaia is best known in the West for her 1987 novel, *Zhenskii dekamaron* (*The Women's Decameron*), sometimes referred to as *Damskii dekamaron*, which by 1992 had been translated into thirteen languages. The novel was finally published in Russia in 1992. While borrowing its framework from Giovanni Boccaccio's famous fourteenth-century work, Voznesenskaia's novel was unique in that it told its tales from the viewpoint of ten new mothers quarantined in a maternity hospital for ten days. In spite of considerable social and political differences, the novel's ten storytellers traced common, gender-based experiences, and, as Catriona Kelly observed, the novel was a rare example of a Russian work's finding an appropriate language for writing about sex. *The Women's Decameron* has continued to be widely read and taught in the West.

From 1980 onward, Voznesenskaia lived in Munich, where she worked for the Society for Human Rights and Radio Liberty and contributed to the émigré journals *Posev* and *Grani*. Her second novel, *Zvezda Chernobyl'* (*The Star Chernobyl*), also published in 1987, represented her continuing interest in social and political matters. Based on a wide range of documentary materials that Voznesenskaia collected while working for Radio Liberty in 1985 and 1986, like her earlier novel, *The Star Chernobyl* focused on the resourcefulness and humanity of its women characters, though without its predecessor's good cheer and bawdiness. *Letters of Love* marked the author's interest in the role of religion and individuality in the lives of Russian women. Later, Voznesenskaia turned to writing detective novels, including *Rusalka v basseine (Mermaid in a Swimming Pool)* and *Liubimykh ubivaiut vse (Everyone Kills the One They Love)*, both of which were published in Moscow in 1994.

Cross-references: Tatiana Mamonova, *Mariia*, Woman and Russia.

Suggested Readings

Curtis, Julie. "Iuliia Voznesenskaia: A Fragmentary Vision." In *Women and Russian Culture: Perceptions and Self-Perceptions*, edited by Rosalind Marsh, 173–187. New York: Bergahn Books, 1998.

Feinstein, Wiley. "Twentieth-Century Feminist Responses to Boccaccio's Alibech Story." *Romance Languages Annual*, no. 1 (1989): 116–120.

Henry, Kathryn. "Iuliia Nikolaevna Voznesenskaia." In *Dictionary of Russian Woman Writers*, edited by Marina Ledkovsky, Charlotte Rosenthal, and Mary Zirin, 733–735. Westport, CT: Greenwood Press, 1994.

Kelly, Catriona. *A History of Russian Women's Writing*. Oxford: Clarendon Press, 1994, 386–387.

Kolodziej, Jerzy. "Iuliia Voznesenskaia's Women: With Love and Squalor." In *Fruits of Her Plume: Essays on Contemporary Women's Culture*, edited by Helena Goscilo, 225–238. Armonk, NY: M. E. Sharpe, 1993.

Vosnesenskaia, Iuliia. *Liubimykh ubivaiut vse* (*Everyone Kills the One They Love*). Moscow: Mosty, 1994.

Vosnesenskaia, Iuliia. *Rusalka v basseine* (*Mermaid in a Swimming Pool*). Moscow: Mosty, 1994.

Vosnesenskaia, Iuliia. *Zhenskii dekamaron*. Tel Aviv: Izd. "*Zerkalo*," 1987. (Translated as *The Women's Decameron*. London: Quartet Books, 1986, and New York: Henry Holt, 1987.)

Voznesenskaia, Iuliia. "*Zhenskoe dvizhenie v Rossii*" (The Women's Movement in Russia). *Posev*, no. 4 (1981): 41–44.

Vosnesenskaia, Iuliia. *Zvezda Chernobyl'*. New York: Liberty House, 1987. (Translated as *The Star Chernobyl*. London: Quartet Books, 1987.)

Vosnesenskaia, Iuliia, comp. and ed. *Letters of Love: Women Political Prisoners in Exile and the Camps*. London: Quartet Books, 1989. (Russian excerpts published as "*Zapiski iz rukava*." *Iunost'* (*Youth*) 1 (1991): 81–88; 2: 65–69; 3: 45–47.)

Natasha Kolchevska

W

Woman and Russia (*Zhenshchina i Rossiia*) (1979–ca. 1984)

A group of Leningrad feminists who, in the fall of 1979, initiated and published the Soviet Union's first and only independent feminist almanac, also called *Woman and Russia.*

Zhenshchina i Rossiia (Woman and Russia) was a small organization that in 1979 compiled a *samizdat* publication, *Al'manakh zhenshchinam o zhenshchinakh* (*Almanac for Women and about Women*), also known as *Woman and Russia*. Only ten copies of the original *Al'manakh* were produced, and those circulated hand to hand, illegally, through the unofficial Soviet *samizdat* network. A combination of KGB persecution and internal tensions led to the group's breakup into two camps after its initial publishing effort. Nonetheless, *Woman and Russia* caught the attention of Western feminists, and the almanac was translated, published, and widely discussed in England, France, and the United States during the 1980s.

Woman and Russia's founding members were Tatiana Valentinovna Mamonova, Iuliia Nikolaevna Voznesenskaia, Tatiana Mikhailovna Goricheva, and Natalie Malakhovskaia. Mamonova was a committed student and proselytizer of a Western-type model of political feminism, and she approached the others with the idea of publishing a compilation of works "for women and by women" (the almanac's subtitle). Unlike Mamonova, the other three original members based their feminism on their Christian beliefs and, shortly after the group's initial formation, broke with her to found the *Mariia* club. By the summer of 1980 all had emigrated or been forced to emigrate from the Soviet Union. *Woman and Russia* continued to be published in Leningrad, despite Mamonova's departure. The religious feminists also published an almanac, *Mariia* (six issues, 1980–1981) from Paris and Frankfurt and contributed to émigré Russian Christian publications such as *Posev* during the 1980s. Mamonova lived in France for four years before moving to the United States. After her departure from the Soviet Union, she lectured and published widely on women's issues in Russian culture and literature and spoke at numerous international conferences, including, after Perestroika, forums in the Soviet Union and Russia. As of 1994 essays from the series of almanacs produced by Woman and Russia had been translated into eleven languages and published in twenty-two countries.

The different weight given to social and religious agendas was the flash point dividing the Woman and Russia collective. The *Mariia* contingent argued for the unique role of Christianity and of the Virgin Mary as peacemaker, in the regeneration of women's sense of self-worth after decades of attack and erosion by Soviet Communism. Goricheva became the religious feminists' theoretician, arguing in several articles in *Mariia* that Russian women's liberation could be achieved only by finding their faith in God, which, in turn, would lead to altered and enriched relationships with people. The *Mariia* club rejected Marxism and rationalism totally, blaming them for bringing what was once "Holy Russia" to a spiritual, moral, and physical apocalypse. Mamonova, on the other hand, identified with nineteenth-century social radicals and contemporary European and American feminists and sought to promote a program for achieving women's social, political, and sexual rights that was closer to Western models.

In spite of these ultimately irreconcilable differences over the roles of religion and politics, many common concerns drew the Woman and Russia collective together. Foremost among these was their frustration with the unwillingness of both the dominant, official culture and the dissident, or nonconformist, groups to address women's issues seriously. The lack of forums for the discussion of social concerns such as motherhood, divorce, child care, and alcoholism and its role in the disintegration of the family affected Soviet women more directly than men because of women's responsibilities for the family. The Woman and Russia collective suggested that women were discriminated against professionally. They argued that women bore a disproportionate share of the crises in housing and consumer goods and that they suffered alienation, self-hatred, and other forms of psychological harm from living in a "phallocracy" (the first documented use of that word in a Russian publication). These and other issues, such as the treatment of women in prisons, domestic and state violence against women, and women and peace, were often addressed in the almanacs. In addition, poetry and prose were published in every issue. Sexuality, either hetero- or homo-, however, received little attention.

Even after its founders' departure from the Soviet Union, the movement continued to play a role in feminist activism in the Soviet Union. At its peak, *Mariia* had chapters in Leningrad, Moscow, Odessa, and Riga. A 1984 English-language anthology, *Women and Russia: Feminist Writings from the Soviet Union*, edited by Mamonova, incorporated selections from the five issues of *Woman and Russia* published in *samizdat* in the Soviet Union after the departure of its founders. The anthology showed considerable geographical and thematic breadth, with contributions from the Baltic republics, Armenia, and Central Asia, and included essays by, or interviews with, working women, drug addicts, and lesbians.

In retrospect, the first Soviet feminists had more impact abroad than in the

Soviet Union. As Rosalind Marsh and others have pointed out, there has been minimal recognition of their efforts by the recent generation of Russian feminists. Certainly, the KGB easily and effectively neutralized this group of neophytes, yet internal dissension and their lack of a broader social base also played a role in limiting their possibilities for becoming a large-scale organization.

It is also true that the collective's members suffered from a common essentializing, generalizing tendency, shared by their male counterparts in the dissident community, and were often naive or idealistic in the solutions that they proposed for addressing women's issues. Nevertheless, at the beginning of the 1980s, when so many aspects of Soviet life seemed to be mired in despair and cynicism, the handful of members of Woman and Russia presented an accurate reflection of many Soviet women's frustrations and aspirations.

Cross-references: Tatiana Mamonova, *Mariia*, Iuliia Voznesenskaia.

Suggested Readings

Holt, Alix. "The First Soviet Feminists." In *Soviet Sisterhood*, edited by Barbara Holland, 237–265. Bloomington: Indiana University Press, 1985.

Mamonova, Tatiana, ed. *Women and Russia: Feminist Writings from the Soviet Union*. Boston: Beacon Press, 1984.

Marsh, Rosalind. "Introduction" and "The Russian Women's Movement: Anastasiia Posadskaia, the Dubna Forum and the Independent Women's Movement in Russia." In *Women in Russia and Ukraine*, edited by Rosalind Marsh, 1–30, 286–298. Cambridge: Cambridge University Press, 1996.

Morgan, Robin. "The First Feminist Exiles from the U.S.S.R." *Ms*. (November 1980): 49–56, 80–83, 102, 107–108.

Ruthchild, Rochelle. "Sisterhood and Socialism: The Soviet Feminist Movement." *Frontiers* 7, no. 2 (1983): 4–12.

Voznesenskaia, Iuliia. "*Zhenskoe dvizhenie v Rossii.*" *Posev*, no. 4 (1981): 41–44.

Woman and Russia: First Feminist Samizdat (Al'manakh zhenshchinam o zhenshchinakh: Vypusk 1). London: Sheba Feminist, 1980.

Natasha Kolchevska

Women in the Communist Party of the Soviet Union (CPSU) (1922–1991)

Although the USSR proclaimed the equality of men and women, its leading organization, the CPSU, was evidence of the fact that women were not fully represented in all organs of power. Only three women ever sat on the Politburo, and until 1990 women never exceeded 30 percent of the Party's membership.

To some extent, the story of women's progress in the CPSU may be viewed as a barometer of women's progress in Soviet society. From the formation of the USSR in 1922 and before that in the RSDLP/B and the RKP/B, women's participation in the CPSU never equaled that of men. Nevertheless, the number of women did increase over the years. At the time the USSR was formed, women constituted approximately 10 percent of the Party's membership. At the time the USSR was dissolved at the end of 1991, women members made up 33 percent of CPSU membership. In the post-Stalin era, the number of women averaged 25 percent; the official explanation of the imbalance was usually that domestic and family responsibilities prevented women from participating fully in Party life.

In the USSR membership in the CPSU gave one access to political and economic upward mobility possible through no other route in Soviet society, except for a few members of the intelligentsia, such as scientists, writers, musicians, and dancers of international note. The Soviet leadership closed off other paths to political and economic success by consolidating the major positions in society into the *nomenklatura*. The term *nomenklatura* referred to a list of positions in the political and economic sphere filled primarily by CPSU members. To become part of the *nomenklatura* signified that one had achieved considerable success and that, barring a serious political error, a life of comfort and continued success lay ahead. The fact that women were a minority in the CPSU made it difficult for them to achieve the highest-level positions in any profession. At various Party congresses the post-Stalin leaders—N. S. Khrushchev, L. I. Brezhnev, and M. S. Gorbachev—argued that more women should be recruited into the Party and should be promoted to important positions. However, the number of women in the CPSU reached a high of 33 percent only in 1990, at a time when Party membership had declining significance in the changing political climate of the USSR.

In the early days of the Russian revolutionary movement, some women activists occupied important positions within the movement. After the Bolsheviks came to power in 1917, only Aleksandra Kollontai became part of V. I. Lenin's new government. She was appointed as commissar (i.e., minister) of social welfare in the *Sovnarkom* (Council of People's Commissars, later renamed the Council of Ministers), but her appointment was brief. Prior to the October Revolution, Elena Stasova had served as secretary of the Central Committee of Lenin's Bolshevik faction; after the revolution, she worked in the Secretariat of the Party and briefly served as one of several secretaries of the Secretariat. She was never seriously considered for the top position of General Secretary, established in 1919 and redefined after 1922, when Stalin assumed the position. The position of General Secretary was created after the death of Iakob Sverdlov, when the expanding administrative responsibilities of the Secretariat mandated a more formal structure.

In the 1920s, as the USSR was consolidating, a number of prominent women were assigned to work in *Zhenotdel* (the Women's Department of the CPSU). Although the work of *Zhenotdel* was important, it was not a position from which one was likely to be appointed to high political office. Stasova even refused to become involved in *Zhenotdel*, preferring to be part of the Secretariat instead. A few women were on the Central Committee of the CPSU in the 1920s and 1930s, but once Stalin consolidated his power in the later 1920s and 1930s, there were fewer women in major positions. Even after the Purges of the Party (1935–1938), in which many men in high positions perished, or in the post–

World War II era, in which the USSR faced a shortage of men, few women rose to high positions.

In the post-Stalin era, opportunities for women increased in the Party and in society generally. During the Khrushchev years, Ekaterina Furtseva was appointed minister of culture and became the first woman on the Council of Ministers since Kollontai. She also served in the Secretariat and was the first woman to serve on the Politburo.

After Khrushchev, there was a long hiatus before another woman was appointed to the Politburo. In the 1980s Aleksandra Biriukova, who had risen to a leading position in the state trade union structure, became a member of the Party Secretariat under Gorbachev and in 1988 a candidate member of the Politburo. She stepped down at the tumultuous Twenty-eighth Party Congress in 1990, at which numerous prominent officials resigned from their positions, and some, most notably Boris Yeltsin, left the Party. In the larger and less powerful reconstituted Politburo that emerged from the Twenty-eighth Party Congress, Galina Semënova, a well-known journalist, became a member of the Politburo. Her work focused on women's issues, but her appointment lasted only a year, as the CPSU and the Politburo were swept away by the events of August 1991 and the tumultuous collapse of the USSR in December.

The post-Stalin leadership of the CPSU gave mixed messages to women aspiring to be active in the CPSU. Although they gave speeches encouraging women, few changes occurred in Soviet society to facilitate women's entry into Party activism. Apart from speeches, there was little effort to raise consciousness about women's double and triple burdens or to alleviate the situation, all of which made it impossible for women to take on additional responsibilities besides their jobs and their families. The USSR officially distanced itself from Western developments of the 1960s and 1970s, which sought to modify traditional attitudes toward women. Bourgeois feminism was viewed with disdain in the USSR. Gorbachev, whose wife, Raisa Gorbacheva, had continued her professional career until he became General Secretary, was more attuned to women's aspirations than his predecessors, but even he gave mixed signals to women. On the one hand, he placed two women successively on the Politburo, increased the number of women on the Central Committee, and succeeded in recruiting more women into the Party; however, he also talked of returning women to their natural place as mothers and homemakers. Gorbachev's messages about women's natural roles may have had an impact on political developments in the final years of the USSR and later. For example, in the Supreme Soviet (the Soviet parliament), as it existed until 1988, there were no competitive elections; one candidate ran per electoral district. There was a strict quota for the number of women, non-Russians, workers, and so on to be represented in the Supreme Soviet. Approximately one-third of the Supreme Soviet deputies were women. In the reconstituted parliament of 1989, seventy-five seats were allocated for the Soviet Women's Committee in the one-third of the Congress of People's Deputies representing public organizations. The number of women fell from about one-third to 15.7 percent in the new Congress of People's Deputies. Women like Galina Starovoitova, who emerged as leaders in the new Congress of People's Deputies and in its smaller standing body, the Supreme Soviet, were exceptional and owed their victory to their achievements in public life.

The activities of the women in the CPSU tended to be centered on the primary Party organization in the workplace or on the district and local Party organizations; relatively few women were prominent in the all-union CPSU. Women constituted less than 5 percent of the Central Committee (CC) of the CPSU in the post-Stalin era, and many were elected for only one term. It was not uncommon to find a woman factory worker from Central Asia on the CC, thus satisfying three underrepresented groups: women, workers, and ethnic minorities. Of the continuing members of the Central Committee, few were women. Apart from the prominent women mentioned earlier, Valentina Tereshkova, the first woman in space and later head of the Soviet Women's Committee, was one of few women to occupy a perennial seat on the Central Committee. At the Twenty-eighth Party Congress in 1990, thirty-one women were elected to the Central Committee out of 307 full and 105 candidate members, the highest number ever, but the Party itself was rapidly losing ground in the society.

On balance, women in the CPSU were never a major political force; women's participation in the Party cannot really be viewed as a vehicle for a women's movement, except for *Zhenotdel* in the 1920s. At the highest levels, there was briefly heightened attention to women's issues in the declining days of the USSR, but the Soviet Union collapsed before there were concrete results.

Cross-references: Aleksandra Kollontai, Soviet Women's Committee (SWC), Galina Starovoitova, Elena Stasova, *Zhenotdel*.

Suggested Readings

Brown, Archie, ed. *The Soviet Union: A Biographical Dictionary*. London: Weidenfeld and Nicolson, 1990.

Buckley, Mary, ed. *Perestroika and Soviet Women*. Cambridge: Cambridge University Press, 1992.

Buckley, Mary. *Women and Ideology in the Soviet Union*. Ann Arbor: University of Michigan Press, 1989.

Lapidus, Gail. *Women in Soviet Society*. Berkeley: University of California Press, 1978.

Nechemias, Carol. "Democratization and Women's Access to Legislative Seats: The Soviet Case, 1989–91." *Women and Politics* 14, no. 3 (1994): 1–18.

Noonan, Norma C. "Women in the Communist Party of the Soviet Union." In *Modern Encyclopedia of Russian and Soviet History*, edited by Joseph L. Wieczynski, vol. 55, 10–14. Gulf Breeze, FL: Academic International Press, 1993.

Rule, Wilma, and Norma C. Noonan, eds. *Russian Women in Politics and Society*. Westport, CT: Greenwood Publishing Group, 1996.

Smith, Gordon. *Soviet Politics: Struggling with Change*. 2d ed. New York: St. Martin's Press, 1992.

Norma Corigliano Noonan

Z

Zetkin, Klara Eissner (1857–1933)

A German revolutionary and women's advocate who cooperated with the Russian revolutionary movement and was credited with the establishment of International Women's Day. After the Bolshevik Revolution, she became a Comintern official.

In the history of the Russian revolutions, several notable foreigners became identified with Russia and its causes. Klara Zetkin was one of them. Although German by birth and active in the German Social Democratic Party, Klara Zetkin is perhaps best known for her work in the Russian revolutionary movement and in the Comintern.

Klara Eissner was born in Widerau, Germany, on May 7, 1857. Her father was a teacher, and her mother was a feminist. Klara studied at a teacher's institute in Leipzig (1874–1878) and after graduation worked as a tutor and governess. She found friendships among the socialist community in Leipzig and through them met Osip Zetkin (1848–1889), a Marxist revolutionary from the Russian Empire. Zetkin became both her lover and her mentor. Both were active in the German Social Democratic Party (SDP). The party was declared illegal in 1879, and Zetkin was expelled from the country in 1880. Klara followed him to Zurich and then Paris. Although the two never officially married, Klara adopted his name, bore him two sons, and later nursed him through his final illness. Both Klara and Osip contracted tuberculosis during the 1880s, and it proved fatal for Osip. She remained faithful to his memory and adopted his country and its causes as her own.

During her years in Paris in the 1880s, Klara began to cooperate with Karl Marx's daughter, Laura LaFargue, to assist women workers. Zetkin was strongly influenced by the theories of August Bebel concerning women, especially his book, *Women and Socialism*. She began to speak out on woman's rights within the context of socialism. She argued that the cause of revolution could progress more quickly if women participated, and, therefore, it was incumbent on the socialist movement to attract women and serve women's interests. Her argument differed from that of other feminists, who tended to argue that women needed special attention from the movement, without emphasizing the value of women to the movement. Adding to Zetkin's cachet was the fact that she was acquainted with Friedrich Engels during the last years of his life, when he, too, addressed women's issues.

After Zetkin's death, Klara moved back to Germany and worked as editor of *Die Gleichheit (Equality)*, a newspaper for socialist women (1892–1917). Active in the international socialist movement, she help to organize the First International Socialist Women's Congress (1907). Three years later, at another International Conference of Socialist Women, she introduced the motion that March 8 be recognized as International Women's Day. Her motion carried, and the women's holiday was born.

Although a recognized socialist feminist, Zetkin stood aloof from what the Marxists called "bourgeois feminism," which sought reform, rather than revolution. A Marxist with internationally recognized credentials and acquaintances, she understood women's issues in the context of socialist concerns. Nonetheless, her commitment to women may have hurt her with other SDP members, and, prior to World War I, she never obtained a seat on the SDP Executive Committee, which she had wanted for many years. Unlike some of the other German Marxists, Klara Zetkin opposed World War I and eventually lost her editorship of *Die Gleichheit* because of her position against the war.

Klara was acquainted with V. I. Lenin and supported the Bolshevik Revolution and Lenin's establishment of a new Communist International (the Comintern). After World War I, she joined the new German Communist Party (KDP) and became active in the Comintern. She was elected to the German Reichstag in 1920 and reelected until her death, even though she resided in Russia most of the time. In 1920 she also became secretary of the International Women's Secretariat of the Comintern.

Although Zetkin had many achievements in her life, one of the most famous was her conversation with Lenin on women's issues in 1920, which remains one of the more complete and precise statements of Lenin's views on women and gives a snapshot of his views on Soviet policy toward women. Her friendship with Lenin and his wife, Nadezhda Krupskaia, was no doubt a factor in her decision to reside in Russia and devote her efforts to the Comintern. Zetkin's influence somewhat declined after Lenin's death. The new leaders were less internationalist and, particularly in the case of Stalin, less impressed with foreign communists, who had extensive international ties. Her health was failing, but she continued to work. In 1932 she returned briefly to Germany to open the Reichstag as honorary president, because she was its oldest member. She returned to Moscow, where she died in 1933.

Cross-reference: Nadezhda Krupskaia.

Suggested Readings

Foner, Philip S., ed. *Clara Zetkin: Selected Writings*. New York: International, 1984.

Lenin, V. I. *The Emancipation of Women*. (Appendix, "Lenin on the Women Question, by Klara Zetkin.) New York: International, 1966.

Noonan, Norma C. "Clara Eissner Zetkin." In *Modern Encyclopedia of Russian and Soviet History*, edited by Joseph L. Wieczynski, vol. 46, 23–26. Gulf Breeze, FL: Academic International Press, 1987.

Stites, Richard. *The Women's Liberation Movement in Russia.* Princeton, NJ: Princeton University Press, 1978, 1991.

Norma Corigliano Noonan

Zhenotdel (Women's Department of the Communist Party) (1919–1930)

The Women's Department of the Communist Party, established by V. I. Lenin in 1919 and eliminated by J. V. Stalin in 1930. During its years of operation, *Zhenotdel* helped to develop social policies affecting women and children, helped women with the transition to modern life, and recruited women into the Communist Party.

After the Bolshevik Revolution in 1917, Lenin's government declared that women were equal under the law. The declaration did not guarantee women's equality, and it was clear that considerable work was necessary to train women to work in the new society, reconcile women to the new political system, and assist women and families in the difficult economic and health situation. All of these areas were subsumed under the rubric of the "woman question," the favorite socialist term for women's issues. At the time of the revolution, more than 80 percent of the women were illiterate, and few either understood or were sympathetic to the goals of the new regime.

The Russian Social Democratic Labor Party (RSDLP), out of which Lenin's Bolshevik movement had emerged, had always taken the position that revolution would free all oppressed groups, including women. Women like Aleksandra Kollontai and others in the movement had advocated a movement of socialist women, but the Party's leaders, including Lenin, remained resolute in the belief that there should not be a separate women's organization. After the Congress of Women Workers and Peasants in November 1918, it became clear that the Soviet leadership had to address women's issues and respond to women's demands for a greater role in the Soviet system. In 1919 *Zhenotdel* was created as a department within the Russian Communist Party/Bolsheviks (RCP/B), later called the Communist Party of the Soviet Union (CPSU), and Lenin appointed Inessa Armand as its first head.

From the perspective of the Party, *Zhenotdel*'s primary goal was the recruitment of women and political socialization of women so that they could adapt to life in the new order. From the perspective of women working in *Zhenotdel*, helping women to cope with the problems of the new society and developing social policies to help women and children were also important goals. Tension between the Party leadership and the women who ran *Zhenotdel* persisted throughout its history, even though its top leaders were prominent Party members and several served on the Central Committee of the CPSU. The Party was not sympathetic when the department complained about the behavior of Party or Komsomol members toward women and was impatient when *Zhenotdel* demanded more social services for poor women, especially single mothers and their children. The women administrators did as much as possible for women but met continual resistance from the male leadership of the Communist Party.

Zhenotdel focused on women as mothers and workers, in keeping with the basic Bolshevik approach to women. The first head, Inessa Armand, worked in *Zhenotdel* only a year before she died of cholera. Aleksandra Kollontai became the leader of *Zhenotdel* in 1920 and aggressively pursued policies to benefit women until her dismissal in 1922. During the next eight years, three prominent women headed *Zhenotdel*: Sofia Smidovich, Klavdiia Nikolaeva, and Aleksandra Artiukhina. Perhaps the most effective leader was Aleksandra Artiukhina, but even her efforts were not enough to save the department. The latter three had a lower public profile than Armand and Kollontai, although each had a long history in the revolutionary movement and the Communist Party. Unlike Kollontai and Armand, Nikolaeva and Artiukhina had a working-class background and could relate personally to the hardships that women faced.

Although numerous prominent Bolshevik women were involved in *Zhenotdel*'s work, to some degree, a few well-known women chose not to associate with the department, because they feared that their role in the Party would be compromised. Perhaps the most famous of these was Elena Stasova, who consciously refused to be involved with *Zhenotdel*, even after she was dismissed from the Secretariat of the Communist Party. Even Nadezhda Krupskaia, Lenin's wife, had an advisory role in *Zhenotdel*, no doubt because of her early writings on the "woman question" and perhaps to be Lenin's eyes and ears within this department, which from its earliest days met with suspicion from the male leadership of the Party.

Zhenotdel's local affiliates, called *Zhenotdely*, tried to reach out into the regions of the newly created Soviet Union. There was also a training program for recruiting and training women to work in the regions. The trainees, called *delegatki* (delegates), were assigned to local areas to train others to work with women. In Muslim areas, such as Central Asia, which were incorporated into the Soviet Union with difficulty, *Zhenotdel* met particular resistance, and a number of *Zhenotdel* workers perished in their work. Local women who attended *Zhenotdel* meetings, even though they were called women's "clubs" in the remote areas, were often beaten by their husbands or worse.

During its decade-long existence, the goals of recruitment and socialization of women were never far from the center of *Zhenotdel*'s work, but the department also developed programs to assist women and served as an advocate for women's interests. *Zhenotdel* tried to improve health care services for women and children, develop day-care facilities for working mothers, and address issues of discrimination in the workplace. Included under *Zhenotdel*'s purview was the publication of several journals for women, including *Rabotnitsa (Working Woman)*, *Krestianka (Peasant Woman)*, and *Kommunistka (Communist Woman)*. *Rabotnitsa* and *Krestianka*, which had roots in the revolutionary movement, continued to be the primary women's magazines throughout the entire Soviet era.

Stalin terminated *Zhenotdel* as a national organization in 1930 and declared that the woman question had been solved. This was far from the truth. The rationale for disbanding *Zhenotdel* was never fully explained, but there were several plausible and possible reasons. In the program for rapid industrial growth initiated by Stalin's First Five-Year Plan in 1929, there was little interest in developing special social and health services for women; all resources had to be directed toward industrial growth. Second, by 1930 society had acquiesced to Soviet rule, so special socialization campaigns for women did not appear necessary. Furthermore, some Party leaders had for years believed that *Zhenotdel* was unnecessary and that no practical benefits could be derived from the department. Stalin himself had never been a supporter of *Zhenotdel*, which perhaps finally sealed its fate. Nonetheless, after 1930 *Zhenotdel*'s work continued in Central Asia and other areas where traditional cultures prevented women from playing an active role in Soviet society.

In the seventy-four years of the Soviet regime, *Zhenotdel* was the most concerted attempt to have a special agency dedicated to the problems of women. The *Zhensovety* introduced by N. S. Khrushchev in the 1950s adopted a few of *Zhenotdel*'s functions but were limited in their scope.

Cross-references: Inessa Armand, Aleksandra Artiukhina, Family Protection and Women's Well-Being, Aleksandra M. Kollontai, Nadezhda Krupskaia, Legal Equality in the 1920s, Soviet Women's Committee, *Zhensovety, Zhensovety* in the Soviet Army.

Suggested Readings

Clements, Barbara E. *Bolshevik Feminist*. Bloomington: Indiana University Press, 1979.

Clements, Barbara E. *Bolshevik Women*. Cambridge: Cambridge University Press, 1997.

Farnsworth, Beatrice. *Aleksandra Kollontai: Socialism, Feminism, and the Bolshevik Revolution*. Stanford, CA: Stanford University Press, 1980.

Hayden, Carol Eubanks. "*Zhenotdel* and the Bolshevik Party." *Russian History* 3, no. 2 (1976): 150–173.

Lenin, V. I. *The Emancipation of Women*. New York: International, 1966.

Noonan, Norma C. "Two Solutions to the Zhenskii Vopros in Russia and the USSR—Kollontai and Krupskaia: A Comparison." *Women and Politics* 11, no. 3 (1991): 77–99.

Stites, Richard. *The Women's Liberation Movement in Russia: Feminism, Nihilism and Bolshevism, 1860–1930*. Princeton: Princeton University Press, 1978, 1991.

Norma Corigliano Noonan

Zhensovety (*Zhenskie sovety*, or Women's Councils) (1958–ca. 1991)

Women's local organizations created during the Khrushchev period that attempted to address some women's issues, particularly those identified by the government and Communist Party of the Soviet Union (CPSU).

During the Soviet period, the CPSU established and sometimes abolished women's movements in order to mobilize women in support of the state and to encourage them to fulfill the need for women as workers or women as mothers; the *zhensovety* (women's councils) were a notable example of an official women's movement in the late Soviet era. Nikita S. Khrushchev advocated the creation of the *zhensovety* as part of his new approach to politics, which included a broadly defined program for building communism. The establishment of the new women's organizations in 1958 was justified by the fact that other groups targeted specific segments of the population, such as youth and pensioners. The *zhensovety* were created at the oblast, *krai*, and *raion* levels of administration as well as in factories, offices, and farms. In the late 1950s and 1960s, the goals of the *zhensovety* varied by region and perceived need. *Zhensovety* were created to ensure that every woman consciously participated in the creative work of the people and that Marxist–Leninist ideas reached every institution. *Zhensovety* were supposed to encourage women to become politically active and, if they were still housewives, to coax them into the workforce. In some cases, the *zhensovety* were an attempt to understand the life circumstances of each working woman, her interests and her desires.

During the Brezhnev era, the *zhensovety* faded into virtual oblivion. During Perestroika, they were again revived. Mikhail S. Gorbachev envisioned a contradictory role for women. On the one hand, he advocated that women should return to their womanly mission of housework, child care, and homemaking. On the other hand, he advocated that women should achieve a higher profile in public life. According to Gorbachev, the *zhensovety* could contribute to the latter goal. In 1986 the Twenty-seventh CPSU Congress decided to resurrect the *zhensovety*, which were placed under the auspices of the Soviet Women's Committee (SWC), to galvanize support for Perestroika at the local level. To some extent, during Perestroika the CPSU lost some control over social organizations, such as the *zhensovety* and the SWC at the national and local levels.

Although the *zhensovety* and SWC were officially approved organizations, they began to reject the supervision of the corresponding local CPSU committees. By the late 1980s almost 250,000 *zhensovety* existed in most, but not all, of the Soviet republics.

Under the auspices of a new chairwoman of the SWC, Zoia Pukhova, the *zhensovety* hoped to gain greater visibility by criticizing the Soviet system and the status of women within it. The *zhensovety* drew attention to women's working conditions, such as the lack of safety regulations and long hours, as well as the likelihood of high levels of female unemployment as a result of the proposed economic reforms. Despite their new approach, the feminist groups that emerged during Perestroika viewed both the *zhensovety* and the SWC with suspicion since they were official organizations sponsored and supported by the state. The *zhensovety* and SWC were accused of being antidemocratic, of harboring the *nomenklatura*, and of failing to challenge the role of women as subjects, rather than agents, of political change. By 1991, however, the new leader of the SWC,

Alevtina Fedulova, threatened to go into "constructive opposition" if legislative initiatives on women's and children's issues were not considered by government organs. In addition, the SWC, which was reorganized as the Women's Union of Russia (WUR) in 1991, began to prepare women for political office in an attempt to counter the decline in female political participation that accompanied the economic and political reforms. In October 1993, following Boris Yeltsin's dissolution of the Supreme Soviet and Congress of People's Deputies, the electoral bloc *Zhenshchiny Rossii* (Women of Russia) was established in preparation for the parliamentary elections in December 1993. The electoral bloc, which also registered itself as a political movement, was formed by the alliance of three women's organizations, including the Women's Union of Russia.

Although the *zhensovety* were a Soviet institution, they continued to exist in various forms into the post-Soviet era and contributed to the strength of the Women of Russia movement.

Cross-references: Alevtina Fedulova, Soviet Women's Committee (SWC), Women of Russia (WOR), Women's Union of Russia (WUR), *Zhensovety* in the Soviet Army.

Suggested Readings

Browning, Genia K. *Women and Politics in the USSR: Consciousness Raising and Soviet Women's Groups*. New York: St. Martin's Press, 1987.

Buckley, Mary. *Women and Ideology in the Soviet Union*. Ann Arbor: University of Michigan Press, 1989.

Heitlinger, Alena. *Women and State Socialism: Sex Inequality in the Soviet Union and Czechoslovakia*. Montreal: McGill-Queen's University Press, 1979.

Muzyria, A. A., and V. V. Kopeiko. *Zhensovet: opyt, problemy, perspektivy (The Zhensovet: Experience, Problems, Prospects)*. Moscow: Politizdat, 1989.

Waters, Elizabeth. "Finding a Voice: The Emergence of a Women's Movement." In *Gender Politics and Post-Communism: Reflections from Eastern Europe and the Former Soviet Union*, edited by Nanette Funk and Magda Mueller, 287–302. New York: Routledge, 1993.

Cheri C. Wilson

Zhensovety (Women's Councils) in the Soviet Army (ca. 1960–1991)

The *zhensovety* (Women's Councils) played a special role in the Soviet army in the period from 1960 through the 1980s, when troops and their families were dispersed to military bases in remote parts of the USSR. This role ended with the demise of the Soviet Union, but the activism of the *zhensovety* helped to pave the way for the women's movement in the post-Soviet era.

At the end of the 1950s and early 1960s, when the USSR was developing its rocket program, some major changes occurred in the deployment of military personnel within the country. Prior to this period, the majority of military personnel were concentrated in bases on the borders and in the large centers of the Russian Republic, although some troops were on bases in small military communities in the republics. The Khrushchev administration decided that the new bases and military garrisons, where strategic weapons were placed, should be located far from urban centers.

Military men were sent to these centers with their families for long-term assignments. Small military cities, both old and new, were self-contained, with kindergartens, schools, shops, clubs, and the *Dom* (House) of the Officers. Local people, the wives of officers, and people in the lowest ranks of the Soviet army staffed these services.

Life for women in these isolated and self-contained centers was difficult and complex. Housing was not always available, especially when families first arrived. The jobs were not satisfactory. Husbands were often away on assignment for weeks at a time, leaving the women alone in an isolated area. The women had to spend a lot of time with one another, and friction frequently developed among the women or between the women and their husbands.

To address these problems, the Political Administration of the Ministry of Defense of the USSR decided to establish *zhensovety* on the military bases, staffed by special instructors. They developed work plans for the wives residing in the military centers. The plans included lecture series and discussion groups on Marxist–Leninist topics and the creation of sewing, knitting, reading, musical, and drama circles. There were also programs for the children.

In addition to providing programs, the *zhensovety* supervised the condition of apartments, the education of the children, and the relationship between spouses. The *zhensovety* promoted the interests of women living on the bases. The bases were a microworld in which people lived for years without leaving the center. The only hope of escape was the transfer or promotion of their husbands to another post or center.

The *zhensovety* performed a valuable role on the military bases until the late 1980s, when the USSR began to unravel. They helped to make life on the bases livable and also tried to protect the interests of the women living with their husbands in these isolated conditions.

Cross-reference: Zhensovety.

Elvira Ershova

PART III

WOMEN'S MOVEMENTS IN THE TRANSITIONAL AND POST-SOVIET ERAS, 1985–

The transitional period in modern Russia, which began with *Perestroika* in 1985 in the Soviet Union and continued in the independent Russian Federation after 1991, has been a tumultuous era by any measure. On the one hand, it opened opportunities for women to form associations and movements never before possible in their history. On the other hand, the transition took a harsh toll on the entire population, most especially on women. The new conditions created by glasnost and *Perestroika* and their aftermath allowed women to form and develop new organizations outside the strict control of the CPSU. At the same time, restructuring hit women hard, as social policies designed to aid women to combine work and motherhood eroded and as the ideological framework that women belong primarily at home gained ground. Women disproportionately made up the unemployed and suffered discrimination in a workplace that perceived men as more performance-oriented. The mass media turned women into sex objects, and there was an explosion of sexually explicit material in Russian society. On the political front women's representation in the State Duma has declined with each of the elections held since 1993, and few women served in high-level executive positions in the 1990s.

Despite these setbacks, women demonstrated increased activism by creating new women's organizations. In the final decades of communist rule the Soviet state provided two avenues for women's activism: the *zhensovety* (women's councils) and the *Komitet Sovetskikh zhenshchin* (Soviet Women's Committee). By 1998 about 600 independent, nongovernmental women's organizations had registered with the Russian Ministry of Justice, but the number of women's organizations, registered and unregistered, was estimated at close to 2,000. While many of these organizations were no longer active, there nonetheless emerged a rich diversity of social, cultural, and political activity aimed at promoting women's interests and changing women's status. Networking activities increased with the formation and development of new women's organizations, providing clear evidence that a new phenomenon was emerging, an independent women's movement.

Women's organizations addressed a wide array of issues. Many groups focused on legal issues and social rights and provided expert advice or support in areas related to women's social benefits and the rights of army recruits. The widespread *Komitety soldatskikh materei Rossii* (Committees of Soldiers' Mothers of Russia) fall into this category. Other organizations developed educational programs ranging from schools of leadership for women, to summer schools for gender studies and women's studies. Another important focus involved providing information to women throughout the country; a number of organizations included among their activities serving as resource centers to distribute information through publications and electronic mail. Many groups formed as a response to economic distress and sought to alleviate problems of poverty, especially among single mothers, who were raising children without the state subsidies of the past.

Regional and national organizations of women entrepreneurs emerged as market reform opened up opportunities for private enterprise. The variety of women's organizations included crisis centers, organizations for women with disabilities, women journalists, and rural women, and environmental groups. Although few women's groups participated in elections or political campaigning, the experience of *Zhenshchiny Rossii* (Women of Russia, or WOR) in directly contesting the 1993, 1995, and 1999 elections to the State Duma is a noteworthy exception.

Several women's organizations have included regional networks or were themselves networks. The *Soiuz zhenshchin Rossii* (Women's Union of Russia), the successor of the *Komitet Sovetskikh zhenshchin* (Committee of Soviet Women) and the primary constituent unit of WOR, has worked in several policy areas and had many regional and local affiliates based largely on the *zhensovety*. Independent women's organizations, which participated in the *Pervyi nezavisimyi zhenskii forum* (First Independent Women's Forum) in Dubna in 1991, formed a network that evolved into the *Informatsionnyi tsentr nezavisimogo zhenskogo foruma* (Information Center of the Independent Women's Forum), while the *Konsortsium zhenskikh nepravitel'stvennykh ob"edinenii* (Consortium of Women's Nongovernmental Associations) included ninety-one groups in 1998. In 1996 the *Obshcherossiiskoe obshchestvenno-politicheskoe dvizhenie zhenshchin Rossii* (the All-Russian Sociopolitical Movement of Women of Russia) broke off from WOR and created many regional branches. Divisions among women's organizations with respect to ideology and concerns over hierarchical control often prevented joint action and the consolidation of the women's movement. Nevertheless, the first fifteen years of the transition were characterized by an impressive development of women's organizations and movements.

The growth of women's organizations did not take place in a vacuum. Many women's groups, particularly those with a more feminist orientation, participated in the international women's movement, received funding from foreign governments and foundations, and introduced new words and expressions into the Russian language like "gender," "woman's rights are human rights," "equal opportunity," and "women's studies." International contacts spurred the development of a wide array of organizations across diverse groups of women like police officers, the disabled, journalists, entrepreneurs, and scholars. While foreign assistance provided crucial financial support, there has been a concern that the predominance of U.S. funding privileged English-speaking elements of the women's movement and that competitive grants fostered divisiveness rather than consolidation among women's groups eager to secure funding.

The international arena buttressed the efforts of Russian women activists by legitimating attention to women's issues. Women's groups and the Russian government look to United Nations documents like the ILO (International Labor Organization) Convention on Workers with Family Obligations and the UN Convention on the Elimination of All Forms of Discrimination against Women (CEDAW) to identify appropriate standards regarding women's status. International conferences like the United Nations' (UN) Fourth World Conference on Women, held in Beijing in 1995, also stimulated preparatory work and strategizing by both nongovernmental women's organizations and government agencies. The Russian government created the *Kommissia po uluchsheniiu polozheniia zhenshchin* (Commission on Improving the Status of Women) in 1997 to develop measures that would meet international standards, such as those contained with CEDAW. CEDAW also was cited in the introduction to the *Kontseptsiia zakonotvorcheskoi deiatel'nosti po obespecheniiu ravnykh prav i ravnykh vozmozhnostei muzhchin i zhenshchin* (Conception on Legislative Activity to Secure Equal Rights and Equal Opportunity for Men and Women), an important framework for legislative action to promote women's equality proposed by the State Duma's Committee on Women, Family, and Youth and passed by the State Duma in November 1997. International organizations and documents thus assisted Russian women activists and government officials committed to using state power to move society toward greater gender equality.

Traditionally, however, the Russian state has shown greater commitment to declarative statements than to action when questions of women's equality arose. Many women's groups lobbied government to take a more activist stance vis-à-vis issues like women's unemployment, poverty among single mothers, violence against women, the lack of modern contraceptives, and discrimination against women in the workplace. Yet there was a new attitude toward state power and the relationship between women and the state exhibited by many women's groups, particularly those of a feminist bent.

There have been warnings about dependence and against reliance on the state. Thus, women's groups have called on women to demonstrate initiative, to determine their own role in society rather than let the state define "women's place." While both men and women were mobilized in the past in accordance with state objectives, women, especially, have voiced concern over a patriarchal state that often categorized them as a problematic group, like invalids and children, in need of state protection. Women's organizations were divided as to whether "privileges" or welfare benefits targeting on mothers and women should be maintained, since they relegated women to second-class status in the emerging market economy and reinforced traditional divisions of labor between men and women. The contemporary Russian women's movement sought to enlarge women's identity, to define women not solely in terms of motherhood but as individual citizens possessing the right to self-fulfillment, to a full array of opportunities in Russia's economic, cultural, and political life.

The contemporary women's movement chose to link itself with past Russian women's movements when leaders from seventy-four women's organizations, scholars, journalists, political figures, and representatives from foundations, gathered in Moscow on December 9–10, 1998, to mark the ninetieth anniversary of the *Pervyi vserossiiskii zhenskii S"ezd* (First All-Russian Women's Congress), held in St. Petersburg in December 1908. The meeting was organized by the *Konsortsium zhenskikh nepravitel'stvennykh ob"edinenii* (Consortium of Women's Nongovernmental Associations) and other women's groups. It was the first time during the course of ninety years that the anniversary was recognized and honored. The program centered on a series of jubilee readings that included, along with an exhibit of materials from the History Museum, information about the First All-Russian Women's Congress. Women activists took steps toward recovering their past by celebrating a history long ignored by specialists in their own country. The contemporary women's movement thus placed itself within the historical context of Russian feminist traditions and within past as well as ongoing efforts to achieve democratization.

A

Academic Feminism in St. Petersburg (1985–)

Several centers for gender research and the first comprehensive graduate program in gender studies in Russia were established in St. Petersburg. Together with Moscow, St. Petersburg has led the development of academic feminism in Russia.

The rebirth of Russian feminism in the 1980s and 1990s had a strong academic component. The second wave of feminism developed simultaneously in women's groups and in academe. In St. Petersburg (Leningrad until 1991) academic feminism quickly created new institutions. The interaction between women's movements and feminist research followed three steps. First, some women scholars became interested in feminist activism. Second, new centers for gender research emerged. Third, gender research was integrated into programs of higher education.

In the first stage, the establishment of the *Peterburgskii tsentr gendernykh problem* (St. Petersburg Center for Gender Issues, or PCGI) in 1992 influenced several scholars. Although PCGI's profile was not primarily academic, the Center organized lecture series, ran a small library, and coordinated meetings for feminist scholars from throughout Russia. Some St. Petersburg scholars were enticed to combine research with involvement in the women's movement. For instance, historian Irina Yukina (Iukina) worked at PCGI and wrote a history of the Russian women's movement. Psychologist Natal'ia Khodyreva and sociologist Natal'ia Zabadykina founded the Psychological Crisis Center for Women, while continuing to lecture and write about women's issues. Khodyreva also conducted seminars with women's collective memory work based on a research method developed in Germany by the feminist scholar Frigga Haug.

In the next stage, gender research entered academia. Grigorii Tishkin, professor of history at the Academy of Culture in St. Petersburg, organized a series of international conferences about women and culture. Several centers of gender research emerged in the mid-1990s. Among them were the Center for the Integration of Women's Studies, coordinated by Dr. Tatiana Gerasimova, and the

St. Petersburg Scientific Center, Women and Russia, headed by Dr. Valentina Ushakova; both programs were at St. Petersburg State University. The St. Petersburg Institute of Sociology founded a Section for Family and Gender Research. Headed by Dr. Sergei Golod, this section specialized in research on sexuality; for example, Dr. Aleksandr Klëtsin conducted one of the first empirical studies of sexual harassment in the Russian workplace. A Center for Independent Social Research, founded in 1993, had a group focusing on gender research coordinated by Dr. Elena Zdravomyslova. The group actively recruited younger scholars into women's and men's studies.

There were significant differences in the ideological orientation and scholarly productivity among the new research centers. Their degree of integration into the international academic or feminist communities also varied. Some research centers distanced themselves from Western feminism by talking about the science of "feminology," which emphasized women's historical role in Russia and their place in contemporary Russian society. Others saw themselves as part of the international women's movement. From its earliest days, academic feminism in St. Petersburg also tended to emphasize the importance of including men's studies in gender research.

In the mid-1990s, gender studies started to become integrated into higher education. For example, in 1996, a gender studies program for graduate students was launched by sociology faculty at the new European University of St. Petersburg. The three-year graduate program, coordinated by Dr. Anna Temkina and Dr. Elena Zdravomyslova, was the first of its kind in Russia. It featured courses on the gender dimension of classical social theory, Russian gender culture, qualitative methods, and feminist social theory. The program also provided courses in Russian gender culture for foreign students. Another program initiated in 1995, the *Zhenskii gumanitarnyi kollegium* (Women's Humanitarian Collegium), was affiliated with the Nevskii Institute and headed by Galina Fortunatova. The Collegium focused on scholarly conferences and discussions, with the goal of disseminating their findings in publications.

During the 1990s academic feminism in St. Petersburg was institutionalized. It became clearly distinguished from feminist activism, although cooperation and the exchange of ideas continued.

Cross-references: Feminism in Post-Soviet Russia, Gender/Women's Studies in Russia, Ol'ga Lipovskaia, St. Petersburg Center of Gender Issues (PCGI), The Scientific Center "Woman and Russia," Anna Andrianovna Temkina, Women's Humanitarian Collegium, Elena Andreevna Zdravomyslova.

Suggested Readings

Golod, Sergei. *XX vek i tendentsii seksualnykh otnoshenii v Rossii (The 20th Century and Sexual Relations in Russia)*. St. Petersburg: Aleteia, 1996.

Khodyreva, Natal'ia. "Sexism and Sexual Abuse in Russia." In *Women in a Violent World*, edited by Chris Corrin, 27–40. Edinburgh: Edinburgh University Press, 1996.

Klëtsin, Aleksandr, ed. *Gendernye tetradi (Current Gender Research)*. St. Petersburg: Publications of the St. Petersburg Institute of Sociology, Russian Academy of Sciences, 1997.

Temkina, Anna, and Elena Zdravomyslova, eds. *Gendernoe izmerenie sotsial'noi i politicheskoi aktivnosti v perekhodnyi period (Gender Dimension of Social and Political Activity in the Transitional Period)*. St. Petersburg: Center for Independent Social Research, 1996.

Tishkin, Grigorii A., ed. *Feminizm i russkaia kul'tura. Sbornik trudov (Feminism and Russian Culture: A Collection of Works)*. Conference proceedings. St. Petersburg: International Institute for "Women and Management," 1995.

Zabadykina, Elena. "The Range of Women's Organizations in St. Petersburg." In *Women's Voices in Russia Today*, edited by Anna Rotkirch and Elina Haavio-Mannila, 255–266. Aldershot: Dartmouth, 1996.

Anna Rotkirch

All-Russian Sociopolitical Movement of Women of Russia (*Obshcherossiiskoe obshestvenno-politicheskoe dvizhenie zhenshchin Rossii*, or MWR) (1996–)

A federal civic-political organization created by Ekaterina Lakhova in 1996. The All-Russian Sociopolitical Movement of Women of Russia was designed to be a more cohesive organization than the Women's Union of Russia (WUR) and espoused a more reformist and more feminist agenda.

The *Obshcherossiiskoe obshestvenno-politicheskoe dvizhenie zhenshchin Rossii* (the All-Russian Sociopolitical Movement of Women of Russia, or MWR) was a federal civic-political organization registered in November 1996 by Ekaterina Lakhova, chair of the President's Commission on Women, Family, and Demography, deputy of the State Duma, and former chair of the parliamentary coalition Women of Russia. Lakhova created the movement in response to the fact that the Women's Union of Russia (WUR), the largest organization in the Women of Russia electoral bloc, could not persuade its members to vote uniformly in national elections. Many members voted for communists in the parliamentary elections in 1995 and for Gennadii Ziuganov over Boris Yeltsin in 1996. In the wake of these elections, Lakhova felt that a more effective strategy would be to create a unified organization that would join local women's organizations within a vertical structure. By June 1998 the MWR had representatives in sixty-two of the eighty-nine subdivisions of the Russian Federation and over 70,000 individual members.

The chief objective of MWR was to increase women's voice in Russian politics and civil society. Like WUR, MWR promoted the equal rights of women as specified in the Fourth United Nations Conference on Women in Beijing (1995), encouraged women to enter the political process, and advocated more social spending to alleviate women's difficulties in the Russian transition from socialism to a market economy. The MWR, however, more explicitly favored democratic reform and the creation of civil society as the only means to achieve such goals. Unlike WUR, MWR espoused an agenda that bore some similarities to Western feminism; MWR called not only for political and economic equality between the sexes but for social and cultural change as well. MWR was also responsible for persuading representatives of forty different women's organizations to sign a Charter of Women's Solidarity on March 4, 1997, which called for equal rights and equal opportunities for men and women.

The principal governing body of the MWR was a Coordinating Council consisting of organizational representatives from each of twenty regions, which helped to oversee the activities of local organizations that had significance for federal politics and to coordinate joint projects of its local affiliates. There was also a small staff in Moscow (as of 1998, six people), who, among other things, published a monthly newspaper entitled *Zhenshchiny Rossii* (*Women of Russia*).

Many of the local representatives, meanwhile, had their own organizations that pursued independent projects, including an organization to help homeless children in Komi, a group of mothers against narcotics in Irkutsk, and the interuniversity academic program Women of Russia centered in Ivanovo. Most of the support for such activities came from local governments and enterprises, although in some cases MWR offered its affiliates some logistical and even limited financial support. In addition, the close connection between Lakhova and the MWR and the Yeltsin government may have given local affiliates somewhat greater access to government officials at the regional and federal level. Reflecting Lakhova's reformist philosophy, the MWR's Moscow leadership had closer ties with more openly feminist organizations, particularly the Consortium of Russian Nongovernmental Women's Associations, than with Lakhova's erstwhile allies in the WUR. In the regions, however, the situation was more complicated. In some places, the memberships of the MWR and WUR were distinct and even divided; in other places they worked closely together and sometimes included the same people. In the 1999 parliamentary elections, Lakhova did not organize a party list but instead affiliated herself with the *Otechestvo-Vsia Rossiia* (Fatherland-All-Russia) list and was elected.

Cross-references: Consortium of Women's Nongovernmental Associations, Ekaterina Lakhova, Women of Russia.

Suggested Readings

Aivazova, Svetlana G. *Russkie zhenshchiny v labirinte ravnopraviia (Russian Women in the Labyrinth of Equal Rights)*. Moscow: RIK Rusanova, 1998.

Lakhova, Ekaterina F. *Moi put' v politiku (My Path into Politics)* Moscow: "Aurika," 1995.

Lakhova, Ekaterina F. *Perspektivy Paritetnoi demokratii v Rossii (Prospects for a Parity-Democracy in Russia)*. Moscow: Informatik, 1997.

James Richter

Arbatova, Mariia Ivanovna (1957–)

A dramatist, journalist, talk-show hostess and politician, and the best-known feminist in Russia in the 1990s.

Mariia Arbatova was born in 1957 in Moscow. Her mother was a physician, and her father was a teacher of Marxist philosophy at a military high school. In 1975 Arbatova began studying at the Faculty of Philosophy of Moscow State University. She transferred to the Gorkii Institute of Literature to study to become a playwright and graduated from the institute in 1984. Arbatova also belonged to the informal cultural circles of the bohemian intelligentsia. The essential challenge was, as she put it in the short story *"Moi uchitel'ia"* (My Teachers), how to become "both a personality and a woman" against the social conventions of late Soviet society.

From the early 1980s, Arbatova wrote poems, plays, and short stories. Her fiction had an autobiographical quality and dealt with the lives and relationships of artists and writers. She was among the first to describe Soviet institutions, love affairs, and motherhood through the eyes of an intellectually and sexually autonomous woman. For this reason her plays were not staged in the Soviet Union until 1984. Arbatova's writing was direct, passionate and ironic. A typical title of one of her short stories was *"Abort ot neliubimogo"* (Abortion from Somebody You Don't Love). Her fourteen plays have been staged in Russia and in the United States, Great Britain, and Germany.

Since the late 1980s, Arbatova has published articles about feminism and the women's movement and has become a regular columnist in the newspaper *Obshchaia gazeta* (The *Common Newspaper*). Arbatova's opinions remained provocative and controversial. They stressed personal creativity and responsibility, liberal values, and women as agents rather than victims. Unlike many Western feminists with a similar liberal, hedonistic credo, Arbatova also wrote extensively and tenderly about motherhood and men. In real life, she gave birth to twin sons and was married twice. As with most Russian feminists of the 1990s, her revolt against conventions did not imply a refusal of family life or heterosexuality. Arbatova's originality and importance were underscored by the fact that, unlike many famous Russian women activists, she did not work in close cooperation with Western feminists.

In the early 1990s Arbatova led a small women's association called *Klub Garmonii* (Harmony Club). She later coordinated the *Klub zhenshchin, vmeshivaushchieshsia v politike* (Club of Women, Who Mess with Politics). The name referred to the prevalent attitude that women should not mess with politics. The club gathered Moscow businesswomen and female politicians about twice monthly. In 1996 Arbatova participated in the preparation of the section on the rights of women, children, and handicapped for Boris Yeltsin's electoral program. The actual impact of this section, as of the whole electoral program, remained limited.

Arbatova became widely known to the general public through the weekly television talk show *Ia sama* (*I Myself*), which started in 1996. The show featured invited guests who discussed their private lives with two hostesses, one of whom represented "traditional" views on family values and gender roles, while the other, Arbatova, provided a "feminist" opinion. The program was popular among viewers of both sexes, but especially among working-class women. Some Russian intellectuals tended to accuse the program of triviality or of reducing feminism to private and sexual problems. The television show was nevertheless crucial in making the word "feminism" acceptable in Russian public discourse. For most Russians, "feminism" was associated with Mariia Arbatova.

Suggested Readings

Arbatova, Mariia. *Menia zovut zhenshchina (My Name Is Woman: A Collection of Short Stories).* Moscow: Alma Mater, 1997. (The anthology includes the short stories named in the text.)

Arbatova, Mariia. *Mne 40 let: avtobiograficheskii roman (I'm 40 Years Old: An Autobiographical Novel).* Moscow: AST, 1999.

Arbatova, Mariia. *P'esy dlia chteniia (Plays for Reading)* (collected plays). Moscow: Prometei, 1995.

Much, Rita." Feminist Theatre in the Soviet Union: An Interview with Maria Arbatova." *New Theatre Quarterly* 7, no. 27 (August 1991): 284–286.

Rich, Elisabeth. "Mariya Arbatova." *South Central Review* 12, no. 3–4 (Fall–Winter 1995): 108–114.

Smith, Melissa, ed. and trans. *Russian Mirror: Three Plays by Russian Women* (includes *On the Way to Ourselves* by Mariia Arbatova). Amsterdam: Harwood, 1998.

Anna Rotkirch

Association for the Advancement of Women in Science and Humanities (AAWISH) (*Assotsiatsiia v podderzhku zhenshchin v nauke i obrazovanii*) (1996–)

A nongovernmental women's organization established in 1996 uniting women working in the Russian Academy of Science, universities, and other higher educational institutions of the Russian Federation.

For many years women working in the Russian Academy of Science wanted to improve the position of women scholars. In particular, there were perceived needs to improve their opportunities for research and career advancement. With the growth of democratic tendencies in Russia, the idea of establishing an organization for cooperation among women in the sciences received new impetus.

Realization of this initiative became possible with the support of foreign organizations, including American Women in Science (AWIS), European Women in Science and Humanities (EWISH), and the American Association for the Advancement of Science (AAAS). AAWISH, the Association for the Advancement of Women in Science and the Humanities, was organized at a seminar in Moscow supported and organized by AAAS, EWISH, AWIS, and the Russian chapter of EWISH. Participants included women from various cities and regions of the Russian Federation, including Moscow, St. Petersburg, Novosibirsk, Tomsk, Kemerovo, Khabarovsk, Vladivostok, and Sakhalin, where the largest universities and research centers are located.

Major tasks identified for the new organization involved the necessity of establishing links between women in science and humanities and between women employed in research institutions and those in educational institutions. The goals were to establish a women's lobby in the Academy of Science to support women's careers, defend their rights, and develop fair opportunities for promotion and representation in academic administrative structures. Each of the constituencies working separately could not hope to improve the situation for women academics. Furthermore, because of anticipated changes in the Academy of Science and higher education in Russia, closer cooperation between women scholars and women teachers seemed timely.

AAWISH conducted regular meetings in Moscow, maintained correspondence with its members in the regions of the Russian Federation, and published a quarterly newsletter in which news about national and international events was published and women could share both their problems and their achievements. AAWISH's agenda included greater outreach to women in the many regions of the Russian Federation to inform them of research opportunities and to assist them in establishing international contacts. As a longer-term goal, AAWISH planned to organize programs and seminars for women to update their knowledge of science and to arrange training programs for women teaching in the humanities. In the transitional period, regional scholars and university teachers have few opportunities to obtain access to information, books, the Internet, and other resources to update their knowledge of their field.

AAWISH established good ties with other women's organizations, established a network of women in the regions of the Russian Federation, and created a database of women scholars and teachers interested in further cooperation. AAWISH also had permanent contacts with American and European women scholars, and its members participated in international conferences where women's issues were debated.

Cross-reference: Foreign Funding and the Women's Movement in Russia.

Tatiana Shakleina

The Association of Women in Law Enforcement (*Assotsiatsiia zhenshchin sotrudnikov pravookhranitel'nykh organov Sankt-Peterburga*) (1992–)

The Association of Women in Law Enforcement was founded in St. Petersburg in 1992 by Narcotics Squad detective Galiia Mavliutova. The organization sought to combat workplace discrimination and offered support for women who were experiencing difficulties due to the transition from Soviet communism. Mavliutova stressed contact with the West.

The *Assotsiatsiia zhenshchin sotrudnikov pravookhranitel'nykh organov Sankt-Peterburga* (the Association of Women in Law Enforcement) was a St. Petersburg women's organization founded in 1992. The group exposed and combated the discrimination faced by women working in the militia, fire-fighting forces, and law enforcement organizations. Their goal was to create an environment wherein people were valued for the performance of their work. Narcotics

Squad detective, founder, and leader Lieutenant Galiia Sergeevna Mavliutova saw international, professional conferences—contact with women and men from the West—as the most promising vehicle for effective attitudinal change. She attended conferences abroad, and the organization sponsored one in 1994 in St. Petersburg. The group supported members' travel by engaging in private fund-raising by selling clothes, handicrafts, dishes, and kitchen utensils at gala "society parties." Donations from Russian business were neither sufficient nor reliable. Mavliutova was largely responsible for staging fund-raising events and was also committed to using proceeds to benefit city charities. A product of the city's orphanage system, she was particularly sensitive to the many needs in the city. It was not uncommon for single mothers to approach her personally for assistance. She generally obliged and pledged that the organization would benefit not only the women members but also other women working in law enforcement and fire-fighting. Mavliutova believed that women were key political actors, and she perceived a strong relationship between the work of her organization and Russian democracy. The association relied on an active core but had a membership of 300.

The group was significant as an example of a collective, active response to workplace discrimination. It was also an important example of the way women's groups worked to further the goals not only of women members but also of the larger society.

Suggested Readings

Gottlick, Jane F. Berthusen. "From the Ground Up: Women's Organizations and Democratization in Russia." In *Democratization and Women's Grassroots Movements*, edited by Jill M. Bystydzienski and Joti Sekhon, 241–261. Bloomington: Indiana University Press, 1999.

McMahon, Patrice C. "The Effect of Economic and Political Reforms on Soviet/Russian Women." In *Women in the Age of Economic Transformation*, edited by Nahid Aslangeigui, Steven Pressman, and Gale Summerfield, 59–76. New York: Routledge, 1994.

Nechemias, Carol. "The Prospects for a Soviet Women's Movement: Opportunities and Obstacles." In *Perestroika from Below: Social Movements in the Soviet Union*, edited by Judith B. Sedaitis and Jim Butterfield, 73–96. Boulder, CO: Westview Press, 1991.

Racioppi, Linda, and Katherine O'Sullivan See. "Organizing Women before and after the Fall: Women's Politics in the Soviet Union and Post-Soviet Russia." *Signs* (Summer 1995): 818–850.

Jane F. Berthusen Gottlick

The Association of Women Journalists (AWJ) (*Assotsiatsiia zhurnalistok*) (1992–)

An organization formed in 1992 by women journalists concerned with stereotypical images of women in the Russian media.

The *Assotsiatsiia zhurnalistok* (Association of Women Journalists, or AWJ) united women journalists determined to combat stereotypical images of women as sexual objects or as housewives in the print media. The AWJ engaged in several lines of activity. First, seminars for journalists on women's issues were held, with scholars, politicians, and art critics delivering lectures. A second task involved research on women's images in the media. According to a 1995 AWJ study, only 1 percent of all newspaper and magazine space in Russia's mainstream national press was devoted to women. Newspapers preferred to write about women movie stars, prostitutes, alcoholics, and drug addicts. There was an absence of stories that reflected the lives of Russian women. Follow-up research conducted in 1998 revealed that 2 percent of all newspaper space focused on women. Some change was evident, with images of professional women, successful women, and women activists beginning to appear. The AWJ served as a bridge between the mass media and the women's movement, pushing for change in how women were depicted in the media. The organization had a network of more than 300 members in Russia and the Commonwealth of Independent States, and its annual conferences drew women journalists from across Russia's regions. The AWJ also created a special course on Women and Journalism at Moscow State University's Department of Journalism. Additional activities involved sponsoring public meetings and international conferences on topics like women and politics, women in ethnopolitical conflicts, and education for women. AWJ published books and brochures for women journalists and worked with the U.S. National Council for Research on Women on the international women's magazine *Vy i My (You and We)*. Led by cochairs Nadezhda Azhgikhina and Irina Iurna, the organization sought an active role in Russia's political life by providing information to the Russian government and participating in the Russian and international women's movement.

Cross-reference: *Femina.*

Suggested Readings

Azhgikhina, Nadezhda. "Tri goda v 'NG' " (Three Years at NG). *Nezavisimaia gazeta* (November 13, 1998), 15.

Vy i My (You and We) (renamed *We/My* in 1998). <*www.neww.org/vim*>

Nadezhda Azhgikhina

B

The Baikal' Regional Union of Women-"Angara" (*Baikal'skii regional'nyi soiuz zhenshchin-Angara*) (1992–)

An association of women in the Russian Far East, based in Irkutsk but encompassing the entire Baikal' region, that was designed to promote the inclusion of women in sociopolitical-economic transformation. Its work was multifaceted, extending into many areas of life and work.

The *Baikal'skii regional'nyi soiuz zhenshchin-Angara* (the Baikal' Regional Union of Women-"Angara") was founded in 1992 in Irkutsk and officially registered in 1995. "Angara" was a broadly based organization without formal membership requirements, that united women from many occupations and professions. It sought to inform the populace of new developments in various parts of Russia and abroad that would raise the professional and personal consciousness of women about business, politics, health, culture, communication, and other areas. "Angara" united more than thirty women's organizations in the Baikal' region.

Among its achievements was the establishment of a Center for Children's Rights, in which children, medical personnel, and law enforcement organs participated. Its hot line received as many as 1,500 calls a year. "Angara" also established a Crisis Center for Women, which was designed to give women psychological help in the transition to the new economy.

A seminar on the management of noncommercial organizations was sponsored by "Angara"; participants in the seminar formed a United Council of Social and Non-Commercial Organizations of Irkutsk and Irkutsk Oblast. "Angara" created the Irkutsk section of the Association of Women Entrepreneurs of Russia and the "Angara" Women's Business Center. In 1999 eleven women associated with "Angara" received the award Woman Director of the Year at the Third International Forum and Exhibition, "The World, Women, Russia, Moscow." "Angara" also organized the women's forums *Zhenshchiny za vyzhivanie planeta* (Women for the Survival of the Planet) in 1996, 1998, and 2000.

Although "Angara" had some external sponsors, it relied heavily on its women volunteers. "Angara" represented an example of a regional organization that initiated a number of meaningful projects and participated in efforts begun elsewhere in the country, such as the School of Women's Leadership. It worked hard to keep itself abreast of new movements around the nation. In 1999 the association published a book on its work, *Initsiativy zhenshchin Baikal'skogo regiona (Initiatives of Women of the Baikal Region).*

Suggested Reading

Initsiativy zhenshchin Baikal'skogo regiona. Irkutsk: Izdatel'stovo poligraficheskii kompleks TWIN, 1999.

Zoya Edvardovna Molokova

Bronevich, Valentina Tadeevna (1956–)

An attorney and Governor of the Koriak Autonomous Okrug (Kamchatka Oblast) and the Russian Federation's first female governor (1996–).

Valentina Bronevich, an Itel'men, an indigenous people of the Kamchatka peninsula, was born on January 25, 1956. She received a higher education and was trained as a lawyer at Irkutsk State University. She worked as a lawyer and then as a judge in the Koriak Autonomous Okrug (AO), rising to become assistant chair of the okrug court and ultimately chair of the Koriak Autonomous Okrug Ispolkom (executive committee). She served in the latter post for four years, resigning in 1990 over policy differences with other leading Koriak officials. Bronevich was considered a pro-reform, pro-Yeltsin politician.

Bronevich earned a reputation as a strong supporter of the rights of indigenous peoples in the Koriak AO. During the 1990s she served as the head of Kamchatka oblast's Department on National Questions (1990) and later as chair of the Oblast Electoral Committee (1994–1996). While working in Petropavlosvk-Kamchatskii, the capital of Kamchatka oblast, of which Koriak was a part, she set up a legal center for the region's indigenous peoples and organized the publication of textbooks to teach children their local languages, an accomplishment that she particularly relished.

On November 17, 1996, Bronevich was elected governor of Koriak AO, becoming the Russian Federation's first female governor. She defeated the incumbent governor Sergei Leushkin by a margin of 46 percent to 21 percent. Bronevich enjoyed the support of Vladimir Shumeiko's pro-Yeltsin reform movement Reforms—New Course. She also benefited from the actions of another candidate, Nina Solodiakova, who was supported by the *Narodno-patrioticheskii soiuz Rossii* (People's Patriotic Union of Russia) but withdrew from the race and declared her support for Bronevich the day before the election. Bronevich was considered to be among those governors who were strong managers, placing professionalism above political orientation. As governor she focused on economic issues and sought to diversify the okrug's economy by developing the fish industry as well as fur and mineral enterprises.

Following her election in 1996, Bronevich was one of two women on the

Federation Council, where the two top legislators of each region of the Russian Federation had automatic representation. The other woman was Valentina Pivnenko, the Chair of the Chamber of Representatives of the Legislative Assembly of the Karelian Republic, who left the Federation Council in March 1997. Bronevich also served as chair of the Kamchatka Oblast Election Commission as well as assistant chair of the Federation Council Committee on Affairs of the North and Small-Numbered Peoples. On April 19, 1997, she joined the party *Nash Dom—Rossiia* (Our Home Is Russia, or NDR) and became chair of the Council of Regional Branches of NDR. From March 1997 through May 1998 Bronevich was the only woman in the Federation Council.

On May 5, 1999, Bronevich and Kamchatka Oblast Governor Vladimir Biriukov signed a cooperation agreement. The background to this agreement was complex. The agreement was the result of difficult negotiations between the regions, whose relationship had been strained by legal ambiguities due to the fact that the Koriak Autonomous Okrug is simultaneously subordinate to Kamchatka Oblast as well as an equal subject of the Russian Federation, according to the 1993 Constitution. In 1991 the Koriak Autonomous Okrug had unsuccessfully attempted to secede from Kamchatka Oblast with the hope of establishing the Koriak Republic within the RSFSR. At that time, Bronevich, who was then chair of the Okrug executive committee, had argued against secession, contending that it would not be in the best interest of the region's indigenous peoples. She argued that secession would create another expensive bureaucracy that would not serve the native peoples. Bronevich's view of the cooperation agreement was that deepening ties with Kamchatka Oblast, especially in the economic sphere, would be particularly beneficial to the Koriak Autonomous Okrug. Kamchatka denied rumors that the two regions would merge; however, Bronevich conceded that if the two regions were to merge, she would be willing to resign so that there would be only one governor.

In late September 1999 in preparation for the December parliamentary elections, Bronevich, along with twenty-three governors and other politicians, formed a new national political bloc, *Edinstvo* (the Interregional Movement, Unity), known by the nickname *Medved'* (Bear). Unity's goals included "electing a new generation of honest and responsible people to the State Duma." Prime Minister Vladimir Putin supported the bloc, which posed serious opposition to the *Otechestvo-Vsia Rossiia* (Fatherland-All Russia) alliance headed by former prime minister Evgenii Primakov (September 1998–May 1999) and Moscow mayor Iurii Luzhkov. Unity was a surprise success in the parliamentary election, finishing a close second to the *Kommunisticheskaia partiia Rossiiskoi Federatsii* (Communist Party of the Russian Federation, or KPRF) with 23 percent of the overall vote. As of December 1999 Bronevich was once again the only woman in the Federation Council.

Cross-reference: Valentina Pivnenko.

Suggested Readings

Belonuchkin, G. V. "Bronevich Valentina Tadeevna." *Federal'noe sobranie: Soviet Federatsii, Gosudarstvennaya Duma: Spravochnik (Federation Assembly: Federation Council, State Duma: Reference Book).* Moscow: IEG "Panorama," 1996. <http://www.cityline.ru: 8084/politika/bio/bronevic.html> (1997).

"Bronevich Valentina Tadeevna." Spisok chlenov Soveta Federatsii (List of Members of the Federation Council). <http://www.council.gov.ru:8104/sostav/members/deput/d_204783.htm> (November 23, 1999).

"Koryak and Kamchatka Sign Agreement (Izvestiia, May 6, 1999)." The CEN/ASIA Discussion List: [TURKISTAN-N] TEB: Volume 99: 49–16-May 1999. <http://www.soros.org/tajik/cenasia/0457.html> (May 16, 1999).

"A New National Political Bloc." American Russian Center: Russian Far East News. <http://www.arc.uaa.alaska.edu/arc/news11–99.htm> (November 1999).

Orttung, Robert. "Regional Incumbents Suffer Defeat." OMRI Daily Digest. No. 223, Part I. <http://www.rferl.org/newsline/1996/11/1-RUS/rus-181196.html> (November 18, 1996).

Tsukanova, Lyubov. "RUSSIA: Data on 1996-Jan 1997 Regional Elections Published." FBIS Daily Report, FBIS-SOV-97-022 (January 31, 1997).

"Valentina Bronevich." Norsk Utenrikspolitisk Institutt-Norwegian Institute of International Affairs (NUPI). Centre for Russian Studies Database. <http://www.nupi.no/cgi-win/Russland/Personer.exe/902> (1999).

"Valentina Bronevich First Female Governor in Russia." Norsk Utenrikspolitisk Institutt-Norwegian Institute of International Affairs (NUPI). Centre for Russian Studies Database. <http://www.nupi.no/cgi-win/Russland/krono.exe/304> (1999).

Cheri C. Wilson

C

Charter of Women's Solidarity (*Khartii Zhenskoi Solidarnosti*) (1997)

A declaration that sought to consolidate the strength and coordinate the efforts of women's nongovernmental organizations and politicians to advance policies of interest to a broad spectrum of women's groups.

On March 4, 1997, the *Khartii zhenskoi solidarnosti* (Charter of Women's Solidarity) was signed by thirty-nine women's organizations and ten women politicians and public figures. An initiative of Ekaterina Lakhova, the Charter's goals include joint activity to (1) advance the interests of children, women, families, pensioners, and the poor; (2) overcome the socioeconomic crises plaguing Russian society; and (3) secure equal rights and equal opportunity for women. More specific priorities involve seeking guarantees of access to free education, the development of family planning services, ensuring the rights of draftees and those serving in the military, improving the working conditions of rural women, and so on. The diverse goals reflect the variety of women's groups that signed the charter, which ranged from feminist organizations like the *Moskovskii tsentr gendernykh issledovanii* (Moscow Center for Gender Studies), to the *Komitet soldatskikh materei* Rossii (Committee of Soldiers' Mothers of Russia) to the charitable organization *Budushchee—bez SPIDa* (The Future—Without AIDS). Missing from the list of signatories was the *Soiuz zhenshchin Rossii* (Women's Union of Russia, or WUR), an absence that presumably stemmed from the tension between Lakhova and Alevtina Fedulova, former allies in the electoral bloc Women of Russia, as well as the concerns that many women had about cooperation with the WUR, which was perceived by many as an old-line, Soviet-style, hierarchical organization. The charter represented a move by Lakhova to boost her organization, the *Obshcherossiiskoe obshestvenno-politicheskoe dvizhennie zhenshchin Rossi* (All-Russia Sociopolitical Movement of Women of Russia), within the context of fostering greater cooperation among women's groups, and by 1999 more than 300 organizations had signed the Charter. Yet there was little evidence of progress in institutionalizing joint action, and in 1999 Lakhova noted that problems remained in learning how to use instruments like the Charter in the struggle for equal rights.

Cross-references: All-Russian Sociopolitical Movement of Women of Russia, Committee of Soldiers' Mothers of Russia, Alevtina Fedulova, Ekaterina Lakhova, Women of Russia (WOR), Women's Union of Russia (WUR).

Suggested Reading

Il'ina, Nadezhda. "*Zhenshchina Rossii*" (Woman of Russia). *Nezavisimaia gazeta* (March 6, 1999), 9.

Carol Nechemias

Cheboksary Women's Movement (1991–)

The women's movement in Cheboksary, the capital of Chuvashia, provides insight into the development of women's groups in non-Russian areas of the Russian Federation.

Cheboksary, the capital of the ethnic republic of Chuvashia, is situated on the Volga about midway between Moscow and the Ural Mountains, with a population of approximately 500,000. In the early post-Soviet period, Cheboksary was a depressed region dominated by light industry, with some electrotechnical industry and a large tractor-building factory. Like the textile industry in Ivanovo, that in Cheboksary was overwhelmingly dominated by women, who suffered from large-scale unemployment. As of 1995 the women's movement there was relatively new, and the city, perhaps because of its distance from Moscow, had been little exposed to Western feminists and feminist literature.

Although Chuvashia was populated largely by people of Chuvash nationality, with a minority Russian population, the movement in Cheboksary was not significantly divided over ethnicity. In three of the four women's groups existing in Cheboksary as of mid-1995, ethnic Chuvash and Russians worked together without respect to nationality.

The women's movement in Cheboksary was in an embryonic stage as of 1995, organizationally speaking. The movement had expanded from two organizations in 1991, to four in 1994, with about 140 member-activists. Central was the Cheboksary city *zhensovet* (Women's Council), which had existed under the Soviet regime as a branch of the Soviet Women's Committee and reregistered in 1991, under the leadership of the activist Nina Petrova. In 1991 the Chuvash Republic's *zhensovet* also registered; it had operated under the leadership of Iraida Stekolshikova since 1988. Both the city and republic-level *zhensovety* were local subdivisions of the *Soiuz zhenshchin Rossii* (Women's Union of Russia, or WUR), headquartered in Moscow. The *zhensovety* of Cheboksary and the Chuvash Republic predated Russia's economic transition from state-socialism but since its advent had focused heavily on assisting women's adaptation to the economic transition, conducting unemployment counseling and engaging in charitable activities. Their activities included raising the issue of women's unemployment with the local administration, advocating the establishment of retraining courses for women, and urging tax breaks to enterprises that would create new workplaces for women.

Newer organizations included the Chuvashian branch of the *Assotsiatsiia zhenshchin s universitetskim obrazovaniiem* (Russian Association of University Women, RAUW), formed in 1994, with approximately a dozen members. As their first major event, the Cheboksary-based leaders of RAUW sponsored a three-day seminar in May 1995, bringing a team of women's movement activists from Moscow and the United States to Cheboksary to discuss the possible intersections between women's activism and politics in Russia. Economic issues also entered the spectrum of the organization's concerns: the executive director of the group stated that the organization aimed to help solve Russia's economic problems and engage in charity for women in need of assistance.

In 1994 a newly created association called Salam Bi registered at the republic level. *Salam Bi* was Cheboksary's sole women's organization formed on an ethnic foundation; it was based on the a cappella choral group at a local university and had formed to promote Chuvashian culture and protect the environment. Despite its ethnic basis, the group was open to cooperation with the city *zhensovet*, run by Petrova, an ethnic Russian; both groups invited each other's members to their events. With about fifty members, *Salam Bi*'s activities centered around cultural and ecological awareness events, such as a music festival held in a local forest. The association's members included rural teachers, journalists, doctors, singers, and tutors, in essence, talented women interested in Chuvash culture.

In mid-1995, *Klub zhenskaia initsiativa* (the Women's Initiative Club) was organized in Cheboksary, bringing together approximately twenty-five powerful women in the republic. The club's founders were professional women, including republic-level ministers, administrators, and factory directors; its formation was spurred by the woman who served as the Chuvash Republic's labor minister; its goals were to combat unemployment and maximize women's business activity under market conditions. As was the case with the *zhensovety*, the Club's fundamental concerns were motivated by the growing effects of poverty and economic decline on the population and on women and families. As elsewhere in Russia, the leaders of Cheboksary's women's organizations were well educated, several with postgraduate degrees. In Cheboksary the movement was too small to be ripe for coalition building, although the groups were prepared to cooperate with each other. The relatively small size of the city and the small-town feeling contributed to collaboration between the organizations, as did cross-memberships. Nina Petrova, for example, the long-standing activist and chair of the city *zhensovet*, was among the founders of the city's *Klub zhenskaia initsiativa*. Petrova also expressed interest in providing organizational support for the nascent Chuvashian branch of the Russian Association of University Women. Likewise, the RAUW invited the leaders of the city and republic women's councils, as well as Ol'ga Denisova, a founder of the new *Klub zhenskaia initsiativa*, to its seminar.

A lack of resources and distance from other women's organizations elsewhere in Russia were significant constraints on women's group activity and development in Cheboksary. Russia's limited communications infrastructure prevented many groups in outlying provinces from maximizing their potential. The political setting for the movement was positive, in that the Chuvash Republic was small enough that the President of the Chuvashian Republic, Nikolai Federov, attended the charter conference of the *Klub zhenskaia initsiativa*. This suggested that women's issues might be addressed with some concern within the republic's administration.

Cross-references: Soviet Women's Committee, Women's Union of Russia (WUR).

Suggested Readings

Bremmer, Ian, and Ray Taras, eds. *New States, New Politics: Building the Post-Soviet Nations*. Cambridge: Cambridge University Press, 1997.

Mastyugina, Tatiana, and Lev Perepelkin. *An Ethnic History of Russia: Pre-Revolutionary Times to the Present*. Westport, CT: Greenwood Press, 1996.

Smith, Graham, ed. *The Nationalities Question in the Post-Soviet States*. New York: Longman, ca. 1996.

Sperling, Valerie. *Organizing Women in Contemporary Russia: Engendering Transition*. Cambridge: Cambridge University Press, 1999.

Valerie Sperling

Commission on Improving the Status of Women (CISW) (*Kommissia po uluchsheniiu polozheniia zhenshchin*) (1997–)

A commission created in January 1997 to coordinate the activities of the federal government, regional governments, and civic organizations in advancing women's status through implementation of the principles of equal rights and equal opportunities. Emphasis was placed on preparing recommendations for the Russian government that would move society closer to international standards such as the UN Convention on the Elimination of All Forms of Discrimination against Women (CEDAW).

The Commission on Improving the Status of Women (CISW) (*Kommissia po uluchsheniiu polozheniia zhenshchin*) was created in January 1997 as the result of a Russian Federation government decree (N91). The commission engaged in several lines of activity: (1) the promotion of collaborative activity between government agencies and nongovernmental organizations to implement the principle of equal rights and equal opportunities for women; (2) the preparation of recommendations to the Russian government on state policy toward women, including measures designed to meet relevant international standards, such as those contained within CEDAW; and (3) the monitoring of progress toward implementing Russia's national plan of action to improve the position of women by the year 2000. The national plan stemmed from a June 1996 presidential decree (N932) issued in the midst of the presidential campaign.

Initially, the CISW was chaired by the Vice-Chairman of the Russian Federation government, Oleg Sysuev, whose duties centered on social policy, and included representatives of the executive and legislative branches of government and of civic organizations. The commission was granted the right to involve regional government agencies, scientific and educational institutions, and the business sector in its work. Special working teams of experts prepared proposals; the Ministry of Labor and Social Development provided technical and organizational assistance. In December 1998 in the wake of a restructuring of Yeltsin's government, Vice Premier Valentina Matvienko became CISW's chair. Her overall responsibilities within the Yeltsin administration involved social issues. In March 1999 the Commission's members included seven deputy ministers drawn from the Ministries of Labor and Social Development, Culture, Agriculture, Health Care, Secondary and Professional Education, Economy, and Justice; the deputy chair of the State Committee on Statistics; the deputy head of the Department of International Cooperation and Human Rights in the Ministry of Foreign Affairs; the head of the Department on Family, Women, and Children in the Ministry of Labor and Social Development; the chair of the State Duma Committee on Women, Family, and Youth; the chair of the Commission on Women, Family, and Demography; a member of the State Duma Budget Committee; two representatives from regional government agencies; and five representatives from nongovernmental organizations. The number of members from civic organizations, including charitable and trade union organizations, decreased over time. While the *Soiuz zhenshchin Rossiia* (Women's Union of Russia, or WUR) was represented, the independent women's movement generally has not made significant inroads in securing formal membership on the CISW. The commission had more of a decorative character than an activist stance. Its activities were invisible to women's nongovernmental organizations and to the public.

Cross-reference: Commission on Women, Family, and Demography.

Suggested Reading

Sperling, Valerie. *Organizing Women in Contemporary Russia: Engendering Transition.* Cambridge, UK: Cambridge University Press, 1999.

Nadezhda Shvedova

Commission on Women, Family, and Demography under the President of the Russian Federation (CWFD) (*Komissiia po delam zhenshchin, sem'i i demografii pri Prezidente Rossiiskoi Federatsii*) (1993–)

A presidential commission established as an advisory body, focusing on the formulation of policies to improve women's status, protect children and families, and resolve demographic problems.

The *Komissiia po delam zhenshchin, sem'i i demografii pri Prezidente Rossiiskoi Federatsii* (Commission on Women, Family, and Demography, or CWFD) was established by Presidential decree (N1908) on November 15, 1993.

Ekaterina Lakhova, a member of the State Duma and a strong advocate of woman's rights, served as its chair (1993–). An advisory body, the CWFD's role involved the formulation of recommendations and the provision of information to the federal and regional governments and to civic organizations. The commission's goals included a broad list of tasks associated with gender, family, children, and demography.

The CWFD's members were drawn from four different groups. One group consisted of the heads of federal departments associated with the Ministry of Labor and Social Development, the Ministry of Education, and the Ministry of Justice. A second component drew from women's nongovernmental organizations, including representatives of *Planirovanie sem'i* (Russian Family Planning Association), the *Soiuz zhenshchin Rossii* (Women's Union of Russia, or WUR), and the *Informatsionnyi tsentr nezavisimogo zhenskogo foruma* (Information Center of the Independent Women's Forum). The third element involved individuals from such children's public organizations as *Detskii fond* (Russian Children's Foundation). Members also included sociologists, demographers, medical specialists, social workers, and other scientists and scholars. Recommendations were forged as the result of compromise and partnership among commission participants.

The CWFD published an informational-analytical bulletin describing its activities and materials from forums held on women's and family issues. It also made analytical reports to the President of the Russian Federation, some of which were disseminated to regional administrative heads. Lakhova considered the two most important of these reports to be those addressing the issues of the death rate in Russia and the promotion of women's roles in regional government. The Commission sought to improve the qualifications and competence of women in regional government through leadership training. Courses for these women involved interaction with high-level federal executive officials, State Duma deputies, leaders of women's nongovernmental organizations, and well-known scientists and experts. But few of these sessions were held due to a lack of gender consciousness, insufficient funding, and the weakness of the women's movement.

The CWFD organized conferences, workshops, and roundtables on topics like family violence, women and the mass media, rural women, the abandonment of children, and family planning. After the 1995 UN World Conference on Women in Beijing, the commission organized discussions with the aim of implementing the conference's recommendations. A June 18, 1996, presidential decree (N932) on Russia's national plan of action to improve the position of women by the year 2000 also generated CWFD activities focusing on the development of policies that would lead to greater gender equality.

In the aftermath of the August 1998 economic crisis in Russia, there was an effort to abolish the CWFD as a cost-saving measure, an attempt that was resisted with the assistance of women's groups, particularly the Consortium of Women's Nongovernmental Associations.

The CWFD was a point of access for the women's movement to the federal executive branch of government. The Commission channeled communication between the Russian government and women's organizations. Its power depended largely on the strength of the women's movement and the personal commitment of the CWFD's leader to the idea of gender equality in rights and opportunity.

Cross-references: Commission on Improving the Status of Women, Consortium of Women's Nongovernmental Associations, Ekaterina Lakhova.

Suggested Readings

Ladin, Sharon. *WRAW to CEDAW Country Reports. Independent Information for the 14th Session of the Committee on the Elimination of Discrimination against Women (CEDAW).* Minneapolis: International Women's Rights Watch (IWRW), 1995.

"Sotsial'noe partnërstvo: faktor obshchestvennogo soglasiia" (Social Partnership: A Factor in Social Consensus). *Analiticheskii vestnik,* no. 10 (1998). Moscow: Informatsionno-analiticheskoe Upravlenie Apparata Soveta Federatsii.

Sperling, Valerie. *The Women's Movement in Contemporary Russia: Engendering Transition*: Cambridge: Cambridge University Press, 1999.

Nadezhda Shvedova

Committee of Soldiers' Mothers of Russia (*Komitet soldatskikh materei Rossii*) (1989–)

An organization established in 1989 to combat human rights abuses in the military; it advised parents of draftees and killed servicemen on their rights and the rights of servicemen; prominent opponent of the war in Chechnia; nominee for Nobel Peace Prize and winner of the Sean MacBride Peace Prize in 1995.

The *Komitet soldatskikh materei Rossii* (Committee of Soldiers' Mothers of Russia, or CSM) constituted perhaps the most internationally visible women's movement in Russia during the 1990s. From the time of its founding in Moscow in 1989, CSM actively lobbied to stop human rights abuses in the military, end the war in Chechnia, and implement an alternative service bill. The group provided a range of services to parents of drafted soldiers and participated in nonviolent protest. It used a combination of effective strategizing, a compelling cause, and international connections to influence Russian policy making and public opinion.

CSM was founded in 1989 by Mariia Kirbassova to battle human rights violations and, in particular, the practice of *dedovshchina* (hazing), a violent and virtually condoned form of hazing in the military. Kirbassova's involvement came from a callous reaction to an appeal to her son's commander to allow her son to serve in a position relevant to his education. Many of its early leaders were mothers of soldiers in the Afghanistan War who objected to the exploitation of their sons. At the same time, human rights violations in the military worsened in the late 1980s, often manifesting new, nationalist tensions. The incidence of "suicide" among draftees increased rapidly, as *dedovshchina* became more common, prompting other parents to join CSM. Testing new opportunities for political action and growing public opposition to the military, Kirbassova and her colleagues, including later CSM press secretary Valentina Melnikova, began to protest conditions in the military.

New openness in the media and the political system allowed CSM to draw significant attention to the problems that it addressed. While urging military reform, it managed one of its first victories by pushing for legal exemptions from military service to draftees in higher education. The war in Chechnia brought the group international attention. CSM was at the forefront of opposition to the first Chechen war (1994–1996), and although the war's end was probably most attributable to the presidential election of 1996, CSM was crucial in shaping public opinion. CSM then turned its attention to lobbying for legislation implementing the constitutional right to alternative service. The renewal of the Chechen war in the fall of 1999 again raised the primacy of CSM's opposition to the Russian government's military campaign, a role rendered even more difficult due to heightened public support for the war effort.

In addition to urging political change, CSM provided services to the parents of soldiers. It was able to do both effectively because of its structure. Its central office, located at the Moscow Center for Human Rights, was primarily responsible for lobbying the central government and relaying information to and from local groups. The coordinating body also built international ties and won several grants and prizes, including the Sean MacBride Peace Prize, awarded by the International Peace Bureau in Geneva. In addition, hundreds of local affiliated groups provided support services to their areas. They counseled parents on their legal rights and wrote letters on their behalf to responsible authorities. They held sessions advising parents on helping their sons avoid the draft. Although the Moscow office was the central coordinating body, local groups acted fairly independently, in part because of Russia's problematic communications infrastructure.

CSM's political success was attributable to several factors. It gained prominence, in part, because the issues that it addressed were compelling, life-threatening, and new to open discussion. Its leaders used strategies necessary for visibility in Russia's quasi-democratic structure: they held press conferences and issued press releases, using the media to pressure the government. In addition, the group appealed to the public by effectively using Russian ideas about womanhood and motherhood. Its leaders stressed that members act as mothers protecting their children. They focused on ideas about maternal instinct and claimed that mothers suffer in unique ways when their sons are killed in military service. CSM supported this image in its strategic choices as well: during the war in Chechnia, for example, groups of mothers crossed the front lines to reclaim imprisoned soldiers. This action earned them dramatic and sympathetic press coverage. The image that CSM projected appealed successfully to public sentiment by evoking traditional ideas about women's roles. At the same time,

CSM argued that motherly pain and protective instinct were the basis of its right to a political voice. In other words, its ideology of motherhood allowed the group to carve out a space for women's visible and effective political action.

As a movement of women, CSM sometimes cooperated with other women's groups, many of which also supported agendas of peace and antiviolence. However, it did not consider itself feminist, and its leaders expressed skepticism about publicly associating with feminist groups. Thus, its ties to other women's groups were not strong. Nonetheless, CSM's visibility as a women's movement meant that its activities might have had important implications for other groups' success.

Cross-reference: The Committee "The Soldier's Mother" (St. Petersburg).

Suggested Readings

Caiazza, Amy. "Military Service and Maternal Obligation: Gender, Citizenship and Civil Society in Contemporary Russia, 1993–1997." Ph.D. Diss., Indiana University, 1999.

Caiazza, Amy. "Russia Meets Its Matriarchs." *Transitions* 5, no. 1 (1998): 58–61.

Konstantinova, Valentina. "Women's Political Coalitions in Russia (1990–1994)." In *Women's Voices in Russia Today*, edited by Anna Rotkirch and Elina Haavio-Mannila, 235–247. Brookfield, VT: Dartmouth, 1996.

Lipovskaia, Ol'ga. "New Women's Organisations." In *Perestroika and Soviet Women*, edited by Mary Buckley, 72–81. Cambridge: Cambridge University Press, 1992.

Pinnick, Kathryn. "When the Fighting Is Over: The Soldiers' Mothers and the Afghan Madonnas." In *Post-Soviet Women: From the Baltic to Central Asia*, edited by Mary Buckley, 143–156. Cambridge: Cambridge University Press, 1997.

Sakwa, Richard. *Russian Politics and Society*. New York: Routledge, 1993.

Torture, Harsh Treatment, and Incidences of Death in the Russian Army. London: Amnesty International, 1997.

Amy Caiazza

The Committee "The Soldier's Mother," St. Petersburg (*Komitet "Soldatskaia mat' "*) (formerly *Komitet soldatskikh materei*—Committee of Soldiers' Mothers) (1989–)

A woman's group organized in St. Petersburg in 1989 that assisted the Russian state in its effort to draft men into its army. Members provided counseling to men drafted into military service as well as to their families.

The St. Petersburg *Komitet soldatskikh materei* (Committee of Soldiers' Mothers) was founded in 1989 in collaboration with the officials of the city's military district. The group was led by Marina Aleksandrovna Averkina working with ten volunteer members (men and women and including representatives from the city's military and medical committees and a lawyer), who together supported the Russian Federation's military and mandatory military draft of the state's young men. State sponsorship provided for the minimal material needs of the Committee and included meeting space in the House of Officers. Once each week the members provided counsel to men called to the draft as well as to their friends and families, and assistance and support were also provided by members through the mail. The primary objective of the members was to communicate the urgent need to defend order and the Motherland, and money for transportation was provided to recruits or parents as necessary. The Committee was also responsible for seeing new recruits off to their new work and supplying information to parents interested in locating military sons. Averkina reported shaming recruits into service, telling them that no real Russian girl would hold the arm of a coward, a man who rejected his civic duty. While the effectiveness of the service was difficult to measure, the group was significant as an example of a women's organization geared to support the state during the transitional period immediately preceding and following the dissolution of the Soviet Union. This was critical since Russian data estimated that nearly half of the privates and noncommissioned officers viewed service in the army as wasted time and energy, and the same number were reportedly reluctant to perform their military duty conscientiously. It was one of the few examples of a "women's group" that received state support. This group was quite different from the well-known Committee of Soldiers' Mothers, which opposed the treatment of young men in the military. Eventually, the St. Petersburg organization changed its name to *Komitet "Soldatskaia Mat' "* (Committee "Soldier's Mother"), perhaps to avoid confusion with the other, nationwide organization.

Cross-reference: Committee of Soldiers' Mothers of Russia.

Suggested Readings

Gottlick, Jane F. Berthusen. "From the Ground Up: Women's Organizations and Democratization in Russia." In *Democratization and Women's Grassroots Movements*, edited by Jill M. Bystydzienski and Joti Sekhon, 241–261. Bloomington: Indiana University Press, 1999.

McMahon, Patrice C. "The Effect of Economic and Political Reforms on Soviet/Russian Women." In *Women in the Age of Economic Transformation*, edited by Nahid Aslangeigui, Steven Pressman, and Gale Summerfield, 59–76. New York: Routledge, 1994.

Nechemias, Carol. "The Prospects for a Soviet Women's Movement: Opportunities and Obstacles." In *Perestroika from Below: Social Movements in the Soviet Union*, edited by Judith B. Sedaitis and Jim Butterfield, 73–96. Boulder, CO: Westview Press, 1991.

Racioppi, Linda, and Katherine O'Sullivan See. "Organizing Women before and after the Fall: Women's Politics in the Soviet Union and Post-Soviet Russia." *Signs* (Summer 1995): 818–850.

Jane F. Berthusen Gottlick

Consortium of Women's Nongovernmental Associations (*Konsortsium zhenskikh nepravitel'stvennykh ob"edinenii* (formerly US–NIS Women's Consortium, 1993–1996) (1993–)

The Consortium of Women's Nongovernmental Associations (*Konsortsium zhenskikh nepravitel'stvennykh ob"edinenii*, formerly the US–NIS Women's

Consortium, 1993–1996, was significant as a Western-funded coalition organization that contributed to the building of ties within Russia's women's movement and provided assistance to women's organizations in Russia for program work and infrastructural development.

The idea for the Consortium of women's organizations began in Moscow in September 1992, when Moscow activist Elena Ershova met American Elise Smith at a conference initiated by Ershova and several Russian colleagues, called Women and the Market Economy. The Consortium idea originated with Ershova, who sought to create a network of Russian and American women's organizations with a nonhierarchical structure, jointly led by American and Russian coordinators. The Consortium began its activity in 1994, when the Winrock International Institute for Agricultural Development received an initial grant of $95,000 from the U.S. Agency for International Development (USAID), through the Eurasia Foundation, with which to found the consortium. The money was designated for "seed grants" to women's nongovernmental organizations in the former Soviet Union to fund program work, train women for leadership, make available technical services to women's organizations, and establish more reliable communication between women's nongovernmental organizations (NGOs) through the creation of E-mail networks and the establishment of newsletters. The Consortium sought to increase the visibility of women's nongovernmental organizations in the democratic transition process. The original thirty groups in the consortium included women's organizations in the United States, Ukraine, and the Russian Federation.

Through a small grants program, the Consortium helped fund numerous projects for women's organizations, such as program work, conferences, seminars, and publishing. Consortium grantees included the St. Petersburg Crisis Center; the Association of Women Entrepreneurs of Bashkortostan; the Women's Public Association, "Femina," in the city of Naberezhnye Chelny; and the Association of Women Cinematographers, Moscow. The Consortium funded a wide variety of conferences, including a three-day conference held by *Konversiia i zhenshchina* (Conversion and Women), an association of women in Russia's ailing military industry, on Conversion: Myths and Realities (January 1995), as well as a conference on Women and Society in April 1995, sponsored in part by MOLLI (Moscow Organization of Lesbian Literature and Art). The Consortium also helped to finance the publication of the first independent and indigenously produced text treating the issue of sexual harassment in Russia, in an edition of 1,100 copies. The book covered materials from a seminar on Sexual Harassment at Work, organized by the American Bar Association's Central and East European Legal Initiative, the Consortium, and the Moscow Center for Gender Studies (MCGS), in Moscow on May 20, 1995. The Consortium also assisted with distribution of the Russian-language version of the Boston Women's Health Book Collective's volume *Our Bodies, Ourselves* (published by Progress Publishers); this book was the only extant source in Russian of information about women's health from a supportive, feminist perspective.

Recognizing the sometimes divisive effect of foreign grant competitions on the women's movement in Russia, Martina Vandenberg, a talented young feminist hired as the American coordinator of the U.S.-NIS (Newly Independent States) Consortium, made an effort to announce the consortium's grant competitions at a wide variety of women's events to make information about grants available to as many women as possible. Also at the behest of Vandenberg, several foreign-funded foundations held a joint competition to provide travel grants for Russian women hoping to attend the United Nations (UN) Fourth World Conference on Women and the concomitant NGO Forum, held in Beijing (August–September 1995). The competition was administered by an organizing committee with representatives of the four major women's networks in Moscow: the Women's League, the Women's Union of Russia, the Information Center of the Independent Women's Forum, and the U.S.-NIS Consortium. Members of the organizing committee deemed the competition the first positive collaborative experience among Russia's major women's organizations. The Consortium held regular meetings in Moscow during 1994 and 1995, where Vandenberg made valiant attempts to create a real women's movement coalition, bringing together activists from the Women's League with those from the Independent Women's Forum's organizations. The results were somewhat successful, leading to increased collaboration between leaders of both wings of the movement.

USAID-funded grants, such as the one held by the U.S.-NIS Consortium, could not fund lobbying projects, since that would be equivalent to interfering in another country's internal affairs. The Consortium, however, was the inspiration for setting up a June 1995 meeting between women's movement organizations and Women of Russia (WOR) Duma Deputy Galina Klimantova, then head of the Duma Committee on Women, Family, and Youth Affairs, and Maria Gaidash, also a WOR Deputy. This was a significant milestone in the struggle to establish regular channels of contact between women's groups and policymakers. The women's movement representatives discussed international lending agencies' attempts to separate industrial enterprises from the service sphere, the need for gender analysis of such policies and of all Russian legislation, and the issue of state-funded abortion.

Despite the Consortium's positive effects, Ershova's goal of joint Russian–American leadership was not initially met. When the consortium was established, two years after the initial discussion in 1992, the leadership structure included only Americans. This situation changed only in 1996, when power was transferred from the American coordinator of the U.S.–NIS Consortium in Moscow, to Ershova, who was elected unanimously from among the consortium's Russian member organizations. The consortium simultaneously was awarded another major grant, through USAID, which ran through September 1998. The consortium also received a grant from PROWID (Promoting Women in Development, a program under USAID) that ran from October 1997 to January 1999. By 1998 the consortium included ninety-one women's NGOs. The fundamental concerns of the consortium focused on establishing reliable communication among groups within the consortium and with other women's groups, in particular through development of an E-mail network in Russia's regions, and on gaining a greater voice for women in state decision-making processes through advocacy. Several participants in the Consortium were members of the Presidential Commission on Women, Family, and Demography, and many cooperated with the State Duma's Committee on Women, Family, and Youth Affairs. In 1997–1998, the consortium engaged in advocacy work on issues including domestic violence, reproductive rights, the labor code, and the tax code. Members of the Consortium also took an active role in preparing a position paper (*Kontseptsiia*) on legislation concerning men's and women's equal rights and opportunities. The consortium was also active in development and microcredit programs for women's businesses in Russia.

Cross-references: Elena Ershova, Information Center of the Independent Women's Forum, International Women's Center Gaia, Moscow Center for Gender Studies, Women of Russia (WR), Women's League, Women's Union of Russia (WUR).

Suggested Readings

Bozhkova, Elizaveta. *"Chto dni v Pekine nam gotoviat i chto gotovim my v Pekin?"* (What Lies ahead of Us in Peking, and What Are We Preparing for Peking?). In *Strategii vzaimodeistviia: informatsionnvi vypusk (Strategies for Collaboration: Informational Issue)* [based on materials of the third interregional seminar from the series Strategies of the Independent Women's Forum: Before and After Beijing, held in August 1995]. Moscow: (October 1995): 29–31.

Khotkina, Zoia, ed. *Seksual'nye domogatel'stva na rabote (Sexual Importunity at Work).* Moscow: ABA-CEELI, Zhenskii Konsortsium, and MtsGI, 1996.

NEWW (Network of East–West Women). *Newsletter* (Fall 1994): 17.

Sperling, Valerie. *Organizing Women in Contemporary Russia: Engendering Transition.* Cambridge: Cambridge University Press, 1999.

Valerie Sperling

Crisis Centers for Women, Association of (*Assotsiatsiia krizichnykh tsentrov*) (1994–)

An association created to coordinate crisis centers and develop a unified approach to combating violence against women. The association of crisis centers became one of the best-organized and vocal advocates for domestic violence legislation. The association also documented incidents of violence against women in Russia and tried to educate the public about issues of violence and public policy.

The Russian Association of Crisis Centers for Women (*Assotsiatsiia krizichnykh tsentrov*) was founded in October 1994. Created at the initiative of the Moscow-based crisis center ANNA, or *Assotsiatsiia net nasiliu* (Association—No to Violence), the association met for the first time in February 1995 and by 1998 linked thirty-two crisis centers across Russia.

Although the former Soviet Union claimed that it had achieved equality of the sexes, the transition to a new, more democratic Russia highlighted the many problems that already existed and the continued need to promote woman's rights in the Russian Federation. One of the strongest areas of the women's movement in Russia was the development of crisis centers for women and their campaign to combat violence against women. According to the 1998 statistics of the Russian Ministry of Internal Affairs, an estimated 15,000 women were murdered by family members every year. Thirty percent of Russian high school girls were victims of sexual violence annually. Every hour a woman was sexually assaulted in Russia; furthermore, advocates estimated that this statistic represented only 6 percent of the actual crimes committed. Russia has had few legal provisions to protect women from sexual assault or domestic violence or to recognize domestic violence as a crime. There were no specific domestic violence laws under the civil or criminal code; in addition, Russian society was often unwilling to discuss such problems. The lack of social services and societal support often prevented women from receiving protection from the few legal provisions that might be applied to domestic violence situations.

The impetus to form the Association of Crisis Centers came from ANNA. ANNA started as a one-person hot line in 1993 and was initially known as the Family Fund's Women's Crisis Center Project. Although public awareness of domestic violence was low, the center received calls from women all over Russia. In 1994 the organization added a staff person, trained its first group of hot line counselors, and reregistered in December 1995 as ANNA: *Assotsiatsiia net nasiliu* (Association—No to Violence). As of 1998 ANNA had twelve staff members (hot line counselors, lawyers, psychologists, and activists) as well as dozens of volunteers. From 1995 onward, ANNA provided emotional, psychological, and legal support to over 7,500 women and as of 1998 received more than 200 calls a month. In April 1997 ANNA's lawyers and advocates brought the first domestic violence case to court and won, setting a legal precedent for all of Russia. Other pioneer crisis centers, such as *Sëstri* (Sisters), which worked with women surviving sexual violence, and the St. Petersburg Crisis Center for Women provided invaluable training and worked tirelessly with emerging crisis centers across the country.

In 1997 the Association of Crisis Centers launched a campaign entitled Stop Violence against Women to raise public awareness about violence against women and advertise the support services of local crisis centers. In addition, in cooperation with Women, Law, and Development International, the association piloted the Russian Lawyer's Advocacy Project. Working with seven Russian crisis centers from six cities (Moscow, St. Petersburg, Saratov, Irkutsk, Nizhnyi Tagil, and Murmansk), the project provided technical assistance to lawyers and crisis center counselors in an effort to integrate legal professionals into the grassroots movement to combat violence against women. As a result, women victims could receive professional legal counsel in addition to psychological assistance from the crisis centers. The association continued to expand. For example, the Crisis Center in Irkutsk (eastern Siberia) launched a project to develop ten crisis centers across Siberia and Russia's far east. ANNA received financial support from the Ford Foundation, the International Women's Club, and other Western sources. In 1999 the U.S. Agency for International Development (USAID) funded a three-year, $500,000 program to support Crisis Centers for Women (WCC) in Russia; the Interinstitutional Research and Exchange Board (IREX) administered the new grants' program.

Although the Russian government had a weak record of addressing violence against women, grassroots initiatives provided a beacon of hope for women searching for psychological, emotional, and juridical help in surviving the global phenomena of violence against women.

Cross-reference: Foreign Funding and the Women's Movement in Russia.

Suggested Readings

Abubikirova, N. I., T. A. Klimenkova, E. V. Kotchkina, M. A. Regentova, and T. G. Troinova, eds. *Women's Non-Governmental Organizations in Russia and the NIS: A Directory*. Moscow: Aslan, 1998.

Attwood, Lynne. " 'She Was Asking for It': Rape and Domestic Violence against Women." In *Post-Soviet Women: From the Baltic to Central Asia*, edited by Mary Buckley, 99–118. Cambridge: Cambridge University Press, 1996.

Dolan, Tracy. "Women's Crisis Centers: Bringing Violence out of the Home and into the Public Eye." *Frontline* 5, no. 2 (March–April 2000): 1, 4, 6–7.

Israelian, Evgeniia, and Tatiana Iurevna Zabelina. *Kak Sozdat' Krizisnyi Tsentr dlia zhenshchin (How to Start a Women's Crisis Center)*. Moscow: Press-Solo, 1995.

Israelian, Evgeniia, and Tatiana Iurevna Zabelina. *Krizisnyi Tsentr dlia zhenshchin: Opyt sozdaniia i raboty (The Crisis Center for Women: The Experience of Establishment and Work)*. Moscow: Preobrazhenie, 1998.

<http:www.irex.org/programs/wccindex.html>

Sarah Henderson

D

Dement'eva, Natal'ia Leonidovna (1945–)

An archaeologist, museum curator, and Minister of Culture of the Russian Federation (August 1997–September 1998).

Natal'ia Dement'eva, a Russian, was born on September 6, 1945, in Kuibyshev (Samara). She has been married twice. Her first husband, whom she met in college, was the nephew of the director of the Hermitage, Academician Boris Piotrovskii. Her second husband was an engineer. She had one child, a son, from her first marriage.

In 1970 Dement'eva graduated from the History Department of Leningrad State University with a specialization in history and archaeology. From 1970 to 1972, she worked on the Saiano–Tuvinskii expedition of the Institute of Archaeology of the Academy of Sciences of the USSR. She subsequently held a number of positions in the cultural field: senior consultant to the Leningrad branch of the All-Russian Society for the Protection of Historic and Cultural Monuments (1973–1977), chief curator of the Historical Museum of the Leningrad-Shlissel'burg Fortress, "Oreshek" (Hazelnut) (1977–1979), chair of the Leningrad Oblast Regional Inspectorate for the Protection of Monuments (1979–1987), and director of the State Museum of the History of the City of St. Petersburg (1987–1997).

On August 28, 1997, President Boris Yeltsin appointed her minister of culture, in the cabinet of Prime Minister Viktor Chernomyrdin, replacing Evgenii Sidorov (March 1992–1997). The famous St. Petersburg academician Dmitri Likhachev was a key supporter of Dement'eva's candidacy. There were also persistent stories labeling Dement'eva a protégé of Chubais, a rumor that she denied. In St. Petersburg Dement'eva had a reputation as a patron of modern art and as a cheerful and witty lady. She was a member of St. Petersburg's liberal and Western-oriented community.

When she became minister of culture, Dement'eva acknowledged the chronic funding problems of Russian museums and libraries, noting that she hoped "to achieve greater fairness in [the government's] treatment of museums and libraries." She also spoke of how inspired she felt that the "male government" had turned toward women. In addition to her own appointment, women had been chosen to head the Ministry of Health and the Antimonopoly Committee. Dement'eva characterized women as more dynamic and decisive than men, as understanding and feeling some things differently due to their greater burdens in life. She emphasized that women can be trusted with important political posts.

After Chernomyrdin was removed in March 1998, Dement'eva continued as Minister of Culture in Prime Minister Sergei Kirienko's cabinet. After Tatiana Dmitrieva's departure as Minister of Health, she remained one of only two women, the other being Oksana Dmitrieva, the newly appointed Minister of Labor and Social Development, out of the twenty-six ministers in Kirienko's cabinet. In September 1998, when Kirienko was replaced by Prime Minister Evgenii Primakov, Vladimir Egorov, the director of the Russian State Library, replaced Dement'eva as Minister of Culture.

Cross-references: Oksana Dmitrieva, Tatiana Dmitrieva.

Suggested Readings

"Dement'eva Natal'ia Leonidovna." In *Pravitelstvo Rossii (Russia's Government)*. Moscow: Institut sovremennoi politiki, 1997.

"Dement'eva Natal'ia Leonidovna." National News Service-Natsional'naia sluzhba novostei. <http://www.nns.ru/restricted/persons/dement0.html> (1997).

"Dement'eva Natal'ia Leonidovna: Kratkaia biograficheskaia spravka" (Dement'eva Natal'ia Leonidovna: Short Biographical Sketch). National News Service-Natsional'naia sluzhba novostei. <http://www.nns.ru/persons/dement.html> (1997).

Dyogot, Yekaterina. "First Liberated Minister of Culture–Natalya Demtyeva Replaces Yevgeny Sidorov." *Current Digest of the Post-Soviet Press* 49, no. 35 (October 1, 1997): 15; translated from *Kommersant—Daily*, August 29, 1997: 1,3.

"Natalya Dementyeva: Nevzorov Honed His Skills on Me." *Current Digest of the Post-Soviet Press* 49, no. 35 (October 1, 1997): 15–16; translated from *Kommersant—Daily*, August 30, 1997: 1–2.

"Natalya Leonidovna Dementyeva." Norsk Utenrikspolitisk Institutt-Norwegian Institute of International Affairs (NUPI). Centre for Russian Studies Database. <http://www.nupi.no/cgi-win/Russland/personer.exe/981> (1999).

"Women to Head Two Ministries." RFE/RL Newsline. Vol. 2, no. 88, Part I (May 11, 1998).

"Yeltsin Replaces Culture Minister . . ." RFE/RL Newsline. Vol. 1, no. 106, Part I (August 29, 1997).

Cheri C. Wilson

The Disabled Russian Women's Movement (1990–)

Among the many women's movements in Russia, disabled women's movements received little attention outside the Russian Federation, but in the 1990s movements of disabled women began to emerge and asserted their case for equal treatment.

No special studies of disabled women had been done in Russia as of 1999; fragmentary data on the disabled population collected by Natal'ia Shabalina suggested that although there were fewer disabled women than men, the women's handicaps were more severe and that they showed less social adaptation, had less education, and were more frequently unemployed. In the late 1990s disabled women in leadership positions in the All-Russian Society of Disabled began to say that disabled women generally suffered from the dual discrimination of gender and disability.

On June 17, 1999, a *Sovet po problemam zhenshchin invalidov* (Council on the Problems of Disabled Women) of the Moscow City branch of *Vse-Rossiiskoe Obshchestvo invalidov* (the All-Russia Society of Disabled, or ARSD) was formed. Led by the deputy chair, N. V. Lobanova, it was christened *Zhemchuzhina* (Pearl) and was subordinate to the ARSD, which had 2.4 million members throughout Russia, of whom 220,000 were in Moscow. Pearl's aim was to improve the life of disabled women. All eighty regional organizations of the ARSD received letters asking them to facilitate the formation of women's councils, but many letters, signed by men, maintained that such councils were not needed. The reason most frequently given was that women's groups were already functioning in some areas. For example, in Kostroma, where there was an active *Komissiia po problemam zhenshchin-invalidov i ikh semei* (Commission on the Problems of Disabled Women and Their Families), the chair of the Oblast ARSD, A. V. Dubova, organized a conference of leaders of the women's movement within that region. Similar commissions existed in fifteen Russian regions. Their leaders seemed able to reach out into the larger community.

The chair of the Ukhta city branch of ARSD, M. M. Kolpashchikova, reported close contacts with women deputies in the State Duma elected in 1995, who identified with the Women of Russia bloc. The chair of the Ulianovsk Oblast ARSD reported that at their women's meetings, representatives from the government were invited to teas and picnics for an informal exchange of views aimed at finding solutions to pressing social problems. In Perm, where a women's club existed since 1993 and was initially created as a social and recreational center, seminars were held in the late 1990s to prepare leaders and solve problems of daily life. The chair of Perm Oblast ARSD, V. I. Shishkina, reported close ties with Women of the Kama River Area. Nonetheless, disabled women faced many problems connected with their disabilities, which had to be addressed in special ways.

In Moscow's Pearl Club, one special problem was how to help pregnant women in wheelchairs. Such women were normally pressured by doctors to abort. The doctors cited the risk that the child would be born disabled, which appeared to happen frequently even to able-bodied women because of chronic malnutrition, poor health care, and other environmental factors. Doctors suggested that disabled women would be unable to care for the child properly, but in crisis-ridden Russia of the late twentieth century even many able-bodied women were unwilling to bear children, because having even one child put the family below the poverty line. Even family members, neighbors, and coworkers counsel disabled women against becoming pregnant. A Berkeley, California, organization of disabled mothers, Through the Looking Glass, provided the Pearl Club with video examples of adaptive devices that could make caring for children while sitting in a wheelchair much easier. N. V. Lobanova, and I. M. Margulis, who visited Through the Looking Glass, sought sponsors to distribute to everyone who needed it a device to raise and lower a clothesline of laundry. Another project of the Pearl Club was the acquisition of at least one wheelchair-accessible exam table for gynecological use, because there were few or none in Russia.

Although the results were modest, the movements on behalf of disabled women were raising public consciousness and solving concrete, special problems faced by disabled women.

Cross-reference: The Union of Disabled Women.

Suggested Readings

Dunn, Ethel. "The Disabled in Russia in the 1990s." In *Russia's Torn Safety Nets: Health and Social Welfare during the Transition*, edited by Mark Field and Judyth Twigg. New York: St. Martin's Press, 2000.

Dunn, Stephen P., and Ethel Dunn. "Everyday Life of the Disabled in the USSR." In *The Disabled in the Soviet Union*, edited by McCagg and Siegelbaum, 99–234. Pittsburgh: University of Pittsburgh Press, 1989.

Dunn, Stephen P., and Ethel Dunn. "Commentary on the Life of the Disabled": ("As If We Defended Another State," "Charity Begins at Home: The Regime Yields a Privilege," "Images: Who Notices the Disabled?" "The Disabled Get Organized," "Ilya Zaslavsky: A Deputy for the Disabled." *The Station Relay: Facts and Views on Daily Life in the Soviet Union* 4, nos. 1–5 (September 1988–May 1989): 76–95.

Oleinikova, Marina. *"Rodilas Moskovskaia 'Zhemchuzhina' "* (Moscow's "Pearl" Is Born). *Nadezhda (Hope)*, no. 8 (1999): 5.

Shabalina, N. B., and T. A. Dobrovol'skaia. *"Osobennosti proizvodstvennoi adaptatsii invalidov"* (Peculiarities of Work Adaptation of the Disabled). *Sotsiologicheskie issledovaniia (Sociological Research)*, no. 3 (1985): 121–125.

Shabalina, N. B., and T. A. Dobrovol'skaia. *"Invalidy i obshchestvo: sotsial'no-psikhologicheskaia integratsia"* (The Disabled and Society: Social-Psychological Integration). *Sotsiologicheskie issledovaniia* (Sociological Research), no. 5 (1991): 3–8.

Shabalina, N. B., and T. A. Dobrovol'skaia. *"Invalidy: diskriminiruyemoe menshestvo?"* (The Disabled: A Discriminated-Against Minority?). *Sotsiologicheskie issledovanie* (Sociological Research) no. 5 (1992): 103–106.

Shabalina, N. B., and T. A. Dobrovol'skaia. *"Sotsial'no-psikhologicheskie osobennosti vzaimootnoshenii invalidov i zdorovykh"* (Social-Psychological Peculiarities of the Interaction between Able-Bodied and Disabled). *Sotsiologicheskie issledovanie* (Sociological Research) no. 1 (1993): 62–66.

Shabalina, N. B., T. A. Dobrovol'skaia, and N. A. Demidov. *"Sotsial'nye problemy in-*

validov" (Social Problems of the Disabled). *Sotsiologicheskie issledovaniia* (Sociological Research), no. 4 (1988): 79–83.

Ethel Dunn

Dmitrieva, Oksana Genrikhovna (1958–)

An economist who served as a Deputy to the State Duma (1993–1998, 2000–) and as Minister of Labor and Social Development of the Russian Federation (April 1998–September 1998).

Oksana Dmitrieva, a Russian, was born on April 3, 1958, in Leningrad. She married and had one son. In 1980 she graduated from the Leningrad Institute of Finance and Economy with a specialization in finance and economics. From 1980 to 1991 Dmitrieva was a scientific researcher at the Leningrad Institute of Economy. In 1991 she was appointed chair of the Laboratory of Regional Diagnostics at the St. Petersburg University of Economics and Finance.

In 1993 Dmitrieva was elected a State Duma deputy from the Yavlinsky (or Iavlinskii)-Boldyrev-Lukin (*Yabloko* or *Iabloko*) Party list, appearing sixth on the list. In 1995 she was reelected a State Duma deputy from the *Yabloko* Party list. In 1996 Dmitrieva's book, *Regional Development: The USSR and After*, was published in English by St. Martin's Press. From January 1996 to April 1998 Dmitrieva served as a member of the Duma Committee on the Budget, Taxes, Banking, and Finance and chaired the Duma Subcommittee on Budget Systems and Extra-Budgetary Funds. In March 1998, when Prime Minister Viktor Chernomyrdin was replaced, Dmitrieva was appointed to Prime Minister Sergei Kirienko's cabinet as Minister of Labor and Social Development. After Tatiana Dmitrieva's departure as Minister of Health, Oksana Dmitrieva remained one of the only two women, the other being Natal'ia Dement'eva, the newly appointed Minister of Culture, out of the twenty-six ministers in Kirienko's cabinet.

Upon accepting the appointment, Dmitrieva suspended her membership in *Yabloko*, the party headed by Grigorii Yavlinsky (Iavlinskii). *Yabloko* viewed Dmitrieva's acceptance of the appointment as a mistake. Political commentator Andrei Piontkovskii viewed her appointment as a government strategy to undermine *Yabloko*, the Duma's staunchest opponent of government policies. According to Yavlinsky, six or seven members of his faction had been approached for the position, and government officials had turned to Dmitrieva only after Tatiana Iarygina, a specialist on social issues, had refused the position. During a 1998 May Day demonstration, Mikhail Shmakov, chair of the Federation of Independent Trade Unions, remarked that Dmitrieva was not an expert on labor relations and thus was not the best choice to head the Ministry of Labor.

While Minister of Labor, Dmitrieva was often at odds with Deputy Prime Minister Oleg Sysuev and Pension Fund Chairman Vasilii Barchuk. For example, in June 1998 she presented a draft law, rejected by the Yeltsin administration, that would have increased the minimum monthly wage from \$13.50 to

$18.00 as of April 1, 1998, and indexed annually the minimum wage. In July 1998 Dmitrieva criticized the management of the Pension Fund and called for a close examination of the fund's finances. Also in July 1998 she strongly opposed a proposal to reduce pension payments in light of the Pension Fund's financial difficulties. In September 1998, when Kirienko was replaced by Prime Minister Evgenii Primakov, Sergei Kalashnikov, a member of Vladimir Zhirinovsky's party, *Libernal'nia demokraticheskaia partiia Rossii* (Liberal Democratic Party of Russia, or LDPR), replaced Dmitrieva as Minister of Labor. In December 1999 she was elected a State Duma deputy with 41 percent of the vote from *Iuzhnyi* electoral district No. 213 in St. Petersburg with *Otechestvo-Vsia Rossiia* (Fatherland-All Russia, or OVR) affiliation.

Cross-references: Natal'ia Dement'eva, Tatiana Dmitrieva.

Suggested Readings

"Dmitrieva Criticizes Management of Pension Fund." RFE/RL Newsline, vol. 2, no. 144, Part I. <http://search.rferl.org/newsline/1998/07/290798.html> (July 29, 1998).

"Dmitrieva Oksana Genrikhovna." National News Service-Natsional'naia sluzhba novostei. <http://www.nns.ru/persons/dmitr.html> (1998).

"Government Rejects Increase in Minimum Wage." RFE/RL Newsline, vol. 2, no. 117, Part I. <http://www.rferl.org/newsline/1998/06/190698.html> (June 19, 1998).

"More on the Formation of the New Government." Norsk Utenrikspolitisk Institutt-Norwegian Institute of International Affairs (NUPI). Centre for Russian Studies Database. <http://www.nupi.no/cgi-win/Russland/krono.exe/2170> (1999).

"Oksana Genrikhovna Dmitrieva." Norsk Utenrikspolitisk Institutt-Norwegian Institute of International Affairs (NUPI). Centre for Russian Studies Database. <http://www.nupi.no/cgi-win/Russland/Personer.exe/103> (1999).

"The Russian Duma Moving towards Economic Compromise, Active in Foreign Policies." Norsk Utenrikspolitisk Institutt-Norwegian Institute of International Affairs (NUPI). Centre for Russian Studies Database. <http://www.nupi.no/cgi-win/Russland/krono.exe/696>(1999).

"Women to Head Two Ministries." RFE/RL Newsline, vol. 2, no. 88, Part I (May 11, 1998).

"Working Pensioners to Keep Pensions for Now." RFE/RL Newsline, vol. 2, no. 139, Part I (July 22, 1998).

Cheri C. Wilson

Dmitrieva, Tatiana Borisovna (1951–)

An important physician and psychiatrist and minister of health of the Russian Federation (1996–1998).

Tatiana Dmitrieva, a Russian, was born on February 21, 1951, in Ivanovo, a regional center a few hours northeast of Moscow. She and her husband, a professor and psychiatrist, had no children.

Tatiana Dmitrieva graduated from the Ivanovo State Medical Institute in 1975 with a specialization in forensic psychiatry. She worked as a psychiatrist at the

Ivanovo Oblast Psychiatric Hospital from 1975 to 1976. In 1976 she moved to the V. P. Serbskii Central, All-Union Scientific Research Institute in Moscow, where she remained until 1996. Dmitrieva completed her clinical residency in 1978 and her graduate work in 1981. She worked as a junior researcher from 1981 to 1983 and a senior researcher from 1983 to 1986. Dmitrieva chaired the Clinical Department of General and Forensic Psychiatry from 1986 to 1989. She was the Assistant Director of Sciences from 1989 to 1990. From 1990 to 1996 she was the Director of the State Social and Forensic Psychiatry Research Center of the Serbskii Institute. That same year, Dmitrieva became chair of the I. Sechenov Medical Academy in Moscow as well as a member of the Teaching Bureau of the Ministry of Health. On August 22, 1996, President Boris Yeltsin appointed her Minister of Health of the Russian Federation. In 1997 Dmitrieva was appointed a corresponding member of the Russian Academy of Medical Sciences.

Upon her appointment as Minister of Health, Dmitrieva warned that the health sector was poorly funded. She stated that her top priorities were fighting AIDS and providing good pediatric and maternity care. She indicated, however, that the government had been unwilling to allocate the necessary funding for such programs. In August 1997 Dmitrieva submitted a report on the restructuring of the public health care system by 2005, which was subsequently approved by the government. According to Dmitrieva's report, basic medical services would still be provided free of charge and would be financed through mandatory medical insurance. Some medical services, such as cosmetic surgery, physiotherapy, and massage therapy, however, would be fee-based. Dmitrieva promised that the poor would still be able to receive such special services free of charge if a doctor prescribed them. In addition, the new system would force publicly funded hospitals and clinics that were closed to the general public to join the national system. According to Dmitrieva, more than twenty federal agencies had special medical facilities funded by the federal budget but closed to the public.

In May 1997 Dmitrieva became the only female member of Prime Minister Viktor Chernomyrdin's cabinet. In August 1997 the number of women ministers in Chernomyrdin's cabinet increased to two when Natal'ia Dement'eva was appointed minister of culture. Dmitrieva's other activities included heading the Russian delegation of the intergovernmental Joint Commission on Economic Cooperation between the Russia Federation and the Benelux countries (Belgium, Netherlands, and Luxembourg) that met in Brussels in July 1997. During her tenure as Minister of Health, she, along with Donna Shalala, the U.S. Secretary of Health and Human Services, served as cochairs of the Health Committee of the Gore–Chernomyrdin Commission. In March 1998 Yeltsin replaced Chernomyrdin with Prime Minister Sergei Kirienko. In May 1998, as part of Prime Minister Kirienko's restructuring of the cabinet, Oleg Rutkovskii, the former head doctor at Moscow's First City Hospital, replaced Dmitrieva as Minister of Health. In December 1999 she was elected a State Duma Deputy from the

Otechestvo-Vsia Rossiia (Fatherland-All Russia, or OVR) party list, where she was listed thirteenth.

Cross-reference: Natal'ia Dement'eva.

Suggested Readings

"Dmitrieva Tatiana Borisovna." *Pravitel'stvo Rossii* (Russia's Government). Moscow: Institut sovremennoi politiki, 1997.

"Dmitrieva Tatiana Borisovna: Kratkaia biograficheskaia spravka" (Dmitrieva Tatiana Borisovna: Short Biographical Sketch). National News Service-Natsional'naia sluzhba novostei. <http://www.nns.ru/persons/dmitat.html> (1997).

"Gore-Chernomyrdin Commission Briefed on Women's Health Program." American International Health Alliance (AIHA). <http://www.aiha.com/english/pubs/fal97/aihadir.htm> (1997).

"Tatyana Borisovna Dmitriyeva." Norsk Utenrikspolitisk Institutt-Norwegian Institute of International Affairs (NUPI). Centre for Russian Studies Database. <http://www.nupi.no/cgi-win/Russland/Personer.exe/1043> (1999).

Cheri C. Wilson

E

Ekaterinburg Women's Organizations (1987–)

Three major groups, each with close ties to local and governmental and business leaders, dominated the women's movement in Ekaterinburg, the largest city of the Urals.

Ekaterinburg, known as Sverdlovsk during the Soviet era, was the political base of Boris Yeltsin, president of Russia 1990–1999, and the center for the defense and mining industries. In the post-Soviet period, the oblast remained one of ten major donor regions to the Russian federal budget. In the 1990s the oblast witnessed fierce political competition between the oblast governor and the Ekaterinburg mayor, and electoral politics played an important role in organizing the region's women's activism. There were three major women's organizations: the *Sverdlovskii oblastnoi soiuz zhenshchin* (the Sverdlovsk Oblast Women's Union), the *Ural'skaia assotsiatsiia zhenshchin* (the Ural Association of Women, or UAW), and *Ekaterina*. Each of the three women's organizations worked closely with local government officials and enterprise managers, and the two most active organizations were created precisely to mobilize support for the political careers of their founders. Local officials were responsive to these women's organizations with grants and other forms of cooperation as a means to win their support in elections.

The oldest, though perhaps least active, of the three was the *Sverdlovskii oblastnoi soiuz zhenshchin* (Sverdlovsk Oblast Women's Union), created as the *Sverdlovsk Oblast' Sovet Zhenshchin* (Sverdlovsk Oblast Women's Council) in 1987, and reconstituted as the Sverdlovsk Oblast Women's Union in 1991. It had branches throughout the oblast and was an affiliate of the *Soiuz zhenshchin Rossii* (Women's Union of Russia, or WUR). Its leader, Ol'ga Leonova, was deputy Mayor of Sverdlovsk under the Soviet regime. The goals of the Sverdlovsk Oblast Women's Union reflected the goals and rhetoric of the national organization of WUR: the elimination of discrimination against women in Russia; the promotion of women into decision-making positions at the local, regional, and federal levels; the social adaptation of women into new economic conditions; and the well-being of the family. The Sverdlovsk Oblast Women's Union's activities included work with the employment office on women's employment, organizing roundtables and conferences for International Women's Day, and providing school supplies and festivals for homeless children. The Women's Union was also involved in a committee consisting of government officials and representatives of women's organizations that helped to resolve specific problems brought to it by women who believed that government agencies had treated them unfairly. For example, a woman prisoner appealed to the committee to obtain visitation rights for her children.

The largest and most influential women's organization in Ekaterinburg, as of 1999, was the *Ural'skaia assotsiatsiia zhenshchin* (the Ural Association of Women, or UAW), founded by Galina Karelova. Karelova, who was named Deputy Minister of Labor and Social Development of the Russian Federation in 1998, began her political career as an activist for cooperative housing under the Soviet regime. In 1993, as Deputy Chair of the Sverdlovsk Regional Council, she brought together a group of women friends, associates, and activists to create the UAW in order to mobilize women to support her attempts to improve the oblast's social policy toward women, children, and families. The UAW was again mobilized to support her candidacy for the State Duma in 1995. With a platform emphasizing education, reform of the pension system, and social support for women, families, and children, Karelova and the UAW put together an impressive grassroots effort and a sophisticated media campaign that defeated seventeen competitors. The campaign mobilized many new women's organizations and activists under the UAW umbrella. Karelova resigned as president of the UAW when she was promoted to her position in the Ministry of Labor, although she remained influential in the organization. She was replaced by Evgeniia Barazgova, a sociologist at Ekaterinburg State University. In 1996 the organization claimed to have 2,000 individual and collective members (including Olga Leonova of the Sverdlovsk Oblast Women's Union) and had branch organizations in other cities and *okrugy* (districts) within the oblast. A council of thirty-five women, which included representatives of the branch organizations as well as many of the original UAW members, was responsible for key policy decisions. Its numerous organizational members included an enterprise fund for women entrepreneurs, a center for sociological research, Women of Russia, and a center for social support of women and families. In the late 1990s the UAW no longer defined itself as a political organization but instead regarded itself as a social organization designed to support women's activism and help women take their rightful place in the oblast's "civil society." The UAW, for example, was the first organization to sign an agreement of social partnership with the oblast governor in order to institutionalize cooperation between the oblast administration and the UAW on the protection of women and children's rights, on women and children's health, and on women's employment and entrepreneurship. It also operated a women's leadership school, created to improve women's administrative abilities and to encourage women to enter politics. In addition, the UAW organized a number of programs on local television entitled *Women's Parliament*, which brought specialists together to speak on pressing social problems such as unemployment and benefits. Finally, in the economic arena, the UAW received a large grant from the oblast government to encourage women's entrepreneurship in the region. As of 1999 its projects included an initiative to create a network of women's organizations throughout the Ural regions as a complement to efforts by the oblast governor to create an economic Association of the Greater Urals. Although the UAW received grants from a variety of Western donors—including a prestigious Democracy and Civil Society Award presented by the United States and European Union in 1998—it relied most heavily on the work of volunteers and material assistance from city and oblast officials and from large local enterprises. Despite its impressive record, representatives from some of the active organizations within its membership expressed skepticism about the organization's ability to make a real impact on women's lives. At best, they thought that the group enabled its members to sustain their contacts with other women's organizations in the region.

Ekaterina, the third major organization, was formed in 1997 by Nadezhda Golubkova, a former member of the UAW as well as a deputy of the City Duma and chair of the City Commission on Social Politics. Like Karelova and the UAW, Golubkova created *Ekaterina* partly to strengthen her political position. As the only woman in the City Duma, she maintained that she needed other women's support to ensure that her advocacy for education and other social programs was taken seriously. Although the organization was not a member of the UAW, the links between the organizations remained close. In fact, Barazgova, the UAW president, was listed as one of *Ekaterina*'s founders. Whereas the UAW increasingly defined itself as a social organization working at the oblast level, *Ekaterina*'s activities were limited to the city of Sverdlovsk and had explicit political connections with the city's mayor. *Ekaterina*'s activities included work with women in industrial enterprises on issues of employment; support of education; work with preschool children to help alleviate the closing of nurseries at factories; and work with the wives of officers. Perhaps *Ekaterina*'s most interesting program, however, was a crisis center run by journalist Liudmila Ermakova. The crisis center provided counseling and juridical advice to women suffering from all sorts of abuse. It was also a member of the Association of Crisis Centers—Ermakova, in fact, was a member of the association's Presidium—and in 1999 planned to begin offering training sessions for crisis center workers throughout the Ural region. Most remarkably, the group gained the active support of the local police chief and in August 1999 began a project training local police officers to deal with issues of domestic violence.

There were also a number of smaller organizations not associated with these three organizations, including Women Communists and Mothers against Narcotics. Most notably, the local chapter of the Committee of Soldiers' Mothers of Russia, led by Dina Solokhina, served as a conduit through which soldiers and deserters whose rights had been violated could make their appeal to government officials. Because women's organizations in Ekaterinburg and Sverdlovsk oblast generally were closely connected with local political and business leaders, it was likely that regional elections would continue to have a substantial impact on their continued activities.

Cross-references: Committee of Soldiers' Mothers of Russia, Crisis Centers for Women, Women's Union of Russia (WUR).

Suggested Reading

Efremova, Irina. "Russian NGO Promotes Women's Involvement in Politics." *Give & Take: A Journal on Civil Society in Eurasia* 1, no. 2 (Fall 1998): 13–14.

James Richter

Environmentalism and Women in Russia (1980s–)

In the late 1980s and 1990s women became actively involved in an environmental movement in Russia, as evidence of a variety of environmental crises became known.

Women have always made prominent contributions to the Russian environmental movement. In the late 1980s, however, a new phenomenon emerged, women's environmentalism. It had a distinct dynamics and specific orientation and was reinforced by the wider women's movement. Women's interest groups devoted to environmental issues have increased in numbers, though not yet in political influence. There was also an increase in the number of environmental groups with a large female membership or female leadership.

Women activists generally had professional backgrounds, with biologists, geographers, and environmental experts forming the core of the green movement. They often became agents of public pressure in order to overcome the inertia of official state agencies charged with responsibility for environmental policy. For example, women experts participated actively in the public struggle over Lake Baikal, the pollution of the Volga River, and unrestrained air pollution in Moscow, Dzerzhinsk, Kuibyshev, and other industrial cities. One of the best-known cases involved a public campaign launched by biologist Mariia Cherkasova in the mid-1980s against the construction of a dam on the Katun' River. Under Cherkasova's initiative, *Komitety spaseniia Katuni* (Committees to Save the Katun' River) were created in six cities; thousands of citizens supported the activities organized by these committees. The massive campaign of public protest halted construction of the dam. Cherkasova became one of the leaders of the *Sotsial'no-ekologicheskii Soiuz* (Socioecological Union), which had a high rate of female membership and served as an umbrella organization for green groups in Russia.

Several environmentally focused organizations were created by women during the 1990s. The early post-Soviet transition was marked by a tendency to exclude women from societal governance. The leaders of large environmental groups and movements followed this trend and became less likely to include women at the decision-making level. Women responded by creating women-only organizations that specified the goal of introducing women's distinct perspectives into the environmental movement. Sociological surveys showed that women approached environmental issues differently than did men. These differences were reflected in the agendas of women-only environmental groups that emphasized environmental health, education, and law.

Environmental health was one of the most prominent spheres of women's civic activism. Economic instability and the breakdown of social programs, including the health care system, resulted in negative demographic trends and the substantial rise of diseases. Women's reproductive health especially suffered: in the 1990s there were a threefold increase in the number of pregnant women suffering from anemia and a 61 percent increase in complications at birth. High rates of premature births, miscarriages, infant mortality, and birth defects were viewed, in part, as stemming from environmental degradation. The death rates for women and men reached unprecedented rates for peacetime in this century; of the generation of girls alive in 2000, only 10 percent are expected to live to pensioner age. Group members provided mutual help and support, lobbied local governments for social programs, distributed educational materials, organized mental health centers, and developed special work programs for families. The proactive position of such groups was exemplified by the *Dvizhenie za iadernuiu bezopasnost'* (Movement for Nuclear Safety, or MNS), an organization launched in 1989 by women from Cheliabinsk, one of the largest Russian military production centers. Routine dumping of radioactive waste into the river system, several accidents, and the day-to-day operation of the nuclear reactor and chemical plant in the region resulted in severe environmental contamination, a situation that local authorities preferred to ignore. MNS members under the leadership of Natal'ia Mironova campaigned for the release of information on the radioactive contamination and the state of the population's health. Facing officials reluctant to disclose full information, the group acquired radiation monitoring equipment and enlisted the help of medical and scientific experts to independently assess the state of the environment and of public health in the area. Local physicians who were active in MNS estimated that more than half the population of childbearing age in the region was sterile. MNS initiated courses on healthy living for women and published brochures on how to reduce contamination. In local politics, the MNS led the civic protest against the plans of local authorities to develop facilities for treating imported plutonium waste. The MNS had more than 150 active members and enjoyed mass public support in the region.

There were many other examples of similar activities on the part of women who found themselves living in environmentally critical areas and chose to fight for the future of their children. In Moscow such groups achieved success in several ways: they closed some polluting factories, prevented the construction of power stations in densely populated areas, and stopped the destruction of park zones. These NIMBY (not-in-my-backyard) groups used political methods of public pressure, including picketing, and generally dissolved soon after attaining their goals.

Some women's associations were created specifically to influence policymakers. This type of women's environmentalism is exemplified by *Ecoiuris*, the first Russian public interest environmental law organization. *Ecoiuris* was created by women legal experts from the Russian Academy of Science and the Moscow Bar Association. Members provided expert advice on environmental issues to other organizations and citizens, worked as legal experts for the State Duma, attended public hearings on large development projects, and offered training in environmental law and public activism. In the courts *Ecoiuris* successfully litigated several cases and drew public attention to violations of environmental legislation. *Ecoiuris* was unique in its sphere; its multifaceted activities have provided inspiration and strengthened the drive to enforce environmental laws.

Other women's organizations placed an emphasis on environmental education. Several groups opened environmental libraries, largely with donations from abroad, and educated the public through publications, mass media programming, and workshops. These groups usually focused on youth and often forged strong connections with schools.

Women's activism in rural communities also had a strong environmental dimension. Agrarian reforms undertaken in the 1990s completely neglected the ecological and social needs of rural communities. Dramatic declines in food production occurred, social service networks disappeared, and living conditions deteriorated. Approximately 70 percent of Russia's rural communities lacked running water or sewage systems, and nearly half had no gas, electricity, or medical facilities. The daily inconveniences of rural life especially affected women, due to the greater strength of patriarchal traditions in the countryside than in the cities. According to selective surveys of rural residents in the mid-1980s, women spent more than eight hours a day on home chores and private garden plots in addition to over seven hours at the workplace. Privatization made this double burden even more arduous and time-consuming. Yet, despite these hardships, rural women took the lead in improving their communities and environment. The *Mezhregional'noe dvizhenie sel'skikh zhenshchin* (Interregional Movement of Rural Women, or IMRW) was created in 1996 to respond to the most pressing needs of women in the Russian countryside. One of IMRW's most prominent projects involved the development of organic farming systems, an approach particularly appropriate for Russia because economic conditions rendered chemical fertilizers and pesticides unaffordable for the majority of farmers. Women from the *Vserossiiskii sel'sko-khoziastvennyi kolledzh* (All-Russian Agricultural College, or ARAC) in Sergeev Posad trained area farmers and students in affiliated institutions in integrated pest management and innovative marketing techniques. ARAC distributed hundreds of textbooks and extension pamphlets to over 250 agricultural colleges in Russia; it also introduced a four-year curriculum focusing on sustainable agriculture. The promotion of sustainable agriculture simultaneously addressed ecological, economic, and social problems.

Divisions among women's environmental organizations occurred over opportunities for foreign contacts and assistance. Some women activists viewed particular "ecofeminist" groups as more adept at forging foreign linkages than achieving concrete results. The problem involved women's organizations that added "green" issues to their agendas, attended countless meetings, traveled to foreign conferences, and published newsletters and reports but remained far removed from grassroots participation or practical work. These charges were leveled at groups connected with the former Soviet *nomenklatura*, like the *Soiuz zhenshchin Rossii* (Women's Union of Russia) and the *Rossiiskaia Akademiia Gosudarstvenennoi sluzhby pri Prezidente Rossiiskoi Federatsii* (Russian Academy of Government Service under the President of the Russian Federation). Some organizations were well versed in how to submit proposals pleasing to Western funding agencies, how to use Western terminology like "conflict resolution," "sustainable development," and "woman's rights." Yet these same groups may have promoted activities that exist primarily on paper. The impact of Western aid thus was an issue, with considerable criticism directed toward the failure of foreign foundations to scrutinize the results of their grants or to reach out to groups working effectively at the grassroots level.

According to Soviet ideology, the oppression of women and the degradation of the environment took place exclusively in market economies. On paper, the USSR introduced comprehensive and progressive environmental legislation as well as measures that guaranteed woman's rights. Glasnost exposed the emptiness of Soviet claims. Russian women, who had the world's highest rates of employment, education, and political representation, turned out to be relatively powerless members of society. Environmental regulations, introduced earlier than most analogous measures in the West, failed to prevent environmental abuses. Women environmental activists perceived similarities between the status of women and that of the environment. Both were treated as objects of governmental policy, as free resources to be manipulated by male leadership in accordance with regime priorities. Both lay outside the realm of central governmental priorities, and both suffered from the failure of socialism to tackle gender oppression and environmental exploitation. The reintroduction of capitalism did not resolve these problems and may even have strengthened them. But the 1990s brought about the intellectual and political liberation of women, and women became an active part of the environmental movement and added "green" issues to the larger women's movement.

Cross-references: Foreign Funding and the Women's Movement in Russia, Women's Union of Russia (WUR).

Suggested Readings

Åhlander, Ann-Mari Satre. *Environmental Problems in the Shortage Economy: The Legacy of Soviet Environmental Policy: New Horizons in Environmental Economics*. Brookfield, VT: Elgar, 1994.

Danilov-Danielian, Viktor, ed. *Ekologicheskie problemy : chto proiskhodit, kto vinovat i chto delat?: uchebnoe posobie (Ecological Problems: What Is Happening, Who*

Is Guilty and What Can be Done? A Study Guide). Moscow: Izd-vo MNEPU, 1997.

Dawson, Jane. "Intellectuals and Anti-Nuclear Protest in the USSR." In *Beyond Sovietology: Essays in Politics and History*, edited by Susan Solomon, 94–124. Armonk, NY: M. E. Sharpe, 1993.

Jancar-Webster, Barbara. *Environmental Management in the Soviet Union and Yugoslavia: Structure and Regulation in Federal Communist States*. Durham, NC: Duke University Press, 1987.

Mirovitskaya, N. "The Environmental Movement in the Former Soviet Union." In *Environment and Society in the Eastern Europe*, edited by Andrew Tickle and Ian Welsh, 30–66. London: Longman, 1998.

Perminova, A. I., ed. *Mezhdunarodnaia konferentsiia: zhenshchiny v ekstremal'nykh situatsiiakh, tom 1–4 (The International Conference: Women in Extreme Situations)*. Vol. 1: *Rossiiskaia Akademiia Gosudarstvennoi Sluzhby pri Prezidente Rossiiskoi Federatsii, Ekologicheskaia Zhenskaia Assambleia, Konfederatsiia delovykh zhenshchin Rossii IuNESKO (Russian Academy for Public Service under the President of the Russian Federation, Environmental Women's Assembly, Confederation of Business Women of Russia, UNESCO)*. Moscow: Izdatel'stvo RAGS, 1997.

Peterson, D. J. *Troubled Lands. The Legacy of Soviet Environmental Destruction*. Boulder, CO: Westview Press, 1993.

Protasov, Vitalii Fëdorovich. *Ekologiia, zdorov'e i prirodopol'zovanie v Rossii (Ecology, Health and the Use of Nature in Russia*). Moscow: Finansy i statistika, 1995.

Pryde, Philip, ed. *Environmental Resources and Constraints in the Former Soviet Republics*. Boulder, CO: Westview Press, 1995.

Wolfson, Ze'ev. *The Geography of Survival. Ecology in the Post-Soviet Era*. Armonk, NY: M. E. Sharpe, 1994.

Yanitskii, Oleg. "Industrialism and Environmentalism: Russia at the Watershed between Two Cultures." *Sociological Research* 34 (1995): 48–66.

Yanitsky, Oleg. *Russian Environmentalism. Leading Figures, Facts, Opinions*. Moscow: Mezhdunarodnyie Otnosheniia Publishing House, 1993.

Natal'ia Mirovitskaia

Ershova, Elena (1934–)

Founder of Gaia and a former senior researcher at the USA–Canada Institute of the Soviet Academy of Sciences with research specialization in peace and women's movements in the United States. Ershova also helped establish the Women's League and in 1998 became coordinator of the Consortium of Women's Nongovernmental Associations.

Elena Ershova was born in Moscow on June 26, 1934. The daughter of engineers, she received her early education in the sex-segregated schools of Stalin's Soviet Union. She was educated at the Institute of International Relations in the 1950s, after which she joined the staff of the journal *Kommunist* in 1957 but did not become a member of the Communist Party of the Soviet Union (CPSU) until 1962. In 1968 she enrolled in postgraduate studies at the Academy of Social Science of the Central Committee; upon completion of her thesis, which dealt with the American peace movement, she was awarded the *kandidat* degree. After completion of graduate work, Ershova became a researcher at the USA–Canada Institute of the Soviet Academy of Sciences. There Ershova continued to work on the U.S. peace movement, writing a definitive study of the Vietnam antiwar movement, and she also conducted research on other social movements, including the women's movement in the United States. The latter work provided her first exposure to feminism. Because of her familiarity with the women's movement in the United States, Ershova served as consultant to the Soviet Women's Committee from 1970 to 1985. During Perestroika, she addressed women's issues in Russia, proposing reforms of the women's movement itself so that it would more directly serve Russian women.

In 1990 she started an organization called *Mezhdunarodnii zhenskii tsentr Gaia*, (International Women's Center Gaia) named after the Greek goddess who created life out of chaos. Ershova, together with several other women, envisioned Gaia as an organization that would directly help women in need in the Soviet Union and, later, Russia. Financial difficulties forced her to shift Gaia's work away from direct assistance to women to educational and political advocacy activities. During the transition, Ershova frequently lectured on women's situation in Russia at many international conferences, such as a major conference on women's organizing in Vienna in 1994 and the NGO [Nongovernmental Organization] Forum in Beijing in 1995. Together with other women, she organized several events in Moscow, including the first conference on Women and the Free Market Economy in 1992. In addition to her work with Gaia, Ershova was one of the founders of the Women's League, an organization of women's groups established in 1992.

In 1993, together with Elise Smith from Winrock International, she initiated the NIS–U.S. Women's Consortium as a network of women's organizations. The goal of the consortium was to foster collaborative activities to improve the status of women in the newly independent states of the former Soviet Union. In 1996 the consortium evolved from a fledgling group of nongovernmental organizations to an international organization including the United States, Russia, Ukraine, Belorussia, and Moldova. Its Russian affiliation was officially registered in 1996 as the Consortium of Women's Nongovernmental Associations, and Ershova was elected its coordinator.

In 1998 Ershova stepped down as President of Gaia and was replaced by her longtime associate and Vice President for International Contacts, Nadezhda Shvedova. Although still affiliated with Gaia, she concentrated her efforts on her new position as coordinator of the Consortium of Women's Nongovernmental Associations in Moscow. In the latter role, she was a key planner of the December 1998 conference commemorating the ninetieth anniversary of the first Women's Congress in Russia.

Cross-references: Consortium of Women's Nongovernmental Associations, First All-Russian Women's Congress, International Women's Center Gaia, Women's League.

Suggested Readings

Noonan, Norma C. "The Bolshevik Legacy and Russian Women's Movements." In *Russian Women in Politics and Society*, edited by Wilma Rule and Norma C. Noonan, 77–93. Westport, CT: Greenwood Publishing Group, 1996.

Racioppi, Linda, and Katherine O'Sullivan See. *Women's Activism in Contemporary Russia*. Philadelphia: Temple University Press, 1997.

Racioppi, Linda, and Katherine O'Sullivan See. "Organizing Women before and after the Fall: Women's Politics in the Soviet Union and Post-Soviet Russia." *Signs: Journal of Women in Culture and Society* 20, no. 4 (Summer 1995): 818–850.

Sperling, Valerie. *Organizing Women in Contemporary Russia: Engendering Transition*. Cambridge: Cambridge University Press, 1999.

Zhenskoe dvizhenie v kontekste rossiiskoi istorii (The Women's Movement in the Context of Russian History). Moscow: Izd. "Eslan," 1999.

Linda Racioppi

F

FALTA/SAFO ***(Feministskaia Al'ternativa/Svobodnaia Assotsiatsiia Feministskikh Organizatzii)*** **(1990–)**

Organized as *Svobodnaia assotsiatsiia feministskikh organizatsii* (Free Association of Feminist Organizations, or SAFO) in 1990, it later metamorphosed into *Feministskaia al'ternativa* (the Feminist Alternative, or FALTA), a cocounseling group based in Moscow, cochaired by activists Marina Regentova and Natal'ia Abubikirova. SAFO was significant for its role as one of the first organizations registered in the USSR to dare to use the term "feminist" in its name, as well as for its support of the First Independent Women's Forum.

SAFO was originally established as the result of a feminist conference in March 1990, where Marina Regentova and Natal'ia Abubikirova became acquainted. The name was more grandiose than the organization; it was a group of approximately a few dozen people, rather than an association of diverse groups. In addition to Regentova and Abubikirova, founding members included Ol'ga Lipovskaia, editor of the journal *Zhenskoe chtenie (Women's Reading)* and later director of the St. Petersburg Center for Gender Issues, and Anna Natal'ia Malakhovskaia of *Mariia*, a dissident group that produced several issues of an underground feminist publication in 1979. SAFO was officially registered with the Ministry of Justice in 1990.

SAFO played a central financial and organizational role in the First Independent Women's Forum, Russia's first nationwide women's conference held independently of the state, which brought over 200 women to Dubna, Russia, in March 1991.

In 1993 the organization's name was changed to FALTA, the Feminist Alternative, in order to emphasize the feminist definition of the group. As the feminist cocounseling group FALTA, they began to produce *FEMINF (Feminist Informational Journal)*. By April 1994 *FEMINF* had appeared four times, in small runs, distributed largely to women who had attended the Independent Women's Forums in Dubna and at seminars of the organization itself. The journals covered thematic issues, including politics and violence.

As of late 1994, FALTA's activities included feminist cocounseling and lectures, for instance, by feminist philosopher Tatiana Klimenkova, who delivered lectures on the history of the women's movement. According to the cochairs, nearly sixty women participated in the group, and approximately twenty-five women considered themselves consistent group members. The weekly, free cocounseling groups lasted three hours; Regentova and Abubikirova injected feminism into the process by including material on sex-based discrimination and oppression to raise consciousness about societal, as well as individual, issues.

Group leaders in 1994 were interested in establishing a center in Moscow to expand into working with teenagers and into other regions that expressed interest in starting similar groups. In 1995 FALTA officially registered with the Ministry of Justice in Russia.

In 1996 FALTA expanded its work to train counselors and lawyers to work with female survivors of violence. FALTA was also a member of the Coordination Council of the Russian Association of Crisis Centers, and its leaders became involved in preparing a college course in the gendered aspects of violence against women. FALTA members continued to develop and conduct workshops on woman's human rights, women's leadership, and conflict resolution.

Cross-references: Crisis Centers for Women, Independent Women's Forum, Ol'ga Lipovskaia, *Mariia*, St. Petersburg Center of Gender Issues (PCGI).

Suggested Readings

Lipovskaia, Ol'ga. "New Women's Organizations." In *Perestroika and Soviet Women*, edited by Mary Buckley, 72–81. Cambridge: Cambridge University Press, 1992.

Lipovskaia, Ol'ga. "Women's Groups in Russia." In *Post-Soviet Women from the Baltic to Central Asia*, edited by Mary Buckley, 186–199. Cambridge: Cambridge University Press, 1997.

Sperling, Valerie. *Organizing Women in Contemporary Russia: Engendering Transition*. Cambridge: Cambridge University Press, 1999.

Valerie Sperling with additional information furnished by Tania Lipovskaia, a member of FALTA

Fedulova, Alevtina Vasil'evna (1940–)

A prominent leader and government official who served in various positions, including director, Young Pioneers (1971–1984); director, Soviet Peace Committee (1984–1987); member, Central Committee of the Communist Party (1990–1991); first deputy director, Soviet Women's Committee (1987–1991); deputy to the State Duma and deputy speaker of the Duma (1993–1995); and chair, Women's Union of Russia (1991–).

Alevtina Vasil'evna Fedulova was one of the most visible and controversial members of the women's movement in the 1990s. As a leader of the *Komitet sovetskikh zhenshchin* (Soviet Women's Committee, or SWC), she had promoted the official, worker–mother image of the Soviet woman. Later, as head of the *Soiuz zhenshchin Rossii* (Women's Union of Russia, or WUR), she pointed out some of the problems of Soviet life. She maintained that the old regime had advanced women's status but did not tell the whole truth about women's status. She acknowledged that women's interests were not always advanced by Soviet policies. An astute politician, she recognized the lack of popularity of former Communist officials and asked that people "not judge her harshly" because of her Pioneer and Komsomol past. In the 1990s she claimed to understand "everything in a new way, despite her completely different past life experience."

Fedulova was born in 1940 in Elektrostal', an industrial city in the Moscow region, where she also lived in her early years. She decided to become a teacher, and, although her mother wanted her to attend the local polytechnic institute, she applied to the Moscow Pedagogical Institute, where she was accepted on her fourth try. After completing her training, she worked as a teacher for a few years. She became a member of the Communist Party of the Soviet Union (CPSU) in 1963 and was soon recognized as a potential leader.

In 1971 Fedulova rose to prominence when she was appointed head of the Young Pioneers, an officially sponsored organization for ten- to fourteen-year-old children, providing them with recreational activities and political education. In 1984 she was appointed head of the Soviet Peace Committee. In 1984 she joined the *Komitet sovetskikh zhenshchin* (Soviet Women's Committee, or SWC), which experienced renewed support in the mid-1980s, when the *zhensovety* (women's councils) were reconstituted. Although the *zhensovety* were officially separate from SWC, SWC exercised leadership over the vertical structure of women's organizations.

In the late 1980s Fedulova also completed a program at the CPSU's Academy of Social Sciences and was headed for a successful political career. From 1981 to 1986 she also worked with the Party Auditing Commission and in 1990 was appointed to the Central Committee of the CPSU.

Despite her range of interests and positions, Fedulova began to focus her efforts on women's issues in the late 1980s and early 1990s. Her interest in women's issues solidified at a time when these problems became more visible to society, and Fedulova was a key figure in the developing women's movement. She began to work full-time for SWC in 1987 as First Deputy Director and then as Director during its transition from SWC to WUR in the early 1990s. She headed the electoral effort of the *Zhenshchiny Rossii* (Women of Russia, or WOR) electoral bloc in 1993 and led its activities in the Duma, where she also served as Deputy Speaker (1994–1995). In that role she promoted legislation to protect women's interests in the privatization process and a new family code with increased alimony rights.

After the defeat of Women of Russia in 1995, Fedulova lost some of her public visibility. However, because WUR continued as an active organization with relatively significant resources and experience, as its head Fedulova could still influence policy concerning women; the public considered her one of the most prominent and recognizable actors involved in women's issues. She also continued to represent Russia at international conferences and meetings. In the

1999 parliamentary elections, she ran as a candidate from the party list of Women of Russia. Women of Russia did poorly in the 1999 parliamentary elections, as other parties competed to draw women's support, and Fedulova was not elected to the State Duma.

Because of her background as a prominent CPSU member, Fedulova's position was controversial among some women activists in the 1990s. Fedulova herself admitted that the SWC had stressed the positive advances of woman's rights under communist rule—workplace rights, child care, maternity leave—without focusing on the problems associated with their lives, such as the double burden and workplace discrimination. SWC had promoted the idea of the Soviet worker–mother, often relying on traditional ideas about women's "natural" role as primary caretakers. Throughout her career Fedulova stressed the "innate" nature of women, their patience and their caring, qualities that she said men lack. These ideas often led her to focus on policies to help women fulfill these roles, rather than modify them.

Nonetheless, Fedulova played an important role in the modern Russian women's movement. WUR was one of the most important women's organizations during the 1990s, and as its leader Fedulova was an important player in the Russian women's movement.

Cross-references: All-Russian Sociopolitical Movement of Women of Russia, Ekaterina Lakhova, Soviet Women's Committee, Women of Russia, Women's Union of Russia.

Suggested Readings

Buckley, Mary. "Adaptation of the Soviet Women's Committee: Deputies' Voices from Women of Russia." In *Post-Soviet Women: From the Baltic to Central Asia*, edited by Mary Buckley, 157–185. Cambridge: Cambridge University Press, 1997.

Konstantinova, Valentina. "Women's Political Coalitions in Russia (1990–1994)." In *Women's Voices in Russia Today*, edited by Anna Rotkirch and Elina Haavio-Mannila, 235–247. Brookfield, VT: Dartmouth, 1996.

Lipovskaia, Ol'ga. "New Women's Organisations." In *Perestroika and Soviet Women*, edited by Mary Buckley, 72–81. Cambridge: Cambridge University Press, 1992.

Lipovskaia, Ol'ga. "Women's Groups in Russia." In *Post-Soviet Women: From the Baltic to Central Asia*, edited by Mary Buckley, 186–197. Cambridge: Cambridge University Press, 1997.

Posadskaya, Anastasia. "A Feminist Critique of Policy, Legislation and Social Consciousness in Post-Socialist Russia." In *Women in Russia*, edited by Anastasia Posadskaya, 164–182. London: Verso, 1994.

Racioppi, Linda, and Katherine O'Sullivan See. *Women's Activism in Contemporary Russia*. Philadelphia: Temple University Press, 1997.

Rule, Wilma, and Nadezhda Shvedova. "Women in Russia's First Multiparty Election." In *Russian Women in Politics and Society*, edited by Wilma Rule and Norma C. Noonan, 40–59. Westport, CT: Greenwood Press, 1996.

Slater, Wendy, "Women of Russia and Women's Representation in Russian Politics." In *Russia in Transition*, edited by David Lane, 76–90. New York: Longman, 1995.

Amy Caiazza

Femina (1990–)

A nonprofit women's organization in the Republic of Tatarstan. Its work was feminist in orientation and sought to improve the status of women in Tatarstan and Russia.

Naberezhnye Chelny, Tatarstan, may not immediately strike the visitor as a city friendly to feminism or conducive to the growth of a women's movement. It was the center of the USSR's heavy-truck industry; the KAMAZ truck factory once employed 77 percent of the local population. Naberezhnye Chelny, like many other regional, heavy-industry cities, struggled to recover from Russia's economic travails in the 1990s. Although the entire population suffered from the waning productivity of the KAMAZ trucking plant, women were hardest hit by the industrial slump and made up nearly 80 percent of the town's registered unemployed. The economic turmoil, however, produced at least one ray of light—the women's group *Femina. Femina* ("woman" in Latin) was established in November 1990 with the purpose of conducting research into the sociological and economic effects of the transition to a market economy on the status of women in a single-industry town. *Femina* reported the results of the study in its first television documentary, *Kamazonka*, in 1991. Inspired by the successful production, *Femina* persevered, using nonprofessional equipment and volunteers to produce videos that portrayed women's condition in Naberezhnye Chelny from the inside.

Following its initial filmmaking success, *Femina* produced fifteen half-hour documentary programs that were broadcast on the local television channel to a viewing audience of 250,000. In addition, *Femina* conducted more than ten sociological studies, published more than twenty scientific and popular articles, and hosted six regional conferences, including its most recent project, the first and second women's video festivals in 1997 and 1998.

Femina focused on film as a means to improve the position of women in society, arguing that women bore the brunt of negative images on television and the mass media. *Femina* believed that by changing the media, one might be able to change both the perception and position of women in society. The organization's two most ambitious projects in the 1990s were the First and Second Russian Inter-Regional Video Festival, Women's Themes, held in Naberezhnye Chelny. The objectives of the festivals included improving the quality of television broadcasts for and about women, raising sensitivity to women's issues among the general public, and strengthening the interaction between women's organizations and the mass media. For the 1998 festival, television journalists, producers, and women's activists from such far-flung regions as Murmansk, Irkutsk, Saratov, and Novocherkassk submitted their work. The videos touched on a wide variety of issues concerning women, ranging from domestic violence, single motherhood, and unemployment, to women's excellence and achievements in the arts, politics, or economics.

In addition to its work with films, *Femina* continued its research agenda. In 1998 the group conducted a broad sociological survey of the gender content in national television programs to document how women were portrayed on Russian state-owned television. *Femina* also helped to assemble a unique journal, *Devochki prociat vnimaniia! (Girls Ask for Attention!)*, a magazine primarily written by girls for other girls. The indefatigable director of *Femina*, Elena Mashkova, also taught self-defense seminars for women, which she conducted all over Russia. *Femina*'s plans for future projects included a full-length film on domestic violence in Russia, as well as the continuation of its work on education on gender issues. Its work was supported by the Ford Foundation, the John D. and Katherine T. MacArthur Foundation, the Eurasia Foundation, Global Fund for Women, and other agencies. *Femina*'s early record of achievement suggested that the organization had a good chance of succeeding and that *Femina* could have a regional and national role in influencing Russia's contemporary women's movement.

Cross-reference: Foreign Funding and the Women's Movement in Russia.

Suggested Readings

Abubikirova, N. I., T. A. Klimenkova, E. V. Kotchkina, M. A. Regentova, and T. G. Troinova, eds. *Women's Non-Governmental Organizations in Russia and the NIS: A Directory*. Moscow: Aslan, 1998.

Kobaeva, E. V. *"Sotsial'naia zashchishchennost' i zaniotost' zhenshchin v usloviiakh monopromyshlennogo goroda"* (Social Protection and Women's Employment in a Monoindustrial City). In *Zhenshchiny i sotsial'naia politika: Gendernyi aspekt*, edited by Zoia Khotkina, 68–78. Moscow: Institut sotsial'no-ekonomicheskikh problem narodnonaseleniia, 1992.

Mashkova, Elena Valentinovna, ed. *Devochki prociat vnimaniia! (Girls Ask for Attention!)*. A quarterly journal.

Mashkova, E. V., E. V. Loginova, and A. G. Kosurov. *Otchët po siuzhetnomu analizy peredach tsentralnykh televisionnykh kanalov. Genderniie stereotipy i televizionaia reklama (Report of the Content Analysis of Programs of the Central Television Channels. Gender Stereotypes and the Television Commercial)*. Naberezhnye Chelny, 1998.

Zhenskii bloknot. Occasional newsletter, published by *Femina*.

***Unpublished* Femina Papers and Reports**

Femina. "Differentsiatsiia oplaty truda muzhchin i zhenshchin v AO KAMAZ" (Differences in Salaries for Men and Women at KAMAZ). 1991.

Femina. "Otnosheniie zhenshchin k uvelicheniiu otpuska po ukhodu za det'mi." 1992.

Femina. Praktika zhenskogo predprinimatel'stva" (Experience of Women in Business). 1994.

Femina. "Problemy zaniosti zhenshchin" (Problems of Employment of Women). 1991.
Femina. "Zhenshchiny i trud" (Women and Labor). 1990.

Sarah Henderson

Feminism in Post-Soviet Russia: Emergence and Development (1990–)

A new development in Russia in the transitional and post-Soviet period, feminism was concentrated in a few cities and among the intelligentsia. The emergent feminist groups received Western funding and support and became a small, but vital, political presence in the 1990s.

With the exception of a small, dissident feminist movement in Leningrad in 1979 whose members were forced to emigrate in 1980, feminism arose in Russia during the late 1980s and early 1990s during the time of monumental societal change prior to the collapse of the USSR in 1991 and during the transitional period in the new Russia. In many ways, 1990 may be viewed as the starting point of contemporary Russian feminism. Although feminist groups developed in other cities, including St. Petersburg, Tver, Naberezhnye Chelny, Myrnyi, and elsewhere, the hub was Moscow. Most feminist organizations received financial support from Western foundations in the late 1990s.

Because of the longtime prejudice against the term "feminism" in the former Soviet Union, one of the obstacles to overcome in identifying feminists was the historical disdain for the term. The term was often used pejoratively in the USSR and regarded as a Western phenomenon irrelevant to the realities of Soviet life. In post-Soviet Russia, the reluctance to use the term persisted. Most, but not all, Russian feminists of the first post-Soviet cohort, that is, those women who began movements in the early 1990s, identified, at least to some degree, with Western feminism. By the late 1990s the Russian feminist movement included varieties of organizations with differing political orientations; their specific agendas grew out of the experience of Russian women in the Soviet period and during the transformation. The feminist-oriented research and information centers attempted to network the women's groups that identified themselves as feminist.

In a biographical research study conducted by the author, most feminists of the first cohort appeared to come from families within the intelligentsia, and most were socialized into the Soviet political system but subsequently reached a level of consciousness that led them to break with established patterns and beliefs. In most instances, their parental families were characterized by a strong, authoritarian mother who governed the home. During the Soviet era, the young girls were often leaders in the Young Pioneers but turned away from official groups during their teenage years, even though some were nominally Komsomol members. Most feminists had university degrees and could be found in a variety of professions. Most feminists had married young, borne children early in their marriage, and endured unhappy relationships. Many were divorced.

The developments surrounding Perestroika (1985–1991) inspired some women to become political or social activists, but many were disillusioned by the results of Perestroika because of the insensitivity to women's issues and the sexist attitudes toward women in the democratic movement and new democratic institutions. Activism during the mobilization encouraged by Perestroika resulted in the cognitive liberation of the first-cohort feminists. At the same time, international contacts were expanded, thus opening doors previously closed to them. The knowledge of foreign languages, especially English, proved invaluable for women seeking to cement contacts outside their immediate experience. Despite the failures of some aspects of Perestroika, it created an atmosphere in which women questioned all the realities in which they had been socialized, including the political system, the economic structure, their personal relationships, marriage, and so on. Some women declared their independence from Soviet-style gender relations in the family. Their gradual metamorphosis was soon given the name of feminism.

When women realized that their changing views were not unique, some began to organize into research groups or support groups to share experiences and conduct research into the changes affecting women in Soviet and, since late 1991, Russian society. The emerging research organizations and other women's groups met at two national forums organized in Dubna by the Moscow Center for Gender Studies in 1991 and 1992. Not all groups were feminist, but the feminist groups were among the most determined. As the 1990s progressed, a number of the feminist groups were able to obtain foreign assistance to pursue their agendas.

Among the notable organizations and networks were the Moscow Center for Gender Studies, the St. Petersburg Center for Gender Issues, the Women's League, the Consortium of Women's Nongovernmental Associations, the Information Center of the Independent Women's Forum, and many regional groups. Some of the most active regional groups were in Ivanovo, Rostov-on-Don, and Murmansk. The mass media also became an important resource of the women's movement. Radio *Nadezhda*, the television program *Ia sama* (*I myself*), and women's sections of publications such as *Ogonëk* were important in informing the public on women's agenda. The women-only publications, such as *Moskvicha (Moskovite)* and *Preobrazhenie (Transformation)*, provided necessary information and relevant statistics, accompanied by commentary.

In 1998 the coalition strategy of women's organizations formed the Network Women's Program, headquartered in Moscow, under the auspices of the Open Society Institute and sponsored by the Soros Foundation. The network identified as its priorities woman's rights, reproductive rights, women and education, women's public participation, information and media, and problems of women's organizations. The new coalition represented a new stage in the evolution of Russian women's movements and Russian feminism.

Cross-references: Consortium of Women's Nongovernmental Associations, Foreign Funding and the Women's Movement in Russia, Ivanovo Women's Movement, Tatiana Mamonova, *Mariia*, Moscow Center for Gender Studies, St. Petersburg Center of Gender Issues, Iuliia Voznesenskaia, Woman and Russia.

Suggested Readings

Lipovskaia, Ol'ga. "New Women's Organizations." In *Perestroika and Soviet Women*, edited by Mary Buckley, 54–72. Cambridge: Cambridge University Press, 1992.
Marsh, Rosalind, ed. *Women in Russia and Ukraine*. Cambridge: Cambridge University Press, 1996.
Noonan, Norma C. "The Bolshevik Legacy." In *Russian Women in Politics and Society*, edited by Wilma Rule and Norma C. Noonan, 77–93. Westport, CT: Greenwood Publishing Group, 1996.
Racioppi, Linda and Katherine O'Sullivan See. *Women's Activism in Contemporary Russia*. Philadelphia: Temple University Press, 1997.
Rimashevskaia, Natal'ia. "The New Women's Studies." In *Perestroika and Soviet Women*, edited by Mary Buckley, 118–123. Cambridge: Cambridge University Press, 1992.
Rotkirch, Anna and Elina Haavilo-Mannila, eds. *Women's Voices in Russia Today*. Brookfield, VT: Dartmouth, 1996.
Sperling, Valerie. *Organizing Women in Contemporary Russia: Engendering Transition*. Cambridge: Cambridge University Press, 1999.
Zdravomyslova, Elena. "Feminist Recruitment: Reconstruction from the Life Stories of Russian Feminists." Unpublished paper presented at the International Conference Biographies and the Division of Europe. Berlin, Germany, February 17–20, 1999.

Elena Zdravomyslova

Fonareva, Natal'ia Evgen'evna

Chair of the Russian Federation State Anti-Monopoly Committee (1997–1998). First Deputy Minister for Anti-Monopoly Policies and Support of Small Business (MAP) (1998–).

Little is known of Fonareva's early life and personal background, but she came into the limelight in 1997. On August 25, 1997, Natal'ia Fonareva was appointed chair of the Russian Federation State Anti-Monopoly Committee, a cabinet-level post in Prime Minister Viktor Chernomyrdin's cabinet. In October 1997 she became a member of the Russian Federation State Commission on Operational Questions. As Chair of the State Anti-Monopoly Committee, Fonareva also was a member of the Interagency Commission on Economic Security of the Russian Federation Security Council. On December 18, 1997, President Yeltsin appointed her to the State Representatives' Collegium of the 40 percent state-owned gas monopoly *Gazprom*.

In January 1998 Fonareva urged the government to try to block efforts by some Duma deputies to weaken the ban on television advertising of alcohol and tobacco products. In March 1998, when Prime Minister Chernomyrdin was removed in favor of Sergei Kirienko, Fonareva was one of only three women, together with Irina Khakamada, head of the State Committee on Development and Support for Small Businesses, and Tatiana Regent, head of the Federal Migration Service, who retained positions in the new cabinet. In September 1998, when Prime Minister Kirienko was replaced by Evgenii Primakov, she kept her post. In November 1998 Fonareva headed the Commonwealth of Independent States (CIS) Interstate Anti-Trust Council and served as the acting chair of the Russian State Anti-Trust Committee. Also in November 1998 Gennadii Khodyrev, the minister for Anti-Monopoly Policies and Support of Small Business (MAP), appointed her first deputy minister for MAP. Fonareva's appointment came at the expense of Irina Khakamada, who lost her position as head of the State Committee for the Support and Development of Small Businesses, when it merged with the newly created Ministry for MAP. Khakamada had declared her interest in the position of First Deputy Minister for MAP, which was given instead to Fonareva. In March 1999 Fonareva was nominated one of the state's candidates to the Board of Directors of the 52 percent state-owned RAO (Russian joint-stock company) *Edinaia energeticheskaia sistema Rossii* (Unified Energy System of Russia, or UESR).

Cross-references: Irina Khakamada, Tatiana Regent.

Suggested Readings

"Culture Minister on Women in Government." RFE/RL Newsline. Vol. 1, No. 107, Part I. <http://www.rferl.org/newsline/1997/09/010997.html> (September 1, 1997).

"Government Calls for Tougher Advertising Standards." RFE/RL Newsline. Vol. 1, No. 193, Part I. <http://www.rferl.org/newsline/1998/01/120198.html> (January 12, 1998).

"Women to Head Two Ministries." RFE/RL Newsline. Vol. 2, No. 88, Part I. <http://www.rferl.org/newsline/1998/05/110598.html> (May 11, 1998).

"Yeltsin Replaces Culture Minister . . ." RFE/RL Newsline. Vol. 1, No. 106, Part I. <http://www.rferl.org/newsline/1997/08/290897.html> (August 29, 1997).

"Yeltsin Replaces Representatives in Gazprom . . ." RFE/RL Newsline. Vol. 1, No. 183, Part I. <http://www.rferl.org/newsline/1997/12/191297.html> (December 19, 1997).

Cheri C. Wilson

Foreign Funding and the Women's Movement in Russia (ca. 1991–)

Foreign funding, particularly from the West, played an important role in supporting women's organizations in post-Soviet Russia.

Women's nongovernmental organizations (NGOs) in Russia were targeted by many Western funding agencies as a key component to a healthy and flourishing civil society. The funding of NGOs was due, in part, to the desire to foster "Western-style" gender equality, as well as to bolster women's sagging status in Russian society. Foundations such as Eurasia, Ford, Soros, MacArthur, the Global Fund for Women, and U.S. Agency for International Development (USAID)/ Women in Development (WID) were key players in assisting women's groups as they developed skills related to starting and running an NGO. The embassies of Northern European countries also provided crucial grant assistance.

Many Russian organizations subsisted primarily on Western grants during the late 1990s and, if fortunate, received small subsidies or grants from Russian sources. In a 1998 survey of women's groups across Russia, about half of the respondents reported that they had received a grant or assistance from a Western foundation. Thus, the effects of aid on women's groups were substantial, in both positive and negative ways.

Foreign funding opened a myriad of possibilities for women's groups that would not have existed without such aid; grants and assistance from the West provided a wealth of experiences and opportunities not normally available to NGOs in Russia. On a tangible level, grants brought support in terms of organizational infrastructure. Grants supplied computer equipment, money for salaried employees, or office space. In the 1998 survey, of the organizations that had received Western assistance, two-thirds reported having used the money for office equipment, 48 percent used grants to pay staff, and 43 percent received grants for the purchase of books and other literature. Foreign funding seemed to provide the basics that groups needed to build organizational infrastructure.

In addition, grants funded domestic and international conferences on women's issues. Drawing from the 1998 survey, of the women's groups that had received Western aid, 63 percent received grants to organize workshops, seminars, and training sessions, and 37 percent received grants to travel abroad for a conference or workshop. For example, the Ford Foundation supported Russian women's participation in the NGO Forum during the UN Fourth World Conference on Women in Beijing in 1995. The Soros Foundation was also active in promoting international conferences around the themes of woman's rights as human rights, domestic violence, and the trafficking of women. Foreign funding also supported training seminars to teach women leaders practical skills about running an NGO.

Grants also supported feminist research on women's issues and financed many newsletters and journals of individual women's groups. The Russian version of *Our Bodies, Ourselves*, published as *O vas i vashem tele*, perhaps the only Russian medical text addressing women's health issues, was subsidized by the MacArthur Foundation and published in Russia by Progress Publishers. The Moscow Center for Gender Studies (MCGS) conducted research and offered programs with the assistance of the MacArthur Foundation, the Ford Foundation, and USAID. Assisted by the Ford Foundation, MCGS ran a gender studies summer school from 1996 to 1998. In 1998 MCGS published a two-volume work on woman's rights in Russia and books on several policy areas. In 1998, with assistance from USAID, it published a series of monographs as part of the Gender Expertise Project, analyzing the impact of legislation on women.

Some grants were used to strengthen networks and ties with women's groups in Russia's regions. The Ford Foundation, through the NIS-U.S. Consortium, and the Network of East-West Women, actively funded projects that involved obtaining access to E-mail and the Internet; such access enabled women to discuss issues on a global level via electronic networking.

In the late 1990s foundations appeared to focus on continuing outreach to Russia's regions and building ties among women's groups. In addition, issues revolving around domestic violence rose to the forefront. The Ford Foundation supported the work of ANNA, a network of crisis centers, and the establishment of new crisis centers across eastern Siberia. Soros, USAID, and the U.S. State Department also sponsored projects on this theme.

Foreign grants opened a world of opportunity for some groups in a troubled Russian economy that had little to offer women's organizations. In 1997 the Eurasia Foundation assigned almost $.5 million in grants to women's groups or to projects with a woman-centered focus. The Ford Foundation in the 1996–1997 fiscal year distributed over $600,000 to support seven different projects on women's issues across Russia. Although the size of the grants was small when compared to the foreign aid given for economic restructuring, the money was useful in assisting the work of women's groups. As the 1998 survey of 150 women's organizations indicated, the grants enabled groups to solidify their organizational base, network with other groups, and participate in a wide array of opportunities not readily available to others. Without foreign assistance, most women activists would not have been able to travel to Beijing or to Prague for conferences, and many organizations would not have been able to plan and organize the multitude of conferences that were made possible through grants.

Foreign funding had negative results as well. Funding widened the distance between groups with access to foreign funds and those without such grants. One of the largest differences was the widening gap between those with access to technology and those without technology. Groups that had received funding were more likely to have an organizational infrastructure. In the 1998 survey, funded groups were more likely to have the communication basics: computers (83 percent), fax machines (55 percent), E-mail service (55 percent), and Web pages (16 percent). Groups that had never received Western assistance were less able to communicate with the outside world except by telephone and conventional mail.

Funding from Western foundations overwhelmingly was given to groups that professed a feminist agenda or that focused solely on women's issues. In the 1998 survey, funded groups were much more likely to focus on issues that related directly to women, while unfunded groups often worked with other segments of society, such as soldiers, the disabled, or the poor, or worked within a religious framework. Unfunded groups were also more likely to consider the goals of working for economic and political development as "very important," while funded groups rated these goals low on their list. Even though the majority of women's groups operated within a charitable mission, feminist groups had a disproportionate share of foreign funding. Part of this was due to the fact that many charitable women's groups did not seek funding. On the other hand, many foreign grant organizations operated within the general mandate of "democratization." Russian groups that provided charitable services had difficulty learning the specific language that Western foundations use, such as "civil society," "democratization," or "the third sector." As a result, groups that did not adapt their activities to the established rubrics were often overlooked in the funding process.

Although foreign aid facilitated networking and communication, networking sometimes excluded groups that did not receive foreign aid. According to the 1998 survey results, organizations that received Western funding reported a higher level of interaction with other women's groups and other NGOs on a national as well as international level. Funded groups maintained regular communication with other women's organizations and NGOs and attended conferences with greater frequency than groups that never received Western funding. Thus, there was a widening separation between groups that had access to seminars, networking opportunities, and potential funding sources and groups that were unable to make connections. Although several women's groups received grants to lessen this divide, it appeared likely to remain for many years.

Although funding opened up a myriad of opportunities for the women's movement, it also widened the gap between groups within the women's movement. In the context of extreme economic uncertainty in the late 1990s, the money provided by foreign aid exacerbated tensions between groups with access to aid and those without such aid. In the light of government inaction on most women's issues in Russia, foreign funding remained the only form of viable monetary assistance to the women's movement in Russia.

Cross-references: Consortium of Women's Nongovernmental Associations, Gender Expertise Project, Information Center of the International Women's Forum, Moscow Center for Gender Studies, Women's Information Network.

Suggested Readings

Abubikirova, N. I., Klimenkova, T. A., Kotchkina, E. V., and Regentova, M. A. "Women's Organizations in Russia Today." In *Women's Non-Governmental Organizations in Russia and the NIS: A Directory*, edited by N. I. Abubikirova et al., 9–23. Moscow: Aslan, 1998.

Adams, Francis. "USAID's Democracy Initiative: Recipient Needs or Donor Interests." *International Studies Notes* 23, no. 3 (Fall 1998): 9–14.

Diamond, Larry. *Promoting Democracy in the 1990s: Actors and Instruments, Issues and Imperatives*. A Report to the Carnegie Commission on Preventing Deadly Conflict. New York: Carnegie Corporation of New York, 1996.

Henderson, Sarah. "Importing Civil Society: Western Funding and the Women's Movement in Russia." Unpublished Paper presented at American Political Science Association (APSA) Annual Meeting. Boston: APSA, September 4, 1998.

O vas i vashem tele (About You and Your Body). Moscow: Progress, 1996. (A translation of the U.S. publication *Our Bodies, Ourselves*. New York: Simon and Schuster, 1984.)

Sperling, Valerie. "Foreign Funding of Social Movements in Russia." *Policy Memo* # 26. Program on New Approaches to Russian Security Policy Memo Series, David Center of Russian Studies. Cambridge: Harvard University, January 1998.

Sperling, Valerie. *Organizing Women in Contemporary Russia: Engendering Transition*. Cambridge: Cambridge University Press, 1999.

Struyk, R. J. *Making Aid Work: Lessons from Successful Technical Cooperation in the Former Soviet Bloc*. Washington, DC: Urban Institute Press, 1997.

Sarah Henderson

G

Gender Expertise Project (*Proekt gendernaia ekspertiza*) (1997–1998)

A project conducted by scholars associated with the *Moskovskii tsentr gendernykh issledovanii* (Moscow Center for Gender Studies, or MCGS) that focused on conducting gender analyses in selected policy spheres and on integrating women's interests into Russian reforms.

Although the *Moskovskii tsentr gendernykh issledovanii* (Moscow Center for Gender Studies, or MCGS) was involved with the gender analysis of public policy since 1990, the *Proekt gendernaia ekspertiza* (Gender Expertise Project) represented a formal effort to develop a base for public advocacy for women by providing the Russian government as well as women's nongovernmental organizations with in-depth analyses of selected public policy issues. Headed by project director Elena Kochkina and project coordinators Elena Kulagina and Tatiana Tomilina, the Gender Expertise Project received funding from U.S. AID (U.S. Agency for International Development), channeled through the program Women in Development (PROWID). The Gender Expertise Project focused on four issue areas: women and employment, women and the mass media, reproductive rights, and refugee policies. Roundtable discussions were held, recommendations were prepared for government agencies, and articles were written for various bulletins and for the mass media.

An array of scholars headed research on particular policy areas. The philosopher Ol'ga Voronina focused on women's issues in the mass media, including sexism in advertising, sexist language, and the publication of erotic and pornographic material. The economist Natal'ia Kosmarskaia completed a study of how refugee and migration problems impact women, while the philosopher Elena Ballaeva examined reproductive rights within the Russian context. The economist Marina Baskakova explored how labor laws and regulations affected women in the labor market. In addition, the Gender Expertise Project played an important role in working on the Conception on Securing Equal Rights and Equal Opportunities *(Kontseptsiia po obespecheniiu ravnykh prav i ravnykh voz-*

mozhnostei muzhchin i zhenshchin), a measure passed by the Duma in 1997 that outlined legal strategies for achieving gender equality.

The work of the Gender Expertise Project demonstrated the importance of monitoring public policy and integrating women's interests into the policy process.

Cross-reference: Moscow Center for Gender Studies.

Suggested Readings

Ballaeva, E. A. *Gendernaia Ekspertiza zakonodatel'stva RF: reproduktivnye prava zhenshchin v Rossii (Gender Analysis of Russian Federation Legislation on Women's Reproductive Rights)*. Moscow: MTsGI (MCGS), 1998.

Baskakova, M. E. *Ravnye vozmozhnosti i gendernye stereotipy na rynke truda (Equal Rights and Gender Stereotypes in the Labor Market)*. Moscow: MTsGI (MCGS), 1998.

Gendernaia ekspertiza zakonodatel'stva RF o sredstvakh massovoi informatsii (Gender Analysis of Russian Federation on the Mass Media). Moscow: MTsGI (MCGS), 1998.

Kosmarskaia, N. P. *"Zhenskoe izmerenie" vynuzhdennoi migratsii i migratsionnoe zakonodatel'stvo Rossii (The Women's Dimension of Forced Migration and Russian Migration Policy)*. Moscow: MTsGI (MCGS), 1998.

Carol Nechemias

Gender/Women's Studies in Russia (1990–)

The development of gender or women's studies in Russia occurred later than in the United States and Western Europe. Most program development began in the 1990s but grew quickly, especially when considered against the backdrop of the economic hardships that beset the country.

In the later Soviet period, social scientists had studied women's issues for some years, but constraints were imposed on conclusions derived from their studies. In particular, studies in the 1980s increasingly focused on the double and triple burdens that women faced as workers, mothers, and wives. Whatever women's difficulties, it was expected that published research would emphasize the positive achievements rather than the shortcomings of Soviet society. Individual scholars, especially in the major cities, had acquired respect for their research work, but the first major attempt to merge their talents into a center occurred with the establishment of the *Moskovskii tsentr gendernykh issledovanii* (Moscow Center for Gender Studies, or MCGS) in 1990. The MCGS was created within the Institute for the Study of Population Problems of the Academy of Sciences. It gathered scholars from a variety of institutes of the Academy of Sciences to study women's problems. In 1996 the MCGS initiated an annual summer school program to promote gender and women's studies. Several other institutes within the Academy of Sciences also established separate programs or departments to focus on women's issues.

By the mid-1990s women's studies had been established at several universities. One of the best-known programs was the interuniversity research program established by the Russian government and located in Ivanovo. The program was designed to coordinate women's studies programs in thirty Russian universities and institutes. Its chief administrator was Ol'ga Khasbulatova, who had started the Ivanovo Center for Gender Research and a program of "feminology" at Ivanovo State University. The Ivanovo program focused on the study of feminology, an approach that may be described as the study of women's historical role in Russia and their place in Russian political, economic, cultural, and social life.

In Moscow several universities established women's studies programs and conducted research on women. In St. Petersburg, several universities endeavored to include women's studies in their curriculum; in particular, the European University in St. Petersburg established a master's-level program in women's studies. Women's studies programs also developed at a number of regional universities.

By the late 1990s women's studies had made significant inroads in Russia. Methodologies varied. Some programs tended to be influenced by Western women's studies, whereas others continued the more traditional emphasis on women's economic and social issues. Some programs tried to develop new methodologies, such as feminology, which were uniquely Russian. Financial constraints on all universities limited access to materials and resources, but with determination women scholars managed to establish a firm base for women's studies.

Cross-references: Academic Feminism in St. Petersburg, Ivanovo Women's Movement, Moscow Center for Gender Studies, Anastasiia Posadskaia, St. Petersburg Center of Gender Issues.

Suggested Readings

Koval, Vitalina. "Russia." In *European Women's Studies' Guide 11*, edited by Claudia Crops, 168–172. Utrecht: WISE, 1997.

Mamonova, Tatiana. *Russian Women's Studies: Essays on Sexism in Russian Culture*. New York: Pergamon Press, 1989.

Martynova, E. I. *Osnovy feminologii (The Basics of Feminology)*. Krasnoiarsk: Krasnoiarsk State Trade-Economics Institute, 1998.

Moscow Center for Gender Research. *Materialy konferentsii, "Gendernye issledovaniia v Rossii: Problemy vzaimodeistviia i perspektivy razvitiia, 24–25 ianvaria 1996 goda" (Materials of the Conference: Gender Research in Russia: Problems of Collaboration and Perspectives for Growth)*. Moscow: 1996.

Posadskaia, Anastasiia, ed. *Women in Russia: A New Era in Russian Feminism*. London: Verso, 1994.

Rimashevskaia, Natal'ia. "The New Women's Studies." In *Perestroika and Soviet Women*, edited by Mary Buckley, 118–122. Cambridge: Cambridge University Press, 1992.

Vitalina Koval, with assistance from Norma Noonan

I

Independent Women's Forums (*Nezavisimyi zhenskii forumy* or IWF) in Dubna, First, March 29–31, 1991, and Second, November 27–29, 1992

The First and Second *Nezavisimyi zhenskii forumy* (Independent Women's Forum, or IWF) held in Dubna marked the birth of an independent women's movement during the final years of perestroika and within the Russian Federation following the breakup of the USSR. The forums brought together nonstate-sponsored women's groups and furthered the development of an informational network among previously isolated organizations.

The *Nezavisimyie zhenskie forumy* (Independent Women's Forums, or IWF) were historic events in the creation of a women's movement in post-Soviet Russia. The First Forum, held March 29–31, 1991, broke new ground as the first major, publicly advertised conference on women's issues that was not under the control of the official Soviet Women's Committee of the Communist Party of the Soviet Union (CPSU). Both Forums took place in Dubna, a town near Moscow, and brought together women involved in independent, unofficial women's groups.

The first IWF occurred before the breakup of the USSR and included about 200 women, representing forty-eight organizations from twenty-five cities in the USSR, plus twenty-six foreign guests from the United States, Canada, England, India, Sweden, Austria, Germany, and France. The idea for the forum originated with activists from the *zhensovet* (women's council) of the *Ob'edinennyi institut iadernykh issledovanii* (Joint Institute for Nuclear Research) in Dubna. An organizing committee of nineteen members was formed, which was dominated by women from the Joint Institute for Nuclear Research, the *Moskovskii tsentr gendernykh issledovanii* (Moscow Center for Gender Studies, or MCGS), and the *Svobodnaia assotsiatsiia feministskikh organizatsii* (Free Association of Feminist Organizations), more generally known by its acronym, SAFO. The organizing committee included many of the earliest activists in the feminist movement, like Anastasiia Posadskaia, director of the MCGS; Ol'ga Voronina, a future MCGS director; MCGS scholars Zoia Khotkina and Valentina Konstantinova; and Ol'ga Lipovskaia, Natal'ia Abubikirova, Natal'ia Filippova, Tat'iana Klimenkova, and Marina Regentova, all active with SAFO at that time.

The first IWF adopted the broad theme "Democracy Minus Women Is Not Democracy." The conference covered a broad array of topics: the process of social transformation in the USSR; the women's movement; the United Nations (UN) Convention on the Elimination of All Forms of Discrimination against Women (CEDAW); women and the market economy; women and the arts; stereotypes of women in the mass media; and women as objects of consumption. Although violence against women was not on the conference agenda, it was raised as an issue at the forum, and an unscheduled workshop was organized. This was significant because the issues of rape and wife battering had been taboo subjects for public discussion in the USSR. Another controversial matter involved sexual preference. Two days before the first IWF, the daily newspaper *Moskovskii komsomolets* published a lurid article depicting the conference as a gay and lesbian gathering. The Forum almost had to be canceled, as permission for the meeting to be held at the Joint Institute of Nuclear Research was withdrawn and reinstated only after protests and explanations. Some of the forum organizers believed that the newspaper article was inspired by the KGB, and two KGB agents apparently attended the conference. The conference's final statement avoided any comment on sexual preference and lesbian rights.

The Forum's concluding document was unanimously adopted (with two abstentions) and declared that women are the objects of economic, political, sexual, and cultural discrimination. Key proposals included the establishment of a public body to ensure the implementation of CEDAW; the proportional representation of women in parliament and state power at every level; the setting up of a fund and training programs to support women in business; the initiation of a campaign against stereotyped representations of women; and the formation of new educational ventures such as sex education and women's studies. Although there was disagreement over the formation of a coordination center, with many Forum participants fearing the creation of new, top-down, hierarchical organizations, there was consensus over the need to develop an independent women's information network.

The second IWF was held under changed circumstances. The USSR had collapsed, and the fears and risks connected with organizing an independent women's conference had abated. There were far more participants, over 500 people representing sixty organizations in the Commonwealth of Independent States (CIS), and a lengthy list of domestic and foreign sponsors. The conference was devoted to the theme "From Problems to Strategy." The Forum attracted considerable media coverage and demonstrated that an independent women's movement had become a reality. Sessions focused on topics like women in business, women's unemployment, rural women, women and electoral campaigns, women and mass media, women and violence, women and health, women's international collaboration, management of nonprofit organizations, and women in religion. The forum called on the government to collect and disseminate information about the status of women and to evaluate all proposed policies for their impact on women.

A major result of the second Forum involved the decision to create an independent organization to administer a women's information network. This led to the creation of the *Informatsionnyi tsentr nezavisimogo zhenskogo foruma* (Information Center of the Independent Women's Forum, or ICIWF), which was registered by the Moscow government in 1994 and represented one of the first women's networks in Russia/CIS. The ICIWF has played a major role in establishing information networks among women's organizations and has promoted a variety of activities in the area of education, the arts, and political lobbying.

The First and Second Independent Women's Forums demonstrated a keen interest in fostering and perpetuating a women's movement. Both forums were pioneering events in the development of networking among the independent, nongovernmental women's organizations that emerged during perestroika and in the wake of the breakup of the USSR.

Cross-references: Information Center of the Independent Women's Forum (ICIWF), Ol'ga Lipovskaia, Moscow Center for Gender Studies (MCGS), Anastasiia Posadskaia, SAFO.

Suggested Readings

Cockburn, Cynthia. " 'Democracy without Women Is No Democracy': Soviet Women Hold Their First Autonomous National Conference." *Feminist Review*, No. 39 (Winter 1991): 141–148.

Rusakova, N. "*Ona v otsutsivie liubvi i deneg*" (She: In the Absence of Love and Money). *Sovetskaia kul'tura* (May 25, 1991): 5.

Schultz, Debra. "At Independent Forum, Women's Groups Move from Problems to Strategy." *Surviving Together* (Spring 1993): 57–58.

Shcherbanenko, E. "*Feminizm v otechestennykh tonakh*" (Feminism: Native Voices). *Pravda*, May 8, 1991, 3.

Sperling, Valerie. *Organizing Women in Contemporary Russia: Engendering Transition.* Cambridge: Cambridge University Press, 1999.

Trylowsky, Ulana. "A Firsthand Report from the Independent Women's Forum." *Surviving Together* (Spring 1993): 59.

Carol Nechemias

The Information Center of the Independent Women's Forum (ICIWF) (*Informatsionnyi tsentr nezavisimogo zhenskogo foruma*) (1994–)

A Moscow-based organization that has provided independent, feminist-oriented women's groups in Russia with information services, educational seminars, and support in political campaigns.

The *Informatsionnyi tsentr nezavisimogo zhenskogo foruma* (the Information Center of the Independent Women's Forum, or ICIWF) was founded in 1994 by Marina Liborakina and Elizaveta Bozhkova to continue and expand the work of the first two Independent Women's Forums held in 1991 and 1992. From

1991 to 1993, the Forum had worked as a loose umbrella of women's organizations and activists across the country, facilitating collaboration and providing a voice for its members in national policy debate.

The Information Center served as a support center for women's organizations and as a clearinghouse for information on women's issues, woman's rights, and women's opportunities. Its extensive library, planned by Larisa Fëdorova, contained approximately 2,000 publications and an archive of approximately 200 documents. As part of its outreach activities, the ICIWF published through the Internet a weekly *Informatsionnyi listok (Information Bulletin)*; a paper version, *Vestnichka (Little Herald)*, compiled monthly on the basis of the E-mail bulletins; and a quarterly journal, *Vestnik (Herald)*, which contained forty to sixty pages of news, analysis, and feature articles related to the women's movement.

In 1996 the Information Center began to expand its work with women's groups outside the Moscow region. With support from the Ford Foundation, the ICIWF provided initial start-up capital to establish regional information centers that would strengthen horizontal links between women's groups across Russia. The cities that were chosen—Mirnyi, Snezhinsk, Petrozavodsk, Pskov, and Voronezh—possessed strong, independent women's organizations and provided a diversity of geographic locations across the Russian Federation. In 1998 three new centers, Irkutsk, Zhukovskii, and Dubna, were added. These independent branch centers supplied information to their own constituencies and requested from the center information on issues that most affected women living outside the capital.

The activities of the ICIWF included seminars, conferences, and a variety of projects related to regional social policy, ecological problems, equal opportunity, domestic violence, women and the arts, and training in coalition building, lobbying, and running political campaigns. The Information Center sought dialogue with the Russian government through its participation in preparations for the United Nations (UN) global conference in Beijing in 1995 and its ongoing contacts with state agencies dealing with women's issues. The Information Center also provided expertise and advice on legislation being considered by the State Duma.

As of 1998 the ICIWF had five full-time employees and about forty member organizations, including several from the newly independent states of Ukraine, Kazakhstan, and Belarus. It received financial support from the Ford Foundation, the British Embassy, AWID (Association of Women in Development), and other organizations. Although based in Moscow, the Information Center established itself as one of the few Russian nongovernmental organizations with a truly broad grassroots network. Its explicit, antihierarchical ideology helped it sustain a flexible, multifaceted network that has reached out to feminist activists in the regions.

Cross-references: Foreign Funding and the Women's Movement in Russia, the Independent Women's Forums, Mariia Liborakina.

Suggested Readings

Abubikirova, N. I., T. A. Klimenkova, E. V. Kotchkina, M. A. Regentova, and T. G. Troinova, eds. *Women's Non-Governmental Organizations in Russia and the NIS: A Directory*. Moscow: Aslan, 1998.

Kuznetsova, Larisa, ed. *Sami o Sebe (About Ourselves)*. Moscow: ICIWF, 1998.

Liborakina, Marina. *Obretenie Sily: Rossiiskii Opyt (Finding Strength: The Russian Experience)*. Moscow: CheRo, 1996.

Liborakina, Marina, and Tatiana Sidorenkova, eds. *NET nasiliu v sem'e (NO to Domestic Violence)*. Moscow: Information Center of the Independent Women's Forum, 1997.

Vestnichka (Little Herald). E-mail bulletin of ICIWF.

Vestnik (Herald). Quarterly Journal of ICIWF.

Sarah Henderson and Anna Rotkirch

The Institute for Development of International Business (*Institut razvitiia mezhdunarognogo predprinimatel'stva*) (1988–)

Founded in Leningrad in 1988, the *Institut razvitiia mezhdunarognogo predprinimatel'stva* (Institute for Development of International Business) was the city's first independent women's group to offer women instruction to prepare for work in a market economy and provide support for women's efforts in the difficult transition to a market economy.

The *Institut razvitiia mezhdunarognogo predprinimatel'stva* (the Institute for Development of International Business) was the first independent women's organization in Leningrad to offer business and English-language training. The organization sought to prepare Russian women for work in the market economy. Specific training in finance and business planning supplemented general business education and business-language preparation. It was initially organized in 1988 and registered in St. Petersburg in 1992 by Leah Moiseevna Lerner. Lerner was concerned about the disproportionately severe impact on women of the transition to a market economy. The majority of the newly unemployed were women. The institute offered intensive six- and ten-day certification programs at different levels of competence as well as international internship opportunities. Lerner's broader goal was to construct a support network for women business leaders. The fifteen institute members met with over 200 past and current students monthly in order to create a community of support and recruited prospective students from failing plants and enterprises. The Institute encouraged its students to become involved in the political life of the city and Russian state, and students were nominated and ran for election during the 1993 races. Members were also involved in the International Women's League, which promoted women's roles in politics. Funding from private Western sources provided the initial opportunity for organization. For example, Lerner received a grant from the Universal Women's Fund, based in New York, to support the purchase of a computer system and access to the Internet. The Institute achieved self-financing by 1993.

The group was significant not only for its work of retraining Russian women workers but also for its commitment to creating operating structures that allowed the voices of those involved to be heard. The group had a complex organizational structure that facilitated the individual involvement of many women. Lerner adopted many of the institute's governing concepts from seminar instructors in the United States, Japan, and Spain and cited her work with women outside Russia as the impetus for her organization. The organization was significant as evidence of women's successful efforts to create work for other women and provide retraining for unemployed or underemployed women. It was also an important example of Western influence on emerging Russian institutions.

Cross-references: Foreign Funding and the Women's Movement in Russia, *Missiia*, St. Petersburg Association of University Women (VERA), *Sovremennaia zhenshchina*, Women and Business in Russia.

Suggested Readings

Gottlick, Jane F. Berthusen. "From the Ground Up: Women's Organizations and Democratization in Russia." In *Democratization and Women's Grassroots Movements*, edited by Jill M. Bystydzienski and Joti Sekhon, 241–261. Bloomington: Indiana University Press, 1999.

McMahon, Patrice C. "The Effect of Economic and Political Reforms on Soviet/Russian Women." In *Women in the Age of Economic Transformation*, edited by Nahid Aslangeigui, Steven Pressman, and Gale Summerfield, 59–76. New York: Routledge, 1994.

Nechemias, Carol. "The Prospects for a Soviet Women's Movement: Opportunities and Obstacles." In *Perestroika from Below: Social Movements in the Soviet Union*, edited by Judith B. Sedaitis and Jim Butterfield, 73–96. Boulder, CO: Westview Press, 1991.

Racanska, Luba. "The Yeltsin Presidency, Economic Reform, and Women." In *Russian Women in Politics and Society*, edited by Wilma Rule and Norma Noonan, 108–109. Westport, CT: Greenwood Publishing Group, 1996.

Racioppi, Linda, and Katherine O'Sullivan See. "Organizing Women before and after the Fall: Women's Politics in the Soviet Union and Post-Soviet Russia." *Signs* (Summer 1995): 818–850.

Jane F. Berthusen Gottlick

The Institute "Woman and Management" (*Institut "Zhenshchina i upravlenie"*) (1992–)

A woman's organization founded in St. Petersburg in 1992 to provide education for women in the transitional period. Several St. Petersburg women leaders were among the students of the institute's educational courses. The group was also able to secure funding by offering courses to unemployed women, whose work was subsidized by the city. It was a good example of the important roles that men played in "women's organizations."

The *Institut "Zhenshchina i upravlenie"* (Institute "Woman and Management") was founded in St. Petersburg in 1992. It was established as an educational organization and nominally led by Elena Ivanovna Kalinina. In its attempt to serve the educational needs of women in post-Soviet Russia, the Institute offered courses in business, economics, and, periodically, women and politics. Specific courses on Russian politics, women in Russian politics, and aspects of political campaigning encouraged women to become directly involved in the emerging political structures of the Russian Federation. Members also offered lecture series, supported student exchanges, and conducted professional scientific research for various city and state authorities, including the State Education Committee and the State Assets Company. State funding purportedly given in return for the institute's willingness to train unemployed women supplemented the registration fees of students to support the program. The six faculty included men and women, and while ultimate authority remained in the hands of the male sector, the institute allowed some of the city's women leaders to become acquainted. Not only did women leaders find out that other women leaders and women's organizations existed, but a few constructed joint conferences and cooperated on various projects, and several former students became candidates for city office in 1994. The organization's influence appeared to be limited, however, by other women leaders' concerns about Kalinina's relationship with the former *Komitet sovetskikh zhenshchin* (Soviet Women's Committee) and her notable Communist past. Some women leaders, of varying background, saw her as a potential threat to the infant Russian democracy and as evidence of the continued power of the former Communist Party members. The Institute's office in a beautiful building in the center of the city on Staryi Nevskii (Nevsky) Prospekt was evidence for some that women, too, were ready to take advantage of the pain of the people in the post-Soviet period. Others focused on the fact that men headed three of the four educational departments in the institute. Only the Department of the Healthy Way of Life was directed by a woman. The Department of the Economy and Business, the Department of Management, and even the Department of Feminology were headed by men. The institute provided a significant example of organized attention to women's unemployment. The inner workings also revealed the conscious manipulation of public relations on the part of male (and female) leaders and power brokers.

Cross-reference: The St. Petersburg Association of University Women.

Suggested Readings

Gottlick, Jane F. Berthusen. "From the Ground Up: Women's Organizations and Democratization in Russia." In *Democratization and Women's Grassroots Movements*, edited by Jill M. Bystydzienski and Joti Sekhon, 241–261. Bloomington: Indiana University Press, 1999.

McMahon, Patrice C. "The Effect of Economic and Political Reforms on Soviet/Russian Women." In *Women in the Age of Economic Transformation*, edited by Nahid Aslangeigui, Steven Pressman, and Gale Summerfield, 59–76. New York: Routledge, 1994.

Nechemias, Carol. "The Prospects for a Soviet Women's Movement: Opportunities and Obstacles." In *Perestroika from Below: Social Movements in the Soviet Union*, edited by Judith B. Sedaitis and Jim Butterfield, 73–96. Boulder, CO: Westview Press, 1991.

Racioppi, Linda, and Katherine O'Sullivan See. "Organizing Women before and after the Fall: Women's Politics in the Soviet Union and Post-Soviet Russia." *Signs* (Summer 1995): 818–850.

Jane F. Berthusen Gottlick

The International League of Women Writers (*Mezhdunarodnaia liga pisatel'nits*) (1989–)

An outgrowth of an association of writers initially created by the women writers in the Soviet Writers' Union. Larisa Vasil'eva, the association's founder, reorganized the group as the International League of Women Writers in 1992. The purpose of the organization was to promote the interests and concerns of women writers.

In 1989, in response to the exclusion of women from the Editorial Board of the publication, *Sovetskii pisatel' (Soviet Writer)*, an official organ of the Soviet Writers' Union, Larisa Vasil'eva, a respected Russian poet, led a spontaneous movement to organize women writers. She recognized that exclusion of women from the Editorial Board was part of the marginalization of women writers. Although individual women writers were respected, women had little voice in the Writers' Union. The women organized as the Federation of Soviet Women Writers within the Writers' Union. The Federation developed ambitious goals, which included creation of a publishing house and establishment of a women's perspective in policy making, especially in the areas of ecology, ethics, and important social issues. The federation had approximately 500 members before the August 1991 coup against M. S. Gorbachev and the subsequent dissolution of the USSR.

When the Soviet Union collapsed, the Writers' Union also disintegrated. The Federation lost most of its non-Russian members as pressure grew for each independent Republic to cut its ties with Russia. In 1992 the Federation was reconstituted as the *Mezhdunarodnaia liga pisatel'nits* (International League of Women Writers), accepting membership of writers from Russia, the Commonwealth of Independent States (CIS), and foreign countries. In post-Soviet Russia, the League faced the same limitations as most other groups: many talented people but few resources and limited finances. With each devaluation of the ruble, their potential role and outreach lessened. The League continued to exist and offered advice to writers within its orbit, but its role was curtailed, and its efforts were not widely known.

Cross-reference: Larisa Vasil'eva.

Norma Corigliano Noonan

International Women's Center Gaia (*Mezhdunarodnyi zhenskii tsentr* Gaia) (1990–)

A women's group established in 1990 to provide support for women during the transition from communist rule. As it became increasingly difficult for small organizations like Gaia to support themselves, as well as grassroots projects, the group's focus shifted to education and political advocacy.

Elena Ershova, the founder of the *Mezhdunarodnyi zhenskii tsentr* Gaia (International Woman's Center Gaia), usually referred to as Gaia, was a senior researcher at the USA–Canada Institute of the Academy of Sciences with research specialization in peace and women's movements in the United States. She was joined by women such as Nadezhda Shvedova, who became Vice President for International Contacts, Zhenia Israelian, Tamara Sychevskaia, Ekaterina Zhukova, Tatiana Zabelina, and Natal'ia Iogansen, many of whom were scholars at the USA–Canada Institute.

Gaia activists began working to support women and their families in concrete ways, through projects such as a sewing center, an English-language instruction and arts training center for children, a traditional folk arts program, and a women's fine arts support project. In the early 1990s Gaia, like many other grassroots organizations, faced the difficulty of securing funds for its operation. When the organization was initially established, it was partially supported by the MIR (Peace) Association; later it received some support for its projects from international sources such as the Sam Rubin Foundation, World Learning, and other private groups in the United States. Gaia's projects, however, failed for lack of funds and because of the new taxation system, whose unrealistic tax rates forced many firms into bankruptcy.

Increasingly, Gaia activists focused their attention on public education, political advocacy, and development of international contacts. With Ershova taking a lead in the establishment of the Women's League, Gaia became one of the founding member organizations of that "organization of organizations." In 1992 Gaia cosponsored the conference Women and the Free Market Economy, an important event that brought together academic specialists, policymakers, and activists to discuss how women were faring in the emerging market economy. Gaia activists were also visible in the international conference scene. Ershova, for example, attended conferences on women's organizing in Vienna in 1994 and the NGO Forum in Beijing in 1995, and Gaia members spent considerable time lecturing and attending domestic public forums and conferences on women's rights and status in Russia. In 1993 Gaia registered as an official women's organization. The organization did not nominate candidates for political office; however, some Gaia members, including Shvedova, ran for elected office, but no one was successful. Ershova steered clear of direct involvement in politics. She did become active in the Consortium of Women's Nongovernmental Associations, and as her role within the latter organization grew, she gave up her position as President of Gaia. Nadezhda Shvedova became head of the organization in 1998.

Cross-references: Consortium of Women's Nongovernmental Associations, Elena Ershova, Women's League.

Suggested Readings

Ershova, Elena, Linda Racioppi, and Katherine O'Sullivan See. "Gender, Social Movements and Multilateralism: A Case Study of Women's Organizing in Russia." In *Innovation in Multilateralism*, edited by Michael G. Schechter, 303–334. New York: United Nations University/St. Martin's Press, 1998.

Noonan, Norma C. "The Bolshevik Legacy and Russian Women's Movements." In *Russian Women in Politics and Society*, edited by Wilma Rule and Norma C. Noonan, 77–93. Westport, CT: Greenwood Publishing Group, 1996.

Racioppi, Linda, and Katherine O'Sullivan See, *Women's Activism in Contemporary Russia*. Philadelphia: Temple University Press, 1997.

Racioppi, Linda, and Katherine O'Sullivan See. "Organizing Women before and after the Fall: Women's Politics in the Soviet Union and Post-Soviet Russia." *Signs: Journal of Women in Culture and Society* 20, no. 4 (Summer 1995): 818–850.

Linda Racioppi

Ivanovo Women's Movement (1991–)

The Russian women's movement was not confined to Russia's largest cities. Ivanovo, a city a few hours northeast of Moscow, gave birth to some of the most interesting developments in the post-Soviet women's movement and in gender studies.

Ivanovo, a city of approximately 400,000 people, had a small, but active, women's movement in the 1990s. Known as the "city of brides" because of its female-dominated textile industry, Ivanovo suffered a severe industrial decline during the economic transition. Many factories found themselves without raw materials and had to stop or curtail production as Central Asian countries sought world market prices for their cotton. During much of the 1990s the Ivanovo oblast had the highest unemployment rate of all Russia's provinces. Not surprisingly, economic issues became a central focus of the Ivanovo women's movement.

Even during the Soviet era, the local *zhensovet* (women's council), an offshoot of the *Komitet sovetskikh zhenshchin* (Soviet Women's Committee, or SWC), had a reputation for committed activism on behalf of women. The local branch of the *Soiuz zhenshchin Rossii* (Women's Union of Russia, or WUR), led by Natal'ia Kovaleva, registered with the provincial Ministry of Justice in June 1991 to continue the *zhensovet*'s work for the welfare of women and families. The *Gorodskoi sovet zhenshchin* (City Women's Union) provided a consultation service for women needing assistance with employment or with issues relating to the receipt of welfare benefits. It also worked with the local municipal administration to obtain subsidies for child-care centers and to reduce apartment rents and transportation costs for multichild families. The group also had success in electing three of its members, including Kovaleva, to the city council in 1996, ensuring that the city budget addressed at least some of women's welfare needs.

Finally, the city Women's Union also held charity events and a Mothers' Week with the support of the city administration.

According to its charter, the Ivanovo Women's Union may have both individual and collective members. In 1995–1996, the Ivanovo Women's Union had four district-level subdivisions and also acted as an umbrella organization under which the *Komitet mnogodetnykh semei* (Committee of Multichild Families), *Komitet nepolnykh semei* (the Committee of Single-Parent Families), and a local branch of *Komitet soldatskikh materei Rossii* (Committee of Soldiers' Mothers) operated. The Committee of Single-Parent Families was founded in 1993, a group of seven activists led by Larisa Nazarova, a widowed single mother, to cater to the needs of Ivanovo's 2,300 single-parent (*nepolnye*) families. Similarly, the Committee of Multichild Families, which encompassed the approximately 2,300 families with three or more children, was run by a group of eight activists, headed by Nina Temnikova, herself the mother of ten children. Both organizations' constituencies included young mothers, many of whom had lost their jobs in the textile industry and remained unemployed.

Ivanovo's branch of the Committee of Soldiers' Mothers of Russia formed in response to the war in Chechnia. Their activities included sending humanitarian aid to Chechnia as well as holding informational meetings about soldiers' rights and obligations for the mothers of young men about to come of age and be drafted into the Russian army. The Committee itself was small, with a group of eleven core activists, although dozens more had attended its meetings.

Ivanovo's City Women's Union also sponsored a monthly lecture series between October and April, entitled the University of Women, a program of the local Center for Culture and Leisure. As of 1995, the "University" had been operating for over a decade. Attracting approximately 400 people each time, the lectures focused on the creative arts. Audience members paid a small fee to hear these lectures, which were occasionally presented by renowned figures.

In 1992 the women's movement in Ivanovo separated into two different directions, though members of the two directions still cooperated closely. While the Ivanovo Women's Union continued to emphasize social welfare, a second group formed the *Klub delovaia zhenshchina* (Business Women's Club), led by Margarita Razina, which sought to empower women to deal with the new economy. In some ways, this organization resembled an exclusive women's rotary club, in which approximately twenty-five notable women of the community met regularly to share information about their activities and other news. The Club also encouraged women's industry in Ivanovo in various ways. It sponsored an annual fair entitled Women's Creative Activity and Enterprise, organized competitions among promising local clothing designers for an opportunity to exhibit their creations in the famous Moscow salon of Slava Zaitsev, and held annual seminars for designers and textile painters.

The Businesswomen's Club also helped found the *Tsentr sotsial'noi podderzhki zhenshchin i semei* (Center for Social Support of Women and Families), created in 1994 at the initiative of Ol'ga Khasbulatova, a former party official and historian of the early twentieth-century Russian women's movement. This organization offered unemployed women psychological counseling and job retraining courses in a variety of subjects, including secretarial work, bookkeeping, social work, entrepreneurship, and handicrafts. The center maintained an exhibition hall where local craftswomen could display their wares. Supported, in large part, by the local division of the federal employment service, the center had eight staff members at its height in 1995–1996. When that support ceased in 1996, the center could no longer offer retraining courses.

An energetic activist for woman's rights, Ol'ga Khasbulatova also founded the local chapter of Ekaterina Lakhova's organization the *Obshcherossiiskoe obshestvenno-politicheskoe dvizhenie zhenshchin Rossii* (All-Russian Sociopolitical Movement of Women of Russia) in January 1997. Khasbulatova also helped Ivanovo become an important site for the study of "feminology" and gender studies outside Moscow and St. Petersburg. In March 1996 the *Ivanovskii Tsentr gendernykh issledovanii* (Ivanovo Center for Gender Research, or ICGR) was created as part of Ivanovo State University and was registered as an autonomous social organization in 1997. Under Khasbulatova's leadership, the university became the administrative center for the interuniversity program, the Women of Russia: Problems of Adaptation to New Socio-Economic Conditions. The interuniversity program published a quarterly journal, *Zhenshchina v rossiiskom obshchestve (Woman in Russian Society)* and sponsored an annual conference that attracted scholars from all over Russia and abroad. In 1998 the program was reconstituted as *Feminologiia i gendernye issledovaniia v Rossii* (Feminology and Gender Research in Russia). The interuniversity program included thirty institutions and was sponsored by the Russian Federal Ministry of General and Professional Education, with additional support from Lakhova's All-Russian Sociopolitical Movement of Women in Russia and, in the initial stages, the United Nations Educational, Scientific, and Cultural Organization (UNESCO). The theme of the May 1999 conference was Feminology and Gender Studies in Russia.

Despite differing philosophies, the different strands of Ivanovo's women's movement worked well together. The leadership was highly educated, many with advanced postgraduate degrees, and often had previous contacts with each other in various Soviet-era institutes, including the Communist Party and Komsomol organizations at their academic institutes or through other professional ties. Finally, though poor in resources, the ability of the Ivanovo Women's Union to elect representatives to the city council, as well as Khasbulatova's past political connections, created a political environment that allowed the organization to operate with some success.

Cross-references: Committee of Soldiers' Mothers of Russia, Gender/Women's Studies in Russia, Ekaterina Lakhova, Women's Union of Russia (WUR).

Suggested Readings

Browning, Genia. "The *zhensovety* Revisited." In *Perestroika and Soviet Women*, edited by Mary Buckley, 97–117. Cambridge: Cambridge University Press, 1992.

Khasbulatova, Ol'ga. *Opyt i traditsii zhenskogo dvizheniia v Rossii (1860–1917) (The Experience and Traditions of the Women's Movement in Russia)*. Ivanovo: Ivanovo State University, 1994.

Khasbulatova, Ol'ga. *Zhenskie organizatsii v novykh usloviakh (Women's Organizations under New Conditions)*. Ivanovo: Znanie, 1991.

Sperling, Valerie. *Organizing Women in Contemporary Russia: Engendering Transition*. Cambridge: Cambridge University Press, 1999.

Valerie Sperling and James Richter

K

Karelian Center for Gender Studies (*Karel'skii tsentr gendernykh isledovanii*, or KCGS) (1995–)

A nonprofit women's organization in Petrozavodsk, Republic of Karelia. Feminist in orientation, the Center posited that woman's rights were an integral part of human rights, as stated and upheld by various United Nations documents and conferences.

The *Karel'skii tsentr gendernykh isledovanii* (Karelian Center for Gender Studies, or KCGS) was a pioneering feminist center in Karelia. The first openly feminist group to form in the republic, the center was founded after the 1995 United Nations (UN) Women's Conference in Beijing. Prior to the UN Conference, Larisa Boichenko headed an organization in Petrozavodsk called Artemis, Association of Women in Sciences. Dissatisfied with Artemis and inspired by the experience of other women leaders, Larisa Boichenko returned to Petrozavodsk and established the Center for Gender Studies, consciously choosing the term "gender studies" over the less controversial "women's studies." The Center was officially registered as a nongovernmental association in 1995; its activities were aimed at advancing gender studies, establishing a database on women's organizations in the Republic of Karelia, providing seminars to women in the region, and serving as an information center for women's groups as well as other nongovernmental organizations in the region.

In 1996 KCGS received grants from the Ford Foundation and the Eurasia Foundation to establish the Information and Education Center of the Women of the Republic of Karelia in Petrozavodsk. Since 1996 they have organized many seminars for Karelian women on topics such as women of Karelia and their role in society, women against violence, and computer courses for women.

According to the Center for Gender Studies, overcoming most women's groups' isolation from one another was one of its biggest challenges. The Republic of Karelia was sparsely populated; as a result women's groups operated with little knowledge of others' activities. The Center for Gender Studies hoped to overcome its isolation by continuing its work with seminars. As of the late

1990s, its goal was to obtain funding to start a computer network with other women's groups in the region.

Although the Center was explicitly feminist, it worked with a wide array of women's groups in the region that represented more traditional interests. The Center also served as a regional hub for the Information Center of the Independent Women's Forum.

Cross-reference: Information Center of the Independent Women's Forum.

Suggested Readings

Abubikirova, N. I., T. A. Klimenkova, E. V. Kotchkina, M. A. Regentova, and T. G. Troinova, eds. *Women's Non-Governmental Organizations in Russia and the NIS: A Directory*. Moscow: Aslan, 1998.

Kuznetsova, Larisa. *Sami o sebe (About Ourselves)*. Moscow: ICIWF, 1998.

Sarah Henderson

Khakamada, Irina Mutsuovna (1955–)

An important female politician in the Russian Federation and a state official. Khakamada was recognized as an economic specialist and as a leading advocate for women's economic affairs.

Irina Khakamada, a Russian Japanese, was born April 13, 1955, in Moscow. Her father, Mutsuo Khakamada, a Japanese communist, immigrated to the USSR for political reasons in 1939 and took Soviet citizenship. He died in 1991. Her mother, Nina Iosifovna Sinel'nikova, was a retired schoolteacher. Khakamada's maternal grandfather perished during the Stalinist Purges, and her maternal grandmother committed suicide when her family was sent to Khabarovsk in the Far East, where Khakamada's parents met. Khakamada has been married several times and has two children.

In 1978 Khakamada graduated from Patrice Lumumba Friendship of Peoples University in Moscow with a degree in international economics. In 1981 she completed her graduate work in the Economics Department of Moscow State University. From 1981 to 1982 Khakamada worked as a junior researcher at the Scientific Research Institute for the Automated System of Administration of Gosplan (the State Planning Committee) of the Russian Republic. From 1982 to 1989 she was an assistant professor and the assistant chair of the Department of Political Economy at the Technical College of the ZIL automobile factory. In 1984 Khakamada successfully defended her dissertation for the *kandidat* degree.

In 1989, after achieving the rank of docent with a specialty in political economy, she left academe to become assistant chair of a cooperative, Systems and Programs, headed by Konstantin Borovoi and founded on the basis of several Moscow cooperatives and several district-level divisions of the Red Cross. At the end of 1989 Khakamada and Borovoi helped to create a Russian raw materials commodity exchange. In October 1990 she became a member of the Exchange Council of the *Rossiiskaia tovarno-syr'evaia birzha* (Russian Raw

Materials Commodity Exchange) as well as the chief researcher and director of the exchange's Information-Analytical Center. In 1991 Khakamada and Borovoi helped to establish the *Rossiiskii natsional'nyi kommercheskii bank* (Russian National Commerce Bank) and the *Agenstvo ekonomicheskikh novostei* (Economic News Agency). That same year, she also became the chief researcher for the Russian investment company, Rinako.

Khakamada became a member of the Communist Party of the Soviet Union (CPSU) in 1984 and left the Party in 1989. In 1990 she was a candidate for the Mossovet (Moscow City Council) from the Sverdlovsk district of Moscow but was not elected. In December 1992 Khakamada was elected general party secretary of the *Partiia ekonomicheskoi svobody* (Party of Economic Freedom, or PES), which Borovoi had founded in May 1992. PES supported both establishment of a system of separation of powers and effective coordination and cooperation among the various branches of power. The party also supported the development of an effective market economy and the creation of social funds and scientific centers for the realization of humanitarian programs. Lastly, the party advocated national accord among the peoples of the Russian Federation.

In October 1993 Khakamada was a candidate for the State Duma from the electoral bloc August, created by PES and the *Partiia konstitutsionnyh demokratov* (Party of Constitutional Democrats, or PKD). In December 1993 she was elected to the State Duma, with PES affiliation, representing Kashirsk electoral district No. 194 in Moscow. From 1994 to 1997 she served on the Duma Committee on Economic Policy and its Subcommittee on Macroeconomic Policy. In addition, Khakamada served as a member of the delegation of the State Duma of the Russian Federation to the Parliamentary Assembly of the Council of Europe. In February 1994, following a split with Borovoi, she withdrew from PES. She co-organized the electoral bloc the *Liberalno-demokraticheskii soiuz 12-ogo dekabria* (Liberal-Democratic Union of December 12, or LDSD) together with Boris Fëdorov, Minister of Finance of the RSFSR (July–December 1990) and Minister of Finance of the Russian Federation (1993–1994). LDSD sought to unite parliamentarians elected from single-member constituencies all over Russia but was dissolved in the spring of 1995 in the wake of a parliamentary crisis. In 1994 Khakamada organized the Liberal Women's Fund, whose Board of Trustees of five women included Ella Pamfilova. Her motto was that women must become independent in all aspects of their lives: in work, in politics, and in everyday life.

In May 1995 Khakamada announced the creation of the nonparty electoral bloc *Obshchee delo* (Common Cause), which united the Liberal Women's Fund, the Russian Women's Association for New Social Policy, the Liberal Youth Union, and other student groups. Common Cause, which was pro-reform, called for the support of the educational and health sectors of the Russian economy, sectors in which an overwhelming majority of the employees were women. In June 1995 Khakamada, the only woman, along with politicians from several democratic parties and movements, founded a watchdog organization, For Honest Elections. The group proposed to set up its own network of election observers to supervise the tabulation of votes so that the official results of the December 1995 parliamentary elections would reflect the actual voting. In December 1995 she was elected as a deputy to the State Duma from the single-member district No. 197, the Orekho-Borisovskii electoral district of Moscow, as a member of Common Cause.

In early January 1996 Khakamada joined the Duma faction *Rossiiskie regiony* (Regions of Russia), a "centrist" faction that represented the interests of the regions in the State Duma. In May 1996 she, along with Marina Sal'e and the leaders of several other democratic parties, including Sviatoslav Fedorov's *Partiia samoupravleniia trudiashchikhsia* (Party of Worker's Self-Government), and Boris Fedorov's *Vperëd, Rossiia!* (Forward Russia!), signed an agreement not to support Anatolii Sobchak, the mayor of St. Petersburg, in his reelection bid. In late September 1996 Khakamada's Common Cause joined forces with Egor Gaidar's *Vybor Rossii* (Russia's Choice), Galina Starovoitova's *Demokraticheskaia Rossiia* (Democratic Russia), and four smaller parties to offer a "liberal alternative to bureaucratic capitalism." From 1996 to 1997 she served on the State Duma Committee on the Budget, Taxes, Banks, and Finances. Her legislative interests included new social and economic technologies, budgetary and tax politics, and government finances.

On November 10, 1997, Khakamada left the Duma faction Regions of Russia when President Boris Yeltsin appointed her Chair of the State Committee for the Support and Development of Small Businesses. She supported policies to alleviate three major obstacles that faced small businesses in Russia: the heavy tax burden, the pressure to pay criminal groups for protection, and the high costs of office space and equipment. She also hoped to attract more media interest in small businesses and noted that Russian, financially oriented publications focused primarily on banking or industrial "giants." After Prime Minister Chernomyrdin was removed in April 1998 and replaced by Sergei Kirienko, Khakamada was one of only three women, the other two being Natal'ia Fonareva, chair of the State Antimonopoly Committee, and Tatiana Regent, chair of the Federal Migration Service, who retained cabinet-level posts in Kirienko's cabinet. She, along with Fonareva, was a member of the Russian Federation State Commission on Operational Questions. In November 1998 she lost her position when the State Committee for the Support and Development of Small Businesses merged with the newly created Ministry for Antimonopoly Policies and Support of Small Business (MAP), with Gennadii Khodyrev as minister. At that time, Khakamada stated that she would accept only the post of first deputy minister for MAP. That position, however, went to Natal'ia Fonareva, who had been head of the State Committee on Antimonopoly Policies. After leaving the government in November 1998, Khakamada served as president of a private institute for the development of businesses.

In 1999 she joined pro-Kremlin young reformers as one of the leaders of the *Soiuz pravykh sil* (Union of Right Forces, or SPS) and was a candidate for the

State Duma from single-member district No. 207, the Vostochnyi District of St. Petersburg, as a member of SPS. Khakamada occupied the third place on SPS' candidate list, after former prime minister Sergei Kirienko (April–August 1998) and former First Deputy Prime Minister Boris Nemtsov (March 1997–March 1998). SPS cleared the 5 percent hurdle with 8.71 percent of the overall vote, and she won the single-member district with 23.37 percent of the vote.

The Russian public has always been fascinated by Khakamada because of her beauty and exotic appearance. In March 1994 the French company Christian Dior introduced onto the Russian market a new perfume, *Nezhnyi puazon* (Tender Poison), a variant of the famous perfume Poison. The company chose Khakamada as its Russian spokesperson because, in its eyes, she represented the modern Russian woman.

Although Khakamada never formally allied herself with other Russian women's political organizations, such as Women of Russia, she gained broad respect both in Russia and abroad as a voice for women's economic interests and as a knowledgeable politician. In 1995 *Time* magazine named her "Politician of the Twenty-First Century." At the end of 1996 *Time* also named her one of the most famous women in the world. In the May 4–5, 1996, issue of *The Australian Magazine*, a supplement to *The Weekend Australian*, Khakamada ranked ninetieth among the 100 most powerful women in the world.

Cross-references: Natal'ia Fonareva, Ella Pamfilova, Tatiana Regent, Marina Sal'e, Galina Starovoitova.

Suggested Readings

"Irina Mutsuovna Khakamada." Norsk Utenrikspolitisk Institutt-Norwegian Institute of International Affairs (NUPI). Centre for Russian Studies Database. <http://www.nupi.no/cgi-win/Russland/Personer.exe/68> (1999).

Khakamada, Irina. *Devich'ia familiia*. Moscow: Podkova, 1999.

"Khakamada Irina Mutsuovna." Irina Khakamada's Home Page. <http://www.hakamada.ru/> (1999).

"Khakamada Irina Mutsuovna: *Kratkaia biograficheskaia spravka*" (Khakamada Irina Mutsuovna: Short Biographical Sketch). National News Service-Natsional'naia sluzhba novostei. <http://www.nns.ru/persons/hakamada.html> (1995).

"Khakamada Irina Mutsuovna: Pravitel'stvo Rossii (Biografii)" (Khakamada Irina Mutsuovna: Government of Russia (Biography). <http://www.panorama.org:8101/gov/gov20063.shtml> (1999).

"Khakamada to Run from St. Pete in Duma Elections." RFE/RL Newsline. Vol. 3, no. 180, Part I. <http://www.rferl/newsline/1999/09/15099.html> (September 15, 1999).

"The Liberal-Democratic Union of December 12." Norsk Utenrikspolitisk Institutt-Norwegian Institute of International Affairs (NUPI). Centre for Russian Studies Database. <http://www.nupi.no/cgi-win/Russland/polgrupp.exe/The+Liberal-Democratic+Union+of+December+12> (1999).

McCauley, Martin, ed. *Longman Biographical Directory of Decision Makers in Russia and the Successor States*. Harlow, U.K.: Longman, 1993.

"Party of Economic Freedom." Norsk Utenrikspolitisk Institutt-Norwegian Institute of International Affairs (NUPI). Centre for Russian Studies Database. <http://www.nupi.no/cgi-win/Russland/polgrupp.exe/ Party+of+Economic+Freedom> (1999).

"Soiuz pravykh sil" (Union of Right Forces). Union of Right Forces' Home Page. <http://www.pravdelo.ru/MainPage.htm> (1999).

"St. Petersburg Democrats Refuse to Back Incumbent Mayor." OMRI Daily Digest. No. 91, Part I. <http://solar.rtd.utk.edu/friends/news/omri/1996/05/960510I.html> (May 10, 1996).

Cheri C. Wilson

Klimantova, Galina Ivanovna (1944–)

A regional and national leader who served as director, Udmurtiia Children's Affairs Department (1980s), Duma deputy and chair of the Committee on Women, Family, and Youth Affairs (1994–1995), and staff member, Federation Council (1996–).

Galina Ivanovna Klimantova was born in 1944 in the town of Novianskoe in the Alanaevskii region of Sverdlovsk. After graduating from Ural State University in 1967 with a linguistics degree, she worked in Udmurtiia as a radio editor, editor in chief of the regional youth paper, and secretary of the local trade union.

A member of the Communist Party of the Soviet Union (CPSU), she completed the journalism program of the Higher Party School of the Central Committee in 1977. Klimantova gradually shifted her focus to children's and then women's issues. In the late 1980s she served in the Udmurtiia bureaucracy as head of the local children's affairs department and chief of staff of the Council of Ministers. When the *Soiuz zhenshchin Rossii* (Women's Union of Russia, or WUR) was officially founded in 1990, she became involved and eventually directed the Women's Union of the Udmurtiia Republic.

Klimantova did her most visible work in the 1990s. She participated in drafting a program on women's health and family planning in Udmurtiia. In 1993 in the first elections to the new Duma, she won a seat representing Udmurtiia's single-member district as a member of the Women of Russia bloc. In the 1994–1995 Duma session she chaired the Committee on Women, Family, and Youth Affairs. In this position she completed what she considered her most important achievement: she helped to draft a new, controversial family code, drastically changing the systems of alimony and of property ownership in marriage. Concerned with the dropping Russian birthrate, she also pushed a pro-natalist demographic policy. These positions often put her and the Women of Russia bloc in conflict with feminist groups, which generally emphasized women's reproductive choice over maintaining Russian population levels. For feminists, while pro-natalist policies could result in benefits for women, ultimately, such policies sought to use women's bodies for the state's demographic purposes.

In 1995 Klimantova was the third name on Women of Russia's party list, which guaranteed her a seat in the State Duma if Women of Russia passed the

5 percent threshold. The party did not, however, and Klimantova lost. In 1996 she began to work as a staff member of the Federation Council. Although she continued work on women's issues, her visibility dropped. She attended international conferences—including the United Nations Conference on Women in Beijing—and continued to work with WUR on women's issues.

Cross-references: Women of Russia, Women's Union of Russia (WUR).

Suggested Readings

Buckley, Mary. "Adaptation of the Soviet Women's Committee: Deputies' Voices from 'Women of Russia.' " In *Post-Soviet Women: From the Baltic to Central Asia*, edited by Mary Buckley, 157–185. Cambridge: Cambridge University Press, 1997.

Konstantinova, Valentina. "Women's Political Coalitions in Russia (1990–1994)." In *Women's Voices in Russia Today*, edited by Anna Rotkirch and Elina Haavio-Mannila, 235–247. Brookfield, VT: Dartmouth, 1996.

Lipovskaia, Ol'ga. "New Women's Organisations." In *Perestroika and Soviet Women*, edited by Mary Buckley, 72–81. Cambridge: Cambridge University Press, 1992.

Lipovskaia, Ol'ga. "Women's Groups in Russia." In *Post-Soviet Women from the Baltic to Central Asia*, edited by Mary Buckley, 186–197. Cambridge: Cambridge University Press, 1997.

Posadskaya, Anastasia. "A Feminist Critique of Policy, Legislation and Social Consciousness in Post-Socialist Russia." In *Women in Russia*, edited by Anastasia Posadskaya, 164–182. London: Verso, 1994.

Racioppi, Linda, and Katherine O'Sullivan See. *Women's Activism in Contemporary Russia*. Philadelphia: Temple University Press, 1997.

Rule, Wilma, and Nadezhda Shvedova. "Women in Russia's First Multiparty Election." In *Russian Women in Politics and Society*, edited by Wilma Rule and Norma C. Noonan, 40–59. Westport, CT: Greenwood Press, 1996.

Slater, Wendy. "Women of Russia and Women's Representation in Russian Politics." In *Russia in Transition*, edited by David Lane, 76–90. New York: Longman.

Amy Caiazza

Kola Peninsula, Women's Congress of the (*Kongress zhenshchin Kol'skogo poluostrova* (1992–)

An umbrella group uniting seventy-three women's organizations in the northernmost Arctic recesses of Russia. Its mission was to promote the development of women's initiatives and participation of women in the political realm in the region, as well as in Russia as a whole.

The Kola Peninsula is a massive knob of tundra and forest between the White Sea and the Arctic Barents Sea. Its main center is the city of Murmansk. Until 1990 in Murmansk, as in the rest of Russia, the *Komitet sovetskikh zhenshchin* (Soviet Women's Committee, or SWC) was the only organization with official status as a women's organization. An "independent" women's initiative was launched in Murmansk in the summer of 1992, when Liubov Shtyleva and Irina Fogt organized the first Women's Congress of the Kola Peninsula *(Kongress zhenshchin Kol'skogo poluostrova).* The congress brought together 252 women representing twenty-seven independent, as well as Soviet-era, women's organizations in the Kola Peninsula. Many of the groups had sprung up since 1990 as self-help/support groups in the wake of harsh economic changes. Initially, the Congress was created to address shortcomings in state social policy during the transition. The founding member organizations included organizations for families with handicapped children, groups for pensioners, clubs for large families, women's needlework circles, and others. The groups attempted to compensate for the lack of government services by providing them themselves. While most groups in the Congress were not overtly political, they had to provide moral and sometimes economic support for groups that traditionally received government protection, such as the elderly or the disabled. The leadership of the Congress was more overtly political in its projects and plans by pushing for long-term change, such as the promotion of women to political office.

In the spring of 1994 the Women's Congress launched a variety of programs to provide assistance to women, as well as to the general population of Murmansk. The congress conducted seminars to train women as high-level market specialists, financial managers, bank clerks, and insurance experts; this program was organized for unemployed, yet educated, women wishing to upgrade and update their existing skills. The Congress opened a women's hot line to provide psychological, medical, legal, and social support for rape victims and victims of domestic abuse. It also launched the following programs: a Special Child studio for the development and adaptation of disabled children; a Center for Women's Politics, formed to provide systematic training and education for the development of female political leaders; and a café-club, Retro, to alleviate the social isolation of senior citizens.

In the late 1990s the Congress tried to expand its outreach to other cities in the Kola Peninsula, with the assistance of the Ford Foundation and the Soros Foundation. Although the Congress developed networks of women's groups throughout the region, many groups remained isolated and out of reach in Russia's northernmost territory. Historically, the Murmansk region has often been isolated from the rest of Russia due to its extreme northern location. People lived far from each other; thus, establishing E-mail communication between the cities in the region was crucial. As a result, the Congress established a regional network of resource centers for nongovernmental organizations in nine cities across the region. By linking most of the centers with E-mail, the Congress hoped to provide informational and reference support to other civic organizations and to the population as well. The Congress also conducted a special education program for women journalists in the region. Members of the Congress kept in close contact with other women's groups throughout Russia through conferences, seminars, and E-mail. They published and electronically distributed their monthly newsletter.

Although the Congress was led by ardent feminists, they worked hard to maintain a broad coalition of women's groups, which mirrored all aspects of women's experiences in Russia. Thus, they presented a broad spectrum of women's activism, reflecting both Western as well as traditional Russian influences and concerns.

Cross-reference: Foreign Funding and the Women's Movement in Russia.

Suggested Readings

Abubikirova, N. I., T. A. Klimenkova, E. V. Kotchkina, M. A. Regentova, and T. G. Troinova, eds. *Women's Non-Governmental Organizations in Russia and the NIS: A Directory*. Moscow: Aslan, 1998.

"Informatsionnii Listok" (The Informational Leaflet). Organizational Newsletter. Murmansk. Published on E-mail, monthly.

Parshkova, Svetlana, Nadezhda Khlebnikova, and Lyubov' Shtyleva, eds. *O chem dumaiut zhenshchiny (What Do Women Think About)*. Murmansk: KRTsOZh, 1998.

Sarah Henderson

L

Lakhova, Ekaterina Fillipovna (1948–)

A prominent leader in post-Soviet Russia who served as state counselor and chair, Coordinating Committee on the Affairs of Family, Motherhood, and Childhood (1991–1993); Duma deputy (1993–); chair, Women of Russia Duma faction (1993–1995); chair, President's Commission on the Affairs of Women, Family, and Demography (1994–), and head, All-Russian Sociopolitical Movement of Women of Russia (1996–).

Ekaterina Fillipovna Lakhova was born in 1948 in Sverdlovsk (present-day Ekaterinburg). She experienced an unhappy childhood; her mother died before she reached the age of two as a result of an infection from an abortion, and Lakhova described her relationship with her father as strained. Lakhova decided to devote her life to health issues, especially in children's medicine.

Lakhova completed her medical training at the Sverdlovsk State Medical Institute in 1972 and worked as a pediatrician throughout the 1970s, serving in her clinic's administration from 1976. From 1981 to 1987, she worked in the Sverdlovsk local health administration, a position that served as a bridge to her political career. In 1987 she moved to Moscow to become a People's Deputy in the Supreme Soviet of the RSFSR (Russian Republic) and headed the Committee on the Affairs of the Family and Demography of the Supreme Soviet. During that period she also worked in the leadership of the state health administration. In 1991 the Supreme Soviet eliminated the Family and Demography Committee, and, as compensation, Gennadii Burbulis, then Secretary of the Russian Federation, appointed Lakhova state counselor and chair of the Government's Coordinating Committee on the Affairs of Family, Motherhood, and Childhood. In 1992 the committee became part of President Yeltsin's administration. As head of the committee, she initiated the Children of Russia program designed to improve conditions in schools, home, and society for Russian youth.

Since President Yeltsin (1990–1999) also came from Sverdlovsk, many rumors suggested a connection between them. Lakhova denied rumors that her rise in politics resulted from personal connections to Yeltsin. In her autobiography, she claimed that she did not meet Yeltsin until well after coming to Moscow and that she had never worked as his children's pediatrician, as rumors maintained. In fact, she argued that the rumors, promulgated by the Communist Party of the Russia Federation, were spawned as a reaction to a woman's trying to advance in politics.

Lakhova's position in the Supreme Soviet and as adviser to the government marked the beginning of her work in women's policy issues. Lakhova became involved with the political bloc Women of Russia (WOR) and ran on its proportional representation list in the 1993 elections. This affiliation allied her with Alevtina Fedulova's Women's Union of Russia (WUR), a major sponsor of WOR. Lakhova joined WOR to combat the lack of female voices in Russian politics. Like Alevtina Fedulova, her assumptions about women's voice often reflected traditional ideas about gender roles in Russia. She wanted women to bring peace to politics and argued in an interview in *Nezavisimaia Gazeta (Independent Newspaper)* that as politicians, "women and mothers should be good and should cool the sometimes unnecessary and emotional passions to which men are subject." She supported protectionist policies for women workers because of their roles as mothers. These positions reflected Soviet-era approaches to women and their interests and often put Lakhova in conflict with Russia's emerging feminist movement.

Once elected to the Duma, Lakhova became chair of the WOR faction. In 1994 she also became chair of Yeltsin's Commission on the Affairs of Women, Family, and Demography, which replaced the former Coordinating Committee that she had headed. Although WOR lost in 1995, Lakhova won a seat from a single-member district in Ul'anovskaia oblast.

Although, as previously noted, in the early 1990s feminist groups and WOR were skeptical of each other's politics, Lakhova began to work more closely with various feminist groups, and her views changed to reflect her exposure to feminist ideas. She lobbied Yeltsin to accept quotas in the executive branch, a measure supported by feminists, and worked for similar quotas in party lists for Duma elections. She was heavily involved in the Russian Family Planning Association and supported increased availability of contraception and sex education. Lakhova's increased cooperation with feminist groups, however, sparked conflict with the leaders of WOR and WUR, especially Fedulova. As a result, in November 1996 she created her own women's organization, the *Obshcherossiiskoe obshestvenno-politicheskoe dvizhenie zhenshchin Rossii* (All-Russian Sociopolitical Movement of Women of Russia). As its head, Lakhova argued for a "women's line" of "dialogue, compromise and agreement" as opposed to current Russian politics, "cruel, aggressive, male." On the other hand, she pledged to build cooperation among Russian women's movements. She initiated and signed the 1997 Charter of Women's Solidarity, designed to promote harmony among feminist groups. Fedulova and WUR did not sign that document. Lakhova's new organization also published a newspaper, *Women of Russia*, often featuring leaders from various women's and feminist groups.

In 1996 Lakhova endorsed Boris Yeltsin's reelection as president. In 1995 she published her memoirs, *Moi put' v politiku (My Journey into Politics).* In her official Duma biography (part of a guide to the Duma published by the National News Service over the Internet), she described her ideological and professional changes as part of a larger personal transformation. She talked about her feelings of "personal involvement in history, trying to affect what happens around me and change it for the better."

In the 1999 parliamentary elections, Lakhova ran on the *Otechestvo-Vsia Rossiia* (Fatherland-All-Russia) list headed by Iuri Luzhkov and Evgenii Primakov. She actively campaigned for the party and was elected to the State Duma in December 1999.

Lakhova may be regarded as one of the most important figures in the Russian women's movement of the 1990s.

Cross-references: All-Russian Sociopolitical Movement of Women of Russia, Charter of Women's Solidarity, Commission on Women, Family, and Demography, Alevtina Fedulova, Women of Russia, Women's Union of Russia.

Suggested Readings

Azhgikhina, Nadezhda. "*V Rossii budet zhenskaia politicheskaia partiia*" (In Russia There Will Be a Women's Political Party)." *Nezavisimaia gazeta*, January 23, 1997.

Buckley, Mary. "Adaptation of the Soviet Women's Committee: Deputies' Voices from 'Women of Russia.' " In *Post-Soviet Women: From the Baltic to Central Asia*, edited by Mary Buckley, 157–185. Cambridge: Cambridge University Press, 1997.

Konstantinova, Valentina. "Women's Political Coalitions in Russia (1990–1994)." In *Women's Voices in Russia Today*, edited by Anna Rotkirch and Elina Haavio-Mannila, 235–247. Brookfield, VT: Dartmouth, 1996.

Lakhova, E. F. *Moi put' v politiku (My Journey into Politics).* Moscow: Aurika, 1995.

Lakhova, E. F. *Zhenskoe dvizhenie v gody reformy: problemy i perspektivy (The Women's Movement in the Years of Reform: Problems and Prospects).* Moscow: "Informatik," 1998.

Lipovskaya, Ol'ga. "New Women's Organisations." In *Perestroika and Soviet Women*, edited by Mary Buckley, 72–81. Cambridge: Cambridge University Press, 1992.

Lipovskaya, Ol'ga. "Women's Groups in Russia." In *Post-Soviet Women: From the Baltic to Central Asia*, edited by Mary Buckley, 186–199. Cambridge: Cambridge University Press, 1997.

Posadskaya, Anastasiia. "A Feminist Critique of Policy, Legislation and Social Consciousness in Post-Socialist Russia." In *Women in Russia*, edited by Anastasia Posadskaya, 164–182. London: Verso, 1994.

Racioppi, Linda, and Katherine O'Sullivan See. *Women's Activism in Contemporary Russia.* Philadelphia: Temple University Press, 1997.

Rule, Wilma, and Nadezhda Shvedova. "Women in Russia's First Multiparty Election." In *Russian Women in Politics and Society*, edited by Wilma Rule and Norma C. Noonan, 40–59. Westport, CT: Greenwood Press, 1996.

Slater, Wendy. "Women of Russia and Women's Representation in Russian Politics." In *Russia in Transition*, edited by David Lane, 76–90. New York: Longman, 1995.

Amy Caiazza

Liborakina, Marina Ivanovna (1960–)

A Moscow feminist scholar and activist specializing in the development of civil society and social policy. Liborakina was the founder of the Feminist Orientation Center and cofounder of the Women's Information Center.

Marina Liborakina was born in Magnitogorsk in 1960 and grew up in the northern Russian town of Norilsk. Her mother was a teacher of Russian, and her father was a mountain engineer. Liborakina graduated from the Moscow Institute for Management in 1983 with a degree in economics. In 1991 she completed the *kandidat* degree at the State University of Management in Moscow.

In the late 1980s Liborakina became involved with an intellectual movement called the Moscow methodological circle. The circle was an original Russian combination of systems theory, social planning, and action research. It organized "activity games" based on the Russian theory of activity (*teoriia deiatel'nosti*) for enterprises around the country. Later it also provided postgraduate education through the School of Cultural Policy, an experimental institution headed by the Moscow philosopher Piotr Shchedrovitskii in 1989–1995. This institution trained many influential consultants in city planning and judicial and educational innovations. Liborakina graduated from the School of Cultural Policy in 1995 with a B.A. equivalent in sociocultural studies.

In 1991 Liborakina became associated with the Russian Institute for Cultural Research, which introduced contemporary cultural studies in Russia. In 1994 she completed the work for the European Diploma for Cultural Managers, a one-year program organized by the Council of Europe. She was a visiting scholar at the Center for the Study of Philanthropy in New York in 1995 and in 1997–1998 and at the University of Helsinki in early 1999.

During her studies at the School of Cultural Policy, Liborakina organized one of the first Russian women's consciousness-raising groups. Some female students had experienced gender discrimination in their otherwise open-minded intellectual community. They founded a small group in order to reflect on their experiences. In 1991 the group established the *Feministskii orientatsionnyi tsentr* (Feminist Orientation Center, or FOC). It was one of the first organizations in postsocialist Russia that used the word "feminist" instead of the less challenging "women," "feminology," or "gender." In 1993 FOC was officially registered as a nongovernmental association. FOC introduced new values and methods for women's personal and professional development. It hosted a Finnish-Russian seminar on collective memory work and gave courses in women's assertive behavior and self-defense. FOC participated in the second Independent Women's Forum in Dubna in 1992 and in the formation of the feminist platform for the Russian parliamentary elections in 1993. FOC also organized workshops on Art against Violence in Moscow and at the United Nations global women's conference in China in 1995.

The Center was among the very first to raise publicly the question of sexual violence in Russia. Liborakina circulated a petition to protest the rapes of Bosnian women during the war in former Yugoslavia in the early 1990s. Although limited in scope, the action challenged the solidarity that many Russians felt with Serbia. It also raised the issue of sexual war crimes, which had previously not been discussed in Russia.

In the mid-1990s FOC became involved in larger educational projects. The emerging Russian civil society had an acute lack of knowledge about the principles of nonprofit management, fund-raising, and project design. Liborakina organized a series of regional seminars in support of nongovernmental organizations. Between 1994 and 1998 seminars were held in Vladivostok, Irkutsk, Tomsk, Ekaterinburg, Cheliabinsk, St. Petersburg, and other cities. Liborakina also wrote about the history and current revival of Russian women's activism.

Together with Elizaveta Bozhkova and others, Liborakina founded and became codirector of the Information Center of the Independent Women's Forum in 1994. They wanted to create a flexible structure for regular informational exchange among small women's organizations. The Center provided a database, Web page, newsletters, and thematic seminars and served as a medium for various campaigns.

In 1997 Liborakina became increasingly involved with social policy issues. She took part in the evaluation of a proposed law on domestic violence in 1997. At the Institute of Urban Economics in Moscow, a think tank founded in the early 1990s, she combined social research and consulting for municipal authorities in different cities. In 1998–1999 she was a researcher in the international program Protecting Women during Privatization, administered by Women, Law, and Development International and financed by the U.S. Agency for International Development (USAID). As part of her work for the Institute of Urban Economics, she created a program for municipal development after the financial and social crisis of August–September 1998 and participated in its implementation in the city of Iaroslavl.

Marina Liborakina represented the younger generation of contemporary Russian feminists in the 1990s. She was among the first to adopt an explicit feminist identity and among the first to integrate successfully gender and feminist concerns into the larger contexts of education, social policy, and civic activism in Russia.

Cross-references: Independent Women's Forums, Information Center of the Independent Women's Forum.

Suggested Readings

Liborakina, Marina. "A Bridge between Past and Future." In *The Simulation and Gaming Yearbook*, edited by Danny Saunders, Fred Percival, and Matti Vartiainen, vol. 4, 41–48. London: Kogan Page Ltd., 1996.

Liborakina, Marina. *Obretenie sily: Rossiiskii opyt. Puti preodoleniia diskriminatsii v otnoshenii zhenshchin: kulturnoe izmerenie (Empowerment: The Russian Experience. Ways to Overcome Discrimination of Women—a Cultural Perspective).* Moscow: "CheRo," 1996.

Liborakina, Marina. "The Unappreciated Mothers of Civil Society." Transitions 5, no. 1 (January 1998): 52–57.

Liborakina, Marina. "Women's Voluntarism and Philanthropy in Pre-Revolutionary Russia—Building a Civil Society." *Voluntas* 7, no. 4 (1996): 397–411.

Liborakina, Marina, Mikhail Fliamer, and Vladimir Iakimets: *Sotsial'noe partnërstvo (Social Partnership).* Moscow: School of Cultural Policy, 1996.

Liborakina, Marina, and Vladimir Iakimets, eds. *Grazhdanskie initiativy i budushchee Rossii (Citizen's Initiatives and the Future of Russia).* Moscow: School of Cultural Policy, 1998.

Liborakina, Marina, and Tatiana Sidorenkova, eds. *NET nasiliu v sem'e (NO to Domestic Violence).* Moscow: Information Center of the Independent Women's Forum, 1997.

Liborakina, Marina, and Leila Simonen. "The First Menstruation—Bodily Memories of Finnish and Russian Women." In *Women's Voices in Russia Today*, edited by Anna Rotkirch and Elina Haavio-Mannila, 88–106. Aldershot: Dartmouth, 1996.

Anna Rotkirch

Lipovskaia, Ol'ga (1954–)

A journalist, translator, and interpreter by profession, Lipovskaia became one of the most visible and prominent feminist leaders in Russia during the 1990s; she is best known for her leadership of the St. Petersburg Center for Gender Issues.

Ol'ga Lipovskaia was born on February 9, 1954, in the village of Elets-Gora in the Kirov region in Northeast Russia. Her mother was a graduate of the Institute of Foreign Languages in Leningrad, and her father was a mining engineer. After completing secondary school in 1971, she worked in a variety of jobs in Leningrad (present-day St. Petersburg). She was briefly married and divorced from her first husband in 1975. With her second husband, Armen Airapetian, she had a son, Marat, born in 1976, but the couple divorced in 1978. She and her third husband, Ildar Nassyrov, had a daughter, Diliara (1984), and they divorced in 1991. From 1979 to 1984 she worked as a secretary in the School Department of the Executive Committee of the Kuibyshev district of Leningrad. In 1984 she began a three-year course in the French language at a special program of the Officers Club in the Leningrad Military District (*Dom Ofitserov Leningradskogo Voennogo Okruga*) and graduated in 1987.

In 1985 she turned her attention to women's issues when a friend gave her a book on feminist issues; the book, *Sweet Freedom* by Beatrice Campbell and Anne Coote, was dedicated to the British women's movement. In late 1987 she began work on a *samizdat* feminist journal, *Zhenskoe chtenie (Women's Reading)* and became active in the Union of Independent Publishers of Samizdat.

With the beginning of unofficial political parties under Gorbachev's policies of Glasnost, Perestroika, and *Demokratizatsiia* (democratization), Lipovskaia became active in the opposition party, *Demokraticheskii Soiuz* (the Democratic Union) and from 1988 to 1992 served both on its editorial board and on the Coordinating Committee of its Leningrad organization.

In the early 1990s she was one of the founding members of SAFO, later renamed FALTA. In 1992 she founded and became the director of the *Peterburgskii Tsentr Genderskikh Problem* (St. Petersburg Center of Gender Issues, or PCGI). From 1992 onward, her work with PCGI commanded her full-time attention. Through her articles and activism, Lipovskaia became one of the best-known Russian feminists both in her own country and in the West.

Cross-references: FALTA/SAFO, St. Petersburg Center of Gender Issues (PCGI).

Suggested Readings

Lipovskaia, Ol'ga. "The Mythology of Womanhood in Contemporary 'Soviet' Culture." In *Women in Russia: A New Era in Russian Feminism*, edited by Anastasia Posadskaya, 123–134. London: Verso, 1994.

Lipovskaia, Ol'ga. "New Women's Organizations." In *Perestroika and Soviet Women*, edited by Mary Buckley, 72–81. Cambridge: Cambridge University Press, 1992.

Lipovskaia, Ol'ga. "Women's Groups in Russia." In *Post-Soviet Women: From the Baltics to Central Asia*, edited by Mary Buckley, 186–199. Cambridge: Cambridge University Press, 1997.

Norma Corigliano Noonan

LOTOS (*Liga osvobozhdeniia stereotipov*, or League for Emancipation from Stereotypes) (1988–1990)

One of Russia's first women's organizations, LOTOS was created primarily by four women who identified as feminists, and it was significant as one of the first organizations to emerge under the rapidly changing political opportunities for feminist organizing in the Soviet Union's final years.

In the mid-1980s the discussion of women's issues began in earnest, evidenced by seminars on women's issues initiated by state and Communist Party of the Soviet Union (CPSU)-related organizations. These events provided a forum in which feminist academics, previously isolated from each other, became acquainted. Natal'ia Zakharova, Ol'ga Voronina, and Valentina Konstantinova, all working at different academic research institutions, met at one such seminar, held in the fall of 1987 under the auspices of the Academy of Social Sciences of the Central Committee of the CPSU. After encountering each other repeatedly at such seminars, the three began to meet as a group in their free time to discuss feminism and ways to counter the reassertion of sexist stereotypes, in particular, the "return women to the home" campaign that was spreading in late 1980s Russia. In April 1988 Zakharova introduced her new coworker, Anastasiia Posadskaia, to the group. In early 1989 Posadskaia formulated a declaration that became the foundation for their tiny new organization: *Liga za osvobozhdenie ot stereotipov*, or LOTOS (the League for Emancipation from Stereotypes). The document called for enriching perestroika with an egalitarian ideology, undoing the sex-based stereotypes that pervaded the political and economic spheres, and creating a new ethos whereby women could play a worthy role in the workforce, and men could enjoy a worthy role in the family.

LOTOS members continued to speak out at academic events, where their critical remarks on women's status in the Soviet Union met with disapproval. In 1989 the Congress of People's Deputies approved the idea of preparing a state program on improving women's status and protecting the family, maternity, and childhood. Natal'ia Rimashevskaia, Director of the Institute of Socioeconomic Population Problems within the Soviet Academy of Sciences, was given the task of collecting a group of researchers and formulating a position paper (*konseptsiia*) on the subject. Under Rimashevskaia's direction several LOTOS members took part in writing the position paper. The document focused on creating a new, more egalitarian policy that considered emancipation a "bilateral" issue: freeing women to take a more extensive role outside the home and men to play a greater role in the family sphere. In 1990 the position paper was presented to the Soviet Council of Ministers, and Rimashevskaia's institute was allotted five staff positions to form the first Soviet women's studies research laboratory. The new *Moskovskii tsentr gendernykh issledovnii* (Moscow Center for Gender Studies, or MCGS) was thus created, with Posadskaia as its Director; other LOTOS members, except Zakharova, who had accepted a position in Vienna, were on the staff. LOTOS thereby folded into MCGS and did not appear to continue its existence as a discrete organization.

Cross-references: Moscow Center for Gender Studies, Anastasiia Posadskaia.

Suggested Readings

Buckley, Mary, ed. *Perestroika and Soviet Women*. Cambridge: Cambridge University Press, 1992.

Memorandum LOTOSA/LOTOS: Liga za osvobozhdenie ot stereotipov (Memorandum of the Organization, LOTOS: The League for Emancipation from Stereotypes).

Moskovskii tsentr gendernykh issledovanii: 1990–1995 (Moscow Center for Gender Studies, 1990–1995). Moscow: 1995.

Noonan, Norma C. "The Gorbachev Leadership: Change and Continuity." In *Russian Women in Politics and Society*, edited by Wilma Rule and Norma C. Noonan, 108–119. Westport, CT: Greenwood Publishing Group, 1996.

Posadskaia, Anastasiia, ed. *Women in Russia: A New Era in Russian Feminism*. London: Verso, 1994.

Valerie Sperling

M

Matvienko, Valentina Ivanovna (1949–)

Ambassador of the Russian Federation to Malta (1991–1994), ambassador of the Russian Federation to Greece (1997–1998), Deputy Prime Minister of the Russian Federation (September 1998–). As of 1999 she was the highest-ranking woman in the Russian government.

Valentina Matvienko was born April 7, 1949, in the town of Shepetovka, Khmel'nitskii oblast of the Ukrainian Republic. Her husband, Vladimir Vasil'evich Malyshev, is a colonel and head teacher at the Russian Army Medical Academy (RVMA), named for S. M. Kirov. She has a son, Sergei.

In 1972 she graduated from the Leningrad Chemical-Pharmaceutical Institute. From 1972 to 1977 Matvienko served as a department head, secretary, and first secretary of the Petrograd *raikom* (raion committee) of the *Vsesoiuznogo Leninskogo kommunisticheskogo soiuza molodezhi* (All-Union Leninist Young Communist League—Komsomol, or VLKSM) of the city of Leningrad. From 1977 to 1984 she was the secretary, second secretary, and first secretary of the Leningrad *obkom* (oblast committee) of the VLKSM. From 1984 to 1986 Matvienko was the first secretary of the Leningrad, *Krasnogvardeiskii raikom* of the Communist Party of the Soviet Union (CPSU). In 1985 she graduated from the Academy of Social Sciences of the Central Committee (CC) of the CPSU. From 1986 to 1989 Matvienko was Deputy Chair of the Executive Committee of the Lensovet (Leningrad City Council) on cultural and educational matters. From March 1989 to January 1992 she was a People's Deputy of the USSR Supreme Soviet, member of the Presidium of the USSR Supreme Soviet, and Chair of the USSR Supreme Soviet Committee on Women, Protection of the Family, Maternity, and Childhood. Matvienko was a member of the CPSU until 1991.

In May 1991 Matvienko completed advanced courses in diplomacy at the Diplomatic Academy of the USSR Ministry of Foreign Affairs. She was the Soviet Union's Ambassador to Malta from 1991 to 1992 and the Russian Federation's Ambassador to Malta until 1994. From 1994 to 1995 Matvienko was Ambassador for Special Missions and a member of the Group of Ambassadors for Special Missions. From 1995 to 1997 she was the director of the Ministry of Foreign Affairs' Department for Relations with Russian Federation Members, the Federal Parliament, and Social and Political Organizations, a position in which she served as a lobbyist for former Foreign Minister Evgenii Primakov (1996–1998). Matvienko was also a member of the Collegium of the Russian Federation Ministry of Internal Affairs from 1995 to 1997. In March 1997 she represented the Russian Federation at the Forty-first Session of the United Nations (UN) Commission on the Status of Women held at the UN Headquarters in New York City. From October 1997 to September 1998 Matvienko was Ambassador of the Russian Federation to Greece.

On September 22, 1998, Matvienko was appointed to Prime Minister Evgenii Primakov's government as Deputy Prime Minister of Social Policy. Matvienko's social portfolio was quite extensive and included coordinating questions on social policies, labor relations, social security, the system of social guarantees, privileges and payments, the social protection of the poor segments of the population, and the guarantee of pensions; overseeing questions of general and professional education, health protection, culture, and government youth policies; guaranteeing the cooperation of the government with trade unions, social organizations and associations, religious organizations, and the means of mass information; and overseeing the question of the Russian trilateral commission on the regulation of social–labor relations. In Moscow her appointment was viewed as a tactical attempt by Primakov to limit his new government's vulnerability in the social sector. In addition, Primakov's successful confirmation as Prime Minister was partially attributed to Matvienko, who had gained support for him from a broad spectrum of Duma deputies. On October 18, 1998, she was appointed cochair of the Estonian–Russian Intergovernmental Commission, replacing former Deputy Prime Minister Oleg Sysuev. The Commission was established to improve Estonian–Russian relations. Several obstacles existed to improved relations, including the status of Russians in Estonia and the fact that the Russian Federation did not acknowledge that Estonia had been forcibly incorporated into the Soviet Union in 1940 as a result of the Molotov–von Ribbentrop Pact. In addition, Matvienko was cochair of the Russo–Austrian Commission for Trade and Economic Cooperation.

In January 1999 she reported that Russia was dissatisfied with International Monetary Fund (IMF) loans because they had no impact on Russia's economic situation. On February 8, 1999, Matvienko received an honorary doctorate from RVMA and became the first woman to possess a diploma, medal, and mantle from the academy, which perhaps can be attributed to her husband's position there. During her tenure as Deputy Prime Minister in Primakov's cabinet, she was credited with improving the situation with the payment of delayed salaries and pensions. For example, from the time Matvienko was appointed in September 1998 through May 1, 1999, the level of unpaid pensions—16.5 billion rubles ($670 million)—dropped by almost half compared with the figure of 30.5 billion rubles registered on October 1, 1998. In May 1999, when Primakov was replaced by Prime Minister Sergei Stepashin, she was reappointed Deputy Minister in charge of the Ministries of Labor, Health, Education, and Culture. In June 1999 Matvienko joined the Board of Directors of *Obshchestvennoe Rossiiskoe Televidenie* (Russian Public Television, or ORT). In August 1999, when Stepashin was replaced by Prime Minister Vladimir Putin, she was again reappointed Deputy Prime Minister. As of 1999 she was the only female member of the Presidium of Council of Ministers of the Russian Federation, which included the prime minister, the two first deputy prime ministers, and the ministers for interior, defense, foreign affairs, economy, finance, and state property, as well as eight governors.

Suggested Readings

Helmer, John. "Russia: Woman to Administer Social Affairs Portfolio." RFE/RL Weekday Magazine. <http://www.rferl.org/nca/features/1998/09/F.RU.980923132801.html> (September 23, 1998).

"Matvienko Valentina Ivanovna." *Pravitel'stvo Rossiiskoi Federatsii* (Government of the Russian Federation). <http://www.pravitelstvo.gov.ru/government/ministers/matvienko.html> (1999).

"Matvienko Valentina Ivanovna: *Kratkaia biograficheskaia spravka*" (Matvienko Valentina Ivanovna: Short Biographical Sketch). National News Service-Natsional'naia sluzhba novostei. <http://www.nns.ru/persons/matvien.html> (1999).

Kto est' kto v Rossii i v blizhnem zarubezh'e: spravochnik (Who's Who in Russia and the Near Abroad: A Directory). Moscow: Izd. Novoe vremia: Vse dlia Vas, 1993.

Schulz-Torge, Ulrich-Joachim, ed. *Who's Who in Russia Today: A Biographical Dictionary of More than 2,100 Individuals from the Russian Federation including the Other Fourteen Former USSR Republics*. Munich: K. G. Saur, 1994.

"Valentina Matvienko." Norsk Utenrikspolitisk Institutt-Norwegian Institute of International Affairs (NUPI). Centre for Russian Studies Database. <http://www.nupi.no/cgi-win/Russland/Personer.exe/1117> (1999).

Cheri C. Wilson

Missiia (Mission) (1990–)

A women's organization formed in Moscow in 1990 as a support system for women entrepreneurs during the transition from a planned to a market economy.

The all-union Russian women's association *Missiia* (Mission) was formed in 1990 to assist and promote women in the developing market economy of the USSR and later of Russia. The founder and head of *Missiia* was Tatiana Luk'ianenko. *Missiia*'s work was based on policies adopted by the United Nations Convention on Abolishing All Forms of Discrimination against Women, ratified by the USSR in 1981, as well as on policies adopted at the United Nations Conference on Women in Nairobi (1985). *Missiia* had several goals, including assistance to women's businesses, establishment of educational centers and business schools to increase women's professional skills, organization of a data bank on women's issues and the women's movement, and the organization of a network of women's crisis centers.

In the early 1990s *Missiia* undertook a number of projects. Among the projects was research about women in rural areas where there was a high birthrate. To try to improve the status of those women, research was conducted on their problems and needs and conditions in hospitals, kindergartens, maternity hospitals, schools, children's activity centers, and other regional services in order to suggest to local authorities methods to improve conditions. Their methods and policy suggestions were approved in Kazakhstan by 1992 but were applicable also to other regions.

In the early 1990s *Missiia* also supported women's small businesses, which sought to create jobs for women. *Missiia* worked especially with two firms headed by women, LITT, located in Moscow, which produced women's accessories, porcelain souvenirs in "Dzhel" style, and other types of small souvenirs, and Vera, a firmed based in Riazan. About 1,000 women worked for LITT.

A third area of activity was the publication of information bulletins on women's activities, which served as advertisements for women's businesses and established contacts between women's businesses and women's organizations.

Missiia also helped to sponsor a conference of Russian–American women in 1993 entitled Women of Russia: Yesterday, Today, and Tomorrow. The conference papers were published in a bilingual book of the same title in 1994. In 1994 *Missiia* sponsored an international conference of women artists. *Missiia* also created a data bank on women's businesses to assist them to expand contacts with other businesses.

During the economic crisis that Russia faced in the late 1990s, *Missiia* functioned primarily on the local level, continuing its activities in Moscow, Norilsk, Rostov-on-Don, and Kamchatka. The crisis center work was curtailed. The need to reduce the scale of operations characterized numerous organizations in the late 1990s.

Cross-references: Women and Business in Russia, Women in Business in Russia.

Suggested Reading

Ershova, Elvira, ed. *Zhenshchiny Rossii: vchera, segodnia, zavtra. (Women of Russia: Yesterday, Today, Tomorrow).* Moscow: "Rossiia Molodaia," 1994.

Elvira Ershova

Moscow Center for Gender Studies (MCGS) (*Moskovskii Tsentr Gendernykh Issledovanii*) (1990–)

The first scholarly center established in the USSR by feminists committed to promoting gender research and reducing gender discrimination. The MCGS has contributed to the advancement of women's studies, played a coordinating role in the independent women's movement, and sought to influence public policy through contacts with officials and the mass media.

The *Moskovskii Tsentr Gendernykh Issledovanii* (Moscow Center for Gender Studies, or MCGS) had its roots in the late 1980s, when the Soviet government invited the *Institut Sotsial'no-Ekonomicheskikh Problem Narodonaseleniia* (Institute of Socioeconomic Population Problems, or ISEPP), directed by Natal'ia Rimashevskaia, to prepare a position paper for a government program on the improvement of the Status of Women and the Protection of Family, Maternity, and Childhood. Anastasiia Posadskaia and Natal'ia Zakharova worked closely with Rimashevskaia on this project, injecting as much feminist thinking as possible. Their framework broke with the traditional Soviet ideology of state protectionism with respect to women and pointed to the goal of liberating individuals and achieving gender equality within the family. In the course of this work the need to establish gender research as an independent field within Soviet academe became evident. In April 1990 the Presidium of the USSR Academy of Sciences, responding to a proposal from Zakharova, Posadskaia, and Rimashevskaia, issued a resolution establishing the MCGS as part of ISEPP. Zakharova left shortly thereafter to accept a position in Vienna. Posadskaia became the Center's first director, heading a group of five individuals. At the core of MCGS was a small group of women scholars who had studied the "woman question" in the USSR and had all participated in LOTOS, the *Liga Osvobozhdeniia ot Obshchestvennykh Stereotipov* (League for Emancipation from Social Stereotypes), an organization founded in 1988. In April 1994 the MCGS registered as an independent, nongovernmental research and cultural institution, although it continued to enjoy a warm, supportive relationship with ISEPP. As the result of Posadskaia's marriage to an American citizen in 1995 and consequent move to the United States, two philosophers, Olga Voronina and Tatiana Klimenkova, became the codirectors of MCGS. By 1995 the number of scholars associated with MCGS had grown to fourteen; researchers held *kandidat* degrees in economics, philosophy, history, sociology, and geography.

Since its founding in 1990, the MCGS has engaged in an impressive list of activities. Its scholars produced a rich array of publications on women's issues, sponsored seminars and conferences, lobbied government officials and provided them with expert analysis, and actively participated in furthering the development of an independent women's movement. In 1990–1992 the MCGS conducted a series of open seminars related to the theme of Women in Politics and Politics for Women. Over the years that followed, many conferences, seminars, and training programs have been conducted, all aimed at promoting knowledge about women's issues, women's political activism, and women's integration into the market economy.

The networking that occurred at the MCGS spurred a parallel line of activity: the Center's associates became active members in the emerging independent women's movement. The beginning of one of the first independent women's organizations, *Nezavisimaia zhenskaia demokraticheskaia initsiativa* (Independent Women's Democratic Initiative), whose acronym, *NeZhDi*, means "Don't wait," can be traced to an MCGS seminar in the summer of 1990. The MCGS, in collaboration with other women's organizations, organized the first and second Independent Women's Forums, held in Dubna in 1991 and 1992. The Forums brought together many new, nongovernmental women's groups and advanced the development of horizontal cooperation among women's groups. The MCGS has continued to play a major role in fostering the growth of institutions that contribute to the institutionalization of the women's movement, including work with the East–West Women's Network to develop an electronic mail network among women's groups in Russia.

By the late 1990s MCGS scholars were frequently pursuing major projects on their own. For example, the economist Zoia Khotkina was instrumental in developing a series of summer schools designed to promote women's and gender studies within Russia. These annual summer programs began in 1996 with financial backing from the Ford Foundation. Another key MCGS scholar, the philosopher Tatiana Klimenkova, received support from the MacArthur Foundation to complete her book, *Zhenshchina kak fenomen kul'tury (Woman as a Cultural Phenomenon).* From 1996 to 1998 the philosopher Marina Malysheva coordinated a major research project supported by the MacArthur Foundation on the enforcement of woman's rights in Russia. An additional important project involved the Gender Expertise Project, carried out in 1997–1998 under the direction of sociologist Elena Kochkina and funded by the U.S. Agency for International Development (USAID). While MCGS had a substantial history of providing expertise on women's issues to government agencies, this project represented a systematic effort to examine public policy from a gender perspective.

The MCGS has brought together feminist scholars who have played a key role in the development of research on women and who have actively participated in advancing the women's movement in Russia. The Center has functioned as a major hub of feminist research and activism in Russia.

Cross-references: Foreign Funding and the Women's Movement in Russia, Gender Expertise Project, Gender/Women's Studies in Russia, Independent Women's Forums, Information Center of the Independent Women's Forum, LOTOS, Anastasiia Posadskaia.

Suggested Readings

Ballaeva, E. A. *Gendernaia ekspertiza zakonodatel'stva RF: reproduktivnye prava zhenshchin v Rossii (Gender Analysis of Russian Federation Legislation on Women's Reproductive Rights*). Moscow: MTsGI (MCGS), 1998.

Baskakova, M. E. *Ravnye vozmozhnosti i gendernye stereotipy na rynke truda (Equal Rights and Gender Stereotypes in the Labor Market*). Moscow: MTsGI (MCGS), 1998.

Khotkina, Z. A., N. L. Pushkareva, and E. I. Trofimova. *Zhenshchina gender kul'tura (Women—Gender—Culture).* Moscow: MTsGI (MCGS), 1999.

Klimenkova, T. A. *Zhenshchina kak fenomen kul'tury: Vzgliad iz Rossii (Women as a Cultural Phenomenon: A View from Russia).* Moscow: "Preobrazhenie," 1996.

Kosmarskaia, N. P. *"Zhenskoe izmerenie" vynuzhdennoi migratsii i migratsionnoe za-*

konodatel'stvo Rossii (The Women's Dimension of Forced Migration and Russian Migration Policy). Moscow: MTsGI (MCGS), 1998.

Mezentseva, Elena, and Natal'ia Kosmarskaia, eds. *Moskovskii tsentr gendernykh issledovanii: 1990–1995 (The Moscow Center for Gender Studies, 1990–1995).* Moscow: MTsGI (MCGS), 1995.

Posadskaya, Anastasia, ed. *Women in Russia.* London: Verso, 1994.

Prava zhenshchin v Rossii: issledovanie real'noi praktiki ikh sobliudeniia i massovogo soznaniia, tom 1, tom 2 (Women's Rights in Russia: Enforcement Practice and Public Opinion, vols. 1, 2). Moscow: MTsGI (MCGS), 1998.

Racioppi, Linda, and Katherine O'Sullivan See. *Women's Activism in Contemporary Russia.* Philadelphia: Temple University Press, 1997.

Rimashevskaia, N., A. Posadskaia, and N. Zakharova. *Kontseptsiia gosudarstvennoi programmy uluchsheniia polozheniia zhenchshin, sem'i, okhrany materinstva i detstva (Framework for a Government Program to Improve the Position of Women, the Family, and Protect Motherhood and Childhood).* Moscow: Institut Sotsial'no-ekonomicheskikh Problem Narodonaseleniia, 1992.

Rimashevskaia, N. M. *Zhenshchina v meniaiushchemsia mire (Women in a Changing World).* Moscow: Nauka, 1992.

Voronina, O. A. *Gendernaia ekspertiza zakonodatel'stva RF o sredstvakh massovoi informatsii (Gender Analysis of Russian Federation Legislation on the Mass Media).* Moscow: MTsGI (MCGS), 1998.

Zakharova, N., N. Rimashevskaia, and A. Posadskaia. "*Kak my reshaem zhenskii vopros*" (How We Decide the Women Question). *Kommunist*, no. 4 (March 1989): 56–65.

Carol Nechemias

Mother's Right Fund (*Fond Pravo Materi*) (1990–)

A nonprofit, nongovernmental organization to protect the legal rights and interests of parents whose sons have been killed in the army in Russia in peacetime.

The conditions of military service for young soldiers were a topic of widespread public concern in Russia throughout the 1990s. The first war in Chechnia (1994–1996) further highlighted the abysmal conditions of Russia's deteriorating military might; official estimates reported 3,800 dead, 17,900 injured, and 1,900 missing. However, in addition to the losses incurred in the two wars in Chechnia, 4,000 soldiers have died each year without ever entering a conflict zone as victims of poor living conditions, inadequate medical care, hazing, or disease. In some units, there were even reports of starvation. Poor safety procedures have led to numerous fatalities during training. In addition, hazing and brutality toward new recruits were widespread, and suicide became a common response to the brutality of military service. In response, several grassroots groups, such as *Fond Pravo Materi* (the Mother's Right Fund), the Committee of Soldiers' Mothers of Russia, and the Moscow Research Center for Human Rights emerged to protest the brutality endured by Russia's military conscripts. The Mother's Right Fund protected the rights and interests of parents whose sons had been killed in the Russian army while serving within Russia's borders. Veronika Marchenko, a young journalist, set up the organization in 1990 and registered it in 1993. The Fund educated Russia's public, particularly soldiers' families, about their rights and about ways to use the law to protect these rights. The Fund also conducted research on violations of the rights of soldiers and their families and made the information available to the families, policymakers, and the press. Its publications included the well-known series "One Hundred of Fifteen Thousand." Each volume provided photographs and brief biographies of 100 dead soldiers. The Fund's monthly bulletin contained an advice column for families, a list of soldiers killed during the past month, and information about events and activities of interest. The Fund also dispensed free legal advice to parents in personal consultations in Moscow and by letter and telephone from Moscow and the regions. Consultation and direct aid were given to parents who brought their cases to court, and the Fund provided material aid to several severely disadvantaged families. The Fund received increasing amounts of media attention as it expanded and as its public audience multiplied. For example, in 1997 it received almost 2,000 letters from parents of dead soldiers and from public organizations; it also received almost 2,000 calls and 300 visitors. The Fund attempted to respond to each request for information and plea for help. The Mother's Right Fund was governed by a five-member board and was a member of the Moscow Research Center for Human Rights, an umbrella group for human rights groups. Since 1994 the Fund has participated in an advisory capacity in the work of the State Duma committee responsible for developing legislative proposals on military service and on the rights of veterans and their families. The fund has received financial support from the Ford Foundation, the Open Society Institute, the Konrad Adenauer Stiftung, United Way International, and the Swiss government, among others.

Cross-reference: Committee of Soldiers' Mothers of Russia.

Suggested Readings

"One Hundred of Fifteen Thousand." A series of reports. Moscow: Fond Pravo Materi.
Pravo Materi. (Mother's Right). Monthly news bulletin. Moscow.

Sarah Henderson

P

Pamfilova, Ella Aleksandrovna (1953–)

Minister of Social Protection of the Population (1991–1994) and one of the best-known and most highly respected female politicians in the Russian Federation.

Ella Pamfilova, a Russian, was born on September 12, 1953, in Moscow. She is married and has a daughter. In 1976 she graduated from the Moscow Institute of Energy with a degree in electronic engineering. From 1976 to 1989 Pamfilova worked as an engineer and supervisor at the Central Mechanical-Repair Plant of the Moscow Energy Industrial Association (Mosenergo). In 1986 she was elected Chair of the Trade Union Committee for the Central Mechanical-Repair Plant of Mosenergo.

In March 1989 Pamfilova was elected to the USSR Congress of People's Deputies representing the trade unions. In her preelection manifesto, Pamfilova emphasized the importance of treating all workers equally and pointed out the lack of social justice in Soviet society. In order to resolve social problems, she suggested that the bloated bureaucracy be drastically reduced. In addition, Pamfilova suggested that officials should be subject to a code of honor that stressed moral issues. She served on the Credentials Commission of the First USSR Congress of People's Deputies and was a founding member of the Interregional Deputies Group, which she left in October 1989. In the summer of 1990 Pamfilova was elected to the USSR Supreme Soviet and served on the Committee on Ecology and the Rational Use of Natural Resources as well as the provisional Committee for Combating Crime. From January through November 1991 she chaired the USSR Supreme Soviet Commission on Privileges and Benefits. She also organized an inspection of the financial and economic administration of the USSR Supreme Soviet.

In November 1991 Pamfilova resigned from the Communist Party of the Soviet Union (CPSU) and was appointed Minister of Social Protection of the Population of the Russian Republic, a position that she continued to hold in the early post-Soviet Russian Federation. Her main goal was to establish a safety net for the poor in order to prevent an outburst of discontent. She also advocated that all CPSU social facilities should be utilized to serve the people. In addition, she established an administration to recommend the most efficient use of social facilities. Pamfilova became well known for refusing to utilize any of the benefits that accompanied her ministerial post, while continuing to live on the outskirts of Moscow in a Khrushchev-era apartment (*Khrushchëby*). During her tenure, legislation was passed to improve the status of the poor. She also asserted that charitable organizations should be established at the ministerial and local levels if state revenues proved inadequate. In July 1992 she was appointed Russian Federation President Yeltsin's official representative to a committee drafting the law to change state pensions. In December 1992 Pamfilova resigned as Minister of Social Protection of the Population to protest Yeltsin's removal of Acting Prime Minister Egor Gaidar. Yeltsin persuaded her to reconsider, and she was reappointed as minister of social protection of the population in Prime Minister Viktor Chernomyrdin's cabinet on December 23, 1992.

In December 1993 Pamfilova was elected a State Duma deputy from Kaluga electoral district No. 87 (Kaluga oblast) as a leading figure of *Demokraticheskaia vybor Rossii* (Russia's Democratic Choice, or DVR), the party that Egor Gaidar headed. In January 1994 she resigned as Minister of Social Protection of the Population because of her disagreement with Chernomyrdin's economic policies and the slow pace of reform. Pamfilova's resignation came with the condition that she would remain actively involved with social policy. From January 1994 to May 1994 she served on the State Duma Committee on Labor and Social Policy. In May 1994, when the Council on Social Policy was created under the auspices of the presidential administration, Pamfilova was appointed its head. The Council prepared an antipoverty program that included a plan to reform wage and employment policies. The government rejected the program, however, and the Council was secretly dissolved in November 1994, an act that Pamfilova learned about only in the press. In 1994 she resigned from Russia's Choice because of its continued support for the government's social policies. She also served on the Board of Trustees of the Liberal Women's Fund, which Irina Khakamada founded in 1994.

In 1995 Pamfilova joined the *Respublikanskaia partiia Rossiiskoi Federatsii* (Republican Party of the Russian Federation, or RPRF), which had been founded in November 1990 and was headed by Vladimir Lysenko and Grigorii Bondarev; it was a subdivision of the umbrella organization *Demokraticheskaia partiia Rossiia* (Democratic Party of Russia, or DPR). The DPR, established in 1990 as a political alternative to the CPSU, was headed by Nikolai Travkin. The RPRF adopted a social-democratic program and advocated the rebirth of the Russian Federation on the basis of solidarity, economic freedom, and individual liberties. In August 1995 Pamfilova formed and topped the party list of the Pamfilova-Gurov-Vladimir Lysenko electoral bloc in anticipation of the December 1995 parliamentary elections. In December 1995 she was elected a State Duma deputy from Kaluga electoral district No. 86 (Kaluga oblast) atop the

Pamfilova-Gurov-Vladimir Lysenko party list. In January 1996 Pamfilova, along with forty other State Duma deputies, formed the "centrist" faction *Rossiiskie regiony* (Regions of Russia) to represent the interests of the regions in parliament. Some of Pamfilova's other activities in the State Duma included assistant chair of the Committee on the Affairs of Women, Families, and Youth and the State Duma Security Commission, dealing specifically with social security issues.

In 1998 and 1999 Pamfilova concentrated her efforts on expanding the national movement, *Za zdorovuiu Rossiiu* (For a Healthy Russia), whose aim was to unite public forces capable of formulating a reasonable, adequate social policy. The movement chose to concentrate on several problems: childhood, informational support for the social sphere, social pharmacy, medicosocial rehabilitation, ecological rehabilitation, and psychological and medicopsychological rehabilitation. According to Pamfilova, the movement's program would consist of two stages. In the first stage, the movement would identify the most successful elements and tie them into an integral system. The second stage of the program would eventually entail joint efforts on the part of the public, businesses, and the state.

In preparation for the 1999 parliamentary elections, Pamfilova initially had hoped to consolidate several movements, *Otechestvo* (Fatherland), *Golos Rossii* (Voice of Russia), and *Vsia Rossiia* (All Russia). Unfortunately, this hope never came to fruition, as *Otechestvo* and *Vsia Rossiia* formed an alliance (*Otechestvo-Vsia Rossiia*) instead. As a result, she topped the party list of her movement, *Za grazhdanskoe dostoinstvo* (For Civil Dignity), followed by Aleksandr Dondukov and Anatolii Shkirko in the second and third positions, respectively. The movement, however, failed to clear the 5 percent barrier. Since Pamfilova chose not to run from a single electoral district in 1999, in contrast to the 1993 and 1995 elections, she was not elected to the State Duma. Pamfilova was a candidate for President of the Russian Federation in the election of March 2000. She chose to run, although she knew her chances of winning were negligible; she thus became the first woman to appear on the presidential ballot in Russia. Pamfilova obtained only 1 percent of the vote but made history with her candidacy.

At various times, Pamfilova served as an unofficial ambassador representing women's interests to the government, although she participated in none of the women's organizations of the post-Soviet era. She was highly respected by both women and men as both a woman leader and an incorruptible politician.

Cross-reference: Irina Khakamada.

Suggested Readings

Belonuchkin, G. V. "Pamfilova Ella Aleksandrovna." In *Federal'noe sobranie: Soviet Federacii, Gosudarstvennaya Duma: Spravochnik* (Federation Assembly: Federation Council, State Duma: Reference Book). Moscow: IEG "Panorama," 1996. <http://www.cityline.ru:8084/politika/bio/pamfil.html> (1997).

"Commission Releases Final Results." RFE/RL Russian Election Report, no. 5, April 7, 2000.

Dikun, Yelena. "The Star-Crossed Mission of Ella Pamfilova." *PRISM: A Bi-Weekly on the Post-Soviet States* (A Publication of the Jamestown Foundation) 2, no. 16. <http://www.jamestown.org/pubs/view/pri_002_016_005.html> (October 1, 1996).

"Ella Aleksandrovna Pamfilova." Norsk Utenrikspolitisk Institutt-Norwegian Institute of International Affairs (NUPI). Centre for Russian Studies Database. <http://www.nupi.no/cgi-win/Russland/Personer.exe/61> (1999).

Kachalova, Iuliia. "Politics Is for People: An Interview of Ella Pamfilova." Woman Plus (A Publication of the East–West Women's Innovation Fund). <http://www.owl.ru/eng/womplus/1998/pamfil-e.htm> (1998).

Kto est' kto v Rossii i v blizhnem zarubezh'e: spravochnik (Who's Who in Russia and the Near Abroad: Directory). Moscow: Izd. Novoe vremia: Vse dlia Vas, 1993.

McCauley, Martin, ed. *Longman Biographical Directory of Decision Makers in Russia and the Successor States.* Harlow, U.K.: Longman, 1993.

Morozov, Vladimir, ed. *Who's Who in Russia and the CIS Republics.* New York: Henry Holt, 1995.

"Pamfilova Ella Aleksandrovna." National News Service-Natsional'naia sluzhba novostei. <http://www.nns.ru/persons/pamfil.html> (1995).

"The Republican Party of the Russian Federation." Norsk Utenrikspolitisk Institutt-Norwegian Institute of International Affairs (NUPI). Centre for Russian Studies Database. <http://www.nupi.no/cgi-win/Russland/polgrupp.exe/The+Republican+Party+of+the+Russian+Federation> (1999).

Schulz-Torge, Ulrich-Joachim, ed. *Who's Who in Russia Today: A Biographical Dictionary of More than 2,100 Individuals from the Russian Federation including the Other Fourteen Former USSR Republics.* Munich: K. G. Saur, 1994.

Cheri C. Wilson

Pivnenko, Valentina Nikolaevna (1947–)

An economist and sociologist, Chair of the Chamber of Representatives of the Legislative Assembly of the Karelian Republic (1995–1996), and one of two women in the Federation Council of the Russian Federation (January 1996–March 1997, May 1998–).

Valentina Pivnenko, a Russian, was born on June 14, 1947, in Petrozavodsk (Karelian Republic). She graduated from the Petrozavodsk State Timber Industry Technical Secondary School, the Petrozavodsk State University named for O. V. Kuusinen, and the Moscow Academy of Labor and Social Relations. She was married and had two children and a grandchild.

She worked in the Karelian Branch of the State Timber Industry as a technician, engineer, and head of the Department of Labor and Wages. She was a member of the Communist Party of the Soviet Union (CPSU) from 1971 to August 1991. In 1979 she was elected secretary of the Karelian Oblast Committee of Trade Union Workers, a position that she held until 1990. She also headed the Department of Economic Protection of the Council of Trade Union

Workers. From 1990 to 1991 she worked on the staff of the trade union worker groups in their negotiations with the government. In April 1992 out of seven candidates, she was elected chair of the Karelian Republic Trade Union Council. She represented the trade unions of the Russian Federation as a member of the staff of the Trilateral Commission on the Regulation of Social–Labor Relations. In April 1994 she was elected a deputy to the First Session of the Chamber of Representatives of the Legislative Assembly of the Karelian Republic from the Prionezhskii electoral district. She was elected its Chair in May 1994. In January 1996 she entered the second session of the Federation Council of the Russian Federation. She was the only woman in the Federation Council until November 1996, when she was joined by Valentina Bronevich, who had been elected governor of the Koriak Autonomous *Okrug*. During that period, Pivnenko served on the Federation Council Committee on the Budget, Tax Policies, Finances, Currency, Customs Regulations, and Banking Activities and was elected assistant Chair of the Committee in mid-1996. She was also a member of the Control-Budget Committee of the Interparliamentary Assembly of the Commonwealth of Independent States (CIS). In February 1997 she represented the Russian Federation at the Inter-Parliamentary Specialized Conference on Towards Partnership between Men and Women in Politics, held in New Delhi, India. In April 1998 she was reelected a deputy to the Second Session of the Chamber of Representatives of the Legislative Assembly of the Karelian Republic from the Prionezhskii electoral district. In May 1998 she was reelected its chair. In June 1998 she rejoined Bronevich in the Federation Council after both chambers of the Karelian Legislature elected her to represent them again. This vote was particularly significant since the Karelian legislators could have chosen Natal'ia Kotsiuba, who had been director of the Karelian Branch of the Federal Bankruptcy Service and chair of the Karelian Republic House of the Republic, to represent the Karelian Republic in the Federation Council. On October 15, 1998, Pivnenko was appointed chair of a Temporary Commission established by the Federation Council to investigate the August 1998 financial crisis. In December 1999 she was elected a State Duma deputy from Karelian electoral district No. 16 in the Karelian Republic with 30 percent of the votes over incumbent Larisa Zlobina, a member of the Russian Socialist Party, who received only 8 percent of the votes. In early November 1999 the Karelian Republic Central Election Commission had denied Zlobina's registration for candidacy, which she alleged was an attempt to improve Pivnenko's chances for election. Although Pivnenko ran as an independent, she was reportedly backed by Karelian Prime Minister Sergei Katanandov, a member of *Otechestvo* (Fatherland), as was the chairman of the election commission. Zlobina appealed to the Karelian Supreme Court, which overruled the Election Commission's decision and deemed its action illegal. Pivnenko's election to the State Duma left Valentina Bronevich the only woman in the Federation Council as of 2000.

Cross-reference: Valentina Bronevich.

Suggested Readings

Belonuchkin, G. V. "*Komitet SF po biudzhetu, nalogovoi politike, finansovomu, valiutnomu, i tamozhennomu regulirovaniu*" (Federation Council Committee on the Budget, Tax Policies, Finances, Currency, and Customs Regulations). In *Federal'noe sobranie: Soviet Federacii, Gosudarstvennaya Duma: Spravochnik (Federation Assembly: Federation Council, State Duma: Reference Book).* Moscow: IEG "Panorama," 1996. <http://www.cityline.ru:8084/politika/fs/sf2kombu.html> (1996).

"Karelia: One Female Candidate Too Many." RFE/RL Russian Federation Report. Vol. 1, no. 40. <http://www.rferl.org/russianreport/1999/12/40-011299.html> (December 1, 1999).

"*Pivnenko Valentina Nikolaevna: Kratkaia biograficheskaia spravka*" (Pivnenko Valentina Nikolaevna: Short Biographical Sketch). National News Service-Natsional'naia sluzhba novostei. <http://www.nns.ru/persons/pivnen.html> (1996).

"Pivnenko Valentina Nikolaevna: Biograficheskaia spravka" (Pivnenko Valentina Nikolaevna: Biographical Sketch). Republic of Karelia: Official Server of the Organs of Government Power. <http://www.gov.karelia.ru:80/LA/Person/pivnenko_a.html> (1999).

"Prichiny i posledstviia finansovogo krizisa v Rossii kontsa 90-H godov." <http://www.council.gov.ru:8104/inf_sl/inf_iau/98–10.htm> (1999).

"Pivnenko Valentina Nikolaevna." *Spisok chlenov Soveta Federacii* (List of Members of the Federation Council). <http://www.council.gov.ru:8104/sostav/members/deput/d_204405.htm> (November 23, 1999).

"Verit', liubit', deistvovat': Valentina Pivnenko, Zhenshchina—Senator" (Believe, Love, Act: Valentina Pivnenko, Woman—Senator). <http://pivnenko.karelia.ru/index.html> (1999).

"Women Gain Top Positions in Karelian Legislature." RFE/RL Newsline. Vol. 2, no. 95, Part I. (May 20, 1998).

Cheri C. Wilson

Political Participation by Russian Women in the Transitional Period (1985–)

Since 1985 women's participation in politics, first in the USSR and later in Russia, was transformed as part of the broader societal transition. The results were mixed since women lost much of their former titular status but also made significant gains in learning how to organize political movements.

In the Soviet era, women were not important political actors, even though they were represented in the formal government institutions. Women constituted approximately 33 percent of the Supreme Soviet, the parliament in which candidates were elected without opposition. Women also had guaranteed representation on the local Soviets, but these formal organizations had little power. The system of elite recruitment and socialization did not foster a climate encouraging women's participation. Furthermore, women's involvement in domestic tasks and jobs left little time for politics. Insofar as women were interested in politics, they tended to focus on health issues, social welfare, education, and other issues that impacted their lives. During the transitional period that began with Perestroika and continued into the 1990s, there were increased opportunities for political activism, and women were able to participate in politics under new conditions. New consciousness developed among women about politics. At the end of the 1980s, the reorganized *zhensovety* (Women's Councils) gave new, but limited, opportunities for women's participation; the limitations lay in the restrictive principles of organization of the *zhensovety* and in the absence of debate about gender issues in society. In the elections for the Congress of People's Deputies in 1989, only 15.7 percent of the elected deputies were women (352 out of 2,250). In this first contested national election in the Soviet system, women's representation fell to under one-half of what it had been in the Supreme Soviet prior to the reforms.

The period of economic reform (1992–1995) did not provide a favorable climate for increasing mass political participation, since both interest and trust in politics fell sharply. Nonetheless, there were some successes. The political bloc Women of Russia (WOR) received 8 percent of the vote in the 1993 elections to the new State Duma. Although it failed to reach the 5 percent threshold for participation in the 1995 election, several women were elected from single-member districts. WOR fared even worse in the December 1999 parliamentary elections, securing just over 2 percent of the party-list vote and failing to elect any candidates from single-member districts. At the regional level, organizations such as Women of St. Petersburg were unsuccessful in gathering support for women candidates. For example, in the 1994 city elections in St. Petersburg, only one woman was elected to the city assembly. The assembly had fifty seats, and more than 750 candidates competed for those fifty seats, among them ninety-seven women. Sociological inquiries explored the reasons for women's poor showing in the polls, which appear to result from differences in resources, education, and political experience between men and women. Most of the women candidates did not consider themselves politicians and did not seek a political career. They considered themselves only temporary players in the political arena.

The differences seemed to reflect differences in the recruitment channels between men and women and between the political generations in Russia. In the transitional period, there were two distinct generations of people in politics: those who began a political career during the Soviet era and those who became involved in politics in the transitional era. The opening of new career opportunities meant that some people entered politics through either the old channel or the new. The old, or Soviet, channel included people who had held positions in government; the new, post-Soviet channel was reflected in careers in business or other careers developed in the transitional period. Among women active in post-Soviet politics were women for whom politics was a career under the old system and whose career path included work in the Komsomol, the Communist Party of the Soviet Union (CPSU), or local government. Liudmila Shvetsova, who occupied an important position in the government of Moscow in the late

1990s, provided an example of a woman successful in the new system whose career originated through the old channel. At the local and regional level, there were numerous such women, whose successful participation in Russian politics could be traced to the positions that they held in the Soviet system. Also active in post-Soviet Russia were women who were outsiders in the old system and who sought to promote the reform process. Galina Starovoitova was a notable example of a woman who entered politics during the transitional period. Starovoitova's early success was based on her advocacy of the rights of ethnic minorities. She came to exemplify a politician of principle, until her career was violently cut short in 1998 by an assassin's bullet.

In the transitional period, some women also entered politics because of heightened gender consciousness. These women sought to change public policy concerning women. Several women's groups around the country encouraged such activity, and in some cases members of those groups chose to become candidates as a way to fulfill their goals. For example, in Ivanovo the Union of Women was headed by Natal'ia Kovaleva, who also held a seat in the city's legislature; in other cities, like Cheboksary and Ekaterinburg, and in the Kola Peninsula, women's activism included the promotion of women's participation in the political realm. In 1997 in the legislatures of the eighty-nine federal units of the Russian Federation, women held only nine percent of the seats. That figure, however, masks widespread variation in women's success: in fourteen federal units women held twenty percent or more of the legislative seats; in four legislatures, women held thirty percent or more of the seats.

Nevertheless, because of women's extensive responsibilities with their families, women who were politicians were still an exception in Russian political life. In addition, societal attitudes were not conducive to encouraging women to enter the political arena. Women were viewed as "keepers of the hearth," not as politicians, and as such would enter politics only to create or preserve the "hearth." Negative attitudes persisted against women's entering the political arena, even among women who wished to consider such a step. Women's role in politics, insofar as it was recognized, tended to be seen as limited to issues such as education, health-care, and related concerns.

Cross-references: All-Russian Sociopolitical Movement of Women of Russia (MWR), Ekaterinburg Women's Organizations, Alevtina Fedulova, Kola Peninsula (Women's Congress of the), Ekaterina Lakhova, Liudmila Shvetsova, Galina Starovoitova, Women of Russia, *Zhensovety*.

Suggested Readings

Browning, Geni. "Soviet Politics: Where are the women?" In *Soviet Sisterhood*, edited by Barbara Holland, 207–236. Bloomington, IN: Indiana University Press, 1985.

Konstantinova, V Valentina. *"Vlast' i Zhenshchina: Zhenshchina vo vlasti."* (Power and Woman: Woman in Power). In *Prava zhenshchin v Rossii: Issledovanie real'noi praktiki ikh sobliudeniia i massogo soznaniia (The Rights of Women in Russia: Research on the Reality of their Observance and Mass Consciousness)*, edited by Marina Malysheva, 190–245. Moscow: Moscow Center for Gender Studies, 1998.

Sillaste, Galina. *"Zhenskie elity v Rossii."* (Women Elites in Russia). In *Zhenshchina i svoboda (Women and Freedom)*, edited by V. M. Tishkov, 27–40. Moscow: Nauka, 1994.

Temkina, Anna. *"Zhenskii put' v politiku: gendernaia perspektiva" (Women's Path into Politics: a Gender Perspective)*. In *Gendernoe ismerenie sotsial'noi i politicheskoi aktivnosti v perekhodnyi period (The Gender Dimension of Social and Political Activism in the Transitional Period)*, edited by Elena Zdravomyslova and Anna Temkina, 9–32. St. Petersburg: Trudy TsNSI, no. 4, 1996.

Temkina, Anna. "Entering Politics: Women's Ways, Gender Ideas and Contradictions of Reality." In *Women's Voices in Russia Today*, edited by Anna Rotkirch and Elina Haavio-Mannila, 206–234. Aldershot: Dartmouth, 1996.

Uspenskaia, Valentina. *"Stereotipy na puti zhenshchin k liderstvu"* (Stereotypes in the Path of Women to Leadership). In *Feministskaia teoriia i praktika: Vostok-Zapad (Feminist Theory: East–West)*, edited by Iuliia Zhukova, 25–32. St. Petersburg: St. Petersburg Gender Center, 1996.

Voronina, Olga. "Soviet Women and Politics: On the Brink of Change." In *Women and Politics Worldwide*, edited by Barbara Nelson et al., 722–736. New Haven, CT: Yale University Press, 1994.

Anna Temkina and Norma Corigliano Noonan

Posadskaia, Anastasiia (*Posadskaia-Vanderbeck*) (1958–)

A central figure in the emergence of the independent women's movement during Perestroika and in post-Soviet Russia, founding member and former director of the *Moskovskii Tsentr Gendernykh Issledovanii* (Moscow Center for Gender Studies, or MCGS), and a leading feminist scholar.

Anastasiia Posadskaia was born in Moscow in 1958 and grew up as the only child in a family consisting of her mother and her maternal grandparents. Her grandmother had graduated from Moscow State University's Chemistry Department; her grandfather had worked as a journalist; and her mother was a pharmacist. Her parents never married or lived together. The family's circumstances were difficult: three adults and a child in a single room in a communal apartment. The family strongly supported high educational aspirations, and from the beginning Posadskaia was an excellent student who loved school. As a child she served for several years as the leader of the Pioneers in her school class, though by adolescence, when it became time to join Komsomol, she found herself bored with the organization, considering its activities time-consuming and meaningless.

In 1974 she finished her secondary education in nine years rather than the standard ten, convinced that all roads in life were open to her. Her efforts to enter Moscow State University's Department of Economics taught her otherwise. She found the competition to gain admission to the Economics Department fraught with political favoritism, based on personal connections rather than merit. Lacking a father and coming from a poor family, her application was rejected despite her outstanding academic credentials. Ultimately, she gained admission through the "back door": working as a typist in the Economics Department in 1974, entering the department's night school program the next year, and finally transferring to the full-time, day program in 1976. But the experience sensitized her to double standards and differences between official rhetoric about society and reality.

Further disillusionment with social reality came as the result of an early marriage to a fellow student. One of the first among her classmates to marry, Posadskaia became a wife at age eighteen and shortly thereafter the mother of a baby girl. She moved in with her in-laws and took a ten-month leave from Moscow State University to care for her baby. This new situation turned Posadskaia's attention to women's issues. She had grown up in a family setting where women and men were equal, but at her in-laws' she found that her mother-in-law did all the housework. Posadskaia found her husband, despite her urgings, unwilling to share in household tasks. The marriage failed, and Posadskaia moved back to her family's flat, now made up of four generations of women (her grandfather had died in 1974), and continued her undergraduate studies at Moscow State University.

In 1981 Posadskaia completed her undergraduate program with a "red diploma," the approximate equivalent of a summa cum laude degree. She used every opportunity to write research papers on themes related to women. Her diploma thesis was on women's employment in the United States, a topic that stimulated her interest in women's economic situation in the USSR. Posadskaia was determined to pursue postgraduate work on women's employment in the USSR. When she applied to various institutes of the Academy of Sciences, she confronted sexism: men were preferred over women, and research on women's issues was considered unimportant. Despite these difficulties, Posadskaia secured the support of Professor Mikhail Sonin, who recommended her entry into the Institute of Economics and supervised her work from 1981 until his death three years later. By 1984 Posadskaia completed work on her dissertation on "Socioeconomic Issues of Women's Employment in the USSR" and searched for a position that would allow her to continue research on women. But no one in the Academy of Sciences was interested in her topic. Moreover, Posadskaia did not receive the *kandidat* degree until 1989, as her dissertation defense was delayed due to Sonin's death and the unwillingness of other professors to supervise her work.

From 1984 to 1988 the only positions that Posadskaia obtained involved part-time employment teaching political economy at two industrial institutes, the Moscow Institute of Chemical Technology and the Moscow Institute of Aviation Technology. In June 1988 Posadskaia's goal of finding a position where she could work on women's issues was met: she was offered full-time employment at the newly created *Institut Sotsial'no-Ekonomicheskikh Problem Narodonaseleniia* (Institute of Socioeconomic Population Problems, or ISEPP), headed by Natal'ia Rimashevskaia. In addition, she became acquainted with three women scholars familiar with feminist thought: Natal'ia Zakharova, who worked with Rimashevskaia; Olga Voronina at the Institute of Philosophy; and Valentina

Konstantinova from the Social Science Academy of the Central Committee. These three women opened Posadskaia's eyes to feminist literature, and she began to identify herself as a feminist. The women met informally and formed the group LOTOS, the *Liga Osvobozhdeniia ot Obshchestvennykh Stereotipov* (League for Emancipation from Social Stereotypes).

At ISEPP opportunities to conduct research focusing on women quickly developed. In August 1988 the USSR Council of Ministers requested ideas on how to change women's situation. A revised version of that report, written by Zakharova, Rimashevskaia, and Posadskaia, was later published in *Kommunist*, the theoretical journal of the Central Committee of the CPSU, in March 1989. The government then asked for a more developed position paper, an opportunity that the three women scholars utilized to request the creation of a new center for gender studies. The Presidium of the Academy of Sciences agreed to the new Moscow Center for Gender Studies (MCGS), and Posadskaia became its first director. Except for Zakharova, who had taken a position with the United Nations in Vienna, the LOTOS group went to work at the newly formed Center. Under Posadskaia's leadership, the Center grew in terms of staff, conducted research on women's issues, and participated actively in the emerging women's movement.

Posadskaia was a central player in the development of the Russian women's movement. She served as a member of the Organizing Committee of the First Independent Women's Forum in Dubna in 1991, cochaired the Organizing Committee of the Second Independent Women's Forum in Dubna in 1992, and was a founding member of the Information Center of the Independent Women's Forum. She also forged linkages with the Russian government, serving from 1993 to 1995 on President Yeltsin's Presidential Commission on Women, Family, and Demography and from 1993 to 1995 on the National Committee on the Preparation for the 1995 United Nations (UN) World Conference on Women in Beijing. She frequently represented the independent women's movement abroad: she spoke at foreign universities and at numerous conferences on women's issues, and she participated as a member of the Board of Directors for organizations like the Global Fund for Women (since 1991), the International Women's Health Coalition (since 1994), and the European Network of Women's Studies (1990–1994). Fluent in English, Posadskaia assisted the MCGS in establishing relationships with the international women's movement and with Western foundations like Ford and Eurasia.

In 1995 Posadskaia's career took a new direction after her marriage to an American businessman and subsequent move to the United States. A new name, Posadskaia-Vanderbeck, and a new country did not end her scholarship on Russian women's issues or her social activism. In 1995 she was a Fellow at the Institute for Research on Women (Rutgers University) and a Fellow at the Institute for Advanced Study (Princeton University); in 1996–1997 she was a Fellow at the Center for Russian, Central, and East European Studies (Rutgers University). In 1997 Posadskaia became Director of the Soros Foundation's

Network Women's Program at the Open Society Institute, responsible for the coordination of new programs focusing on women's issues in twenty-six post-socialist countries. Network-wide programs included projects in the areas of violence against women, women's health, and trafficking in women. For 1999–2000 Posadskaia took a leave of absence to teach at Swarthmore College as the Julian and Virginia Cornell Distinguished Visiting Professor.

Posadskaia combined a commitment to scholarship with a commitment to social activism that exemplified the work of MCGS. She was a key leader in the development of gender studies and of the independent women's movement in Russia during perestroika and the post-Soviet period.

Cross-references: Commission on Women, Family, and Demography, Information Center of the Independent Women's Forum, LOTOS, Moscow Center for Gender Studies.

Suggested Readings

Engel, Barbara Alpern, and Anastasia Posadskaya-Vanderbeck, eds. *A Revolution of Their Own: Voices of Women in Soviet History*. Boulder, CO: Westview Press, 1998.

Marsh, Rosalind. "Anastasiia Posadskaia, the Dubna Forum and the Independent Women's Movement in Russia." In *Women in Russia and Ukraine*, edited by Rosalind Marsh, 286–297. Cambridge: Cambridge University Press, 1996.

Molyneux, Maxine. "Interview with Anastasya Posadskaya (25 September 1990)." *Feminist Review*, no. 39 (Winter 1991): 133–140.

Posadskaia, Anastasiia. "The Feminine Dimension of Social Reform: From One Forum to the Next" (Speech at the Second Independent Women's Forum, Dubna, November 1992). In *Women in Russia and Ukraine*, edited by Rosalind Marsh, 298–304. Cambridge: Cambridge University Press.

Posadskaia, A. I. "*Tendentsii Izmeneniia Zakonodatel'stva v Oblasti Sotsial'noi Zashchity Materinstva*" (Gender Changes in Law concerning Social Defense of Motherhood). In *Zhenshchiny i sotsial'naia politika: genderny aspeckt (Women and Social Policy: Gender Aspects)*, edited by Z. Khotkina, 79–88. Moscow: Institut Sotsial'no-ekonomicheskikh Problem Narodonaseleniia, 1992.

Posadskaia, A. I. "*Zhenskie issledovaniia v Rossii: perspektivy novogo videniia*" (Women's Studies in Russia: Prospects for the New Vision). In *Gendernye aspekty sotsial'noi transformatsii (Gender Aspects of Social Transformation)*, edited by M. M. Malysheva, 11–24. Moscow: Institut Sotsial'no-ekonomicheskikh Problem Narodonaseleniia, 1996.

Posadskaya, Anastasia, ed. *Women in Russia*. London: Verso, 1994.

Racioppi, Linda, and Katherine O'Sullivan See. *Women's Activism in Contemporary Russia*. Philadelphia: Temple University Press, 1997.

Rimashevskaia, N. A., A. I. Posadskaia, and N. Zakharova. *Kontseptsiia gosudarstvennoi programmy uluchsheniia polozheniia zhenchshin, sem'i, okhrany materinstva i detstva (Framework for a Government Program to Improve the Position of Women, the Family, and Protect Motherhood and Childhood)*. Moscow: Institut Sotsial'no-ekonomicheskikh Problem Narodonaseleniia, 1992.

Zakharova, N., N. Rimashevskaia, and A. Posadskaia. "*Kak my reshaem zhenskii vopros*" (How We Decide the Woman Question). *Kommunist*, no. 4 (March 1989): 56–65.

Carol Nechemias

R

Regent, Tatiana Mikhailovna (1950–)

Director of the Federal Migration Service of the Russian Federation (June 1992–February 1999).

Tatiana Regent, a Russian, was born on August 21, 1950, in Omsk. She and her husband, Nikolai Ivanovich Regent, had one daughter, Valeriia. In 1974 Regent graduated from Moscow State University with a specialization in economic geography. From 1974 to 1985 she worked as a junior researcher and senior researcher in the Central Research, Development, and Project Institute on Planning and Civil Construction in Rural Areas (*TsNIIEGrazhdanselstroi*). From 1986 to 1990 Regent worked as an assistant professor at the Moscow Oblast N. K. Krupskaia Pedagogical Institute. From 1990 to 1991 she headed the laboratory of the *Institut problem zaniatosti* (Institute of Employment Problems) of the Russian Academy of Sciences. From January to June 1992 Regent served as first deputy chair of the Committee on Migration Affairs, which was under the auspices of the Ministry of Labor and Social Development of the Russian Federation (RF).

On June 14, 1992, she was appointed head of the Federal Migration Service (FMS) of the RF. Regent's duties were particularly difficult considering the numerous waves of forced migration that the RF experienced from 1992 to 1999. The dissolution of the Soviet Union brought concerns about large migrations of Russians from the near abroad (the Newly Independent States, or NIS) of the former USSR. The first Chechen War (1994–1996) displaced numerous people in Chechnia, Dagestan, and Ingushetia. For example, by April 1, 1996, FMS had registered about 437,000 refugees from Chechnia, about one-third of its prewar population.

In 1996 the United Nations High Commission on Refugees (UNHCR) reported that there were an estimated 164 territorial disputes "based on ethnic issues" in the Commonwealth of Independent States (CIS). The UNHCR also described migration trends within the CIS as a potential threat to regional stability. In October 1997 Regent stated that the Russian Federation served as the main transit route for illegal immigration to Central and Western Europe. On

February 15, 1999, President Boris Yeltsin dismissed Regent and several other government officials for no apparent reason. The length of Regent's tenure was especially noteworthy considering the fact that she survived numerous cabinet shake-ups and served in the cabinets of Prime Ministers Egor Gaidar, Viktor Chernomyrdin, Sergei Kirienko, and Evgenii Primakov.

In February 1999 she became the Deputy General Director of "*Gazspetsresurs*" (Gas Special Resource Limited Liability Company). In December 1999 Regent was a candidate for the State Duma on the *Zhenshchiny Rossii* (Women of Russia, or ZhR, or WOR) list, where she was listed sixth. Since Women of Russia failed to reach the 5 percent barrier, Regent was not elected.

Cross-reference: Women of Russia (WOR).

Suggested Readings

"Costs of Chechen War." *OMRI Daily Digest*, no. 67, Part I. <http://www.rferl.org/newsline/1996/04/030496.html> (April 3, 1996).

Kto est' kto v Rossii i v blizhnem zarubezh'e: spravochnik (Who's Who in Russia and the Near Abroad: A Directory). Moscow: Izd. Novoe vremia: Vsë dlia Vas, 1993.

Schulz-Torge, Ulrich-Joachim, ed. *Who's Who in Russia Today: A Biographical Dictionary of More than 2,100 Individuals from the Russian Federation including the Other Fourteen Former USSR Republics*. Munich: K. G. Saur, 1994.

"UN, Russia on CIS Migration." OMRI Daily Digest, no. 102, Part I. <http://www.rferl.org/newsline/1996/05/270596.html> (May 27, 1996).

"Yeltsin Dismisses Three More Officials." RFE/RL Newsline. Vol. 3, no. 32, Part I. <http://www.rferl.org/newsline/1999/02/160299.html> (February 16, 1999).

Cheri C. Wilson

Reproductive Rights (1985–)

Discussions of reproductive rights during perestroika and the post-Soviet era occurred in the midst of political, economic, and demographic crises that complicated efforts to introduce modern contraception and sex education. Access to modern means of contraception remained unavailable to the bulk of Russian women due to problems of access, cost, and cultural attitudes.

The post-Soviet era witnessed economic recession, political crises, and the widespread impoverishment of the population. Debate over reproductive rights occurred in a setting unparalleled in peacetime in modern history: since 1989 the birthrate has dropped sharply, while the death rate has surged upward, leading to actual declines in the size of the Russian Federation's population. In the 1990s women of childbearing age gave birth at the rate of thirteen children per ten women, far below the twenty-one to twenty-two range needed to ensure the mere replacement of the population. These conditions led nationalist and communist politicians to decry what was perceived as the dying out of the nation and to resist family planning and sex education on the grounds that these measures would further lower the birthrate.

In the late 1980s the Soviet approach to birth control differed little from practices predominant in the early 1930s, a reliance on abortion rather than information, services, and contraception. In 1920 the Soviet Union was the first country to legalize abortion with virtually no restrictions and was also the first, sixteen years later, to reverse that position and ban abortions as Stalin sought to boost birthrates and stabilize family life. In 1955, two years after Stalin's death, abortion was once again legalized.

By the 1990s the abortion culture was deeply rooted in Russia. Abortion was regarded as acceptable, whereas other forms of contraception were viewed with suspicion. The production of contraceptive devices, from condoms to birth control pills, remained severely underdeveloped within Russia. This meant reliance on imported products or on one or two factories within Russia. The importing of low-quality birth control pills from Hungary and flaws in Russian intrauterine devices (IUDs) produced in Kazan soured the public and doctors alike to the safety of contraception, particularly hormonal (birth control) pills. In the post-Soviet era, roughly 80 percent of women used abortion as the primary method of family planning; the abortion rate in Russia during the 1990s was the highest in the world, with two abortions occurring for every live birth and the average Russian woman having five abortions in her lifetime.

Perestroika and the post-Soviet transition introduced new developments with respect to reproductive rights and reproductive health. There was open recognition that maternal and infant mortality rates were unacceptably high. In the late 1980s it was revealed that Soviet maternal mortality rates were six times higher than those of the United States, and infant mortality stood at 17.3 per 1,000 births compared with 6.9 in Finland. In the 1990s growing economic distress and the erosion of free health care, along with other factors like harmful environmental conditions, poor diet, alcoholism, and smoking, also contributed to a decline in women's reproductive health. Some 75 percent of all pregnant women in Russia suffered from serious complications during their pregnancies, particularly from anemia but also from sexually transmitted diseases other than AIDS. Infertility increased and affected 15 to 20 percent of all couples by the late 1990s. Women's health also was harmed by abortions carried out in unsanitary conditions and with backward technology.

In addition to a more open acknowledgment of health problems, the post-Soviet era generated efforts to introduce the concept of family planning. Ekaterina Lakhova, as chair of President Yeltsin's *Komissiia po delam zhenshchin, sem'i i demografii* (Commission on Women, Family, and Demography) and former chair of the State Duma faction "*Zhenshchiny Rossii*" (Women of Russia), was a key proponent of family planning and assisted in establishing *Planirovanie sem'i* (Family Planning) as a unit within the multifaceted *Deti Rossii* (Children of Russia) program. By the mid-1990s, however, the federal government ceased to fund the family-planning program due to increased opposition from politicians and religious leaders, who were convinced that it would reduce the Russian population and/or foster immorality.

After the collapse of the Soviet Union in 1991, there was a growth of legalized commercial abortions in private clinics, offering women with money greater personal attention, assurances of secrecy, and the availability of anesthesia. By 1994 private clinics began to advertise sterilization services, which had been declared methods of family planning by the Ministry of Health in 1993, but only for individuals over the age of thirty-five who had at least two children, unless special medical indications were present and the person consented. With the end of the state monopoly on health care, official data on abortion rates and the use of contraceptives became more problematic as private sector activity in the 1990s was not systematically incorporated into official state statistics.

The creation of independent women's organizations in the early 1990s included several working in the field of reproductive rights. The most prominent of these was the *Rossiiskaia assotsiatsiia "Planirovanie sem'i"* (Russian Association of Family Planning, or RAFP). The RAFP, often with the cooperation of foreign assistance, the Ministry of Health, and regional governments, sponsored educational programs for health workers, started family planning clinics, prepared sex education programs for children and youth, and conducted research on public attitudes toward family planning. Access to modern contraception remained difficult, however, due to problems of cost, access, and negative cultural attitudes. In the mid-1990s only 18 percent of women aged fifteen to forty-nine used IUDs, and 6 percent used birth control pills, while 40 percent relied on methods with high failure rates, like the rhythm method and withdrawal.

The promotion of family planning was in its initial stages in the 1990s. Surveys showed that conversations between medical professionals and women about birth control took place often after a woman arrived at the doctor's office seeking an abortion rather than before. At the same time, political forces opposed to abortion emerged, which were often also unfriendly toward the introduction of sex education in public schools and the development of family-planning clinics. The Right to Life Movement and the Russian Orthodox Church conducted campaigns against abortion. A 1998 survey, however, revealed that only 9 percent of men and 6 percent of women favored prohibiting abortion. Yet there was some evidence that support for abortion rights, while still high, has eroded: during the 1990s support for the legal right to interrupt pregnancy declined among women from 88 percent to 67 percent and among men from 73 percent to 50 percent. Several factors may have contributed to this decline: increased information about the harmful effects that abortion, particularly multiple abortions, has had on women's health; increased knowledge about alternative forms of birth control; and increased opposition to abortion from the Pro Life Movement, the Russian Orthodox Church, and "patriotic" politicians concerned about low fertility rates.

The rules governing abortion in the late 1990s allowed the procedure with a physician's referral up to twelve weeks. Such referrals were granted upon request. Between thirteen and twenty-two weeks, medical or social indications were used to justify the request; after twenty-eight weeks only medical indications received consideration. Teenagers between the ages of fifteen and eighteen did not need parental consent. Abortion no longer was free everywhere in the

Russian Federation: in some regions fees were charged, with insurance coverage only for miniabortions and for prescribed medical and social reasons. These reasons included women who already had three or more children, women prisoners, or women over the age of forty-five. In the mid-1990s in Moscow the cost of having an abortion equaled the average monthly wage.

A working group, including deputies drawn from the State Duma Commission on Women, Family, and Youth, RAFP, the Russian Academy of Medical Science, the Ministry of Health, and the Moscow Center for Gender Studies introduced a draft law in 1996, On Citizens' Reproductive Rights and Guarantees of Their Exercise. This draft law represented an effort to create a "constitution" of reproductive rights, but it was stalled in the State Duma, as growing opposition and obstacles clouded the future of the reproductive rights movement in Russia.

Russian conditions prevented the realization of citizens' reproductive rights. There was no guarantee of the right to information and to family planning services or access to modern means of preventing pregnancy. For the bulk of Russian women, abortion did not reflect a choice but rather the absence of alternative forms of contraception.

Cross-references: Commission on Women, Family, and Demography, Family Protection and Women's Well-Being under Communism and Later, Foreign Funding and the Women's Movement in Russia, Ekaterina Lakhova, Moscow Center for Gender Studies.

Suggested Readings

Bodrova, Valentina. "Russian Attitudes on Sex and Youth." *Choices* 25, no. 1 (1996): 9–14.

Popov, A. A. "Family Planning in Russia: The Role of NGOs in De-Monopolizing Population Policy." *Planned Parenthood in Europe* 24, no. 2 (1995): 26–30.

Popov, Andrej A., and Henry P. David, eds. "Russian Federation and USSR Successor States." In *From Abortion to Contraception: A Resource to Public Policies and Reproductive Behavior in Central and Eastern Europe from 1917 to the Present*, edited by Henry P. David with the assistance of Joanna Skilogianis, 223–277. Westport, CT: Greenwood Press, 1999.

Valentina Bodrova

S

SAFO (1993–)

An organization based in St. Petersburg designed to address the needs and pursue the interests of lesbian women. SAFO sponsored lectures and special information programs and various activities to support lesbian women.

SAFO was founded in 1993 by a small group of women, but over time several hundred women have been involved with this informal organization. SAFO established a small community center where it sponsored lectures, seminars, and information sessions on themes such as lesbian and women's movements, health, prevention of AIDS, family and children, and lesbian psychology. The organization organized museum excursions, hikes, one-day marches, and sporting events; it sponsored showings of films directed by women or having feminist or lesbian themes. The walls of its community center were decorated with lesbian and gay artwork, providing a forum to exhibit works that would otherwise not be seen, given the negative societal attitude toward homosexuals. The organization also tried to provide legal assistance, free psychological counseling, and a confidential phone line to deal with women's and lesbian issues.

SAFO worked with the Chaikovskii Fund for Sexual Minorities, an organization of gay men. The two organizations shared funding from foreign human rights, feminist, and homosexual organizations. In 1996 the two organizations, with Western funding, opened the St. Petersburg Public Center for Sexual Minorities; the new center, called Victoria, housed both groups; it had a seminar room, a resource library, a conference room, and a small café. Revenue for the operation came from the café and a disco operated on weekends. The name of the center was noteworthy since women called it Victoria, and men called it Victor and Me (*Viktor i ia* in Russian).

The center was located in an unmarked apartment within an apartment building in the city. One could find it only if told where the apartment was located, since there was no sign or other indication. Publicly, the two organizations were invisible, but, in the center, lesbian women could find self-expression and respect.

Suggested Readings

Essig, Laurie. *Queer in Russia: A Story of Sex, Self, and the Other*. Durham, NC: Duke University Press, 1999.

Gessen, Masha. *The Rights of Lesbians and Gay Men in the Russian Federation: An International Gay and Lesbian Human Rights Commission Report*. San Francisco: International Lesbian Gay and Human Rights Commission, 1994.

Wendy Guyot

The St. Petersburg Association of University Women, or VERA (*Mezhvuzovskaia Rossiiskaia assotsiatsiia zhenshchin s universitetskim obrazovaniem*) (1991–)

The St. Petersburg Association of University Women (VERA) was a women's organization founded in 1991 by Nina Petrovna Andreeva. The organization was educational and philanthropic, and members offered not only direct support to women and children but a market for women's handicrafts.

The *Mezhvuzovskaia Rossiiskaia assotsiatsiia zhenshchin s universitetskim obrazovaniem* (St. Petersburg Association of University Women, or VERA) was founded in 1991 by Nina Petrovna Andreeva. (Nina Petrovna Andreevna should not be confused with the perhaps more famous Nina Andreeva, a Leningrad chemistry lecturer who published a powerful letter in *Sovetskaia Rossiia* in 1988 attacking Gorbachev's reform program.) VERA was probably the largest organization of women in post-Soviet St. Petersburg and claimed over 200 members. VERA was admitted to the International Federation of University Women in California in 1992.

The organization's goal was to revive the traditions of the Russian intelligentsia: culture, morality, charity, and science. A veteran of the *Komitet sovetskikh zhenshchin* (Committee of Soviet Women), Nina Petrovna Andreeva and other volunteers did charitable work, organized educational programs for universities and alternative schools, and facilitated the sale of women's handicrafts and secondhand clothing. The members were committed to retrieving Russian art stolen during World War II and supported the city's efforts in that work. Additional activities included assistance to unemployed women, support for homeless children, and celebrations in honor of survivors of the 900-day siege of Leningrad during World War II. A grant from a Japanese fund allowed the group to support the educational costs of eight children of one city orphanage. Western aid supplemented income from sales and seminars to support the group's programs. Andreeva's contacts in the city and abroad were important in providing access to resources necessary for the group's work. She traveled widely in the West and had rather close ties in England, France, Germany, and the United States. Andreeva was absolutely central to VERA's operation and reported making many decisions single-handedly. VERA had close ties to the International Institute of Women and Management, and together the two groups sponsored a 1994 Conference, Education in the Modern World: Crisis or Development? VERA also worked with the Institute for the Development of International Business to create a business center for women in St. Petersburg. Furthermore, Andreeva relied on the services of the Club-Café *Sudarynia* for catering the various association functions. The organization provided a significant example of a post-Soviet women's organization that capitalized on the assets of women who had risen through the Soviet Women's Committee (SWC) and successfully mobilized Western resources to support not only members but also women and children in the city.

Cross-references: The Institute for Development of International Business, Institute "Woman and Management," Soviet Women's Committee, Union of Soviet Women of Leningrad and Leningrad Oblast, The Women's Club-Café *Sudarynia.*

Suggested Readings

Gottlick, Jane F. Berthusen. "From the Ground Up: Women's Organizations and Democratization in Russia." In *Democratization and Women's Grassroots Movements*, edited by Jill M. Bystydzienski and Joti Sekhon, 241–261. Bloomington: Indiana University Press, 1999.

McMahon, Patrice C. "The Effect of Economic and Political Reforms on Soviet/Russian Women." In *Women in the Age of Economic Transformation*, edited by Nahid Aslangeigui, Steven Pressman, and Gale Summerfield, 59–76. New York: Routledge, 1994.

Nechemias, Carol. "The Prospects for a Soviet Women's Movement: Opportunities and Obstacles." In *Perestroika from Below: Social Movements in the Soviet Union*, edited by Judith B. Sedaitis and Jim Butterfield, 73–96. Boulder, CO: Westview Press, 1991.

Racioppi, Linda, and Katherine O'Sullivan See. "Organizing Women before and after the Fall: Women's Politics in the Soviet Union and Post-Soviet Russia." *Signs* (Summer 1995): 818–850.

Jane F. Berthusen Gottlick

St. Petersburg Association of Widows and Their Families (Valita, or *Assotsiatsiia vdovi ikh semei*) (1991–)

Founded in 1991, Valita provided a forum through which members assisted one another and created work for themselves. Members were also active in lobbying.

The *Assotsiatsiia vdov* (St. Petersburg Association of Widows, or Valita) was founded in late 1991 by Valentina Ivanovna Egorova. Egorova was inspired to organize Valita after reading about an organization of British widows in a local St. Petersburg newspaper. The organization's goal was to provide support to families who lost one parent through death. Most families lost the male parent (hence the Association of Widows), but men and their children were welcome to join. The 500 member families provided moral support to one another, and Egorova coordinated day-care circles for the working parents. Members even cooperated to support their families economically by selling abroad goods they had knit and sewn. There were plans for a bakery or laundry to supplement donations received from Russian business. The members dreamed of opening a center capable of providing not only meeting space but also counseling and support services, and Egorova traveled abroad to international conferences to gather information and ideas. She encouraged her members to become politically active and to defend the cultural and legal rights of their families. Letter-writing campaigns informed local officials that the group existed and demanded action and support. The organization was significant as an example of a post-Soviet "self-help" group and as a women's group that brought members together to form a commercial center capable of supporting themselves. The group was also an interesting example of the influence of non-Russian organizations and people, for the encouragement for organization and even subsequent support came from abroad.

Cross-reference: Foreign Funding and the Women's Movement in Russia.

Suggested Readings

Gottlick, Jane F. Berthusen. "From the Ground Up: Women's Organizations and Democratization in Russia." In *Democratization and Women's Grassroots Movements*, edited by Jill M. Bystydzienski and Joti Sekhon, 241–261. Bloomington: Indiana University Press, 1999.

McMahon, Patrice C. "The Effect of Economic and Political Reforms on Soviet/Russian Women." In *Women in the Age of Economic Transformation*, edited by Nahid Aslangeigui, Steven Pressman, and Gale Summerfield, 59–76. New York: Routledge, 1994.

Nechemias, Carol. "The Prospects for a Soviet Women's Movement: Opportunities and Obstacles." In *Perestroika from Below: Social Movements in the Soviet Union*, edited by Judith B. Sedaitis and Jim Butterfield, 73–96. Boulder, CO: Westview Press, 1991.

Racioppi, Linda, and Katherine O'Sullivan See. "Organizing Women before and after the Fall: Women's Politics in the Soviet Union and Post-Soviet Russia." *Signs* (Summer 1995): 818–850.

Jane F. Berthusen Gottlick

The St. Petersburg Center of Gender Issues (*Peterburgskii Tsentr Genderskikh Problem*, or PCGI) (1992–)

A women's organization founded in 1992. It was primarily an educational and research organization and was led by Ol'ga Gennadevna Lipovskaia, who was also interested in greater cooperation among St. Petersburg's women's organizations.

Ol'ga Gennadevna Lipovskaia founded the *Peterburgskii Tsentr Genderskikh Problem* (St. Petersburg Center of Gender Issues, or PCGI) in 1992. The organization's primary goal was the eradication of gender discrimination, and the center's educational program was the primary vehicle through which the organization operated. PCGI sought to uncover, expose, and destroy gender stereotypes. The educational and research programs consisted of lectures, seminars, political activities, and cultural programs offered by specialists from Russia and the West. Subjects included women's self-defense, women's psychology, women in politics, and women in literature, and women leaders in St. Petersburg were invited to the Center's activities, which were scheduled approximately twice a month. Periodically, PCGI has also held more intensive seminars, such as the international conference Feminist Theory and Practice: East-West (June 9–12, 1995) and the international seminar on Women and the Media (June 20–22, 1997). PCGI also funded special research projects from time to time, such as a study of sexual harassment conducted by two sociologists (1993–1995).

The Center also published a newsletter, *Posidel'ki* (a term meaning women's gathering in Russian villages), which was distributed widely among libraries, academic institutions, and women's organizations. PCGI maintained a database with the names of all the officially registered St. Petersburg women's organizations and their leaders.

Ol'ga Lipovskaia's work and contacts were crucial to the organization. She had important contacts in the West and had published essays in American books and journals. Her publication *Zhenskoe chtenie (Women's Reading)*, with selections from Russian and Western scholars, had established her reputation even before PCGI was established. Lipovskaia was one of the few women leaders to adopt the "feminist" label for herself and her work. PCGI benefited from her fluency in English and her access to contacts and international visits and visitors.

The Center was perhaps the most financially secure woman's group in the city. PCGI has had financial support from a German foundation, Heinrich Boll Stiftung, but some of its projects have also been supported by the Soros Foundation, the MacArthur Foundation, the Democracy Program of the European Union, the Eurasian Fund, and the Global Fund for Women.

The Center was significant for its attempt to bring the city's women leaders together, not only at lectures and seminars but also to foster closer cooperation among women. A 1994 conference (cosponsored by a European counterpart and the St. Petersburg Association of University Women) focused on possibilities for greater cooperation among the city's women's organizations. Some women leaders rejected the Center's feminist platform and were critical of its German funding and of Lipovskaia for her avowed feminism. The Center continued its work throughout the 1990s with foreign support, despite increasingly adverse circumstances in the 1990s.

Cross-references: Feminism in Post-Soviet Russia, Gender/Women's Studies in Russia, Ol'ga Lipovskaia, The Scientific Center "Women and Russia."

Suggested Readings

Buckley, Mary, ed. *Perestroika and Soviet Women*. Cambridge: Cambridge University Press, 1992.

Gottlick, Jane F. Berthusen. "From the Ground Up: Women's Organizations and Democratization in Russia." In *Democratization and Women's Grassroots Movements*, edited by Jill M. Bystydzienski and Joti Sekhon, 241–261. Bloomington: Indiana University Press, 1999.

McMahon, Patrice C. "The Effect of Economic and Political Reforms on Soviet/Russian Women." In *Women in the Age of Economic Transformation*, edited by Nahid Aslangeigui, Steven Pressman, and Gale Summerfield, 59–76. New York: Routledge, 1994.

Nechemias, Carol. "The Prospects for a Soviet Women's Movement: Opportunities and Obstacles." In *Perestroika from Below: Social Movements in the Soviet Union*, edited by Judith B. Sedaitis and Jim Butterfield, 73–96. Boulder, CO: Westview Press, 1991.

Posadskaya, Anastasia, ed. *Women in Russia: A New Era in Russian Feminism*. London: Verso, 1994.

Posidel'ki (Village Women's Gathering). A periodical of PCGI.

Racioppi, Linda, and Katherine O'Sullivan See. "Organizing Women before and after the Fall: Women's Politics in the Soviet Union and Post-Soviet Russia." *Signs* (Summer 1995): 818–850.

Jane F. Berthusen Gottlick

Sal'e, Marina Evgen'evna (1934–)

Doctor of geology and mineralogy. A liberal activist; founder and chair of the *Svobodnaia demokraticheskaia partiia Rossii* (Free Democratic Party of Russia, or SvDPR) (1990–).

Marina Sal'e, a Russian, was born on October 19, 1934, in Leningrad. Her father was a mining engineer. Her mother, Natal'ia Bure, was a dental technician. In the spring of 1942, after her father was wounded on the front, her family was evacuated to Kuba-Sai in Uzbekistan. After the family returned to Leningrad in 1944, her mother was tragically killed.

In 1957 Sal'e graduated from the Geology Department at Leningrad State University with a specialization in geology and geochemistry. From 1957 to 1958 she worked first as a laboratory assistant and then as a junior researcher at the Institute of Geology and Pre-Cambrian Geochronology of the USSR Academy of Sciences, where she remained until 1987. From 1957 to 1959 she was secretary of the Institute's Komsomol organization. From 1960 to 1963 Sal'e attended graduate school and successfully defended her dissertation on "Pegmatites in Chupinskii raion (North Karelia) and the Laws Governing the Place of Deposition of Muscovite in Them" for the *kandidat* degree in 1963. From 1963 to 1979 Sal'e worked as junior researcher at the Institute. In 1977 a negative review from the Central Mineralogical Institute persuaded her to postpone the defense of her doctoral dissertation. From 1979 to 1986 she worked as a senior researcher and, in 1986, successfully defended her doctoral dissertation on "Metallogenes in the Regressive State of Regional Metamorphism." From 1986 until 1989 Sal'e worked as head researcher. From 1989 to August 1990 she served as a research consultant to the institute. During the course of her career, she participated in twenty-five geological expeditions, including in Central Asia, the Caucasus, Karelia, Iakutia, the North Baikal Region, Kola Peninsula, the Ukraine, and the Far East.

Sal'e joined the Communist Party of the Soviet Union (CPSU) in 1971. In

February 1988 she founded and headed the Leningrad club of admirers of the journal *Ogonëk*. In 1989 she was an unsuccessful candidate for the Congress of People's Deputies, campaigning on a platform of a radical approach to Perestroika in order to deprive the *nomenklatura* of its power and privileges. She advocated greater power to the people, a multifaceted economy and transition to a market economy, and new laws on elections, the press, and the leasing of land. From 1989 to early 1990 she served as leader of the *Mezhregionalnaia assotsiatsiia demokraticheskikh organizatsii* (Interregional Association of Democratic Organizations, or MADO). In June 1989 Sal'e helped to organize the *Leningradskii narodnyi front* (Leningrad Popular Front, or LNF) and was elected a member of its Coordinating Council with the highest number of votes. She was an author of the LNF's program and was a member of the editorial board of the LNF's newspaper, *Nabat (Alarm)*. Sal'e remained a member of the Coordinating Council until the LNF dissolved in 1991. In December 1989 Sal'e resigned from the CPSU.

In March 1990 she ran for the RSFSR Congress of People's Deputies (CPD) from Vasileostrovskii territorial district No. 107 in Leningrad. During the elections, Sal'e was supported by the *Demokraticheskie vybory-90* (Democratic Elections 90) platform, and she, in turn, supported the Green Party. Her platform advocated universal human values, ecological wisdom, personal and public responsibility, respect for diversity, decentralization, and lack of violence. This time, Sal'e's campaign was successful. In 1990 she was also elected to the *Lensovet* (Leningrad City Council). Sal'e aspired to be elected chair of the *Lensovet*, but her strict and uncompromising attitude eliminated her chances for election. From April 1990 to June 1991 she was a member of *Na Platforme Narodnogo Fronta* (Platform for the Popular Front, or NPNF). Sal'e left the NPNF, however, because it did not agree with her opposition to Anatolii Sobchak's election as Mayor of Leningrad. She joined the faction *Svobodnaia demokraticheskaia partiia Rossii* (Free Democratic Party of Russia, or SvDPR), a proponent of radical democratic reforms, which stood in staunch opposition to the president and federal government, and the bloc *Demokraticheskaia Rossiia* (Democratic Russia) of the *Lensovet*. From May 1990 to June 1991 Sal'e was a member of the Presidium of the *Lensovet*. During that period, she chaired the Commission on Food, which examined the declining food supply in the city of Leningrad as well as other large-scale industrial centers. In spite of the respect she gained for her political activities, her disagreements with Mayor Sobchak hurt her popularity in Leningrad. In May 1990 Sal'e, together with Il'ia Konstantinov and Nikolai Travkin, founded the *Demokraticheskaia partiia Rossii* (Democratic Party of Russia, or DPR) as an alternative to the CPSU, but she left the founding congress because of a disagreement with Travkin over the hierarchical, organizational structure of the party. In June 1990 she became a member of the *Radikal'nye demokraty* (Radical Democrats, or RD) faction of the Congress of People's Deputies of the Russian Federation (RF) as well as one of the faction coordinators. In July 1990 Sal'e was elected cochair of the northwest division of the SvDPR and later served as a member of its organizing committee. In November 1990 Sal'e was a delegate to the first congress of the *Dvizhenie Demokraticheskaia Rossiia* (Democratic Russia Movement, or *DemRossii*) and was elected a member of its Council of Chairs representing SvDPR. *DemRossii* was a proponent of market reforms and a supporter of the Russian president.

In January 1991 the Lithuanian attempt to overthrow the legally elected organs of power was the impetus for the creation in Leningrad of the *Dvizhenie grazhdanskogo soprotivleniia* (Movement for Civil Disobedience), based on the SvDPR and the *Demokraticheskii soiuz* (Democratic Union), which operated on a parallel basis with *DemRossii*. From February to May 1991 Sal'e and the SvDPR collected signatures on a petition requesting a referendum on the nationalization of the property of the CPSU, but the attempt fell 400,000 short of the 1 million signatures necessary for the referendum. In June 1991 she put forth her candidacy for election to the Presidium of the Leningrad *Gorsovet* (City Council) but was rejected. At the founding congress of the SvDPR in July 1991, Sal'e was elected cochair and was recognized as its de facto leader and ideologue of the party, which is often referred to as Sal'e's party. In August 1991 Sal'e headed the temporary staff of the Leningrad *Gorsovet*, which struggled against the hard-liners' coup against Gorbachev. In the fall of 1991 she participated actively in the movement *DemRossii* and in November was reelected to the Council of Chairs at the second congress of *DemRossii*.

In January 1992 she became a member of the *Malyi sovet* (Small Council) of the St. Petersburg City Council. In January 1992 Sal'e also became cochair of *DemRossii*. On April 14, 1992, she became the Chair of the St. Petersburg City Council. Sal'e, along with the other leader of the radical wing of *DemRossii*, Professor Iurii Afanas'ev, organized an extraordinary congress of *DemRossii* in Moscow. The movement's leadership, Lev Ponomarev, Il'ia Zaslavskii, and Gleb Iakunin, however, opposed the congress, and many regional *DemRossii* organizations refused to participate as well. Sal'e announced that the St. Petersburg branch of the movement would become a formal opposition group to the Yeltsin–Gaidar leadership, which she accused of moving away from democratic reforms. In contrast, the party's leadership expressed its intent to transform *DemRossii* into a presidential party. In November 1992 she left *DemRossii* to head the newly formed Russian Constitutional Union, which regarded itself as a "democratic-liberal opposition to the regime." The Union did not support Yeltsin because it regarded him as a potential dictator, and it called for the dissolution of the parliament, which it considered Bolshevik. In December 1992 Sal'e, along with Congress of People's Deputies Aleskei Manannikov and Viacheslav Volkov, began collecting signatures to urge the congress to create a special Constitutional Assembly to prepare a new Russian Constitution. Earlier, she and Gavriil Popov, leader of the Russian Movement for Democratic Reforms, had proposed that the Constituent Assembly replace the Congress. However, they tempered their proposal and instead stated that the Assembly could be dissolved once the new Russian Constitution was adopted.

At the second congress of the SvDPR in January 1993, Sal'e was reelected the party's cochair. She served as a People's Deputy until October 1993, when President Boris Yeltsin dissolved the parliament. In October 1993, Sal'e suggested that presidential rule be extended throughout the Russian Federation and that the parliamentary elections be postponed until after the referendum on the new Constitution. In 1994 SvDPR was weakened by the departure of many members for the *Demokraticheskii vybor Rossii* (Democratic Choice of Russia, or DVR) and the *Rossiiskii khristiansko-demokraticheskii soiuz* (Russian Christian Democratic Union, or RKDS). In preparation for the December 1995 parliamentary elections, Sal'e's party formed a bloc with Transformation of the Fatherland, headed by Ekaterinburg Governor Eduard Rossel', who headed a bloc of the same name, and Nikolai Arzhannikov's, Safety of Man Party. Sal'e was one of the top three candidates but was not elected. In May 1996 Sal'e along with the leaders of several other democratic parties, including Sviatoslav Fedorov's *Partiia samoupravleniia trudiashchikhsia* (Party of Worker's Self-Government, or PST), Irina Khakamada's *Obshchee delo* (Common Cause, or OD), and Boris Fedorov's *Vperëd, Rossiia!* (Forward Russia, or VpR!), signed an agreement not to support Sobchak's reelection bid.

Sal'e represents an interesting example of a Russian woman who would again and again accept defeat rather than compromise her beliefs. Her leadership was recognized, but she also failed to prevail in numerous political conflicts during the turbulent transition period.

Cross-references: Ekaterinburg Women's Organizations, Irina Khakamada.

Suggested Readings

"Democratic Deputies Lobby for Constitutional Assembly." OMRI Daily Digest. No. 232. <http://solar.rtd.utk.edu/friends/news/omri/1992/12/921203.html> (December 3, 1992).

"Democrats Compete." OMRI Daily Digest. No. 203. <http://solar.rtd.utk.edu/friends/news/omri/1993/10/931021.html> (October 21, 1993).

Geron, Leonard, and Alex Pravda, eds. *Who's Who in Russia and the New States*. New York and London: I. B. Tauris, 1993.

"Marina Yevgenyevna Salye." Norsk Utenrikspolitisk Institutt-Norwegian Institute of International Affairs (NUPI). Centre for Russian Studies Database. <http://www.nupi.no/cgi-win/Russland/personer.exe/529> (1999).

McCauley, Martin, ed. *Longman Biographical Directory of Decision Makers in Russia and the Successor States*. Harlow, U.K.: Longman, 1993.

Morozov, Vladimir, ed. *Who's Who in Russia and the CIS Republics*. New York: Henry Holt, 1995.

"Radical Democrats Form New Organization." OMRI Daily Digest. No. 223. <http://solar.rtd.utk.edu/friends/news/omri/1992/11/921119.html> (November 19, 1992).

"Radical Wing of Democratic Russia Holds Congress." OMRI Daily Digest. No. 142.

<http://solar.rtd.utk.edu/friends/news/omri/1992/07/920728.html> (July 28, 1992).
"St. Petersburg Democrats Refuse to Back Incumbent Mayor." OMRI Daily Digest. No. 91, Part I. <http://solar.rtd.utk.edu/friends/news/omri/1996/05/960510I.html> (May 10, 1996).
"Sal'e Marina Evgen'evna." National News Service-Natsional'naia sluzhba novostei. <http://www.nns.ru/persons/ Salye.html> (1995).
"Sal'e Marina Evgen'evna." National News Service-Natsional'naia sluzhba novostei. <http://www.nns.ru/restricted/persons/ Salye0.html> (1995).
"Sal'e Marina Evgen'evna: Zhizhennyi put'." National News Service-Natsional'naia sluzhba novostei. <http://www.nns.ru/restricted/persons/ Salye5.html> (1995).
Schulz-Torge, Ulrich-Joachim, ed. *Who's Who in Russia Today: A Biographical Dictionary of More than 2,100 Individuals from the Russian Federation including the Other Fourteen Former USSR Republics*. Munich: K. G. Saur, 1994.

Cheri C. Wilson

Savkina, Irina Leonardovna (1953–)

A literary critic focusing on gender and a leading organizer of the feminist organization *Mariia*, based in Petrozavodsk.

Irina Savkina is a literary critic born in Perm on September 15, 1953. Relatively little has been published on her early background and education. As a literary critic, Irina Savkina has focused on gender and its place in Russian women's prose since the nineteenth century. She is associated with the cultural group *Mariia*, one of the few organizations of its kind outside Moscow and St. Petersburg. *Mariia* is best known for issuing two editions (1990, 1995) of the literary anthology of the same name and contributing to a 1993 collection of works by women writers from Finland and northwest Russia: *Zhena, kotoraia umela letat' (The Wife Who Could Fly). Mariia* is a rare attempt to unite provincial women authors under a single publication. There is no connection between this group and the Leningrad-based *Mariia* Club founded in 1979. Savkina has participated in the *Rossiiskie letnie shkoly po gendernym issledovaniiam* (Russian Summer Schools on Gender Studies).

A lecturer at the University of Tampere (Finland), she has also taught on the literature faculties of Karelia and Vologda State Pedagogical Universities and worked with Frank Göpfert at Potsdam University. Savkina received degrees from Leningrad State University (1975), Vologda State Pedagogical University (1982), and the University of Tampere (2000). *Mariia* influenced Savkina's early career: she worked with the group's founder, Galina Skvortsova-Akbulatova, to bring together women writers from northwest Russia in the late 1980s and early 1990s. *Mariia* produced both literary anthologies and a local television broadcast, *Komnata sestry Shekspira (Shakespeare's Sister's Room).* In 1992 Savkina and several other group members attended the *Nezavisimiy zhenskii forum* (Independent Women's Forum) in Dubna, where she first encountered feminist criticism as a distinct academic discipline. Savkina's texts contain an unusually well formulated definition of the problem of gender as a category in *analyzing*

Russian literature. In *Provintsialki russkoi literatury: zhenskaia proza 30–40-x godov XIX veka (The Provincial Women of Russian Literature: Women's Prose of the 1830s and 1840s)*, she notes that feminist investigations must not obscure literature with universal generalization. The works of Michele Foucault, Jacques Lacan, and Jacques Derrida allow feminism to challenge the prescriptive biologism of traditional approaches to women's literature. Discussing early nineteenth-century literature, Savkina mediated between incorporating women into the existing canon of works (as exemplified by Catriona Kelly) and efforts to construct a more discrete corpus of women's works (a methodology ascribed to Barbara Heldt). For Savkina, a feminist critique of literature must examine how gender operates within given texts. Such a critique endeavors to destroy the stereotypical image of women offered by traditional literary history.

Savkina stresses women's space in literature. Her *"Govori, Mariia!: Zametki o sovremennoi russkoi zhenskoi proze"* (Speak, Mariia!: Notes on Contemporary Russian Women's Prose) describes women as existing in a perennially unstable state between home and grave, inhabiting transitory zones such as lines, trains, dormitories, and hospitals. What is enduring in women's literature is the cult of suffering and victimization.

Discussing contemporary Russian women's writing in *"Kto i kak pishet istoriiu russkoi zhenskoi literatury"* (Who Writes the History of Russian Women's Literature), Savkina noted that the anger often marking this writing was only temporary. This description challenged the prevalent criticism of women's literature as unnecessarily embittered and angry, a criticism selectively applied to women authors allegedly unworthy of Russian literature's long tradition of satire and protest.

Savkina has written literary criticism on nineteenth-century women's travel, memoiristic, and prose writing, as well as late- and post-Soviet women's writing by both northwestern and national authors. She has combined literary analysis and activism and made contributions in each field.

Cross-references: Independent Women's Forum, Information Center of the Independent Women's Forum.

Suggested Readings

Savkina, Irina. " '*Govori, Mariia!': Zametki o sovremennoi russkoi zhenskoi proze*" (Speak, *Mariia*!: Notes on Contemporary Russian Women's Prose). *Preobrazhenie (Transformation)* 4 (1996): 62–67.

Savkina, Irina. "*Kto i kak pishet istoriiu russkoi zhenskoi literatury*" (Who Writes the History of Russian Women's Literature). *Novoe literaturnoe obozrenie (New Literary Review)* 24 (1997): 359–372.

Savkina, Irina. "*Mar'ia Zhukova: epizody iz zhizni zhenshchin*" (Mar'ia Zhukova: Episodes from the Life of Women). *Mariia* 2: 211–225. Petrozavodsk: Izdatel'stvo Petrozavodskogo Universiteta, 1995.

Savkina, Irina. *Provintsialki russkoi literatury: zhenskaia proza 30–40-x godov XIX veka (The Provincial Women of Russian Literature: Women's Prose of the 1830s and*

1840s). FrauenLiteraturGeschichte. Series edited by Frank Göpfert. Wilhelmshorst: Verlag F. K. Göpfert, 1998.

Savkina, Irina. "*Da, zhenskaia dusha dolzhna v teni svetitsia . . .*" (A Woman's Soul Should Shine in the Darkness). In *Zhena, kotoraia umela letat': proza russkikh I finskikh pisatel'nits (The Wife Who Could Fly: Prose by Russian and Finnish Women Writers)*, edited by Galina Skortsova, 389–403. Petrozavodsk: Agenstvo INKA, 1993.

Benjamin Sutcliffe

The Scientific Center "Women and Russia" (*Nauchnyi tsentr "Zhenshchiny i Rossiia,"* also *Zhenshchiny Rossii*) (ca. 1990–)

A women's organization founded in St. Petersburg in the early 1990s. It evolved into the city's first women's studies program and demonstrated the creativity of male and female academics during the transition from Soviet communism.

The twenty male and female members of the St. Petersburg *Nauchnyi tsentr "Zhenshchiny i Rossiia"* (Scientific Center "Women and Russia") have encouraged research on the "woman question" at St. Petersburg State University since the early 1990s and founded the city's first women's studies program at the University in 1994. The primary goal of the Center was to encourage research on issues important to Russian women. In addition to their work as teachers and students, the members gathered women's studies bibliographic information from research conducted abroad, built a women's studies library, and participated in professional conferences in Europe and the United States. As part of the effort to survive financially, faculty also arranged student exchange programs and solicited donations only from Russian businesses. The founder and leader Valentina Grigorevna Ushakova saw the work of the Center as intimately connected to the construction of Russian democracy; she was determined that the Center facilitate the cooperation of men and women and promote the recognition that all people are political animals. The work of the Center was significant, and the approach of the members was noteworthy. The members believed that women's "natural sense of responsibility" (Ushakova's words) was essential to Russia's survival. In their view the strong Russian scientific tradition provided a basis for greater political participation for women, which was critical not only for Russian democracy and for Russian women but for Russia as a whole. Ushakova focused the energy of the Center on male–female cooperation and "real work," while avoiding the controversial label "feminism." Although the Center was comfortable in the web of international academe and scholarship, the members were committed to using their work to strengthen contemporary Russian society. They were able to accomplish their work because they uncovered resources, both donated and earned, to support it. In the late 1990s the organization changed its name slightly to *Nauchnyi tsentr "Zhenshchiny Rossii"* (The Scientific Center "Women of Russia") perhaps to capitalize on the national women's movement of that name.

Cross-references: Academic Feminism in St. Petersburg, Gender/Women's Studies in Russia, St. Petersburg Center of Gender Issues, Women of Russia.

Suggested Readings

Gottlick, Jane F. Berthusen. "From the Ground Up: Women's Organizations and Democratization in Russia." In *Democratization and Women's Grassroots Movements*, edited by Jill M. Bystydzienski and Joti Sekhon, 241–261. Bloomington: Indiana University Press, 1999.

McMahon, Patrice C. "The Effect of Economic and Political Reforms on Soviet/Russian Women." In *Women in the Age of Economic Transformation*, edited by Nahid Aslangeigui, Steven Pressman, and Gale Summerfield, 59–76. New York: Routledge, 1994.

Nechemias, Carol. "The Prospects for a Soviet Women's Movement: Opportunities and Obstacles." In *Perestroika from Below: Social Movements in the Soviet Union*, edited by Judith B. Sedaitis and Jim Butterfield, 73–96. Boulder, CO: Westview Press, 1991.

Posadskaya, Anastasia, ed. *Women in Russia: A New Era in Russian Feminism.* New York: Verso, 1994.

Racioppi, Linda, and Katherine O'Sullivan See. "Organizing Women before and after the Fall: Women's Politics in the Soviet Union and Post-Soviet Russia." *Signs* (Summer 1995): 818–850.

Jane F. Berthusen Gottlick

Shvetsova, Liudmila Ivanovna (1949–)

A prominent political official in the Soviet Union and post-Soviet Russia who served as chair of the Committee on Family and Women of the Soviet Government (1991), chair of the Committee for Public and Interregional Relations of the Moscow Government (1994–) and First Deputy Premier of the Moscow Government (2000–).

Liudmila Ivanovna Shvetsova was born on September 24, 1949, in Alma-Ata, Kazakhstan; her father was a military officer, and her mother was a secondary school teacher of English. She successfully completed a special mathematical secondary school in Rostov-on-Don as a silver medalist and graduated from the Kharkov Aviation Institute in 1973. In 1997 she received the *kandidat*'s degree in political science from Moscow State Social Sciences University. Shvetsova was also honored as a member of three academies within the Russian Academy of Science: Social, International Teachers, and Creative Work.

Like many others of her time, Shvetsova's early political career was shaped by the Komsomol. Shvetsova worked for the Komsomol for fourteen years, rising from secretary of a regional Komsomol Committee (1975–1976) to Secretary of the Central Committee of the Komsomol of Ukraine (1976–1978) and then a Secretary of the Central Committee of the Komsomol of the USSR (1981–1989). Her positions in the Komsomol also included serving as chair of the Central Council of the All-Union Young Pioneers Organization (1985–1988).

She chaired the Department of Rewards of the Supreme Soviet Secretariat and in the late 1980s was in charge of the Department of the Apparatus, which provided services to the Congress of People's Deputies. Her responsibilities included assistance to the deputies in preparing their speeches, questions, or other documents to departments and ministries of the executive branch of the government or to regional authorities and analyzing and preparing responses to letters from constituents. Her work for the Congress of People's Deputies involved technical support services and public relations.

During the Soviet era, she was awarded three orders: *Znak pocheta* (the Decoration of Merit) in recognition of her work for the 1980 Olympics; *Trudovogo Krasnogo Znameni* (the Red Banner of Labor) for organizing the Tenth World Youth and Student Festival in Moscow; and the *Orden druzhby* (Order of Friendship) for organizing the Celebration of the Fiftieth Anniversary of the Victory in World War II. She also twice received the *Blagodarnost' Presidenta* (President's Gratitude Award) and *Pocheta gramota* (the Certificate of Merit of the Russian Federation Government), and one star in the Libra Constellation was called "Liudmila Shvetsova."

Liudmila Shvetsova entered into the history of the "woman question" as the first and last chair of the Committee on Family and Women of the Soviet Government (1991). Shvetsova worked on policy concerning youth, women, and the elderly within the Council of Ministers. Her efforts led to the establishment of the Committee on Family and Women of the Soviet Government in May 1991; it existed only a few months due to the collapse of the USSR in December 1991.

In post-Soviet Russia, Shvetsova was unemployed for a brief time. During that period, she established the *Zhenskii initsiativ fond* (Women's Initiative Foundation) and the public movement *Konfederatsiia zhenskaia liga* (Confederation Women's League).

In 1994 Shvetsova was appointed Chair of the Committee for Public and Interregional Relations of the Moscow government. The goals of the Committee were to involve the public in decisions of economic and social issues of the city, research the attitudes and needs of Moscow citizens for the Moscow government, and inform the Moscow population about the activities of the Moscow government. Shvetsova's work involved the creation of systems of cooperation and collaboration between the authorities and the residents and the formation of a network of interregional contacts and relations. She wanted to create new types of relationships with the regions, based on principles of transparency, cooperation, and mutual understanding among equal partners, instead of authoritarian dictatorship over the regions.

Shvetsova and her committee developed a system of civic-state councils, the first national grants program, a bill, *O sotsialnom partnërstve* (On Social Partnership), and the project *Resursny tsentr* (Resource Center), together with the United Nations Development Programs.

As of 1999 there were more than 5,000 civic and 15,000 nonprofit organizations in Moscow. The Committee was the first to encourage implementation of the national grant system in Moscow. The Committee was responsible for delivering grants among applicants. For the first time in its history, the Moscow budget had a budget line "For Projects of Public Organizations" (*Na proekty obshestvennikh organizatsii*). The Committee supported social and civic initiatives in various fields such as care for veterans, interactions with women, and children's and youth organizations, as well as organizations for disabled people. The Committee's collaboration did not substitute for social protection functions but tried to support the socially important activities of people in volunteer organizations. In 1997 the Committee financed thirty projects and sponsored and organized 550 public events for the people in Moscow.

In early 2000 Shvetsova was appointed *Prevyi zamestitel' Premier Pravitel'stva Moskvi* (first deputy premier of the Moscow government), making her one of the most important officials in the Moscow region.

Shvetsova stated that she preferred to work with a team of like-minded persons. She believed that her experience with the Committee on Family and Women during the late Soviet period served as a good basis for developing policies to advance the status of women. She also thought that segments of her experience in the Komsomol could be a positive force in the new Russia.

Shvetsova should be viewed as a pragmatic politician and statesperson who supported the promotion of women in the decision-making process and the integration of women into the political process of society. She considered that women's active participation in all spheres of Russian life would strengthen democracy in Russia and benefit society. In 1999 she became the head of the Women's Initiative, an organization that evolved from the Women's League.

Knowledge of the country, striving for professional perfection, the experience of working at state institutions, commitment to ideals of friendship and cooperation, and personal charm were the principal features that made Shvetsova a strong player in the Russian political arena. As of 2000 she was working on a book that expressed appreciation to women activists for their role in Russia's development.

Cross-reference: Women's League.

Suggested Readings

Barulin, Victor. "*Sem' let bez komsomola*" (Seven Years without the Komsomol). *Moskvicha* (Moscow Woman), no. 40 (307) (October 1998): 4–5.

Doklad o vypolnenii v Rossiiskoi Federatsii Konventsii o likvidatsii vsekh form diskriminatsii v otnoshenii zhenshchin. Piatyi periodicheskii (The Report on Implementation of the Convention on the Elimination of All Forms of Discrimination against Women in the Russian Federation). Moscow: Izdatel'stvo "Prava cheloveka," 1999.

Korniak, Valentina, ed. *Integratsiia zhenshchin v protses obshestvennogo razvitiia (The Integration of Women in the Process of Public Development).* Moscow: Academy of Management and Ministry of Social Protection of the Russian Federation, 1994.

Mishkin, V. M., et al., eds. *Rossiia Molodaia. Vek XX (The Young Russia: Century XX).* Moscow: Molodaia Gvardiia, 1998.

Shvetsova L. I. *"Integratsiia zhenshchin v politiku. 70–90-e gody"* (The Integration of Women into the Political Process. (1970s–1990s). Abstract of a *kandidat*'s diss., Moscow State Social University, 1997.

Torgashova, Tatiana. *"Gosydarev Chelovek: Atlantida Liudmily Shvetsovoi"* (The Stateswoman. Atlantida of Liudmila Shvetsova). *Sudarushka (Madame)*, no. 17 (350) (May 19, 1998): 1, 6–7.

Nadezhda Shvedova

The Socioeconomic Transition in Post-Soviet Russia: The Impact on Women

The postcommunist transition to a market economy in Russia severely affected women's status in the workplace, particularly with respect to unemployment, the demise of welfare guarantees, and discrimination.

When Perestroika began in the late 1980s, economists and demographers approached the market economy optimistically. The "egalitarians" hoped that the market would promote equal opportunities for men and women. Traditionalists, who favored a "back to the home" movement for women, thought that the market economy would allow men to earn more and thus permit women to reduce their labor force participation and focus more on home and family. With respect to mass public opinion, survey research suggested that the economic realities of the 1990s eroded public support for a traditional role for women: although 54 percent of respondents favored a homemaker role for women in 1990, only 30 percent did so in 1997. The percentage opting for an egalitarian path for women in the economy climbed from 37 percent to 46 percent during the same period. In reality, neither group's expectations were realized, as economic difficulties virtually precluded women from voluntarily assuming the role of homemaker.

Since 1992 Russia has undergone sweeping socioeconomic changes, including the end of Soviet-style socialism. The social transformations associated with the efforts to construct a market economy and a civil society had a dramatic impact on all of Russia's citizens, but some processes especially affected the status of women. The move to a market economy generated higher levels of unemployment for women than for men, the curtailment of social programs and guarantees, and an intensification of discrimination against women.

Starting in July 1991, the USSR began to record unemployment figures. Studies of the unemployed in the Russian Federation during the 1990s revealed that women constituted 70–80 percent of the unemployed. Despite women's high level of formal education, women's job skills lagged behind those of men. A large proportion of women were involved in unskilled, often heavy physical labor. Well-educated women working in feminized branches of the state economy like education and health care traditionally were poorly paid compared to skilled workers in heavy industry. Among groups of employees most likely to be laid off were middle-aged women and near-pension-aged women working as engineers. Young women with or without small children also faced severe obstacles in the market economy; employers were reluctant to hire them because of the social guarantees associated with motherhood. Men were more successful than women in securing employment in the emerging private sector, where pay scales significantly exceed those of the public sector.

Women's entrepreneurship in the nonstate sector was concentrated in small businesses in spheres of traditional feminine activity. In the realm of business, women lacked access to the main sources of power and finance. As of 1995 women owned or managed only two of Moscow's 125 largest companies.

For working women, the challenge of combining work and family responsibilities increased as the social welfare system collapsed. Many benefits existed on paper rather than in reality; for example, child allowances not only were inadequate but often were not paid. The demise of the heavily state-subsidized child-care system meant skyrocketing prices for places in preschools and summer camps. The guarantee of free health care became a fiction for much of the population, given the severely underfunded health-care system.

Political leaders showed little concern for women's labor force difficulties. Indeed, in post-Soviet Russia, women frequently were viewed as a group that should leave the workplace in light of the economic stresses associated with the transition to a market economy.

Cross-reference: Political Participation by Russian Women in the Transitional Period.

Suggested Readings

Bridger, Sue, Rebecca Kay, and Kathryn Pinnick. *No More Heroines? Russia, Women and the Market*. London: Routledge, 1996.

Posadskaya, Anastasia, ed. *Women in Russia: A New Era in Russian Feminism*. London: Verso, 1994.

Racanska, Luba. "The Yeltsin Presidency, Economic Reform and Women." In *Russian Women in Politics and Society*, edited by Wilma Rule and Norma Noonan, 120–134. Westport, CT: Greenwood Publishing Group, 1996.

Valentina Bodrova

Sovremennaia zhenshchina (The Contemporary Woman) (1994–)

An integrated training program and a reference work for women, both designed to help women adapt to the changing Russian economic system.

The *Sovremennaia zhenshchina* (Contemporary Woman) program, its training center, and the accompanying reference book were all developed by Zoia Edvardovna Molokova in the 1990s to assist women in adapting to the changing Russian economy. Molokova, a technical specialist and professor, realized the need to assist women to acquire skills to work in the new society. In the post-Soviet era, women workers have borne the brunt of unemployment. Few were qualified to undertake entrepreneurship. As the economy shifted its focus away from the military-industrial complex, which had dominated the Soviet economy for many years, unemployment rose in the society. Approximately 70 percent of the unemployed workers in post-Soviet Russia were women. In addition, the difficult economic conditions that arose in the transitional economy forced many women to seek full-time or part-time employment to augment their family incomes, even pensioners (women over fifty-five) and mothers of young children, who had earlier stayed at home with extended maternity leaves.

During an internship in France in 1990, Molokova was inspired to develop a basic reference encyclopedia for women. The underlying assumption of the work was that many women lacked the basic understanding of the changing conditions of modern work life, especially in the transition from socialism to a more competitive market economy. The resulting volume contained the contributions of numerous specialists and provided basic advice on many topics, ranging from legal advice, to makeup basics, from how to organize a small business, to coping with the many details of daily life. The book offered advice on legal rights, including working rights and the basics of starting a business.

In 1995 Molokova began a training program for the women at the *Akademiia narodnogo khozaistva* (Academy of the National Economy) in Moscow. The training focused on how to start one's own business. Both women and men have taken the training program and successfully started businesses or found new employment. As of mid-1999, 119 people had completed the program. From 1996 to 1998 the program had a contract with the government of Moscow for training. The program received grants from the Eurasia Fund (1995–1997) and the government of Moscow (1996–1998). Molokova directed the entire project since its inception and used a variety of specialists for the training. Under her direction a new edition of the book *Sovremennaia zhenshchina* was published in 1999.

Molokova's work was widely recognized, and in 1999 she was named one of the outstanding Woman Directors of the Year in a national competition at the fair the World of Women, Moscow, Russia.

The *Sovremennaia zhenshchina* program emerged as one of the few practical, successful movements to help women improve their skills and find new employment in post-Soviet Russia.

Cross-references: The Institute for the Development of International Business, The Institute "Women and Management," *Missiia*, Women and Business in Russia.

Suggested Reading

Molokova, Zoia Edvardovna, ed. *Sovremennaia Zhenshchina: Entsikopedicheskii spravochnik. (The Contemporary Woman: An Encyclopedia Handbook).* Moscow: Glas, 1994; 2d ed. "The Contemporary Woman" Center, 1999.

Norma Corigliano Noonan

Starovoitova, Galina Vasil'evna (1946–1998)

A prominent human rights activist and scholar who entered the political arena during Perestroika and held a variety of leadership positions prior to her untimely death in November 1998. Cochair of Democratic Russia (1990–1998), people's deputy of the USSR (1989–1991) and Russia (1990–1993), adviser to President Yeltsin on nationality issues (1991–1992), and Duma Deputy (1995–1998).

Galina Vasil'evna Starovoitova was born in 1946 in Cheliabinsk. She attended several institutes of higher education. She completed three years at the Leningrad College of Military Engineering in 1966, earned a degree in psychology from Leningrad State University in 1971, and earned a *kandidat* degree at the Ethnography Institute of the Academy of Sciences in 1976. From 1977 to 1991 she worked as a researcher at the Ethnography Institute and at the Center for the Study of Interethnic Relations under the Presidium of the USSR Academy of Sciences.

An expert and published writer on interethnic problems, an outstanding speaker, and a democrat, Starovoitova became a significant figure in Russian politics. Because of her expertise in ethnic relations, she won respect as an authority on the movements for autonomy of the late 1980s and 1990s. Her articulate support for many of those movements, in turn, led to her popularity among their leaders and supporters. As a result of her championing the Armenian cause in Nagorno-Karabakh, she was elected to the USSR Congress of People's Deputies in 1989 from a district in Erevan, the capital of Armenia. Starovoitova gathered an amazing 76 percent of the vote, despite the fact that she was Russian by nationality and resided in the Russian Republic. As a deputy Starovoitova joined the Interregional Deputies Group (*Mezhregional'naia deputatskaia gruppa*), an alliance of legislators committed to more reform and more freedom.

Starovoitova gained fame for her democratic views as an active participant in the drive to democratize the Soviet system. In 1989–1990 she became a leader in the political club *Moskovskaia tribuna* (Moscow Tribune), which included many influential members of the intelligentsia. In June 1990 she was elected to the Congress of People's Deputies of the Russian Republic from a Leningrad district, where she amassed 75 percent of the vote. She became a founding member of the political party Democratic Russia, one of the leading groups of democrats. As a result of the party's success, from 1990 to 1993 she served as a member of the Congress of People's Deputies of the Russian Republic (Russian Federation after December 1991) and cochaired *Democraticheskaia Rossiia* (Democratic Russia). She also became a member of the Committee on Human Rights in the Russian Supreme Soviet. A committed democrat, during Democratic Russia's troubles between 1991 and 1993, Starovoitova often criticized elements of her bloc for being less than democratic.

As an expert on ethnic issues and a democrat, Starovoitova became Yeltsin's adviser on interethnic relations in 1991. Her work in this position was highly visible and controversial because it coincided with a time of ethnic crisis in Russia. After the Soviet Union dissolved, Russia faced claims of self-determination by various national groups, and as Yeltsin's main adviser, Starovoitova promoted a peaceful solution, a federalist system with fairly high levels of autonomy for national groups. She hoped this route would lead to less violence. With escalating events and Russian nationalist reactions from some quarters, she was criticized for formulating a reactive, rather than a proactive, policy and was removed from her post in 1992.

Even after her dismissal, Starovoitova continued to criticize the president's actions in Chechnia from her position at the Laboratory on Ethnological Problems of the Transition Period, a part of the Institute for Economic Problems of the Transition Period, directed by former Prime Minister Egor Gaidar. She also worked in the West as a researcher, writer, and teacher at Brown University's Watson Institute for International Studies, the Kennan Institute, and the U.S. Institute for Peace. Upon her return to Russia, she reentered the political arena, and although Democratic Russia had diminished in prominence and experienced disarray, Starovoitova won a Duma seat from a single-member district in St. Petersburg in the 1995 parliamentary elections. Starovoitova was the only woman nominated as a candidate for president in 1996, although the Central Electoral Commission rejected her registration.

In the early 1990s Starovoitova stood out from many women figures in Russian politics because she was a female politician with no demonstrated interest in women's issues. She was most interested in nationality issues and the democratic movement. She was at times critical of the Women of Russia bloc's activity in the Duma, because she claimed that it was unnecessary in a democracy, and she did not call herself a feminist. Later, she changed her ideas about the need for a Russian women's movement, claiming that she had experienced sexism in her political life. While not an activist in the women's movement, she supported it vocally. In addition, Starovoitova was a rare figure—a successful and respected woman politician whose power did not originate in active membership in the Communist Party—and thus she played an important, if informal, role in the Russian women's movement.

On November 20, 1998 Starovoitova's life ended unexpectedly when she was murdered in the stairwell of her St. Petersburg apartment. The impetus for the murder was believed to be her outspoken opposition to corruption and her promotion of democratic values and candidates. In the wake of her death, numerous political figures decried the chaos of Russian politics and society, and thus her death continued her legacy of calling attention to the problems of crime and corruption plaguing Russian politics in the 1990s.

Cross-reference: Women of Russia.

Suggested Readings

Buckley, Mary. "Adaptation of the Soviet Women's Committee: Deputies' Voices from 'Women of Russia.' " In *Post-Soviet Women: From the Baltic to Central Asia*, edited by Mary Buckley, 157–185. Cambridge: Cambridge University Press, 1997.

Lane, David, ed. *Russia in Transition*. New York: Longman, 1995.

Lipovskaya, Ol'ga. "Women's Groups in Russia." In *Post-Soviet Women: From the Baltic to Central Asia*, 186–199. Cambridge: Cambridge University Press, 1997.

McFaul, Michael, and Nikolai Petrov, eds. *Russia's 1995 Parliamentary Elections*. Washington, DC: Carnegie Endowment for International Peace, 1995.

Rule, Wilma, and Nadezhda Shvedova. "Women in Russia's First Multiparty Election." In *Russian Women in Politics and Society*, edited by Wilma Rule and Norma C. Noonan, 40–59. Westport, CT: Greenwood Press, 1996.

Sakwa, Richard. *Russian Politics and Society*. New York: Routledge, 1993.

Starovoitova, Galina. *Etnicheskie gruppy v sovremennom sovetskom gorode: sotsiologicheskie ocherki (Ethnic Groups in a Contemporary Soviet City: Sociological Essays)*. Leningrad: Nauka, 1987.

Starovoitova, Galina. *Sovereignty after Empire: Self-Determination Movements in the Former Soviet Union*. Washington, DC: U.S. Institute of Peace, 1997.

Amy Caiazza

T

Temkina, Anna Adrianovna (1960–)

A sociologist specializing in the study of social movements and women's political and professional activity and a teacher of gender studies.

Anna Temkina was raised in a family of the higher technical intelligentsia in Leningrad. She graduated from the Department of Economy of Leningrad State University in 1983. The same year, she was employed at the Institute of Socioeconomic Problems of the Academy of Sciences in Leningrad. During Perestroika, the Institute had a Sector for the Study of Social Movements, headed by Vladimir Kostiushev. The sector gathered democratically oriented younger scholars who closely followed and supported the development of new social movements. In 1989 the part of the Institute in which Temkina worked became the Institute for Sociology. Early in her career, Temkina specialized in the new workers' movements. She studied Western social theory during a 1992–1993 International Research and Exchanges Board (IREX) fellowship at Columbia University in New York.

In the mid-1990s Temkina turned to feminist activism and research. She wrote and lectured about Western feminist classics by authors like Betty Friedan and Juliet Mitchell, who were little known in Russia. She conducted research on the self-perceptions and obstacles facing women politicians in St. Petersburg. Temkina also studied at the new Eastern European Institute of Psychoanalysis in St. Petersburg during 1993–1994 and wrote about Russian women and psychoanalysis. Since 1997 she also conducted research on gender and sexuality.

In 1995 and 1996 Temkina was a visiting scholar at the University of Helsinki in Finland. In 1997 she defended her Ph.D. dissertation at the University of Helsinki on the topic Russia's new collective actors and collective actions. In 1996 she began to teach at the new European University in St. Petersburg, founded by Director Boris Firsov. Together with Dr. Elena Zdravomyslova, Temkina started the first comprehensive graduate program in gender studies in Russia.

Through her rigorous and analytical work, Temkina contributed to the establishment of academic feminist research and to better understanding of Western feminist social theory in Russia.

Cross-references: Academic Feminism in St. Petersburg, Gender/Women's Studies in Russia, Elena Zdravomyslova.

Suggested Readings

Rotkirch, Anna, and Anna Temkina. "What Does the (Russian) Woman Want? Women Psychoanalysts Talk." In *Women's Voices in Russia Today*, edited by Anna Rotkirch and Elina Haavio-Mannila, 49–70. Aldershot: Dartmouth, 1996.

Temkina, Anna. "Entering Politics: Women's Ways, Gender Ideas and Contradictions of Reality." In *Women's Voices in Russia Today*, edited by Anna Rotkirch and Elina Haavio-Mannila, 206–234. Aldershot: Dartmouth, 1996.

Temkina, Anna. *Russia in Transition: The Case of New Collective Actors and New Collective Actions*. Helsinki: Kikimora, 1997. (in English)

Zdravomyslova, Elena, and Anna Temkina. "*Feministskaia epistemologicheskaia kritika*" (Feminist Epistemological Criticism). In *Zhenshchina, gender, kultura (Woman, Gender, Culture)*, compiled by the Russian Summer School of Gender Studies, 66–82. Moscow: Center for Gender Studies, 1999.

Zdravomyslova, Elena, and Anna Temkina, eds. *Gendernoe Izmerenie Sotsial'noi i Politicheskoi Aktivnosti v Perekhodnyi Period (The Gender Dimension of Social and Political Activity during Transition)*. St. Petersburg: Center for Independent Social Research, 1996.

Zdravomyslova, Elena, and Anna Temkina. "*Sotsial'noe konstruirovanie gendera*" (The Social Construction of Gender). *Sotsiologicheskii zhurnal*, nos. 3–4 (1998): 171–182.

Zdravomyslova, Elena, and Anna Temkina. "*Sotsial'noe konstruirovanie gendera kak feministskaia teoriia*" (The Social Construction of Gender as Feminist Theory). In *Zhenshchina, gender, kultura (Woman, Gender, Culture)*, compiled by the Russian Summer School of Gender Studies, 46–65. Moscow: Center for Gender Studies, 1999.

Anna Rotkirch

Trofimova, Elena Ivanovna (1948–)

A feminist literary critic, editor, and scholar active in major projects related to women's writing, including *Preobrazhenie (Transformation)* and the anthology *Chego khochet zhenshchina (What a Woman Wants)*.

Elena Trofimova was born in Moscow on November 13, 1948, but relatively little is known about her early life. She is best known as a literary critic analyzing connections between feminism, culture, and Western poststructuralist criticism in twentieth-century Russia and editor of the feminist cultural journal *Preobrazhenie (Transformation)*. A member of the Moscow branch of *Soiuz rossiiskikh pisatelei* (Russian Writers Union), after 1995 Trofimova lectured in the Department of Culturology of the Philological Faculty at Moscow State University. Trofimova has been affiliated with *Moskovskii tsentr gendernykh issledovanii* (Moscow Center for Gender Studies) and involved with *Rossiiskie letnie shkoly po gendernym issledovaniiam* (Russian Summer Schools on Gender Studies).

Trofimova has been involved with two projects influencing the Russian and international Slavic feminist community: the Moscow Center for Gender Studies, Russian Summer Schools on Gender Studies and the international prose competition, which produced the women's anthology *Chego khochet zhenshchina (What a Woman Wants).*

In 1998 the Moscow Center for Gender Studies third summer program involved seventy scholars, professors, and graduate students from the Commonwealth of Independent States (CIS), Europe, and the United States. The program, funded by the Ford Foundation and held in Taganrog, lasted approximately two weeks and involved both women and men. Consistent with the Summer School's interdisciplinary focus within the humanities and social sciences, in 1998 new seminars discussed the representation of women in literature and history, mass media, and advertising. Trofimova edited those sections of the 1998 program publication dealing with depictions of women in literature, working alongside Natal'ia Pushkareva (historian), Nadezhda Azhgikhina (journalist), Elena Goroshko (specialist in law), and Zoia Khotkina (economist and general editor).

In judging the international competition forming the basis of *Chego khochet zhenshchina*, Trofimova worked alongside the authors and critics Fazil' Iskander, Vladimir Makanin, Zoia Boguslavskaia, Lev Rubinshtein, Galina Belaia, and Marina Mikhailova from Russia and U.S. scholars Marina Ledkovsky and Helena Goscilo. The seventeen anthologized winning entries were from both metropolitan and provincial Russian authors, as well as from Russian-speaking authors and critics abroad. As noted by *Preobrazhenie*'s sponsor, many of the narratives discuss results of gender inequality and its effect on women's character.

Positing an inextricable link between authors and social context, Trofimova also saw a beneficial relationship between postmodernism and feminism. In *"Feminizm i zhenskaia literatura v Rossii"* (Feminism and Women's Literature in Russia), she noted that feminism must reject masculine paradigms connoting culture as a male construct. In her view, postmodernism challenged the "phallogocentric" norm, critiqued existing canons, and ensured that feminist efforts themselves did not ossify into a new canon. Discussing the contemporary poet Nina Iskrenko, Trofimova asserted that unusual language and "deconstruction" of public and private spheres promoted escape from the oppressive quotidian.

In critiquing established categories of Russian cultural and literary life, Trofimova joined Mikhail Bakhtin's theory of folk laughter to her appropriation of Western postmodernist discourse: both destabilized stagnant norms that Trofimova paired with the gendered inequality of late twentieth-century Russia. Despite her postmodernist inclinations, Trofimova's literary criticism was heavily influenced by the biographical approach still prevalent in Russia.

For Trofimova, women's prose was a distinct category whose right to exist stemmed from the innate differences between male and female literary styles.

In *"O knizhnykh novinkakh russkoi zhenskoi prozy"* (Recent Additions to Russian Women's Prose), Trofimova characterized women's writing as more intuitive and polyphonic than the "strict logic" of male authors. This characterization was fairly typical of Russian feminists arguing for a distinctly female canon of modern literature and had resonance in the works of French poststructuralist feminists.

Trofimova's publications and conference presentations discussed irony in Russian poetry, connections between women and culture, changes in the Russian language, and gender divisions in the emerging field of *kul'turologiia* (culturology). In 1999 the Association for Women in Slavic Studies (AWSS) awarded her the Mary Zirin Prize for her achievements.

Cross-references: Gender/Women's Studies in Russia, Moscow Center for Gender Studies.

Suggested Readings

Trofimova, Elena. "*Feminizm i zhenskaia literatura v Rossii*" (Feminism and Women's Literature in Russia). In *Materialy 1-oi rossisskoi letnei shkole po zhenskim i gendernym issledovaniiam (Materials from the First Russian Summer School on Gender Studies)*, 47–51. Moscow: Moscow Center for Gender Studies, 1997.

Trofimova, Elena. "*Fenomen russkoi zhenshchiny: literatura i zhizn' (materialy diskussii)*" (Russian Woman as Phenomenon: Literature and Life: Discussion Material). In *Russkaia zhenshchina: prednaznachanie i sud'ba (The Russian Woman: Destiny and Fate)*, 61–63. Ekaterinburg: Ural'skii Universitet, 1998.

Trofimova, Elena. "*O knizhnykh novinkakh russkoi zhenskoi prozy*" (Recent Additions to Russian Women's Prose). *Preobrazhenie (Transformation)* 3 (1995): 105–111.

Trofimova, Elena. "*Russkii postmodernizm: aksiologiia poezy Niny Iskrenko*" (Russian Postmodernism: Axiology of the Poetry of Nina Iskrenko). *Preobrazhenie (Transformation)* 4 (1996): 68–74.

Trofimova, Elena. "The Soviet Woman of the 1980s: Self-Portrait in Poetry." In *Gender and Russian Literature: New Perspectives*, translated and edited by Rosalind Marsh, 206–225. Cambridge: Cambridge University Press, 1996.

Trofimova, Elena. "*Zhenskaia literatura i knigoizdanie v sovremennoi Rossii*" (Women's Literature and Publishing in Contemporary Russia). *Obshchestvennye nauki i sovremennost'* 5 (1998): 147–56.

Trofimova, Elena, ed. *Chego kochet zhenshchina (What a Woman Wants)*. Moscow: Linor, 1993.

Trofimova, Elena, ed. *Zhenshchina. Gender. Kul'tura. Sbornik nauchnikh stat'ei I esse. (Woman, Gender, Culture: A Collection of Articles and Essays)*. Moscow: Moscow Center for Gender Studies, 1999.

Benjamin Sutcliffe

U

The Union of Disabled Women (*Soiuz zhenshchin invalidov*) (1990–)
A St. Petersburg women's organization that provided material assistance to homebound members and marketed their handmade crafts.

The *Soiuz zhenshchin invalidov* (Union of Disabled Women) was founded in 1990 in Leningrad. The group supported homebound, physically disabled women materially by facilitating communication and friendship and organizing home labor. Its leader, Marina Aleksandrovna Makhorskova, a retired teacher who was disabled but could walk, provided members with food and clothing that she solicited from Russian businesses and an opportunity to sell homemade handicrafts. The de facto sewing and knitting cooperative, made possible, in part, by sewing machines that Makhorskova secured through donations, allowed the women to produce goods that could be sold for profit to supplement their meager pensions. Makhorskova also negotiated an arrangement with a collective farm that allowed the group to have access to small plots of land to grow vegetables and fruits. Regular, if infrequent, outings were made possible by a wheelchair-accessible bus donated by a German sponsor, and Makhorskova dreamed of opening a rest home and making specialized equipment available to the members. Her assistance reached over 100 invalids. Extra goods were donated to a city orphanage.

The organization was significant as an example of a "self-help" group. Its members, all in need themselves, cooperated to support themselves and one another. The leadership, for this group especially, was important, for without Makhorskova, who herself traveled between the apartments of members, contacts would have been limited to phone conversations. While she reported accepting the largest share of the organization's responsibility, she acknowledged holding meetings over the telephone to make group decisions. Tireless and devoted, Makhorskova relied largely on the goodwill donations of local, small-scale philanthropists to take care of her group's members. For example, a fish shop sold her fish at reduced prices, and one company gave her juice and fruit for members' children at a discount. Even as the state's safety net collapsed, groups such as Makhorskova's came together to provide for the needs of the disabled in St. Petersburg.

Cross-reference: The Disabled Russian Women's Movement.

Suggested Readings

Gottlick, Jane F. Berthusen. "From the Ground Up: Women's Organizations and Democratization in Russia." In *Democratization and Women's Grassroots Movements*, edited by Jill M. Bystydzienski and Joti Sekhon, 241–261. Bloomington: Indiana University Press, 1999.

McMahon, Patrice C. "The Effect of Economic and Political Reforms on Soviet/Russian Women." In *Women in the Age of Economic Transformation*, edited by Nahid Aslangeigui, Steven Pressman, and Gale Summerfield, 59–76. New York: Routledge, 1994.

Nechemias, Carol. "The Prospects for a Soviet Women's Movement: Opportunities and Obstacles." In *Perestroika from Below: Social Movements in the Soviet Union*, edited by Judith B. Sedaitis and Jim Butterfield, 73–96. Boulder, CO: Westview Press, 1991.

Racioppi, Linda, and Katherine O'Sullivan See. "Organizing Women before and after the Fall: Women's Politics in the Soviet Union and Post-Soviet Russia." *Signs* (Summer 1995): 818–850.

Jane F. Berthusen Gottlick

The Union of Soviet Women of Leningrad and Leningrad Oblast (1992–)

A pro-Communist and anti-Western women's organization formed in St. Petersburg in 1992. The goal of the group was to resurrect the Soviet Union and, especially, the benefits of the welfare state.

The Union of Soviet Women of Leningrad and Leningrad Oblast was formed after the dissolution of the Soviet Union in 1991 and was led by Valentina Vasilievna Ostrova. The union aspired to assist in the reconstruction of the Soviet Union and opposed the government of President Boris Yeltsin and the transition to democracy and capitalism. Both were described as examples of "betrayal from within" and as Western explanations for Russian unemployment and poverty. Members argued fiercely against the critical, revisionist view of Soviet history and for the reconstitution of the safety net provided by Soviet communist governments, insisting that the rights to child day care, work, education, living space, health care, and culture were responsibilities of the state and that the majority of Russians were suffering from the effects of the Western, capitalist influence that had begun to dictate Russian domestic policy. Ostrova described the early 1990s as the most recent example of Russia's colonization and believed that Russia had become an occupied territory, victim not only of the power of Western capital but of international Jews. The organization relied on the voluntary contributions of members to fund its protests and rallies (such as the 1993 Empty Pots March). The organization utilized a complex network of thirty-eight regional departments. The number of members was undisclosed for fear of retaliation. The organization was St. Petersburg's most prominent, conservative, nationalist women's group, whose goal was to resurrect the Soviet structure and agenda and to limit foreign access and influence. It was also an interesting case insofar as it provided insight into the workings of the budding, democratic, free press. Ostrova insisted that the organization's work was hampered by the media's refusal to provide coverage and publicity.

Suggested Readings

Gottlick, Jane F. Berthusen. "From the Ground Up: Women's Organizations and Democratization in Russia." In *Democratization and Women's Grassroots Movements*, edited by Jill M. Bystydzienski and Joti Sekhon, 241–261. Bloomington: Indiana University Press, 1999.

McMahon, Patrice C. "The Effect of Economic and Political Reforms on Soviet/Russian Women." In *Women in the Age of Economic Transformation*, edited by Nahid Aslangeigui, Steven Pressman, and Gale Summerfield, 59–76. New York: Routledge, 1994.

Nechemias, Carol. "The Prospects for a Soviet Women's Movement: Opportunities and Obstacles." In *Perestroika from Below: Social Movements in the Soviet Union*, edited by Judith B. Sedaitis and Jim Butterfield, 73–96. Boulder, CO: Westview Press, 1991.

Racioppi, Linda, and Katherine O'Sullivan See. "Organizing Women before and after the Fall: Women's Politics in the Soviet Union and Post-Soviet Russia." *Signs* (Summer 1995): 818–850.

Jane F. Berthusen Gottlick

V

Vasil'eva, Larisa Nikolaievna (1935–)

Poet, publicist, essayist, novelist, and popular historian, Larisa Vasil'eva was famous for her work in several genres. In the transitional era in the USSR/Russia, Vasil'eva became a leader of women writers, gaining national recognition as a spokesperson for women. A brilliant and original woman who followed no particular popular movement, she gained success as a uniquely Russian literary voice.

Larisa Nikolaevna Kucharenko was born in Kharkov, Ukraine, on November 23, 1935, the daughter of an engineer who later won fame and a Stalin Prize as codesigner of the Soviet tank T-34, which played an important role in World War II.

Larisa wrote poetry as a child and published her first works at age twelve. She graduated from Moscow State University (MGU) in 1958 with a major in Russian literature. In January 1957 she married Oleg Vasiliev (1931–1993), a journalist and translator, the great love of her life. Their son, Georgi (Egor), was born in 1962 and, like his father, became a translator. Oleg's career as journalist for *Izvestiia* took the family to England for several years, where Larisa wrote an anthology, widely read in the USSR, *Al'bion i taina vremeni (Albion and the Secret of Time)* (1978), chronicling her impressions of British life.

For many years, Larisa considered herself primarily a poet and a wife. When glasnost opened the door to greater freedom of expression among Soviet writers, Larisa emerged as a leader of women writers within the Soviet Writers' Union, when the women realized that the male writers were little interested in having female voices represented in the union's leadership. She was instrumental in establishing the International League of Women Writers in 1989. She gained a national audience not only as a poet but also as a spokesperson for women. Her intention to lead a sustained women's movement, growing out of the Writers' League, was limited both by her writing and by her husband's illness. Oleg's struggle with pancreatic cancer intervened and occupied her energy and attention for several years. During her husband's illness and after his death, Larisa engaged in an intense schedule of writing popular history and novels. Her books, *Kremlëvskie Zhëny (Kremlin Wives)* and *Deti Kremlia (Kremlin Children)* achieved considerable success.

In the mid-1990s, she launched a woman's publishing house and a journal, *Atlantida*. The magazine was short-lived, but the publishing house succeeded. In the crisis-ridden early years of post-Soviet Russia even the most successful intellectuals lost the financial security that they had in the later years of the USSR. Work became the means for survival as well as a response to one's creative urge. Larisa had always been a workaholic, often writing late into the night. In the years after her husband's death, she worked almost to the point of exhaustion. Her megahistory of Moscow, *Dusha Moskvy*, written in honor of its 850th anniversary, reflected her lifelong love affair with the city. Her novel *Pierre and Natasha*, a sequel to *War and Peace*, published under the pseudonym Vasili Staroi, was cowritten with a friend.

A strongly charismatic woman, Vasil'eva had the potential to be one of the most important leaders of the Russian women's movement, but her creative work as a writer has always taken first place. As with other successful authors, personal appearances in Russia and abroad as well as radio and television interviews occupied much of her time when she was not writing. There was little time left over to engage in the organizational work that sustained leadership in the women's movement entailed. A heart attack in 1999 slowed her hectic work pace.

Her occasional essays on the role of women in society and her leadership of women writers since the late 1980s led to invitations to serve on several advisory committees on women in Russia and were often discussed in the media. Her distinctive philosophy about women's role separated her from feminists and from traditional women. Her ideas focused on *Garmoniia* (harmony) and *Partnërstvo* (partnership) with men. She believed that men and women had different roles to play in society and that women should not involve themselves in men's political games. The theory recommended that women do the things that they do best and not try to emulate men. She wanted to leave politics to men and preferred to concentrate on social issues that concerned women, the family, and cultural life. Vasil'eva's theory may be viewed as an important voice within the Russian female intelligentsia, but not as a feminist voice.

Cross-reference: International League of Women Writers.

Suggested Readings

Noonan, Norma C. "Does Consciousness Lead to Action?" *Journal of Gender Studies* 3, no. 1 (1994): 47–54.

Vasil'eva, Larisa Nikolaievna. "Evangelie ot Vasilisy," *Pravda*, Moscow no. 66 (26514), March 18, 1991, 4.

Vasil'eva, Larisa N. *Deti Kremlia (Kremlin Children)*. Moscow: Atlantida, 1997.

Vasil'eva, Larisa Nikolaievna. *Dusha Moskvy (The Soul of Moscow)*. Moscow: Atlantida, 1997.

Vasil'eva, Larisa Nikolaievna. *Izbrannye proizvedeniia (Selected Works)*. 2 vol. Moscow: Khudozhestvennaia Literatura, 1989.
Vasil'eva, Larisa N. (Vasil'eva, Larissa). *Kremlin Wives*. Translated by Cathy Porter. New York: Arcade Press, 1994.
Vasil'eva, Larisa Nikolaievna. "*Niet doma bez khoziaiki*" (There Is No Home without a Housekeeper). *Pravda*, August 10, 1990.
Vasil'eva, Larisa N. *Zhëny russkoi korony (Wives of the Russian Throne)*. 2 vols. Moscow: Atlantida, 1999.
Vasily Staroi (Starostin, Alexander, and Larisa Vasil'eva). *Pierre and Natasha*. Moscow: Vagrius, 1996.

Norma Corigliano Noonan

Vladimir Region, Women's Movement in (1990s)

Vladimir, a region with a rich historical tradition about three hours east of Moscow, presented an interesting case study of women's activism and its limitations in the transitional era. It also reflected differences between the provincial regions and Moscow or St. Petersburg.

The development of the women's movement in the Vladimir region of Russia faced many economic and social problems in the transition from the Soviet era to a new political and economic system. This region of central Russia was the site of numerous enterprises involved in the Soviet military-industrial complex. Women were employed in both military and light industries. After the demise of the Soviet Union, many enterprises closed. The Vladimir region was also part of the famous tourist complex the Golden Ring of Russia, and many women were involved in its tourist industry. The decline of tourism in post-Soviet Russia adversely affected women's employment in the region.

The demographics of the region indicated the severity of its problems. In the late 1990s approximately 65 percent of the unemployed in the region were women, a statistic that mirrored the national unemployment rate for women. Many unemployed women possessed a degree in higher education and good qualifications. Vladimir also had a high divorce rate and many single-parent families headed by women, although precise data were not available. The high inflation rates in the 1990s severely decreased real family income. Two-thirds of all pensioners were women, and the pensions were inadequate for survival. The government was often five or six months in arrears in pension payments and child allowances. In addition, working women in the Vladimir region usually had to care for sick and aging parents and relatives since state services did not provide adequate aid to the elderly. As a consequence, the women were responsible not only for their nuclear family but also for their parents, thus creating a triple responsibility of a job, child care, and preservation of the larger family. The situation was also characterized by the increased rivalry for jobs and fair wages with men and sex discrimination in hiring both in the state and private sectors, although hard data were not available on the exact situation.

These conditions created a basis for the development of a women's movement in the region to protect woman's political, social, and civil rights. One factor hindering the development of women's activity was the traditional Russian mentality with its negative reaction to women's political activity; there was a widespread belief that activism would make a woman forget her family and children. This attitude was shared by many women, who disapproved of a women's movement and considered it an unfavorable development. At the same time, politicians often recruited women to participate in campaigns and to promote their proposals on family protection issues but did not commit themselves to improve social conditions.

The women's movement began in the Vladimir region in 1990. By 1991–1992 six nongovernmental associations founded by women were registered in the Vladimir region. Their activities were directed at the improvement of the large family's position in the region, for example, the association *Semia* (Family), led by Natalia Gorbach; *Semeinyi Ochag* (The Family Hearth) and *Zaria* (Dawn) in the towns of Vyaznikiand and Selivanovo; and the Vladimir branch of the *Blagotvoritelnyi fond sotsialnoi zashchity materinstva i detsvo* (Motherhood and Childhood Social Protection Charitable Fund). These organizations sought to protect large families' rights and coordinate efforts to protect mother and children in the region.

Eight nongovernmental organizations were formed from 1993 to 1995 to address problems in the Russian military. The main purpose of the *Komitet soldatskikh materei Rossii* (Committee of Soldiers' Mothers of Russia) and the *Komitety roditelskoi obshchestvennosti i semei voennosluzhashchikh* (the Committees of Parents and Families of Military Servicemen) was to protect the rights and interest of young soldiers and military families. Most activists in these organizations were women.

In 1995, with the creation of the *Oblast'noi sovet zhenshchin* (Regional Women's Council), headed by Valentina Khiger, collaboration among women's groups increased. Council members conducted charitable campaigns, discussed problems of environmental protection, and collected and distributed contributions for indigent families, orphans, and invalids.

Between 1995 and 1997 the founding of public associations and movements, such as *Kongress sovetskikh zhenshchin* (the Congress of Soviet Women), headed by Irina Fedorova, and a branch of the *Soiuz zhenshchin Rossii* (Women's Union of Russia, or WUR), headed by Liubov Kozina, were vivid examples of women's political activity in the Vladimir region. The Congress of Soviet Women sought the realization and the constitutional protection of women's civil, political, economic, social, and cultural rights and freedoms; it also supported the restoration of the USSR. The membership of the Women's Union of Russia (WUR) consisted of independents, members of the Communist Party of the Russian Federation (KPRF), and active and ex-deputies of local soviets. The organization, however, did not maintain an official dues-paying membership; its activities were carried out by its coordinating council. WUR sought to consolidate the women of the Russian Federation on the platform of strengthening Russian statehood, its defense potential, restoration of the national, state-regulated economy, state control of prices, state ownership of land and natural resources, and the preservation of national spiritual and cultural traditions. The Congress of the Soviet Women and WUR worked in close cooperation, and both were politically oriented toward the KPRF.

The Vladimir branch of the organization, *Obshcherossiiskoe obshchestvenno-politicheskoe dvizhenie zhenshchin Rossii* (the All-Russian Sociopolitical Movement of Women of Russia, or MWR) was established in 1996. Its main aims were to stimulate women's participation in public and political life in Russia and enlarge their representation at all levels of the state structure. The official documents of the movement stated that the women's movement is the basis on which to form a civil society in Russia. The Vladimir branch of Women of Russia tended to support *Otechestvo* (Fatherland), the bloc headed by Iuri Luzhkov, the mayor of Moscow, and *Iabloko* ("Apple"), the party headed by Gregory Iavlinskii (Yavlinsky). Women of Russia supported the idea of "equal rights—equal possibilities" for women and sought to implement quotas for women in state and local government.

As of 1999 sixteen women organizations, unions, and associations were registered in the Vladimir region. Women were also active in a variety of public movements, such as *Oblast'noi fond kultury* (Regional Cultural Fund) and *Semia—zalozhnitsa Chernobylia* (The Family Is Chernobyl's Hostage) and of activist organizations that promoted the interests of special groups, such as invalids. The leaders of three women's organizations, WUR, the Congress of the Soviet Women, and Women of Russia, participated in the *Politicheskii Konsultativnyi Sovet* (Political Consulting Council) of the Vladimir region governor. Thus, they had an opportunity to participate in discussions and influence decisions concerning regional problems and women's issues.

The women's conference held in Vladimir in April 1998, devoted to problems of social partnership and cooperation between the state authorities and women's organizations and associations, reflected the growing understanding of the importance of women's political and social activism. Nongovernmental women's organizations were declared to be a unique instrument to express women's views in all spheres of Russian life and to mobilize social activity and creative potential of the women. The conference focused on a series of goals. It emphasized the need for women to have a greater voice in local decision making and in the implementation of social programs. It advocated women's active participation in elections to gain more seats in the *Zakonodatel'noe sobranie* (regional legislature), governmental offices, commissions, and boards. The conference pointed to the need to improve women's political education through schools for women's leadership and to support women candidates through special public committees, such as *Zhenshchina i politika* (Women and Politics). *Zhenshchina i politika* was a committee created to advance discussion and education, but not a women's organization as such. The conference emphasized the need to shape public opinion in the spirit of equality of sexes and partnership, create a positive image of the modern woman in the mass media, and overcome patriarchal stereotypes of women's role in society. It called for sociological studies on the problems of the family and on women's role in public life in the region. The conference stressed that cooperation between state authorities and women's organizations and associations can be achieved through women's participation in examination of documents and proposed legislation. There should be cooperation between state and public women's associations on the regional, municipal, and district levels in the work of the *Oblast'naia mezhvedomstvennaia komissiia po uluchsheniiu polozheniia semii, zhenshchin i detei* (Regional Interdepartmental Commission on the Improvement of the Position of the Family, Women, and Children). The conference also urged the creation of working groups made up of governmental officials and representatives of women's associations. These recommendations opened the possibility for greater cooperation between state organs and women's nongovernmental associations.

Although there was considerable progress in the 1990s, the Vladimir region women's movement did not gain enough authority and influence among the public to be regarded as a serious political force. At the same time, the need to find adequate solutions to the social and political problems of the region and the country and to express women's interests suggested that women's political activism would continue to develop.

Cross-references: All-Russian Sociopolitical Movement of Women of Russia (*Obshcherossiiskoe obshchestvenno-politicheskoe dvizhenie zhenshchin Rossii*), Committee of Soldiers' Mothers of Russia, Women's Union of Russia (WUR).

Irina Lapshina and Anna Levitskaia, with assistance from Andrei Levitskii.

W

Woman and Development Association *(Zhenshchina i razvitie)* (1992–)

A Russian research group focusing on women's social and economic status.

The association *Zhenshchina i razvitie* (Woman and Development), headed by Dr. Galina Sillaste, a prominent sociologist, was established in Moscow in 1992. The primary focus of the association was research on women's political, economic, and social role in society. Most of the scholars associated with the project were sociologists. Their research tended to be practical in orientation and directed at analysis of contemporary problems. Twice a year, the association held roundtables to discuss the results of the research and sent its findings to the press, government organizations, and other groups that could put the findings to practical use in solving social problems.

Although the organization was based in Moscow, it cooperated with groups in various regions of Russia and in Kirgizia and Kazakhstan.

Cross-reference: Gender/Women's Studies in Russia.

Norma Corigliano Noonan

Women and Business in Russia *(Zhenshchiny i biznes v Rossii)* (ca. 1990–)

Founded in St. Petersburg in the early 1990s, Women and Business in Russia had the goal of providing a cooperative forum for businesswomen. Members were also interested in politics and offered candidates for election through the Russia's Choice Party.

The association *Zhenshchiny i biznes v Rossii* (Women and Business in Russia) provided a support network for businesswomen in post-Soviet St. Petersburg from its inception in the early 1990s. The twenty-two members owned small businesses, and the group served as a forum for consultation, problem solving, and cooperation. While the group members were already successfully working in the new market economy, efforts were made to include in their meetings women who were unemployed. In this way, the group provided help not only to its members but also to women who suffered the costs of the transition to the new economic system. The group's members also acted as intermediaries between Russian and foreign businesses considering cooperation by providing a variety of services such as locating potential partners, performing background checks, presenting proposals, and even mediating difficulties in partnership arrangements. Liudmilla Nikolaevna Chubatyk, the leader of the organization, was also asked to act as an intermediary between unemployed city women and the city's mayor's office and to construct, together with the St. Petersburg Association of University Women, a database containing information about unemployed St. Petersburg women. The group was committed to the emerging political process, and in 1993 several members were offered as candidates for the democratic Russia's Choice Party. The organization exemplified women's successful participation in the emerging market economy and women's cooperation. It was further proof of the commitment to support unemployed women and of the city's attention to the underemployment of its women. In creating this organization, Chubatyk was dramatically influenced by the time that she had spent abroad. She cited a friend's Italian organization as the model for her own and reported encouraging students to spend time abroad because her own life was changed so radically by living in Sweden for an extended period. From her foreign experience she concluded that while Russian people were not worse than other people, their structures were.

Cross-references: Missiia, The St. Petersburg Association of University Women, Women in Business in Russia.

Suggested Readings

Gottlick, Jane F. Berthusen. "From the Ground Up: Women's Organizations and Democratization in Russia." In *Democratization and Women's Grassroots Movements*, edited by Jill M. Bystydzienski and Joti Sekhon, 241–261. Bloomington: Indiana University Press, 1999.

McMahon, Patrice C. "The Effect of Economic and Political Reforms on Soviet/Russian Women." In *Women in the Age of Economic Transformation*, edited by Nahid Aslangeigui, Steven Pressman, and Gale Summerfield, 59–76. New York: Routledge, 1994.

Nechemias, Carol. "The Prospects for a Soviet Women's Movement: Opportunities and Obstacles." In *Perestroika from Below: Social Movements in the Soviet Union*, edited by Judith B. Sedaitis and Jim Butterfield, 73–96. Boulder, CO: Westview Press, 1991.

Racioppi, Linda, and Katherine O'Sullivan See. "Organizing Women before and after the Fall: Women's Politics in the Soviet Union and Post-Soviet Russia." *Signs* (Summer 1995): 818–850.

Jane F. Berthusen Gottlick

Women in Business in Russia (ca. 1987–)

Women began to participate in business in the emerging market economy in Russia in the late 1980s and early 1990s. Their participation took various forms.

Because of the complexities of Russia's market economy and the nearly confiscatory system of taxation, a number of firms went bankrupt, but the healthiest survived.

Women first entered the business arena during Perestroika, without much background or experience, since entrepreneurship was a new endeavor for everyone in socialist Russia. They established commercial banks, opened shops, organized training programs and refresher courses for women, or became lobbyists, trying to influence the political process. Most women in business were involved in small or medium-sized business, producing personal products and accessories or consumer goods for the home, such as window shades. Since the majority of businesses were established in the closing days of the USSR and early days of the new Russian political system, many did not thrive in the difficult conditions of the transitional period. Bankruptcies were frequent, and only the hardiest firms survived. Some of those included LITT, Souvenir, Zhaliusy, Veleny, and others.

Women entrepreneurs, according to researchers, faced many common problems and challenges. Among common problems were the need for initial capital, the limited rights of entrepreneurs under Russian law, the complex tax laws, which were difficult to interpret and apply, and the existence of criminal groups, which extorted approximately 20 percent of the profits. In the 1990s the political system of the Russian Federation did not create an infrastructure to protect entrepreneurs from extortionists, nor did local governments provide conditions in which small businesses could survive, such as subsidized rents for fledgling businesses. The system of taxation tended to hamper all entrepreneurs since taxes often had to be paid before revenue for products was received. Women entrepreneurs remained optimistic that they could succeed if the central and local governments would provide the necessary support to improve the political climate for business. Among needed measures were laws to improve the tax system and to protect entrepreneurs from criminal organizations. Some measures to assist small business took effect in 1999.

Women entrepreneurs focused primarily on consumer goods and services, as well as training programs for women. This was the niche that women carved for themselves and in which they appeared determined to succeed in the first decade of the Russian Federation.

Cross-references: Missiia (Mission), Women and Business in Russia.

Elvira Ershova

Women in Global Security, or WINGS *(Zhenshchiny za global'nuiu bezopasnost')* (1990–)

A Russian nonpartisan association uniting women scholars specializing in the study of international relations and security issues.

The origins of Women in Global Security (WINGS) *(Zhenshchiny za global'nuiu bezopasnost')* can be traced from a December 1990 bilateral meeting of American and Russian women involved in security studies. The meeting was organized at the initiative of the American association Women in International Security (WIIS) and the Committee of Soviet Scientists for Peace against the Nuclear Threat. Catherine MacArdle Kelleher, the President of WIIS, Academician Roald Sagdeev, at that time President of the Committee of Soviet Scientists, and Professor Sergei Kapitsa, then President of the *Phizicheskoe obshchestvo* (Physics Society) initiated the idea of organizing a network of women scholars in the USSR. At the initial meeting, the discussion focused on ways to unite women who had a strong desire for an academic and political career and who supported more active involvement of women in foreign policy decision making. Participants at the conference were women researchers from various academic institutions who were interested in greater cooperation among women scholars. A working group developed a charter and set goals for WINGS.

In the early stages of its development, WINGS enjoyed substantial moral and financial support from American women in WIIS. Official presentation of WINGS as a Russian nongovernmental association occurred in 1992 at the annual convention of the International Studies Association (ISA) held in Atlanta, Georgia, and at a special WIIS seminar in Washington, D.C. Collaboration between WIIS and WINGS resulted in several international conferences: Ethnic Conflict Resolution in Eastern Europe and the Former Soviet Union (1992, Prague); The Role of Ethnic Factors in Russian–Estonian and Russian-Ukrainian Relations and Its Impact on European Security (1993, Tallinn); Women in Conflict (1993, Moscow); Politics, Foreign Policy, and Civil–Military Relations in a Post-Cold War World (1994, Moscow); and Ethnic Conflict and European Security: Lessons from the Past and Implications for the Future (1995, Washington, D.C.).

Within the Russian Federation, WINGS established a network of women engaged in security studies, primarily in academic institutions in different republics, oblasts, and cities. WINGS was active in organizing regional Russian conferences and seminars on security issues. It took part in interinstitutional and interdisciplinary research projects on ethnic issues, both national and international. WINGS encouraged professional development and helped women from the regions of the Russian Federation to develop and undertake research projects and receive international recognition and financial support from foreign and Russian foundations. As a result, women from various regions of the Russian Federation became well known in the Russian and international scientific communities and established their own professional contacts at home and abroad.

WINGS encouraged active participation of its members in political debates about important policy issues and greater involvement in the activities of federal and local power structures. Some members of WINGS served as deputies or staff members of federal and local legislative bodies, as consultants to presidential and government structures, and as experts writing analytical papers for federal executive and parliamentary agencies. Their publications on urgent security problems in the Russian Federation are noteworthy; their expertise and analyses are taken into account in debates and decision making on ethnic, ecological, economic, and human rights issues.

WINGS members were committed both to strengthening cooperation among women scholars in Russia and to developing international cooperation. They actively participated in national and international conferences, including those cosponsored with WIIS. Within the Russian Federation, WINGS helped to organize conferences on Women and Freedom (1996, Moscow) and Women in Politics (1997, Moscow). Educational efforts were central to their agenda since the professional development of the women scholars was viewed as a key to their effectiveness as educators.

WINGS established and tried to maintain contacts with women from the Ukraine, Belarus, Moldova, Armenia, Azerbaijan, Estonia, and Latvia. It is a member of the Consortium of Women's Nongovernmental Organizations of Russia, which affords an opportunity to participate in woman's rights debates and activities. WINGS developed a database of women scholars in Russia specializing in security studies.

The difficulties encountered during Russia's transformation in the 1990s hampered WINGS from achieving all of its goals. The organization did not have secure financing and was, therefore, limited in the assistance that it could offer to women in the regions and to younger scholars.

Despite its difficulties, WINGS remained the organization that maintained and promoted the presence of women in the formulation of a new Russian approach to security policy. It played an important role in the professional development of women scholars and indirectly in the training and preparation of the next generation of women scholars.

Cross-reference: The Consortium of Women's Nongovernmental Associations.

Tatiana Shakleina

Women in the Russian Military since 1992

Due to manpower shortages the Russian military has accepted more women as contract soldiers, and more than one-half of all volunteers are now women. However, no efforts were made to facilitate the entry of women into military ranks.

The Russian military officially came into being on May 7, 1992, in the newly formed Russian Federation. The structure of the Russian military remained that of the former Soviet military. It was composed of four branches, the Strategic Rocket Forces, the Ground Forces, the Air Defense Forces, and the Navy. The power and prestige of the Russian military, however, were much lower than those of its Soviet predecessor. After its deployment in the first war in Chechnia (1994–1996), the Russian military faced many serious problems, including low morale, budget cuts, corruption, draft dodging, and a poor image due to the indiscriminate use of force in Chechnia. According to some estimates, the combat readiness of the Russian army was so low in 1997 that it could field and supply only one of its seventy-eight divisions.

In 1994 there were more than 161,000 women in uniform in the Russian military. They represented 8.5 percent of the total number serving in the military (women were not subject to the draft in Russia). Of these, only four were colonels. None were generals. The absence of women from leadership positions in the Russian army coincided with another tendency in Russia in the post-Soviet period. The female political elite has been shrinking rather than expanding. The sociopolitical crisis resulted in growing unemployment among women. According to 1992 data, more than 70 percent of Russia's unemployed were women. Many women, particularly those who worked in the defense industry and other state-subsidized industries, lost their jobs. The troubled Russian army, however, became a new source of employment for women in Russia. In 1996 women constituted more than one-half of the army volunteers in Russia. Most were the wives of soldiers already serving in the army. They enlisted because their husbands' salaries were so low (ranging from 400 to 800 rubles per month, approximately US $80 to $160 prior to the 1998 devaluation) that they did not even cover the cost of housing. After the economic crisis of 1998, the salary situation worsened. Although salaries were raised 1.6 times in early 1999, the actual salary dropped in terms of its purchasing power. In 1999 the average officer's salary was 650 to 750 rubles (about US $30 per month).

Women's participation in the military tends to increase during times of national emergency and manpower shortages and when a society's values and the structure of its labor market are egalitarian. In the post-Soviet period, Russia experienced enormous manpower shortages. In late 1993, when soldiers conscripted for service in the Soviet army completed their duty, the Russian armed forces became seriously understaffed. The armed forces shrank from about 3 million in 1992, to 1.5 million by the mid-1990s. To compensate for part of the shortfall, in 1992–1993 about 120,000 volunteers joined the military on two- and three-year contracts. About 40,000 more volunteers were added in early 1994. In 1996, 230,000 contract soldiers (i.e., volunteers) constituted 15 percent of the Russian military. Contract soldiers, however, sometimes went for months at a time without receiving any pay due to budgetary constraints and bureaucratic inefficiency, so many of them left the military as soon as they could find employment elsewhere.

During January and February 1997, 2,755 people were accepted for service in the Russian military on a contractual basis; however, 5,942 left during the same period, thus creating more opportunities for women to join. In 1997, 25 percent of the positions to be filled by contract soldiers were vacant. The decision whether to accept women to fill these vacancies could be made by the leaders of military units on a case-by-case basis. Women could apply directly to the units. Besides women, other applicants were mostly former draftees and career military personnel who had previously left the military in search of better-paying jobs but had difficulty finding employment in the civilian job market.

Despite eighty years of Soviet socialism, neither the society nor the labor market in Russia became egalitarian. Despite a shortage of draftees and volunteers, women were not welcome in the Russian military. Even though President

Yeltsin decreed in 1996 that the Russian military would consist entirely of volunteer forces by the year 2000, the consensus among Russian military leaders and analysts has been that "the army needs, first of all, men." Since 1992 the Russian military has not taken any steps to facilitate the integration of women into its ranks. The military reform plans devised in 1996–1997 did not address the question of gender at all. Although the Russian Constitution stated that men and women "have equal rights and equal freedoms and equal opportunities to use them" (Article 19.3), the revised Labor Code of July 1996 limited the scope of professions that women can pursue. It listed 400 jobs for which women fifteen to forty-nine years old were ineligible for employment. Those were jobs considered harmful to their health and their reproductive functions. The Labor Code reflected a tendency to divide professions into "feminine" and "masculine" in Russian society. It was, therefore, no surprise that most women were confined to the support sectors of the Russian military.

Suggested Readings

Addis, Elisabetta. *Women Soldiers: Images and Realities*. New York: St. Martin's Press, 1994.

Azhgikina, Nadezhda. "A Movement Is Born." *The Bulletin of the Atomic Scientists* 51, no. 4 (July/August 1995): 47–53.

Dandeker, Christopher, and Mady Wechsler Segal. "Gender Integration in Armed Forces: Recent Policy Developments in the United Kingdom." *Armed Forces and Society* (Fall 1996): 29–47.

Karasik, Theodore W., ed. *USSR Facts and Figures Annual*. Vols. 21–23. Gulf Breeze, FL: Academic International Press, 1996, 1997, 1998.

Meek, James. "The Military: Thugs in Ragged Uniforms: Poverty, Corruption, and Brutality." *World Press Review* 44, no. 1 (January 1997): 11–13.

Rutland, Peter. "Most Army Volunteers Are Women." *OMRI Daily Digest*, Part I (October 21, 1996); World Wide Web edition www.rferl.org (archives).

"Shootings, Suicides Point to Crisis in the Army." *The Current Digest of the Post-Soviet Press* 59, no. 24 (July 16, 1997): 1–2.

Sillaste, Galina. "Female Elites in Russia and Their Distinctive Features." *Russian Politics and Law* 33 (May/June 1995): 68–82.

Dovile Budryte

The Women of Russia Political Movement *(Politicheskoe dvizhenie Zhenshchiny Rossii)*, or WOR (1993–)

The Women of Russia (WOR) electoral bloc unexpectedly won a place for itself in the State Duma elected in December 1993 but suffered electoral defeat two years later in the December 1995 elections and again in the 1999 elections. WOR rejected feminism in favor of a more pragmatic, softer approach, that emphasized the need to strengthen social programs and the positive benefits that would flow from an increase in the number of women in political decision making.

In the late Soviet era women usually held 33 percent of the seats in the USSR

Supreme Soviet and 36 percent of the seats in the Union Republic Supreme Soviets. Democratization overhauled Soviet-style legislatures by transforming symbolic facades of democracy into working parliaments. This process ended a system of quotas and unopposed candidates that had ensured high proportions of women deputies in favor of competitive elections. As a result, in 1990 women secured only 5.4 percent of the seats in the newly created Congress of People's Deputies in the Russian Republic; this body became the Congress of People's Deputies of the Russian Federation in 1992.

In the fall of 1993, with the first parliamentary elections in the newly independent Russian Federation scheduled for December, three women's organizations, the *Soiuz zhenshchin Rossii* (Women's Union of Russia, or WUR), the *Assotsiatsiia Zhenshchin-Predprinimatelei* (Association of Women Entrepreneurs), and the *Soiuz Zhenshchin Voenno-Morskogo Flota* (Union of Women of the Naval Fleet), formed the electoral bloc—the Political Movement Women of Russia. The impetus did not come from the new, independent women's organizations but rather from the dominant element in the bloc, WUR, the direct successor of the old-line Soviet organization the Soviet Women's Committee. WUR's leader, Alevtina Fedulova, had long worked within the Communist Party of the Soviet Union (CPSU), a fact that generated considerable suspicion and wariness on the part of feminist groups. Listed second after Fedulova on WOR's party list ballot was Ekaterina Lakhova, who had been elected to the Russian parliament in 1990 but had left that position to become President Yeltsin's adviser on family policy.

The WUR had reviewed the programs of thirty political parties in the fall of 1993 and concluded that not one of them had defined a position with respect to the "woman question." Nor were many women included on party lists, a sign that few would be elected through that pathway, an ominous sign in an electoral system in which half the deputies were elected through party list balloting and half through single-member districts. The disinterest of other parties in women's affairs, the alarm generated by the negative impact of economic change on women's lives, and societal rhetoric that women belonged at home provided impetus for direct political action.

To the astonishment of virtually all political observers, WOR gained 8.1 percent of the party list ballots, finishing fourth among twenty-one parties and blocs and electing twenty-one women to the State Duma. WOR stressed a moderate, centrist position, eschewing positions that appeared to pit men against women. At its first press conference, WOR put forward the slogan "Democracy without women is not democracy," only to drop it in favor of the softer "Women of Russia—for Russia." The bloc's appeals were largely populous in nature, emphasizing the need to make social policy the main state priority. WOR also highlighted the idea that the "fair sex" could bring conciliation, compromise, and stability to a Russian political scene wracked by shattering crises.

Within the State Duma, the WOR fraction maintained its independence, asserting that it would work with other parties on particular issues but not align itself with any other political grouping on a permanent basis. Fedulova was elected deputy chair of the State Duma, leaving Lakhova head of the fraction. WOR's major accomplishments involved the creation of the State Duma Committee on Women, Family, and Youth, a new family code, and the Children of Russia program. The Children of Russia program promoted a number of social policies, including family planning; funding, however, was not sufficient to bring modern contraception to Russian women or to achieve the other goals associated with the program. Although the fraction's efforts focused on social policy, WOR Deputy Liudmila Zavadskaia served on the Committee on Legislation and Legal Reform and promoted the idea of "equal rights and equal opportunity" for women.

While in the Duma, WOR periodically published a booklet, *Informatsionnyi biulleten' Zhenshchiny Rossii (Informational Bulletin—Women of Russia)*, and a small monthly newspaper, *Zhenshchiny Rossii (Women of Russia)*, which appeared between April 1995 and June 1996.

In 1995 centrist political blocs fared poorly in the parliamentary elections. WOR finished fifth in the party-list balloting, but with forty-three parties and blocs competing, the popular vote was so fractured that WOR gained only 4.6 percent of the vote. This was insufficient to pass the 5 percent threshold to secure seats through the party-list ballot. Three WOR women, including Lakhova, were elected from single-member districts and joined other fractions in the Duma. WOR's political life as a fraction in the Duma ended. The movement, however, continued to exist. In April 1999 Fedulova announced that WOR would not independently contest the December 1999 parliamentary elections and threw the organization's support behind Moscow's mayor, Iurii Luzhkov, and his electoral bloc *Otechestvo* (Fatherland), which, in turn, later joined forces with former prime minister Evgenii Primakov to form the electoral bloc *Otechestvo—Vsia Rossiia* (Fatherland-All Russia). On September 1, 1999, WOR withdrew from the electoral alliance on the grounds that too few women had been included on the party-list ballot and that a traditional, conservative approach had been taken toward women's role in society. WOR contested the December 1999 parliamentary elections on its own but fared poorly, securing only 2.04 percent of the party-list vote, less than one-half its 1995 percentage, and failed to elect any candidates from single-member districts.

In the years between 1995 and 1999, WOR suffered from internal divisions that compromised its chances for electoral success. Commentary in the Russian press suggested that part of the reason for WOR's decision to withdraw from *Otechestvo—Vsia Rossiia* stemmed from the poor relationship between Fedulova and Lakhova. In 1996 Lakhova left WOR and created a new organization with a name strikingly close to that of WOR, *Obshcherossiiskoe Obshchestvenno-Politicheskoe Dvizhenie Zhenshchin Rossii* (the All-Russian Sociopolitical Movement of Russia). Fedulova complained that the virtually identical names confused the populace and led many to associate WOR, incorrectly, with Lakhova's organization. Lakhova had joined Luzhkov's electoral bloc later than

Fedulova and was placed in the fourth position on the *Otechestvo—Vsia Rossia* party list of candidates. The original electoral bloc, Women of Russia, thus had split into two movements whose leaders were widely regarded as unable to cooperate.

WOR's success in the 1993 parliamentary elections was one of the high points of women's political activism during the 1990s. Within the State Duma, WOR worked to advance social programs designed to promote the well-being of children, families, and women. After the narrow loss in 1995 and the severe electoral setback in 1999, women-only electoral blocs as a strategy for advancing women's causes appeared an unlikely future option.

Cross-references: All-Russian Sociopolitical Movement of Women of Russia, Alevtina Fedulova, Ekaterina Lakhova, Political Participation by Russian Women in the Transitional Period, Women's Union of Russia (WUR).

Suggested Readings

Buckley, Mary. "Adaptation of the Soviet Women's Committee: Deputies' Voices from 'Women of Russia.' " In *Post-Soviet Women: From the Baltic to Central Asia*, edited by Mary Buckley, 157–185. Cambridge: Cambridge University Press, 1997.

Buckley, Mary. "From Faction Not to Party: 'Women of Russia' in the Duma." In *Women and Political Change: Perspectives from East-Central Europe*, edited by Sue Bridger, 151–167. New York: St. Martin's Press, 1999.

Koriakin, Vera. "Zhenshchiny Rossii" (Women of Russia). *Moskvichka*, no. 4 (August 1999): 4.

Lakhova, Ekaterina. *Moi put' v politiku (My Path into Politics)*. Moscow: Aurika, 1995.

Racioppi, Linda, and Katherine O'Sullivan See. *Women's Activism in Contemporary Russia*. Philadelphia: Temple University Press, 1997.

Slater, Wendy. " 'Women of Russia' and Women's Representation in Russian Politics." In *Russia in Transition: Politics, Privatization and Inequality*, edited by David Lane, 76–90. New York: Longman, 1995.

Carol Nechemias

"Women of the Don" Union (*Soiuz "Zhenshchiny Dona"*) (1993–)

A union of organizations with a strong, but not exclusively women's, orientation in the Rostov region of southern Russia.

Soiuz "Zhenshchiny Dona" ("Women of the Don" Union) was established in Novocherkassk in 1993 as the outcome of the first forum for women of the region. Over 100 attended the forum, representing thirteen cities in the region. The principal goal involved promoting women's participation in the political, economic, social, and cultural life of the region. Novocherkassk was not the regional capital and, with a population of about 300,000, was considered a provincial town; nonetheless, "Women of the Don" emerged as one of the two or three best-known, most influential, and most effective women's groups in Russia's regions. Because of the proximity of Rostov to Chechnia, where war had cost 80,000 lives of servicemen and civilians by 1996, an important part of the Union's mandate also included protecting human rights and promoting peace. Many of the union's member organizations, such as the local affiliates of the Committee of Soldiers' Mothers, were involved in counseling soldiers and their families.

"Women of the Don" excelled at citizen diplomacy, hosting international conferences on the theme Women for Life without War or Violence, which received widespread favorable publicity. Members also participated as peace envoys to Chechnia and engaged with women and women's organizations from the breakaway republic. The work of "Women of the Don," nevertheless, was much broader than conflict resolution. It collected and distributed information on the social status of women, encouraged women to assume leadership roles in government and society, analyzed the work of local governments, including their administrative budgets, and aided disadvantaged individuals whose rights had been violated. An example of the ways in which "Women of the Don" assisted those in need was sponsorship of regular public meetings that offered social and legal counseling. The purpose of such gatherings was to protect the rights of individuals from the least advantaged groups within the population by educating them of their rights, advising them of legal procedures, and intervening on their behalf when possible. The primary target groups for these meetings were women, the elderly, the poor, the disabled, orphans, and military conscripts.

Several other organizations within the Union housed similar consulting centers that focused on various target populations. *Sudarynia* (Madame) in Taganrog, for example, dealt primarily with women's issues, including domestic violence and child support. The needs of the elderly were the primary concern of *Nadezhda* (Hope) in Kamensk-Shakhtinskii. Additional counseling centers were scattered across the Rostov region. In 1998 the Union was awarded a grant of $74,000 from the Ford Foundation to strengthen the development of a network of social and legal consulting centers in seven cities in the Rostov region.

The "Women of the Don" Union worked on issues that involved and affected both men and women. It provided an invaluable bridge between those who focused on women's issues and those who focused on human rights, the elderly, and the disabled.

Cross-references: Committee of Soldiers' Mothers of Russia, Foreign Funding and the Women's Movement in Russia.

Suggested Readings

Abubikirova, N. I., T. A. Klimenkova, E. V. Kotchkina, M. A. Regentova, and T. G. Troinova, eds. *Women's Non-Governmental Organizations in Russia and the NIS: A Directory*. Moscow: Aslan, 1998.

Sal'e, M., ed. *Zhenshchin za Zhizn' bez Boyn i Nasiliia (Women for Life without War and for Peace)*. Rostov-na-Donu, 1998.

Soiuz "Zhenshchiny Dona." Informatsionnyi Vypusk (Informational Bulletin). Novocherkassk. Monthly publication.

Sarah Henderson

The Women's Club-Café *Sudarynia* (ca. 1990–)

An organization founded in St. Petersburg in the early 1990s by Liudmila Nikolaevna Ivanova. Ivanova creatively drew on her networks to create a women's group and philanthropic projects that also provided salaried work for several members.

The St. Petersburg's Women's Club-Café *Sudarynia* was founded in the early 1990s by Liudmila Nikolaevna Ivanova after she left the crumbling Soviet Women's Committee (SWC). Ivanova was a well-connected, former Intourist guide who used contacts with Westerners and SWC to open a women's café. The goal of the café-club was to provide a small number of members with a living and to create a structure to support philanthropic efforts on behalf of women and children. Ivanova's prior experience working with children, especially abandoned babies, had made her aware of the serious problems that existed, and she was committed to using the café to benefit others in the city. The café served traditional Russian cuisine and sold women's handicrafts. The proceeds from *Sudarynia* were given to unemployed women, women in hospitals, and children at City Orphanage Number 10. The women from the club-café also read to the children and made routine visits to deliver books, crayons, and candy. Each month, members held birthday parties for children at the orphanage and celebrations honoring the survivors of the World War II 900-day siege of Leningrad. City singers, dancers, clowns, and storytellers assisted in the celebrations as members served homemade meals and sweets. Café *Sudarynia* earned its money to support such events by serving primarily foreign tourist groups. The café provided full-time work for five Club members. Contacts with the mayor's office, which frequently requested catering, Intourist, and the former SWC proved crucial to the club's success. Former SWC members, for instance, helped Ivanova locate and refurbish the café. Ivanova's efforts reflected well on her leadership but also illustrated the significance of the SWC network in post-Soviet society.

Cross-reference: Soviet Women's Committee (SWC).

Suggested Readings

Gottlick, Jane F. Berthusen. "From the Ground Up: Women's Organizations and Democratization in Russia." In *Democratization and Women's Grassroots Movements*, edited by Jill M. Bystydzienski and Joti Sekhon, 241–261. Bloomington: Indiana University Press, 1999.

McMahon, Patrice C. "The Effect of Economic and Political Reforms on Soviet/Russian Women." In *Women in the Age of Economic Transformation*, edited by Nahid Aslangeigui, Steven Pressman, and Gale Summerfield, 59–76. New York: Routledge, 1994.

Nechemias, Carol. "The Prospects for a Soviet Women's Movement: Opportunities and Obstacles." In *Perestroika from Below: Social Movements in the Soviet Union*, edited by Judith B. Sedaitis and Jim Butterfield, 73–96. Boulder, CO: Westview Press, 1991.

Racioppi, Linda, and Katherine O'Sullivan See. "Organizing Women before and after the Fall: Women's Politics in the Soviet Union and Post-Soviet Russia." *Signs* (Summer 1995): 818–850.

Jane F. Berthusen Gottlick

Women's Humanitarian Collegium (*Zhenskii gumanitarnyi kollegium*) (1995–)

A St. Petersburg organization of academic women established to support and promote research on women and create favorable conditions for women to enhance their academic careers.

The *Zhenskii gumanitarnyi kollegium* (Women's Humanitarian Collegium) was founded in St. Petersburg in 1995 by a group of women actively engaged in the organization and development of the nongovernmental higher education system in Russia. The founders included Galina A. Fortunatova, Nataliia N. Chekmareva, Marina I. Dibrova, Nataliia A. Fedorova, Lubov A. Shilnikova, and Nina A. Tishkina. This group of women also established, at the same time, a nongovernmental educational institution, the Nevskii Institute of Linquistics and Culture. The Collegium and the Nevskii Institute worked together closely, and the Collegium was located in the Institute. The Collegium and the Nevskii Institute shared the goal of addressing women's problems in St. Petersburg and other regions of Russia. Among the key areas of concern were education, career development, and nurturing the next generation of women scholars. A women's studies program was started at the Nevskii Institute in September 1998.

As a general policy, the Collegium cooperated with governmental and nongovernmental organizations whose goals and missions it shared. As of late 1998, the collegium had organized three major research conferences. The Nevskii Institute was the principal sponsor of the conferences, and the students majoring in public relations organized and managed the events. The themes were Education in the Contemporary World (1996), From the History of the Woman Question in Russia (1997), and the Woman Question in the Context of National Culture (1998). Three books, edited by Ol'ga R. Demidova and Galina A. Fortunatova, resulted from the scholarly conferences held from 1996 to 1998. In July 1999 the conference theme was Women in a Man's World: Finding Her Path.

In addition to the major conferences the Collegium participated regularly in roundtables and scholarly discussions pertaining to women's issues. The Collegium was also involved in ten conferences in other cities sponsored by the Nevskii Institute, and it published several articles in the journal *Zhenshchina v rossiiskom obshestve (Woman in Russian Society*), published by Ivanovo State University.

As part of its ongoing activity, the Collegium maintained contacts with researchers in other countries and welcomed the participation of foreign scholars in its activities. The institute also cooperated with other women's studies programs. As part of its broader mission, the Collegium participated in the work of the Department for Foreign Students at the Nevskii Institute, organizing lectures, excursions, and student conferences devoted to women's issues.

As with other women's projects in Russia in the late 1990s, funding was a crucial issue. The collegium was actively seeking funds to help support its projects and seminars. As of the late 1990s, it was one of St. Petersburg's most important academic organizations focused on women.

Cross-references: Academic Feminism in St. Petersburg, Gender/Women's Studies in Russia, Ivanovo, Women's Movement.

Suggested Readings

Demidova, O. R., ed. *Ei ne dano prokladyvat' novye puti? Iz istorii zhenskogo dvizheniia v Rossii. Vipusk 2. Sbornik nauchnih trudov (Is Not She the One to Pave New Ways? From the History of the Women's Movement in Russia. Issue 2. Collected Works)*. St. Petersburg: Dorn, 1998. (This work arose from the 1997 conference.)

Demidova, O. R., ed. *Zhenskii vopros v kontekste natsional'noi kul'turi. Tezisi dokladov Mezhdunarodnoi nauchnoi konferentsii (The Woman Question in the Context of National Culture: Theses of Reports from an International Conference)*. St. Petersburg: St. Petersburg State Academy of Culture, 1998. (This work was based on the 1998 conference.)

Fortunatova, Galina A., et al., eds. *Obrazovanie v sovremennom mire. Sbornik tezisov po materialam mezhdunarodnoi nauchnoi konferentsii (Education in the Contemporary World: A Collection of Theses Based on Materials from an International Conference)*. St. Petersburg: St. Petersburg State Academy of Culture, 1996. (This work was based on the 1996 conference.)

Ganelin, R. M., ed. *O blagorodstve i preimuzchestve zhenskogo pola. Iz istorii zhenskogo voprosa v Rossii. Sbornik nauchnikh trudov (On the Nobility and Advantages of the Female Sex: Out of the History of the Woman Question in Russia: A Collection of Scholarly Works)*. St. Petersburg: St. Petersburg State Academy of Culture, 1997.

Tishkin, G. A., et al., eds. *Zhenshchini serebrianogo veka: zhizn' i tvorchestvo. Tezisi dokladov 3-ii nauchnoi konferentsii "Rossiiskie zhenshchini i evropeiskaia kul'tura" (Women of the Silver Age: Life and Work: Theses of Reports to the Third Conference, "Russian Women and European Culture")*. St. Petersburg: St. Petersburg State Academy of Culture, 1996.

Norma Corigliano Noonan

Women's Information Network (*Zhenskaia informatsionnaia set'*, or *Zhenset*) (1996–)

A Moscow-based organization, that maintained a database on the women's movement, disseminated information on women's projects, organized seminars, and published a quarterly journal.

The *Zhenskaia informatsionnaia set'* (Women's Information Network, or *Zhenset*) was founded in Moscow in 1996 by Tatiana Georgievna Troinova. *Zhenset* evolved out of the Women's Information Project (1993–1996), a resource center funded with aid from the German Ministry of Social Affairs. This project, in which Troinova was actively involved, in cooperation with several other women leaders, developed a database of organizations in the women's movement and organized seminars for women from various regions of Russia several times a year. The seminars focused on topics to assist women's social and political development during Russia's transition. Themes included women's participation in elections, regional and national mechanisms to improve women's situation in post-Soviet Russia, and women in politics. In 1996, when the project ended, the organization was dissolved by mutual agreement. Troinova formed the Women's Information Network, which was officially registered at the federal level. *Zhenset* continued the work of the Women's Information Project, with assistance from the U.S. Agency of International Development (USAID), the Eurasia Foundation, the Embassy of the Netherlands, the Global Fund for Women, and the Moscow city government. Maintenance and expansion of the database of women's organizations were a primary goal of the group, as well as disseminating information about the groups. Several prominent women involved in other organizations, including N. I. Abubikirova, T. A. Klimenkova, E. V. Kochkina, and M. A. Regentova, together with Troinova, cooperatively edited and published in 1998 the invaluable reference work *Zhenskie nepravitel'stvennye organizatsii Rossii i SNG: Spravochnik (Women's Nongovernmental Organizations in Russia and the NIS: A Directory*). One of *Zhenset*'s most important activities was the publication of a journal, *Prava zhenshchin v Rossii: Zakonodatel'stvo i praktika (Women's Rights in Russia: Legislation and Practice).* Zhenset also sponsored translations of Western works into Russian and served as a consultant on the Russian women's movements to various organizations, including the State Duma. The organization also published a newsletter, *About Us and about Our Cause.* Troinova and a small staff operated *Zhenset*, which was located in central Moscow. Troinova was trained in math and later in structural linguistics. Prior to entering full-time work on women's issues, she worked in the State Planning Committee (*Gosplan*) and in academic institutions.

In the late 1990s, *Zhenset* played a pivotal role in developing and maintaining information about women's organizations.

Cross-reference: Consortium of Women's Nongovernmental Associations.

Suggested Readings

Abubikirova, N. I. et al., eds. *Zhenskie nepravitel'stvennye organizatsii Rossii i SNG: Spravochnik* (translated as *Women's Non-Governmental Organizations in Russia and the NIS: A Directory*). Moscow: Aslan, 1998. (Published with the assistance of USAID and the Embassy of the Netherlands.)

Prava zhenshchin v Rossii: Zakonodatel'stvo i praktika (Women's Rights in Russia: Legislation and Practice). A quarterly journal. Moscow.

Norma Corigliano Noonan

Women's League (*Liga zhenshchin*) (1992–1999) and Women's Initiative (*Zhenskaia initsiativa* (1999–)

A confederation of women's and other nongovernmental organizations, founded in 1992. As a result of various political developments within the women's movement, it was transformed into a new organization in 1999.

The Women's League was formed in 1992, uniting large foundations, centers, and associations as well as small groups. The original membership included the *Fond zhenskie initsiativy* (Women's Initiatives Foundation), *Mezhdunarodnaia liga zhenshchin-pisatel'nits* (International League of Women Writers), *Mezhdunarodnyi zhenskii tsentr Gaia* (International Women's Center Gaia), *Zhenskaia organizatsiia "Zhenshchina i konversiia"* (the Organization "Women and Conversion"), *Assotsiatsiia "Tvorchestvo"* (the "Creativity" Association), *Moskovskii tsentr zhenskikh remeslel* (the Moscow Center of Women's Handicrafts), *Soiuz zhenshchin iuristov* (the Union of Women Lawyers), *Mezdunarodnyi tsentr "Budushchie zhenshchiny"* (the "Women's Future International Center"), and the *Assotsiatsiia zhenshchiny-predprimatel'nits* (Association of Women Entrepreneurs).

All the member organizations retained their independent status but agreed to form a cooperative partnership in order to promote equal rights and equal opportunities for women. The Women's League cooperated with official organs of government, political parties and movements, and other organizations. The Women's League was headed by five cochairs, drawn from the member organizations, and a Coordinating Board.

The members of the Women's League worked together to implement social projects and programs. In December 1993, the League was one of the organizers of the exhibition, *New Professions*, aimed at the promotion of women in business through stimulation of joint ventures throughout Russia and Europe.

The League inspired the *Belyi tanets* (White Dance) Festival in 1993. The concept of the White Dance referred to an old Russian custom in which women could invite men to dance. In this case, the phrase was intended to connote women's initiative and was an appeal to the whole society. The Festival was held in conjunction with the All-Russia Conference on Russia and the World Economy in Moscow. The festival included exhibits of women's crafts and business, concerts of children's groups, and folk art displays. Even more important, it included a *Politicheskaia tribuna dlia zhenshchin* (Political Tribunal for Women). The participants were women from the new political parties and blocs and women activists. At this forum, it was decided to establish the organizational committee to prepare for the All-Russia Women's Congress in 1994.

The League worked with the Ministry of Social Defense, with the Commission on Women, Family, and Demography of the President of the Russian Federation, and with commissions organized to prepare and accomplish the goals of the United Nations (UN) International Year of the Family and the Beijing UN Fourth World Conference on Women. In particular, the League was a member of the organizing committee for the All-Russian Women's Congress held in Moscow in 1994, which discussed the national report for the Beijing Conference in 1995.

The organizations in the League attempted to inform one another of new developments, exchange expertise on women's issues, offer consultation on parliamentary bills and other official documents, and participate in political activism on behalf of women, children, and the family. The League participants also advocated women's active involvement in electoral politics.

As an organization of organizations, the League depended on the commitment of active women's groups. Some of the participating organizations accomplished their designated goals and projects, but others did not survive Russia's difficult transition in the 1990s. Some organizations left the League because their focus and activities changed. As a result, the League was inactive for a time in the late 1990s. In 1999 it was reorganized under the leadership of Liudmila Shvetsova, an important figure in Moscow government, into the *Zhenskaia initsiativa* (Women's Initiative) and was registered under the new name.

Cross-references: Commission on Women, Family, and Demography, Elena Ershova, the International Women's Center Gaia, International League of Women Writers, Liudmila Shvetsova.

Suggested Reading

Racioppi, Linda, and Katherine O'Sullivan See. *Women's Activism in Contemporary Russia*. Philadelphia: Temple University Press, 1997.

Nadezhda Shvedova

Women's Union of Russia or WUR (*Soiuz zhenshchin Rossii*) (1990–)

An organization founded in 1990 by former leaders of the Soviet Women's Committee; cosponsor of Women of Russia electoral bloc; adviser to the President of the Russian Federation and the State Duma on women's issues.

The *Soiuz zhenshchin Rossii* (Women's Union of Russia, or WUR) was one of the few 1990s Russian women's movements with official roots in the Soviet era. Its leaders, members, organizational network, and even ideology were derived from the *Komitet sovetskikh zhenshchin* (Soviet Women's Committee, or SWC), founded during the Communist era. Thus, it held a controversial position among other women activists, particularly among feminists. Nonetheless, because its members filled positions of power in the legislative and executive branches of government, WUR played a prominent role defining women's issues in Russia during the 1990s.

According to WUR's literature, the Union officially began its activities in 1990, when it held a founding conference in Moscow. As an organization, however, WUR was in many ways simply a renaming of the SWC. Many of the group's leaders were leading members of the SWC; the WUR chair, Alevtina Vasilevna Fedulova, for example, had been SWC president. In 1989–1990 SWC experienced massive cuts in its state-provided budget and was forced to look for outside funding. It also needed to shed its association with the Communist Party of the Soviet Union (CPSU), which was in increasing disfavor among both elites and ordinary people. As a result, SWC's leaders formed WUR on the foundations of the old structure.

Thanks, in part, to these roots, the union played an important role in making women's issues visible during the transitional period. It vocalized concern about the dismantling of child-care centers, the de facto nonpayment of maternity leave, and the drop in women's political representation in political organs. In 1993 WUR jointly sponsored the electoral bloc Women of Russia, which, by appealing to disenfranchised women, garnered more than 8 percent of the proportional representation vote. WUR's success was, in part, contingent on resources from its previous incarnation. WUR had connections, political skills, and insider knowledge that other groups did not possess.

The SWC legacy was also evident in WUR's approach to women's issues. Promoting the communist model of worker–mother, SWC often equated women's issues with family or children's issues. WUR also stressed child care, maternity leave, and other benefits that would ease women's roles rather than change gender roles and end men's lack of involvement in the home. WUR's approach put it at odds with newer women's and feminist movements. WUR called its philosophy "closer to real women," but Russian feminists pointed out that protective policies could disadvantage women in the workplace by making them expensive, inefficient workers for employers to hire. Conflicts between WUR and feminists over such issues were at times quite pointed.

Nonetheless, WUR did focus on advancing the status of women and ran myriad programs designed to promote this goal. WUR sponsored clubs for female small-business owners and women workers in various professional arenas, as well as schools for unemployed women. In cooperation with a Spanish firm, it ran a cosmetology school. Its Democracy for All campaign supported women's political participation through roundtables and campaign training, and, under this rubric, it supported the Women of Russia bloc. It was concerned with mobilizing women throughout Russia and raising consciousness of women's status. To this end, it had hundreds of local affiliates acting as relay points between its central offices and its members. These offices organized training sessions, raised awareness, and provided information on woman's rights. WUR also lobbied actively, calling for government support of the family, extended social benefits, quotas for women in leadership positions, and other policies.

Because WUR worked actively on women's issues, at times it cooperated with other women's groups, including feminists. As a result WUR edged slowly toward ideological positions closer to those of other activists. For example, WUR gradually began to call for equality in family roles and responsibilities, in addition to government assistance for women's roles. In 1997, in cooperation with other women's groups, including the Moscow Center for Gender Studies and the Independent Women's Forum, WUR helped the Duma Committee on the Affairs of Women, Family, and Youth draft and pass a comprehensive position paper, *Kontseptsiia zakonotvorcheskoi deiatel'nosti po obespecheniiu ravnykh prav i ravnykh vozmozhnostei muzhchin i zhenshchin* (Legal Framework on Protecting the Equal Rights and Opportunities of Men and Women). Its negotiations with other women's groups were difficult and at times tense, but, overall, WUR began to cooperate successfully with some of them. WUR emphasized, however, that it was not a feminist group but supported the interests of the "real" or "common" woman.

WUR's ideological position was important because its representatives held significant positions in the Russian government during the 1990s. For example, Ekaterina Lakhova, a leading member of WUR in the early 1990s, was chair of the President's Commission on Women, Family, and Demography. Through her position, WUR played an important role defining women's issues in the Russian Federation.

WUR began to experience internal conflict in the mid-1990s. In November 1996, Lakhova ended her affiliation with the Women of Russia bloc and thus with WUR and Fedulova. Her new organization, the All-Russian Sociopolitical Movement of Women of Russia, became a separate entity and began to solidify connections with feminist groups. Although its programmatic goals were similar to WUR's, Lakhova was more aggressive about building ties to other groups. In March 1997, for example, Lakhova signed the Charter of Women's Solidarity, designed to promote cooperation and harmony among various feminist groups, but Fedulova did not. The charter was written by Lakhova's close friend and colleague Svetlana Aivazova, also part of the new group.

WUR's prominence meant that its fate was important to the development of women's and feminist movements in Russia. Despite its conflict with other groups and within its own membership, its activities helped promote women's issues and advance women's status.

Cross-references: Charter of Women's Solidarity, Alevtina Fedulova, Ekaterina Lakhova, Commission on Women, Family and Demography, Moscow Center for Gender Studies, Independent Women's Forum, Soviet Women's Committee, Women of Russia.

Suggested Readings

Buckley, Mary. "Adaptation of the Soviet Women's Committee: Deputies' Voices from Women of Russia." In *Post-Soviet Women: From the Baltic to Central Asia*, edited by Mary Buckley, 157–185. Cambridge: Cambridge University Press, 1997.

Caiazza, Amy. "Military Service and Maternal Obligation: Gender, Citizenship and Civil Society in Contemporary Russia, 1993–1997." Ph.D. Diss., Indiana University, 1999.

Konstantinova, Valentina. "Women's Political Coalitions in Russia (1990–1994)." In *Women's Voices in Russia Today*, edited by Anna Rotkirch and Elina Haavio-Mannila, 235–247. Brookfield, VT: Dartmouth, 1996.

Lipovskaia, Ol'ga, "New Women's Organisations." In *Perestroika and Soviet Women*, edited by Mary Buckley, 72–81. Cambridge: Cambridge University Press, 1992.

Lipovskaya, Ol'ga. "Women's Groups in Russia." In *Post-Soviet Women: From the Baltic to Central Asia*, edited by Mary Buckley, 186–197. Cambridge: Cambridge University Press, 1997.

Posadskaya, Anastasia. "A Feminist Critique of Policy, Legislation and Social Consciousness in Post-Socialist Russia." In *Women in Russia*, edited by Anastasia Posadskaya, 164–182. London: Verso, 1994.

Racioppi, Linda, and Katherine O'Sullivan See. *Women's Activism in Contemporary Russia*. Philadelphia: Temple University Press, 1997.

Rule, Wilma, and Nadezhda Shvedova. "Women in Russia's First Multiparty Election." In *Russian Women in Politics and Society*, edited by Wilma Rule and Norma C. Noonan, 40–59. Westport, CT: Greenwood Press, 1996.

Slater, Wendy. "Women of Russia and Women's Representation in Russian Politics." In *Russia in Transition*, edited by David Lane, 76–90. New York: Longman, 1995.

Amy Caiazza

Z

Zdravomyslova, Elena Andreevna (1953–)

A sociologist specializing in Russian women's movements who helped develop gender studies in St. Petersburg.

The daughter of famous Soviet sociologist Andrei Zdravomyslov and school director Nadezhda Afanasieva, Elena Zdravomyslova grew up in a liberal and cultivated Leningrad family. She studied at an English-language school and in 1970, at the age of sixteen, entered the Department of Philosophy of the Leningrad State University. During her student years, Zdravomyslova mingled with the bohemian intelligentsia. She graduated in 1975 and finished her graduate studies in 1978 in the sociology of knowledge. Later she specialized in the theory of social movements, and she defended her doctoral dissertation in 1997.

In 1978 Zdravomyslova became a researcher at the Institute of Socioeconomic Problems in Leningrad, but she lost her job for political reasons in 1984. In 1988 liberalization of society under Perestroika and Glasnost made it possible for her to return to the Institute; she was employed in the Sector for the Study of Social Movements, headed by Vladimir Kostiushev. In 1989 part of the Institute of Socioeconomic Problems became the Institute of Sociology, and Zdravomyslova joined this new Institute. As part of her research, Zdravomyslova studied political symbolism and women's movements, including feminist organizations and the Committee of Soldiers' Mothers of Russia. She was also able to supplement her education with study abroad; she was a visiting scholar at the University of California, Berkeley, in 1991, at Stanford University in 1994, and in Dortmund, Germany, in 1994 and 1995.

In 1993 Zdravomyslova organized a sector for gender research in the new Center for Independent Social Research in St. Petersburg. The Center specialized in qualitative research methods and life-story interviews. Zdravomyslova belonged to the few scholars who managed to integrate research and teaching in the unstable postsocialist conditions. Her Sector for Gender Studies chose promising young Russian sociologists and trained them in gender studies through empirical research. Among the young scholars recruited were Tatiana Baraulina,

Zhanna Chernova, Sofiia Chikina, Katerina Gerasimova, and Andrei Khanzin. Research topics included unemployed women, young people, child socialization, male drinking, and female and male sexuality. From 1996 the mission to train graduate students continued at the European University of St. Petersburg, where Zdravomyslova taught gender studies together with Anna Temkina.

Cross-references: Academic Feminism in St. Petersburg, Committee of Soldiers' Mothers of Russia, Gender/Women's Studies in Russia, Anna Temkina.

Suggested Readings

Baraulina, Tatiana, and Andrei Khanzin. "Gender Differences in the Life Strategies of Russian Youth." In *Women's Voices in Russia Today*, edited by Anna Rotkirch and Elina Haavio-Mannila, 107–123. Aldershot: Dartmouth Press, 1996.

Chuikina, Sonya. "The Role of Women Dissidents in Creating the Milieu." In *Women's Voices in Russia Today*, edited by Anna Rotkirch and Elina Haavio-Mannila, 189–205. Aldershot: Dartmouth Press, 1996.

Gerasimova, Katarina, Natalia Troyan, and Elena Zdravomyslova. "Gender Stereotypes in Pre-School Children's Literature." In *Women's Voices in Russia Today*, edited by Anna Rotkirch and Elina Haavio-Mannila, 71–87. Aldershot: Dartmouth Press, 1996.

Voronkov, Viktor M., and Elena Zdravomyslova, eds. *Biographical Perspectives on Post-Socialist Societies*. St. Petersburg: Center for Independent Social Research, 1997.

Zdravomyslova, Elena. "Opportunities and Framing in the Transition to Democracy. The Case of Russia." In *Comparative Perspectives on Social Movements. Political Opportunities, Mobilizing Structures and Cultural Framings*, edited by D. McAdam, J. McCarthy, and M. Zald, 122–140. Cambridge: Cambridge University Press, 1996.

Zdravomyslova, Elena. *Paradigmy issledovaniia obshchestvennykh dvizhenii (Paradigms of Social Movement Research*). St. Petersburg: Nauka, 1993.

Zdravomyslova, Elena. "Prerequisites of Civil Society in Soviet Russia: Café 'Saigon' as Public Sphere." In *Civil Society in the European North*, edited by Elena Zdravomyslova and Kaja Heikkinen, 116–120. St. Petersburg: Center for Independent Social Research, 1996.

Zdravomyslova, Elena. "Problems of Becoming a Housewife." In *Women's Voices in Russia Today*, edited by Anna Rotkirch and Elina Haavio-Mannila, 33–48. Aldershot: Dartmouth Press, 1996.

Zdravomyslova, Elena, and Anna Temkina, eds. *Gendernoe Izmerenie Sotsial'noi i Politicheskoi Aktivnosti v Perekhodnyi Period (Gender Dimension of Social and Political Activity during the Transitional Period*). St. Petersburg: Center for Independent Social Research, 1996.

Zdravomyslova, Elena, and Anna Temkina, eds. *"Sotsial'noe konstruirovanie gendera"* (The Social Construction of Gender). *Sotsiologicheskii zhurnal*, nos. 3–4 (1998): 171–182.

Anna Rotkirch

Glossary of Abbreviations and Major Terms

All Russian terms are given in Library of Congress transliteration. With the names of a few very famous people, the common English spelling is given.

All-Russian: a term used since 1992 to mean a policy or organization that applies to the entire Russian Federation.

All-Union: a Soviet term meaning a policy or system that prevailed throughout the USSR; roughly equivalent to the term "national" or "federal" in the United States.

Bolshevik Revolution: See October Revolution.

Brezhnev, L. I.: first, General Secretary of the CPSU (1964–1982), then president of the USSR (1977–1982).

Chernomyrdin, Viktor: Prime Minister of the Russian Federation, 1992–1998.

Chin'i (ranks): the system of professional classification used in Russia prior to 1917, which established one's salary, benefits, and even status in society.

CIS: Commonwealth of Independent States.

Comintern: acronym for Third Communist International, created by V. I. Lenin in 1920 after the establishment of Soviet Russia as the organization to promote communist revolution. The Comintern was disbanded in 1943 by J. V. Stalin as part of the new image of international cooperation that the USSR wanted to convey during the war. In 1947 the Cominform (Communist Information Bureau) was established, but it did not have very much influence.

Commonwealth of Independent States (CIS): the loose confederation of the independent republics of the former Soviet Union. Formed in December 1991, it includes the former republics, except Latvia, Estonia, and Lithuania, although some of the former republics do not participate in specific aspects of the CIS.

Communist Party of the Russian Federation (CPRF or KPRF): the reconstituted Communist Party in post-Soviet Russia.

Communist Party of the Soviet Union (CPSU): the name of the Russian Communist Party after the formation of the USSR.

Congress of People's Deputies: name for the Soviet parliament, 1989–1991, and for the Russian parliament, 1991–1993. The tripartite legislature, made up of deputies who were popularly elected and those elected from official organizations, in turn, elected a smaller Supreme Soviet.

CPSU: Communist Party of the Soviet Union.

Demokratizatsiia (democratization): a policy pursued during the years of perestroika in order to begin the process of democratization of Soviet politics. It involved a fundamental restructuring of the Supreme Soviet and reformulation of the chief executive's office from the titular chairman of the Presidium of the Supreme Soviet into the president of the USSR. The majority of the new Congress of People's Deputies was selected in competitive elections, as opposed to the former practice of nominating one person for each seat in the Supreme Soviet.

D.o.b.: date of birth.

El'stin, Boris: See Boris Yeltsin.

February Revolution: the overthrow of the tsar in late February 1917 (March 1917 in the Western calendar). Led by moderates who wanted a more viable government, this revolution was the first of two major revolutions in 1917. *See also* the October Revolution.

Federal Assembly: the bicameral parliament of the Russian Federation (1993–), which is divided into the popularly elected State Duma and the upper chamber, the Federation Council, which is made up of officials from Russia's constituent units.

Feminology: a uniquely Russian term for the study of women's historical role in Russia and their place in Russian political, economic, cultural, and social life. This term is often preferred to women's studies or gender studies. Its use also avoids reference to a concept more controversial in Russia, namely, feminism.

Gaidar, Egor (Yegor): Acting Prime Minister of the Russian Federation (May–December 1992) and a leading reformer in the post-Soviet era; Gaidar was the founder of the party Russia's Choice, which was important in the early post-Soviet era.

Glasnost (openness): the more liberal policy introduced after Gorbachev came to power in 1985. It referred to greater openness to revealing problems in society and more freedom in literature and the arts.

Guberniia: an administrative district; the term was used in Russia prior to the Bolshevik Revolution. After the revolution, the former *gubernia* became the oblast.

Gymnasium (*gimnazium*): a Russian high school with a strongly academic curriculum. This was the prevailing system of preuniversity education available before the November 1917 revolution.

Iabloko or *Yabloko*: the reform party headed by Grigorii Iavlinskii (also Yavlinsky). In Russian *Iabloko* means apple, and the nickname was chosen because of its similarity to Iavlinskii's last name.

Iavlinskii (also Yavlinsky), Grigorii: leader of a liberal reform party nicknamed *Iabloko (Yabloko)*.

International Women's Day: a holiday established in 1910 at an international congress of socialist women. Klara Zetkin was instrumental in its establishment. March 8 was established as International Women's Day among women socialists. It became a major commemorative day in the USSR. Subsequently, the holiday has been celebrated by feminists around the world.

Izpolkom (Executive Committee): a general term for the administrative unit of Soviet/ Russian government. The executive committee is headed by a mayor at the local level and by a governor at the regional or provincial level.

Izvestiia (News): Soviet newspaper published under the auspices of the government of the USSR; in the post-Soviet period, the newspaper continued publication under private auspices.

Kadet Party (Constitutional Democratic Party): a liberal, reformist political party active prior to the Bolshevik Revolution of 1917; it supported a limited constitutional democracy led by a representative national legislature.

Kandidat (Candidate): a Russian graduate degree, generally considered to be approximately equivalent to a Ph.D. It is the basic graduate degree needed if one wishes to pursue a career in higher education or research.

Khrushchev, N. S. (Nikita Sergeevich): first secretary of the CPSU (1953–1964) and Prime Minister of the Soviet government (1958–1964).

Lenin, V. I. (Vladimir Ilich): founder of the Soviet system, 1917–1991.

Leningrad: the name used for St. Petersburg, 1924–1991. After Lenin's death in 1924, the city was renamed for him. In 1991 the name was again changed to St. Petersburg.

Newly Independent States (NIS): refers to all the republics of the former Soviet Union.

NIS: Newly Independent States, the fifteen republics of the former USSR.

Nomenklatura: in the Soviet period, the CPSU's list of positions with political significance. Appointment to these positions was controlled by Party organs and usually reserved for CPSU members.

Oblast (province): a large administrative subdivision used in the Soviet period and afterward. The oblast superseded the former *guberniia.*

October Revolution: the Bolshevik Revolution occurred on October 25, 1917, under the Russian calendar, which was November 7, 1917, under the Western calendar. Sources often refer to it as the October Revolution.

Otechestvo (Fatherland): a political movement formed in the late 1990s around the personality of the popular mayor of Moscow, Iuri (Yuri) Luzhkov.

Perestroika (restructuring): Gorbachev's strategy for transforming the Soviet economy, 1985–1991.

Pravda (Truth): the official newspaper of the CPSU, established as the newspaper of the RSDLP/B before the revolution. In post-Soviet Russia, the newspaper continued publication under the auspices of the Communist Party of the Russian Federation (KPRF).

Primakov, Evgenii: Prime Minister of the Russian Federation, 1998–1999 and founder of the 1999 electoral bloc *Vsia Rossiia* (All-Russia).

Putin, Vladimir: Prime Minister of the Russian Federation (August–December 1999) and Acting President of the Russian Federation (January/2000–March/2000); elected President March 26, 2000.

RSDLP/B (also RSDRP/B): the Bolshevik faction of the Russian Social Democratic Party before the 1917 Revolutions.

RSFSR: Russian Socialist Federated Soviet Republic, the official name of the Russian republic within the USSR.

Russian Communist Party/Bolsheviks (RCP/B): the renamed Bolshevik faction after V. I. Lenin came to power in November 1917. The RCP/B became the ruling party of Russia. (In Russian publications, it is listed as RKP/B.)

Russian Federation: the official name of post-Soviet Russia.

Russian Social Democratic Labor Party (RSDLP or RSDRP): the Marxist Party in Russia, established in 1898. It split into several factions. The Bolshevik faction, headed by V. I. Lenin, came to power on November 7, 1917 (October 25, 1917, in the Russian calendar).

St. Petersburg: a city with an interesting history of name changes. Founded by Peter the Great in the early eighteenth century, it was renamed Petrograd (the Russian form of "Peter's city") during World War I in 1915. After Lenin's death, it was renamed Leningrad. In 1991 the name was changed to St. Petersburg in a popular election. It is sometimes called Peter or Peterburg.

Samizdat (self-publishing): the practice of privately circulating manuscripts to limited circles in the USSR. Intellectuals circulated typewritten manuscripts that could not be published in the Soviet Union. The term and the practice became well known in the Brezhnev years.

Soiuz Pravykh Sil (Union of Right-Wing Forces): a party formed in 1999 by former prime minister Sergei Kirienko, Irina Khakamada, and other younger political figures.

Sovet (or soviet): council; the name used for local organs of popular participation prior to the Bolshevik Revolution, which became the cornerstone of the name of the country, Union of Soviet Socialist Republics. The term Soviet was also widely used for legislative organs at all levels, from the national parliament—the USSR Supreme Soviet—to city councils.

Sovnarkhoz: acronym for the council of the people's economy; this was a term used for the local economic councils after the Bolshevik Revolution; the term was revived by Khrushchev in the 1950s to describe the economic districts that he established around the country.

Stakhanovites: workers who excelled and set production records. The term was derived from the achievements of a miner named Stakhanov, who in the 1930s set a record for coal extraction.

State Duma: since 1993, the popularly elected lower house of the reorganized Russian parliament, the Federal Assembly. The term was also used for the parliament of the Russian Empire, 1905–1917, and has roots in Russian history.

Subbotniki: Soviet-era term for the "voluntary days" on which workers contributed their labors to public works of social significance to the community on their day(s) off. Although nominally voluntary, there was great pressure to participate in the projects. The *subbotniki* were instituted during the Stalin era.

Supreme Soviet: the bicameral parliament of the USSR; in 1988 the structure was modified, and the term Supreme Soviet was used for the smaller, working legislative body indirectly elected by the Congress of People's Deputies. The term was used for the early post-Soviet parliament until 1993, when the parliament was renamed the Federal Assembly, and its chambers were renamed the State Duma (the elected lower house) and the Federation Council.

The Unity Electoral Bloc (also called Medved' [Bear]): an electoral bloc formed in 1999 that was associated with high-level officials in the Russian government, including Sergei Shoigu, and was supported by then Prime Minister Vladimir Putin.

Yeltsin, Boris: President of the Russian Republic (1990–1991) and of the Russian Federation (1992–1999).

Zemstvo: elective rural organization in pre-1917 Russia. The zemstvo served as a district council and handled administrative functions at the local level and also was one of the first examples of Russian local self-government.

Selected Bibliography

Abubikirova, N. I., T. A. Klimenkova, E. V. Kotchkina, M. A. Regentova, and T. G. Troinova, eds. *Zhenskie nepravitel'stvennye organizatsii Rossii i SNG: Spravochnik* (English edition: *Women's Non-Governmental Organizations in Russia and the NIS: A Directory*). Moscow: Aslan, 1998. (Published with the assistance of USAID and the Embassy of the Netherlands)

Aivazova, Svetlana. *Russkie zhenshchiny v labirinte ravnopraviia (Russian Women in the Labyrinth of Equal Rights)*. Moscow: RIK Rusanova, 1998.

Arbatova, Mariia. *Mne 40 let: avtobiograficheskii roman*. Moscow: AST, 1999.

Atkinson, Dorothy, Alexander Dallin, and Gail Warshofsky Lapidus, eds. *Women in Russia*. Stanford, CA: Stanford University Press, 1977.

Attwood, Lynne. *The New Soviet Man and Woman: Sex-Role Socialization in the USSR*. Bloomington: Indiana University Press, 1990.

Babaeva, L.V. *Zhenshchiny Rossii v usloviiakh sotsial'nogo pereloma: rabota, politika, povsednevnaia zhizn'*. Moscow: N.p., 1997.

Babich, N. Sh., G. N. Grishina, A. A. Denisova, and V. A. Rychagova. *Internet zhenshchinam: Katalog informatsionnykh resursov*. Moscow: Informatsiia-XXI Vek, 2000.

Baranskaya, Natalya. *A Week like Any Other: Novellas and Stories*. Translated by Pieta Monks. New York: Seal Press, 1989.

Belyakova, A. M., et al., eds. *Soviet Legislation on Women's Rights*. Moscow: Progress, 1978.

Bergman, Jay. *Vera Zasulich: A Biography*. Stanford, CA: Stanford University Press, 1983.

Bridger, Susan. *Women in the Soviet Countryside: Women's Roles in Rural Development in the Soviet Union*. Cambridge: Cambridge University Press, 1987.

Bridger, Sue, Rebecca Kay, and Kathryn Pinnick. *No More Heroines? Russia, Women and the Market*. New York: Routledge, 1996.

Browning, Genia K. *Women and Politics in the U.S.S.R.: Consciousness Raising and Soviet Women's Groups*. New York: St. Martin's Press, 1987.

Buckley, Mary. *Perestroika and Soviet Women*. Cambridge: Cambridge University Press, 1992.

Buckley, Mary. *Post-Soviet Women: From the Baltic to Central Asia*. Cambridge: Cambridge University Press, 1997.

Buckley, Mary. *Women and Ideology in the Soviet Union*. Ann Arbor: University of Michigan Press, 1989.

Chirkov, P. M. *Reshenie zhenskogo voprosa v SSSR (1917–1937)*. Moscow: *'Mysl'*, 1978.

Clements, Barbara Evans. *Bolshevik Feminist: The Life of Aleksandra Kollontai*. Bloomington: Indiana University Press, 1979.

Clements, Barbara Evans. *Bolshevik Women*. Cambridge: Cambridge University Press, 1997.

Clements, Barbara Evans. *Daughters of Revolution: A History of Women in the USSR*. Arlington Heights, IL: Harlan Davidson, 1994.

Clements, Barbara Evans, Barbara Alpern Engel, and Christine D. Worobec, eds. *Russia's Women: Accommodation, Resistance, Transformation*. Berkeley: University of California Press, 1991.

Demidova, O. R., et al., eds. *"Ei ne dano prokladyvat' novye puti . . . ?" Iz istorii zhenskogo dvizheniia v Rossii*. St. Petersburg: "*Dorn*," 1998.

Du Plessix Gray, Francine. *Soviet Women: Walking the Tightrope*. New York: Doubleday, 1989.

Edmondson, Linda Harriet, ed. *Feminism in Russia, 1900–1917*. Stanford, CA: Stanford University Press, 1984.

Edmondson, Linda Harriet, ed. *Women and Society in Russia and the Soviet Union*. Cambridge: Cambridge University Press, 1992.

Einhorn, Barbara. *Cinderella Goes to Market*. London: Verso, 1993.

Elwood, R. C. *Inessa Armand: Revolutionary and Feminist*. Cambridge: Cambridge University Press, 1992.

Engel, Barbara Alpern. *Mothers and Daughters: Women of the Intelligentsia in Nineteenth Century Russia*. Cambridge: Cambridge University Press, 1983.

Engel, Barbara Alpern, and Anastasia Posadskaya-Vanderbeck, eds. *A Revolution of Their Own: Voices of Women in Soviet History*. Boulder, CO: Westview Press, 1998.

Ershova, Elena Nikolaevna, and El'vira Evgen'evna Novikova. *SSSR—SshA: Zhenshchina i obshchestvo*. Moscow: Profizdat, 1988.

Ershova, El'vira B., ed. *Zhenshchiny Rossii—vchera, segodnia, zavtra*. Moscow: *Rossiia Molodaia*, 1994.

Farnsworth, Beatrice. *Aleksandra Kollontai: Socialism, Feminism, and the Bolshevik Revolution*. Stanford, CA: Stanford University Press, 1980.

Farnsworth, Beatrice, and Lynne Viola, eds. *Russian Peasant Women*. Oxford: Oxford University Press, 1992.

Figner, Vera. *Memoirs of a Revolutionist*. Introduction by Richard Stites. DeKalb: Northern Illinois University Press, 1991.

Fomicheva, L. N. *Nadezhda Konstantinovna Krupskaia: Zhizn' i deiatel'nost' v fotographiiakh i dokumentakh*. Moscow: Politizdat, 1974.

Foner, Philip S., ed. *Klara Zetkin: Selected Writings*. New York: International, 1984.

Fong, Monica. *The Role of Women in Rebuilding the Russian Economy*. Washington, DC: World Bank, 1993.

Funk, Nanette, and Magda Mueller, eds. *Gender Politics and Post-Communism: Reflections from Eastern Europe and the Former Soviet Union*. New York: Routledge, 1993.

Ganelin, P. Sh. *O blagorodstve i preimushchestve zhenskogo pola: Iz istorii zhenshogo voprosa v Rossii*. St. Petersburg: St. Petersburg State Academy of Culture, 1997.
Goldman, Wendy. *Women, the State and Revolution: Soviet Family Policy and Soviet Life, 1917–1936*. New York: Cambridge University Press, 1993.
Goscilo, Helena. *Fruits of Her Plume: Essays on Contemporary Russian Women's Culture*. Armonk, NY: M. E. Sharpe, 1993.
Goskomstat Rossii. *Zhenshchiny i muzhchiny Rossii: Kratkii statisticheskii sbornik*. Moscow: Goskomstat, 1998.
Goskomstat SSSR. *Zhenshchiny v SSSR 1989: Statisticheskie materialy*. Moscow: *Finansy i statistika*, 1989. (An annual publication.)
Gromova, S. *Lady Leader—Ledi Lider: Daidzhest*. Moscow: Press-Solo, 1997.
Hansson, Carola, and Karen Liden. *Moscow Women*. New York: Pantheon, 1983.
Heldt, Barbara. *Terrible Perfection: Women and Russian Literature*. Bloomington: Indiana University Press, 1987.
Holland, Barbara, ed. *Soviet Sisterhood*. Bloomington: Indiana University Press, 1985.
Jancar, Barbara Wolfe. *Women under Communism*. Baltimore: Johns Hopkins University Press, 1978.
Kay, Rebecca. *Russian Women and Their Organizations: Gender, Discrimination and Grassroots Women's Organizations, 1991–1996*. New York: St. Martin's Press, 2000.
Khotkina, Z. A., N. L. Pushkareva, and E. I. Trofimova, eds. *Zhenshchina, gender, kul'tura*. Moscow: MCGS, 1999.
Klimenkova, T. A. *Zhenshchina kak fenomen kul'tury: vzgliad iz Rossii*. Moscow: "Preobrazhenie," 1996.
Kollontai, Alexandra. *Selected Writings*. Introduction and commentaries by Alix Holt. New York: Norton, 1977.
Kostygova, T. M., and I. Ia. Kosheleva, eds. *My-zhenshchiny*. Moscow: Politizdat, 1989.
Kotliarskaia, E. M., ed. *Zhenshchiny v SSSR: shtrikhi k portetu*. Moscow: "*Russkii iazyk*," 1988.
Kuslikova, I. S., et al. *Zhenshchiny strany Sovetov: Kratkii istoricheskii ocherk*. Moscow: Politizdat, 1977.
Lakhova, E. F. *Moi put' v politiku (My Path into Politics)*. Moscow: Aurika, 1995.
Lakhova, E. F. *Zhenskoe dvizhenie v gody reformy: problemy i perspektivy*. Moscow: "*Informatik*," 1998.
Lapidus, Gail Warshofsky. *Women in Soviet Society: Equality, Development, and Social Change*. Berkeley: University of California Press, 1978.
Ledkovsky, Marina, ed. *Russia according to Women*. Tenafly, NJ: Hermitage, 1991.
Ledkovsky, Marina, Charlotte Rosenthal, and Mary Zirin, eds. *Dictionary of Russian Women Writers*. Westport, CT: Greenwood Publishing Group, 1994.
Lenin, V. I. *The Emancipation of Women*. (Selections from the Writings of Lenin. Appendix by Klara Zetkin). New York: International, 1966.
Liborakina, Marina. *Obretenie sily: rossiiskii opyt (Put' preodoleniia diskriminatsii v otnoshenii zhenshchin)*. Moscow: *"CheRo,"* 1996.
Mamonova, Tatyana. *Russian Women's Studies: Essays on Sexism in Soviet Culture*. New York: Pergamon Press, 1989.
Mamonova, Tatyana, ed. *Women and Russia: Feminist Writings from the Soviet Union*. Boston: Beacon Press, 1984.
Marsh, Rosalind, ed. *Women in Russia and Ukraine*. Cambridge: Cambridge University Press, 1996.

Martynova, E. I. *Osnovy feminologii: Uchebnoe posobie*. Krasnoiarsk: Krasnoiarsk State Trade-Economics Institute, 1998.

Marx, Karl, Frederick Engels, V. I. Lenin, and Joseph Stalin. *The Woman Question: Selections*. New York: International, 1970.

Maxwell, Margaret. *Narodniki Women: Russian Women Who Sacrificed Themselves for the Dream of Freedom*. New York: Pergamon Press, 1990.

McNeal, Robert H. *Bride of the Revolution: Krupskaya and Lenin*. Ann Arbor: University of Michigan Press, 1972.

Mints, I. I., and A. P. Nenarokov, eds. *Zhenshchiny—revoliutsionery i uchënye*. Moscow: "Nauka," 1982.

Molokova, Zoia Edvardovna. *Sovremennaia zhenshchina*. 2d ed. Moscow: 1999.

Mullaney, Marie Marmo. *Revolutionary Women: Gender and the Socialist Revolutionary Role*. New York: Praeger, 1983.

Murmantseva, V. S. *Sovetskie zhenshchiny v Velikoi Otchestvennoi voine*. Moscow: *"Mysl',"* 1974.

Muzyria, A. A. and V. V. Kopeiko. *Zhensovet: opyt, problemy, perspektivy*. Moscow: Politizdat, 1989.

Posadskaya, Anastasia, ed. *Women in Russia: A New Era in Russian Feminism*. London: Verso, 1994.

Racioppi, Linda, and Katherine O'Sullivan See. *Women's Activism in Contemporary Russia*. Philadelphia: Temple University Press, 1997.

Rotkirch, Anna, and Elina Haavio-Mannila, eds. *Women's Voices in Russia Today*. Brookfield, VT: Dartmouth Press, 1996.

Rule, Wilma, and Norma C. Noonan, eds. *Russian Women in Politics and Society*. Westport, CT: Greenwood Publishing Group, 1996.

Rzhanitsina, L. *Female Labour under Socialism: The Socio-Economic Aspects*. Moscow: Progress, 1983.

Sergeeva, G. P. *Professional'naia zaniatost' zhenshchin: Problemy i perspektivy*. Moscow: *"Ekonomika,"* 1987.

Sokolov, Boris. *Armand i Krupskaia: Zhenshchiny vozhdia*. Smolensk: *Rusich*, 1999.

Sperling, Valerie. *Organizing Women in Contemporary Russia: Engendering Transition*. Cambridge: Cambridge University Press, 1999.

Stishova, L. I., ed. *Oktiabrem mobilizovannie: Zhenshchiny-kommunistki v bor'be za pobedu sotsialisticheskoi revoliutsii*. Moscow: Politizda, 1987.

Stishova, Lidiia, ed. *V budniakh velikikh stroek: Zhenshchiny-kommunistki, geroini pervykh piatiletok*. Moscow: Politizdat, 1986.

Stites, Richard. *The Women's Liberation Movement in Russia: Feminism, Nihilism and Bolshevism, 1860–1930*. Princeton, NJ: Princeton University Press, 1978, 1991.

Tishkin, G. A., ed. *Feminizm i rossiiskaia kul'tura: Sbornik trudov*. St. Petersburg: International Institution, "Women and Management," 1995.

Trofimova, Elena, ed. *Chego kochet zhenshchina (What a Woman Wants)*. Moscow: Linor, 1993.

Vasil'eva, Larisa. *Kremlëvskie zhëny. (Kremlin Wives)*. Moscow: Vagrius, 1992.

Vasilieva, Larissa. *Kremlin Wives*. New York: Arcade Press, 1992.

Vishneva-Sarafanova, N. *Soviet Women: A Portrait*. Moscow: Progress, 1981.

Woman and Russia: First Feminist Samizdat. London: Sheba, 1980.

Zhenshchiny i muzhchiny Rossii 1998: ofitsial'noe izdanie. Moscow: *Goskomstat*, 1998.
Zhenshchiny v SSSR 1991: Statisticheskie materialy. Moscow: *Goskomstat*, 1991.
Zhenskoe dvizhenie v kontekste rossiiskoi istorii (The Women's Movement in the Context of Russian History). Moscow: Izd. *"Eslan,"* 1999.
Zhuravskaia, I. A., ed. *Nasha sovremennitsa*. Moscow: "*Znanie*," 1989.

Index

Boldface page numbers indicate the location of main entries.

Abortion, 133–34, 312–15
Abubikirova, Natal'ia, 245–46, 364
Academic Feminism in St. Petersburg, **199–201**, 319–21, 337–38, 362–63
Aivazova, Svetlana, 368
Alarchin Courses, 52
Alexander I (Tsar), 84, 94
Alexander II (Tsar), 21, 30, 53, 95, 96, 99, 106, 113
Alexander III (Tsar), 61
All-Russian Congress for the Struggle against the Trade in Women, **3–4**, 34, 59–61
All-Russian Society of the Disabled, 229
All-Russian Sociopolitical Movement of Women of Russia (MWR), 196, **201–2**, 212, 272, 284, 348, 358–59, 368
All-Union Conference of Wives of Executives and Engineering-Technical Workers, 164
American Academy of Social Sciences, 68
Andreeva, Nina Petrovna, 317
Andropov, Iurii, 136, 140
Angara, 208–9
Anti-semitism. *See* Judaism
Arbatova, Mariia Ivanovna, **202–4**
Ariian, Praskov'ia Naumovna Belenkaia, **4–6**, 53–55, 85, 121
Armand, Inessa, 75, **127–29**, 137, 189
Artels (communes), 23, 47–48, 52, 90, 118–19
Artiukhina, Aleksandra Vasil'evna, **129–31**, 189
Association for the Advancement of Women in Science and Humanities (AAWISH) (in Russian, the name differs: *Assotsiatsiia v podderzhku zhenshchin v nauke i obrazovanii*), **204–5**
Association for Women in Slavic Studies (AWSS), 340
Association—No to Violence (ANNA), 224–25, 256
Association of Women Entrepreneurs, 357, 365
The Association of Women in Law Enforcement, **205–6**
The Association of Women Journalists (AWJ), **206–7**
Astrov, Nikolai Ivanovich, 51
Avilova, Evgeniia, 24
Azhgikhina, Nadezhda, 206–7

Baian, 44, 111
The Baikal' Regional Union of Women-"Angara," **208–9**
Bakunin, Mikhail, Bakuninists, 11
Bakunina, Ekaterina, 25
Bazankur, O., 44, 111

Bebel, August, 171, 186
Benckendorff, General, 94
Benni, Arthur, 47
Bervi-Kaidanova, Olga, 43
Bestuzhev Courses (Bestuzhevskie Courses), 4, 22, 30, 54, 66, 72, 83, 85, 90, 91, 121
Bezrodnaia, Iuliia (Iakovleva, Iuliia Ivanovna), 16
Birth rates. *See* Demographic issues
Bizenko, Anastasiia, 19
Black Hundreds, 33, 82
Blandova, Mariia, 24
Boane, Anna, 44
Bochkareva, Mariia Leont'eva (1889–1920), **7–9**, 103, 105, 122
Bogel'man, Sof'ia Zakharovna, **9–10,** 111–12
Boguslavskaia, Mariia, 107
Bolshevik Faction of the RSDLP, 66, 172,
Bolshevik Revolution. *See* October (November) Revolution 1917
Bolsheviks, 66, 132, 172
Borodin, A.P., 68
Bozhkova, Elizaveta, 263
Breshko-Breshkovskaia, Ekaterina Konstantinovna, **10–12**, 101–2
Brest-Litovsk Peace Treaty, 83
Brezhnev, Leonid, 135, 183
Bronevich, Valentina Tadeevna, **209–11**
Brusilov, Aleksei, 103, 105
Business, women in, 293–94, 350–52
Butler, Josephine, 91
Byloe (*The Past*), 74

CEDAW. *See* Convention on the Elimination of All Forms of Discrimination against Women
Central Committee of the CPSU, 185
Central Council of Trade Unions (VTsSPS), 159, 164, 170
Chaikovskii Circle, 52
Champseix, Leodile (aka Andre Leo), 90–91
Charnotskaia, Anna, 61
Charter of Women's Solidarity, 202, **212–13**, 284, 368
Cheboksary Women's Movement, **213–15**, 306
Chebysheva-Dmitrieva, Evgeniia, 24
Chechens, 134
Chechnia (Chechnya), 335. *See also* War in Chechnia
Chekhov, N.V., 64, 78
Chekhova, Mariia Aleksandrova Argamakova, **13–15**, 34, 38, 40, 73, 75, 78, 80–81
Chekhova, Mariia Ivanovna, 111
Cherkasova, Mariia, 238
Chernenko, Konstantin, 136
Chernomyrdin, Viktor, 227–28, 233, 253, 300
Chernyi peredel (Black Repartition), 116,
Chernyshevskii, Nikolai, 46, 47, 78
Chicago World's Fair (1893), 85
Childcare: nurseries, kindergartens, 4, 14, 23, 50, 133, 332
Children, abandoned/homeless, 133, 136
Chiumina, Olga, 44
Chuvash, 213, 214
Civil rituals, 132; Red Weddings, 146; Wedding palaces, 135
Civil War (1918–20), 8, 50–51, 104, 128, 145, 168
Collectivization, 133, 146
Comintern, 187
Commission on Improving the Status of Women (CISW), 197, **215–16**
Commission on Women, Family, and Demography under the President of the Russian Federation (CWFD), 201, **216–18**, 224, 283, 309, 313, 365, 368
Committee of Soldiers' Mothers of Russia, 136, 196, 212, **218–20**, 221, 237–238, 271, 297, 347, 360
Committee of Soviet Women. *See* Soviet Women's Committee
Committee on Family and Women (USSR), 329, 330
Committee on Women, Family, and Youth. *See* State Duma Committee on Women, Family, and Youth
The Committee "The Soldier's Mother," St. Petersburg, **220–21**

Committee to Help Russia's Political Prisoners, 21
Commonwealth of Independent States (CIS), 268, 311
Communist Party of the Russian Federation (KPRF), 210, 347–48
Communist Party of the Soviet Union (CPSU), 125, 139, 140, 146, 149, 151, 153, 154, 176, 182–85, 188, 190, 267, 276, 291, 299, 302, 321, 357, 366
Conception on Legislative Activity to Secure Equal Rights and Equal Opportunity for Men and Women, 197, 224, 258–59, 307
Congress of People's Deputies (Russian Federation), 334, 357
Congress of People's Deputies (USSR), 184–85, 290, 299, 305
Consortium of Women's Nongovernmental Associations, 196, 198, 202, 217, **221–24**, 243, 269, 354
Constituent Assembly, 12, 40, 77, 92
Constitutional Democrats (Kadets), 49, 50, 79, 91, 92
Convention on the Elimination of All Forms of Discrimination against Women (CEDAW), 197, 215, 262, 293
CPSU. *See* Communist Party of the Soviet Union
Crisis Centers for Women, Association of, **224–26**, 237, 246, 255–56

Damskii listok (*Ladies Pages*), 113
Damskii mir (*Ladies' World*), 44, 55, 109–10
Damskii mir kalendar' (*Ladies World Calendar*), 44, 55
Damskii vestnik (*Ladies Herald*), 107
Davydov, Karl, 16
Davydova, Aleksandra Arkad'evna, **16–18**
Decembrist Women in Siberia in the 1830s–1850s, **18–19**, 94–95
d'Hericourt, Jenny, 89
Deich, Lev, 116
Delegatki (delegates) program, 130
Dement'eva, Natal'ia Leonidovna, **227–28**
Demidova, Ol'ga R., 362
Demographic issues, 133–36, 217, 279, 312–15
DemRossii (Democratic Russia) Movement, 323
Denikin, General, 50–51
Denisova, Ol'ga, 214
The Disabled Russian Women's Movement, **228–31**
Discrimination against women in the workplace: post-Soviet era, 205, 268; Soviet era, 153
Divorce, 133–34
Dmitrieva, Oksana Genrikhovna, 228, **231–32**
Dmitrieva, Tatiana Borisovna, 228, **232–34**
Domashnaia portnikha (*Domestic Seamstress*), 112
Domestic violence. *See* Violence against women
Dostoevskii, Fëdor, 73
Drug zhenshchin (*Women's Friend*), 107
Dubna. *See* Independent Women's Forum
Duma, imperial period (1905–1917), 14, 38, 39, 60, 75–76, 79
Duma, post-Soviet period (1993–), 197, 224, 277, 279, 300, 305, 315, 357–59, 367. *See also* State Duma
Dzerzhinskii, Felix, 83

Edinstvo, 210
Education, 1, 5. *See also* First All-Russian Congress on Women's Education; Higher Education for Women in Nineteenth- and Early Twentieth-Century Russia; Higher Courses for Women; Women's Medical Courses
Efimenko, Aleksandra, 40
Egorova, Valentina Ivanovna, 318–19
Ekaterina, 237
Ekaterinburg Women's Organizations, **235–38**
Engel'gardt, Anna Nikolaevna, 85
Environmentalism and Women in Russia, **238–42**
Ershova, Elena, 222, **242–44**, 269

European University in St. Petersburg, 200, 260, 337, 371

FALTA/SAFO, **245–46**, 261, 289
Family Protection and Women's Well-Being under Communism and Later, **132–37**, 175, 188–89, 198, 248, 332, 342, 347
Fatherland-All-Russia bloc, 202, 232, 233–34, 285, 301, 348. *See also Otechestvo-Vsia Rossiia*
February (March) Revolution 1917, 40, 56, 101, 103, 104–5. *See also* Provisional government
Federation Council of the Russian Federation, 210, 280
Federation of Soviet Women's Writers, 268
Fedulova, Alevtina Vasil'evna, 175, 192, 212, **246–49**, 284, 357–59, 366
Femina, 222, **249–51**
Feminism: pre-Soviet, 25, 34, 71, 73, 75, 78, 81, 110, 111, 112, 117, 142–43, 150, 186–87; Soviet era, 151, 155–56, 157–58, 177–78, 180–82. *See also* Feminism in Post-Soviet Russia; Gender/Women's Studies in Russia
Feminism in Post-Soviet Russia, Emergence and Development, 202–4, 245–46, **251–53**, 256, 281, 286–87, 289, 337–40
Feminist Informational Journal (FEM-INF), 245
Feminist Orientation Center (FOC), 286, 287
Feminology, 200, 260, 272
Figner, Vera Nikolaevna, 5, 19, **20–22**, 40, 76, 116
Filosofova, Anna Pavlovna, **22–24**, 61, 84, 85, 89, 92, 118
First All-Russian Congress of Women Workers, 66, 128, 130, **137–38**
First All-Russian Congress on Women's Education, 39
First All-Russian Women's Congress, 5, 23, **24–27**, 37, 65, 68, 70, 91, 92, 143, 198
First Conference of Women Workers, 66
First Russian Women's Battalion of Death, 7, 8, 103, 105, 122
First Woman's Calendar, **53–55**
First Women's Pharmacy, 36
First Women's Technical Institute, 5
Five-Year Plans (*Piatiletka*), 146, 147, 190
Flekser, Akim, 16–17
Fonareva, Natal'ia Evgen'evna, **253–54**, 277
Foreign Funding and the Women's Movement in Russia, 197, 222–23, 237, 250, 252, **254–57**, 264, 265, 269, 274, 281, 287, 296, 298, 320, 353, 360, 363. *See also* United States Agency for International Development
Fortunatova, Galina A., 362
Free love, 25, 132, 143, 150
Frichi Movement (aka Frichi Circle), 20
Furtseva, Ekaterina, 184

Gabrilovich, Ol'ga, 97
Gaia, 242–43, **269–70**, 365
Gay and lesbian issues, 62, 222, 262, 316
Gender Expertise Project, **258–59**, 350
Gender/Women's Studies in Russia, 197, 199–200, **259–60**, 272, 274–75, 337–40, 350, 359–60, 370–71
Gintsburg, Baron Goratsii, 59
Glasnost, 148–49, 195, 241, 370
Gorbachev, Mikhail S., 125, 136, 139–41, 148, 174, 183, 184, 191, 288
Gorbacheva, Raisa Maksimovna, **139–41**
Goricheva, Tatiana Mikhailovna, 157, 180–81
Gorolits-Vlasova, L.M., 40
"Great Retreat," 133
Grech Commune, 48
Grinevskaia, Izabella, 44
Guerrier Courses, 30, 42, 72
Gurevich, Anna, 73, 78, 81
Gurevich, Liubov', 17, 73, 79, 85

Health, women's, 54, 222, 233, 239, 312–15
Herwegh, Georg, 29

Herzen, Alexander, 28, 89
Herzen, Natal'ia Alexandrovna, **28–29**
Higher Courses for Women, 5, 30–31, 49, 54, 69, 90
Higher Education for Women in Nineteenth- and Early Twentieth-Century Russia, **30–32**

Iabloko Party, 231
Iakobi, Aleksandra Nikolaevna. *See* Peshkove-Toliverova, Aleksandra Nikolaevna
Ia sama (*I Myself*), 203
Independent Women's Democratic Initiative, 295
Independent Women's Forums (IWF), 196, 245, 252, **261–63**, 286, 295–96, 309, 325, 367
The Information Center of the Independent Women's Forum (ICWF), 196, 217, 263, **263–65**, 275, 286, 287, 309
The Institute for Development of International Business, **265–66**
The Institute "Woman and Management," **266–68**, 317
International Committee of Women for Permanent Peace, 40
International Congress of Women in London (1899), 17, 42
International Council of Women (ICW), 23, 62
The International League of Women Writers, **268**, 344, 365
International Woman Suffrage Alliance Congress, 43
International Women's Center Gaia, 242–43, **269–70**, 365
International Women's Day, 151, 187
International Women's League of Peace, 68
Interregional Movement of Rural Women, 240
Iskra (*The Spark*), 116–17
Iskusstvo i zhizn' (*Art and Life*), 4
Iukina, Irina, 199
Ivanova, Liudmila Nikolaevna, 361
Ivanovo Center for Gender Research, 260
Ivanovo Women's Movement, 259–60, **270–73**
Ivanovo Women's Union, 271
Ivasheva, Vera, 84, 118
Iz istorii zhenskogo dvizheniia v Rossii (*From the History of the Women's Movement*), 43

Journalism, women in: Post-Soviet, 206–7; Pre-1917, 106–14
Judaism, 9, 33, 59; anti-Semitism, 30, 39, 43, 112, 113, 342. *See also* Black Hundreds

Kachovskaia, Irina, 19
Kadets, 49, 50, 79, 91, 92
K.G.B. (Committee of State Security), 135, 182
Kalacheva, Elizaveta, 59, 60
Kalinina, Elena Ivanovna, 267
Kal'manovich, Anna Andreevna, **33–35**, 38, 73, 81
Kalmykova, Aleksandra, 14, 40
Kaplan, Fania, 19
Karelian Center for Gender Studies (KCGS), **274–75**
Karelova, Galina, 236, 237
Kashevarova-Rudneva, Varvara, 87, 96
Kerenskii, Alexander, 7, 103, 105
Khakamada, Irina Matsuovna, 253–54, **275–79**
Khasbulatova, Ol'ga, 260, 272
Khotkina, Zoia, 262, 296, 339
Khoziaika (*Homemaker*), 113
Khrushchev, Nikita, 134–35, 148, 183, 184, 190, 191, 192–93, 300
Kippar, Elena Ivanovna, 112
Kirbassova, Mariia, 218
Kirienko, Sergei, 228, 232, 233, 253, 278, 312. *See also* Russian Federation; Union of Right Forces
Klimantova, Galina Ivanovna, 223, **279–80**
Klimenkova, Tatiana, 246, 262, 295, 364
Klirikova, Ol'ga, 79
Klub delovaia zhenshchina (Business Women's Club), 271
Klub Garmonii (Harmony Club), 203

Klub zhenskaia initsiativa (the Women's Initiative Club), 214–15
Kochkina (Kotchkina) Elena, 296, 364
Kogda chasy zhizni ostanovilis' (*When the Clock of Life Stopped*), 21
Kola Peninsula, Women's Congress of the, **280–82**, 306
Kollontai, Aleksandra Mikhailovna, 25, 66, 73, 75, 130, 137, **142–44**, 150, 183, 189
Kommunistka (Communist Woman), 189
Komsomol (VLKSM), 144–49, 291, 328
Komsomolka, **144–49**
Konradi, Evgeniia, 85, 90, 108
Konstantinova, Valentina, 262, 289, 308
Kovaleva, L.A., 97
Kovaleva, Natal'ia, 306
Kovalevskaia, Sofia, 46–47
Krest'ianka (*Peasant Woman*), 148, 164, 189
Kropotkin, Peter, 23
Krupskaia, Nadezhda Konstantinovna, 75, 127, 137, 140, 145, **149–51**, 176
Kudelli, Praskov'ia, 39
Kuprin, Aleksandr, 17
Kuskova, Ekaterina, 14, 40, 73

Lakhova, Ekaterina Fillipovna, 201–2, 212–13, 217, 272, **283–85**, 313, 357, 358, 359, 368
Lavrov, Peter, 11, 23, 85
Lavrova, Liubov Nikolaevna, 97
League for Women's Equal Rights. *See Liga ravnopraviia zhenshchin*
League of Women Writers, 268, 344, 365
Legal Equality in the 1920s, Women's Pursuit of, **152–54**
Legal Framework on Protecting the Equal Rights and Opportunities of Men and Women, 197, 224, 258–59, 367
Lenin, V.I., 66, 116, 127–29, 137, 149, 150, 176, 187
Lenin's *Last Testament*, 150
Leo, Andre (aka Leodile Champseix), 91
Lerner, Leah Moiseevna, 265
Lesnevskaia, Antonina Boleslavna, **36–38**, 97
Lettres de Femmes (*Letters of Women*), 44
Liborakina, Marina Ivanovna, 263, **286–88**
Liga ravnopraviia zhenshchin (League for Women's Equal Rights), 14, 34, **38–41**, 65, 75, 81, 111
Ligov People's House, 49
Lipovskaia, Ol'ga, 245, 262, **288–89**, 319–20
LITT, 294, 352
Lobanov, Aleksandr Viktorovich, 110
LOTOS, **289–90**, 295, 309
Luk'ianenko, Tatiana, 293
Luzhenovskii, G.N., 82
Luzhkov, Iurii, 202, 285, 348, 358
L'vov, Prince, 40, 56, 63, 92

Makhorskova, Marina Aleksandrovna, 341
Malakhovskaia, Natal'ia, 157, 180, 245
Mamonova, Tatiana Valentinovna, 135, **155–57**, 157, 180
Mar, Anna, 44, 45, 111, 113
Mariia (aka Maria), 155, **157–58**, 177–78, 180, 181
Mariia (Petrozavodsk), 325–26
Marriage: companionate, 13; fictitious, 47; marital law, 39, 132–35; George Sand and, 28–29. *See also* Civil rituals
Martov, Iurii, 66
Martsinkevich, Feliks Vasilievich, 113
Marxism, 116–17, 142–43, 186–87
Mass media, post-Soviet, 203–4, 207, 249–50, 252
Matova, Anna, 111
Matvienko, Valentina Ivanovna, 216, **291–93**
Mavliutova, Galiia, 205–6
Medical-Surgical Academy, 68, 98, 99
Medved' Party, 210
Mensheviks, 117
Merezhkovskii, Dmitri, 16
Messarosh, Anna Borisovna, 107
Mikhailov, Mikhail Larionovich, 106
Mikhailovskii, Nikolai, 16
Military, 354–56, 192–93

Miliukov, Paul, 78, 79
Miliukova, Anna, 75, 77, 78
Mill, John Stuart, 42, 90
Mirbach, V., 83
Mir Bozhii (*God's World*), 16
Mironova, Natal'ia, 239
Mirovich, Zinaida Sergeevna Ivanova (aka N. Mirovich and Zinaida Mirovich), 34, 38, 40, **42–44,** 65, 78
Missiia (Mission), **293–94**
Modnyi kur'er (*The Fashion Messenger*), 113
Modnyi svet (*The World of Fashion*), 113
Molokova, Zoia Edvardovna, 332–33
Moscow, government of, 328–30
Moscow Center for Gender Studies (MCGS), 212, 222, 252, 255, 258, 259, 261, 290, **294–97**, 307, 309, 310, 338, 339, 367
Moscow Center for Human Rights, 219, 298
Moscow Pedagogical Circle, 14
Moscow Teachers' Courses, 14
Moskvicha (Moscovite), 252
Mother Heroine medals, 134
Motherhood, 147, 151, 219–20, 367
Mother's Right Fund, **297–98**
Movement for Nuclear Safety (MNS), 239
Movement of Women of Russia, 359
Muravieva, Countess Aleksandra Zakharovna, **44–45**, 110

Nagrodskaia, Evdokiia, 44, 112
Na Poroge Zhizne (*On the Threshold of Life*), 70
Narodnaia rasprava (Popular Punishment), 70
Narodnaia volia (the People's Will), 21, 52, 116
Narpit (Union of People's Food Service and Dormitory Workers), **159–62**, 170
Nash Dom—Rossiia (Our Home Is Russia) Party, 210
National Council of Russian Women, 25, 63, 68
Nechaev, Sergei, 70, 115
Nechaeva, Ol'ga K., 101
Nedelia (*Weekly*), 108
Nekrasov, Nikolai, 20
Nevskii Institute, 352, 363
New Economic Policy (NEP), 133, 160
Nezavisimaia gazeta (Independent Newspaper), 284
Nicholas I (Tsar), 18, 94, 95
Nicholas II (Tsar), 100
Niglistki (*Nihilists*), **46–48**, 67, 90
Nikolaeva, Klavdiia Nikolaevna, 66, 137, 189
Novoe delo (*New Affairs*), 107–8

Obshchaia gazeta (*Common Newspaper*), 203
Obshchee delo (Common Cause), 276, 277, 324
Obshchestvennitsa Movement, **163–67**
Obshchestvo dostavlenniia deshevykh kvartir i drugikh posobii nuzhdaiushchimsia zhiteliam S-Peterburga (Society for Cheap Lodging and Other Aid to Needy Residents of St. Petersburg), 23, 84, 89
Obshchestvo vzaimopomoshchi rabotnits (Society for the Mutual Aid of Women Workers), 117
October (November) Revolution 1917, 63, 66, 67, 73, 83, 104, 105–6, 120, 122, 132, 143, 144, 152, 188
Ogonëk, 322
Ol'denburgskaia, Princess Evgeniia, 37, 58
On the Subjection of Women, 42, 90
Ordzhonikidze, Grigorii, 163
Orlova-Davydova, Countess Mariia, 59
Ostrogorskii, Victor, 16
Ostrova, Valentina Vasilievna, 342–43
Osvobozhdenie (Liberation), 92
Osvobozhdenie truda (Liberation of Labor), 116
Otechestvo-Vsia Rossiia (Fatherland-All-Russia) bloc, 202, 232, 233–34, 285, 301, 348, 358, 359
Our Bodies Ourselves, 222, 255

Pamfilova, Ella Aleksandrovna, **299–302**
Panina, Countess Sof'ia Vladimirovna, **49–51**, 75
Pankhurst, Christabel, 34, 40, 43. *See also* Suffrage
Pearl Club, 229–30
Perestroika, 191, 195, 251–52, 288, 331, 333–34, 352, 370
Perovskaia, Sof'ia L'vovna, **51–53**, 116
Pervyi zhenskii kalendar' (*The First Women's Calendar*, or PZhK), 4–5, **53–55**
Peshkova-Toliverova, Aleksandra Nikolaevna, 107–8
Petrovskaia, D.F., 113
Pivnenko, Valentina Nikolaevna, **302–4**
Plekhanov, Georgi V., 116–17
Pokrovskaia, Mariia Ivanovna, 40, **55–57**, 77, 81, 92, 110, 120, 121–22
Poles, 37, 96, 97
Politburo, women in, 182
Political Participation by Russian Women in the Transitional Period since 1985, 174–75, 201–2, **304–7**, 362–64
Populism, 20, 21, 48, 52, 72
Posadskaia, Anastasiia, 261, 289, 290, 295, **307–10**
Posidel'ki, 320
Posle Shlussel'burga (After Schlusselburg), 21
Pravda, 66
Prechistenskie courses ("Workers University"), 64
Preobrazhenie (Transformation), 252, 338
Primakov, Evgenii, 210, 228, 232, 253, 285, 292, 358
Professional Union of Home Employees, 159, **168–70**
Prostitution, 25, 34, 50, 55–56, 58–61, 122
Protective legislation. *See* Family Protection and Women's Well-Being under Communism and Later
Provisional government, 14, 49, 56, 76, 82, 101, 104–6, 122
Przhibytek, S.A., 37
Psychological Crisis Center for Women, 199
Pukhova, Zoia, 175, 191
The Purges, 133, 183–84
Pushkin, Alexander, 95
Putin, Vladimir, 210. *See also* Russian Federation

Quotas, 126, 175, 184, 257, 284, 304

Rabotnitsa (Woman Worker), 113, 130, 164, 189
Raikh, Mariia, 43
Rassvet (*Daybreak*), 106
Reed, John, 83
Regent, Tatiana Mikhailovna, 253, **311–12**
Regentova, Marina A., 245, 262, 364
Regions of Russia (*Rossiiskie regiony)* factions of Duma, 277, 301
Reisner, Larisa, **171–73**
Religion: combating influence on women, 132, 189; Islam, 98, 189; religious feminists, 157–58; restrictions on, 134. *See also* Judaism; Russian Orthodox Church
Reproductive rights, **312–15**
Republican Union of Democratic Women's Organizations, 40
Revolution, 31, 40, 62, 117, 129. *See also* February (March) Revolution, 1917; October (November) Revolution, 1917
Revolutionary Tribunal (Bolshevik), 50
Revolution of 1905, 31, 40, 62, 117, 129
Rimashevskaia, Natal'ia, 290, 295, 308
Rodionov, Lev Mikhailovich, 112
Rodzianko, Mikhail, 7, 103, 105
RSDLP. *See* Russian Social Democratic Labor Party
Rukhadze, Zoia, 22
Russian Association of Family Planning (RAFP), 314
Russian Association of University Women (RAUW), 214
Russian Communist Party/Bolsheviks (RCP/B), 113, 132, 176
Russian Federation: government of, 136, 175, 216, 220, 233, 272, 291, 292–93, 299, 301, 302, 303, 306, 311–12, 322, 352, 354; women in, 209–10, 227–28,

231–34, 236, 253–54, 275–78, 283–85, 291–93, 333–35
Russian National Council of Women, 25, 63, 68
Russian Orthodox Church, 25, 134, 157, 158, 166, 314
Russian Social Democratic Labor Party (RSDLP), 66, 113, 142, 171, 176, 188
Russian Society for the Protection of Women (RSPW), 3, 50, **58–61**
Russian Summer Schools on Gender Studies, 325, 339
Russian Women's Mutual Philanthropic Society, 5, 6, 13, 23, 24, 38, 39, **61–64**, 68, 70–71, 83–84, 85, 113, 120
Russkaia mysl' (Russian Thought), 108
Russkii ochag (Russian Hearth), 51
Russkoe bogatsvo (Russian Wealth), 17
Russkoe zhenskoe vzaimnoblagotvoritel'noe obshchestvo. See Russian Women's Mutual Philanthropic Society
Ruttsen (Von Ruttsen), Liudmila Nikolaevna, 34, 38, **64–65,** 73, 78

SAFO, 261. *See also* FALTA/SAFO
SAFO (St. Petersburg), **316–17**
The St. Petersburg Association of University Women or VERA, **317–18**, 320, 351
St. Petersburg Association of Widows and Their Families (Valita), **318–19**
The St. Petersburg Center of Gender Issues (PCGI), 199, 245, 252, 288–89, **319–21**
St. Petersburg First Women's Technical Institute, 5
St. Petersburg Women's Medical Institute, 30–31, 74, 99, 100
Saksen-Al'tenburgskaia, Princess Elena, 59
Salam Bi, 214
Sal'e, Marina Evgen'evna, **321–25**
Saltykov-Schedrin, Mikhail E., 68
Samizdat, 181, 288
Samoilov, Arkadi A., 66, 67
Samoilova, Konkordiia Nikolaevna, **66–67**, 137
Sand, George, 28–29, 46
Savkina, Irina Leonardovna, **325–27**
School of Women's Leadership, 209
The Scientific Center "Women and Russia," **327–28**
Serno-Solov'evich, Alexander A., 90
Severnyi vestnik (Northern Herald), 17, 81
Sex education, 314
Sexual conduct, 47, 146. *See also* Free love
Sexual harassment, 153–54, 222
Sexual preference, 262, 316. *See also* Gay and lesbian issues
Shabanova, Anna Nikolaevna, 23, 24, 40, 62, 63, **67–69**, 70, 77, 92, 99
Shapir, Ol'ga Andreevna (née Kislaikova), 24, **69–72**
Shchepkina, Ekaterina Nikolaevna, 38, 40, **72–74**
Shishkina-Iavein, Poliksena Nestorovna, 38–39, 40, **74–77**, 92
Shvedova, Nadezhda, 269
Shvetsova, Liudmila Ivanovna, 305–6, **328–31**, 366
Sillaste, Galina, 350
Sleptsov, Vasily, 48
Smith, Elise, 222, 243
Sobchak, Anatolii, 322
Socialist Revolutionary Party (SR), 11, 82
Society for the Preservation of Women's Health, 37
Society for the Treatment of Chronically Ill Children, 68
The Socioeconomic Transition in Post-Soviet Russia: The Impact on Women, **331–32**, 346, 352
Soiuz ravnopraviia zhenshchin (Women's Equal Rights Union), 13, 24, 25, 34, 38, 42, 62, 64, 71, 72, 73, **77–80**, 80–82, 111, 120
Soiuz zhenshchin (Union of Women), 34, 38, 64, 73, 79, **80–82**, 109, 111
Solov'ev, Vladimir, 73
Soviet Committee of Soldiers' Mothers, 136. *See also* Committee of Soldiers' Mothers of Russia

Soviet Women's Committee (SWC), 140, **174–75**, 184, 191–92, 195, 246–48, 261, 280, 317, 361, 366
Sovremennaia zhenshchina (*The Contemporary Woman*), 113–14, **332–33,**
Sovremennik (*The Contemporary One*), 86, 87
Sovremennyi mir (*Contemporary world*), 17
Spiridonova, Mariia Aleksandrovna, 19, **82–83**
Spousal abuse. *See* Violence against women
Stakhanovites (Stakhanovitism), 147
Stalin, Joseph, 133–34, 144, 146, 150, 164, 190, 313
Starovoitova, Galina Vasil'evna, 277, **333–36**, 306
Stasova, Elena Dmitrievna, 4, 75, **175–76**
Stasova, Nadezhda Vasil'evna, 61, **83–86**, 89, 118–19
State Duma Committee on Women, Family, and Youth, 197, 224, 279, 315, 358, 367
Stolypin, Petr, 75
Suffrage, 34, 38, 39, 43, 71. *See also* International Women's Suffrage Alliance Congress
Sunday School Movement, 85, 176
Supreme Soviet (USSR), 184, 283–84, 291, 299, 304, 329
Surovtseva, Klavdiia, 163
Suslova, Nadezhda Prokofievna, 68, **86–88**, 98
Suvorin, A.S., 109
Sverdlovsk Oblast Women's Union, 235

Tarnovskaia, Varvara, 85
Temkina, Anna Adrianovna, 200, **337–38**, 371
Ten Days That Shook the World, 83
Tereshkova, Valentina, 175, 185
Terrorism, 21, 82, 115, 116. *See* Figner, Vera; *Narodnaia Rasprava*; *Narodnaia Vol'ia*; Mariia Spiridonova; Trial of the 193
The "Thaw," 134
"Thick" Journal(s), 81, 105
Tolstoy Foundation, 51
Trepov, General, 115
Trial of the 14, 21
Trial of the 193, 11, 52, 116
Trofimova, Elena Ivanovna, **338–40**
Troinova, Tatiana Georgievna, 363–64
Trotsky, Leon (Trotskii), 92, 172
Trubetskaia, Ekaterina, 94
Trubnikova, Mariia Vasil'evna, 23, 83, 84, **89–91**, 118–19
Tuchkova, Natal'ia, 29
Turgenev, Ivan S., 99
Tyrkova, Ariadna, 34, 38, 73, 75, 77, 78, 79, 81, **91–93**

Unemployment, 213, 267, 331–33, 346, 355
The Union of Disabled Women, **341–42**
Union of Right Forces (*Soiuz pravikh sil* or SPS), 277
The Union of Soviet Women of Leningrad and Leningrad Oblast, **342–43**
Union of Women of the Naval Fleet, 357
United Nations World Conference on Women in Beijing, 197, 217, 243, 264, 274, 280, 286, 309
Unity Party (*Edinistvo,* aka *Medved'*), 210
United States Agency for International Development (USAID), 222, 223, 226, 254–55, 258, 287, 364
Ural Association of Women (UAW), 236
Ushakova, Valentina Grigorievna, 327
US–NIS Women's Consortium. *See* Consortium of Women's Nongovernmental Associations
USSR Congress of People's Deputies, 184–85, 290, 299, 305

Vandenberg, Martina, 223
Vannovskii, Pëtr, 99
Vasil'eva, Larisa Nikolaievna, 268, **344–46**
Verbitskaia, Anastasiia, 112
Vestnik (*Herald*), 264
Vestnik inostrannoi literatury (*Herald of Foreign Literature*), 44, 108
Vi i My (You and We), 207

Violence against women, 136, 224–26, 237, 246, 262, 281, 286–87
Vladimir Region, Women's Movement in, **346–49**
Vladimirskie Courses, 69
Vol'kenshtein, Ol'ga Akimovna, 38, 78, 81
Volkonskaia, Mariia Nikolaevna, 18, **94–95**
Volkova, Anna Ivanova, 107
Volynskii, A.I. (pseudonym: Akim Flekser), 16–17
Von Ruttsen, Liudmila. *See* Ruttsen, Liudmila
Voronina, Ol'ga, 258, 262, 289, 308
Voznesenskaia, Iuliia Nikolaevna, 157, **177–79**, 180
Vserossiskoe Zhenskoe Obshchestvo (All-Russian Women's Society), 63

War. *See* Civil War; War in Afghanistan; War in Chechnia; World War I; World War II
War in Afghanistan, 218
War in Chechnia, 136, 218–19, 297, 335, 354, 359–60
WIIS, 353
Williams, Harold, 92, 93
Woman and Development Association, **351**
Woman and Russia, 155–56, 157, 177, **180–82**
Women and Business in Russia, **350–51**
Women in Business in Russia, **351–52**
Women in Global Security or WINGS, **352–54**
Women in the Communist Party of the Soviet Union (CPSU), **182–85**
Women in the military, 354–56
Women in the Russian Military since 1992, **354–56**
Women of Russia (WOR). *See* Women of Russia Political Movement
The Women of Russia Political Movement, 192, 196, 201, 212, 223, 246–48, 278, 279, 284, 305, 312, 313, 335, 348, **356–59,** 367
"Women of the Don" Union, **359–60**
Women pharmacists in late imperial Russia, 36–38, **96–98**
The "Woman Question," 106, 150, 190, 329
The Women's Club-Café *Sudarynia*, **361–62**
Women's Equal Rights Union, 42, 73
Women's Humanitarian Collegium, 200, **362–63**
Women's Information Network (*Zhenset*), **363–64**
Women's League and Women's Initiative, 223, 242, 243, 269, 330, **364–66**
Women's Medical Courses, 96–97, **98–101**
Women's Medical Institute, 30–31, 74, 96, 99, 100
Women's Military Congress, **101–2**, 104
Women's Military Movement of World War I, **102–4**
Women's Military Units of World War I, **104–6**
Women's Periodical Publishing in Late Imperial Russia, **106–9**
Women's Periodicals in Early Twentieth-Century Russia, **109–14**
Women's Progressive Party. *See Zhenskaia progressivnaia partiia*
Women's Publishing Artel, 118–19
Women's Publishing Cooperative, 84, 118–19
Women's Studies. *See* Gender/Women's Studies in Russia
Women's Union of Russia or WUR, 175, 192, 201, 212–13, 213, 216–17, 235, 241, 246–48, 270, 284, 347–48, 357, **366–69**
World War I, 7, 63, 101, 102–4, 122. *See also* the First Russian Women's Battalion of Death
World War II (Great Patriotic War), 147–48, 174, 358

Yeltsin, Boris, 277, 283–84, 300, 312, 334–35, 342, 355–56, 362
Yukina, (Iukina) Irina, 199

Zakharova, Natal'ia, 289, 290, 295, 308
Zasulich, Vera Ivanovna, 52, **115–18**

Zdravomyslova, Elena Andreevna, 200, 337, **370–71**
Zemlia i Volia (Land and Freedom), 21, 52, 87, 116
Zemstvos (local government organs), 97, 98
Zetkin, Klara Eissner, **186–88**
Zheliabov, Andrei, 53
Zhenotdel (Women's Department of the Communist Party), 67, 128, 129–31, 137–38, 142, 143, 150, 183, 185, **188–90**
Zhenshchina (*Woman*), 9–10, 109–10, 113
Zhenshchina i khoziaika (*Woman and Homemaker*), 113
Zhenshchina i voina (*Women and War*), 113
Zhenshchina v rossiiskom obshchestve (Women in Russian Society), 272, 302
Zhenshchiny Rossii (Women of Russia), 202, 305, 313, 358
Zhenskaia initsiativa (Women's Initiative), 364–66
Zhenskaia Izdatel'skaia Artel' (Women's Publishing Artel), **118–19**
Zhenskaia mysl' (*Women's Thought*), 110, 113
Zhenskaia Progressivnaia Partiia (Women's Progressive Party), 24, 56, 62, 110, **119–21**, 122
Zhenskii vestnik (*Women's Herald*), 34, 55–56, 73, 80, 107, 108, 109, 110, 120, **121–23**
Zhenskoe bogatsvo (*Women's Wealth*), 112
Zhenskoe chtenie (*Women's Reading*), 320
Zhenskoe delo (Women's Cause), 107–8, 110, 112, 113
Zhensovety (Women's Councils), 190, **190–92**, 193, 195, 213, 261, 270
Zhensovety (Women's Councils) in the Soviet Army, **192–93**
Zhurnal dlia xoziaek (*Magazine for Housewives*), 110, 112
Zhurnal dlia zhenshchin (*Magazine for Women*), 110, 112, 113

Contributors

NADEZHDA AZHGIKHINA, Nezavisimaia Gazeta, Moscow

LAURIE BERNSTEIN, Rutgers University at Camden, New Jersey

VALENTINA BODROVA, WCIOM, Moscow

DOVILE BUDRYTE, Brenau University, Gainesville, Georgia

AMY CAIAZZA, Institute for Women's Policy Research, Washington, D.C.

RHONDA CLARK, Mercyhurst College, Erie, Pennsylvania

MARY SCHAEFFER CONROY, University of Colorado, Denver

MICHELLE DENBESTE, California State University, Fresno

RUTH A. DUDGEON, History Associates Incorporated, Rockville, Maryland

ETHEL DUNN, Highgate Rd. Social Science Research Station, Berkeley, California

ELVIRA ERSHOVA, State University of Management, Moscow

REBECCA FRIEDMAN, Florida International University

JANE F. BERTHUSEN GOTTLICK, University of Wisconsin-Whitewater

LISA GRANIK, Attorney and independent scholar, New York

WENDY GUYOT, Independent scholar, working in Russia

JANE GARY HARRIS, University of Pittsburgh

SARAH HENDERSON, University of Colorado

PETER JUVILER, Barnard College, Columbia University

NATASHA KOLCHEVSKA, University of New Mexico, Albuquerque

VITALINA KOVAL, Get Institute, Russian Academy of Science

IRINA LAPSHINA, Vladimir State Pedagogical University, Vladimir, Russia

ANNA LEVITSKAIA, Vladimir State University, Vladimir, Russia

ANDREI LEVITSKII, Vladimir State University, Vladimir, Russia

ADELE LINDENMEYR, Villanova University

NATAL'IA MIROVITSKAIA, Duke University

ZOYA EDVARDOVNA MOLOKOVA, National Academy of Management, Moscow

REBECCA BALMAS NEARY, Columbia University

CAROL NECHEMIAS, Pennsylvania State University, Harrisburg

NORMA CORIGLIANO NOONAN, Augsburg College

LINDA RACIOPPI, James Madison College, Michigan State University

JAMES RICHTER, Bates College

ANNA ROTKIRCH, University of Helsinki

ROCHELLE GOLDBERG RUTHCHILD, Norwich University

CARMEN SCHEIDE, University of Basel

THOMAS G. SCHRAND, Philadelphia College of Textiles and Design

TATIANA SHAKLEINA, Institute for the Study of USA and Canada, Russian Academy of Sciences, Moscow

NADEZHDA SHVEDOVA, Institute for the Study of USA and Canada, Russian Academy of Sciences, Moscow

REBECCA SPAGNOLO, University of Toronto

VALERIE SPERLING, Clark University

LAURIE STOFF, University of Kansas

EVA-MARIA STOLBERG, University of Bonn, Germany

BENJAMIN SUTCLIFFE, University of Pittsburgh

ANNA TEMKINA, European University of St. Petersburg, Russia

KLAWA N. THRESHER, Randolph-Macon Women's College

R. CONNIE WAWRUCK-HEMMETT, Dalhousie University

CHERI C. WILSON, Loyola College of Maryland

IRINA YUKINA (IUKINA), Nevskii Institute of Linguistics and Culture, St. Petersburg, Russia

ELENA ZDRAVOMYSLOVA, European University of St. Petersburg, Russia

LIUDMILA ZHUKOVA, State University of Management, Moscow